British Caribbean Enterprises

by

Dr. Christopher Johnson

To: The Parker Family
Tracy inclusive, Happy
Reading!
From: Dr. Christopher Johnson
19th November 2014

First published in Great Britain in 2008
by C.A. Johnson

A CIP Catalogue of this book is available
from the British Library

ISBN 978-09561028 -1-2

Cover design by GarviDesign.uk

The front cover depicts the diversity of the British Caribbean business sector. Medicare pioneer, Trinidadian-born Dr. John Alcindor who established the first black medical practice in Britain, is pictured on the top right hand corner.

Printed in Great Britain by
Berforts Information Press Ltd.

The publisher's policy is to use paper manufactured from sustainable forests

"This is a great book; it provides a rich historical context for understanding minority firms in the UK"

London Development Agency.

"Congratulations to the author on a splendid work; it is needed to showcase the contribution of British Caribbean people over a century"

Mahogany Arts Ltd.

"This publication is indeed revolutionary; not only will it achieve its objective, but will also help bridge the generation divide between the younger, British-born Caribbean and the older, migrant population"

Kim Leevy, Canada.

"This book makes an excellent reference resource. The author has dealt with a topic that is rarely known in mainstream literature"

Professor Sonny Nwankwo, University of East London.

"A scholarly work that combines various disciplines such as commerce, culture, demography, economics, geography, politics, sociology and technology located within a British Caribbean context"

An Education Foundation, England.

"The author has provided an invaluable reference book, and far as I know, the first really comprehensive insight into the British Caribbean business community"

Bill Kirkman MBE, Cambridge.

"Dr Johnson's timely book on Caribbean entrepreneurship in Britain addresses an important, yet often neglected topic within the field of ethnic minority enterprise. With an admirable grasp of history, economics and enterprise, Chris Johnson presents a detailed portrait of Caribbean business owners in a variety of contexts. This book is to be welcomed as a valuable addition to the academic and policy community"

Professor Monder Ram OBE, Director CRÈME Initiative, De Montfort University.

Contents

Section III

British Caribbean Business Strategy

List of Tables, Charts and Minicases

Chapter 3 Overview of the UK Economy

Chapter 4 Challenges facing Entrepreneurs

Chapter 5 Cultural Industries

Preface

Over a century ago since Caribbean people migrated to the UK to improve their economic and financial condition, the issue regarding their contribution to the host society remains a strong focus of attention and intrigue. As we move closer to the first decade of the 21st century, some sections of British society view the presence of migrant communities as a hotbed of social tension whilst others agree that they are producers of wealth; that is, they have brought economic and social benefits to the country.

Behind these views, lies a remarkable variety of explanations as to why this is so. A commonly held view in the past was that people from the Caribbean were likely to be less qualified than the indigenous population even though foreign settlers were found to be skilled, hardworking, experienced and capable of integrating into the host society, despite racial prejudice and other forms of discriminatory practices meted out against them by individuals and institutions.

Historically, politicians complained that the non-white population would affect the way of life of ordinary Britons; in essence values would be corroded. Yet, communities have benefited from the presence of Caribbean settlers particularly their social entrepreneurial activities.

Sections of Big Business perceive that foreigners will impinge on employment opportunities for the resident community even though in the immediate post-war period, the UK had an extraordinary, underclass of jobless and unskilled labour force exceeding tens of thousands. The deliberate recruitment campaign of Commonwealth citizens in the first half of the 20th century was a clear justification that Britain didn't have sufficient labour to tackle problems created by the two World Wars. The collapse of the transport, health, hotel and other utilities meant that overseas skills were a desirable option.

The media argued in favour of laws to reduce the number of non-whites coming into Britain since this situation was creating fear and exacerbating tensions within poorly resourced neighbourhoods, although Britain like the US, always had a history of immigration and/or foreign settlement. Perhaps in the subconscious reaction to this approach, policy makers could not make their minds up whether or not the presence of Caribbean migrants would make a real difference to British prosperity and stability.

Those of religious persuasion particularly the Church of England held mixed views of non-white migrants who were part of the British Empire. The liberal wing of the church favoured an equitable, tolerant and balanced approach to immigration. As was noticeable, sections of the mainstream church showed distaste for `coloured' worshippers, treating them as outcasts, and this resulted in the subsequent formation of black churches in the 1950s as a response to this selective type of `Christian worship rebuff'.

While there is an element of over-statements if not speculations, in the presentation of these views, each has to be engaged in present day British Caribbean communities in the UK. As the first book of its kind, *British Caribbean Enterprises: A Century of Challenges and Successes* seeks to articulate the commercial and social enterprise rhythms which have given rise to the Caribbean presence in the UK and the various public policies which have shaped such a constructive response. This it is hoped, will not only contribute to a better understanding of the contribution Caribbean people make to the British economy, but also their impact on diversity, cultural pluralism and inclusivity.

This book would not have been completed if, I hadn't received support from others: the scores of business owners, social entrepreneurs, enterprise networks, public agencies and institutions, created the occasion for this vital work to be done, by demonstrating through their practices, the necessity for a modern approach to profiling immigrant firms, whilst adding new knowledge to existing literature on SME policy development. I had to consider it a vital necessity given the scarcity of education materials in this area. The multi-sector approach adopted in this book is unusual in the field of business economics and has clearly been recognised and amplified by the works of namely; the Institute of Employment Studies, Institute of Fiscal Studies, Regional Development Agencies, as well as campaigns pursued by employer-business organisations such as the Confederation of Business and Industry, the Federation of Small Businesses, the Trades Union Congress and more recently, Business in the Community.

Additionally, I couldn't research, compile and publish this book either, without the support of business associations and trade networks in London, the Southeast, the Midland Counties, Yorkshire and Humberside and development agencies stretching as far as Scotland and Wales. The opportunity to compile case studies on African and Caribbean firms for Loughborough University's European-funded black business initiative was invaluable, and I am grateful to Professor Geoff Chivers, Ron Chapman, Malcolm Cumberbatch, Mike Atkins and Elaine Harris, all of whom made that memorable initiative, possible. To Professor Monder Ram OBE, who invited me countless times to the CRÈME procurement initiative spearheaded by De Montfort University.

Among those who I would like to mention here, in deep appreciation for their help are: Bill Kirkman MBE, Professor Chris Mullard CBE, Dr. Kimani Nehusi, Andy Bailey MBE, Lee Wiliams MBE, Clarence Cole, Arif Ali, Patrick Lewis, Punam Kharbanda, George Martin, Tony Wade MBE, Lena Hartley, Wesley De Mendonca and several other colleagues and friends who gave of their time, experience and wisdom to help make this work possible.

To my parents Clement and Brenda Johnson, whose love and belief in my quest for excellence, kept me going in times of doubt and uncertainty. To my brothers, Tony and Mikey and sister, Arla, for their dignified support in difficult circumstances. Most importantly I dedicate the labours of this book to my loving children, Angela, Latoya, Mark and Kamara, as well as my grandchildren for whom this book represents an enduring legacy of global Caribbean civilisation.

C. A. Johnson

Acronyms	Definition
ABTA	Association of British Travel Agents
ACBN	African Caribbean Business Network
ACE	African Caribbean Enterprise Consortium
ACER	African Caribbean Education Resource
ACLT	African Caribbean Leukaemia Trust
ACMC	African Caribbean Millennium Centre
ACP	African and Caribbean Pacific
ACS	Association of Caribbean States
ACTV	African Caribbean Television
AGCAS	Association of Graduate Careers Advisory Services
BBA	Black Business Association
BBC	British Broadcasting Corporation
BBI	Black Business Initiative
BCA	Black Contractors' Association
BERR	Department for Business, Enterprise & Regulatory Reform
BFA	British Franchise Association
BHAs	Black Housing Associations
BHRCA	British Hotels, Restaurants and Caters' Association
BME	Black and Minority Ethnic
BPS	Business and Professional Services
BTEG	Black Training and Enterprise Group
CABE	Commission for Architecture and the Built Environment
CBE	Commander of the Order of the British Empire
CEO	Chief Executive Officer
CRER	University of Warwick
CTO	Caribbean Tourism Organisation
DPS	Dinnall Property Services
DIY	Do It Yourself
CARICOM	Caribbean Community and Common Market
CARDI	Caribbean Agricultural Research Development Institute
CARIFTA	Caribbean Free Trade Association
CBE	Commander of the Order of the British Empire

CBI	Confederation of British Industry
CCCU	Caribbean Confederation of Credit Union
CD	Compact Disc
CDM	Construction Design Management
CETA	Community Education and Training Academy
CFE	Caribbean Food Emporium
CIDT	Caribbean Indian Dance Troupe
CIS	Cultural Industries Sector
CITB	Construction Industry Training Board
CIT	Chartered Institute of Transport
CMMB	Caribbean Money Market Brokers
CoVE	Centres of Vocation Excellence
CPA	Community Participatory Approach
CRB	Criminal Records Bureau
CRE	Commission for Racial Equality
CRÈME	Centre for Research in Ethnic Minority Entrepreneurship
CSME	Caricom Single Market and Economy
DBC	Dreadbeat Broadcasting Corporation
DCMS	Department of Culture, Media and Sport
Defra	Department for Environment, Food and Rural Affairs
DETR	Department of Transport and the Regions
DTI	Department of Trade and Industry
EEC	European Economic Community aka the European Union (EU)
EDS	Enterprise Data Systems
EFBWO	European Federation of Black Women Business Owners
EU	European Union
FDI	Foreign Direct Investment
FHSCA	Future Health and Social Care Association
FM	Frequency Medium
FSA	Financial Services Authority
GCSE	General Certificate of School Examination
GDP	Gross Domestic Product

GEM	Global Entrepreneurship Monitor
GLA	Greater London Authority
GP	General Practitioner
GIDC	Grenada Industrial Development Corporation
GPI	George Padmore Institute
GVHC	Grenada Voluntary Hospital Committee
HABIA	Hair and Beauty Industry Authority
HCIMA	Hotel and Catering Institutional Management Association
HEART	Human Employment and Resource Training
HIV	Human Immunodeficiency Virus
HTAs	Hometown Associations
IADB	Inter-American Development Bank
ICE	Inner City Enterprise
ICT	Information Communications Technology
ILO	International Labour Organisation
IMF	International Monetary Fund
IPU	The Inter-Parliamentary Union
IATA	International Airline Transport Association
IT	Information Technology
ITT	Institute of Travel and Tourism
ITVS	Informal Value Transfer Systems
JAMPRO	Jamaican Promotions Corporation
LAC	Latin American and Caribbean
LDA	London Development Agency
LCP	League of Coloured People
LMI	Labour Market Information
MBE	Member of the Order of the British Empire
MIS	Management Information Systems
MOBO	Music of Black Origin
MORI	Market and Opinion Research International
MP	Member of Parliament
MSL	Maurice Sedwell Limited
NCVO	National Council for Voluntary Organisations
NEA	Nichols Employment Agency

NGOs	Non-Governmental Organisations
NHCL	Notting Hill Carnival Limited
NHS	National Health Service
NLBDA	North London Business Development Agency
NTCG	The New Testament Church of God
NTO	National Training Organisation
NVQ	National Vocational Qualification
OBE	Order of the British Empire
OECD	Organisation of Economic Co-operation and Development
OECS	Organisation of Eastern Caribbean States
ONS	Office for National Statistics
PATH	Positive Action Traineeships in Housing
PC	Personal Computer
PCTs	Primary Care Trusts
PFI	Private Finance Initiative
PCU	The Pentecostal Credit Union
PR	Public Relations
RAF	The Roselle Antoine Foundation
RCN	Royal College of Nurses RCP
	Royal College of Physicians
RDA	Regional Development Agency
R&D	Research and Development
RACE	Reading Afro Caribbean Elderly Housing Association
RIBA	Royal Institute of British Architects
RISE	Regional Infrastructure for Social Enterprise
ROI	Return on Investment
SADACCA	Sheffield and District African Caribbean Community Association
SAPI	Search, Analyse, Plan and Implement
SATs	Standard Assessment Tests
SCL	Satellite Consortium Limited
SEEDA	South East Economic Development Agency
SDEM	Supplier Development East Midlands
SED	Sector Excellence Model

SEMTA	Science, Engineering and Manufacturing Technologies Alliance
SET	Science, Engineering and Technology
SFI	Striving for Independence Group
SIC	Standard Industry Classification
SLEMBA	South London Ethnic Minority Business Association
SME	Small and Medium-sized Enterprise
SOBA	Society of Black Architects
SYAC	South Yorkshire African and Caribbean Enterprise and Training Centre
TCS	Tutorial Consultancy Services
TV	Television
UEP	United Evangelical Project
UK	United Kingdom
UKCC	United Kingdom Caribbean Chamber of Commerce
UKTI	United Kingdom Trade and Investment
UN	United Nations
US	United States
USS	Universal Service Solutions
USP	Unique Selling Point
WEB	Women's Education Building
WIOC	West Indian Organisation Co-ordinating Committee
WISC	West Indian Standing Conference
WTO	World Trade Organisation
VOE	Visions of Esteem

Introduction

The task of writing this book, *British Caribbean Enterprises: A Century of Challenges and Successes,* is challenging and exciting, particularly since there is no published account on the organisation and performance of Caribbean firms based on a sectoral approach. Information is patchy and limited to labour market studies on ethnic firms generally. To date, the work of British Caribbean firms is located within a largely immigration versus racial minority framework. Practical solutions are almost non-existent and the norm is to use the firm-size argument to justify the importance of this small and medium-sized enterprise (SME) sector to the UK economy. This means that as an important part of the development process, Caribbean entrepreneurship is rarely considered as essential to economic policy. This fact is further evident from information and data kept by agencies involved in urban regeneration and enterprise development across the UK.

The term *`British Caribbean* ' is used deliberately to rebrand Caribbean settlers who came to the UK by invitation and whose children and succeeding generations, have not only established firm roots, but contribute to British society. Although small, this section of the UK population is a major ethnic group, and so the term *`Afro'* or *African Caribbean' is* a simplification, since this group of migrants are from island-nations such as Barbados, Guyana, Jamaica, Trinidad and Tobago, as well as smaller territories in the eastern Caribbean (Antigua, Dominica, Grenada, Montserrat and St. Lucia to name a few). Caribbean women are successful in terms of both (paid) public sector and self-employment activities. On the basis of these two trends, members of this community thereby compare favourably to other migrants in the UK.

The term `*Black British'* was widely used and accepted by second-generation Caribbean people born to post-war settlers. Although being born in the country made them British, they were born into communities that were relatively closed and isolated. The black community relates this to discrimination while many Britons feel it resulted from the isolation that accompanied migration or British Caribbean `settlership'. A `Black British' culture also developed in the post-war period although there are still notable differences in culture and social mixing involving black Britons of different national backgrounds, including Caribbean people of African background and black Africans respectively. Since that period, a combined culture of similarity and difference has evolved, nurtured and found shared acceptance by those from other ethnic backgrounds.

However, it is important to give more than just token identity status to Caribbean people in the UK. The fact that their contribution is equated with economic prosperity and social cohesion is sufficient to give the refined term `British Caribbean' the recognition it deserves. Surely, the achievements of this community are a lasting triumph for positive integration and social harmony.

Nonetheless, efforts to raise the profile of minority enterprises are usually met by a mixture of disbelief and hesitancy, and it is not surprising therefore, that at events such as annual *Black History Month* observances, the *Black Enterprise Awards* and the *Federation of European Black Women Owners* gala ceremonies, there is bewilderment at the tremendous talent among African and Caribbean people in the UK. Yet they're sections of society that acknowledge the contribution of British Caribbean people's efforts in the post-war reconstruction in health, transport, hotel and other utility sectors. It is known that apart from original Caribbean migrants, members of second-generation families have achieved much individually, as this book illustrates.

Indeed, black men and women lived in Britain as early as the 12th century, but it was not until the 17th and 18th centuries that this population grew rapidly, resulting from the expansion of the British Empire. Between 1500 and 1870, it is estimated that at least 12 million African people were forcibly shipped across the Atlantic to work as slaves in the Americas. Britain's trade in African slaves for 300 years helped make it a world power. In the process, the trade contributed to the creation of reputable British companies such as Lloyd's insurance market, Imperial Tobacco and Midland Bank (**Gyekye 2004**).

Jamaican Francis Barber came to Britain as a child to join Britain's founder of the `English Dictionary', Dr. Samuel Johnson's household as a servant. Barber spent the rest of his life in England. It was not only slavery that Britain profited from its colonies, but also food and munitions during World War I. These events and others, prove like North America and Europe, that Britain is a land of immigrants; a fact endorsed by the British Government in its immigration timeline covering 200 years. The chronological sequence below shows the migrant communities from other countries that are impacting on family life, cultural identity, economic activity and other facets of British society as a whole: -

- 19th century – Jewish arrivals fleeing persecution in Russia and Poland; Irish settlers escaping poverty and trade brings Indians and Chinese to main ports;
- 1930s – Refugees from Nazi oppression arrive in the UK;
- 1948 – The boat, *SS Empire Windrush*, brings 492 Jamaicans in the UK with thousands more to follow; immigration from the Caribbean encouraged to help rebuild post-war Britain;
- 1950s and 1960s – Settlers from other new Commonwealth nations arrive: India, Pakistani and Bangladesh; and
- 1970s – East African-Asians and Vietnamese arrive.

However, there were early signs of business activity by British Caribbean professionals in 1907 when Trinidadian, Dr. John Alcindor, who after having worked with hospitals in England, decided to establish a private medical practice in London. His pioneering efforts inspired other general practitioners to follow suit and it is from the early 20th century period that this book will trace the formal beginnings of Caribbean business development in the British Isles, spanning 100 years.

The curator of the Jewish Museum referred to Britain's attitude to foreigners and other newcomers to the UK, arguing consistently that the vast majority of nationals who entered the country are assets to society. At a London exhibition to commemorate a century of immigration in 2005, she made these sobering comments, and in the process, put the presence of Caribbean people in the UK, in its proper historical context:

People travelling from the Caribbean to post-war Britain were not actually immigrants, they were being invited to come to Britain, and they were an essential part of rebuilding the post-war economy. Many of them had served in World War II and they were coming to the 'Mother Country' looking for a welcome which they didn't always find. The legislation was designed to keep out people from the new Commonwealth, not the old. Those `new' Commonwealth countries were those which had become independent in the 1960s and 70s **(Jillings 2005).**

Apart from importing more British coal as a contribution to the war effort, the (British) West Indian colonies had a more direct input into the European conflict. According to Dyde's *The Empty Sleeve,* when the "West Indian Regiment returned to the Caribbean in 1898, they became part of the garrison of territories"; namely, Barbados, Jamaica and St. Lucia (**Dyde 1997**). In effect, soldiers and other military conscripts from both Africa and the Caribbean displayed unique fighting qualities and skills, as well as an equally fierce commitment to 'King and Country' during the two World Wars of 1914-1919 and 1939-1945.

Many years later after the war; that is, in 1956 London Transport began a recruitment programme in Barbados and one year on, extended it to Trinidad and Jamaica. The arrival of *SS Empire Windrush* in June 1948 in Tilbury Dock, with 492 passengers from Jamaica, most of whom were ex-servicemen seeking work, marked the beginning of post-war mass migration.

Later, Conservative Health Minister, Enoch Powell, from 1960-1963, invited women from the Caribbean to Britain to train as nurses. In reality however, the call for labour was minimal and by 1958, only 125,000 workers had arrived in Britain from the Caribbean. America was the preferred destination for most Caribbean nationals because of its attractiveness and vast economic opportunities due to the Farm Work Programme. Interestingly, it was Powell who later criticised the flow of immigrants to the country with his famous '*Rivers of Blood*' speech in April 1968. Tory Leader, Edward Heath, sacked the controversial Powell after describing his remarks as 'racialist in tone and liable to exacerbate racial tensions'.

Since the 1990s, I have been profiling the work of African and Caribbean firms and this was further expanded in the form of a doctoral thesis. Later, considerable time was spent, in a consulting capacity, boosting enterprise support services, regeneration initiatives, and economic development and strengthening the funding capacity of minority firms. Extensive reviews on the organisation structure and performance systems of hundreds of firms were undertaken to improve strategic competence and market share. During the 1980s and 1990s, Hansib Publishing was the market leader in publishing success stories on minority businesses in titles such as *Third World Impact, Caribbean Times, African Times* and *Asian Times*. A focus of the Hansib Community Awards, was celebrating the achievements of Caribbean people in commerce, industry and civic affairs. I was part of a small group of persons who interviewed scores of business people including young entrepreneurs, to publicise their enterprise activities in the British Isles. Hansib also produced a brief account of African and Caribbean firms to complement news and features on minority enterprise.

Therefore, this book crystallises 25 years of entrepreneurship, business management, market intelligence and partnership experience, using a multi-sector approach to capture themes of a segment of `unsung' captains of commerce and industry who made a positive difference to diversity in Britain, with their own brand of creativity and genius.

By nature, Caribbean people are entrepreneurial, a well-known survival strategy used to overcome injustice over centuries, sometimes referred to as a main armour in their staying power. Beginning with traditional farming or agriculture, enterprises ranging from micro processing, marketing and sales to small-scale distribution and supply chains were established. This approach was further refined, utilising trading networks to promote and sustain commercial and social enterprises in villages, towns and districts. These contributed to a further expansion into mainstream economic activity evidenced by the number of Caribbean firms that have developed since the 1970s when enterprise growth took off in this community.

In this book, the word *`British Caribbean'* refers to people born in either the Caribbean or Britain of Caribbean parentage or descent. The term *`British Caribbean business or firm'* is used to mean businesses founded, owned and controlled by members of this group in the UK. The English-speaking Caribbean, which was dominated by successive European powers, including Britain for over 150 years, has evolved as relatively peaceful. Its culture reflects the political and socio-economic values which influence its diasporic communities in Britain, Europe, North America and elsewhere.

This book endorses the view that the Caribbean is a melting pot of diverse communities and not restricted to one particular group, a myth that is peddled frequently in mainstream and other literature dealing with issues regarding ethnicity, but more principally on Caribbean people as a whole. The blanket term *`African-Caribbean'* or *`Indo-(Indian) Caribbean'* is inapplicable and unacceptable in this context, and so too, is the generic term Black and Minority Ethnic (BME) which is even more suggestive because it appears to give primacy to generalisation; that is, anything other, than white mainstream. The limitation of such approaches undermines the true contribution of Britain's `minorities' and in the case of Caribbean entrepreneurs, their efforts are suppressed within the dominance of other minorities, meaning that as a growth sector, they remain invisible and unfocused. The aim of this book is therefore to publicise British Caribbean firms by assessing their visibility, contribution and competitiveness in the British economy.

Another reason for the preferred use of *`British Caribbean'* stems from the fact that Asian businesses (Chinese, Indians and others from the Indian sub-continent and/or the Asian peninsula in general) are given legitimate primacy in research in mainstream research where success and general profiling are conducted. I can't but view my business experience through the lens of the British Caribbean character since I can't deny my heritage. The fact that I was born in a polyethnic country, Guyana (former British Guiana), is further proof of the importance of this book to both Caribbean people and other minorities experiencing racial discrimination and institutional prejudice daily. My collective African, Chinese, Indian and Portuguese ancestry indeed, makes me, in colloquial terms, a virtual `Guyanese Pepperpot' (or `cook-up').

Another interesting feature of the British Caribbean community is this group's diversity in faith enterprises as is evident in Chapter 15. In London, two organisations have influenced much of what is described in Britain today, as multi-faith groupings. **The North**

London Islamic Cultural Society (1983) was formed by Muslims from the Caribbean, predominantly, Guyanese. It is considered as Haringey's first purpose-built mosque. In South London, the **Caribbean Hindu Cultural Society** (1950s) was also set up by the Guyanese diaspora in the UK to promote Hinduism and education advancement. To their credit, these Societies have helped unite and preserve the work of Caribbean and other `faithists' beliefs within a broader community context.

To be fair, when issues of a British Caribbean business nature are discussed, a selective approach is applied in areas such as crime, anti-asocial behaviour and health matters. In fact, the issues pertaining to race, immigration and social welfare are part of mainstream agenda and these have become the norm for studies on Caribbean communities, globally.

Since the 1980s, studies on BME businesses have reflected the dominance of Asian firms to the exclusion of others, despite the significant contribution of African and Caribbean firms respectively. On the one hand, in the majority of available literature on minority firms in Britain, there is overemphasis on the success of entrepreneurs of Indian, Chinese and other Asian origin.

On the other hand, not only are British Caribbean businesses `hidden' in the rubric `Black' ethno-profile, but their firm-sectors are not subjected to any rigorous analysis; that is, challenges facing owners and prospects for improving organisational performance. This is evident in reports by universities, think-tanks and public authorities like the Small Business Service. Thus, the limited or non-existent categorisation of British Caribbean firms and their sectoral specificity has become problematic and a reality that reflects poorly on national initiatives aimed at improving overall business competitiveness in the UK. For the purposes of flexibility, the terms *`British Caribbean'* and *`Caribbean'* are used interchangeably in this book, to describe members of this community who are involved in the economic and social development of the UK.

Census figures show that Caribbean residents are both enterprising and culturally adaptive to the challenges and opportunities in the UK and these facts explain why:

- They comprise 560,000 or just over 1% of the population and represent just over 12% of minority communities in the UK.
- British Caribbeans live mostly in London/Greater London, the Southeast, the Midland Counties, Yorkshire and Humberside, as well as Scotland and Wales.
- They are more likely to be engaged in enterprise start-ups than any other ethnic group, except the Indian community.
- In terms of economic activity, 9% are in manufacturing; 4% in construction; 13% in retail; 5% in food; 9% in travel and logistics; 3 % in financial services; 14% in property development and 18% in health and social care.
- Caribbean women have a high rate (64%) of economic activity and a low rate (7.8%) of unemployment. Male economic activity is around 66%, but unemployment is about 14% and in some deprived areas of the country, this rate is higher.
- There are nearly 15,000 businesses owned by Caribbean men and women combined, with 51% operating as '*sole proprietor*' and 48% as '*partnerships/companies*' (**Small Business Service 2006**).
- The market share of this group's commercial sector varies from 7% to 11% and social enterprise 6.9%, thereby contributing an estimated £5billion per annum (£3bn for commercial firms and nearly £2bn for social enterprises combined) **(Small Business Service 2003, Labour Force Survey 2004: 2005, GEM 2005:2006).**
- The major obstacles affecting black businesses are obtaining finance (21%), recruiting quality staff (12%), regulations (12%) and cash flow (9%) – **Small Business Service 2006**.

While British media houses are tentative about publicising (consistent) success stories of the Caribbean SME sector, a few commercial institutions have highlighted important enterprise features of this section of the population. Based on informed studies, Lloyds, Barclays and Natwest banks have suggested that despite severe challenges, Caribbean firms are still among the fastest growing concerns in the UK. A Bank of England report stated that the lack of investment capital was a main burden to black business start-ups and there was a need to investigate allied constraints, further:

*The main conclusions of our work are that, firstly, notwithstanding a lack of clearly documented evidence, some ethnic minority businesses, particularly African-Caribbean, perceive access to finance to be a disproportionate problem; secondly, the response to this perception needs to come from various quarters, including not only banks and other finance providers but also Government support agencies and ethnic businesses themselves; and thirdly, there are encouraging signs of action on all these fronts. But what is also clear is that much more research needs to be done in this area (*Bank of England 1999).

Barclays Bank plc also announced that the minority business start-ups had increased considerably from 32,000 in 2000 to 50,000 in 2004. It claimed that these firms comprised 11% of all new enterprise start-ups in the UK. Although the research showed that British Caribbean people had the lowest self-employment rate of 7%, the findings acknowledged that 8% of Caribbean firms were likely to be involved in the property/finance market and 19% in the retail trade **(Barclays 2005)**.

Notwithstanding the ongoing challenges, it is important to recognise from an ethnically stratified position, that Caribbean societies are a blend of African, Amerindian, Chinese, European, Indian and other mixed races due to centuries of slavery, indentureship and colonialism. It is for that reason that Caribbean people are easily adaptive to complex multicultural settings, since their history was moulded by this type of communal situation'.

Current perceptions of British Caribbean firms are therefore a mixture of partial support and stereotyping, with this sector narrowly defined along the lines of culture (mostly music) and sport, yet the evidence disproves this myth. Throughout Britain, there are firms operating in key sectors – construction, personal care, health and social care, computing, training, to name a few. Owners have broken into mainstream markets with new products and services to meet the needs of a more enlightened consuming public. Accordingly, this book illustrates that notwithstanding multiple disadvantage, Caribbean entrepreneurs have utilized their knowledge and experiences often described as '*opportunity* structures' for business start-ups throughout Britain **(Waldinger, Aldrich & Ward 1990)**.

Basically, opportunity structures are created when market conditions tend to favour products or services oriented towards particular ethnic groups in which a wider, non-ethnic market might be served. These structures consist of the channels which access to business is obtained and group characteristics include the particular group's response to conditions in the host society and the mobilisation of resources – a feature of such communities. Aldrich and Ward argued that ethnic strategies emerge from the interaction of all these factors, as ethnic entrepreneurs adapt to the resources made available in opportunity structures and attempt to carve out their own niches **(1990)**.

When the Government Office for London was asked to explain the process of data collection with reference to British Caribbean firms, and generally, monitor the performance of ethnic firms in the capital, a senior policy official was at pains to point out that there were no definite statistics 'stored' for Caribbean firms. "*We don't distinguish between different ethnic groups,*" the official added. Yet, Gol explained that there were perceived barriers affecting these very firms:

- Lack awareness of contracts being tendered;
- Lack of pre-start up help and tailored support from mainstream agencies;
- Poor marketing due to limited finances; and
- Lack of investment, including access to finance/funding **(2004)**.

In addition, GoI made these crucial, but timely observations:

At present there is a lack of awareness and understanding as to what support is available. There are too many support services, and many intermediary organizations that lack sufficient resources to deal with demand for products. London is broken up into boundaries for particular streams of funding where support is provided according to postcode. This discriminates against those who require the same funding that is available in neighbourhood Boroughs, but are excluded because they fall outside the logistical boundary. There is not enough ring-fencing for government funding. BME communities are not very familiar with the required conditions for securing European funding and capacity building is vital in this regard **(2004)**.

Up until 2006, official figures showed that the £2.5 billion per year was allocated for the SME sector, with £1.8 billion or 72% of this allocated for business support services – the aim being to help people start their own or grow existing firms. Millions more are spent on administrative staff, bureaucracy and consultancy, but only a small percentage of minority firms benefit from this provision. Black firms are `signposted' to other agencies that are often unable to advice properly, on either start-ups or provide technical assistance to existing business owners planning on expansion. Research throughout the UK found evidence of this problem even in areas where public institutions were funded to offer support to minority communities interested in enterprise development.

In the 1980s two studies in London pointed to gaps in enterprise support for black businesses, with a quarter of all owners suggesting that it was a deliberate policy by banks to impose restrictions on lending. Most of the owners who were interviewed had a relatively high level of education. Respondents said that their entry into businesses was due to the "considerable need felt to escape from the racial discrimination and frustration that they had experienced in their previous employment" **(Kazuka 1981)**.

The Lambeth study confirmed the Hackney findings, highlighting major areas in which non-white enterprises faced particular difficulties such as owners' inability to obtain enough financial capital for start-ups, premises, lack of managerial experience; lack of knowledge of the assistance to small businesses; racial prejudice; abuse and harassment; vandalism/burglary and other security issues, as well as problems in dealing with the local authority (**Leo 1981**).

In 1996, the Black Business Association of Waltham Forest commissioned a review of its operations in view of reduced statutory funding and the association's failure to access regeneration contracts. Even with a 250-strong membership, the organization did not have the financial capacity to bid for large contracts and therefore seemed to have stuck in a grant-aid time warp. Besides the occasional training contract for new start-ups, the association couldn't advance its agenda of offering all-round support for its membership. There were genuine concerns about the lack of a long-term strategy that should have included a marketing and self-financing plan. The review findings revealed some of the major issues that members thought were urgent: -

- 50% of members rated the association as fairly viable;
- 80% suggested information, training, counseling and financial services;
- 66% suggested a proper marketing plan; and

- 66% supported self-financing initiatives to sustain the BBA's future **(1997)**.

The review also questioned whether the association's aim, `*to promote the development of, and to represent the interests of Black and ethnic businesses*', could be realized since it was faced with increasing challenges such as limited financial resources and lack of a 10-15 year plan for its future.

Business owners are aware that minority firms in Britain have been researched extensively over a 30-years period along the lines of problem-issues and conflict principles. They feel that there has been a collective `dress rehearsal' of causes, symptoms and prescriptions, yet enquiries fail to capture or highlight enterprise success within the British Caribbean community. Even more perplexing, reputable think-tanks responsible for monitoring economic policy, including enterprise support, are seemingly reluctant to acknowledge the value of Caribbean firms to the UK economy, let alone solutions to address underperforming firms.

Amid the growth of `live-theories' and numerous studies on problems affecting minority firms, the British Caribbean SME sector has been struggling to compete. The notion of underperformance is tied to the population ratio of this community and figures in parts of England show, that compared with their geographic presence and their relative dominance in key sectors locally, British Caribbean firms are underperforming compared to the national (industry standards) average.

Business Link reported in 2005 that there were more than 1,200 black firms in the West Midlands, but their performance did not match that community's potential for increased enterprise growth. Notwithstanding this, there are unusual growth patterns in the wider British Caribbean SME sector, at local and regional levels, a factor that has not been maximised for competitive advantage and enterprise sustainability overall.

In 2001, the Small Business Service commissioned a series of literature reviews on ethnic minority SMEs. In examining this area, Ram and Smallbone used the term *'mixed embededness'* to evaluate the impact of ethnic businesses on the British economy **(2002)**. Mixed embededness involves various processes and patterns which, when brought together, are interconnected in different ways. This instrument was not utilised to examine the contribution of British Caribbean firms and their corresponding effect on the UK economy. The use of the case study method is vital in initiatives of this sort and should be applied when dealing with various minority-grouping businesses because of cultural and racial variations.

As an important tool of analysis, the case study method is not often considered by mainstream establishments in relation to Caribbean firms, and yet as this book proves, it is a credible way of studying the operational practices of minority firms on a sector-by-sector basis. Case studies tend to be effective in instances where data is problematic or when sample-sizes are very limited even though they may have a broad sector-type representation. They help bring to light examples of operational processes and organisation practices, considered unique to Caribbean enterprises in various cultural settings. Valuable insights into the strategies by founder-owners to keep their firms afloat in the first three or so years are also gained from this process.

Experience shows that the complexity of businesses and social enterprises require a combination of methods to examine their performance output. A series of measures include case studies, participant observation, questionnaires and field work can all offer scope for quality intelligence which in turn, can help public institutions to better understand and appreciate the workings of Caribbean firm sector in Britain. Some of these methods have been applied in this book to illustrate the organisation and performance of British Caribbean firms.

In 2004, the Greater London Authority published the findings of a commissioned study on black businesses in the capital from a telephone survey of 4,000 firms. Although the sample size was 107, it acknowledged that the exercise was bigger than any other comparable survey containing this information, but it was not large enough to permit detailed analysis – for example, the sub-categories of black-owned businesses. In effect, the study highlighted these major conclusions:

- Over 10,000 black firms employ 70,000 people.
- About 3% of these represent London's labour force.
- Firms make up 4% of economic activity in London.
- Under-representation of firms compared to black population (12%).
- Firms have estimated turnover of £4.5 billion.
- Business and professional services, retail and wholesale are dominant.
- Owners have shown great resilience in recession periods in Britain; and
- Innovation is quite common involving goods and services **(LDA Agency 2004).**

Interestingly, the study authors employed the use of a particular ethnic-cultural term to describe the ethnic origin of owners from different Caribbean backgrounds. In categorising the proportion of businesses owned by African and Caribbean people in London, the GLA used the phrases `mixed (white and black) Caribbean' and `Black Caribbean' to differentiate groups or segments of the Caribbean community. Thus mixed Caribbean people comprised 20% and `Black Caribbean' entrepreneurs reflected 22% in terms of business representation.

The use of creative-based ethnic terms, apart from providing a confused or distorted picture of Caribbean societies generally, also illustrated the complexity of the term `Caribbean' when applied to business and economic pursuits, especially if members are largely segmented along ethnic, cultural, social and geographic lines. This should not affect the fact that British Caribbean entrepreneurs use their cultural skills and ethnic diversity to make advances in the UK by increasing business activities year-on, with women performing at nearly 30% of the national average (22%) for female entrepreneurship.

In 2005, Birmingham Chamber of Commerce and Industry commissioned a review of the local BBA with the aim of recommending a medium-term strategy. The review showed the level of sector differences among Caribbean business owners in the West Midlands. It showed too, the hurdles they faced in maintaining competitive advantage against the background of underinvestment, lack of procurement opportunities, restrictive practices, limited enterprise support, and lack of professional training in leadership, management, customer care, financial planning, public relations and strategic marketing **(BBA: West Midlands 2005)**. Generally, the review highlighted the following:

- Black firms were represented in about 24 different sectors;
- Caribbean businesses comprised 75% of all economic activity in the Midlands;
- The total contribution of black firms was in excess of £100 million;
- About 4% of all firms were involved in a University procurement scheme;
- 100% of firms required information services;
- 60% of owners needed sector-based funding and technical support;

- 75% of owners believed in partnership with public and private agencies;
- 50% recognised that contracts were essential to growth; and
- 80% felt business meetings were vital to sharing best practice.

As most studies on black businesses have shown, issues affecting owners remain in areas such as finance, restrictive practices and the inability to access lucrative contracts from large companies. Here, the issue of finance relates primarily to initial capital investment for starting a business. It is a contentious issue that attracts more problems-analysis than viable solutions. For instance, attitudes among financial advisers employed in mainstream institutions need changing. Business advisers require expert training in cultural sensitivity and conflict management. The reasons why few if any British Caribbean firms have not penetrated into (large-scale) agricultural, engineering, science and technology industries, the hospitality sector, export trade and heavy manufacturing, are due to owners' lack of sufficient knowledge about these sectors, high entry barriers, lack of (substantial) capital investment and market monopoly. Accessing procurement opportunities is still a nightmare for black entrepreneurs though as evidence suggests, this situation is changing slowly for the better in some respects.

In 2002, it was reported that over 20% of business owners had difficulty in business start-ups because of a lack of sustainable support from enterprise agencies. A major factor in the equation was the perception of *institutional racism*, a phrase contained in the findings of the Macpherson Inquiry set up to investigate the death of British Caribbean teenager, Stephen Lawrence, who was murdered in 1993. Additionally, only 21% of African and Caribbean businesses secured start-up finance from commercial houses compared with 34% of enterprises owned by white and Pakistanis, as well as 49% for those owned by Chinese people. This situation existed, even though evidence showed that black entrepreneurs had more formal management qualifications – 46% - than either whites or Asians. Neil Kilnock of Choice FM obtained a start-up loan only when a white director fronted the application. The British Bankers Association insisted that:

While we were unable to prove that discrimination exists, there is clear evidence of disadvantage which cannot be satisfactorily explained in terms of other characteristics of the businesses or their owners. It was important for banks to win customers from among the minority-owned businesses, since these institutions can lose out **(2002)**.

In responding to criticisms of racial prejudice and related discriminatory practices meted out to Caribbean business people, the Department of Trade and Industry (DTI) appeared unable to offer a tangible explanation as to the reasons for this social malaise in British society. The following response bore though, concerns for and recognition of, the multiple disadvantage continuously experienced by British minority firms, including Caribbean-owned enterprises:

The Government is committed to ensuring that all ethnic minority businesses can achieve their potential. There is a need for financial institutions to better explain and signpost their products to ethnic minority customers. There is also a need for ethnic minority businesses to better understand requirements of financial institutions. The Government will continue to engage with key financial institutions to ensure that the needs of ethnic minority businesses are fully addressed **(Griffiths 2002)**.

In an effort to find practical solutions to the intractable problems affecting minority firms, I have collaborated with professionals, business owners and multi-sector agencies and organisations to promote the Caribbean SME sector in the UK, using a variety of approaches. In June 1998, delegates who attended the first ever *Windrush Economic Conference*, supported the idea of a black business strategy, and in October 2001, participants at a business symposium supported the setting of a national commission to implement such a strategy. At the historic Queen's Golden Jubilee celebrations in June 2002, to celebrate the *Caribbean Contribution to the Britain and the Commonwealth* representatives agreed to the development of a broad-based program showcasing the contribution of the British Caribbean SME sector to the UK economy.

Whilst there have been a torrent of conferences, seminar-workshops and other initiatives on minority business development, there has not been sufficient focus on broad-based national representation for the British Caribbean SME sector. From available evidence, a plausible solution lies in the establishment of a national authority to adequately represent the hopes and aspirations of African and Caribbean business communities. This idea should not be seen as a separatist agenda, but as a logical, progressive step towards ensuring that that these two business groups have better access to resources in order to grow, expand and sustain their respective firms. Their continued exclusion from mainstream policy-making because of the `hard-to-reach' lament, is a sad reflection on those who believe in political liberty, economic freedom, social justice and cultural diversity. It does Britain no favours either, since more than 10% of a section of the business community continues to be deprived from boosting wealth-creation endeavours and creating opportunities for greater choice in the range of products and services in the marketplace.

Certainly a major hindrance to the actual representation, more so public acknowledgement and recognition of Caribbean businesses, is the lack of a national body to reflect an economic progressive agenda. In the 1970s, there were two novel projects; namely, a banking venture and the formation of the UK Caribbean Chamber of Commerce. Both were aimed at strengthening the financial capacity and level of national representation and advocacy respectively, of black and other minority firms. The fact that they were short-lived illustrates the necessity for a long-term strategy for Caribbean enterprise development in the UK. These initiatives would be elaborated upon in chapter 15.

In areas where there are local and regional business associations and other enterprise networks in Birmingham, Bristol, Leicester, London, Manchester and Sheffield, to name a few, they can barely articulate a credible policy for businesses from a sector angle. For one thing, even though these networks are business-led in part, and are limited companies with charitable objectives, statutory bodies control their finances and by extension their material existence. So that the capacity of business associations for growth is affected by a dual partnership-patronage system that is flawed. Furthermore, it means that as formal trading organisations, they cannot fully exercise their rights, duties and responsibilities to control the vital area of funding. The effect obviously on membership will be disastrous.

To a large extent, all BBAs in England are experiencing this problem which has resulted in dwindling membership, confused or a distorted sense of direction, perceived lack of purpose and a dent in credibility and public image. Apart from routinely publicizing the difficulties experienced by entrepreneurs, very seldom have major studies analysed the strategic value of independent bodies to lobby and generally articulate a vision for black economic progress in the UK. Such a dilemma can offer business associations a viable alternative to pool their resources to achieve genuine, lasting economic self-sufficiency. It could also provide businesses an opportunity to maximise sector markets to increase profit margins, thereby stabilising businesses that are at risk of collapsing or underperforming.

From the standpoint of the cumulative contribution of black firms to the economy to the tune of about £5 billion, it is rather surprising that efforts to establish a full-scale national authority to represent the more than 20,000 black firms countrywide, was not a priority until a few years ago. A group of business leaders including this author, met in late 2004 to examine the concept of a national body since it was felt that the time had come to end the 'talking shop' and instead, bite the proverbial 'bullet'. After preliminary discussions with public officials and business owners in London and the Midlands, a meeting was convened under the auspices of the Treasury. A small steering committee made a presentation in the presence of then Chief Secretary to the Treasury, Paul Boateng MP. The aim of the proposed business council was:

To establish a national authority that represents the interests and concerns of the African and Caribbean business sector, whilst developing new frontiers of constructive engagement and partnership between this sector's communities and mainstream in all areas of economic planning and development **(NACBC 2005).**

The Chief Secretary and his team were impressed by this overdue initiative, bearing in mind that business owners had a lot of `enterprise grievances' and the opportunity to vent their feelings couldn't have been timelier. This wasn't the case, however, as they convinced the Treasury of their positive intentions. Surely my colleagues and I will cherish January 2005 as a momentous occasion, dictated by a `giant leap of enterprise faith' by a group of dedicated business men and women who were determined to change the image of the British Caribbean SME sector for the better. The Treasury acknowledged this fact in its exhortation to the business group:

It is important to see this in terms of problems and opportunities. To be an effective organisation, the Council needs to remember that it will have to provide support to member-firms and help them to address their problems. You have to help them exploit opportunity because that is what business is all about. You are going to ask people to give resources and time; it is a challenge that local Chambers of Commerce have been unable to respond to. My experience is that (as mainstream organisations) they are withering because members are far too busy involved in their own business to believe that they can help the organisation. You will no doubt be asking businesses to give up time and resources. It means that you have to be disciplined in terms of focus – the membership benefits that would be offered. The Council needs to look seriously at the policy context such as issues around skills development, procurement, business leadership and management, as well as market focus. The Government has placed enterprise as a top priority and there are many initiatives which the NACBC can be involved through a series of collaborative partnerships **(Boateng 2005)**.

One main drawback of enterprise development in relation to strategic planning is the level of spatial distribution among African and Caribbean communities particularly, and its implications for regeneration initiatives across various communities, especially since each area differs from one to another in terms of need. Thus the fragmentation and duplication of support services in the UK remain a challenge in dealing with critical issues on enterprise support for underperforming firms. In London for example, over 10 Boroughs; namely, in the North, South, East and West of the capital, have a high concentration of Caribbean firms, most of which serve minority communities. This justifies the point that such `separation' is often `portrayed in the argument that self-employment provides an alternative method to deal with disadvantage and discrimination, although it has been shown that the motivation for self-employment differs among ethnic groups' **(Noon 2005).**

In other English cities, except Birmingham, Liverpool, Manchester and Sheffield, there are smaller Caribbean groups and though mixed in some areas; there is a greater desire for focused representation and support for economic activities rather than token or symbolic gestures. In northern England, Scotland and Wales, entrepreneurs lobbied representatives of the NACBC to discuss support measures in remote business areas. There was an interest to participate in activities to boost their firms' competitiveness and generally, sustain local economies. This response came long before the Council was formalised. The idea of a national body to represent black businesses seemed to have heightened expectations never before and scores of owners were eager to take part in this new dynamic.

More than 12 businesses were represented at the Treasury meeting and agreed with officials that the groundwork was done to mobilise initial interest, more attention had to be paid towards creating a `critical mass' of membership-firms across the country to `buy-in' to the NACBC `product idea'. This view was forcibly expressed by one of the UK's leading international change management consultancy firms, Focus Consultancy Ltd. This company played an integral part in the formation of the business council, and its head, Professor Chris Mullard, set out methodically, the prerequisites that were necessary for the organisation to attain its laudable aims and objectives:

I believe that any organisation that represents the issues and overall concerns of the black business community is vital, and essentially crucial for advancing philosophically, the Black Economic Agenda. As members, we have a stake and we should ensure that it is shared collectively by other African and Caribbean entrepreneurs in the country. We should consider capital investment, organisational management and staff attainment levels, corporate procurement and the development of appropriate services for member-firms, with a built-in sectoral component. Our main task is to formulate, co-ordinate and implement a realistic strategy that can help our businesses to be sustainable in a global environment that impacts on every aspects of our lives **(Mullard 2005).**

At the time of writing, Loughborough University had completed a European-sponsored black research project covering the UK. This venture that lasted for more than two years, demonstrated a range of methods in evaluating the organisation and performance of the African and Caribbean SME sector. Apart from utilising in-house resources, the university recruited prominent professionals with knowledge and experience in economic affairs and community leadership, along with extensive public sector experience, to lead on the project.

The research was ground-breaking from two perspectives; firstly, the recognition given to firms and their communities; and secondly, the utilisation of experts from the community in the form of educators, consultants, social entrepreneurs, and businesses. I played a vital role in the project by conducting interviews, writing case studies and collating lists of firms in London, the Southeast and the West Midlands. Using the law of comparison, unlike previous undertakings, the Loughborough's European business project demonstrated excellence in the following ways: -

- Partnership co-ordination involving public and private sector;
- A sector-led approach to maximise quality responses from interviewees;
- Channels of advocacy and representation for business associations;
- A thematic framework for accessing information and data on black firms; and
- A UK-wide conference to discuss challenges and prospects of black firms.

For some time now, there has been a common perception that the status of black firms in Britain is comparable to those of African-American companies, fuelling the notion that such comparison may not be necessarily convincing because of differences in the political and economic systems on both sides of the Atlantic. Yet ideally, these differences do not amount to much in theory, but in practice determine the impact of policies aimed at improving the competitive standing of minority firms excluded from the UK mainstream. The saying that `money has no colour' is not always true, and certainly when it comes to hard-nosed business transactions, this view bears no real relevance, particularly if the basis for market competition favours a dominant racial group.

Nevertheless, there are similarities and differences in other parts of the world where Caribbean firms operate; for example, in Canada's minority enterprise sector. A study in Toronto showed how entrepreneurs took advantage of their kinship network and how equally, their experience as migrant entrepreneurs is very similar to other visible minorities - Chinese, Japanese or South Asians in Canada. The analysis revealed important factors which influenced the overall success or failure in business life. These were:-

- Caribbean people were influenced or restricted by the currency regulations of their countries of origin, which prevented the outflow of capital. This was particularly true of Jamaicans and Guyanese during the 1970s when currency controls allowed only a modest $200 to be taken out of the country. Thus, the country of origin may in certain cases control access to capital.
- Some owners were successful because they maintained two business outlets, one in the Caribbean and another in Canada. Maintaining connections in the Caribbean was particularly important for those in the retail food and record importing business that rely on Caribbean suppliers for their produce or records. Often these suppliers are kin. Thus, for foreign entrepreneurs, the problems with suppliers have to do with the effectiveness of their home networks.
- The ability to acquire capital through family/friend networks, usually interest free or at very modest rates of interest was instrumental to many. Initial capitalisation came from relatives and/or from the entrepreneurs relatives operated maintaining his or her job while the business.
- Maintaining a business operation depended also on the use of unpaid spouses/partners and other relatives for labour, as well as very long hours for the proprietor themselves. By using spouses, children and other relatives, the entrepreneur does not have to pay employees and the net profits of the business are used to maintain the family **(Poole 1979: Rhyne 1983)**.

In the American context, the situation is complex and varied, with legislation in the form of *Affirmative Action* helping to cushion the blows experienced by African-Americans, although since the Bush (Jr) Administration has been in office, elements of the powerful Republican Lobby have questioned the legality of positive discrimination. Yet, over the past 30 years the US government has promoted the creation and expansion of minority-owned businesses, a principled goal pursued largely by adding minority components to existing public programmes and establishing the Minority Business Development Agency. The programmes have dealt with capital availability and technical assistance. Limits on majority involvement in minority firms and the risky nature of investment in small business, however, have rapidly depleted the ability to provide money through these firms.

African-Americans comprise 12.9% of the US population and today they still suffer from low rates of business formation because issues like credit and access to capital remain problematic. Overall, black businesses are still characterised by apparent dominance in human services and retail trade which represents no more than 1% of sales receipts of business activities combined. According to the US Department of Commerce, the number of these firms grew by 46% between 1987 and 1992, and with two-thirds operating as a service or retail trade level. Revenues for black-owned enterprises expanded by 63% during that period, from $19.8 billion to $32.2 billion. That compares to a 67% increase, to $3. 3 trillion, for all businesses. These firms are building strategic alliances while positioning themselves to procure government and private sector contracts (***The Black Collegiate Magazine* 2005**).

This is rather significant considering that in recent years, there has been a steady rollback on *Affirmative Action* and minority set-aside programs in several states in America. Meanwhile, the Small Business Administration (SBA) is looking to play a larger role in facilitating African-American entrepreneurship by assembling an aggressive plan to double the volume of business it does to African-American entrepreneurs. For example from 1998 through to 2000, the SBA wanted to guarantee 9,300 loans valued at $1.4 billion.

The original intention of the US government programmes was to increase the number of black firms both in areas where they live and in the large community, but studies have shown that minority-owned businesses are being established within non-white communities rather than in the general community. Of course, there are reasons for the concentration of minority firms in these communities; past discrimination has limited the choice of location of older firms and many are retail and service firms which base their business on being able to provide for the special needs and desires of the minority group.

If the above is true, then the likelihood of developing successful minority businesses is linked to the growth in the non-white market. These firms are being asked to compete in a market with a below average share of the America nation's income. For most black firms, this means that the chances for success are not relatively good. The political reality is that in the US, majority firms are likely to object to any government programmes which subsidise competing non-white firms. They are more likely to support the financing of minority business development, if these firms are not seen as a direct threat to their own market (white consumers – the author's emphasis).

Generally, on both sides of the Atlantic, there are common issues affecting the growth and expansion of black firms (be they African Americans or Caribbean Americans etc.,) and yet encouraging non-white firms to compete in the mainstream market should be a long-term goal to success and economic prosperity. As experts rightly acknowledge, not only will these firms have a better chance of success, but the flow of profits to non-whites would help reverse the flow of money out of their communities. More than anything else, the poverty gap would be reduced and wealth creation could be maximised equally, to benefit whole communities **(Zeller 1981)**.

Apart from investigating the Caribbean and broader minority enterprise sector across the globe, especially in America, Canada and the Caribbean region, as well as reviewing business and economic trends in African and Asia particularly, much of the work done on this book resulted from extensive research and other forms of investigation into the operations of British Caribbean firms dating back to 1907. Primary data was sourced from postal questionnaires and visits to businesses, along with in-depth interviews. I had considerable access to 700 businesses and social enterprises combined, during the period 1997-2007 and identified nearly 300 to be used as case study material for this book.

Above all, besides traditional sources, information and data were accessed through a series of interventions:-

- Business profiles in the ethnic media;
- Consultancy support to firms;
- Policy research for public agencies;
- Performance reviews of business associations;
- Organising/co-hosting conference-workshops;
- Ongoing work into the contribution of minority firms; and
- Dedicated website to promote ideas on human advancement.

Throughout this book, I have used sampled data, along with other methods of inquiry, to obtain information since ethnic monitoring was especially weak in areas where British Caribbean communities were perceived to be small or marginal. Annual employment surveys' persistent use of the 1991 and 2001 census figures also constrained the accuracy of self employment and economic activity among minority firms in the UK. Data from the Office of National Statistics and the nine English Regions with a sector-type distribution showed little distinction between the self employed and those employed in public institutions and private sector agencies.

In several instances, the term `*Black*' was used to lump other ethnic category series; namely, *`Black African' Black British' `Black Caribbean'* and *`Black Other'*. The SBS' Annual Survey of 2003 of minority firms stuck to the term `Black' to describe both African and Caribbean business performance and the persistence of its use prevented an accurate representation of these two groups' overall performance from a sector perspective. Not only did this approach prejudice the accuracy of information and data, but it also demonstrated a continuous flaw in mainstream research when investigating matters pertaining to ethnicity, nationality and cultural diversity.

Accordingly, the various charts and other illustrations in this book were configured using official estimates and sampled data - case studies, data collection on firms by sectors and demography and anecdotal evidence of various issues affecting British firms in general.

In an effort to cover as many issues as possible, I divided this book into three sections, each dealing with specific concerns on commerce and industry from a British Caribbean perspective. Case studies are included to illustrate the importance of the organisation and performance of key enterprise sectors, added to which owners have brought new insights into enterprise practices such as innovation, creativity and strategies for longevity. *British Caribbean Enterprises* is therefore divided into the following sections: -

Section I comprises four chapters 1, 2, 3 and 4. **Chapter 1** sets the scene by outlining a fairly detailed history of the Caribbean landscape, highlighting the effects of slavery, indentureship, self-government and external power politics had on the region as it attempts to create opportunities for further economic and social development, through entrepreneurship and trade. The terms 'West Indian' (colonial) and 'Caribbean' (modern) are used interchangeably to explain the problems experienced by commentators when attempting to describe Caribbean people, ethnically and culturally.

Chapter 2 looks at the development of the Caribbean economy by highlighting various steps taken by National Governments to encourage and stimulate enterprise among the region's populace particularly in light of the effects of globalisation on small-nation states. The activities of Caricom, the regional trading body, are also examined to show its significance and relevance to intra and extra-regional finance and trade.

Chapter 3 provides an overview of the UK economy by tracing the origin and development of Great Britain and how its current structure has created challenges and opportunities for the growth and development of minority firms in key industry sectors and segments in the 12 UK Regions. The political and social value system is nevertheless analysed, to identify the critical nature of institutional discrimination and racial prejudice and their constraining effects on the potential viability of commercial and social enterprises, operated by minorities.

Chapter 4 explores the different challenges affecting owners in their quest to secure market advantage. They range from insufficient, start-up capital, lack of procurement opportunities, poor location and premises, difficulty in recruiting quality staff, limited budget for advertising and promotion, generation issues, too much regulation and limited technical assistance to enterprise support. The chapter suggests a proper system of market intelligence for business owners since it will enable them to plan more strategically according to trends in consumer and financial markets, worldwide.

Section II is a critical part of this book, as it analyses the composition and performance of leading industry sectors and segments of commercial firms and social enterprises, owned and managed by three generations of British Caribbean professionals and entrepreneurs covering a century-period in the UK. This section consists of **Chapters 5 to 15** which look at critical areas of the UK economy by highlighting challenges faced by business owners and their future prospects for increasing market share in the commercial, industrial and service sectors

Chapter 5 examines the growth and development of various segments of the cultural industries sector that dominate the British Caribbean enterprise sector based on both a commercial and entertainment value. It demonstrates the influence settler communities have on the artistic and cultural landscape including appearance, language, speech and social interaction in the UK. This chapter further discusses that this sector will contribute more to the regeneration of diverse communities, with profound changes that, in the end, will help foster economic prosperity and social cohesion in inner-cities.

Chapter 6 assesses the value of the construction industry and the small but vital role played by British Caribbean firms in their desire for financial independence, self-help and contributing to the building of their community and the country as a whole. Issues affecting the building and allied trades are also discussed; they include public sector (housing associations inclusive) contract opportunities, new technologies and the decline in the number of non-white apprentices in the trade. Various challenges and opportunities are presented to show the dynamism of this sector.

Chapter 7 takes a slice at the personal care sector and shows how entrepreneurs are influencing changes in the trade through innovation and enterprise. It examines the pioneering efforts of Dyke & Dryden, resulting in hundreds of hairdressing salons, fashion houses and other personal care enterprises, established throughout the UK since the early 1960s. The comparative low market share of 10% in the personal care sector by Caribbean operators is also looked at against the background of the intense competition from other minority retailers in the industry.

Chapter 8 looks at areas of manufacturing and motoring trades primarily, where Caribbean businesses have an average market share. Segments such as food production, the medicare industry, glassworks, vehicular manufacturing, cultural products and other semi-processing units are profiled, to emphasise the innovative nature of the British Caribbean production-led market.

Chapter 9 examines up to eight key segments in the food trade where business owners are competing to maintain market advantage, as well as improving the quality of food produce. Innovative features such as creative marketing using informal networks, non-processed (raw) materials for production, entry into co-ethnic markets and the use of mainstream distribution and supply chains are scrutinised to illustrate the unique selling point of British Caribbean firms operating in the UK.

Chapter 10 is set in the context of actions taken at the national level to increase the prospects for business and professional services, as well as the corresponding rise in the number of minority enterprises in this sector at the beginning of the mid-1980s to the present time. In exploring this development, over 20 British Caribbean firms are sampled, with a profile of half a dozen segments, to portray the resourcefulness of non-European business owners who, in the face of labour market discrimination and racial prejudice, converted their (public/private sector) experiences and knowledge to set up successful entities in diverse markets. A challenge-prospects framework is also presented to show the highly competitive nature of this sector.

Chapter 11 focuses on the complexity of the travel market in the UK and the effects of international competition on tour operators, airlines and other industry operators. The skill, innovation and the sustainability of Caribbean-owned travel agents, tour operators and other firms are highlighted. Issues affecting the operations of this sector are examined in some detail, showing how retailers have repositioned their companies to maximise growth prospects in the tropical and fairly stable Latin American and Caribbean travel market. This chapter also draws on the technical and cultural skills and industry networks owners have developed to remain competitive.

Chapter 12 reflects on the complex world of the knowledge economy that consists of information technology and its application to almost every facet of human activity. Its benefit as a resource for advancing knowledge and productivity is described in the context of emerging Caribbean-owned and managed technology firms that are underpinned by a sizeable number of Caribbean people (37%) who are computer literate. This section investigates IT segments such as recruitment, cultural heritage services, e-commerce and training to form a picture of the British Caribbean contribution to the knowledge economy of the UK.

Chapter 13 assesses how the standards of education and training are being aided by the presence of settler communities whose members are both professional and entrepreneurial in outlook. The constant lament about underachievement affecting Caribbean boys in particular since the 1960s, was the catalyst for the establishment of a variety of educational organisations and groups – some of which became formal instruction centres. The increase in training firms by Caribbean professionals turned entrepreneurs, has also added stimulus to the necessity for employee or staff development training, with a culturally sensitive approach. This chapter considers the work of over a dozen firms that are market leaders in education and training in the UK, and looks at the challenges and opportunities in this sector, as well.

Chapter 14 focuses on the global recognition the NHS enjoys since its creation in the 1940s. It highlights too, the contribution by Caribbean settlers to medicare at the start of the 20th century (1907), although seen in the wider context of Imhotep, the real *`Father of Medicine'* and the healthcare enterprise legacy left by Mary Seacole. Various industry segments are profiled, emphasising the diversity, professionalism and experience of operatives in the UK, providing services to clients from a multi-ethnic background. The disadvantage black professionals face in gaining entry into the more scientific and technology-based medicare market is also examined. A framework showing both challenges and prospects is presented as a future strategy for small-scale operators who are keen to increase market share in their respective segments of health and social care.

Chapter 15 looks at the emergence of social enterprise by defining its role and function in the context of American and European operating models. The concept of social enterprises as not-for-profit, trading companies with social objective aims, is also defined in a British situation. This evolution is further evident by a diverse range of British Caribbean community organisations and groups operating throughout the UK since the early 1930s, starting with the League of Coloured People. This penultimate chapter profiles 100 different groups consisting of faith organisations, community centres, professional associations, business networks and a variety of other community-based organisations that have all demonstrated amazing longevity despite limited funding, slender resources and competition by reputable charities that possess huge budgets. This chapter demonstrates once again, the vitality of Caribbean professionals and activists who are among Britain's leading social entrepreneurs, as they seek to bolster diverse communities with their latent creativity and resilience.

Section III consists of **Chapter 16** that unveils a British Caribbean SME Strategy for the 21st century by providing a foundation for sustaining this sector. This section recommends a comprehensive business planning and development model that business leaders should pursue to improve their economic participation in the British economy and the world as whole. Much of the elements are applicable to multi-sector agencies, institutions and organisations across the political and social divide, covering culture, education, enterprise, regeneration, social affairs, skills training, spatial planning, skills training and the environment.

Noteworthy, when this book was first planned in the late 1990s, the general idea was to write an expansive account on Caribbean businesses, but having scrutinized existing material and collaborated with businesses, customers, and worked with public agencies and institutions and a range of networks, I recognised that an indepth look at the British Caribbean firm by a sector-by-sector approach was urgent. Further, it was apparent because of the recognition by leading commercial banks such as Barclays, NatWest and Lloyds regarding the increasing formation of Caribbean firms, and the implicit Central Government directive, instructing Regional Development Agencies to include minority firms in regional strategy. Of course, there are primary aims and objectives of this book and they include:

- To provide valuable information and data on British Caribbean firms;
- To document the contribution of Britain's modern entrepreneurs;
- To profile growth sectors of British Caribbean firms;
- To publicise the work of minority business leaders; and
- To show the impact of British Caribbean firms on the UK economy.

In 2002, while addressing a public meeting including Party faithfuls, then Minister for Small Business, Nigel Griffiths MP, publicly declared and endorsed the growth of the British Caribbean SME sector and its contribution to the UK. He emphasised that it was equally important that this sector be further investigated and studied to give it greater credence and recognition, acknowledging that British Caribbean entrepreneurs led in `business formation rates' and were among the most `highly qualified and experienced business people' in the country:

My government takes very seriously the concerns of small businesses, including Caribbean firms, in their quest for excellence. We don't have sufficient evidence to determine the extent to which their contribution affects every sector of the economy. My department is committed to ensure that all SMEs are provided support so that they can realise their real potential and value. I am therefore happy to work with these businesses through their various networks to ensure that members and their organisations enjoy sustainable growth **(Griffiths 2002)**.

Indeed, the Scottish-born Minister's intervention couldn't have been more opportune; in effect, his timing was absolutely perfect since the idea of publicly acclaiming British Caribbean entrepreneurial success was not in vogue - regarded as insignificant and somewhat irrelevant from a media purview. Whether the official line was a sign of things to come, was another matter, but what remains now, is for the history and contribution of British Caribbean businesses and social enterprises to be fully publicised within a sectoral framework. Effectively, this book is a valid representation and a major triumph of this enterprise fact.

Selected References

1. Gyekye, Elizabeth: Black History Month, *Guardian Unlimited Limited* September 3, 2004, London.
2. Jillings, Sarah: London exhibit marks immigration century, *BBC Caribbean* March 23, 2005).
3. Dyde, Brian (1997): *The Empty Sleeve: The story of the West Indian Regiments of the British Army,* Hansib Caribbean, St. John's Antigua, WI.
4. Office for National Statistics, London 2005.
5. *Employment and Ethnicity*, Commission for Racial Equality Fact File 1, 2005.

6. Global Entrepreneurial Monitor, London 2006.

7. Report on Financing Ethnic Minority Firms, Bank of England 1999.

8. Waldinger, R; Aldrich, H and Ward, R (1990): Ethnic Entrepreneurs, Sage, London.

9. Kazuka, Martin w (1981): *Why so few Black Businesses*? Hackney Council for Racial Equality, London.

10. Leo, F (1981): *Ethnic Minorities and Small Firms*, London Borough of Lambeth.

11. Johnson, C.A. and Kayada, B (1997): Challenges and Prospects, Review of the Black Business Association 1987-1997, London.

12. Ram, Monder and Smallbone, D (2001): *Ethnic Minority Enterprise: Policy in Practice*, Final Report for the Small Business Service', London.

13. *Ready for Business: The contribution of black businesses to the London economy*, London Development Agency, 2004.

14. *Performance Review: Final Report,* Black Business Association, West Midlands, England 2005.

15. *Engaging Ethnic Enterprise*: speech delivered by Nigel Griffiths MP, 13th February 2002.

16. Policy Development Plan 2005-2010, National African and Caribbean Business Council.

17. Noon, Mike (2005): Ethnic minorities in work: conceptual and empirical challenges, De Montfort University, Leicester, England.

18. Poole, G (1979): Development in the West Indies and Migration to Canada, PhD Dissertation, Department of Anthropology, Mc Gill University.

19. Rhyme, D: `Some Factors Facing Non-White Entrepreneurs in Toronto', Currents, Vol 1, No. 1, 1983.

20. `100 Years of Black Business', Part II, *The Black Collegiate Magazine*, USA 2005.

21. Zeller, R.E (1981): Minority Economic Development and the Entrepreneur: Government Policies for the Location of Minority Businesses, Florida State University USA.

22. The Changing Face of Britain: Ethnic Minorities in the UK, Lloyds TSB 2004.

23. Johnson, C.A (2002): *The Caribbean Contribution to Britain and the*

Commonwealth, paper presented on the occasion of the Queen's Golden Jubilee, TCS Tutorial College, London.

24. Sullivan, Wilf (2006): `The place of race at work', *The Voice*, April 10-16, p 42, London.
25. Gilroy, P (1987): *There Ain't No Black in the union Jack: The Cultural Politics of Race and Nation*, Chicago, Chicago University Press.
26. Hall, Stuart (1980): `Race, Accumulation and Societies Structured in Dominance' in UNESCO, Ed, *Sociological Theories: Race and Colonisation*, Paris: UNESCO, pp 305-45.
27. Layton-Henry, Zig (1992): *The Politics of Immigration*, Oxford, Blackwell

Chapter 1

Historical Background

Introduction

Businesses Caribbean Enterprises: A Century of Challenges and Successes couldn't be written without reference to the history of the Caribbean Region. It is important to assess the impact of the political and socio-economic systems there during the colonial period, on the one hand, and the post-independent era on the other hand. The main aim is to provide a brief account of the events that shaped the Caribbean over the past 500 years.

The term `*Caribbean*' derives from the Amerindian word `*Carib*' (the original inhabitants). It also refers to the `*West Indies*' a term that was first used in the late 15th century. Caribbean history is complex and at first glance it may seem easy to tell, but further study reveals something far different – a mixture of legend, myth and distortion. From Columbus' so-called "discovery" to the development of a "tourist paradise", (the earlier period of) Caribbean history is characterised by (cultural) genocide, destruction, slavery, indenturehip and colonisation. In fact, if anyone "discovered" the Caribbean, it was the aboriginal groups, not Columbus. For reader identification, the terms `Caribbean' and `West Indian' will be used interchangeably to explain various periods of development – the pre-colonial, colonial and post-colonial, independent epochs. Notably, the region is comparatively, the most stable zone of peace and stability, worldwide.

The Caribbean is located at the southern equator of the Americas in the Caribbean Sea and its geography is extremely intricate because of European colonialism which created links and barriers between the island-territories without regard for their actual distances from each other, and left the region split into Spanish, British, French and Dutch entities. The Caribbean territories are curve southward from the bottom tip of Florida to the northwest of Venezuela to South America. There are at least 7,000 islands, islets, reefs and cays in the region.

In defining the Caribbean it is important to combine historical, cultural, linguistic and geographical features. While there are many factors which distinguish individual or groups of islands from each other, all have a similar geography. For example, with the exception of Guyana, the shores of all Caribbean countries and their territories are washed by the Caribbean Sea. The other similarity is their colonial past.

Although the English-speaking Caribbean has a population of over six million, the wider Caribbean Island Nations have an overall population of more than 30 million comprising Africans, Indians, Amerindians, Chinese, Portuguese and other ethnic groups. In effect, therefore, the region is a melting pot of cultures, histories and geography **(Table 1.1**).

Table 1.1 Selected Caribbean Countries by Population and Languages

(Source: World Factbook 2005)

Country	Population	Official Language	Spoken Languages
Anguilla *	13, 155	English	English, some Spanish
Antigua and Barbuda	71, 823	English	English and local dialects
Bahamas	330,602	English	English and Creole
Barbados	266,731	English	English
Belize	301,746	English	English, Spanish, Mayan, Garifuna and Creole
Bermuda *	65,365	English	English and Portuguese
British Virgin Islands	21,998	English	English
Cayman Islands *	48,859	English	English
Cuba +	11,326,354	Spanish	Spanish
Dominica	71,369	English	English and French patois
Grenada	110,429	English	English and French patois
Guyana	767, 245	English	English and Creole (African, Hindu)
Haiti	8,301,478	French	French, Creole
Jamaica	2,692,569	English	English, Patois (Creole)
Montserrat	9, 439	English	English
Saint Kitts and Nevis	39,487	English	English
Saint Lucia	168,458	English	English, French patois
Saint Vincent and The Grenadines	117,848	English	English, French patois
Trinidad and Tobago	1,088, 644	English	English, Hindustani, Spanish, Creole, French
Turks and Caicos Islands *	20,566	English	English

Notes: The above countries are members of the regional grouping, the Caribbean Community or Caricom which was established in July 1973 in Port-of-Spain, the capital of Trinidad and Tobago. Those countries with the asterisks hold membership of the Association of Caribbean States or the ACS which was formalized in July 1994 in Cartagena de Indias, Colombia, comprising 25 Members States and three Associate Members. Eight other non-independent Caribbean countries are eligible for associate membership. Although most of the Caribbean states' official language is English, even in former British colonies, citizens speak a variety of 'Englishes' ranging from Standard English to local and national Creole dialect forms.

In their attempt to gain ultimate control of the natural resources of the non-industrialized world, Europeans used racism to plunder and commit genocide which led to the near decimation of the Amerindian population and the eventual colonization of peoples of African and Indian origin in particular. Other racial groups including the Chinese, Portuguese and other mixed groups became part of the wider assimilated nationalities across the region. Scholars - Eric Williams, Clive Thomas and George Beckford - have written extensively on slavery, indentureship and colonialism. Explaining the turbulent events during that period, Thomas wrote:

All these events took place during the commercial phase of capitalist development in Europe, when the emphasis was on market expansion, the simple exchange of commodities already produced and the seizure of treasure and surplus produce from others. In this phase, the Caribbean provided an important source of primitive accumulation for Europe (**Thomas 1988**).

Eric Williams also pointed out that:

The slave trade kept the metropolitan industry turning; it gave sustenance to new industries based on the of processing of colonial raw materials; it yielded large profits which were ploughed back into the metropolitan industry; and it gave rise to unprecedented commerce in the West Indies and made the Caribbean territories among the most valuable colonies the world has ever known (**Williams 1970**).

Colonization and Independence

Some islands changed hands more than 20 times during the Caribbean wars. Europeans waged war among themselves and with the Carib Indians. Spanish explorers wiped out the Arawak tribe as they plundered the Caribbean for gold in the 16th century. It wasn't until the Emancipation Act of 1834 ended slavery and Europe no longer relied on the islands for sugar production that the Caribbean became less of a fighting prize; however, the lasting European influence in the Caribbean is evinced by this colonization timeline:

- 1496 – the Spanish founded settlements in Hispaniola;
- 1508 - the Spanish founded settlements in Puerto Rico;
- 1515 - the Spanish founded settlements in Cuba;
- 1554 – the Dutch plundered Santiago de Cuba;
- 1555 – the French plunder Havana;
- 1586 - Santo Domingo surrendered to the British;
- 1595 - the British took over San Juan;
- 1628 - the Dutch captured the Spanish silver fleet off Cuba;
- 1634 – the Dutch seized Curacao;
- 1635 - the French acquired Martinique;
- 1655 – the British commandeered Jamaica from Spain; and.
- 1565 – the French occupied half of Hispaniola and called it Haiti.

Forced Labour

Slavery began in the 18th century when European importers demanded high quantities of sugar, the product of sugarcane, which grew easily in the Caribbean's temperate weather. As demand for sugar increased, so did the demand for plantation labor. The indigenous Arawaks were the Europeans' original slaves but they were quickly dying out. By this time slavery was a fixture in European and Arab countries. Many new slaves from Africa's Guinea coast were shipped to the West Indies via the notorious Middle Passage -a horrendous mode of transport in which slaves were packed into the ship's hold so tightly that they could not move freely and sometimes suffocated to death. They were used as pawns in the infamous Triangular Trade: European ships set sail for the Caribbean colonies with bartering goods, arms, and liquor for African slave traders; slaves were captured and shipped from Africa to the islands; and in the final step, sugar and rum were exported from the Caribbean back to Europe **(Barreiro 1990).**

In the 1770s, anti-slavery movements began to take shape in Europe. The Society for the Abolition of Slavery was established in 1787 to raise public awareness of the inhumane treatment of slaves. It wasn't until 1807, however, that a law was passed banning the trade of slaves on British ships. A massive anti-slavery rebellion in Jamaica destroyed many sugar estates, motivating Parliament to sanction the Emancipation Act of 1834. After a four-year "apprenticeship" during which the slaves were still bound to plantation life, they were released unconditionally. Cuba was still importing slaves until 1865, and did not officially abolish slavery until 1888.

Despite their appalling condition including their inability to exercise (freedom of) choice as normal human beings, there was an aspiration to become liberated one day through the access of land property. And so it was, many freed slaves purchased land for subsistence farming, but on some of the smaller Caribbean islands, there was little land left to buy, so free labourers had to return to the plantation. Slavery was then followed by indentureship – the importation of Indians from the Southern part of India, Chinese from Hong Kong and Portuguese from Madeira.

Indentureship

According to the planters in Britain's tropical territories, there was a 'crisis' of labour in the colonies in the post-Emancipation period, after 1834. The problem originated at the time of the abolition of the African Slave Trade, in 1807. Britain faced the problem of acquiring continuous supplies of cheap and easily controlled labour for its slave-less colonial plantations.

One of the problems the planters encountered was the reluctance of freed Africans and their descendants to work on the plantations. 'How could sugar be produced without slaves?' remained the nagging question. By 1838, plans were already underway to exploit the labour resources of India by means of indentureship. Observers, such as the

Anti-slavery Society feared that this form of labour control would be abused, coming as it did so soon after emancipation.

Thus in the wake of the African slaves, there followed a traffic involving 'Coolie ships' from India, which carried Indian indentured labourers to replace African slaves on the Caribbean plantations. From the time the first shipment of indentured Indians arrived in Guyana in 1838 until 1917, more than half a million Indians were transported to the Caribbean. During the early years of this emigration, the long and hazardous voyages were undertaken in relatively small ships, and the mortality rate was high, reaching its peak in the 1850s.

In Trinidad where the first batch of Indians had arrived in 1845, there was provision made under the system of indentureship on key issues, for example, labour and wages, leave and desertion, free wage-labour and indentured labour, grievance procedure, relations between employers and labourers, and free labour. Despite new reforms, the deplorable social and economic conditions of Indians subject to the indentureship system led to official inquiries and reports detailing the Indians' problems such the one in 1914 report on the condition of Indian immigrants in Jamaica and in Trinidad. Today, Indians can be found in Guyana, Jamaica, Trinidad and Tobago and the smaller English-speaking Caribbean territories.

As bonded labourers, poorly paid Indians were caught in a cycle of poverty and indebtedness to their employers and often, like their predecessors the African slaves, they were engaged in continuous resistance against their oppressors. Perhaps surprisingly, the experience of indentureship strengthened the resolve of the majority of Indians (approximately two-thirds) to remain in the Caribbean and make their homes there. Through schools and churches set up by the Canadian missionaries - John Morton and Kenneth Grant – most indentured Indians were educated and many were converted from Islam and Hinduism to Christianity both during indentureship and after its abolition in 1917 **(Royal Geographical Society 1931).**

Although slavery and indentureship were over, Europeans still contested for control of the region and the Caribbean economy remained virtually agricultural in nature, tied to the fetters of European capitals, with little thought given to the process of industrialization by modernizing the agricultural or plantation economy to revitalize the regional economy. Today, the Caribbean is suffering from the side-effects of colonialism, added to the poor returns for exports which have a corresponding impact on under-investment in goods and services. It was left to the Caribbean `elite' – the well-educated and committed nationalists, political activists and trade unionist and professionals- to start the campaign to secure Political Independence from Britain.

It should be noted however, that the Caribbean was dominated for centuries by European powers; namely, the British, French, Spanish, Dutch and Portuguese; however, it was Spain that devised a formula for European conquest, including the infamous `*mercantile system'* that exploited and decimated Amerindians. With a reduced population, the Spanish transported slave labour from West Africa, thereby forming the bedrock of Europe's *Industrial Revolution* during much of the 17th and 19th centuries.

The Industrial Revolution originally referred to the developments that transformed Great Britain, between 1750 and 1830, from a largely rural population making a living almost entirely from agriculture to a town-centered society engaged increasingly in factory manufacture. Other European nations underwent the same process soon thereafter, followed by others during the 19th century, and still others (such as Russia and Japan) in the first half of the 20th century. In some countries this transformation is only now taking place or still lies in the future. **(BBC 2005)**

Self-Government

In 1876 the British attempted a quasi-type Federation in the West Indies to maintain political control over the colonies. Only about three per cent (mostly the elite class) in the Caribbean were entitled to vote. By the 1930s the world suffered the Great Depression which was triggered by the stock market crash in the US after a boom in the market in the 1920s. Businessmen and economists alike felt that the Federal Reserve would stabilise the economy, but this bet did not pay off. The crisis threw the American economy in turmoil, with cost of living rising, consumables increased, workers were sacked and the recession affected fragile regional economies like those in the West Indies.

Elsewhere in the non-English speaking Caribbean, Cuba and Puerto Rico were ceded to the United States in the late 19th century, and Cuba gained its independence in 1901, but independence for all the island nations wasn't a legitimate prospect until the 1960s. The French possessions remained departments of France; citizens of these islands have the same rights and privileges as citizens of Burgundy or Province. In 1962, Jamaica and Trinidad and Tobago became independent states within the British Commonwealth; Barbados did the same four years later. Next came independence for Antigua, Barbuda, Redonda, Anguilla, St. Kitts and Nevis, St. Lucia, St. Vincent, and Dominica.

Today, the islands continue to build on this self-reliance. Led by trade unionists and would-be statesmen - T.A. Marryshow (Grenada), Hubert Nathaniel Critchlow (Guyana) Alexander Bustamante (Jamaica) and Albert Cipriani (Trinidad) the first blow was struck for political freedom. In effect, the labour movement became a catalyst for self-rule in the Caribbean. Self-government became a necessity for the following reasons:

- The need for an independent political system;
- The establishment of an economic union;
- Cultural unity and social cohesion; and
- The dismantling of British rule.

However, if the Caribbean thought it had seen the back of colonialism with the collapse of the British Empire, it witnessed neo-colonialism in disguise with the resurgence of US imperialist expansionism in the Americas. To illustrate its ambitions, the US Government ordered military intervention in Panama (1979) and Grenada (1983) under the pretext of protecting US interests. On December 17, 1989 U.S. President George Bush (Snr) ordered troops to Panama, with the subsequently announced aims of seizing Noriega to face drug charges in the United States, protecting American lives and property, and restoring Panamanian liberties.

The American invasion of Grenada was the first major U.S military operation since the Vietnam War. In part, it may have been a test of the so-called "Vietnam syndrome," the purported "affliction" that makes it difficult for the American public to support U.S. military intervention without a just cause. In Grenada's case, the justification was the protection of American lives and the Reagan administration falsely claimed that the island's only operating airport – Point Salines - was closed. By limiting the ability of Americans who wished to depart from leaving, the US could then use its continued presence in Grenada as an excuse to invade (**Zunes 2002**).

A New Dawn

Nevertheless, this imperial nightmare did not daunt the spirit of hopeful West Indians, even in the face of the collapse of both the West Indian Federation and the Caribbean Free Trade Association (CARIFTA). In spite of the fragile economy and low-skilled workforce, the educated middle class comprising the political elite, broke through and in 1973, the Caribbean Community and Common Market (CARICOM) was established. **(Table 1.2)**

Table 1.2 The Post-independent Caribbean

*(**Source:** The London Diplomatic List, 2003, Foreign & Commonwealth Office)*

Independent Territories	European Overseas Territories
Antigua and Barbuda	**France:**
Bahamas	Dominican Republic
Barbados	Guadeloupe
Belize	Martinique
Cuba	
Dominica	**Netherlands Antilles:**
Grenada	Aruba
Guyana	Bonaire
Haiti	Curacao
Jamaica	St. Maarten
Saint Lucia	
Saint Kitts & Nevis	**Britain:**
Saint Vincent & The Grenadines	Anguilla
Suriname	British Virgin Islands
US Protectorate	Cayman Islands
Bermuda	Montserrat
Puerto Rico	St. Helena
US Virgin Islands	Turk & Caicos

Notes: Apart from Haiti and Cuba, several other colonies in the Caribbean Region secured political independence from the British, Dutch and French, with more than a dozen others operating as either departments or protectorates of American and European powers. Nationals have used this situation to great advantage by claiming dual or multiple identities in their quest for political, economic and social advancement – either in their own country or overseas.

Such was the achievement of both the trade union movement and the diplomatic skills of the fast rising political leadership, that prior to Caricom, Trinidad (1962) Jamaica (1962) and Guyana (1966) gained independence from Britain. This solidarity rekindled the belief in political and economic unification, a vision that activated an unprecedented burst of enterprise in the modern Caribbean region, which migrants brought to the shores of the metropolis in North America and Europe, including Britain. Even by today's standards, political independence is not a palliative cure for the economic ills of the Caribbean society, a fact that was recognized by regional `independent emancipators' such as T.A. Marryshow (Grenada) and Alexander Bustamante (Jamaica), Captain Arthur Andrew Cipriani (Trinidad and Tobago), Hubert Nathaniel Critchlow (Guyana) and Sir Grantley Adams (Barbados)

Political Traditions

The vibrant political traditions of the Caribbean could be classified into two broad categories: the Anglo-Caribbean and the Latin American traditions. The Anglo-Caribbean tradition includes those systems influenced by British political culture and institutions – Barbados, Guyana, Jamaica, Trinidad and Tobago, as well as the Eastern Caribbean territories. The Latin-Caribbean tradition refers to political systems which are influenced by continental Europe, specifically Spain, France and the Netherlands. Cuba, Haiti and Surname are part of Caricom.

In contrast to the Latin American arena, the Anglophone-Caribbean has a long history of stable democratic government and in the 17th century; a form of representative government was instituted under an old representative system of planter class. Later, the countries moved to self-government under nationalist leaders. The Governments of Latin America have tended to be less democratic, with Haiti, Suriname, the Dominican Republic and Cuba (until 1959), experiencing military upheavals during the 19th and 20th centuries respectively.

With respect to forms of state, like most regions of the world, the Caribbean is divided into monarchies and republics, with the majority of states maintaining monarchial rule with the Queen of the United Kingdom as ceremonial Head of State. However, there are some republics; namely, Cuba, Dominican Republic, Guyana, Suriname, Trinidad and Tobago. Guyana has an Executive Presidency, with the Prime Minister as head of the Cabinet. Suriname has a Presidency that is vested with extensive powers, while Trinidad and Tobago has a ceremonial-type Presidency, with many powers falling under the office the Prime Minister. Other island-states have a combination of Governor-Generalships and Prime Ministers who have executive powers in their respective provinces. Interestingly, only the twin-island of St. Kitts and Nevis has a federal state system of government **(Table 1. 3).**

Proportional Representation or `PR' has been a contentious issue since the beginning of the Independent Movement in the Caribbean and Latin America. It is generally accepted that while it may be workable, even appropriate for the UK and other Western democracies, it has failed to provide the necessary structures for the socio-economic advancement of smaller states in the Caribbean. The dominance of the two-party system is evident in both Britain (Conservative versus Labour) and the US (Democrats versus the Republicans). The system excludes smaller parties that are at the mercy of `tribal' politics and the media's obsession with sound-bites. In 2002, the Guyanese People's National Congress Reform Party submitted a proposal for shared governance to widen participation and representation in the legislative, executive and administrative arms of the State. This proposition reflected the dilemma which the PR system poses for English-speaking Caribbean countries in particular.

Ministerial portfolios will be allocated proportionally to those parties who get at least five per cent of the vote so if one party gets fifty-one per cent of the votes, another 43% and the rest less than five per cent each, the first two will divide ministerial portfolios between them. This will be done by agreement if possible but if discussion fails to produce agreement, the selection process will be achieved by alternate picks, the party with the largest vote having the first pick. There will be a non-executive president as head of state appointed by a multi-party vote in parliament for a term of seven, which, to use the language of the document, "straddles the holding of national elections and reduces the pressure the office-holder to pander to the parties in hopes of reappointment." The parties involved in the government will sign a Coalition Agreement that will include a policy platform based on the national development programme and ideas from party manifestos, portfolio allocation and party responsibilities and the decision-making structure and procedures in the executive **(Hinds 2002).**

Table 1. 3 Model Political Systems by Caribbean Countries

(World Factbook, 2005)

Country	System of Government
• Barbados	Parliamentary democracy with executive authority invested in the Prime Minister who is appointed by the Governor General. The bicameral Parliament consists of an Upper House or the senate and a Lower House.
• Guyana	Democratic Republic with the President as head of state and Prime Minister, head of government – a British -style Proportional Representation system is entrenched in the political culture.
• Jamaica	Constitutional parliamentary democracy with a Governor General representing the Queen as Head State. The Prime Minister presides over the Senate and House of representatives.
• Trinidad and Tobago	Republic, President elected by an electoral college consisting of the Senate and House of Representatives.

• Organisation of Eastern Caribbean States (*Antigua and Barbuda, Dominica, Grenada, Montserrat, Saint Kitts and Nevis, Saint Lucia, Saint Vincent and the Grenadines. Anguilla an Overseas Territory of the UK, is an Associate Member*	Inherited the Westminster model of governance, anchored on a two-party system of popular representation which forms the basis of a parliamentary house involving the ruling government and an official opposition.

Note: Almost every Caribbean country has a multi-party system in which there is an official Opposition, with regular elections held to ensure that Governments are accountable to the electorate and are monitored by various segments and sections of their respective societies. .

Gender Politics

Since the last half of the 20th century women have dominated global politics, with the Caribbean fashioning exemplary leadership in times of economic crisis, social disunity and other structural difficulties. The elections of Jamaican Portia Simpson-Miller as the first female Prime Minister of the ruling People's National Party in the early part of 2006, was a unique development in the shifting role of gender politics in the Americas. The fact that non-European women are making inroads in a still, conservatively male-dominated institution is illuminating in the modern Caribbean. The veteran Simpson-Miller was elected as result of her grassroots credentials and voter confidence, coupled with her political savvy. In 2007, she subsequently lost the General Elections to the main Opposition Party. Yet instinctively, Caribbean women politicians demonstrate qualities of leadership, management, creativity and style in different settings – much of these were evident during the post-independent era, the 1980s and 1990s when agro-dependent economies suffered decline in export commodities and protectionist measures imposed by the developed North. This period was marked too, by strict conditionalities imposed by Western financial institutions such as the IMF/World Bank.

Besides, the new Jamaican leader, other women have made significant inroads into the highly contested political theatre in the Caribbean and they include Janet Jagan (Guyana) Kamla Persad-Bissessar (Trinidad and Tobago), Billie Miller (Barbados), Grace Duncan (Grenada), Cynthia A. Pratt (Bahamas) and Dame Lois Marie Browne-Ewans (Bermuda).

The indomitable Dame Eugenia, who was the first female PM in the Caribbean, was dubbed the *`Iron Lady of the Caribbean'* because of her ambition, drive and doggedness. American-born Janet Jagan was the first female President of an English-speaking Commonwealth country until 1999 after succeeding her late husband, Dr. Cheddi Jagan. Bissessar was the first woman in Trinidad and Tobago to serve as acting PM in 2000 while holding the position of Attorney General. Billie Miller was Deputy Leader of the Barbadian Opposition in 1993-94, and was replaced recently by the amiable Attorney-General, Mia Mottley. Dame Hilda Bynoe became the first Governor of the Caribbean Commonwealth, having served her native Grenada from 1968-1974. Dame Nita Barrow was Governor General of Barbados 1990 -1995.

Africa's remarkable history of female-dominated Royal personages as early as the 14th century Egyptian period is experiencing a resurgence with the 2005 election of Liberia and Africa's first female modern head-of-state, Ellen Johnson-Sirleaf. And since the latter part of the 20th century, the Indian-subcontinent has produced leaders such as Indira Gandhi (India), Benazir Bhutto (Pakistan), Srimavo Bandaranaike and daughter, Chandrika Kumaratunga (Sri Lanka), as well as Khaleda Zia and Sheikh Hasina (Bangladesh). Indeed women in Africa, the Caribbean and the Indian subcontinent recognize that they have to compete in a male-dominated political atmosphere, but it is often the poor, the powerless and the voiceless that gravitate towards their human touch. In Western capitals, this trend is evolving too, as sections of the world's population show an increasing appetite for altering the masculine character of global politics, in a further attempt to preserve their strained democracies.

Generally, women have served with distinction in several capacities: Heads of State and Government, Chiefs of Governments of External Territories (British, Dutch, French, US), and Permanent Representatives and Ambassadors of the UN. According to the *World Classification List,* of the 137 states surveyed to date, women's representation in Caribbean Parliaments is rated at 11% or 15 countries. Before 1945, Austria was the only state to have elected a woman to the presidency of one of the Parliament's Chambers **(Table 1.4).** From that time to 1997, only 42 states of the 186 with a legislative institution have, at one time or another in recent history selected a woman to preside over Parliament: this has occurred 78 times. Of the 22 countries with `*Women Speakers of National Parliaments'*, the Caribbean polled 31% or 7 women speakers. The world figures suggested that overall; women occupied only 9.5% of the total number of 236 posts of Presiding Officers of Parliament or one of its Houses **(International Parliamentary Union 2006**).

Table 1.4 Women Parliamentarians in the Caribbean

(Source: Women in National Parliaments, the Inter-Parliamentary Union, Switzerland, March 2006)

Country	Lower House	Upper House or Senate	Number
• Antigua and Barbuda	10%	17%	5
• Bahamas	20%	43%	15
• Barbados	13%	23%	9
• Belize	6%	25%	5
• Cuba	36%	-	219
• Dominica	12%	-	4
• Dominican Republic	17%	6%	28

• Grenada	26%	30.8%	8
• Guyana	30%	-	20
• Haiti	3%	25%	10
• Jamaica	11%	19%	7
• Saint Lucia	5%	36%	5
• Saint Vincent & The Grenadines	18%	-	4
• Suriname	25.5%	-	13
• Trinidad and Tobago	19%	32%	17

Note: The Inter-Parliamentary Union (IPU) is the international organisation of Parliaments of sovereign States, established in 1889 with a membership of 140 countries. The Union is a focal point for world-wide parliamentary dialogue and works for peace and co-operation among peoples and for the firm establishment of representative democracy.

Noteworthy, if the increase of women in public life is anything to go by, then the rise in the number of British Caribbean women into commercial activities, illustrates the universal trend that despite continued inequalities, women have gradually crossed barriers to succeed. Official estimates on minority businesses in the UK suggest that Caribbean women have a high level of enterprise successes – up to 25% of the national average which is 22%.

In addition, numerous agencies and institutions influence political and socio-economic development in the Caribbean Region. They perform diverse functions such as enabling governments to access intellectual and professional resources, as well as facilitating non-governmental organizations (NGOs) or civic groups to input into a range of activities. The major institutions include the:

- *Caribbean Disaster Emergency Response Agency (1991)* to make an immediate and coordinated response to any disastrous event affecting any Caribbean State.
- *Caribbean Agricultural Research and Development insitute (1975)* – to serve the agricultural research and development needs of the Caribbean.

- *Caribbean Examinations Council* (1972) – to replace overseas secondary exams; regulates the conduct of exams and prescribes qualfication requirements of candiates.
- *Caribbean Epideomology Centre* (1975) – public health information, service and consulting organisation dedicated to improving the health status of Caribbean people.
- *Caribbean Meterological Institute* (1967) – to improve, develop meterological/ hydrological services, awareness of these benefits to Caricom Member States.
- *Caribbean Food Corporation* (1976) - a lead agency to implement the Regional Food Plan, invest in traditional-non-traditional agricultural, as well as as other enteprrises.
- *Association of Caribbean Community Parliamentarians* (1989) – to encourage and stimulate Caribbean democracy through various structures and processes.
- *Caribbean Food and Nutrition Institute* (1967) – set up to develop a regional approach towards solving the decline in nutritional, health standards among the poor.
- *Caricom Regional Organisation for Standards and Quality* (2003) – an inter-governmental organization mandated to harmonise and implement standards to facilitate international competitiveness.

Migration Issue

Caribbean citizens make up a significant segment of the population in Britain and Canada. In the US, they number over 22 million, in Canada 800,000 and in Britain over 500,000. Population analysts suggest that these figures will rise over the next 10 to 20 years, even though unofficial reports refer to a trickling return of nationals who have made good, financially. Caribbean communities are concentrated in cities, towns and suburbs. In Britain for example, they are dotted around inner cities and areas where there are relative '*comfort zones*' (residential areas where peace, security and community safety are guaranteed **(*Caribbean Business Community Island* 2003).**

The outflow of Caribbean nationals to `*greener pastures*' in North America and Europe resulted from several factors; the downturn of the regional economy, poor pay, unemployment, coupled with the urge to improve personal economic well-being. Since 1991, Caribbean governments have been working relentlessly to reduce public sector bureaucracy, including the removal of subsidies from loss-making state enterprises. However, it is doubtful whether in such circumstances, sufficient labour can be found to compensate for deficits in the economy and the continued out-migration of skilled professionals.

Another important reason for the contraction of the Caribbean economy in recent times was the decline in exports such as oil and sugar and other agricultural products, textiles and other raw materials. Thus migration is seen as a safety valve (**Maingot 1994**). A solution to deal with this crisis seems to be hinged on the following: -

- Enhance the productive capacity of non-traditional sectors of the economy.
- Re-skill displaced employees or create actual deployment.
- Invest more in growing businesses to rekindle enterprise in poor areas.

Caribbean Governments recognise that reducing migration is not a simple solution, since there is a parallel relationship between the nature of development and the numbers leaving the region. The approaches mentioned above are being pursued as part of an ongoing process of restructuring various economies. Compared to other regions and countries, Caribbean migration rates exceed 80% among nationals in Guyana, Grenada, Haiti and St. Vincent and The Grenadines **(Table 1.5)**.

In a study covering more than 300 countries during 1990 and 2000 to measure the levels of emigration `stocks' and rates of educational attainment among migrants, the authors noted that proportionately, the Caribbean labour force showed the *'highest skilled migration rates'* among developing states, followed by Central America, Western and Middle and Eastern Africa. **(Docquier and Marfouk 2005)**

Table 1. 5 Caribbean countries with emigration rates and educational attainment

(Source: National Fund for Scientific Research, March 2005)

Country	Emigration rates	Educational attainment
• Antigua & Barbuda	66.8%	48.3%
• Bahamas, The	61.2%	52.4%
• Barbados	63.5%	43.3%
• Belize	65.5%	41.3%
• Cuba	28.7%	38.6%
• Dominica	64.2%	37.8%
• Dominican Republic	21.6%	26.5%
• Grenada	85.1%	40.9%
• Guyana	89%	44.2%
• Haiti	83.6%	39%
• Jamaica	85.1%	42.8%
• St. Kitts & Nevis	78.5%	44.4%
• St. Lucia	71.1%	36.8%
• St. Vincent & The Grenadines	84.5%	42.7%
• Suriname	47.9%	18.4%
• Trinidad & Tobago	79.3%	51%

Notes: the above represents higher level of emigration rates and high 'selection rate' of educational attainment for the 2000 period, all of which reflect the extent to which Caribbean émigrés, since the early 20th century, have been investing their intellectual, professional and other resources into Western capitals to improve their general well-being despite the prejudices confronting most of them. The Caribbean countries above, hold membership of the Caricom Community.

While it is overstated that the *brain-drain* is nothing new to the Caribbean, the price is great, since it represents wasted investment in human capital. During the 1970s and 1980s, between 6% and 7% of the total workforce in the region emigrated overseas. In the case of Jamaica, migration to the US and Canada showed an increase. Of the 5,000 emigrants from Guyana each year, nearly 300 were high-level skilled persons and professionals (**Sackey 1978; Boodhoo and Baksh 1981: 59**).

In Trinidad and Tobago the proportion of skilled migrants in the 1960s were higher and it was estimated the general trend with 17,200 rising slowly at first in 1962, showed the largest movements among clerical and administrative employees, teachers, along with healthcare personnel, engineers and technicians (**Harewood 1983: 25**).

With respect to the UK, migratory trends among Caribbean nationals have decreased following the removal of the 1962 open entry regulations for Caribbean Commonwealth citizens. Specific categories include the dependants of previous migrants and those with work permits in required occupations, or recruited employees such as nurses and more recently, teachers. The number of Commonwealth Caribbean citizens fell from just over 30,000 between 1955 and 1962 to approximately 15,000 by 1966, subsequently to 5,000 in the early 1970s and about 3,000 by 1984. there was an increase in 1986 to about 6,000 and then the numbers fell a year later to an annual volume of approximately 4,000 **(British Migration Census Division 1994)**.

Experts claim that migration has both a cost and benefit to the sender countries and recipient countries alike. Caribbean peoples' knack for upward mobility ensures the revitalisation of communities and their increasing tendency towards higher education and the propensity for risk-taking through enterprise is evidenced in the metropolis. Given their multicultural and multi-ethnic backgrounds, Caribbean people are not only a cementing force in industrialised societies, but they add to many strands to the fabric of the cultures. As a nation with nations, Caribbean peoples' rate of growth is faster than the national average. According to the North American media;

In effect, Caribbeans are now a very visible feature on the American, British, Canadian landscape especially, but elsewhere also. Indeed the Caribbean community has been a sleeping behemoth that is beginning to awaken (***The Caribbean Impact* 2003, USA).**

Remittances

The economic significance of Caribbean diasporic communities is further underscored by the fact that countries 'back home' receive more monies from financial remittances than from foreign investment and international aid. In territories like Jamaica and the Dominican Republic, remittances account for up to 10% or more of the GDP of emerging economies. Several studies have been done on this growing economy and many conclusions have been made in favour of remittances being used a 'development tool'. Remittances constitute a critical flow of foreign currency in the whole of Latin America and the Caribbean (LAC) Region. They have a great effect on national economies and a corresponding impact on domestic revenue, consumption and investment which are significant in reducing levels of poverty and deprivation, although money transfers, unregulated as they are, may not be the total answer to long-term stability in the Caribbean.

As migration patterns increase and reporting mechanisms from central Banks improve, remittance flows to the LAC Region reached over $US38 billion in 2003 from all parts of the world, implying 180 million transactions a year. Studies show that money transfers have substantially exceeded development assistance inflows to 19 countries and equal more than 150% of the interest paid on the total LAC external debt during the past five years. Accordingly, the Inter-American Development Bank reported that remittances account for at least 10% of GDP in six countries; namely, Haiti, Nicaragua, El Salvador, Jamaica, the Dominican Republic and Guyana **(IADB 2005).**

Overall, worker remittances flows to the LAC Region jumped from $US23 billion in 2001 to $US45 billion in 2004, demonstrating that migrants do invest in their home countries, both economically and socially, though the latter seems more of the case. At the current growth value projected, total remittances to LAC countries for 2000-2010 will be US$500 billion. In one particular international study, figures showed that the Caribbean had a market share of 7.5% between 2002 and 2003 of the total money transfers done during that period **(Table 1. 6).**

Table 1. 6 Caribbean: Trends in Remittances by Selected Countries

(Source: Lapointe, Michelle: Diasporas in Caribbean Development, the World Bank Report, August 2004

Year	2001	2002	2003	2004
Belize	N/A	N/A	73	77
Cuba	930	1,265	1,194	N/A
Dominican Republic	1,807	2,206	2,217	2,438
Guyana	N/A	119	137	143
Haiti	810	931	977	1,026
Jamaica	967	1,288	1,425	1,497
Trinidad and Tobago	N/A	59	88	93
Caribbean	4,514	5,868	6,038	N/A

Note: The above figures are quoted in $US millions. The absence of remittance figures for Belize in 2001-2002, Cuba 2004 and Trinidad and Tobago illustrates the complexity of this growth industry. Jamaica has the highest number of money transfers than any other English-speaking Caribbean country, with Guyana and Trinidad and Tobago coming second and third respectively. The Dominican Republic is the leading non-English speaking country n the region that has the highest number of remittances per annum, followed by Haiti. Countries with populations in excess of one million tend to have the greater volume of money transfers because of the larger number of nationals abroad.

Remittances and other (diasporic) exports are only one side of the diasporic economy and though it is an expanding source of income and resources to otherwise impoverished countries there is no clear evidence that these inflows outweigh the cost associated with migration. The cost of out-migration of and 'return' migration of nationals could also have adverse effects on the Caribbean.

Notable examples are (new) security and health risks associated with the deportation of criminals from the US and with the spread of HIV/AIDs from mobile populations like tourists, sex workers and migrants.

Yet, the notion of how remittances should be invested in `back home' economies remains a challenging prospect. Only in the last four years has there been any real attempt by international institutions to examine ways of regulating this growth industry. The fact is Caribbean Governments can assist the process by improving the efficiency of money transfers and setting up measures to ensure that such investments benefit recipients and others at risk of poverty or experiencing deprivation and exclusion in the labour market. For a start, the creation of a Micro enterprise Investment Fund (MIF) that stimulates both inward and investment opportunities and formalize the activities of the informal or parallel economy in certain parts of the Caribbean is critical. The following outcomes could be achieved by the MIF measure: -

- Promote entrepreneurial activities for the rural and suburban poor.
- Address the lack of enterprise skills, market access and critical seed capital.
- Open new possibilities the new use of information technology.
- Mobilize savings and turn earnings into equity.
- Securitize remittance flows to create low cost and longer-term capital.
- Research impact of senders especially women who comprise the bulk.

On a broader scale, national governments in collaboration with international agencies and institutions and multinational corporations, should investigate these possibilities:

- *SME Sector Development:* Help develop the capacity of SMEs in the Caribbean by providing producers more extensive information about the export market according to sectors.
- *Social investment funds:* Hometown Associations or HTAs should be involved in rural development and social investment programmes that are currently financed in the Caribbean.
- *Human Development:* Attention should be focused on health, education reform, and on vulnerable population affected by emigration including at-risk youth, female-headed households, and the elderly). Financial institutions should engage government agencies dealing with education, health and social welfare.
- *Banking sector reform:* Specialists in the World Bank and other such institutions should be consulted to see how their work on financial sector development can complement existing efforts to expand access to financial institutions in the Caribbean.

However, the presence of Caribbean diasporic communities plays a valuable role beyond remittances as markets for tourism as well as ethnic, specialty and niche exports. These resource-communities have long been key markets for artistic and cultural products that generate annual exports worth over US$ 100 million in Jamaica, Trinidad and Tobago and the Dominica Republic **(Nurse 2003a).** The growth of diasporic exports is also reflected in the migration of professional sports players, for example, baseball players from the Dominican Republic and track and field athletes, along with footballers and cricketers from the Anglophone Caribbean.

The main negative associated with migration is the problem of brain-drain of which the Caribbean has the highest in the world. The share of total migrants with tertiary education ranges from 22 percent in the case of the Dominican Republic to as much as 46 percent in Trinidad and Tobago. Importantly, the migration rate among the well educated is tremendous. In the case of Guyana, the migration rate among the well-educated classes is estimated at over 70 percent.

Other Anglophone Caribbean territories like Jamaica and Trinidad and Tobago also have migration rates over fifty percent (**Carrington and Detragiache 1998*)*.

The shift in labor markets in the core economies towards services also signals the 'feminization of migration' as women out-number men from labour exporting territories like Jamaica and the Dominican Republic. The departure of highly skilled migrants reduces productivity and creates labour gaps. This is illustrated by the loss of human resources that are not easily replaced, as is the case with the migration of teachers and medical professionals from the Caribbean such as the case of Guyana, Jamaica and Trinidad and Tobago that have lost nurses and teachers to the US and the UK in the last decade. Some of the labour gaps have been filled by the importation of doctors and nurses from Cuba that has a surplus in this sector.

While Caribbean people use formal channels to transfer monies to their home countries, the use of remitting agencies reduce costs to nationals on low income and help provide more efficient and trustworthy services than banks or formal money-sending services. Money transfer services, banks and credit unions have the potential to cut costs and introduce migrants and their families to the formal banking system. Some regional officials disagree that remittances should not be regarded as foreign aid, since an improvement in the region's stock exchanges can help accelerate business expansion in the Single Market Economy.

Caribbean people are increasingly better educated than before. Countries in the region have invested a lot of resources in their training and education. You must bear in mind the cost of educating people. So what we are seeing now is a return on that investment. It is absolutely the furthest thing you can get away from foreign aid. I suspect that as real foreign aid falls people are looking at ways to say that it doesn't matter. But it does matter when foreign aid falls because remittances are not a replacement for that. It's a return on our investment, which others took and which should be added to the aid that we get. A couple of years ago when official aid was falling some people said it didn't matter because foreign investment was taking its place. But foreign direct investment doesn't take the place. That should have been an additional element so that when you get the two together you can have enough capital (**Blake 2004).**

In addition, by forming *"hometown associations*" (HTAs) overseas nationals have retained cultural ties to their country of birth. The structures of these organizations however, vary depending on the nature of project activities in either the overseas-based country or in a specific Caribbean territory. While there is no published record of Caribbean HTAs performance in Britain, the geographic distribution of these associations is significant in terms of locational activities.

In an effort to include remittances as a contributory factor to labour and enterprise, surveys were conducted with different organizations to assess their linkages with their `back home' countries and the challenges to this new form of enterprise creativity. Most of the associations from the English-speaking nations of the Caribbean have more than half-a-dozen groups involved in different projects in Britain and in their home-countries. Some of the main features that emerged from these organizations were: -

(a) They offered a range of charitable support;
(b) Formed by people from the city and suburbs;
(c) They invest in education or relief help from natural disasters;
(d) They raise less than £20,000 per year; and
(e) Groups work with larger British-overseas based charities in the Caribbean **(Fig 1.1).**

Yet, despite the opportunities for out-migration, what is particularly frustrating for the Caribbean in general is not the number of nationals who leave, but the massive loss of well-educated professionals the region can ill-afford. It seems that a solution to the problem lies in greater solidarity between Caribbean citizens at home and nationals abroad and the linkages sender and recipient government institutions create. According to the World Bank:

Caribbean communities are increasingly transnational; they are no longer bounded by strict national borders. Diaspora members can play a role in the advancement of their home countries. There are a range of opportunities for the World Bank to take advantage of diaspora groups in development activities. Addressing the related but distinct issues of private family transfers, community donations, nostalgic markets, migrant investment and return migration will require flexible and innovative strategy – and a new dialogue among different sectors of the Bank and between the Bank and overseas communities **(World Bank 2004).**

Figure 1.1 British Caribbean Associations by UK Locations

(Source: Independent Surveys on Caribbean Organisations, 2002/2007)

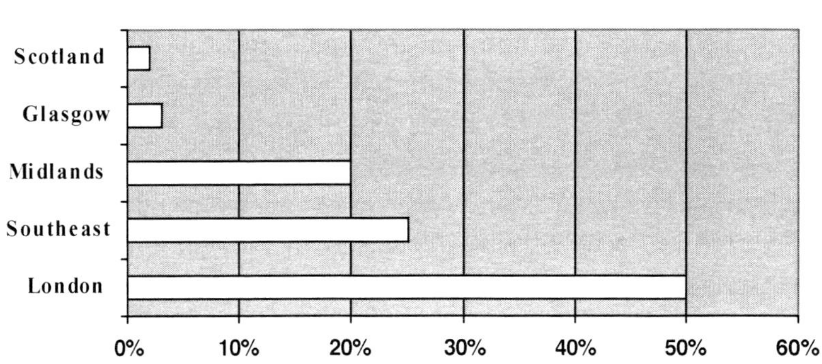

Notes: *Most Caribbean organizations are located in London, with less than a quarter operating in other cities – Liverpool, Manchester, Birmingham, London and Leeds; others are in Glasgow and Scotland.*

Conclusion

This chapter examined briefly, the origin, growth and development of the Caribbean Region and the various processes that interplayed in its progressive route to economic and social development. This overview also shows the links between the psychological levels of thinking and doing business in the region has impacted on survival strategies in a 'host' environment with specific reference to business enterprise development among Caribbean men and women in Britain.

Epochal events such as slavery, indentureship, emancipation, colonization and political independence were examined to provide the context of the Caribbean's economic relationship, both intra and extra-regionally, especially with the industrial North, including Britain. The challenging, but persistent democratic traditions, including emerging and potentially viable political institutions along with an instinctive desire to advance enterprise, were also looked at to explain the region's level of advancement since the early 1960s, despite continued pressure on export commodities to trade fairly and equitably in global markets.

As globalization takes its toll on developing states, issues around migration; namely their consequential effects on both the recipient and sender nations are assessed. International institutions acknowledged that that the Caribbean Region has one of the highest emigration rates based on equal levels of educational attainment although this situation contributed to the growing brain drain problem in the Americas.

The practice of money transfers was also highlighted in this chapter and it was recognized that money transfers were a significant proportion of domestic revenue among Caribbean countries. It was suggested that a revolving fund should be set up, pooling a percentage of remittances into a revolving fund for micro business development. This will be of particular befit to villages and districts that bear the brunt of poverty and other inequalities due to structural adjustment in national economies. In this next chapter we will take a look at the performance of the Caribbean business economy, to further contextualize the organization and performance of Caribbean businesses in Britain.

Chapter Notes

The Caribbean Region – is named after the Caribs, one of the dominant Amerindian groups in the Americas at the time of European colonization in the late 15th century. The analogous `West Indies' originates from Christopher Columbus' idea that he had landed in the Indies (then meaning all of south and east Asia, when he actually reached the Americas. Both terms are used interchangeably to mean persons from the English-speaking Caribbean.

Caribbean History – Professors Clive Thomas, Norman Girvan, George Beckford, Rex Nettleford and Dr. Eric Williams are among the foremost chroniclers of Caribbean history during the intervening period leading up to political independence and also during the socialist experiment and the Cold War in much of the 1970s and 1980s. Apart from refreshing insights, Caribbean historians are noted for their creativity, sincerity and missionary zeal in contrast to the Western preoccupation of the Caribbean being an exotic paradise and its people having a `laid-back' attitude.

Slavery and Indentureship – although slavery is given much prominence in the lives of both the Caribbean and elsewhere, indentureship also served to perpetuate the racial hierarchical divide where people from the non-European countries are still categorized according to colour, race, religion and other economic and social backgrounds.

Regional Integration – early attempts at a political federation and an economic union did not expunge the determination of the region's populace to pursue the formation of the Caribbean Community (Caricom) in July 1973. Since that period, there has been a succession of regional initiatives such as the sub-regional grouping, the Organisation of Eastern Caribbean States (1981), the Association of Caribbean States (1994) and the South American Common Market Community (2004) and the creation of multiple institutional arrangements to progress political, trade and other relationships within and without the region.

Proportional Representation – also known politically, as `first past the post' is quite controversial in fledging democracies where voter apathy has the potential to undermine the most efficient electoral system. With an increase in political parties and other mass movements in the Caribbean, it is likely that some point, a viable alternative may be found to this politically controversial issue.

Remittances - are a cushion for domestic earnings in most developing countries including the Caribbean where in some states, money transfers comprise up to 10% of GDP. It is estimated that Caribbean nationals in the UK alone, remit in excess of £400 million per year to their `homeland', while for Canada and the US, the sum runs into billions of dollars.

African American Business Success – was spurred due to brutal racial segregation during the first 30 years or so in the 20thcentury. Economic empowerment was viewed as another vehicle for equality and therefore, there was an unquenchable desire to set up black banks, insurance companies, newspapers and various enterprises that served the black community. It was the black church and fraternal organizations that nurtured and channeled that economic spirit. Initially churches didn't have businesses in the traditional sense, but they owned buildings representing the only major assets owned by African Americans at the time (**Brooks 2005**).

Hometown Associations – migration and globalization have transformed the relationship between Western nations and the developing world, with hometown associations (HTAs) becoming major players in promoting local development, both within the `host' society and `back home'. Since their creation dating back as far as 50 years in some instances, Caribbean-type HTAs have shown a relatively stable lifecycle, maintaining a core of active members who in turn, are able to draw support from hundreds of supporters both within and outside of their communities.

Selected References

1 Thomas, Clive (1988): *The Poor and the Powerless*, Latin American Bureau, London p18.

2 Williams, Eric (1970); *From Columbus to Castro: The History of the Caribbean 1492-1969*, Andre Deutsch, London p148.

3 Breinburg, Petronella (1986): *Language attitudes: The case of Caribbean language*, in Sutcliffe & Wong, eds., 136-148.

4 Dalphinis, Morgan (1991): 'The Afro-English Creole community', in S. Alladina and V. Edwards, eds., *Multilingualism in the British Isles*, Vol. 2: Africa, the Middle East and Asia, 42-46, London, Longman.

5 Barreiro, Jose (1990): 'Caribbean History: Whither Progress?' *Northeast Indian Quarterly,* Caribbean Web Designing pp 66-77.

6 Migration Histories, Indentureship by Dr. Ron Ramdin, *Migration Histories from a Caribbean Family,* Trinidad, Royal Geographical Society, January to December 1931.

7 Society and Industrialization, BBC October 2005

8 *Women in National Parliaments*, the International Parliamentary Union, Switzerland March 2006.

9 The Caribbean Immigrant Population in North American, *Caribbean Business Community Islands* Newsletter, September 1, 2003.

10 *Emigration to North America from Jamaica,* 1970-1980, National Planning Agency, Kingston Jamaica 1992.

11 Thomas-Hope, Elizabeth (2002): *Skilled Labour Migration from Developing Countries: Study on the Caribbean Region*, International Labour Programme, Geneva, Switzerland.

12 O'Neil, Kevin, Hamilton, Kimberly and Papademetriou, Demetrios (2005), *Migration in the Americas*, paper presented for the Policy Analysis and Research Programme of the Global Commission on International Migration, Migration Policy institute, Washington, D.C.

13 Salt, John and Millar, Jane (2006): *Foreign Labour in the United Kingdom: current patterns and trends,* Migration Research Unit, University College London, appeared in Office of National Statistics, Labour Market Trends October 2006.

14 *Remittances as a Development Tool in Latin America and the Caribbean,* Inter-American Development Bank, Washington, D.C., January 2005.

15 Docquier, Frederic and Marfouk, Abdeslam (2005): *International Migration by Educational Attainment 1999-2000*, National Fund for Scientific Research, Catholic University of Louvain, Belgium.

16 Lapointe, Michelle (2004): *Diasporas in Caribbean Development*, World Bank Report.

17 Nurse, K (2003a): *The Caribbean Music Industry*, Caribbean Export Development Agency, Barbados.

18 Carrington, W.J and Detragiache (1998): *How Big is the Brain Drain*? IMF Working Paper 98/102, Washington D.C.

19 Orozco, Manuel and Lapointe, Michelle, `Mexican Hometown Associations and their Development Opportunities', Research Series, *Inter-American Dialogue*, Remittances Project, September 2003.

Chapter 2

The Caribbean Business Economy

Introduction

This chapter will address the challenges of Caribbean states and the opportunities that national Governments have, in their collective quest to transform traditional agriculturally-based economies to modern and open trading markets, by introducing new products and services. This section will illustrate that despite their size and unevenness, Caribbean states are enjoying modest, but significant growth rates even against the backdrop of natural disasters and unfair terms of trade for export commodities on the world market. It should be noted that the Caribbean business environment has changed since the 1990s from an almost restricted enterprise zone to a highly competitive regional economy. This is due to policy measures such as financial incentives, market access, better commodity pricing, funding opportunities, as well as technical assistance and support for product development.

Yet formidable challenges remain as structural problems affect economies such as Guyana, Haiti and the Dominican Republic and several other Eastern Caribbean countries. Unemployment is as high as 10% among the youth and this has resulted in poverty, widening gap in income distribution, drug trafficking and addiction. Migration poses a serious challenge to governments and businesses and is seen as a two-edged sword, since it serves as a reminder that many educated people lack access to significant economic opportunity and therefore opt for the more `greener pastures' in the industrialised North.

Another major hindrance to sustainable development is the recurrence of natural disasters especially the hurricane season – the last of which in 2004 devastated 90% of Grenada, a once thriving island reputed for its world class spices. Insufficient aid and lack of technical expertise have slowed the island's recovery programme, but Grenadians are optimistic that their once 'spice paradise' will be reborn, and become a highly competitive market for investors. The country attracts hundreds of overseas students who attend the popular medical school in St. George's, the capital. This institution represents one of the Caribbean's finest offshore medical facilities in the 21st century.

Prior to independence and the post-independent era, average growth for a median Caribbean country was just under 3% (2.8%) higher than Latin America in every decade, but lower than East Asia. However, this reasonable growth performance was blighted by intervening factors. First, average growth began reducing in each decade since the 1970s, with 10 Caribbean states suffering a decline in economic fortunes – Antigua and Barbuda, Dominica, St. Lucia, and St. Vincent and the Grenadines. The Dominican Republic, Guyana, Suriname and Trinidad and Tobago experienced increased economic growth in the 1990s, having suffered major downturns in the 1980s.

Second, the gap between the 'haves' and 'haves-not' has widened with growth performance varying widely within the Caribbean than in Latin America. Over the 1960-2002 periods, the slowest growing countries in the region were Haiti, Jamaica, Guyana and Suriname, also four of the five poorest in terms of per capita Gross Domestic Product (GDP). These countries are also categorised as 'low income' states, while the middle and high income countries are Barbados, Antigua and Barbuda, St. Lucia, Jamaica and Trinidad and Tobago.

In 1988 the Caricom Secretariat announced the '*Year of Small Business*', stressing that businesses should *"aspire first to be successful regional traders before taking on the rest of the world,"* but by the 1990s, there was evidence of low productivity as mineral products, textiles, bananas and tourism fell considerably. One contributory factor was reduced public investment especially in the smaller territories.

The continued debt burden in the region also impeded investment into new products and services. Countries within the Eastern Caribbean sub-region suffered decline in productivity as foreign debt caused governments to increase capital and current expenditures. For Guyana and Jamaica debt has been a protracted issue since the 1980s, and while debt has been reduced in the former, the latter has decided to maintain very high primary surpluses in the medium-term to stabilise and reduce its debt. In an attempt to control their foreign exchange rate mechanism, the governments of Guyana and Jamaica introduced 'Cambios' a free-market, but somewhat regulated 'exchange windows'.

Today, Jamaica and Guyana have fluctuating exchange rates, with Guyana having the largest exchange rate (to the US Dollar and Pound Sterling) than any other English speaking Caribbean nation. The Eastern Caribbean states' currencies are pegged to the OECS currency, one that has been stable for nearly 20 years (and possibly one of the few stable currencies in the world). This situation offers these states some degree of flexibility in the exchange rate mechanism, reasonable per capita growth and modest investments in public services and a gradual reduction in foreign debt.

A 2004 World Bank Study of 159 firms showed that foreign investors in the Caribbean recognised that if a climate for investment was to be effective, critical factors had to be addressed. Performance ratings covered the legal environment, labour issues, taxation and customs, among others. Within each category, there were sub-components which were of major importance to firma. Some of these factors included political stability, exchange rate stability, and attitude towards productivity, telecommunications, power supply and shipping. Firms in different sectors, however, attach varying degrees of importance to the various factors affecting investment climate (**World Bank 2004**).

On the one hand, manufacturing companies tend to be more export-oriented; they are concerned with exchange rate stability and shipping services and modern technology inputs. On the other hand, service sector firms because they are more geared towards the local market, tend to focus on political and administrative stability and local market size, but less on the availability of unskilled labour. **(Fig 2.1)**

Figure 2.1 Sample Ratings of the Investment Climate in the Caribbean

(Source: World Bank Survey, 2004)

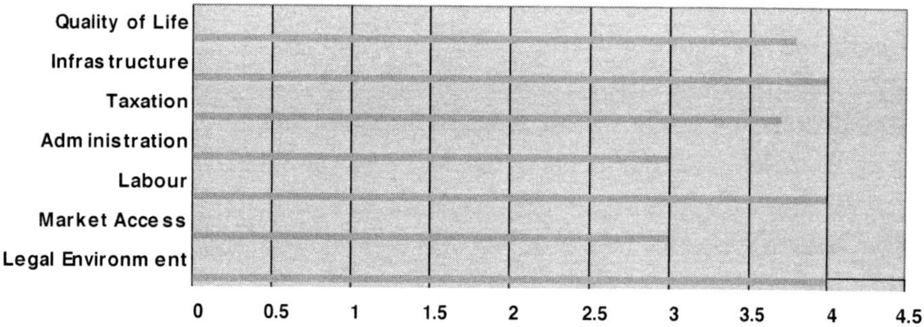

Note: Importance rating scale: 3= moderate importance, 4= major importance, 5= critical importance

In the 1980s, the value of agricultural products amounted to about 17% of GDP in the region and declined to 8% in 1998. During that period, tourism receipts increased from a little more than 7% of GDP to about 11% of GDP in 1994 to 1997. Construction activity contributed significantly to growth as the Bahamas, Barbados, and St. Kitts and Nevis modernized their tourism plants and as Guyana, Belize and Trinidad and Tobago upgraded their physical infrastructures. While sugar output increased, banana output fell reflecting the uncertainties of the WTO ruling against the European Union proposals for banana imports from the Caribbean. The manufacturing sector also performed well while mining performances were mixed with adverse effects from falling prices of gold and bauxite and increases in prices from oil in 1999-2000 which benefited Trinidad and Tobago.

After securing political independence from the British in the 1960s, the new governments in Barbados (the Barrow Administration), Guyana (the Burnham Administration), Jamaica (the Manley Administration), and Trinidad and Tobago (Williams' Administration) introduced centralised planning to control the major product sectors of the economy. Several decades later, with growing structural problems, these countries began in the late 1990s, a major shift towards private-sector led, market-based development strategies, and to reform their public services. This approach was driven both by internal economic pressures and direct external forces brought about by conditions imposed by international financial institutions such as the IMF/World Bank. In short, `privatisation' or the `free-market' became the new economic doctrine as the 21st century dawned upon the Caribbean region and other parts of the developing world.

By opening its economy, the Caribbean demonstrated that like smaller countries such as Singapore, Cyprus and Ireland, it was possible to successfully diversify and increase the production chain to higher value-added products. Already there are offshore education and IT-enabled activities with potential growth, particularly in Barbados and Antigua and Barbuda. The Dominican Republic and Trinidad and Tobago have seen some increase in manufacturing activities. Belize has increased exports of shrimps and other states are trying to diversify their tourism products, beyond the sun-and-sea related services.

Indeed, Caribbean governments believe in self-employment as a viable alternative to unemployment, but they are also conscious of critical factors blighting growth. The persistent flight of skills to Europe and North America, inadequate technology and a narrow economic base, have reduced the market share of companies in the region. Success is likely to be achieved when there is greater emphasis on the development of entrepreneurial and technical resources for new firms. An urgent task facing Caribbean business owners is the acquisition of appropriate technology and the mastery of techniques to deal with international competition. (**West Indian Commission Report, 1992**)

In addition, there are other exciting prospects for businesses that are market-driven; for example, the travel industry, modern telecommunications, international trade and other growth sectors. Proactive strategies by Caribbean governments have resulted in growing competition within these sectors. A recent study by the Caribbean Development Bank (CDB) showed that a large percentage of businesses supported the policy of free trade aimed at stimulating the regional economy.

The study highlighted the diversity of the Caribbean market and its effect on international trade. Export growth strategies are central to firms in securing competitive advantage in a global economy. It is therefore necessary for governments to facilitate the right type of business environment by implementing the right mix of "*incentives and support measures that would favour achievement of agreed goals*" (**Caricom 1992**). With such a growth strategy, Caribbean businesses would be in a better position to trade in goods, capital and other resources in emerging markets across the world (**Fig 2. 2**).

Figure 2. 2 Export-led Growth Strategies

- Extra-regional Trade – benefits small firms to improve market advantage
- Manufacturing and Diversification – improves technology competence
- Niche Markets – increase market share and profitability
- Development Finance – access to new and flexible types of funding
- Concessional Credit – maximum credit and borrowing opportunities
- Stock Market - engage with viable and reputable intermediaries to support investment

(Source: Textual analysis based on trends in the Caribbean Region 2000-2006)

Niche Markets

On a more general level, the Caricom Secretariat has encouraged businesses to take advantage of currency conversion, movement of labour and removal of trade barriers, in an effort to gain maximum advantage in lucrative markets. The emphasis is on the acquisition of high-order skills to compete in both regional and international markets. At the time of writing, the Single Market Economy was introduced with several states working towards repositioning their economies to maximise financial and trade opportunities throughout the Caribbean and Latin America. According to a Caricom study:

The integration movement should encourage the development of a skills-intensive manufacture and service exports base. These areas will rely heavily on the quality of the region's human resource. New institutions will need to be developed to generate skilled labour to improve the levels of finance and trade between Caribbean businesses and other regional and international companies. **(West Indian Commission Report 1992)**

Like Europe and North America, the Caribbean has created new markets for investment and trade. Changes in the economy have stimulated art and craft, the cottage industry, food processing and housing. Private investments have created opportunities for access to resources to increase output in energy, information technology, transportation and allied services. Although the pace of regional economic integration has been slow, the extent of regional programmes in health and education is staggering. Caribbean institutions are creating conditions for efficient, low-cost provision of common services, and Caribbean entrepreneurs are looking to expand their operations and will therefore welcome joint venture partners with capital and technology. Recent estimates suggest that areas of investment are wide and varied – ranging from manufacturing and services to stock markets and other multiple sectors according to countries' profile **(Table 2.1)**

It should be stressed that in spite of a narrow economic base, the Caribbean has adapted to international trends. By repositioning, the region is a beneficiary of emerging markets in Africa, Europe, Latin America and North America where products and services are traded, using the cultural touch. British Caribbean businesses can thus maximize strategic advantage by developing mutually beneficial contracts with their counterparts 6,000 miles away. Over a quarter of all British Caribbean entrepreneurs in the UK originate from the Caribbean and this has long term benefits since both groups can gain from technology transfer, best practice, product knowledge, customer profiling, cost efficiency, risk management and knowledge of import/export techniques.

Generally critics including nationals, who left the region prior or after political independence, are often unwilling to appreciate and understand the impact of the colonial legacy on the region. The Caribbean has never conquered any part of the world or showed any such inclinations, unlike the West. It has never been involved in land-grabbing or military expansionism and though its citizens fought in World War II as British subjects, the regional structure historically, was based on a plantation model where agriculture remained the major bedrock for the Industrial Revolution in Britain and Europe. For instance, it took Britain the best part of a century to become an industrialized, advanced nation – politically, economically, financially and militarily. To therefore compare the 40-odd year Caribbean independent group of nations with Britain and its European allies is a lesson in short-sightedness.

Table 2.1 Major investment opportunities in the Caribbean

(Source: World Bank Report, 2004)

Sector	Investment Opportunities
Manufacturing	export oriented exchange rate stability reliable shipping quality port facilities anti-monopoly practices

Services	strong labour market political stability sound economic policies.
Stock Market	proper financial procedures quality administration attractive incentives excellent location portfolios
All Sectors	quality infrastructure overall effective laws and regulations positive attitude towards investment labour productivity attractive tax incentives quality telecommunications quality power supply.

In addition, although the region is a signatory to the trade protocol involving two other regional bloc countries – Africa and the Pacific – agricultural and textile producers have had a raw deal on export commodities since the 1980s. The African, Caribbean and Pacific Group of countries also known as the `ACP' signed the European Lome Convention in 1977 to have access to European markets, with guaranteed concessions for bananas, sugar, textiles and other raw material-products. With the growing enlargement of the EU in 1992 and the mass production of artificial sweeteners (beet sugar), as well as large-scale competition from Latin American banana growers (with support from US multinational corporations), not only did Caribbean producers suffered, but the region's already small market share in agriculture, textiles and other export commodities, shrunk even further which consequently dented the coffers of Member States. Developing countries have expressed concern over the unfair practice of subsidising farmers in America and Western Europe particularly. This practice has a knock-on effect on traders markets since it creates price distortions and severely weakens the profit margins of small farming communities, including micro food retailers.

However, against the backdrop of resource limitations, the growing out-migration of skilled professionals and structural weaknesses in their economies, Caribbean governments are doing their utmost to introduce open-market policies whilst adopting greater transparency in their dealings with financial and trade markets –regionally and internationally **(Table 2.2).**

Table 2. 2 Competitive profile of selected Caribbean countries

(Source: World Bank, 2006)

Country	Strengths	Weaknesses
Barbados	strong policy & legal structure attractive investment possibilities reliable utilities	high rate taxes weak tax administration poor on customs and taxation
Dominican Republic	low cost labour force skilled labour advanced communications quality shipping	unreliable power supply exchange rate instability
Grenada	availability of unskilled labour potential for multiple enterprises	limited managerial-technical skills high taxes high import tariffs complicated customs-tax clearance
Guyana	variety of investment possibilities attractive exchange rate educated workforce investment policy	limited management skills inefficient custom clearance unreliable power supply high costs of crime

Jamaica	macro economic stability quality seaports and airports access to skilled labour	low labour productivity high crime
Trinidad and Tobago	macro economic stability abundant power supply	high crime anti-competitive practices

Trading Activities

The Caribbean Region has excellent trading links with principal trading partners and the rest of the world, including Britain, the EU and the USA. The region's total imports expanded from EC$22.9 billion in 1996 to EC$27.0 billion in 2001 at an average growth rate of 3.4% over the period. Earnings from total exports moved from EC$15.5 billion in 1996 to EC$17.9 billion in 2001, at an average growth rate of nearly 3% over the period. Throughout the period, the UK has been a major trading partner of the region – with imports of the 20 commodities accounting for 55.6% of Caricom's total imports from the UK. The top 16 commodities accounted for an average 94.2% of Caricom's total domestic exports to the UK, with region's four domestic exports to the UK in 2001 being:

- Raw cane sugar;
- Bananas;
- Aluminum oxide, other than artificial corundum; and
- Methanol. **(Caricom 2006)**

These items contributed to a collective 89.7% to the region's domestic exports to the UK in 2001. Raw cane sugar and banana maintained their top positions with average percentage contributions of 49.1% and 26.1% respectively over the period. These two commodities contributed to more than 75% of Caricom's total exports to the UK over the 1996-2001 periods **(Table 2.3 & Fig 2.3).**

Table 2. 3 Value and Distribution of Caricom's Total Exports: 1996-2001

(Source: Caricom Secretariat, April 2006)

(EC$'000)

Year	Domestic Exports	Total Exports	%
1996	11,871,588	12,580,141	100
1997	13,314,287	14,023,041	100
1998	12,165,159	12,962,037	100
1999	13,346,672	14,043,820	100
2000	17,864,870	18,562,683	100
2001	16,148,183	16,849,494	100

Note: Exports to the United Kingdom between 1996 and 2001 come up to 41.5% of total commodity exports by Caricom, while exports to the Rest of the European Union totaled 51.6% over the same trading period.

Figure 2. 3 Major Destinations of Caricom's Exports: 2001

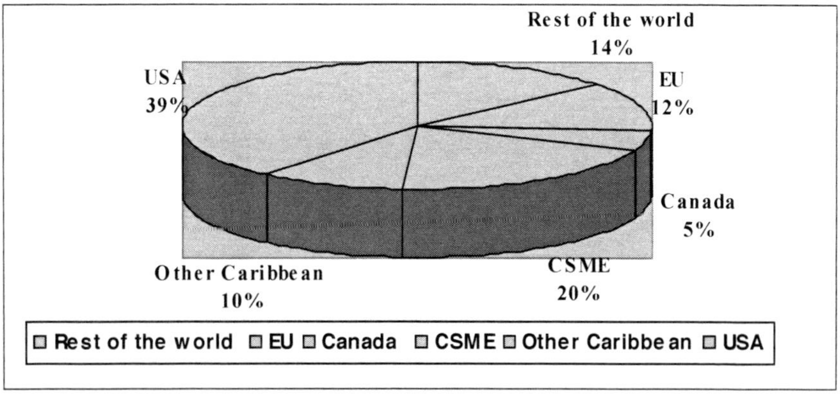

Notes: The USA because of its close proximity was the top major destination (39%) for all Caricom exports for 2001, followed by Caribbean countries in the Caricom Single Market Exchange (CSME) area.

In spite of its current trade deficit (a fact that is common among the most developed and industrialized countries today) due primarily to its reduced market share in agricultural products such as bananas and other commodities, the Caribbean has the potential to consolidate and improve its present portfolio of exports such as:

- Food and live animals;
- Beverage and tobacco;
- Crude materials;
- Mineral fuels – lubricants and related materials;
- Animal and vegetable oils;
- Chemicals and related products;
- Manufactured goods;
- Machinery and transport equipment;
- Other commodities and transaction; and
- Tourism products (package tours etc).

However, even though the region's share of exports has fallen short of projected targets, in recent years, Britain has attempted to provide some measure of support through its international aid programme. In 2004, the British Government launched a Regional Assistance Plan for the Caribbean to cover that period until 2007. The plan sets out how the UK Government expects to contribute £36 million to help countries in the region make progress towards achieving the UN Millennium Development Goals over the period.

The plan has two principal aims; to help reduce poverty and vulnerability and to ensure that British development assistance, as well as others, is provided in a way that helps achieve Caribbean development goals. According to the British Government, 'The Plan will address the challenges posed by the changing world trade environment and the needs for ever more efficient use of the region's human resources' **(Department for International Development 2004).**

Financial Services

In so far as the financial services sector is concerned, offshore banking is regarded as one of the fastest growth industries in the region. The opportunities that exist in the evolving stock exchange market are indicative of the possibilities for additional investment in other commodity markets as evidenced by the number of foreign banks with eastern Caribbean countries, including the popular location of The Bahamas. If the definition of financial services is extended to the facilitation of offshore businesses, it is also important to note that in the Cayman Islands, it was estimated that more than 40,000 offshore companies were registered as of 1997 including almost 600 banks and trust companies. The associated banking assets amounted to somewhat more than US $500 billion.

In the British Virgin Islands, 250,000 companies were on the offshore registry at the end of 1997. The adoption of a comprehensive insurance law in late 1994, which provides a blanket of confidentiality with regulated gateways for investigation of criminal offences, is expected to make the British Virgin Islands even more attractive to international business.

The formal domestic Caribbean markets for equities are relatively small and restricted to three countries; namely, Barbados, Jamaica and Trinidad and Tobago where there are active stock exchanges. Surname and The Bahamas have stock exchanges with limited trading activity. In other territories such as Guyana and some of the eastern Caribbean states, there are informal markets in stocks and bonds – over the counter operations at trust companies and at central banks, but yet the stock market performance in the region especially in the first half of 2005, was reasonably impressive **(Table 2. 4).**

Table 2. 4 Summary performance of the Caribbean Stock Market

(Source: CMMB Stock Market Quarterly, Issue 9, April, 2005)

Country	Trade Volume	Sector Performance
Barbados	Volume traded B$10,831,808 with the first quarter of 2005 – showing volume of trade equals 10.8 million shares	Banking, insurance, manufacturing, tourism, trading, food retailing, utilities
Jamaica	Market capitalisation of J$818,930,209 with a trade volume of J$704,424,216	Communications, manufacturing, retail and tourism
Trinidad and Tobago	Market capitalisation of TT$115,169,931 with a trade volume of TT$54,114,558	banking, manufacturing, property, non-banking finance
International Markets	N.A.	Equity markets around the world got off to a reasonable start in the first quarter of 2005 in light of global economic growth projected at 3.6%. European and Asian equities outperformed US markets.

Note: The Stock Market continued its golden run in the first quarter of 2005, with over 54 million shares in 27 company stocks with investors spending $1,026 million. In the same period in 2004, a little over 92 million shares traded for a market share of $518 million.

Deposits which remain the major means of capital mobilisation, account for about 75% of the liabilities of the commercial banks. In the wake of the uncertainties that followed instability in the exchange rates in the Caribbean economies in the 1970s and 1980s, commercial banks, in particular Jamaica, offered the option of deposits in foreign currencies, mainly in US dollars. Guyana also followed suit with its `Cambios' (businesses authorised by the Government to change foreign currencies), and since that period, these one-stop financial supermarkets have mushroomed also in Trinidad and Tobago and the Dominican Republic where the indigenous banks assume larger proportions of deposit transactions. In supporting business start-ups in the Caribbean, commercial banks utilise overdrafts and loans as lending instruments, since the lack of finance for long-term investment and for the capitalisation of small enterprises remains a challenge for the region. According to the World Bank,

Permanent overdrafts are the predominant form of business finance in Jamaica, Trinidad and Tobago and Suriname. This practice is, of course, hazardous both to banks and borrowers. The lack of term finance is particularly acute for small businesses and for farmers. In the Dominican Republic the unavailability of long-term finance is one explanation for the decline in agriculture **(World Bank 1996).**

The solution to this problem seems to be for the development of a secondary market in the Caribbean, to assist with providing long-term business finance. A genuine secondary market exists only in Jamaica where a group of commercial banks, merchant banks and money market brokers are prepared to provide underwriting of new issues of private debt. There is some venture capital finance available in Caribbean states such as Barbados as well as Trinidad and Tobago - financed directly by the contributions of donor community and the governments. It should be noted however, that traditionally the focus for most international analysts has been on Asia and America. Yet, the Caribbean has demonstrated that while it may have smaller markets, it can match or better the returns offered by developed stock markets in North America and Europe.

Enterprise Development

Enterprise has been a historic feature of economic development in both urban and rural parts of the Caribbean, and for years, women in particular, have combined domestic chores with micro (commercial) trading activities. These activities were often aimed at augmenting income or improving the quality of family life, while in other instances, the choice was to be financially self-sufficient. One notable feature in the 1980s - 1990s, was the latent creativity of low-income public servants who used their people skills to set up subsidiary firms to boost incomes. Many soon left their once `proud' vocation to become successful entrepreneurs in either traditional commercial ventures or to provide innovative services to satisfy a set of social needs. Caricom has estimated that the region's micro and small enterprise: -

- account for about 45% of jobs created;
- account for 70% of agricultural exports;
- play a leading role in marketing farm produce;
- provide transportation for commuters and tourists;
- are leaders in manufacturing sub-sectors like wood products; and
- has a lead role in construction, equipment repair, maintenance and retail.

A more regional definition adopted by the Caribbean Technological and Consultancy Services of the Caribbean Development Bank and endorsed by policy experts, is `Micro enterprises' meaning: it is owner managed with less than five employees, less than US$25,000 investment in equipment and usually a home based operation **(Table 2. 5)**. Accordingly, `small enterprises' are defined in the Caribbean regional context, as businesses with the following characteristics:

- Less than 25 employees;
- Less than 4,000 sq. ft. of manufacturing area;
- Less than US$50,000 investment in equipment (excludes real estate); and
- Less than US$125,000 annual sales.

Table 2. 5 Enterprise definitions by Caribbean countries

Country	Definition
Barbados	Not more than US$5000,000 authorised or paid capital, under 25 staff
Grenada	Income not exceeding US$300 per month, net asset under US$18,518
Guyana	Up to 15 persons with an investment up to US$9,036 in equipment
Jamaica	Less than 10 staff with under US$5,480 initial capital investment
Trinidad & Tobago	Owner manager 1-5 employees, with assets up to US$15,873

(Source: National Baseline Survey Reports, Barbados, Grenada, Guyana, Jamaica, Trinidad & Tobago, 1995-97)

The issue of defining small enterprises is not altogether problematic for policy makers in the Caribbean since it allows agencies not only to be sophisticated in dealing with various forms of enterprise sectors, but they can also offer greater flexibility to challenge stereotypes and conventions which are prescriptive and are unworkable in instances where micro firms and small business conduct a range of activities compared to their original intentions or general purpose.

With regard to the ratio of business activity in both domestic and regional market, figures suggest that between 70% and 85% of all business activity is conducted by enterprises employing less than 25 persons. Even though their individual levels of activity may be comparatively small, collectively their importance to the general economic entrepreneurial class cannot be overemphasised. The environment that these firms operate within has the following features:

- a small and limited domestic market
- non-availability of high cost of principal raw materials
- diversion of demand to import substitutes
- lack of hands-on technical support
- high financial/labour costs resulting in uncompetitive pricing
- lack of co-ordination among enterprise support bodies
- poor information on opportunities for SMEs.

Constraints aside, SMEs are a vibrant distinct sector in the Caribbean and can be classified in the following sub-sectors:

- Food and agro-processing;
- Marine and fishing;
- Woodwork and furniture;
- Light engineering and electronics;
- Garments;
- Handicrafts;
- Tourism and service related industries; and
- Emerging technologies (telecommunications).

The size and composition of business sectors be they agricultural, manufacturing and/or services have an impact on the value of job creation, skills development, new technologies, innovative products, new production processes and segmented markets. A major strategic problem though, is a large gap in the knowledge of the detailed structure and performance of firms. Statistical information about the size and distribution of employment is sketchy, particularly since there is no regional monitoring and registration agency. There are of course, various public sector-type agencies that carry out country-wide studies in the region; they comprise urban development commissions, industrial development corporations, enterprise development institutes and private sector-led bodies. These agencies also examine the constraints affecting the SME sector as a whole. Constraints are classified as follows: -

- ***Legal*** – the importance of the enterprise sector has been recognised and articulated; no specific legislation aimed at the establishment and the development of micro and small enterprises. The Caribbean Association of Industry of Commerce does little policy research on the regional SME sector.
- ***Institutional*** – agencies provide support, but there is no institutional framework for facilitating the planning, implementation, co-ordination and valuation of activities in the SME sector. There is considerable duplication of services; small business associations are weak and non-existent, lacking financial and human resources.
- ***Infrastructural*** – unavailability of economically priced factory and warehouse commercial space – a major hindrance to enterprise growth and development.
- ***Financial*** – lack of accessible and affordable financing facilities remain problematic; no collateral, low credit, low capitalisation, high risk/unproven management capability.
- ***Non-availability of proper training and technical assistance*** – owners from various educational backgrounds with limited business experience, have little access to quality enterprise training; materials are complex and irrelevant; core function of agencies is not training but credit provision; absence of technical skills training and upgrading in the sector.
- ***Marketing*** – except in the agricultural sector, there is no formal institutional arrangement for marketing the products and services of SMEs in the national, regional and international markets; little access to market information-data on opportunities for new markets; lack of financial and human resources, SMEs do not have the capacity for sustained advertising and promotion of their products.

Culture of Entrepreneurship

Historically, there has always been an enterprise culture imbedded in the Caribbean psyche as part of its survival strategy, to deal with poverty, alienation and class differences. Yet the region has experienced similar problems to developing or emerging democracies that were once colonised especially as it relates to formal education and training curricula activities. Nationals were trained to be good 'public servants' – employees and managers – rather than 'good employers'. In fact, most business schools teach students how to be good managers or employees within large organisations as against how to manage their own business. At secondary education level, there is little effort towards creating awareness and orientation for business start-ups. The situation is worse at university level where students are encouraged to take up jobs in the Civil Service, professional or larger private sector firms.

Since the mid-1980s and more so, the early 1990s, Caribbean governments have collaborated with non-governmental organisations and the private sector to undertake a stream of initiatives to encourage and promote enterprise culture **(Table 2. 6)**. Barbados, Jamaica, Guyana, Trinidad and Tobago and other smaller territories are in the forefront of disseminating and fostering information culture among the business community in the region.

Table 2. 6 Enterprise Initiatives among Caribbean Countries

Country	Major Enterprise Initiatives
Barbados	Youth Entrepreneurship, Institute of Management and Productivity
Grenada	Small Enterprise Development Unit, Employers' Federation
Guyana	Institute for Private Enterprise Development, public sector schemes
Jamaica	Human Resource Training Trust, Entrepreneurial Centre University

Trinidad and Tobago	Youth Training &Employment Partnership, Small Business Development
Other Caribbean States	Junior Achievers Business Laboratories and Business Associations
Caribbean Region	Chambers of Commerce, Development Foundations, other schemes

(Source: Small Enterprise in the Caribbean, Caricom Secretariat, 2000)

On top of the agency support system as evidenced in Table 2. 6, there are other vital institutions that encourage and stimulate enterprise development in the Caribbean; they include: -

- *Barbados* – with a few information services in the public, quasi-public and private sectors – library services, a small business centre, an export development agency resource centre and business information centre for young entrepreneurs.
- *Grenada* - has a Chamber of Commerce and an employers' federation – regarded as important resource centres on the island.
- *Guyana* - no information resource centre that provides relevant information and data on SMEs, except for GO-Invest, a public agency that promotes foreign investment and provides trade and market information mainly for foreign investors.
- *Jamaica* – has an economic development agency; a one-stop shop for investors, exporters and the business community, national and international. Information covers investment opportunities, the prevailing economic and market trends, as well as cost models and data on various types of investment.
- *Trinidad and Tobago* – its National Business Information Centre is located within the state-owned small business centre and was established with assistance from the European Union (EU). The centre has provision for customer service, information resources and computer database systems for entrepreneurs.

The twin-island of Trinidad and Tobago is the first country in the Caribbean that embarked on a national policy, `*A total quality nation*' along the lines of the Singaporean model. In other countries, consumer groups and associations, together with Government Consumer Affairs Departments are actively involved in ensuring that local and imported products are of proper quality, labelling, weights and measures etc. in terms of labour practices and working conditions, these are still in their development stages in the region. Few SMEs comply with certain basic practices according to legislation and regulations in general. There are too few monitoring mechanisms in place to supervise enterprise owners' compliance with labour legislation and practices.

Notwithstanding structural problems affecting the continued growth and development of enterprise in the Caribbean, Governments have put in place a range of existing infrastructure and support services aimed at employment generation, creation of new markets and the development of premises and so forth. To some degree, economic problems have contributed to declining manufacturing and other production firms.

Apart from temporary political and economic setbacks, countries of the Caribbean are considered overall, as safe-havens for investment opportunities because of their proximity to North American markets. The financial landscape for SMEs is wide and varied and many countries have implemented grant, equity, credit and other financial arrangements to benefit start-ups and existing enterprises in their respective locations. These schemes are operated and facilitated through, and by public, private and civic sector bodies, and tend to be supported by international agencies such as the Canadian International Development Agency (CIDA) and the EU **(Table 2.7)**.

Table 2.7 Financial measures for supporting enterprise in the Caribbean

Countries	Existing Measures
Barbados	Debt financing, equity financing, grant-aid support
Grenada	Commercial loans, credit union schemes
Guyana	Loans, business credit and credit union saving schemes
Jamaica	Micro credit, loan scheme, credit union program
Trinidad and Tobago	Credit aid scheme, commercial loans and credit union program
Caribbean (general)	Blend of trade and community-type loan and grant-aided schemes

(Source: Caricom Secretariat, 2003)

In addition, there are exemplary models of enterprise support programmes across the Caribbean especially among the `Five' countries in **Table 2.7**. Individual entrepreneurs are benefiting from most of these initiatives and have witnessed not only physical growth in their firms, but also growth in market share and profitability. Agencies have taken into account essential sectors such as the cultural industries, garment manufacturing, agricultural, export promotion and food retailing, having recognised that both inter and extra regional markets have tremendous potential for product diversification. Above all, public agencies and private sector institutions are keen to collaborate on joint ventures to ensure that businesses maximise both finance and market trading opportunities **(Minicases 2.1)**.

At the regional level, the Caribbean Export Development Agency has been promoting and marketing Caribbean products both at the regional and international levels. In a drive to diversify into non-traditional export market niches, many Caribbean countries have put measures in place to ensure ready access to export financing, access to primary and non-trading inputs at reasonable prices and an adequate institutional infrastructure for trade. This institution is responsible for collecting information and data in internal and external markets and processes same for individual enterprises in the Caribbean, via Chambers of Commerce and other enterprise networking groups. Routine seminars, conferences and workshops are also held to update business owners on new legislation such as tax harmonisation policies resulting from the Single Market Economy.

Therefore, for a variety of reasons, the Caribbean SME sector required dedicated assistance and technical support in marketing their products for both domestic as well as overseas markets. The services that are mostly needed include:

- researching market and developing sector specific trade information systems;
- participating in relevant trade show and trade missions;
- developing joint marketing arrangements among members;
- building their organisational capacity to promote specific goods; and
- developing the basics of small scale export marketing finance and management.

At the beginning of 2006, there was evidence that the Caricom Single Market was taking shape, with several countries taking part in the initial process. Critics have stated that the uneven nature of national economies will prevent an efficient convergence of the overall regional economy. Issues to do with currency valuation, banking regulations and other financial arrangements will influence the pace of reforms in national economies such as the '*Big Four*' - Barbados, Guyana, Jamaica and Trinidad and Tobago, which have individual currencies plus their own exchange rates.

Since the early 1980s, the Eastern Caribbean States' currencies have been pegged to the OECS Currency and this situation will allow smaller states to have possibly, a smoother and effective transition towards integrating within a regional single market. This new regional development is an acid test to public officials, institutions set up to promote enterprise advancement, as well as potential and existing entrepreneurs.

Minicases 2. 1 Sector-based activities in the Caribbean

(Economic Developments in the Caribbean, Caricom Secretariat, 2004)

- ***Small Business Incubator in Grenada*** – The Small Enterprise Development Unit in association with the Grenada Industrial Development Corporation (GIDC) decided to effectively use and make the dormant factories operable once more. Two factory shells of 15,000 sq. ft were identified and subdivided into 13 units. For the first time, the objective of providing SMEs access to industrial park with common facilities such as secretarial accounting, technical and business counselling under one roof was achieved. The Incubator houses 13 different units (garments, agro-industrial, fish packaging for exports, small engine repairs, printing etc) and employs 35 persons. The GIDC developed other facilities around thc island and it expects to attract local entrepreneurs. This institution is part of the country's micro and small business sector.

- ***Crafting for Success in Jamaica*** – Jamaica is a destination for almost one million tourists annually, and a ready-made market for locally produced handicraft. The products offered, however, lacked both artistic and utility value from the tourist point of view. High Gate Dolls and Crafts began in 1994 with two women producing one type of doll. By 1998, with help from JAMPRO, the national economic development agency, the business expanded to 18 individuals working as a group producing three lines of dolls as a cottage industry whereby 85% of the manufacturing process is carried out in the producers' homes. The firm operates as a co-operative society, producing (a) Syni – a line of Rastafarian Reggae dolls, (b)

Panchita and friends is the educational line and consists of children characters and (c) Folk line is strongly cultural with a secondary theme of an environmental awareness, consisting of characters. The total sales in 1998 were estimated at J$1.20 million (US$328,767).

- ***Music and Technology in Trinidad & Tobago*** - Neil Swantson has been involved in the music industry for many years as a disc jockey and sound systems engineer and he recognised that with new technology and more sophisticated recording techniques, there was potential in the one billion dollar music industry market in T&T. In 1996, after 12 years in the USA, he returned to Trinidad and launched his business, Electro Sounds, which is involved in principally, the manufacture of compact discs. The company completes all stages of production in-house and is the first to introduce CD recording in the country. Swanston has overcome initial problems – mainly a reluctance to accept new technology – by adopting innovative marketing strategies and identifying his own trust and professional integrity. With a modest beginning, Electro Sounds has grown from TT$69,000 (US$10,950) to over half a million dollars (US$80,000) in 1998. The business has helped to promote big names in Calypso and Chutney music in the international market. In 1999, Electro Sounds participated at the International Entertainment Trade Show in Paris – a mecca for the music business. Swanston's advice for potential entrepreneurs is this: firstly, get the necessary knowledge in the field you wish to enter; secondly, prepare yourself for whatever comes along and thirdly, be patient as things unfold.'

Besides, the impact of globalisation such as restricted markets for certain essential commodities and other unfair trade practices, increasing environmental concerns, the flight of key skills from the region, structural poverty, debt problems and the drug menace, all add to the typical challenges facing an eventual Caribbean Single Market Economy (CSME). Yet a regional single market is a provider of benefits for the more than 50,000 firms in the Caribbean. It will harmonise the financial system and strengthen trade, whilst creating employment opportunities to improve standards of living, especially among the rural poor, deprived and excluded communities. In the main, the benefits of the CSME far outweigh predicted losses. The benefits include the following:

- *Trade in goods and services in mass consumer markets* – greater opportunities to improve trade and enhance profitability in key sectors, nationally and regionally.
- *Harmonisation of taxes, business agreements, incentives etc* – a better deal for national economic reforms as they seek to strengthen the collective fabric of existing financial and other fiscal systems and procedures.
- *Competitive products* – better quality and prices, application of innovative technology and state-of-the art production techniques and building on modern processes of marketing and competitive pricing techniques.
- *Improved services by persons and businesses* – higher levels of efficiency to maximise production and productivity targets through the facilitation of target markets and the development of new market segments.
- *Export support to business enterprises* – incentives for targeting specific regional and international markets, as well as improving the competitiveness of existing firms and those with the potential for enhancing the export portfolio of the region.
- *Common external and economic trade policy* – a collective set of regimes beneficial to the negotiated trade agreements with foreign investors and multilateral institutions involved in overall finance and trade protocols.
- *Increased employment and improved standards of living* – contributory rise in the number of job creation opportunities and

positive indices with respect to better wages and salaries, high quality social amenities and the modernisation of economic and social systems of governance.

Emerging Opportunities

Notwithstanding the multiple challenges – political, economic, social and otherwise – affecting the Caribbean region, there are emerging sectors in which entrepreneurs could access, if the right systems and procedures are in place, coupled with the appropriate mix of national-regional policies and programmes. These potential sectors reflect the growing sophistication among various types of customers (families, young people, professionals and consumer groups etc) and the influence they bring to bear on the introduction of innovative goods and services. Clearly, while agriculture and manufacturing are also essential to material prosperity, in an open market regime, small economies such as those in the Caribbean tend to compete more effectively by maximising their (services) strengths. This sector includes information communications technology (ICT)-enabled products and services, cultural tourism, offshore education and health services, to name a few.

Ireland and Singapore are among two leading countries that have demonstrated an intelligent mix of policy measures to facilitate the growth and development of services especially in areas where there have been industrial decline. In such a setting, run-down sites have been either redeveloped or regenerated by introducing a variety of measures to create modern services that meet the demands and needs of mass consumers. In the long run, these services, apart from stimulating creativity, will increase investment opportunities in the Caribbean, thereby improving the organisation and performance of businesses and social enterprises **(Table 2. 8)**.

Table 2. 8 Potential growth sectors of the Caribbean Economy

Services Sector	Impact Opportunities
ICT	An essential ingredient for attaining competitiveness in both services and niche manufacturing sectors in the Caribbean. *Unique Jamaica,* a cluster of small hoteliers and attractions used ICT to launch a cost effective marketing campaign.
Cultural Tourism	Will revitalise the tourism sector and deepen linkages with the rest of the economy. Existing niches such as St. Lucia's Jazz Festival, Dominica's Creole Festival and Barbados' upscale resort, Sandy Lane could be further developed.
Offshore Education	Medical schools represent a small but growing services sector in terms of offshore education, with Dominica and Grenada among Caribbean countries that have 23 such institutions in the Region.
Healthcare	Growth in the delivery of cross-border provision of health services has created opportunities for Caribbean health service providers. Examples of these services include Le Sport in St. Lucia and Island Dialysis in Barbados, among others. This sector can foster linkages between offshore medical education and provision of medical services could generate higher economies of scale, mutually beneficial for both sectors.

(Source: Caricom Secretariat, Guyana, South America, 2005)

Conclusion

Since the 1980s, the Caribbean has emerged as a developing democracy with honed instincts towards advancing entrepreneurship.

Governments have sought to implement market-oriented policies that are acceptable to international markets. The legacy of a plantation-type or agriculturally-based narrow economy has impeded the region's growth potential, not forgetting the persistent balance of payments issues experienced by Guyana and Jamaica particularly during much of the 1970s and into the 1980s. Currency devaluations affected sustainable levels of foreign revenue for investment in national infrastructure.

This chapter highlighted the trading relationship the Caribbean has with the Britain, Europe and North America and the real threats faced by small producers because of the growing enlargement of the EU since the early 1990s. The production of artificial sweeteners or beet sugar has also resulted in the decline of sugar exports coming from Guyana, Suriname, Trinidad and Tobago especially. The special relationship that still exists between the Caribbean and the UK is invaluable in terms of the existing trade protocol with the EU. The 1977 *Lome Convention's* successor, the *Contonou Agreement* which needs to be negotiated on mutually, agreeable terms; that is favourable to the participating countries in the African, Caribbean and Pacific group.

This section also looked at the importance of maximising opportunities in emerging sectors such as IT, cultural tourism, offshore medical education and healthcare, in order to counter the effects of globalisation and its effects on regional consumer markets, product segmentation, new technologies and expanded financial and trading zones. Undoubtedly, owners and managers have to face the task of learning new leadership and management techniques of innovation, whilst having to deal with the wider structural problems, irrespective of their firms' size and composition. The next chapter will overview the UK economy and show the impact of British Caribbean SME sector in helping the country to sustain its level of global competitiveness in the 21st century.

Chapter Notes

Small Business – Heads of Government declared 1988 as the `*Year of Small Business*' and the Caricom Secretariat organised several workshops and regional consultations while many studies were conducted. The period also saw the setting up of new Micro and small Enterprise (MSE) institutions.

ILO – the International Labour Organisation was founded in 1919 to advance opportunities for women and women to obtain decent and productive work in conditions of freedom, equity, security and human dignity.

Investor Survey – the Caribbean Investor Perception Survey was conducted by the Foreign Investment Advisory Service of foreign companies operating in the Caribbean to determine the various factors influencing foreign investors' location decisions in the region, as well as attractiveness of the different countries for foreign direct investment (FDI).

Single Market – January 2006 witnessed the component of the Caricom Single Market and Economy (CSME), a move aimed at deepening the integration movement to better respond to the challenges and opportunities presented by globalisation.

Growth Potential - about 14 leading sectors in the Caribbean have tremendous growth potential if they receive the right level and type of investments in terms of their size, composition and export-orientation of investments.

Major Commodities – during the period 1996-2001, machinery and transport dominated Caricom's imports from the UK while food dominated the region's export commodities to this trading partner.

Stock Market – with over $US1 billion in assets under management, CMMB has emerged as a pioneer in regional financial services and has raised the level of awareness and sophistication of the capital markers in the Caribbean through its publications such as the *Bond Guide, Fixed Income Quarterly* and *Stock Market Quarterly*.

Associated States – in July 1994 the Association of Caribbean States (ACS) was established to strengthen regional co-operation and the integration process, with a view to creating enhanced economic space in the region, among other things. Members comprise both the English-speaking and non-English speaking Caribbean states in the Americas.

Singaporean Model – this approach involves developing top notch national companies that can aggressively secure market share with continuous integration of productive factors to ensure national competitiveness based on an optimum mix of internal and external financial and business resources.

Selected References

1 *Benchmarking FDI Climate in the Caribbean*, Foreign Investment Advisory Service, World Bank, June 2004.

2 *Selected Indicators of Caricom Member States*, Caribbean Community Secretariat, Georgetown, Guyana March 2004.

3 *Stock Market Quarterly*, Issue 9, April 2005ue No. 9, CMMB Securities Limited, Port of Spain, Trinidad.

4 *Small enterprise development in the Caribbean*, International Labour Organisation, Caribbean Office 1999.

5 Best, Lloyd (1999): *Economic Theory and Economic Policy in the 20th Century West Indies: The Lewis Tradition of Town and Gown*, Basseterre, Eastern Caribbean Central Bank, November 3, 1999.

6 Yew, Lee Kuan (2000): *From Third World to First – The Singapore Story*: 1965-2000, Kuala Lumpur, Times Media Print Limited.

Chapter 3

Overview of the UK Economy

This chapter examines in some detail, the composition of the United Kingdom and the influence minority communities, including the British Caribbean population, have on overall governance. It shows the diversity of the country and how existing structures and systems have given rise to various meanings and expectations through both individual and collective forms of identity between the State and its citizens.

The second half of the 20th century witnessed the dismantling of the British Empire which controlled one-fourth of the world – Africa, the Caribbean, the Indian sub-continent and Hong Kong, among other parts of the world. The UK is a leading trading power and financial centre and is one of the quartet of trillion dollar economies of Western Europe, with a population of around 60 million (**2004 estimates**) comprising White, Black and Asian other ethnic groups. Geographically, the country is located along Western Europe, islands including the northern one-sixth of the island of Ireland between the North Atlantic Ocean and the North Sea, northwest of France.

The UK is a constitutional monarchy with executive power invested in an elected government headed by the Prime Minister (who is also Lord of the Treasury) and his Cabinet. After 18 years in opposition the Labour Party rebranded itself, `New Labour', moving the Party to the centre ground of politics, to become electable with a massive majority in the 1997 elections over the ruling Conservatives. Labour won again in 2005, but with a reduced majority. The Iraqi conflict contributed much to this debacle, with nearly half of all voters demonstrating their distrust of the government's handling of the situation, and one which has fuelled further controversy in other parts of the world, especially when Britain joined the US in the `war on global terror'.

The absence of a formal or written constitution has partly corrupted law-making in Britain and created several anomalies. One the one hand, people born in Britain or naturalised Britons are unsure whether they are subjects or citizens. In a traditional monarchy everyone governed by the Crown is supposedly a subject, but this situation has become complex with *Citizenship Studies* introduced in the National Curriculum at the beginning of this century. It is a reminder of the 1950s-1970s when `Civics' and later `General Knowledge' were integral to the Caribbean colonial education system. The curriculum covered the duties and responsibilities of citizens; these were applicable to most Caribbean colonies on the verge of winning Political Independence from Britain.

The various Acts passed of Parliament during the 1960s-1980s bore much relevance, and according to the Home Office, British nationals include British citizens, British Dependent Territories citizens, British Overseas citizens, British Nationals (Overseas) and British subjects. The law says that all British citizens have the 'right of abode' in the UK, but only a small proportion of other British nationals have this right. A few citizens of Commonwealth countries also have it. The `right of abode' is an unqualified right to enter, live and remain in the United Kingdom. People holding UK permanent residence (Indefinite Leave to Remain) do not hold this right, nor do citizens of other EU countries (including Irish citizens).

Nationality Dilemma

From 1949 to 1962, all Commonwealth citizens, whether they were citizens of the UK and Colonies, British subjects without citizenship, or citizens of Commonwealth countries, had this right. From 1962, even citizenship of the UK and Colonies did not in itself give automatic access to the UK. The British Nationality Act 1981 restored the link between UK citizenship and immigration rights by granting British citizenship only to those citizens of the UK and Colonies with the 'right of abode' in the UK. Other citizens of the UK and Colonies were granted subsidiary categories of British nationality such as British Overseas citizenship which give no right to enter and live in the UK.

The British Nationality Act 1948 created a citizenship of the UK and Colonies for those people who had a link to the UK (as it was in 1948) and the colonies which were British at the time. Citizens of the UK and Colonies, as well as citizens of all Commonwealth nations had the collective status of 'British subject' under the law in both the UK and other Commonwealth nations.

The creation of 'citizenship of the UK and Colonies' in 1949 did not make much difference to civic rights within the UK. Up until 1962, any Commonwealth citizen, or British subject without citizenship, could freely enter the UK to live and work (as could Irish citizens without British subject status). Even after immigration control was imposed in 1962, Commonwealth citizens legally in the UK retained the right to vote or hold public office, and most of these rights remain intact in the UK today, even though other Commonwealth nations like Canada and Australia have abolished reciprocal rights for Britons.

From 1 January 1983, UK nationality law changed again with the British Nationality Act 1981. Commonwealth citizens no longer had the status of British subject, and citizenship of the UK and Colonies was split into three categories: British citizenship, British Dependent Territories citizenship and British Overseas citizenship. People who were British subjects without citizenship retained that status under UK law.

By the early 1980s the fact that Commonwealth citizens were British subjects gave them no immigration access to the UK. This had effectively ended in 1962, and in fact from that date even among citizens of the UK and Colonies there was a division between those who had the right of abode in the UK and those who did not. The 1981 Act finally brought a degree of convergence between the UK's immigration and citizenship laws - only British citizenship in itself would give a right to live in the UK **(Table 3.1).** All other categories of British nationality gave the right to British consular protection and passport facilities, but no automatic right to live freely in the UK (***http://www.reform.org***).

Table 3. 1 Impact of various UK Nationality Legislation by period

Period	Impact of Legislation
1948	British Nationality Act created a citizenship of the UK and British colonies.
1962	Any Commonwealth or British subject without citizenship entered freely into the UK.
1983	British Nationality Act with three categories –British subject, British dependent Territories citizenship and British Overseas citizenship

(Source: Home Office, 2005)

British society is often challenged by issues pertaining to demography and immigration involving `outsiders' or `others' (as minorities) from Africa, the Caribbean, India, China among others, and as ideology and racism collide, the couple – the State and her dependents (the publics) - are locked in fierce competition as to whether to accept the level of immigration or `settlership' or contest on the grounds of keeping `Britain pure'. And yet while ordinary Brits may care less about this fact, it is known that black people have lived in the British Isles for centuries, observers note the presence of black soldiers in the Roman Legions and later, Caribbean nationals fought for `King and Country' and later for `Queen and Rule Britannia Rule'. However, it was not until the first half of the 20th century that significant, large-scale migration of Caribbean people occurred in the post-war period when British companies, in a bid to fill labour shortages, recruited individuals living in the British Commonwealth.

Accordingly, one writer stated that, "These migrations were not numerically the largest in British history, but in important respects they were definitive of the ethnic composition of British today" **(Smaje 1995)**. Numerically, the most important Caribbean migrant groups were Jamaicans, though Barbadians and Guyanese also constituted about 20% of the original migrant population. They were followed later by nationals from other countries including Anguilla, Grenada, St. Lucia, St. Kitts and Nevis, St. Vincent and the Grenadines, as well as Trinidad and Tobago. It should be noted that although most Caribbean people in the UK appear (physically) to reflect African ancestry, they and others have mixed heritage backgrounds.

For example, because Guyana and Trinidad and Tobago, more than any other Caribbean English-speaking country, have a large Indian/Asian population, it is quite misleading to categorise all Caribbean people in the UK as `Afro-Caribbean' (colonial) or `African-Caribbean' (modern). Other countries such as Grenada and Jamaica also have a fair amount of mixed racial groupings. A growing, small, but significant number of Caribbean nationals of Indian and African cultures, are today's reflection of the ethnic strains of British-hood – `African-Caribbean', Black British' British-Asian', `Asian' or significant `others. It is for this reason and more, why defining people of Caribbean background remains problematic, controversial and at worse, confusing. It is worth repeating here that Caribbean forbears and their post-war generation were victims of slavery, indentureship and colonialism (periods in British and Caribbean history that are well documented) respectively. In particular, the Slave Trade was perhaps the most damaging, since it contributed to the forced removal of masses of African people into the Caribbean, followed later by indentured labourers from India, China and Portugal, imported to sustain the plantation economy that was tied to European capitals for centuries. These historical events have therefore given rise to the modern culturally, diverse and plural societies such as the Caribbean Region and they are fast multiplying in the UK. These epochal events have a reference point to which Britain cannot escape or pretend not to have any knowledge of, since it is a shared destiny involving both Caribbean people and their British counterparts.

As the debate continues about changes to the UK system of governance, the concept of Republicanism has been discussed in a few circles as an alternative to the current `patronage' system especially since members of the House of Lords are selected and appointed by the Prime Minister rather than elected. In the first quarter of 2006, there was much furore over `cash for peerage' and for a country that prides itself on preaching to the developing world and minority communities about liberal values, this incident proved that no political system – developed or not – is flawless. The Republican lobby is relatively small and its views are often nullified by opinion leaders and monarchists who, despite calls for a rethink of the hereditary system, have consistently indicated (by their actions) that the tradition of patronage remains at least for the time being.

In addition few minorities discuss constitutional reforms for fear of either upsetting the status quo or they simply don't know what to make of their own presence in a democracy that is seemingly complex to outsiders. If however, Britain is to maintain its position as an influential player in global politics, a concerted effort must be made to implement radical reforms. Indeed, the present state of affairs regarding (Royal) subjects and (modern British) citizens is undermining the democratic values of not only mainstream Britons, but others who wish to make a greater contribution to development and change in the country. The British Caribbean business community's own input is thus a case in point.

Historically, England existed as a unified entity since the 10th century; the union between England and Wales begun in 1284, but it was not formalised until 1536 with an Act of the union. In 1707, England and Scotland agreed to permanently join as Great Britain – the legislative union of Great Britain and Ireland was implemented in 1801, with the adoption of the name the United Kingdom of Great Britain and Ireland. The Anglo-Irish Treaty of 1921 formalised the partition of Ireland, six northern Irish counties remained part of the UK as Northern Island and the current name of the country, the United Kingdom of Great Britain and Northern Island was adopted in 1927 **(ONS 2000-2005)**.

Since the beginning of the 21st century, there has been virtual self-government in Scotland and Wales and in mid-2007, Northern Island finally elected a Power-Sharing Government comprising various factions involved in centuries-old conflict on the island. Today, the notion of an independent Scotland is hotly debated as the Scots move towards greater self-determination.

Nonetheless, the system of devolved government has had mixed fortunes; on the one hand, it has encouraged greater representative and participative democracy in Scotland and Wales. On the other hand, the pattern in England is more complex since the country does not have a separate governing body, but instead, divided into nine Regions complemented by a range of assembly-type bodies, including an elected Mayor of London, as well as Regional Government Offices and Regional Development Agencies.

Regional Demographics

In mid-2005 the resident population in the UK was over 60 million, of which 50,763,000 lived in England. The population increased by 8% since 1971, from 55,928,000. Growth has been faster in more recent years and during the middle of 1991 and the same period of 2006, the population grew by an average of 0.4% and the average growth per since mid-2001 **(Table 3. 2)**. Minority communities are not evenly distributed around the country, but tend to be highly concentrated in more urbanised areas (**ONS 2005**).

Table 3. 2 Population Estimates for the United Kingdom 2004-2005

Whole of the UK	**Population Estimate** *(in millions)*
United Kingdom	60,209,500
England	50, 762, 900
Wales	2,965,900
Scotland	5,116,900
Northern Island	1,741,600
English Regions	**Population Estimate**
North East	2,558.3
North West	6,846.2
Yorkshire and Humber	5,063.9
East Midlands	4,306.3
West Midlands	5,365.4
East	5541.6
London	7517.7
South East	8164.2
South West	5067.8

(Source: Mid-2000 UK Population Estimates, Office of National Statistics, 2005)

Nearly half of all people in Britain of racial origin live in Greater London, compared with less than one in 10 of the white population. People of non-white background are less likely than white people to live in Wales, Scotland and the North East and South West Regions of England. More than 75% of people from Africa, the Caribbean and the Indian-subcontinent who have settled in Britain prefer living and working in the capital or on the suburbs of London. Caribbean people are the third largest ethnic group in the UK.

Yet three quarters of the minority population live in the Metropolitan Counties of: Greater London, Greater Manchester, West Yorkshire and West Midlands. Compared with less than a quarter of the white population, the concentration of individual ethnic groups is even more extreme. Greater London comprises more than 80% of the total African population, with nearly 60% of the Caribbean population and less than 20% of the Pakistani population. The concentration of ethnic groups in particular areas has been explained in terms of `choice' and `constraint' principles. The choice principle argues that Caribbean people for example, prefer to live within concentrated areas where their own `group' reside – for social support and shared linguistic, cultural and religious traditions. The constraint theory argues that minorities have often been prevented from moving outside certain geographical areas by the economic position, lack of information about housing opportunities elsewhere, and by discrimination or fear of discrimination.

The various skill profiles and experience among minorities also led them in their earlier arrival in Britain, to seek employment in key sectors. For example, Caribbean people lived in inner-cities to maximise job opportunities in construction, health care, clothing and other industries. **Table 3. 3** shows the category of minority groups based on actual census figures although the overall population has increased to 60 million since 2006.

Table 3. 3 Population by Ethnic Grouping

Group	No ('000)	%	Minority ethnic population (%)
White	54,154	92.1	-
Mixed	677	1.2	14.6
Indian	1,053	1.8	22.7
Pakistani	747	1.3	16.1
Bangladeshi	283	0.5	6.1

Other Asian	248	0.4	5.3
Caribbean	566	1.0	12.2
African (black)	485	0.8	10.5
Black Other	98	0.2	2.1
Chinese	247	0.4	5.3
Other	231	0.4	5.0
All other minority groups	4,635	7.9	100
All Population	**58,789**	**100**	**-**

(Source: Office of National Statistics, 2001)

For decades, demographers and ethnographers alike have been grappling with spatial distribution among minority communities, all of whom are vital to policy-making from political, economic and social perspectives. Statistics around the country suggest that the black population is the most segregated compared to the rest of the population across districts, although the same could be said for the Indian and wider Asian community, when indices are computed separately for inner-city districts such as Burnley, Leicester, Luton and Southall for example **(Stilwell and Duke-Williams 2005).**

Residents from the British Caribbean community are therefore located in various parts of the country though invariably, in highly concentrated and narrowly defined inner-cities or suburbs of England. More than half of all British Caribbean people reside in London/ Greater London, the Southeast, Midland Counties, the Northwest, Yorkshire and Humberside, with smaller `concentrates' in Scotland and Wales. Caribbean residents are the fourth largest minority group in the South west of England. About 45% of the region's Caribbean population for example, live in Bristol although Gloucester has the highest percentage of this community (**South West Observatory 2003**). Nationally, Lewisham has the highest proportion of Caribbean residents (12.3%). – **Table 3.4**.

Table 3. 4 British Caribbean presence as distributed by Regions

Region	Geographical Distribution
London/Greater London	Brent, Croydon, Ealing, Hackney, Haringey, Hammersmith, Havering, Islington, Kensington & Chelsea, Harrow, Lambeth, Lewisham, Merton, Redbridge, Southwark, Tower Hamlets, Wandsworth, Waltham Forest
Southeast	Reading, Slough, Surrey
Midland Counties	Birmingham, Coventry, Derby, Dudley, Leicester, Nottingham
East of England	Essex County, Luton
Yorkshire & Humberside	Scarborough, Sheffield
North & South West	Bristol, Leeds, Liverpool, Leeds, Manchester
Scotland	Aberdeen, Edinburgh, Glasgow
Wales	Cardiff, Newport, Swansea
Northern Island	Belfast, County Down

(Source: UK-wide Government Offices 2005)

Economic Status

Agriculture plays the smallest role in the UK economy, with farm production about 1.7% of the Gross Domestic Product (GDP), manufacturing about 20% and services 73% of GDP. Large manufacturing and the service sector have an important role in overall economic activity, accounting for 45.5% of total private sector employment (55.4%). There are approximately 3.7 million SMEs in the UK which represent 99.8% of all enterprises in the country. **(DTI 2004)**

About 12% of the labour force is self-employed; women comprise up to 26.5% of all self-employment activities. Female entrepreneurial activity rate was less than half of males – 5.1% - of working age men in 1999, but only 2% of working age women. It was suggested that if female entrepreneurial activity were to match that of UK males, the country's business start-up rates would increase by 50% **(OECD 2000)**.

The UK's industrial policy in the 1960s and 1970s was focused on supporting major heavy industries based on the advent of the Industrial Revolution in the 16th and 17th centuries respectively. In the early 1970s there was a decline in manufacturing with massive lay-offs and economic devastation in towns and regions where industrial plants and other factory installations existed. The need for economic revitalisation and diversification and job creation led to the adoption of a new 'enterprise culture' revolution – a direct move from dependency to self-sufficiency. During the mid-1980s, the Thatcher Government pursued this agenda with the setting up of enterprise development agencies, Training and Enterprise Councils and other far-reaching initiatives designed to stimulate enterprise in various communities.

The country has a long history of SME support and development and the 1971 Bolton Task Force Report on Small Firms recommended measures to support small firms. Local Enterprise Agencies were set up to help with the provision of 'managed workspaces' and were funded by local banks, the private sector and local communities. The introduction of the Small Firms Loan Guarantee Scheme in 1981 was aimed at improving the ability of firms to borrow money from traditional lenders in cases where they did not meet the necessary collateral requirements.

In the 1990s, Business Link was set up to provide counselling and advice to growth-oriented SMEs. The Single Regeneration Budget (SRB) was also established, to tackle economic underperformance in deprived areas. These policy initiatives were not adequate enough to tackle underperforming small firms and the loss of thousands of enterprises that went bust during the 1980s and 1980s. Anecdotal evidence suggests that only about 7% of all minority firms usually access enterprise support agencies and this trend continues.

The Government introduced The Competitiveness White Paper, themed *Our Competitive Future: Building the Knowledge Driven Economy* thereby giving enterprise a more pivotal role in UK public policy. The legislation set out measures to `tackle the fear of failure, increase the rewards of success, raise the level of entrepreneurial opportunity, and open up sources of finance for entrepreneurial ventures' **(DTI 2000)**. Among other things, the paper committed the state to look at ways of improving enterprise education (primary through post-secondary levels), a rebalancing of small business support towards new enterprises, the relaunch of programs to encourage the unemployed into self-employment and the general promotion of enterprise in the UK **(Table 3. 5).**

Table 3. 5 Key SME Policies and Programmes in the UK

Period	Policy Type	Aim
1960s	Government support for heavy industries – manufacturing etc	Improve productivity and spur industrial growth.
1970s	Local Enterprise Agency Scheme	Stimulate start-ups and help with the provision of `managed workspaces'.
1981	Small Firms Loan Guarantee Scheme	Improve the ability of small firms to borrow money from traditional lenders in areas where they had no collateral or security.
1987	Enterprise Allowance Scheme	Promote self-employment as an employment alternative.

1990s	Training Enterprise Councils	Post-16 vocational training and enterprise support to foster economic growth and strengthen community skill base.
1994	Business Link	`One stop shop' to provide counselling and advisory support to SMEs.
1999	SMART Scheme	Help with smaller projects undertaken by micro entrepreneurs by subsidising consultancy costs.
2000	Regional Development Agencies (RDAs)	Business-led, set up to promote sustainable economic development, main tasks to help English regions improve economic performance; reduce social and economic disparities
2000	Small Business Service(SBS)	Be a strong voice for small business in England.
2001	Learning and Skills Council (LSC)	Improve skills of young people and adults; ensure England has a workforce of world class standard.

(Source: DTI Strategic Framework 2000-2001, London, England (www.dti.gov.uk/about.into.htm)

Competition issues have been dogging policy makers for some time and the Government has been working relentlessly to find practical solutions to these hurdles. A combination of structural weaknesses and the consistent under-utilisation of the expertise of minority firms have resulted in the lowering of the UK's competitiveness benchmark over the past two years. The country has slipped from 9th position in 1997 to only 17th position by 2004 according to official sources **(Sheffield University 2005)**.

London, the Southeast and Eastern England performed on average compared to other areas in the UK. Scotland witnessed the `biggest decline in its competitiveness' since 1997 - a fall from 4$^{th}$ in 1997 to 8$^{th}$ position in 2005. The four `bottom' league regions were unchanged from 1997; Yorkshire and the Humber in 9th position followed by Northern Island 11th, Wales and 12th North East England. In North East England and the Midlands, the number of private sector employers was reduced with the public sector accounting for employment growth in these areas. In Scotland (77.6%) and Wales (55.4%) there were job increases in the public sector than in self-employment activities because of the introduction of `Regional Parliamentary' structures. Only London (53.1%) and Northern Island (65.9%) had more jobs created from the private sector, rather than the public sector between 1997 and 2004. The *Competitiveness Report* asserted that there was little evidence of the UK becoming a `more innovative and knowledge-based economy' since 1997, with public expenditure on research and development falling from 0.22% in 1997 to 0.2% in 2002.

Moreover, the desire to stimulate enterprise development in the country has not been matched by any real improvement. The UK's business start-up rate per 1,000 individuals has remained so as in 1997 – 3.2 per 1,000 persons, while self-employment rates fell between 1997 and 2003, from 12.9% of all those in employment to 12.6%. If policy measures for developing entrepreneurship fail to consider the sectoral contribution of minority firms, including the Caribbean segment, then it is likely that the UK will continue experiencing problems that can lead to the undermining of its competitiveness.

In terms of regional economic development, there were variations in the manufacturing and services sector. Manufacturing rates fell in every region between 1988 and 2002, and then increased in most regions in 2003. The impact of these changes on the UK rate for all industries reduced from 11% of business stock in 1998 to 9.5% in 2001, and then increased to 10.6% in 2003 **(Fig 3.1)**.

Figure 3.1 VAT registrations of business stock by selected regions

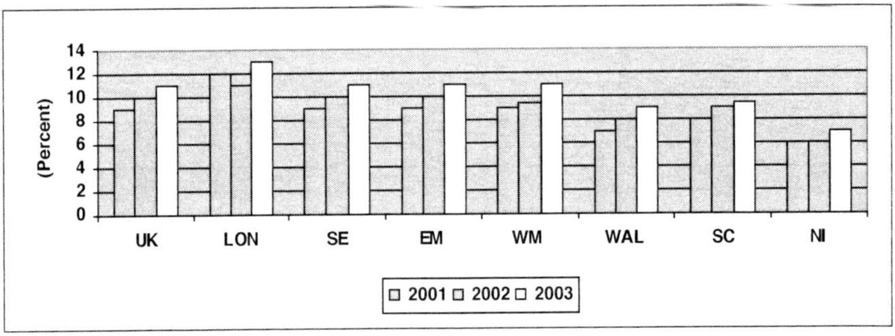

(Source: Small Business Service, DTI, England

Guide to abbreviated UK Regions: UK- United Kingdom, LON-London, SE-Southeast, EM-East Midlands, WM-West Midlands, WAL-Wales, SC-Scotland and NI-Northern Island

Regional Development Agencies

Under the Regional Development Agencies Act of 1998, development agencies came into being with Regional Assembly a title universally adopted by the English authorities as regional chamber. Their original role was to channel opinions to the business-led RDAs. They conduct a wide range of advocacy and consultancy roles with national government bodies ands the European Union, but their public profile is very low. Each acts as a Regional Planning Body with a duty to formulate a Regional Spatial Strategy, replacing the planning function of County Councils.

About two-thirds of Assembly members are appointees from the County and District Councils and unitary authorities in the Region, the remaining one-third are from other Regional interest groups. None is directly elected. The nine English Regions are as follows: East of England (5.3 million); East Midlands (4.2 million); London (7 million); North East (2.5 million); South East (8 million; South West (4.9 million); West Midlands (2.2 million) and Yorkshire & The Humber (5 million).

The English Regions which comprise 80% of the total UK population are more ethnically diverse than other parts of the country. In the 2001 Census minorities made up nearly 10% of the total population in England compared with only 2% in both Scotland and Wales, and less than 1% in Northern Island. About 78% of Africans and 61% of Caribbean people live in London. More than half of the Bangladeshi community (54%) also live in London. Only 19% of Pakistanis reside in London, while 21% live in the West Midlands, 20 % in Yorkshire and Humberside. What the statistics didn't show though, are the levels of economic activity by British Caribbean firms in the UK as **Table 3. 6** shows.

Table 3. 6 Type of employment by ethnicity, Great Britain

	MALES		FEMALES	
Group	**% full time**	**% self-employed**	**% full time**	**% self-employed**
• White	91.0	16.7	56.4	7.2
• Mixed	81.8	11.9	60.9	-
• Indian	88.1	18.2	64.0	6.9
• Pakistani	82.6	25.6	56.1	-
• Bangladeshi	65.2	15.9	65.6	-
• Other Asian	86.9	14.5	70.7	-
• **Caribbean**	**87.7**	**11.0**	**67.7**	-
• African	81.8	9.3	65.5	-
• Black Other	78.6	-	66.3	-
• Chinese	76.2	15.9	62.5	13.0
• Other	83.3	13.5	66.4	7.4
All ethnic groups	**90.4**	**16.7**	**57.0**	**7.1**

(Source: Labour Survey for Spring 2004 to Winter 2004/05

In Scotland and Wales, Caribbean firms comprise up to 12% combined in all entrepreneurial activities but this data has not been analysed and used adequately to target potential entrepreneurs, under-performing firms and existing businesses that need support to stimulate growth and sustainability. In other parts of the country such as the Midlands and Yorkshire and Humberside, there is no sound data and profiling of successful Caribbean firms and their input into local regenerations schemes, let alone the impact they have on regional economic policy.

Table 3. 6 shows the variation between full time employment and self-employment among the various ethnic groups and even though there is a reasonably low self-employment rate (11%) by members the Caribbean community, when compared with (their) 1% ratio of the total UK population, this figure demonstrates a satisfactory level of `economic activity', contrary to mainstream opinion. The figure of 11% is also an increase of 4% prior to 2004 when the figure stood at around 7.1% for a few years; that is, since the last two censuses of 1991 and 2001. To date, studies have failed to capture the full extent of the contribution of black businesses to the UK in general. While sourcing information and data remains problematic, it is vital that greater efforts be made to highlight positive trends in the British Caribbean SME sector by mirroring their performance through annual (country) profiles. I have sampled data of British Caribbean firms by region, percentage of self-employment activities and their area contribution, to illustrate the real net effect of Caribbean firms on the regional and national economic scene, despite limitations in size and composition **(Table 3.7)**.

Table 3.7 Level of self-employment activity by British Caribbean entrepreneurs

(Source: Regional and Country Reports, UK, 2005/2006)

Region	Number	% self-employed	Contribution
London	4,000	22%	£990 million
Southeast	2,734	5.7%	£114 million
East Midlands	1,110	5.5%	Unavailable
West Midlands	1, 937	6%	105 million
Yorkshire & Humberside	300	2.8%	Unavailable
Scotland	83	8.7%	£43 million
Wales	-	3%	-

Note: the above figures are based on actual estimates sourced from the UK Regions with rough calculations using a percentage of the total Caribbean population involved in self-employment activities according to available labour market information. The number of firms along with their contribution to the Welsh economy is unavailable and so is the figure for contribution of firms to the East Midlands.

During 1997 and 2005, this author conducted reviews on hundreds of Caribbean SMEs in London, the Southeast and the Midland Countries, which formed the basis of focused intervention, by examining challenges and prospects of the small firm sector, as well as analysing its organisation and performance. The reviews and audits were also part of a strategy to test new models of enterprise support, management and leadership training, capacity building, funding and procurement and promote best value. Much of the activities, apart from a few, were conducted using a co-ordinated, multiple partnership approach involving local authorities, universities, private sector companies and community sector agencies and organisations.

One initiative that had an enduring effect on both businesses and local authority personnel involved in regeneration and neighbourhood renewal, was a three-year enterprise support program targeting more than 50 African and Caribbean businesses and social firms in the neighbourhood ward of Harlesden, one of London's most deprived areas. This programme showed the effectiveness of genuine partnership-working and public-private sector co-ordination to create mutual benefits for all parties. The initiative also proved that by working strategically, firms can access tailored support despite a history of exclusion from mainstream enterprise agencies (**Minicase 3.1**).

Minicase 3. 1 The BME Business Programme in Harlesden

(Source: Impact Assessment of BME Business Programme, Harlesden, 2002-2005, London

The **BME Business Programme** was the brainchild of TCS Educational Trust Ltd that partnered the London Borough of Brent, west London to deliver an innovative three-year business support programme for African and Caribbean firms that were excluded for years from mainstream enterprise support. The programme was delivered in three phases in a part of London that is culturally diverse, with a large minority population. The three phases consisted of an economic research component, a skills training programme and a final assessment of the entire initiative. The following results showed proof of the programme's success:

Business owners were keen to create a network to further develop minority firms.

- 90% of business owners clamoured for enterprise support and funding.
- More than 50% felt that the business programme helped them.
- Over 25% were troubled by poor public services, high taxes and limited access to markets.
- 78% of firms benefited directly from the program.

- 40% of were sole traders.
- 64% participated in different types of market research.
- 57% of all business sectors had a business plan.
- 50% had a customer care plan.
- 64% expressed their intention to compile a business growth strategy.

The program reflected a positive commitment by the local authority to deal with challenges affecting minority firms in the area and much time was spent consulting with owners and mainstream companies, with several high-profile events organised to celebrate best practice. In the end, the business owners agreed to set up the **NW10 Connect** enterprise network aimed at maximising the opportunities that would arise from regeneration projects including the Wembley Stadium construction project, in the area.

Priorities and Programmes

Since their establishment in 2000, RDAs have implemented policy initiatives to encourage and stimulate greater involvement of minority communities into the decision-making process, with a view to boost enterprise productivity and ensure that regional performance is not affected by an under-skilled labour force and equally, under-performing firms. Priorities geared towards minority communities have been often labelled *`neighbourhood renewal'* *`social inclusion'* and *`community cohesion'*, to name a few slogans. To their credit, Central Government drives most of the RDA agendas, since they are Treasury-funded. The impression is that BME firms are usually too small in size and structural composition to be considered central to economic planning and development, and therefore should be restricted to the fringes of regional-national economic policy. This is evident in the number of deprivation studies that have been done to determine when and how, as well as the level of intervention required for black firms operating in inner-cities where deprivation was quite high. These studies do little to suggest the impact fledging British Caribbean firms have on local economies.

By rolling out programmes to accommodate `hard to reach' minority client-firms, the RDAs ensure that at the end of their fiscal year, they can tick their `equality boxes' and continue receiving subventions for minority business development. Much of the problems associated with black businesses and their continued exclusion from mainstream are contained in numerous studies on deprivation and exclusion – both public and private. This book will ignore the temptation of repeating a litany of `enterprise' woes and instead, acknowledge the significant work done by RDAs in London, East Midlands, Advantage West Midlands, and the Scottish Executive, for diligently analysing the multiple challenges facing small business owners firms and instituting measures to alleviate systemic and market failures that tend to undermine the performance of Caribbean firms particularly.

Sector Markets

Indeed, research around black firms in the UK has tended to be continuously flawed, as both independent agencies and public institutions rehearse problem-issues rather than focus on areas of growth potential and sustainability which are central to economic policy making for the SME sector, and which also serves the purpose of inclusion in terms of urban renewal. This situation however, has not affected much, the presence of traditional and non-traditional commercial and industrial activities by members from the British Caribbean community across the country.

In the decade of 1990-2000 in particular, most Caribbean firms experienced a combination of consolidation and slim, but significant growth and though these developmental cycles were never measured (both qualitatively and quantifiably) or for that matter recognised sufficiently. Barclays reported in 2006 on the level of progress minority firms made during that period, but stopped short to measure the impact these firms made to the UK economy.

In an effort to provide evidence on the performance of the Caribbean SME sector, I appropriated a Sector Excellence Model (SED) to capture relevant information and statistics on the sectoral dominance of firms in various parts of the British Isles. Pure desk research or other empirical methods of investigation are not sufficient to guarantee an objective appraisal of distinctive features on British Caribbean firms across sector categories and market segmentation (performance). If questionnaires, case studies and interviews are used to sample-size growth sectors, high yielding results could be achieved even when a skeletal piece of research is conducted. Several examples of business sectors from selected area regions are presented here to illustrate the effectiveness of the SED approach and its capacity to unearth valuable facts on different sectors and segments of British Caribbean firms, even as owners struggle against formidable challenges: operational obstacles, restrictive practices and market discrimination, as well as other barriers, to succeed **(Table 3. 8)**.

Table 3. 8 Sector Distribution of Caribbean firms in the UK

Region	Dominant Sectors	Time line
London	Building and construction, hairdressing, retail, music and clothing), restaurants, computing, professional services, medicare, social enterprises.	1907 to present
Southeast	Manufacturing, construction, hotels and restaurants, transport and communication, travel and shipping, business services, education and training, healthcare, social enterprises.	1950s to present
East Midlands	Food retailing, construction, services, education, healthcare, distribution and logistics, social enterprise.	1970s to present
West Midlands	Cleaning, travel and shipping, food retailing, construction, multi-media, healthcare, education, training, consultancy, legal services, personal care, publishing, security services, music production and promotion, manufacturing, social enterprise..	1950s to present

Scotland	Restaurants, takeaways, personal care, business services social enterprises, business services.	1990s to present
Wales	Construction, food, personal care, training, business services, consultancy, social enterprise.	1990s to present

(Sources: Independent research and analysis of official business reviews, UK 1999-2006)

In recent times, official studies from banks, research institutes and universities and other independent sources, have been critical of the low formation rate of the Caribbean small firm sector, as well as its underperformance in terms of turnover when compared to this community's population ratio. However, since the distribution of Caribbean communities differ from region to district and from ward to neighbourhood, it is possible that by using a mean average one can test the validity of such assertion. For instance, the British Caribbean firm's national start up rate or level of economic activity is 7% -11% even though the community is only 1% of the total UK population. This translates into one in every seven British Caribbean person is likely to set up a business each year whether it is micro, small or medium-sized. In spite of poor enterprise support and access to finance, along with barriers to entry in certain markets, firms continue to excel beyond their market potential and sectoral limitations in the British economy.

During the period 2004 and 2006, I conducted random surveys to examine the organizational structure and sectoral performance of Caribbean firms in London, the Southeast and Midland Counties particularly. It was recognized that enterprise agencies had more interest in obtaining information around `ethnic profiles' and routine problems affecting black businesses overall, rather than developing excellence models for researching effectively, ethnic firms in Britain. This has been the case for years as published labour market data shows.

The surveys which covered more than 25 key sectors across England also identified several features which pointed to the way owners managed their firms according to age, sectors, products and services, location, growth strategies and profitability. For instance, where information on market share for Caribbean firms was deemed problematic, or in the words of public agencies, clients `are hard to reach', sample-sized surveys and structured interviews were conducted in business clusters showing growth trends. This was done in response to a consistent pattern of evidence showing that the market share of British Caribbean firm was ignored coupled with their annual rate of turnover, all which are central to economic policy-making, regionally and nationally **(Table 3. 9)**.

Table 3. 9 Selected British Caribbean business sectors and turnover profile

Main Sectors/Segments	Estimated Turnover (£)
Consultancy	500, 000 – 3 million plus
Cleaning	500,000 – 1 million
Carnival Arts	50,000 – 400,000
Construction	100,000 – 2 million
Design	150,000 – 300,000
Retail	350,000 – 750,000
Food	20,000 – 5 million
Personal Development	50,000 – 375,000
Events Management	100,000 – 2 million
Transportation	500,000 – 750,000
Public Relations	100,000 – 1 million plus
Hairdressing	20,000 – 300,000
Financial Services	150,000 – 2 million plus
Publishing	350,000 – 4 million
Manufacturing	500,000 – 5 million
Healthcare	100,000 – 1 million

(Source: Independent Research, 2004-2007, England)

If **Table 3.9** is anything to go by, the evidence illustrates that, contrary to popular opinion, the performance of Caribbean firms in consultancy, cleaning, construction, events management, public relations, financial services, publishing and manufacturing, shows the vast potential for further growth especially in non-traditional areas. While the data may have highlighted the relative underperformance in the food (restaurants, takeaways and catering units) and hairdressing sectors due to operational problems and market competition, it can be assumed that if each sector's market share was computed, using the annual turnover divided by the number of clients of each, the figure might vary between 2% and 3% plus for the above industry sectors and segments. If also, the figure for social enterprise is included (the national average for Caribbean start-ups is 6%) then the market share will increase considerably.

As **Table 3.9** also suggests, 17% of the firms in various sectors have a turnover in excess of £3 million, while 11% generate £1 million and over, 23% generate a yearly £500,000, 40% have a profit margin of £100,000 - £350,000 and 9% of firms generate under £100,000. There are variations in profit margins depending on the location of firms; those on the high street tend to do exceptionally well compare to firms trading in the suburbs or deprived neighbourhoods. By industry standards therefore, the British Caribbean enterprise sector can be classified in terms of size and composition, as micro, small and medium-sized in character, even though smaller firms are engaged in enterprise activities equivalent to medium-sized type companies.

In the last five years, there has been significant growth around healthcare firms and professional services such as events management, training, PR and consultancy, with micro and small businesses dominating the scene. Even more interesting, are the number of professionals among the highly creative and asset-valued group of entrepreneurs in Britain today, a fact duly acknowledged by Barclays plc in 2006.

Regional Growth

Further, since the overall BME business sector pumps an estimated £30 billion per annum into the UK Treasury, a reasonable estimate suggests that Caribbean firms which make up between 7% and 11% of all economic activity, contribute approximately between £2-£3 billion annually to the UK economy, with more than 50% or over £1 billion input into the city of London and the Southeast Region respectively, while firms in the Midlands Counties contribute over £100 million, the Northeast and West, Yorkshire and Humberside, along with Scotland and Wales, contributing the remainder of the market value for minority businesses in both the local and regional economies in the UK.

In major cities across the 12 UK Regions, Caribbean businesses have mushroomed, and in some instances have surpassed the regional average in terms of performance and general output, thereby contributing to the Gross Domestic Product in the respective areas. GDP is a measure of the total economic activity in an area and it can be described as the final goods and services produced by the economy. Although the GDP figures used in this book are based on 2002 estimates, they reflect a growing trend in the way in which British Caribbean firms have been contribution to wealth creation in the UK as a whole as the statistics below illustrate (**Table 3.10**).

Table 3.10 Selected city areas of Caribbean self employment activity

Area Region	Number	% self-employed	% of Population
Essex	295	8.2	1.61
Luton	160	5.3	1.3
Birmingham	1,004	6	4
Leicestershire	160	6	0.5
Cambridgeshire	226	2.9	0.82
Sheffield	313	1.3	1.7
Leeds	200	1.7	4

Note: the estimated number of firms has been calculated by dividing the Caribbean population in each area by the percentage of those self-employed. The information was obtained from the 2001 census although some of the figures have been updated based on recent surveys in each of the selected areas above.

Apart from routine statistics and the rehashing of current problems, the real success of Caribbean enterprises from a policy perspective is not considered a media priority. Publicising positive stories on these businesses is worthy, since it provides not only confidence to entrepreneurs, but also enables the wider public to have greater insights into the tangible contribution non-white people are making to the UK economy. Publicising the enterprise success of minority firms is also important to public institutions, especially policy-makers who are keen on learning more about changing patterns in business, consumer, financial and trade markets.

Then again, it should be emphasised that there is no central database for minority firms by sector activity and structural composition in the country. Apart from being a major obstacle, this situation constitutes a real dilemma for local and national strategic planning. Even though current estimates suggest that the cumulative value of minority firms to the British economy is £32 billion per annum and increasing, this fact has not filtered through to the wider society. The fact too, that support agencies keep little strategic information on Caribbean firms is also proof why researching this sector is deemed problematic, and yet there are a host of methods that could be used to secure information and data on this growth sector in the UK.

For the purposes of this book, information on British Caribbean firms and social enterprises was obtained from numerous sources. In the absence of official statistics, case studies were used to examine issues affecting firms, as well as existing and future opportunities owners should exploit for market advantage. In spite of the research dilemma, a range of datasets were utilised to analyse the organisation performance of Caribbean firms from a sectoral perspective. By using multiple sources, it was possible to firstly, testing the validity of official sources of information; and secondly, to cross-reference estimates throughout the UK based on the growth, development and performance of British Caribbean businesses and social enterprises in the various sectors included in this book (**Fig 3. 2**). Data was therefore obtained from the sources below: -

Figure 3.2 Datasets used to access the British Caribbean SME Sector

- Newspaper profiles on small firms;
- Performance Review of local business associations;
- European-funded business support program;
- *Women Into Business* courses;
- European-funded audit of cultural industries;
- Healthcare reviews and business planning sessions;
- *Ethnic Minority Economic Data*, Government Regional Offices;
- Presentations to public institutions that organisation special events;
- Interview owners of commercial firms and social enterprises;
- The *BBC* website;
- *The Blacknet UK* Business Directory; and
- Scientific Commons.

Some ethnic publishers allocate space to promote entrepreneurial success but there is a tendency to simplify entrepreneurial achievement by accentuating greatly, the entertainment value of the minority community. Caribbean firms are diverse and a sector model is required when publicising challenges and opportunities of this sector. Realistically, a `one fit all' strategy is ineffective since businesses are complex operations to manage particularly in a highly competitive global economy where ethnicity, entry barriers and restrictive practices can result in either success or failure. As a former publisher, I am aware of the little appetite mainstream editors have for success stories on black economic achievement.

Yet it is mind-boggling to observe the media's obsession with stories of underachievement affecting Caribbean children in mainstream schools, the use of harmful drugs by a proportion of black youths, allied to the rap/gun culture of inner-city youths across England. Differences aside, civilised societies have an obligation to promote harmony, tolerance and co-existence between and among various communities rather than preaching these essential human values to developing states or emerging democracies. The media has a moral obligation to balance the subjective and objective reporting of news and information on issues affecting communities in the UK. The racial disturbances involving Asian and Caribbean communities in November 2005 in Handsworth, Birmingham was typical of the fear, insecurity, distrust and isolation, partly generated by media frenzy, apart from economic and social problems affecting deprived communities.

Nonetheless, if British Caribbean firms are to compete effectively in the global economy, owners ought to put in place, a market intelligence system to access opportunities in key sectors of the economy. They must exploit the comparative advantage of technology and the integration which the UK economy offers. Such flexibility means that firms can be in a better position to maximise returns by introducing cost effective management practices in staff recruitment, sourcing quality materials and equipment from suppliers (competitively priced) and taking advantage of the UK's advantage in valued-added services in design, financial services and innovation. **(Fig 3. 3)**

Figure 3.3 Comparative advantage of the UK Market

The UK economy possesses a number of strengths which put British-based businesses at an advantage when competing in global markets and which attract businesses to locate in the UK. These include:

- A tradition of **open and competitive markets** – encouraging competition and pushing for free trade in goods and services.
- Strengths in **science** – with just 1% of the world's population, the UK undertakes 4.5% of the world's research, produced 9% of the world's scientific papers and receives 11% of the world's prizes for those papers. UK scientists claim around 10% of internationally recognised scientific prizes every year.
- A highly **creative economy** – the cultural industries account for 8% of the UK gross value added in 2003, with employment in this sector totalling 1.8 million jobs. The sector grew by an average of 6% a year between 1997-2003.
- Historical linkages to **overseas markets** – as a member of the European Union, the UK has access to the world largest marketplace. It also has strong trading links with Africa, the Caribbean, China, India and other Commonwealth countries. Use of English as an international language of business – the main language of books, newspapers, airports and air traffic control, international business and academic conferences, science and technology, diplomacy, sport, music and advertising. Over two-thirds of the world's scientists read in English, 75% of the world's mail is written in English and 80% of the world's electronically stored information is in English.
- **World class universities** – the UK is a global centre for higher education, with several institutions in the top 50 worldwide, London school of Economics, Imperial College, University College London, Cambridge and Oxford, as well as the School of Oriental and African Studies.

(Source: Globalisation and the UK, HM Treasury, Britain, December 2005)

In late 2005 at the annual Treasury Enterprise Conference to discuss the UK's economic challenges in the 21st century, apart from a token British-born Caribbean entrepreneur from Sir Alan Sugar's television programme, '*The Apprentice*', there was no dialogue on the input of Britain's ethnic SMEs to enable the country to meet the necessary global economic challenges. Much of the conference discussions were dominated by 'sparring matches' – Britain versus the EU versus the WTO and the like. With a handful of African, Asian and Caribbean businesses and professionals, little wonder they showed any 'stomach' for such discussions even though the debates were generally informative, illuminating and refreshing.

In studying the Treasury's blueprint for the UK economy, summarised in a document presented by then Chancellor of the Exchequer, Gordon Brown, in November 2005, the prospects made interesting reading. The 60-page document covered topics ranging from the UK's prestigious location to the world as a leading financial centre to the implications for not responding to the global competitive challenge.

The document brought together several policy initiatives, but it was the '*Long-term Global Economic Challenges and Opportunities for the UK*' that was impressive. The challenges are no doubt ideal, for both large and small firms alike, and are even more important to the British Caribbean firm sector; they include:

- Macro economic stability in a more integrated global economy.
- Building an enterprising and flexible business sector where firms can succeed.
- Where firms can seize opportunities in more open and competitive global markets.
- Promoting innovation for scientific research and knowledge-driven industries.
- Opening up the acquisition of skills for the global economy.
- Ensuring fairness and provide financial security to those in need.
- Increasing the energy and resource efficiency of the economy.

Conclusion

This United Kingdom is a trillion dollar economy and over the years it has become a magnet for social, financial and technical capital. Three of the 12 regions have independent Assemblies, including Northern Island with a Power-Sharing Government formed in mid-2007 after centuries-old conflict. There has been some discussion on devolved government involving some English Regions in an attempt to create more local accountability and enhanced democracy particularly for minority and other communities that experience multiple disadvantage in terms of unemployment, poor housing and other social ills associated with exclusion.

This chapter also covered briefly, the migration of Commonwealth citizens to the UK and the legislation that was implemented to reduce the number of settlers from both the African continent and the Caribbean region. With the increase in the minority population over the past 20 years, there been a gradual integration of Caribbean people into the mainstream of British society. This has been achieved despite the persistent racial prejudice and other forms of discrimination experienced by many in this community. The enterprise success of thousands of Caribbean residents was illustrated by information and data from official and independent sources throughout the UK.

It was suggested that annual reviews on the organisation and performance of Caribbean firms like other enterprises, was a necessity to measure the impact of their contribution to local advancement, as well as the UK economy as whole. In the next chapter we will examine the challenges confronting British Caribbean business owners in their quest to maintain a competitive edge in the marketplace.

Chapter Notes

Citizenship Studies – in September 2002 Citizenship Studies became a statutory part of the national curriculum, aimed at helping young people understand their rights and responsibilities and becoming responsible members of society.

Immigrants Act – the Commonwealth Immigrants Act ad a succession of laws passed in 1968, 1971 and 1981 restricting black entry to Britain. This his period saw the emergent struggle against race prejudicc and intolerance by African, Caribbean and Asian people.

Black London – in AD 50 Roman London, Africans served the Roman army – an African craved wooden spoon was found at Southwark Bridge showed the earliest African connection in Southeast London.

Population Growth – the Caribbean population is just over 1% and yet members of this community contribute more than 10% to commercial and social enterprise development in the whole of the UK. Members from this community are concentrated in different pockets of inner-city areas. This situation is also described as spatial distribution, meaning the dispersal of communities across the UK.

Intelligence Observatory – a dedicated website site aimed at improving access to research and intelligence, thereby improving the quality and relevance of research undertaken. Most of the nine English Regions have set up these sites.

Bolton Report – named after its author J.E. Bolton who chaired a national Committee of Inquiry on small firms. The report is reputed to be the first of its kind to consider the role of small firms in the national economy, the facilities available to them and the problems confronting them and to make the necessary recommendations.

Competitiveness Report – a document that contains (evidence-based) indicators such as investment in key skills, cost effective and efficient management practices, quality control systems, market flexibility, premises, infrastructure, trade portfolio and other prerequisites, to measure a country's growth and level of competitiveness.

Best Value – was introduced in 1999 to replace compulsory competitive tendering (CCT). Best Value is founded on the principles of challenge, compare, consult and compete, with the general idea of ensuring that all statutory services should be delivered in manner that befits these principles.

Sector Excellence Model – formulated by this author and applied to a selected group of owners of commercial and social enterprises, operating in traditional and non-traditional sectors and segments of the UK economy. If applied, efficiently, this model can provide vital clues to the problems affecting underperforming firms, locally and regionally.

Selected References

1 Benzeval, M; Judge, K and Smaje, C (1995): `Beyond Class, Race and ethnicity – Deprivation and Health in Britain', *Health Services Research* 30: 163-177.

2 Bolton, J.E (1971): `*Small Firms: Report of the Committee of Inquiry on Small Firms*', Cmnd 4811 (HMSO, London).

3 Regional Economic Profile, Issue 2, September 2006, South West Observatory, South West England.

4 Population Estimates: Components of population change for United Kingdom 2991-2004 and 2004-2005, Office of National Statistics.

5 Stilwell, John & Duke-Williams, Oliver (2005): *Ethnic population, distribution, immigration and international migration in Britain*, School of Geography, University of Leeds, England September 2005.

6 Annual Report of Department of Trade and Industry 2004.

7 Competitiveness White Paper, Department of Trade and Industry December 1998.

8 DTI Strategic Framework 2000-2001.

9 UK Productivity and Competitiveness Indicators 2003, DTI economics Paper No. 6, Department of Trade and Industry.

10 Labour Force Survey for Spring 2004 to Winter 2004/05, Office of National Statistics.

11 Ethnic Minority Businesses economic contribution, Northwest Regional Development Agency, 6 September 2005.

12 Bedfordshire and Luton Employment Study: Final Report, Bone Wells Associates, London April 2005.

13 *The Regional State of Women's Enterprise in England*, Prowess Ltd, England 2005.

14 *Ready for Business; The contribution of black businesses to London's economy*, Greater London Authority December 2004.

15 Foner, Nancy, (1979): `West Indians in New York City and London: A Comparative Analysis', *International Migration Review*, Vol. 13, No. 2, Special Issue: International Migration in Latin America, pp284-297.

16 Ward, Robin and Reeves, Frank *(1980): Racial disadvantage: West Indians in business in Britain,* House of Commons Home Affairs Committee: Race Relations and Immigration Sub-Committee.

17 *Moving on Up? Bangladeshi, Pakistani and Black Caribbean women and work*, Equal Opportunities Commission September 2006.

18 Byron, M (1994): *Post-war Caribbean migration to Britain: The unfinished cycle*, Aldershot, UK: Ashgate.

19 Peach, C (2004) `Caribbeans in the United Kingdom', In, Melvin Ember, Carol R. Ember and Ian Skoggard (eds.) *Encyclopedia of Diasporas*, New York, Kulwer Academic/Plenum Publishers, pp624-633.

20 Fraser, S (2004); `Finance for Small and Medium-Sized Enterprises': *A Report on the 2004 Survey of SME Finances,* Centre for Small and Medium-Sized Enterprises, Warwick Business School, University of Warwick England.

21 *Globalisation and the UK*, HM Treasury December 2003.

Chapter 4

Challenges facing Business Owners

Introduction

This chapter will examine major challenges faced by British Caribbean business owners as they endeavour to adapt new trends in the global marketplace. The survival strategies of owners will help to demonstrate competitiveness in the face of restrictive practices. In effect, this book will showcase selected individuals who became successful entrepreneurs by commercialising ideas into (marketable) products and services to fundamentally change factors of production, distribution and exchange in the UK. Against the backdrop of continued obstacles such as barriers to entry, structural problems, skill issues and access to lucrative contracts, among others, owners and managers have fought relentlessly to overcome. Other challenges faced also involve the generation factor, competence symbols, corporate social responsibility and inadequate enterprise support. Businessman and author, Tony Wade, has said repeatedly that `Caribbean people have to work ten times harder to succeed in the professions and business activities because of systematic racial prejudice and discrimination' **(Wade 1997)**. Yet British Caribbean businessmen and women profiled in this book have shown remarkable resilience and tact by competing in markets that in some instances were considered the main preserve of white companies.

The small firm sector is pivotal to the UK economy because of its culture, flexibility and innovation, as well as its efficient and low-cost operations. There are an estimated 100,000 minority firms, including Caribbean firms which represent between 7% and 10% of all economic activity in the UK. Small firms in general account for 3.2 million self-employed people, reflecting 12% of the total population **(National Employment Panel, England 2005).** Culture and innovation are star qualities that enable British Caribbean businesses owners to develop specialist products and services, new technologies, modernise production techniques and access niche markets in both traditional and non-traditional sectors such as food, manufacturing, security, information technology, publishing, consultancy, to name a few.

Atlantic Comparison

Despite racial prejudice, the sterling achievements of African-Americans are both the pipe dream and aspiration of Caribbean and other non-white communities universally. Yet, the political and social history of America is different. The majority of African-Americans were born in the USA, and the country has a written constitution priding itself on the hallmark of excellence, the renowned *`American Dream'*. The Civil Rights Movement campaigned for *Affirmative Action* legislation that was introduced in 1973 and thereafter, African-Americans took steps to establish their own institutions and lobbied Federal Government for active participation and institutional representation in every facet of US society. Since that period, however, the Republican Lobby (the Bush Jr Administration) has questioned the validity of Affirmative Action; that is whether in its current form, it constitutes a form of `positive discrimination' and one which may have implications for the current political climate in the country.

In contrast, British Caribbean people represent less than two per cent of the total UK population and unlike the USA, there is no formal written constitution; there is instead a `Bill of Rights' convention, with citizens treated as subjects rather citizens, though this fact has been cleverly disguised by the introduction of Citizenship Studies in September 2002. Citizenship education was introduced in all secondary schools in England, catering especially for 11-16 year olds and linked to all relevant curriculum guidance materials in England, Wales, Scotland and Ireland.

The *Race Relations Act* (1976) and the 2000 Amendment, along with the *Equalities Act* (2007), have done little to resolve restrictive practices by some large companies and mainstream institutions. Civil unrests during the decades of the 1950s, 1960s, 1970s, 1980s, 1990s, also did little to change the picture in Britain, apart from streams of high-sounding enquiry reports. The MacPherson Report however did have some impact, when it accused the police of '*institutional racism*' following the inquiry into the horrific death of the school teenager, Stephen Lawrence in 1993.

On the positive side, John Archer was the first black mayor in the UK (Battersea, 1913) whilst Guyanese, Randolph Beresford, was the first Caribbean-born Mayor of a London Borough (Hammersmith & Fulham 1976). Despite the colour bar, sports personalities, professionals and other practitioners were recognised and rewarded for their invaluable contribution to British society. Trinidadian Lord Leary Constantine, former West Indies cricketer, was the first black Peer (1962) followed by Grenadian physician, Lord David Pitt who was the longest serving black Parliamentarian having granted a life peerage in 1975. Bernie Grant (Guyana) and Dianne Abbott (Jamaican parentage) were among the first group of black British MPS to join the House of Commons in 1987. Abbot is still the first black woman to achieve that political feat. Valerie Amos (Guyanese) was the first black woman Cabinet Minister to be Leader of the House Lords (2003-2007).

Other life peers include Dominican-born, Baroness Patricia Scotland who made legal history by becoming the first black female QC at the age of 35 in 1991, is also the first black female Peer. Lord Waheed Alli is the youngest member of the House of Lords of Lords. Another Guyanese, Sir Herman Ousley was the first black head of the Commission for Racial Equality. Grenadian Baroness Ros Howells is another Life Peer who has earned many firsts in her active campaign for justice in the field of race relations. Harvard-trained lawyer, David Lammy, who replaced Grant, is a minister in the Labour Administration. In summing up, the Caribbean 'conquest' of the Lordship system, one leader writer said:

When they first came to Britain a half a century ago to lowly positions in the National Health Service or London Transport, it was hard to imagine that Caribbean immigrants would scale the social heights of the motherland. But with the beach-head they have now on Mount Lords, they are well on the way to getting to that very summit" (**Mair 2001**).

Despite these notable achievements, there is no single authority that can truly articulate a sustained political, economic and social agenda for the British Caribbean community. Loosely coordinated networks including social enterprises, have attempted to plug this gap, but with limited success. In the mid-1980s, the Ethnic Minority Business Initiative was conceived by the Home Office to develop a framework of inclusion for non-white firms affected by racism and prejudice from mainstream companies and institutions. Following the Brixton disturbances in 1981, the Scarman Report recommended greater African-Caribbean participation in business to "earn" their way out of poverty. This scheme also determined the agenda for several agencies between 1982 and 1984 (specifically the Greater London Enterprise Board, the Greater London Training Board, and the London Co-operative Enterprise Board) which were not specifically set up for such purpose, but through which support to minority firms was chanelled for much of the 1980s (**Memon, 1988**).

The London Development Agency is the first such public body in England to include black businesses in its strategic plan, although this has not been widely publicised in the mass media and filtered down to the average minority SME in the capital. Further to that initiative, the Mayor of London instigated the formation of the **African Caribbean Business Network** to act as a regional, representative organisation encompassing the hopes and aspirations of African and Caribbean businesses in the capital. In the launching the organisation in 2001, Mayor Livingstone said this about the ACBN: -

African and Caribbean Business make a vital and growing contribution to London's economy. As a significant players on London's economic scene, African and Caribbean businesses must receive appropriate recognition and support from government institutions such as the Greater London Authority, the London Development Authority, Business Link for London, the DTI and the local Learning Skills Council. By raising their profile of these businesses, African and Caribbean people will take pride in ownership. This newly emerging sector has specific needs which must be addressed. I see the formation of the ACBN as timely. It is a voice positioned to talk directly to and for the African and Caribbean business people **(LDA 2001).**

Some business owners hope that the ACBN would not be limited to a `talking shop' especially since they have got used to witnessing various community ventures scuppered after funding is exhausted. There is also scepticism regarding issues on enterprise support such as the failure of some advisors and brokers to deal efficiently with original business ideas and the cultural sensitivity that underpins their success. For example, only a few agencies are capable of advising young entrepreneurs on start-ups in the multimedia technology segment of the creative industries. There is a belief that the London business organization can be a fresh impetus for the conversion of business ideas into commercially viable products and services for the economic progress of the capital. The success of the GLA study on African and Caribbean businesses **(2004)** in London has reinforced the importance of genuine partnership involving public authorities, businesses and their communities, to achieve common aspirations and goals.

Organisation Structure

Another test confronting British Caribbean businesses is that of organizational structure and general staff profile; all firms are categorized as micro, small and medium in composition. Staff levels usually dictate the nature of firms and their activities. Micro units (with less than 5 persons) such as carpenters, mechanics and engineers in particular, recruit one or more staff depending on the workload involved. Staff may include a business partner or part-time secretary to deal with customer queries and general correspondence. In terms of end-of-year financial reports, owners may hire accountant/auditors to prepare and submit business accounts to Companies House.

The management style of owners and managers is another feature of British Caribbean business development although research remains largely exploratory on this subject. Styles differ depending on the type of firm – manufacturing, production and services. Independent and official research suggests that management styles of non-white businesses change as firms evolve 'as the focus of the founder shifts from passionate commitment to being objective (**Figure 4**). It means that owners need to adopt a more realistic approach to the business rather than a strictly personal one' (**Clifford & Cavenaugh 1985).**

Figure 4.1 Organisation structure of average-type Caribbean firms

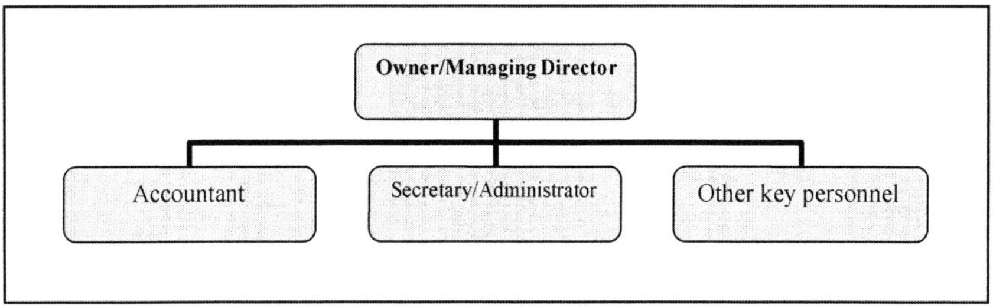

(Source: Adapted from independent research done on UK firms, 1999-2007)

In the British Caribbean SME sector, there is some evidence too, that founder-managers have a reached a 'delegation crisis' in which they are unable or unwilling to relinquish any degree of control over important decisions. This of course is primarily due to the process of transition from founder-ownership to maintaining continuity by passing the mantle to succeeding owners in cases where the business has problems or is faced with winding up **(Churchill & Lewis 1973).** The majority of owners haven't considered succession planning or passing on the business to a next of kin, friend or business partner, as a viable growth strategy. During 2002-2005, one study revealed though, that 5% of owners realised the importance of succession planning as an exit strategy, especially in cases of emergency such as sickness or death **(Brent Council 2002: BBA 2005).**

Human Capital

Recruiting quality staff is a challenge to all businesses today, but more so, it is particularly formidable for minority enterprises because it involves issues such as confidence, managerial authority and control, discipline and the right staff composition, coupled with relevant recruitment selection and placement procedures, all of which can impact positively or negatively on firms. While the Learning and Skills Council estimates that 7 million adults are functionally illiterate, its targets are to help 750,000. A survey of 1.3 million middle and lower level jobs carried out in 1993 by the Institute of Employment Studies found that almost every job requires some competence in basic skills (**Moser 1999: IES/ALBSU 1993**). Poor work ethics, excessive sick leave, frequent time-off and requests for more holidays away from work, are problems faced by employers. Disrespect for functional authority and the abuse of subordinates by supervisory and/or managerial staff are areas of concern that need tackling swiftly to improve employer-employee relationship in the work environment for the benefit of improved levels of production and productivity.

There are persistent skills shortage in almost every sector in the UK, with vacancies in administration, clerical, supervisory, technical and others difficult to fill. Like the developing world, the developed British Isles has its fair share of out-migration too, with hundreds of Britons emigrating to Commonwealth, European and North American destinations. It is estimated that one in 12 British nationals may be living abroad, a total of about 5.5 million. Apart from pensioners looking for retirement in the sun, many leaving each year are young and highly skilled. Experts suggest that this represents four in 10 were in managerial or professional occupations (**Johnston 2007**). Skills shortages are therefore a challenge to all companies including British Caribbean firms, and a problem affecting the UK's global competitiveness as the indicators showed in the last chapter.

In 2004 a study by the GLA showed that black firms employed 70,000 people which represented 3% of the total workforce in the capital. This trend is also prevalent in other regions where minority firms generally, contribute reasonably to local economies, all of which add up to an average cumulative input of 5% to the total UK pool of economically activity employees.

However, research indicates that labour constraints may arise either through a lack of available skilled or unskilled workers or due to the unwillingness or inability of small firms to pay the going market wage rate (**DIUS, HM Government 2007: CBI and DfES 2005).** It has been argued consistently that the main problem experienced by firms considering growth was the recruitment of skilled labour (**Lloyds 2006**). Based on existing research, therefore, it seems reasonable to conclude that labour availability is a problem, especially when the economy is buoyant. It should be noted here, that while skill shortages are a problem for British Caribbean firms, businesses with more than 10 staff usually buck this trend, by using either agency staff or recruiting `quality' referrals as employees. This is evident in sectors such as computing, education, healthcare and professional services which require a high degree of competence and experience.

Small firms (with more than 10 staff) may recruit at least two specialist posts – an administrator/secretary and a technical person to deal with routine tasks. This flat structure is fairly defined in areas such as manufacturing, education, training and related services that are specialist sectors. Medium-sized businesses (with more than 20 staff) demand appropriate staffing. For instance, a typical small to medium-sized firm may have a managing director, operations/project manager, administrator, an accountant and a tier of supervisory and technical support staff. Firms with elaborate structures consist of construction, manufacturing, production, food, social care, education, technology and other service sectors. **Focus Consultancy, Nichols Employment Ltd, Cleone Foods, Universal Service Solutions**, and other such companies fall into this category.

It is estimated that up to 20% of British Caribbean firms are owned and managed by highly skilled and experienced professionals. A third of all owners have between 10-20 years experience and have held management positions in mainstream public institutions and private agencies prior to setting up their own concerns (**Johnson 1999).** It is important that business leaders continuously strengthen their firm's leadership, managerial, technical, financial and strategic competences to be able to compete and improve market share.

Yet the expansion of these enterprises is affected by various risk factors; namely inadequate staff, limited investment, poor technology, restrictive markets (which have a bearing on profit margins) and lack of incentives for expansion. These however, have not affected the ability or desire of owners to continue trading, as this book confirms.

Generation Factor

Age and gender are often used to evaluate the performance of employers and employees and their corresponding effect on the economy, but local labour market statistics have done little to show the influence of the `generation factor' on the overall productivity of minority firms. Independent research suggests that owners fall into three broad age categories: 30-40; 40-50 and 50-60 plus, and despite their varying levels of experience, knowledge, training and or technical competencies, all three groups have success as their main goal. A younger cohort, under-30 are also making inroads with their specialist brand of leadership, products, services and negotiating competence, along with an appetite for affluence and market positioning.

The first generation of Caribbean settlers used their disadvantage to pursue business start-ups: Arif Ali **(Hansib Publishing)**, Tony Wade (**Dyke & Dryden**), Mike Harry (**Sunshine Homes**), Everton Forbes (**Forbes Travel**) and Winston Pickersgill (**New Look Travel),** triumphed, with more than 150 years of combined industry achievement. Ali is in full-time book publishing; Wade has produced two brilliant books, *How They Made A Million* and *Black Enterprise in Britain and* is still active in enterprise activities. Harry has treaded between construction, employment training and financial services. Forbes and Pickersgill are among the leading travel and shipping agents in London.

The second generation of British Caribbean people are among the country's leading minority entrepreneurs. Members from a cohort of 30-50 something, with support from families and friends, have established all types of businesses in key sectors, as they compete for a lion share of the market. Unlike the pioneers of the 1950s and 1960s, these core entrepreneurs comprise professionals, ex-employees of public and private sector agencies, plus social activists who utilise their experience and contacts to improve diverse communities. They all relish the challenge of competing in an open market where they are comparatively, in a better position (unlike their peers) to acquire the necessary skills to manage diverse commercial firms along with social enterprises **Table 4. 1** illustrates the age category of owners and industry sectors they manage and the different competencies they impact on their respective niche markets.

Table 4.1 Characteristics of Business Owners by Age Group

Group	Sector/Segment	Competence	Values
30-40	Cultural industries, consultancy, training, computing, social enterprise, retailing, technology, leisure, catering, personal care	Qualified in areas attractive to both professional and commercial aspirations; they seek to build on these via enterprise activities	Believe in swift wealth acquisition; risk takers and leadership between consultative and co-operative.
40-50	Cleaning, education, training, healthcare, consultancy, business services, legal services, travel/shipping, IT, food retailing, food production, transport and logistics	Multi-qualified often with accreditation from various professional bodies; combine intellectual and entrepreneurial skills to achieve results	Some members of this group tend to see business as a lifestyle affair; others regard it as a serious commitment - beneficial to them and community.
50-60 plus	Construction, financial services, professional services, production, retail, technology, social enterprises	Least qualified though there are exceptions among some; group members have vast experience, maximise the use of contacts and knowledge advance cause	Conservative leadership style, slow to diversify; risk averse; enjoy the respect of public authorities - they have progressive agendas.

(Source: Interviews with business owners, UK 1999/2007)

As the above figure shows, the age groups of entrepreneurs reflect a set of leadership values combined with professional and technical flair that have enabled all three generations to be successful in business. In the last few years, it was noticeable that entrepreneurs from a much younger age group – those under-30 – are quite economically active than let's say the over-40 group. In other minority communities, this development is also apparent, pointing to the importance younger people have attached to self-employment activities. Current business leaders in the 40-50 age group actually started trading in their mid to late-30s, whilst pioneers of the British Caribbean SME sector established companies in their late 30s to early 40s. According to a leading survey on BME firms in the early 21st century:

The rapid growth of young minority entrepreneurs (British Caribbean ones in particular – the author's emphasis) in urban areas, coupled with their propensity to start new firms, could signal an exciting new generation of entrepreneurial talent. A significant proportion of the younger generation (members) are committed to remaining in their communities as their parents. This augurs well for them in providing a fresh impetus in the regeneration of their cities **(GEM 2004).**

Noteworthy, such variations in the generation or age factor demonstrate two things; firstly, the majority of the 11% of the total British Caribbean business population are not only matured or seasoned entrepreneurs, but have adapted well to the economic cycles including recession periods in the UK and the world at large. Secondly, these trends support the evidence contained in numerous studies on the UK small firms sector since the 1980s which explained the resilience and creativity of minority firms in the country, especially their part in boosting growth in the economy.

The challenge for the British Caribbean community is to work with support agencies and organisations to tap into the potential that exist among young black people who are interested in enterprise but who need help with direction. This action will assist in reducing the low level of business formation rate which experts classify as disappointing from an ethnic minority firm sector perspective.

Finance

The lack of accessible and affordable finance remains a major constraint too, for small firms in the British Caribbean context. In fact, obtaining finance and the availability or access of premises is very problematic for minority firms in general. This factor has almost impeded the growth potential of firms especially in sectors with little cost over-runs. The constraints in relation to capital investment (start-up) or expansion funds are mainly due to:

- lack of collateral
- poor credit
- low capitalisation which limits borrowing capacity
- high risk involved in unproven management capability
- inexperience in accessing markets

Coupled with the lack of sufficient start-up funds, many owners are unable to source working capital resulting in premature failures or underperformance in particular industry sectors. In fact, working capital has been identified as perhaps the single most relevant constraint affecting the progress of small (minority) firms. Interestingly, more than 30% of all British Caribbean firms polled by this author since 1999 explained that they used a combination of personal savings, (friends) borrowings and overdrafts to start-up or keep their businesses afloat. In a survey done in the West Midlands covering British Caribbean firms, all 100% owners said finance posed a problem for business start-up. The owner of an IT firm explained how he managed without commercial support:

With an overdraft of £500 I made up my mind that if the bank was not willing to give me a loan I would have to go it alone and luckily, I had some extra cash which I saved from my redundancy package to start the company. I was surprised since this was the 1990s when the government was trying to encourage minority communities to be more active in self-employment. The negative reaction that I received from the bank manager was certainly due to ignorance and prejudice, since he did not think that a Caribbean person was capable of setting up an IT company despite having the knowledge and experience to do it' **(Bailey 2006)**.

Owners representing other sectors voiced similar experiences and only a small percentage since that period had any real banking facility such as overdrafts and access to additional banking facilities. These were only possible when proof of business plans and or formal requests showing reasons for capital investment and so forth were provided. Micro firms have further issues to contend with in this area, most notably, service companies contracting with local authorities. Quite often, client numbers are low and these affect profit margins which in turn, create a `high' risk factor for commercial institutions since lending is not and cannot be a realistic and viable option. The issue of late payment by large institutions do have an adverse effect on the profitability of small firms, let alone their credit-rating capacity from the bank's perspective. It is vital for owners to weigh the cost and benefit when planning strategies for start-up, growth and expansion irrespective of which type of trading sector.

Marketing Campaign

Apart from a host of private concerns, there is no formal institution in Britain that is fully capable of marketing and/or promoting minority firms - their products and services in national, regional and international markets. The presence of an export promotion council has not served these businesses overall, except on the odd occasion when authorities are desperate to show international governments and companies especially in North America, that cultural diversity is alive in the UK. Agencies like Business Links that have responsibility for engaging firms, haven't done enough to help British Caribbean companies to access national and international markets. Less than 5% of owners have regular access to information pertaining to incentives for innovation, export, technology, research and the like. Having membership with Chambers of Commerce, local business associations and trade networks doesn't offer owners an automatic guarantee of technical support, a view commonly shared by British Caribbean business leaders in the country.

In addition, business advisers and enterprise management consultants are not always keen to share information since there is a perception that owners may not need specific types of information. In other instances, it is assumed that owners are unable to use information and data effectively, in which case, it is of little or no value to them. Lack of financial and human resources also restrict British Caribbean entrepreneurs from putting in place a sustained marketing campaign to promote the products and services on offer.

With changes in national consumer markets and developing trends in inter-continental and other global markets, small firms should tailor their strategies to maximize trading opportunities. The challenge therefore, is for SMEs to access total markets by:

- researching market opportunities and developing sector specific information
- participating in relevant exhibitions and trade shows
- developing joint marketing arrangements among members
- building organizational capacity to promote specific goods; and
- developing the basics of small scale export marketing and financial management.

Business Information

Business information plays a key role in helping firms to achieve business competitiveness and success. The ability to access the right information at the right time and at the right price and using it to add value to enterprise activities is a major factor in a firm's ability to compete successfully in export markets. The demand for the supply of information is not often clearly understood by business start-up operatives, particularly if they are poorly advised from the beginning. Availability, access and comparability often make it difficult for enterprises to use information that is available.

With rapid changes in globalization, legislation and general procedures for business operations, owners have to be knowledgeable about the new information age. British Caribbean SMEs are under pressure to improve the quality and consistency of products and services in a market where competition is high in relation to human, financial, technical, distribution and supply, along with procurement chains. These resources are required more than ever, to upgrade and remain competitive in both domestic and overseas markets.

There are several agencies and institutions in which information can be accessed, but the market for business information is perceived to be complex and not quite open. Suppliers of business information range from policy institutes and private research companies to independent brokers. Business owners often take information for granted because they either cannot afford it or disregard its value, until there is an urgent need to conduct market research and /or when there is a marked decline in the firm's competitiveness. Information is required for different reasons – market contracts, customer profiles, new products and services, types of technology, premises availability and a host of other areas that might seem unimportant to enterprise development. Failure to take into account the importance of business information can indeed, make a huge difference between the survival and failure of a firm.

Enterprise Learning

The enterprise culture in the UK is alive but minority firms still lack the kind of orientation which can allow their organizations to become world-class leaders. Despite the recipe of skills training available for start-ups and existing firms, only a fraction of British Caribbean firms have accessed training in areas such as inward and external investment opportunities, financial resources to invest in a variety of business processes, corporate leadership and management techniques, and quality market research, export marketing management, global institutional cultures and markets.

A CBI report suggested that Government should increase the number of women and ethnic minority entrepreneurs in deprived areas of the country. It argued that the ways to tackle the problem should be to:

- Ensure that the regulatory and taxation systems enable and encourage enterprise.
- Make the necessary investments in infrastructure in all regions.
- Improve access to finance for certain groups;
- Enhance support to particular groups to facilitate start-up and growth (**CBI 2006**).

Additionally, the business organisation explained that the number of people with skills and knowledge to start a business varied significantly between ethnic groups including the members from the Caribbean community who had the knowledge and skills and experience rating of over 60% **(Fig 4. 2)**.

Figure 4.2 Knowledge and experience of business start-ups

(Source: Global Entrepreneurship Monitor, 2005)

Note: the above figures represent percentages

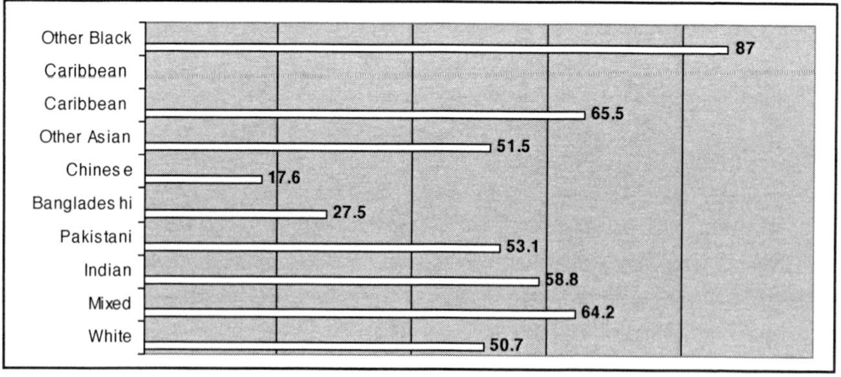

It is known that the majority of mainstream support agencies, as well as independent brokers, have a menu of business programmes that are either generic or routine; that is, they don't often meet the specific needs of minority firms operating in sectors that require a culturally sensitive, specific approach. In an effort to meet the demands of British Caribbean SMEs, an action learning curriculum for entrepreneurial skills development should be implemented with appropriate delivery agencies, supported by local trade associations and related neighbourhood networks, to help create `market acceptable' entrepreneurs in the UK.

Competence Symbols

These have an important role to play in the image and general reputation of a firm; they reflect the organisation's culture and its symbiotic relationship with staff and the wider publics. Symbols also relate to slogans, mottos and generally, customer philosophy. And yet there is little information and data available on this facet of industry in literature dealing with the minority firms sector in the UK. There is a preoccupation with, and over-simplification of, racial and cultural differences, allied to problems affecting this sector. Culture is defined as a code of behaviour, beliefs or simply a way of life. Due to their informal approach, British Caribbean business owners are often described as *`laid back'*, a term that assumes that they're not serious business people; lacking managerial competence to lead firms. Nonetheless, owners reflect their choice of company slogans and their usage to reap commercial success as stated below:

- The motto of TCS Tutorial College Ltd (education) is *`I am Somebody Great';*
- The maxim of Body Classics (personal care) is *`Be generous to customers';*
- The philosophy of DWT (construction) is *`Each situation has to be looked at individually, with a view to designing a solution specifically for that Challenge'; and*

- The customer charter for Hansib Publications (publishing) is *`Our job is to make information to the widest possible reading public'.*

By creating unique slogans, firms have enhanced their brand image and inspire confidence among staff and customers. These slogans also partly explain the leadership of business owners. Production companies have mixed dictatorial and relaxed management styles, while service-based firms have a more consultative style, since owners employ a more people-oriented or human-centred ethos. The dynamics of firms are too fluid to prescribe a rigid leadership style even though an autocratic system might be essential to enforce control and related codes of organisational practice. Independent research suggests that 55% of all British Caribbean business owners and their employees have values similar to mainstream companies **(Table 4.2).**

Table 4.2 Value Profile of British Caribbean Firms

Owners	Staff
Careful	Fitting in
Flexible	Resourceful
Adaptable	Job satisfaction
Stable	Competitive
Innovative	Maximising opportunities
Informal	Creative conflicts
Decisive	High expectations
Collaborative	Sharing information

(Source: Adapted from Strategic Flexibility, Wiley & Sons Ltd, 1998)

Table 4. 2 shows that people who have worked together for some time develop values, traditions and customs, which are then automatically shared and understood by all. This is a secret, but guiding principle by many of today's British Caribbean firms. Indeed, values play a critical role in the way employers and employees interface to achieve the goals and objectives of the firm.

Policy Regulation

Another formidable challenge facing Caribbean SMEs is that of policy regulation. Mention was made in this chapter of a strategic framework for business development, but it is also relevant to policy regulation governing black firms in general. For what its worth, the Government's minority enterprise development policy is largely piecemeal and does not address sectoral performance, productivity and sustainable development of this sector. In the main, black business owners tend to just `get on with it' and will probably `take on board' token policies around social inclusion and community cohesion, bordering on capacity building when the opportunity arises.

With the exception of the London Development Agency, Advantage West Midlands and the Scottish Executive, the policy scope is limited when it comes to British Caribbean businesses in general. The constant lament that they are few in number and do not readily constitute a critical mass, is an inherent failure to recognize that minority communities on the whole, are dispersed throughout the country and their needs require a combination of approaches. The example given in the last chapter on a model enterprise support scheme in West London is one but significant indicator of what is required.

From a legislative point of view, when SME policies are tabled in Parliament there is little evidence to support the actual state of BME businesses. To begin with, case studies on key sectors can be the basis for a performance review of British Caribbean firms, regionally and nationally. Other minority firms face the same dilemma and this situation has existed since ethnic monitoring began over 20 years on sector-based industries in the UK. There isn't much debate either at the regional or sub-regional level and Chambers of Commerce have been slow to react to changes in minority firms; that is, their level of start-ups, sector diversification, customer segmentation, difficulties around investment capital and interventionist strategies to counter the decline or underperformance of potentially viable, firms particularly those trading in low-income neighbourhoods.

Each year, a large chunk - over 60% - of European funds are allocated to deprived and excluded inner-city areas, but less than five percent of black businesses and social enterprises benefit from this resource. Additionally, tens of millions of pounds are allocated for enterprise support - in excess of £2 billion over the past year - and yet there is no definitive policy using a sectoral model for British Caribbean SMEs that are among the fastest growing firms in the UK today. There is insufficient evidence as to how these funds have been spent, their beneficiary values and the impact such investments have on minority firms' levels of production and productivity, and more specifically, in regeneration areas.

In the final section of this book, we shall examine a strategy aimed at British Caribbean businesses in the UK via a long-term policy encompassing among other areas:

- definitional framework;
- sectoral representation of firms and enterprises;
- net contribution of each sector;
- cumulative contribution of firms by region and country;
- percentage ratio of these firms to the UK's GDP;
- mix of incentives for firms contributing to key industry sectors;
- corporation tax relief to companies investing in regeneration;
- incentives for modernization and expansion to meet industry standards; and
- establishment of a national business council.

Social Responsibility

Owners and managers of private companies are encouraged to show greater corporate and social responsibility in the affairs of society. It is argued that their contribution to this effort brings added social benefits to firms and those most in need. For Caribbean SMEs, it is both a challenge and opportunity. The principle of social responsibility was pioneered by the first generation of Caribbean nationals more than 50 years ago. As a counter to racial prejudice, business leaders pioneered social responsibility by establishing social enterprises and community organisations to empower the deprived and the excluded among them.

Initially, social organisations were formed, followed later by business associations, partnerships and other alliances that, in some instances, were mainstreamed, replacing the *'I can go-it-alone'* attitude. Whether it was Birmingham, Manchester, London, Liverpool or any other city, community enterprises blossomed through self-help. It is these changing *'opportunity structures'* that have played a great hand in business formation across Britain (**Waldinger, Aldrich, Howard & Ward, 1990**).

A few examples of this innovation were the founding of the **League of Coloured People (1930s)** by Dr. Harold Moody, the **West Indian Standing Conference (1959),** co-founded by William Trant, the **New Testament Church of God (1953)** founded by Dr. Oliver Lyseight, along with other social enterprise initiatives across the UK. The presence of community finance initiatives or 'CFIs' and business incubator centres in London, Birmingham, Sheffield and Manchester are all testament to the dedication of sections of the Caribbean communities and others who invested time and resources towards improving the welfare of their community and in the process, supporting the modernisation of inner-cities and suburbs. These initiatives prove that modern markets could be initiated by the desire of people to reallocate their value and goods for services and goods for money.

Caribbean communities are known for their latent thrift and for ages, they have used various methods of self-help to secure financial independence. *Su-su* or *box-hand'* involves friends, neighbours, relatives or work mates pooling their finances which are held by an elected fund administrator. Each *`pardner'* (person) is entitled to a weekly *`box-hand'* or sum of money on a rotational basis. A proportion of funds are held in a reserve account. This semi-credit union is similar to *Christmas Club* in many English neighbourhoods. The difference is, in the latter case there are more withdrawals and in-payments than the former.

However, business owners still have to confront the reality of being unable to access sufficient investment capital for start-ups and to fund growth-expansion. By applying the principle of social responsibility, it might be possible to pool a percentage of their returns to set up a revolving for micro firms and social enterprises that deliver essential services in social care, community education (Saturday schools), rehabilitation programmes for ex-offenders and a range of other welfare-oriented ventures. In chapter 15 there will be further discussion and analysis on the performance of British Caribbean professionals regarding the growth and development of social enterprise in the UK.

Contract Tendering

Accessing contract or procurement opportunities is also a formidable challenge for the British Caribbean SME sector. In a predominantly service-based economy, the inability to access lucrative public and private sector contracts could severely hinder growth and affect profitability, which in turn, can impinge on the growth of small firms. Successive British Governments have applied instruments in the Race Relations and the Equal Opportunity Policy Acts to change the attitude of Local Authorities and large companies towards BME firms. Critics have argued that owners should try and understand the contract compliance systems first, before complaining about discrimination. Of course, they are different types of contract-agreements which involve:

- Supplying materials, equipment or artisan labour;
- Professional or consultancy services;
- Plant, supply or design and build; and
- Carrying out management contracts.

Businessman Mike Harry suggested that owners should institute appropriate systems to manage contracts efficiently so that they could ensure positive results in terms of delivery and customer satisfaction:

All businesses whether large or small, must have measures to deal with financial control, labour and supervision, targets, customer satisfaction and referrals. There are pros and cons of contract management that need considering too. Closing a contract is vital to sustaining one's business and a professional approach to monitoring the activities of the contract is key. We must bear in mind that we are competing in a market where trends are changing. Customer choice and client expectations will dictate the way contracts are made and executed, but also the owner's ability and capacity to adapt to the new regulatory business climate (**Harry 2001**).

Restrictive practices also come in the form of racial discrimination and prejudice. So then, how can Caribbean firms fight this twin problem? The transport removal company, **Benjamin Oswald**, uses its database, including repeat customers and information networks, to obtain data and background information on lucrative contracts. Customer referrals and business contacts (including competitors) are also used to secure deals. This process is assessed routinely to measure variations in output and overall company performance. Lee Williams, who owns the cleaning company, **Universal Service Solutions,** explained his experience in the procurement business:

As a company, you cannot take the market for granted. When we first began trading in the 1990s with private companies and later government institutions, we made sure we invested in all-

round technical support. When you don't have specialists in your organisation, as the owner and managing director, you have to consider investing in someone who is good at procurement. In the end, if you recruit a professional person, your investment can pay dividends **(Williams 2006).**

Veteran business leader, Joy Nichols whose firm is a market leader in the healthcare recruitment sector, also viewed access of procurement opportunities as a serious issue:

For years, we have survived as a company by looking at opportunities in both public and private sector markets and structure the company and its systems to suit. We have recruited qualified and experienced people with knowledge of the market, plus created partnerships to deliver contracts. Our company won a lucrative LDA procurement contract to stimulate growth among minority firms in the capital **(Nichols 2004)**.

In responding to allegations of unfairness in the tendering process, Central Government replaced Compulsory Competitive Tendering or CCT with Best Value which has, as its core values – consult, compare and compete. A further effort was made to adopt a fairer tendering system by firstly, piloting two procurement pilots in Haringey and Birmingham. The main purpose was to engage excluded communities and strengthen their organisational capacity to enable access to tender opportunities. There is no concrete evidence to suggest that firms landed major contracts.

In the East Midlands, the notion of procurement has taken on new importance with some large companies pursuing 'supplier diversity' strategies to meet their corporate (social) responsibility objective. Through '*Meet the Buyer*' events and other practical hands-on sessions, the supplier diversity challenge is being championed in that region by De Montfort University, under the leadership of Professor Monder Ram, an expert on ethnic minority business policy.

To date, the work of the Centre for Research into Ethnic Minority Entrepreneurship has attracted minority firms and some Caribbean firms have maximised the opportunity to meet and learn from mainstream buyers about various techniques in contract tendering.

Even so, the majority of British Caribbean businesses consulted, are least interested in ethnic monitoring. Why? There is no guarantee that it will eradicate discrimination in the tendering process simply because recording, checking and verifying procedures are not necessarily full proof, especially when managed by personnel who are unsympathetic to clients from various backgrounds. In short, no amount of regulatory framework could prevent or even isolate temporarily, the inherent racist prejudices of officials.

The flipside of this however, are the extreme commercial pressures on contractors, particularly working with under price-based contracts, particularly in the case of housing associations, contracting firms and local authorities. A merit system is therefore vital to ensure that businesses, irrespective of their ethnicity or nationality, are treated fairly.

Enterprise Support

One of the onerous challenges facing British Caribbean SMEs is accessing quality support including relevant technical assistance in both start-ups and existing firm operations. During 1997- 2005, independent research showed that over 75% of African and Caribbean business owners had no access to quality support from mainstream enterprise agencies. Government figures suggest that less than 10% of all minority firms have access to enterprise support. In the nine English Regions alone, there are hundreds of agencies and brokerage facilities providing services to SMEs. Yet, the vast majority of minority firms don't receive ample help and support needed. Signposting and a bit of information on minimum start-up requirements is often seen as patchy or piecemeal as minority firms (especially new start-ups) require specially, tailored market sector support in order to gain competitive advantage. Advice on premises, export markets and inward invest opportunities is also problematic **(GEM 2004)**.

The advent of CFIs in the late 1980s hasn't solved the problem altogether since much of the work done by these agencies is around start-ups, with existing firms and those at the lifecycle of maturation or decline stage, in a precarious situation with little or no help at all. There is a dire need to establish facilities that cater for specific sector-type firms, with advisers, consultants and other technical personnel adequately trained and experienced to handle a more effective and efficient sector-based approach to enterprise support.

These centres could provide services such as information, consultancy, technology, accounting, quality testing, consumer marketing, designing, packaging and ICT services for businesses at various stages of development. The overall challenge is for British Caribbean firms to look for enterprise support agencies that cater for their cultural, social and business requirements. There is an absolute necessity for a national authority to help facilitate this process – the urgency is therefore sooner rather than later.

Indeed as this chapter highlighted, there are various challenges – personal, official and business – that British Caribbean owners have to grapple with. Overcoming hurdles to achieve enterprise success is a lesson in time, patience and the appropriate level of resources in terms of social capital, market intelligence, goodwill, financial investments, access to consistent, quality and targeted support. Understanding the business market is crucial in deciding the pace of growth and expansion, as well as sustaining the operations.

It is the case that, initially, business owners set several goals and objectives and quite often these targets seem elusive, but by focusing on a clearly defined structure, along with satisfying customer demands for quality and affordable products and services, owners can achieve invariably, the results they aspire to (**Table 4. 3**).

Table 4.3 Challenges of British Caribbean Firms

Challenges	Effect on Firms
Organisation Structure	Firms have flat structures; micro, small to medium; staff levels dictate operations, as well as management and employee values.
Human Capital	Quality staff is a challenge - there is a national skills shortage in Britain with an estimated 7 million unable to read or write properly.
Generation Factor	British Caribbean owners are in age categories: 30-40; 45-50, 55-60 plus, with the under-30s fast emerging as modern entrepreneurs.
Finance	Limited access to investment capital and inability to secure affordable premises affect the growth potential of firms.
Marketing Campaign	No formal institution promotes the products and services of black firms in national, regional and international markets.
Business Information	Accessing the right information is essential to business success.
Enterprise Learning	Quality education and training is vital for world-class entrepreneurship –more than 60% of all British Caribbean people have 'knowledge and experience' of enterprise development.
Competence Symbols	Business owners use competence symbols to highlight quality products and services and customer-expected product values.
Policy Regulation	There is no well articulated and coherent Caribbean SME strategy.
Social Responsibility	Caribbean people have used their disadvantage to set up businesses and social enterprises to create social cohesion in inner-cities.
Contract Tendering	Inability to secure contracts hinders the growth and profitability prospects of small firms. There is no official evidence suggesting that procurement schemes have increased market share and profits for African and Caribbean firms respectively.

Enterprise Support	Challenge to British Caribbean SME sector development. Research shows that a large proportion of Caribbean business owners have no access to quality enterprise support. Official data suggests that less than 10% of all minority firms have accessed enterprise support.

(Source: Textual analysis based on trends in the Caribbean SME sector, 2000-2007)

Conclusion

This final chapter in Section 1 looked in some detail, at the various challenges affecting British Caribbean owners and managers of firms. Issues around organization structure or the structural composition of the firm, the importance of social capital, generation factor, finance, marketing campaigns, business information, competency symbols and policy regulations including enterprise support, were all analysed. It was noted that although there are similarities on the challenges faced by mainstream versus minority firms, the latter's situation was far more intense because of entrenched discrimination and prejudice in British society. It was further recognised that the eventual success of Caribbean-owned firms in the UK was hinged on owners' determination to gather adequate market intelligence, whilst updating it regularly, to stay in contention.

However, the enterprise challenge remains where owners of minority firms are less likely to receive consistent, quality technical assistance and enterprise support for start-ups and existing business especially if owners choose to operate in traditional sectors that were once considered the preserve of white-dominated companies. In the next section, a total of 11 emerging industry sectors would be analysed to show proof of the British Caribbean community's commitment to enterprise and economic development in the UK.

Chapter Notes

Civil Rights – the Civil Rights Act of 1964 was aimed at making discrimination, exercised by governments or employees in the US against any individual because of such individual's race, colour, religion, sex or national origin, unlawful.

Affirmative Action – among other actions, this American law requires `all reasonable steps must be taken to ensure that qualified minority and women candidates have available to them the same educational and job opportunities that are available to non-minority or male candidates' (**Cohen & Sterba: 2003**).

Minority Firms – a Small Business Service survey on BME businesses showed that almost 50% of these firms didn't seek any advice at start-up stage.

John Archer – was the first person of African descent to hold civic office in London; he was of mixed race, Barbadian father and English mother. He won many prizes as a professional photographer. His record to the local community was extraordinary.

Lord Constantine – described as cricket legend, political activist, Lord Leary Constantine was the first black Peer in the House of Lords. He was called to the Trinidad Bar in 1955 and served as that country's High Commissioner from 1961 to 1964. In his book, *The Colour Bar* (1954), he wrote about his experience of Britain and his life within the society.

Lord Pitt – apart from an outstanding career as a physician specializing in medicine, Lord David Pitt was an extraordinary politician and legislator in both the Caribbean and Britain. In 1943 he founded the West Indian National Party and served as its president until 1947. In the 1950s he defended the growing black population against discrimination and prejudice by heading the Campaign Against Racial Discrimination (CARD), an association he founded with the encouragement of Dr. Martin Luther King Jr.

Randolph Beresford- came to Britain in 1953 as an adult and when confronted by prejudice, he joined Hammersmith and Fulham Trades Council and fought hard to stop racial discrimination. This author was privileged to co-author his biography, *A Journey Through Life – from Guyana to Ghana*, Entra Publications, Hertfordshire, England 1995.

Bernie Grant – described as an activist was Britain's first non-white Councillor and one of the first such MPs. Grant was also one of few charismatic political leaders of modern times. Although he courted controversy during his 40 year campaign for racial justice and minority rights, he was a powerful link between British minority communities and African nations particularly, the world over.

Lord Alli – became the youngest Peer age 34 in 1999 and it was thought that he might help the Prime Minister to reach out to a younger generation. He influenced the government policy during the drafting of the Communications Bill in 2003 and took over as chairman of the media rights company, Chorion in the same year.

Workplace Demands – apart from the level of functional illiteracy in the UK, it is estimated that between 65% and 70% of employment opportunities will require a Level 3 qualification by 2010. Only 41% of UK 25-28 year olds held such qualifications in 1998. Of 19-21 year olds, the figure was 43% (**DfEE 2000**).

Britons Emigrate – since 1997, over one million (1.8) Britons have left the country and about 900,000 have returned. At the same time, more than 3 million foreign nationals arrived and about half that number left. Whilst this situation affects levels of immigration, surveys indicate that another million Brits are set to leave permanently over the next five years and a further 500,000 will live overseas for part of the year (**Johnston 2007**).

Boosting Enterprise – the Confederation of Business and Industry (CBI) advised the government to implement suitable measures to boost enterprise across the population, by encouraging more enterprise in minority communities, as well as groups that are disadvantaged and under-represented. The organization forecasted that there will be 2.6 million more self employed men and women by 2020 (CBI 2006).

Regional Action – London Development Agency has an integrated ethnic business development strategy. Advantage Midlands had set up a Centre for Expertise for minority business concerns and the Scottish Executive carried out a series of comprehensive reviews on minority firms throughout Scotland – both in urban and suburban areas.

Christmas Club – a tradition that encourages consumers to set up special savings account at a local bank or credit union or a trust. The money is saved for holiday travel, shopping and generally as means of having extra cash to spend on other consumables. Popular in Britain and America. In the US, a Christmas Club cheque can be automatically transferred into an American Trust account or mailed in late October for consumers' holiday shopping.

***`Meet The Buyer'*** - this De Montfort University initiative is popular with minority firms including a small but significant proportion of Caribbean business owners in the East and West Midland Counties, who have benefited from *`Meet The Buyer'* events such as seminars and conferences to discuss with large companies the techniques of procuring goods and services.

Selected References

1 *Enterprising People Enterprising Places*: A Report by the National Employment Panel, England May 2005.

2 Cohen, Carl & Sterba, *James P (2003): Affirmative Action and Racial Preference* Oxford University Press Inc., New York, USA.

3 Johnson, John H & Bennett Jr, Lerone (1989, 1992) *Succeeding Against the Odds: The Autobiography of a Great American Businessman*, Amistad, New York, USA.

4 Badgett, M.V. Lee, *Economic Perspectives on Affirmative Action*, Washington D.C: Joint Centre for Political and Economic Studies, 1995.

5 Mair, John (2001): Caribbean Peers, *The Caribbean Voice*, NY, USA.

6 Memon, S. (1998) Greater London ethnic minority business development initiatives: A policy review, *Policy and Politics*, 16(1) pp 55-62.

7 *London's African and Caribbean Businesses get Ken's Support*, London development Agency, 4th September 2001).

8 Clifford, D.K & Cavenaugh, R.E (1985): *The Winning Performance*, New York, Bantam Books.

9 Hambrick, D.C. & Crozier, L.M (1985): `Stumblers and stars in the management of Rapid Growth', *Journal of Business Venturing*, Vol. 1, pp 31-45.

10 *Economic Research*, Neighbourhood Renewal Unit, Brent Council, London June 2002.

11 *Performance Review,* Black business Association, Birmingham, England September 2005.

12 *World Class Skills: Implementing the Leitch Review of Skills in England*, Department for Innovation, Universities and Skills July 2007.

13 *Collaborating on skills*: a guide for directors, CBI and DfES, November 2005.

14 *Third of businesses believe skills gap is their biggest threat*, Lloyds TSB November 2006.

15 Johnson, C.A (1999) *Organisation and Performance of African and Caribbean Businesses*, PhD thesis, London.

16 Hamel, Gary, Prahalad, C. K & Thomas, Howard (eds.); *Strategic Flexibility: Managing in a Turbulent Environment*, pp93-115, John Wiley and Sons Ltd, 1988.

17 Total Entrepreneurial Activity by Age', *Global Entrepreneurship Monitor*, London 2004.

18 `Boosting enterprise across the population: `Enabling the enterprise population', *Enterprise Brief*, Issue 5, May 2006, CBI.

19 *Skills for all: Proposals for a National Skills agenda, Final report of National Task Force,* DfEE 2000.

20 Moser, Claus (1999): *A Fresh Start, Improving Literacy and Numeracy*, and *Basic Skills and Jobs,* Institute of Employment Studies/ALBSU 1993.

21 *Skills for Competitiveness,* British Chamber of Commerce 1998.

22 Waldinger, Aldrich, Howard & Ward (1990) *Ethnic Entrepreneurs*, Sage Publications.

23 *Barriers to Survival and Growth in Small Firms*: Report for South West, Federation of Small Businesses, completed by Department of Marketing, University of Strathclyde, Glasgow, Scotland, November 2000.

Chapter 5

Cultural Industries

The power to create and innovate remains the greatest guarantee of respect and recognition – Professor Rex Nettleford, 1970

Introduction

This chapter examines the participation of British Caribbean firms in the cultural industries by highlighting growth segments, showing the challenges facing owners and illustrating the many-sided opportunities in this sector. The terms `*cultural industries sector*' (CIS) and `*creative industries*' will be used interchangeably to mean artistic and cultural forms of creativity. Effectively, the cultural industry describes the role of cultural entrepreneurs and arts enterprises, for profit as well as not-for-profit in the production, distribution and consumption of film, television, books, music, theatre, dance, visual arts, multimedia, animation and so on. The CIS is not just a commercial arena, it is an artistic and social space where spiritual values, psychic meaning and bodily pleasures are displayed, enacted and represented (**Nurse 2000**).

Whilst there is no concrete figure for the total market share of minority firms in the cultural economy because of fragmentation, official data and independent estimates (based on industry standards) were used to show to measure the market share of black firms. Using a 5% ratio of the CIS in Britain, it can be assumed therefore, that Caribbean cultural enterprises have a market share of 12% with a net value of just over £90 million per annum. This will become clear when each sub-sector or segment is analysed in this chapter.

The word `culture' is a subject of intense debate especially when dealing with various shades of political and social opinions. For example, the cultural values of a firm are evident by the disposition of the founder/owner. For the purpose of this book however, culture is a system of beliefs, traditions, values and generally, the way of life of people and societies. On a practical level, culture conveys different meanings to different people and to different circumstances and situations, again depending on the perspective in question.

Caribbean civilization represents an evolution of migrant peoples primarily from three continents – Africa, Asia and Europe – and through a process of adaptation has made the content and form essentially Caribbean **(Carrington 2006)**. The Scottish Executive described culture in a manner embracing both a material and non-material dimension:

Ideas and customs and traditions, beliefs, habits of thinking, religions, languages, identities, mythologies and histories, and the expression of these in myriad forms such as poetry and prose, visual arts, music, song, theatre, comedy, dance, architecture, design, costume, film, photography and a range of crafts. It is represented in the natural and historical landscape; archaeology, buildings; museum, gallery and library collections; archives and records; and shared memories and experiences **(University of Glasgow 2004)**.

This chapter will therefore focus on advertising, carnival arts, design, broadcast media, music, performing arts, publishing and other creative endeavours. On average, the market share for each segment or sub-sector varies from one to five percent and while this may be categorized by industry standards as low or disproportionate, in relation to overall market value, it represents a vital part of the British Caribbean firm sector's input into the UK economy.

The importance of the CIS to the UK economy is illustrated by the composition and size of activities and the variation of businesses constantly evolving. There are conflicting views on the general turnover and the number of people employed in creative enterprises in Britain because of the way the sector operates. Firstly, there is the multi-activity trend of firms where a design firm is likely to engage in marketing, training and a host of other activities, apart from core products and services.

Secondly, flexible employment opportunities make it difficult to obtain accurate information and data on organization structure, wage and salary administration, market portfolio, product types and industry performance. In mapping the sector in the 1990s, the DCMS estimated it at £60 billion, while the latest average figure was put at £112 billion. The sector employs approximately 1.3 million people in 250,000 enterprises, including self-employment, added to a further 100,000 part-time and casual group of workers **(Fig 5.1).**

Figure 5.1 Market value of key CIS growth segments in the UK

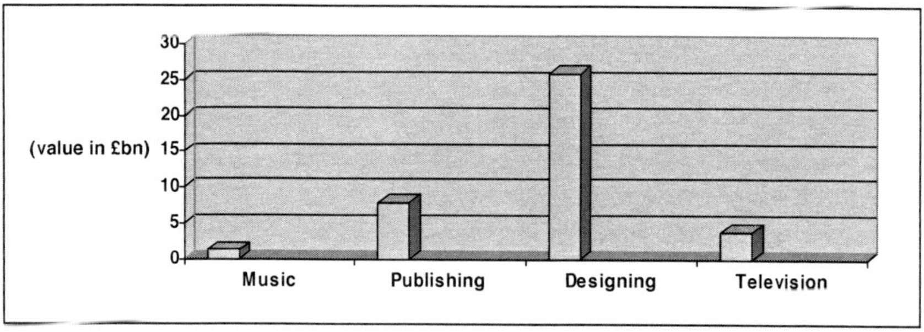

(Source: Mintel, DCMS and independent sources, 2001-2005)

Public bodies such as the National Training Organisation (NTO) provide a more conservative estimate of around £70-£80 billion per annum and this has been used to inform and guide study profiles of the CIS all over the UK (**Respect 2005**). There is little doubt that many segments such as radio, newspapers, design and multi-media technology firms, have grown, as modern technology, refined thinking and new markets have transformed their prospects.

Apart from other emerging creative segments, figure 5.1 makes the point that the UK cultural economy was driven during 2000 and 2005 by four segments. Music (the recording industry) peaked at £1.24 billion in 2005 after the sale of 270 plus million units of pre-recorded musical products. Digital media transformed the industry, added to online facilities for other cultural products, including online newspaper-publications. Newspaper publishing is estimated at billions of pounds per annum. Projections in the publishing industry are based on combined book sales of £3.98 billion and magazine publishing of £3.19 billion in 2004. In 2005, children's publishing was worth £672 million while television had reached £3.7 billion in 2004, a remarkable growth trend of 59.6% since 2000.

As stated at the beginning of this chapter, British Caribbean firms' contribution to the cultural industries in the UK is around 12%. Their impact is measured by the market value estimated at over £90 million in advertising, carnival arts, designing, the broadcast media, music, the performing arts and publishing. The performance of enterprises in these segments vary from low and medium to high even though there is no real yardstick to measure the BME creative industries output as a whole. Informal evidence suggests that non-white professionals are involved in CIS start-ups and grow firms without business support, a fact illustrated by the creative firms set up and the added value they bring to the national economy **(Fig 5.1)**.

Figure 5.1 Leading segments of British Caribbean cultural firms

(Source: Independent estimates based on evaluating official data, 2000-2005)

Sector	Estimated Market Value	Emerging Strength
Advertising	£5 million	Low
Carnival Arts	£16 million	High
Designing	£5 million	Medium
Broadcasting Media	£10 million	High
Music	£20 million	High
Performing Arts	£5 million	High
Publishing	£30 million	High
Total	**£91 million**	

Note: The above estimates have been calculated using a nominal percentage of the BME contribution to creativity from the overall market value of the UK CIS. In the case of advertising, a 5% ratio of £117 billion was used to find the average market share for the Caribbean firm's input into this creative segment.

Advertising

The British Caribbean advertising industry is relatively small (5%) compared with the mainstream equivalent. The emphasis is to change the image of corporate advertisers by encouraging white-owned organisations to maximize the potential of minority consumers. This can result in higher levels of inclusion by minorities in the mass media; for example, Barclays, Natwest and Halifax led the way to improve ethnic images in mainstream advertising. The use of African American actor, Samuel Jackson, the `Lilt Ladies' and the recent Maltesers campaign, was but a tiny fraction of the type of (representative) image that is desirable in multicultural Britain. There is much to be gained by implementing such a strategy and it should be pursued by Caribbean advertisers.

By the 1980s there was a sea-change in the advertising world as Thatcherite free-market policies boosted entrepreneurship in the UK. Members from minority communities took advantage of this opportunity to set up firms that were considered non-traditional. Despite this achievement, black businesses were regarded (and still are) as food shops, beauty salons or routine buying-and-selling activities. Owners were considered incapable of managing (mainstream-type) advertising agencies because of insufficient skills, inexperience and staying power. This perception almost became a permanent fixture in the British psyche, until fast-rising entrepreneur, Yvonne Thompson, founded ASAP, the first black advertising company in the UK (1980s). Earlier, she made a profitable investment in *Choice FM*, the first black radio station in the UK **(Minicase 5.1)**.

Minicase 5.1 ASAP Communications

After working for a major record company for several years without promotion, and instead, being shunted sideways, Guyanese-born Yvonne Thompson established **ASAP Communications Ltd** in 1984. A pre-market survey enabled her to access vital information on the vast potential of the billion-currency ethnic consumer market in the UK. She had though, to convince white companies that her firm could deliver, since a PR agency targeting niche markets by ethnicity was unheard of in the UK at that time.

The unique selling point (USP) of Thompson's company is quality service and dedicated staff and this is reflected in customer service all-round. '*The most pleasurable aspect of my job is putting together a good proposal, carrying it through, and seeing it work. PR companies are there to achieve their clients' wishes, so as to make a client happy. When that happens, my company grows, and a strong company can then make a positive social impact by taking on and training recruits, for example,*' Thompson said.

The firm has grown tremendously with clients from both mainstream and minority sector agencies and organizations, with consumer research, media liaison, advertising and promotion and other events are among the major services offered to scores of clients – public and private. Her advice to graduates is `gain practical skills, since leaving university with book sense and no common sense does not work. Experience is as important as knowledge, so too is determination, sustainability and having a goal.'

Since Thompson had investment of her own, she didn't really need much support from the bank, but sought technical support and advice from industry specialists. With ASAP's multi-million pound turnover, plans are to consolidate the business, to optimize niche markets in advertising and increase market share by an estimated 5% and more in the coming years.

However, entry barriers and access to markets in creative segments for minority firms are comparatively low in advertising, design, music, publishing, crafts, the performing arts and radio, as well as computer technology. The success and commitment of minority entrepreneurs in the CIS are in part, due to these trends. They are confirmed by the prevalence of cultural enterprises – both commercial and non-commercial – in many inner-cities throughout the UK. One particular segment that has tremendous growth potential however, is carnival arts which impacts too, on cultural regeneration.

Carnival Arts

This represents a novel feature in the world of creativity, and by definition, has its genesis in carnival festivity which was brought to Britain by nationals from Trinidad and Tobago. Today carnival festivals are held in more cities in England and Wales than at any other time in history. Much has been written about the annual Notting Hill Carnival (and related festivities) as being the largest street festival in Europe and while this artistic showpiece generates about £93 million per annum, Caribbean arts and cultural groups receive only around £16.2 million **(Minicase 5.2)**.

Minicase 5.2 Notting Hill Carnival

The first carnival – a Caribbean 'fayre' staged in St. Pancras Town Hall in 1959 – was a prelude to this annual festival, organized by the civil rights activist, the late Claudia Jones, founder of the *West Indian Gazette*. The event embodied her political stature and Trinidadian folk traditions.

By 1965, the **Notting Hill Carnival** was born, inspired by mobile steel bands that performed through the streets, and crowds 'Play Mas' in the district of Ladbroke Grove. The British press and the authorities, including the police, showed surprise at the number of black people and their costumed pageantry.

Between 1972 and 1998, several developments occurred as this festival became integral to the British calendar. The Carnival Development Committee was formed and sound systems were introduced for the first time. After a spate of confrontations with the authorities including the police and wrangling involving personalities vying for control of the event, the committee was replaced by the Notting Hill Carnival Limited (NHCL), a company that was formed to regularize the annual festival that is reputed to be Europe's largest street festival.

In an effort to bring greater respectability to the carnival, the organisers appointed political scientist and businessman, Professor Chris Mullard, CBE in 2002. To date, the Notting Hill Carnival has facilitated similar festivities throughout the UK as diverse communities join with hundreds of foreign tourists to celebrate an artistic class act, founded by Caribbean artists and cultural producers in the first part of the 20th century.

Therefore it could be assumed that British Caribbean firms have a market share of 17% in carnival arts, although current information suggests that the productivity of these firms equal almost 70%, considering also the economic and social investments cost borne by the black community in total. Apart from hundreds of enterprises that have mushroomed since the beginning of carnival, in recent years, the white community, along with a growing number of foreign tourists, have benefited from this event. The greatest beneficiary however, has been (and still is) the Treasury.

The LDA's commissioned study on the Notting Hill Carnival in 2004, showed a total income of £93 million producing up to 3,000 full-time equivalent jobs elsewhere in the economy. This study prompted the Arts Council of England to unveil a National Carnival Strategy to help resource professional artists and culture producers, as part of its campaign to introduce greater diversity in cultural regeneration. In making a case for the strategy, the Council provided the following proof:

In the UK there are over 300 samba groups and over 70 carnival events. There are more than 60 carnival groups in London and on the Isle of Wight –host of the second oldest English Carnival – there are over 17 carnival events. Carnival has benefitted nationally from our approach of encouraging risk taking and the wider application of carnival arts (**Arts Council of England 2005)**.

There are hundreds of consultants and firms involved in carnival arts activities such as costume production, design courses and workshops to attract the young unemployed, people with disability and the celebration of inter-faith events on a yearly basis. These firms are located in regeneration areas of London, the Midland Counties and other areas in Britain. The London cultural firm of Mahogany Arts Ltd has revolutionized carnival arts, exported its fertile creativity and showed the true meaning and power of diversity, British-style **(Minicase 5.3)**.

Minicase 5. 3 Mahogany Arts Limited

In 1989, two Trinidadians Clary Salandy and Michael Ramdeen founded **Mahogany Arts Limited.** Their original aim was to use their artistic skills to unify diverse communities, by making carnival arts more accessible to a wider audience. There was at the time, a considerable gap in the artistic and cultural products market.

With no funding and lack of enterprise support, the pair worked long hours to turn the perceived entertainment hobby into a fully-fledged cultural enterprise. They used their (designing, engineering and organizational) skills to mobilize support from other artists and producers and attract various customers who were keen on embracing a new form of `cultural appreciation'.

Other constraints faced were: limited space for costume production, excessive fees by professionals and poor returns from events and insufficient advertising revenue. After the third year in operation, the confidence of the owners grew significantly, and so was the firm's reputation. Members from the community were hired to deal with the increasing orders for costumes for festivals in the UK, Malaysia, Dubai, Qatar, the Caribbean and Europe.

With a turnover of less than a million pounds, Salandy said Mahogany has learnt more about the cultural industries sector from a global perspective, and that the firm's future plan is to transform Carnival into a commercially viable artistic, cultural and kinetic designing industry especially for those interested in pursuing careers in Carnival Arts.

Aside of its entertainment and commercial value, carnival has a remedial, rehabilitative function especially for young artists and potential cultural producers who are unemployed, but whose talent could be maximized through various forms of creative endeavours. Mahogany utilizes about 25% of its resources to deliver vocational training for teenagers and young unemployed people experiencing long-term job loss due to either a lack of qualifications and skills or labour market discrimination. Those who fail the school system are given opportunities to do better, by accessing an alternative course of study and practice, as an apprentice testified.

I found Mahogany quite good for young people like me and while there, I learnt about working in a group. I was able to improve my skills and self-esteem as someone who was born in England to Caribbean parents. I left after doing a 12-week costume design course, a changed person and today I have a job as a salesman. Mahogany's training is absolutely fabulous and its work should be publicized. If it wasn't for Mahogany, my life would have been the same – dull, boring and troubled **(Mahogany 1999)**.

Design

The design industry covers different activities - industrial, manufacturing, packaging and presentational materials and processes with a market share of £26 billion. Enterprises consist of freelance designers, small design consultancies and small organizations. Micro businesses dominate the sector with around three quarters of the companies employing less than 20 people. London companies tend to be slightly larger with up to 30% of firms employing more than 25 people. BME owned and led design enterprises reflect the national pattern more than the UK's outlook with the majority consisting of freelancers, the self-employed and micro firms. About 90% have 10 or fewer employees with firms employing not more than 25 people.

Minority firms have significant clusters in clothing, food and drink, luxury and consumer goods, entertainment and leisure, with an emphasis on textiles, fashion and exhibitions. There is much vitality within British Caribbean designers in personal care, youth entertainment and leisure. Excluding the returns from independent designers and those working in the informal economy, the conservative market share for British Caribbean designers is possibly 2% or £5 million per annum. The vital assets of firms are creativity, social investment and economic support for disadvantaged communities **(Minicase 5. 4)**.

Much of the talent in minority firms has been translated into advertising features used to target audiences from minority ethnic communities. At the same time, major areas of design work notably, the public sector, finance, capital goods and transport, offer few opportunities for black designers. One of the main strengths of British Caribbean firms in the design industry, though, is their artistic talent and product knowledge despite the fact that this is not adequate for sustainable growth. Then there is the constant challenge of securing sufficient capital from commercial institutions whilst maintaining an eye on customer demands. The owner of Adornment Limited described the reality of her firm's growth prospects:

If I did not subsidize my business with another income, the running cost would not have been realized, as I work from home and hardly ever give back what I take out. I employ 30 staff on a part-time basis approximately three months prior to the trade show. I have no idea how we get through it, even with the part-time staff and job sharing in some capacity **(Respect 2005)**.

Minicase 5. 4 Café Couture

Entrepreneur, Dave Roberts combined fashion with food to produce an innovative enterprise in the bustling shopping city in the West Midlands. His bistor, **Café Couture**, offered a new themed concept, hence the cocktail menu contained names such as *Super Model, Kirsty Turlington, Fashion Victim, Blue Denim and Black Suit.*

Roberts closed his clothing shop because of competition from large retailers. "I sold the shops, but I wanted to stick with the fashion element." He was unsuccessful in securing premises on Broad Street, another busy location in the West Midlands and since he had no previous experience in the leisure industry, this ruled him out altogether.

"I want to combine fashion with food and drink thereby doing something different because if you get the leisure market right, it can be a nice trade to be in. The customers are usually between the ages of 25 and 45 years; working professionals who are moving into the Jewellery Quarter's new city apartments," Roberts explained.

Although Café Couture's yearly turnover is just over half a million pounds, Roberts main aim is to satisfy customer demands by offering high quality products and services at reasonable prices. His ultimate goal however, is to open a fashion consultancy in Birmingham. The young entrepreneur is involved in property development and fashion design.

Yet the design industry is not a complete `walk in the park' as other well-meaning entrepreneurs have stated. Members of second generation Caribbean trendy artists have worked with experienced designers like Bruce Oldfield and/or emulated his work by starting their own businesses. In their quest for success, many have suffered humiliating experiences such as liquidation or closure, but despite these hurdles, they have overcome by growing their firms organically. Avis Associates demonstrated the juggling act of maintaining a proper image in design consultancy with a tidy profit margin at the end of it all.

As I was still struggling with cash flow getting a continuous monthly fee coming in from one source was a priority. My first contract was for one year and this was an extremely busy and seemed to overtake my life. However, I reaped the rewards for the business as other companies approached me **(Respect 2005)**.

Famous designers like Oldfield also referred to the challenges in the design industry. A person of mixed parentage (a Jamaican father and white mother), he set a gold standard in the female fashion design industry by outfitting some of the world's famous women, including the late Princess Diana (when she was Lady Diana Spencer). He rose from humble beginning to iconic status, being spurred by ambition and persistence. In 1980 he set up his company and built a fashion empire bit by bit, often making barely enough money to pay bills. His view of Britain's fashion market reflects its state of affairs.

The British fashion industry is a mass market; it doesn't do a great deal for the designers. It brings it down to this kind of high-street mentality which is not really fashion, or it certainly is not creativity. People in France and Italy spend a lot on more clothes and quality manufacturing is prized. It is hard to build a business in Britain, we are just not very good entrepreneurs, it would seem **(BBC 2005)**.

After 30 years in the business, Oldfield's work won academic recognition from the University of Birmingham (England) with an Honorary Doctorate in recognition of his achievements as a fashion designer in February 2005. The award coincided with the work and achievements of students graduating from the Birmingham Institute of Art and Design in that year. Yet it is through the broadcast media that the black community has made a difference to multi-cultural Britain as the following sub-section illustrates.

Broadcast Media

In this sub-section, the effect of British Caribbean firms on the broadcast media; namely, television, films, documentaries and other audio-visual forms of communication, will be shown. The UK cable and satellite market was worth £3.3 billion in 2003, with the market growing by 5.9% since 2000. The industry is set for major changes by 2008 in which time, over 60% of households could be signed up to cable and satellite services with the multi-digital TV home firmly established; that homes that subscribe to both Freeview and a digital cable or satellite TV service.

The British Caribbean market in the broadcast media is around £10 million and increasing, with success rates in films and documentaries despite a low take-up in the television industry (ownership). Start-up costs in this area are quite high with nearly £1 million pounds required for necessities such as license, equipment, staff, premises, broadcast materials and other relevancies. Between 2000 and 2002, total employment and use of ethnic minority media freelancers grew from 116,000 to 151,000 mainly in broadcast TV and radio where freelancers increased from 6.9% to 7.8% over that short period. British Caribbean professionals are increasingly part of broadcast radio, independent production and cinema exhibition where some sources suggest that up to 20% (10% in independent production) of all those working in the sector are from the Caribbean community.

Until now, the success of British Caribbean professionals has been considerable in terms of image and reputation. In the main however, stardom has been down to independence, hard-nosed dealing, professionalism and networks established in both ethnic communities and mainstream agencies and institutions. Norman Beaton of *Desmond's* TV fame was a pioneer whose work and life helped change British television's inclusive programming for the better in many respects. It was his determination and sense of pride that propelled others into mainstream television and who much later, became producers, directors and government advisers **(Minicase 5.5).**

Beaton's remarkable achievement was followed by his contemporaries - Ramjohn Holder, Carmen Munroe, Rudolph Walker – who pushed the boundaries of mainstream television further to ensure that minority concerns remained fixed on the public audio-visual agenda. There are however, ongoing issues around quality black programming and the inclusion of more minorities in the production and direction of news and documentaries. Journalist Russell Myrie argued that the gap in the market for the *Desmond's* TV series for example, should be plugged. The comedy series, *The Crouches*, attempted to satisfy a demand by centering on a family spanning three generations.

Minicase 5. 5 Norman Beaton - Desmond's

Prior to his death in December 1994, Norman Beaton was the most prominent black British television actor for over a decade. His most notable achievement was the ***Desmond's*** television series that attracted more than six million viewers around the globe. Upon his arrival in the UK from British Guiana (now Guyana) in the 1960s as a trained teacher, he worked at a bookshop until his wife and children arrived and then taught in Liverpool, the first black teacher to be employed by that city's education authority. He was soon frustrated with his job and began writing plays.

His first production was the musical, *Jack of Spades*, which centred on the doomed relationship between a black man and a white woman. Its moderate success gave Beaton the confidence to concentrate more on theatre and he wrote and performed the lead role in another musical, *Sit Down, Banna.* In the early seventies, Beaton did other plays, including Shakespeare, and in 1975, he helped establish the Black Theatre of Brixton in south London and a year later, he broke into the television series, *The Fosters.*

Yet, it was his sequence of *Desmond's* (1989-1994) ON Channel 4, the title character that made him a renowned TV personality. In 1991 he appeared as a guest on The *Bill Cosby Show* and in several movies including *The Mighty Quinn* (1989). After years of hard living began to affect his health, he returned to Guyana in 1994 at age 60 where he died.

Even so, it was Trinidadian Horace Ove who broke new ground with films and documentaries that demonstrated his vast experience and skill in balancing comedy with more serious issues such as race and class, with an underlying emphasis on Caribbean cultural traditions. His work ranged from African-American themes, musicals and carnival festivity to institutional racism experienced by black Britons. Reggae (1970), *King Carnival* (1973), *Pressure* (1975) and *Playing Away* (1985) were among his finest works. *Pressure* was the first feature-length film by a non-white director in Britain and though controversial, it became a hallmark of Ove's filmmaking career.

Another success was the **African and Caribbean Television (ACTV),** an all day broadcast media channel launched on digital satellite in the earlier part of this century. ACTV has a subscription of nearly seven million and the station is viewed by 17 million in the UK. It is rated as the first production channel to target the fast growing black population in the country and has received support from a local college. Scores of unemployed people have access to employment opportunities, and through the work of the station, a special course was designed to address the under-representation of minorities in mainstream media.

Founder of the TV channel, Vernon King, a lawyer is conscious of the needs of local communities and endeavoured to publicise their views on local television. After a brief survey, he decided to set up a communications medium that would influence the views of local citizens.

ACTV will provide a new and distinctive voice for a growing population that is poorly served by traditional broadcasters. It will also offer relevant and entertaining programming to an audience that is hungry for content that appeals to them specifically. Our target audience is one that constantly sets trends in fashion, music and sports and the potential is therefore clear to advertisers and ACTV will open up opportunities for them to use the channel to communicate effectively with a key niche audience **(College of North East London 2003)**.

There are other successful media production companies and independent presenters including Lenny Henry, whose television series, *Chef*, became a hit with viewers exposed to the multi-talented and rare professionalism of Caribbean artists within a mainstream setting. Henry who is now actively involved in annual charity shows, was followed by others; namely, **Floella Benjamin Productions**

Ltd, sports personalities Garth Crooks, BBC radio and television, Ian Wright and John Barnes. The sporting legends, Crooks, Wright and Barnes, each combinc television careers with stints in charities, cultural, education and health awareness campaigns among others.

Charles Thompson, founder of the **Screen Nation Film and TV Awards**, the UK's premiere event to mark the achievements of black professionals in the industry, has been making movies for the past 10 years. He believes that the increase in non-white artists in British television is possible if appropriate steps are taken to implement a multicultural strategy by recruiting actors and actresses on merit.

Development is the key to seeing more diversity on the screen. The film and TV sector needs to be developed so that we are not shown a narrow perspective of black people. Audiences need to be given the opportunity to see a wide range of film and television by black people, starring black people. This could capture the public imagination **(*The Voice* 2003)**.

In an effort to find solutions to the problem of minority under-representation, the UK Film Council and British Film Institute tabled proposals to improve the image of the industry but questions remain about the motive of these bodies. The authorities have long recognized the importance of diversity, but there are issues around stereotyping of, and lack of opportunities for black talent. The September 2003 Screen National Film and TV awards captured the emerging talent among black Britons, but according to Thompson, 'they need to aspire to that level and respect what has gone before them.'

Radio

Unlike television, radio stations are fashionable with British Caribbean communities in predominantly inner-city areas. Community radio stations are sometimes referred to as 'pirate' radio stations because of their informal operations, although they serve a useful function by providing news, entertainment, advertisements and promoting important events for the black community. They also encourage talent in media (sound) engineering, production, disc jockeying and presentation to the point where radio operators have either advanced careers in specialist multi-media industries or at best, set up firms with links to institutions such as the BBC.

One popular radio show that stimulated both interest and intrigue was *Black Londoners.* As the first BBC radio magazine program, it was developed later into a host of creative educational activities for diversity in education. Grenadian Alex Pascall was invited to present the program first in 1974. As a founding `Father' of the Notting Hill Carnival, he is a political activist, an accomplished writer and musician. His `finest hour' was his informed views of the terrible tragedy in the New Cross Fire in 1981 which killed 13 children in south London, and which later sparked unrest in the area.

Pascall received the OBE for services to the community and contrary to critics; he is a respected cultural archivist in the diaspora because of his extensive knowledge and experience of Caribbean cultural history. A few years ago, he formed a creative educational publishing company, **Good Vibes Records and Music Limited**, to promote a `global dimension in (arts) education'.

Nonetheless, it should be recalled that it was Caribbean settlers who were in the vanguard of Britain's Community Radio Movement, beginning in the late 1970s. Indeed, members of the Caribbean community had no choice but to establish radio stations because mainstream channels did not cater for the information, education and entertainment needs of the non-white community. Veteran community leader, Vince Hines, explained the background to the black community radio movement in the UK.

One of the first community radio stations was started by a group of African immigrants from the Caribbean in 1979. The station was called "DBC" – Dread Broadcasting 'Co-operation' [Corporation] and broadcast on the FM band. The Station was founded and based in Neasden, the London Borough of Brent and moved subsequently to Ladbroke Grove, in the Royal Borough of Kensington and Chelsea, west London. Pre-recorded taped music and a low level transmitter were placed on high rise buildings and transmitted to Londoners over 10-20 mile radius. DBC audience consisted mostly of immigrants and settlers from the Caribbean. Jamaica's reggae music was very popular with DBC audience. DBC came about partly because main stream radio was not catering for the new immigrants and settlers. The station was founded and operated by volunteers. **(Hines 2004)**

Yet it was commercial radio that became a media triumph for the black community. Described in some quarters as one of `Britain's phenomenal black entrepreneurs', Neil Kelnock, founded *Choice FM* as the original black radio station in the country. Originally, the Jamaican was not keen on pursing a glamorous media career, but was inspired by the 1970s Black Power Movement. He became the movement's official photographer in the UK and the *West Indian World* newspaper. He was motivated to start the radio project after attending the second African Festival of Arts and Culture in Lagos, Nigeria, in 1977 **(Minicase 5.6)**.

Minicase 5. 6 Choice FM

Neil Kelnock played a key role in launching **Choice FM** in 1990. Along with his business partner, Patrick Berry, Kelnock was responsible for the radio's revenue raising effort and his ethnic advertising markets in London. He was described in one authoritative report on the creative industries in London, as `the classic portfolio or serial entrepreneur`.

He spearheaded the successful bid for Choice 107.1 FM North London in 1999 and he oversaw the planning, launch and the set of this new venture. This digital expansion was a key to the future of the radio station and the mainstream competition's attempts to enter the market of minority listeners. Both Kelnock and Berry were conscious of racial discrimination and used enterprise, effective support systems and focused strategies to overcome this vice.

Kelnock's enterprise helped him win a public sector contract with the LDA to produce a *`Business Airwaves'* program aimed at BME-led businesses in London. The success of Choice FM however, was based on the following values:

- Determination to triumph over odds.
- Respect for community needs.
- Considerable knowledge of products and services.
- Belief in self-reliance.
- Recognition of advertising power.
- Quality business practice.
- Commitment to growth and expansion strategies.

In the early part of this century, Capital Radio bought the assets of Choice FM much to the disappointment of the Caribbean community in particular, even though it was stated unofficially, that the deal was a conscious business decision by Kelnock and Berry. Yet for what it is, Choice FM still remains a legendary radio station for the entire Caribbean population in the British Isles.

Despite the career achievements of community radio pioneers in mainstream broadcasting, this media faces immense challenges due to poor funding, unsuitable premises, poor quality programming and inadequate presenters and researchers. The demand for greater diversity in cultural, educational, social and sports programming, is being met by community radio stations in Britain, and though efforts have been made to support them via European and Lottery funding, a better system for co-ordinating resources to make this industry more market acceptable, is necessary.

Music

According to Mintel, over 270 million units of pre-recorded music were purchased in the UK in 2004. The value of the market remained at over £1 billion and it was expected to stand at approximately £1.24 billion (manufacturing selling prices) in 2005. Acquiring, purchasing and listening to music using facilities such as download websites and

MP3 players is popular, and there is evidence that the new digital format has begun eroding CD sales. Other formats such as audio cassette tapes are expected to become more or less obsolete.

Similar to other segments of the cultural industries, music in the British Caribbean community is highly fragmented, a reflection of the current state of the industry. For instance, there is no reliable database or statistics on composers, producers and other artists in the music industry, and with the high level of under-representation in the production, marketing and sales by this section of the UK population; it is extremely difficult to obtain a balanced picture of British music generally. Minorities are involved in core business segments such as: music publishing, composition and song writing; promotion and management, recording, agents and carnival-based ventures.

Just as in the wider cultural industries sector, the majority of music firms are micro and they seldom employ more than five people excluding casual or part-time workers. Scores of venues, for example, include locations operating with different names and under various proprietors, while others have used pubs, restaurants and social clubs.

The Bloomsbury International Society has led the way in classical music fusing British-European, African and Caribbean rhythms. Professor of Music, Ian Hall (the first Caribbean person to study music at Oxford University), is president of the organisation which promotes harmony, using the arts, education, travel and sport. In 2000, the UN appointed the Guyanese to take charge of the World Association of Non-Governmental Organisations, a task that he has fulfilled so far, with dignity and nobility. Through Bloomsbury, he has captured a global market in the arts whilst fulfilling a dream of promoting the strengths of multiculturalism in British society.

Over the past 50 years, we have used our culture to overcome apathy, despair, suffering from a hostile society, reluctant to recognise our contributions and acknowledge them. We have given Britain every schematic range of music including ska, reggae, the blues, calypso, kaiso, dub, jazz, spirituals and rap. While we continue to share our rich heritage with the host society, we must also have a shared commitment to ownership of heritage assets in order to sustain our cultural businesses (***Caribbean Times*** **1994**).

African peoples have influenced Western music since the 16th century when black musicians entertained British audiences. African-Americans, represented by the Fisk University Jubilee Singers, were among the most popular black minstrels in Britain, winning the hearts of many, who listened with `manifest pleasure' to spiritual music. Between the two World Wars, Britain was a major centre for the recording and manufacture of gramophone records. Recordings in London of African and Caribbean music in the 1920s and 1930s demonstrated the important role of settler musicians in the evolution of the UK recording business **(Cowley 1985)**.

Still, one untold story in the British music scene is the legendary **`PAMA Records'**, a record label developed in 1958 in Harrow by the Palmer brothers (Jeff, Harry and Carl) who were in the property business at the time. Having understood the potential wealth of Jamaican music based on weekly parties held in the homes of `new Caribbean arrivals', the brothers capitalised on this lucrative trade and helped change the British music charts forever.

The Palmers' first signings included Joyce Bond, *The Marvels*, *The Crowns*, Norman T Washington and *The Other Brothers*. During the latter part of 1967, they released rock steady, partly in competition to Island/Trojan Records. Jeffrey Palmer founded the London Apollo Club to showcase the talent of existing and potential musical artists and the Palmers were responsible for the overall success of two UK based bands – *The Mohawks*, led by Jamaican keyboardist Graham Hawk, and *The Inner Mind*, led by organist, Ian Smith. After Pama's demise in the early 1970s, it was later renamed Jet Star, which is today, one of the largest distributors of Jamaican music in the UK.

However, Eddy Grant is the leading promoter of universal Caribbean music. As a successful entrepreneur, he has changed the focus and direction of Caribbean music, by creating unique musical brands, setting up a record label company and creating possibly, the widest collection of Caribbean popular music ever. His musical group, The Equals, propelled him to fame and after a number of years, he moved to Barbados to settle **(Minicase 5.7).**

Minicase 5. 7 Ice Records

Eddy Grant is a leading musical authority with more than 35 years experience in show business. As a child, he was exposed to the distinctive sounds of African and Indian music which is indigenous to Guyana along with the music of the surrounding countries Suriname and Trinidad and Tobago.

While still pretty young, Grant's musician father moved the family to London and the fusion of ethnic and commercial pop influences culminated in Grant founding The Equals, probably the finest and first multi-racial pop/rock outfit to achieve international acclaim. The Equals topped the chart with their classic "*Baby Come Back,*" and with Grant as songwriter, lead guitarist and producer, the musical group achieved three more major top 10 hits in the following 18 months.

In 1982, his solo recording *I Don't Wanna Dance*, spent three weeks at No 1 in the UK singles chart. He made other top hits, but *Electric Avenue* was US and UK No 2 in 1983, selling over a million copies, plus a later remix of the song was a UK top ten again in 2001. Grant's musical talent is stunning; he has played every single instrument, sung every vocal part and produced stars such as Sting, Mick Jagger and Elvis Costello. With offices in Barbados, London and America, Grant's company, **Ice Records**, has become in a few short years, the foremost international classic Calypso, Soca and Ringbang record label. Ringbang seeks to develop African rhythms fused with Caribbean cultural artistry which may be applied universally. The company is involved in proactive marketing to keep pace with modern trends in the music world.

In spite of much success however, British Caribbean music is largely undervalued in terms of recognition, due in part to the exclusion of professional musicians, producers and promoters from mainstream. While black musicians have a considerable share of the market in relation to (cover) record sales running into tens of millions of pounds, it is white producers who benefit from super profits. Traditional research into the music industry tends to avoid (financial) inequalities and other disparities between musicians and producers/ promoters on the basis of ethnicity, since expertise in this area is scarce. The partnerships or joint venture model is a viable solution for British Caribbean firms in their efforts to narrow the gap between black musicians, white producers and marketing companies. With his honed experience and knowledge of the music industry, Eddy Grant has shown the way for others to follow.

The formation of numerous organizations to represent BME musical artists has not impacted sufficiently on the industry since these bodies lack financial clout to alter the balance of power in a market driven predominantly, by white self-interest. For instance, black music is perceived by most Europeans as exotic and demonstrative of artists' sexuality, but yet white artists are brilliant at imitating black artists especially if the music appears commercially viable or has market potential. Bob Marley's `*I Shot the Sheriff*' (1973) was a classic, but was undervalued initially, until it became a popular international hit (No. 1) with English artist, Eric Clapton (1974). Self-regulation of the industry has not helped either, and it is therefore time for a proper evaluation of Caribbean producers' contribution to the UK cultural scene.

In the late 1990s the Department of Culture referred to a lack of investment in new talent and suggested that record companies relied on selling catalogues, CDs of established bands, adding that now `collectors are completing their collections, there is a dearth of material to keep the industry alive (**DCMS 1998**). Despite the apparent low value that is placed on British Caribbean music in the

UK, the cumulative worth of Caribbean music is astounding.

The Barbados music industry is driven by soca artists and music bands, as well as earnings derived from festival tourism. Trinidad and Tobago thrives on its different music forms, a major source of revenue. The export of steelpan instruments to educational music markets in North America and Europe has helped strengthen the country's musical assets earning power of over US$50 million **(Nurse 2002)**

The music industry in the Eastern Caribbean is driven by festival tourism such as the St. Lucian Jazz Festival contributes US$14 million in visitor expenditure; the Dominica World Creole Festival and the St. Christopher and Nevis Music Festival which are estimated to earn nearly $2 million annually**.** The figure below shows the range of Caribbean musical products over the past fifty years. Innovation is responsible for the success of artists who have the ability to cross-over the cultural and social divide. Jamaica, the primary source of reggae and dancehall music has gained international recognition such as the American Grammy's **(Table 5.2).**

Despite the apparent shift in popular music, there are moves in various parts of the UK to mainstream traditional music while at the same time, share common values with diverse communities across different generations in Wales and Scotland. It is in these areas where enterprise agencies have taken the initiative to support new and innovative enterprises by sections of the ethnic minority community in an effort to promote sustainable cultural regeneration.

Table 5.2 Caribbean musical forms and their global economic impact

Musical Forms	Key Drivers	Economic Impact
Classical/Popular – jazz, soul (R&B), 'oldies', hip-hop (rapping), garage and metal, influenced by African, American and Caribbean artists and cultural producers.	Live performance, festival tourism, recording industry.	St. Lucian Jazz Festival visitor expenditure US$14.8 million (2000).
Salsa - Originated from Latin America and popular with Caribbean communities at home and abroad.	Record sales, parties and other social functions at clubs, pubs etc.	Unofficial accounts suggest this musical type has a substantial market value running into millions too.
Calypso – popular with Trinidadians, but now a marketable product at carnival festivities in America, Britain, Caribbean, Europe and Latin America.	Festival tourism, live performance, recording industry, music publishing, music instruments.	Earnings for Trinidad and Tobago US$50-60 million. Carnivals in the diaspora: Canada (Caribana) Cnd$200 million, Labour Day, in New York, US$300 million and Notting Hill, London, £93 million.
Reggae - Originated in Jamaica and now has global appeal, with pulsating lyrics based on social commentary, entertainment and other celebratory forms of enjoyment.	Recording industry, live performance, music publishing and festival tourism.	High global earnings and for Jamaica US$80-100 million, reggae music sales estimated at US$300 million.

Soca - Fusion of calypso, blending African, Indian and indigenous Caribbean rhythms originating from Trinidad and Tobago, but is now a musical (artistic) product.	Digital recording, live performance, music publishing, festival tourism and educational events.	Worth tens of millions in the global market – tend to be lumped with the earnings of calypso.

(Source: Bilby, Kenneth: The Caribbean as a Musical Region, The Woodrow Wilson International Centre for Scholars, Washington, D.C., 1981 and Bourne, C., and S.M. Allgrove (1997): `Prospects for Exports of Entertainment Services from the Caribbean: The Case of Music', Caribbean Dialogue 3.3; 1-12)

In December 2005, the **Triple D's Jazzclub**, the brainchild of Barbara Ross, an entrepreneur of Welsh Caribbean origin, was opened. With guidance from the Business Support Programme in Wales, Ross' dream of creating a vibrant jazz venue in Newport became a reality. Budding stars from the local community have live performances as they showcase abundant talent, thereby enriching the multicultural fabric of the Welsh community.

The club fills a gap that consists of traditional pubs, bars and night clubs. It offers young audiences, including upcoming singers, an opportunity to meet successful artists and producers to benefit from their talent and experience in the local music scene. The club is a fulfilment of Ross' dream for many years, but one which needed business advice and encouragement to realise her plans. Said the new club owner,

`Thanks to the Ethnic Business Support Agency, the advisers encouraged me to go ahead even at times when I felt like abandoning my dream. I hope my club will be a big hit and will rapidly get a name as a place where people can have a dance and listen to such diverse genres as jazz, funk-jazz and rhythm `n' blues'
(*Ethnic Enterprise* 2005).

Performing Arts

There are similarities between the performing arts and music – they share common features notably the large number of performers or small groups or companies. Professionals tend to move between firms and art forms and such diversity poses significant challenges for industry analysts. The events in this sector vary in range and scope dance and theatre feature prominently among British Caribbean firms.

There are no real figures for the performing arts sector in the UK, but independent estimates show that the British Caribbean firms have a relative market share of 5% or £5 million per annum based on theatrical productions, dance and other arts celebration by leading organizations and smaller cultural groups. Theatre appears to be a more prominent segment in the Caribbean community at least in number and turnover. The success of black theatre in Britain has been one of great struggle and despair and only in the last 20 years, have there been significant gains resulting from the work of leading campaigners who were first generation Caribbeanists.

Faced with continued discrimination and lack of support, Caribbean artists established agencies to represent diverse creative interests. Trinidadian Pearl Connor-Mogotosi was the first to set up an agency, representing the interests of minority artists. **The Edric Connor Agency** (named after her filmmaker husband) was set up in 1956 and renamed the Afro-Asian Caribbean Agency to represent artists, writers and performers in all areas of the arts.

The agency produced memorable films including *Carnival Fantastique (1959)* and the cricket series, *West Indies vs. England (1963).* In 1963, she led another enterprise, the Negro Theatre Workshop, a company of 30 actors , probably best known for their production in Wole Soyinka's *The Road (1965).*

There was an upsurge in 'alternative' touring theatre companies in the 1970s and 1980s, aiming to reach outside mainstream audiences. Quite rightly, the Arts Council of England duly recognized them and funded organizations such as **Carib, Temba** and **Black Theatre Co-operative** (now Nitro). Caribbean professionals developed lasting theatre companies, with Talawa Theatre seen as a leading light in Britain's diversity quest in the performing arts field. Besides its professional outlook as a cultural enterprise, Talawa enjoys a healthy respect from industry authorities and audiences alike in the UK **(Minicase 5.8)**.

Minicase 5. 8 Talawa Theatre Company

Talawa Theatre Company was the brainchild of Yvonne Brewster and other colleagues in 1986. Prior to that time, prejudice in mainstream theatre companies was widespread and Brewster was the sole black actress with an ambition to be a leading theatrical director in the UK. Her main purpose behind Talawa was to provide an outlet for African, Caribbean and other minority artists and cultural performers in the country.

There were the usual start-up problems: non-support from banks, limited space for performances and the challenge of recruiting quality managerial and technical personnel. Brewster utilized the services of industry specialists since she had a network of dedicated artists, producers and directors to call on.

Mainstream arts bodies refused to fund adequately the work of the organization – there was scepticism as to whether the company could survive, but Talawa grew, producing outstanding performances. Its plays were based on interfacing historical experiences of black communities with those of British and European host societies.

With a turnover in excess of £500,000, the company illustrated diversity excellence and developed sound management practices, alternative program formats for different audiences and a competent marketing team to satisfy the demands of a modern, sophisticated theatre audience. The staff increased from a few to 10 plus and the company has a growth expansion strategy that involves new premises, as well as reaching out to students and like-minded arts organizations.

There is a growing awareness of both the importance of the performing arts and their relative neglect by support agencies and so the Arts Council of England `*Decibel Initiative*' aims to create additional resources, increase recognition and profile, create stronger networks, and develop managerial skill and artistic talent in the culturally diverse arts sector. The BME employment and enterprise sectors including non-commercial are: performance – drama including poetry where around 5,000 people with a turnover of £35 million annually; dance around 10,000 people with a turnover of about £15 million and writing approximately 1,500 people earning about £2 million. Supporting services such as agents are around 100 enterprises, employing around 250 people.

Dance

Since the beginning of time, dance has been associated with people of colour, and in the 1930s, Britain's first black dance company, **Les Balles Negres**, was founded by Jamaican, Richie Riley and Berto Pasuka who were influenced by Marcus Garvey's dream of a spectacular show to celebrate the opening of the amusement park in Kingston, Jamaica. In 1946, both men were united in London, and after being professionally trained, Riley and his partner established the dance company. Riley who died in 1997 said that:

Negro ballet is vital in choreographic art. As conceived by Berto Pasuka, its human emotion in dance form, being the opposite of Russian ballet with its stereotyped entrechats and pointed work (***The Guardian* 1999**).

Although the company folded in 1953, Riley demonstrated that ballet was not limited to European culture, but rather, dance in general, had widespread appeal to societies, irrespective of ethnicity, economic and social, as well as other persuasions. Leon Robinson of **Positive Steps Production** said that there are still problems associated with racial prejudice in this art form even though this ought not to be:

If you are a black dancer and you desire to be in the Royal Ballet, then you should have the opportunity. The truly great companies are cross-cultural. Colour should not be an issue when it comes to dance **(1999)**.

By the mid-1980s, dance was back on the British Caribbean cultural agenda, as professional artists, sensing a change in emphasis and direction of Britain's multicultural society, formed companies and arts groups to tap into this market. The inner-city London Borough of Hackney became a fertile ground for the mainstreaming of universal dance forms, the British-Caribbean way **(Minicase 5.9)**.

Minicase 5.9 The Carol Straker Foundation

In 1987, a young British Caribbean dancer with professional training from the US set up the **Carol Straker Dance Foundation** with a small grant from the Barclays Youth Project. Carol Straker, who founded the institution in her name, provides (regular courses) outlet for dancers and other artists from the black community to showcase their talent.

At first, she encountered major challenges: limited funds, inadequate staff, restricted space and the anxiety of trying to secure bids from regeneration agencies even though the dance company was in one of the most deprived areas in inner-London. With support from her family, colleagues and friends, Straker who is of Barbadian parentage, implemented a long-term action plan to sustain the Foundation.

The enterprise offers dance classes, examinations, information and advice, festivals, film production and related public performances. Through much public exposure, the company learnt about the global dance sector and attracted high-profile patrons, supporters and friends. Straker has implemented specialist training programs for (mainstream) students interested in ballet, jazz and tap dance.

Staff ratio has increased from two to about five persons, with 20 volunteers who contribute to various performances and offer expert advice on managerial, technical and operational matters. In recent times, besides Lottery grants, the company has benefited from European funding and built an excellent portfolio of performing arts projects.

With a turnover of less than £100,000, the company is gearing for expansion. There is a desire to push the multicultural angle of dance, increase engagement with mainstream arts organizations and develop innovative products and services to meet a growing dance clientele. A top priority is introducing new performances, along with hosting dance exhibitions and other cultural shows to raise awareness and obtain the funds to finance the company's growth strategy.

However, a persistent problem affecting performing arts companies, is finding suitable premises - affordable with adequate facilities. Most organizations, be they commercial or charity, operate from run-down industrial estates or cramped offices that inhibit prospects for growth and expansion. There are many incubator centres catering for cultural businesses, but they are not ideally suited for dance companies keen on maintaining quality service and meeting the demands of a diverse clientele.

Having to access shared premises is one way in which performing arts companies can sustain their operations and the Carol Straker Dance Foundation is a wonderful example of this. It occupies a permanent exhibition site in Hackney and this has helped foster a lasting partnership between two distinct groups on the basis of joint bids and other shared programming. Through its annual funding scheme, the Arts Council of England has encouraged commercial and not-for-profit organizations to adopt the `group co-ordination' model as a means of Best Practice in relation to securing additional finance and technical support, whilst benefiting from learning and trusted relationships. In the other following section, there are similar challenges as well as prospects for professionals and firms involved in the publishing industry, another vibrant segment of the CIS.

Publishing

This section deals with the British Caribbean SMEs participation in the newspaper, book and magazine publishing, an important segment of the cultural industries sector. Through case studies, statistics and other methods, the organization and performance levels of firms will be illustrated to show their contribution to both the publishing industry and the UK literature market as a whole.

Traditionally, publishing industries range from book, journal and electronic media through to newspapers and magazines. Publishing is regarded as the third largest sector of the CIS by revenues and the second largest sector by employment in the UK. Although the industry is more active in London (54%) and the Southeast (34%), there are variations in size and revenues compared with other segments in the creative industries in the UK. Although newspapers account for the largest sector in the industry with around 10,000 firms, the sector is dominated by a small number of larger companies – around 250 – that account for two-fifths of all jobs **(AGAS 2005)**.

The UK market value for publishing is wide and varied, with forecasts for revenue sales predicted at nearly 6% in 2005, bearing in mind that a large percentage of newspaper income is obtained from classified advertising, especially in the regional press. Many newspapers maximize the power of the Internet to realize even greater value from this revenue stream, with major acquisitions being made by larger newspaper group-companies. Newspaper sales have also fallen due to the millions of people who use the worldwide web to access information on a large scale, including daily news reports from both newspapers and a variety of news agencies.

Although minorities have a small market share in the billion pound publishing industry with mostly employment concentration in operative, clerical and supervisory levels and poorly represented in the professional and technical occupations, Caribbean firms have a `high' emerging market share in the sector estimated (independently) at 5% or £30 million at any given time excluding operators who own either micro firms or conduct their affairs in the informal economy. This industry has created pioneering enterprises such as **Hansib**

Publishing, **Voice Communications**, **The Ethnic Media Group** and the (Jamaican) **Gleaner Group**, along with countless other publishing houses in Britain.

Contrary to popular opinion, professional writing and publishing have been part of the Caribbean community's traditions for centuries, starting with an oral base or storytelling genre. The first generation of settlers originated from a folk tradition that inspired dialogue and discussion on local and national issues affecting the masses. Later, as these societies emerged during the intervening pre-independent and post-independent periods of the 1930s and 1960s respectively, several authors (self-published) and small publishers emerged both in the Caribbean Region and the diaspora in Britain, Europe and North America.

Apart from the dramatic events that occurred during political independence in Africa, Caribbean and Asia (especially the Indian sub-continent) , writing and publishing were also triggered by the Civil Rights and Black Power Movements respectively in the US, with themes depicting the struggles of black societies worldwide, captured in poetry, song, news bulletins, magazines and small presses. The *Lux* journal and the monthly magazine, *Fraternity*, were the first publications to be published around 1893 in Britain, but it was during the second part of the 20th century, that black publishing took off in the UK. There were many reasons for this trend:

During 1945 and 1975, there was no radio station, film company or television station owned or managed by the black community in Britain. The community depended on the black press to be informed of events at home and abroad. A struggle without its publicity organ was seen as one unlikely to progress very far. Publishing was the first endeavour and it has been the most difficult to sustain. Although some of the earlier publications had a radical and revolutionary stance, they created editorial space for humour, fashion and business, foreign affairs and campaign issues involving the black community **(Hines 1998)**.

This period also witnessed the influence of Caribbean scholars such as C.L. R. James, V. S. Naipaul, Eric Williams, George Padmore, Arthur Lewis and Walter Rodney, all of whom wrote on issues that impacted on the political, economic and social value systems worldwide. They challenged Western systems of domination which resulted in injustices and other State excesses. Though their work was perceived as controversial, their influence could not have been more profound especially in parts of the world where poverty, ignorance and other equalities were rife.

Yet, it was the relentless campaign of Trinidadian political activist, Claudia Jones, that spurred the development of black publishing and its radicalisation. A victim of US racism, she arrived in Britain in the 1950s and edited the *West Indian Gazette* from 1958 to 1963. She also directed the affairs of the Notting Hill Carnival in its formative years.

After Jones' death in 1964, there was a temporary void until Guyanese-born, Arif Ali, established **Hansib Publishing** in 1971, to provide a channel for African, Asian and Caribbean communities to debate political, economic and social issues that affected their general welfare. He built the company into the most reputable minority publishing enterprise in the UK and Europe combined. Such was Ali's potency and consistency for over a generation, until the late 1990s, that the name, Hansib became synonymous with (campaigning for) universal minority rights, social justice and black economic liberation **(Case Study 5.10)**.

Case Study 5.10 Hansib Publishing Ltd

At the height of its success 1971-1996, **Hansib Publishing**, was the most renowned multi-ethnic publishing company in Britain and Europe. Arif Ali who established the family-owned business after arriving in the UK, 1957, had previously owned accounting and food retail firms, and after setbacks in the 1980s, he built a multi-million pound publishing empire comprising newspaper and magazine titles. The *West Indian Digest* was replaced by

Caribbean Times and later, the *African Times* and *Asian Times* were incorporated into the product segments of the business.

All three tabloid publications were known for their informative, campaigning, inspiring and authoritative style. Their coverage of issues was brilliant and controversial at the same time, but such news-reporting style found favour with minority readers. Hansib secured a viable stake in mainstream advertising, thereby enabling large companies and public agencies to access lucrative minority consumer markets that remained largely untapped during that time.

The firm expanded, opening branches in the Midland Counties, Africa, the Caribbean and the US and in 1995, the company had a customer base in excess of 100,000, with a turnover estimated at £2 million plus a market share of 10%. Two years later, Hansib announced the sale of its newspaper titles to the Ethnic Media Group, a moved designed to consolidate its striving publishing operations. The company has over 200 book titles including themes on cricket, education, history, literature and politics and has published country profiles on the Caribbean Region to capture the growing tourism market in the Americas.

The publishing giant also had a social focus, a practice that was unusual for minority firms struggling for recognition and longevity. Ali's continued success is due to close contacts with diverse communities, along with his honed knowledge and understanding of the importance of building constructive partnerships between nations and institutions. He believed also in making a `positive difference' to diverse communities in Britain, and the creation of the *Hansib Community Award* was designed to honour unsung achievers who had contributed to various fields of human endeavour in the UK and elsewhere.

Another significant milestone for Hansib, was its progressive work-study program that benefited a generation of practicing journalists and professional writers (including this author). Today, many are in established careers; namely, public relations and the media, while some have set up agencies to provide customized media services.

Ali's eldest son, Kash, founded *Books of Colour*, a catalogue and publication company, in 1999, and with his vast experience in printing, there is every reason to believe, that he will continue in the footsteps of his father, Hansib-style.

Another reputable publication, is *The Voice* most arguably, a market leader in the ethnic press and recognized as the authoritative voice of the black community and respected for its tireless campaign for black representation in mainstream institutions, as well as economic justice and social equality for non-white communities in Britain. Unlike, Hansib Publishing, *The Voice* is the mouthpiece for a generation of black Britons and its pages are dedicated to domestic issues, international news, entertainment, sports and features on matters of interest to the black community.

The late Jamaican accountant, Val McCalla, founded the newspaper in 1981 using his home at the beginning until he found suitable premises. At first, he struggled to convince large companies to advertise in the newspaper but they soon realized that the publication was useful for promoting essential goods and services to a growing ethnic consumer market. Government departments, public and private sector companies, along with community organizations began (mass) advertising in *The Voice* and soon, the newspaper became an automatic choice of media advertising in Britain. In reflecting on his company's success, McCalla acknowledged that:

When we launched The Voice, the few existing ethnic newspapers were all aimed at, and produced by, the first generation of African -Caribbean peoples to Britain. Their readers were still coming to terms with life in an often hostile society, and news from `back home' was still high on the list of priorities. We must recognize the emerging market of a second generation of black people who had all been born in Britain. The mainstream media tended to treat black people as immigrants, intrusive, problematic and alien (***The Voice* 2002)**.

As a tabloid newspaper, the publishers transformed the format, style and content to reflect a modern readership. In April 1992 the *Weekly Journal*, the first national black broadsheet, was launched with a circulation of 10,000 and a readership of 120,000, mostly aimed at professionals. *The Voice* has won countless awards for its coverage of affairs within Britain's ethnic community and has grown in stature as one of the country's top 100 consumer publications. The Gleaner Group bought the assets of Voice Communications and has since strengthened the newspaper's estimated 15% share of the ethnic media market.

Other Publishing

British Caribbean professionals have succeeded in setting up other publishing houses to cater for other consumer markets ranging from business, children, entertainment, fashion, literature and politics to sports. These markets are largely segmented, catering for professionals and mass consumers alike. Limited capital investment, inadequate premises and inability to attract (sufficient) quality staff, including freelancers are recurring problems that have dented the profits of micro or relatively small publishing houses. The growth of online publishing over the past five years, has not helped traditional `paper-type' publishers either.

Nationally, the UK retail book sales market was £3.98 billion in 2004 which represented a 3.2% increase on 2003. It is estimated that the book market will increase by up to 10.4% by 2009. Magazine publishing was £3.19 billion in 2004, with 3,343 titles produced at the end of that year. A growth in the number of magazines was expected in 2005 by 3% and thereafter, a forecast of 2.5% until 2009. Children's publishing was worth £672 million in 2004, an increase of 5.1% over 2003 and estimates had suggested a further decline of 20% in 2005 over 2004. Booksellers are concerned that this market is oversupplied and that picture books simply do not sell in the UK the same way that they do in Europe and the US markets.

Since newspaper attracts high market entry barriers, some British Caribbean entrepreneurs have opted for small-scale production involving targeted publications at minimum start-up costs, although to sustain any publishing operation still requires a fair amount of capital. Judging from the volume of black publishing houses mushrooming, the national market share is probably in the region of 2%, not bad for a community that represents one percent of the total UK population. Generally, book traders specialize in a variety of subjects or themes, and according to **Table 5. 3,** these markets continue to diversify to cater for the broader literary needs of ethnic consumers.

Table 5.3 Snapshot of leading British Caribbean publishers

Publishers	Areas of Interest
New Beacon Books	Established in 1966 - Black life in Britain, also literature on global communities in Africa, Asia, Latin America, Caribbean and the Middle East.
Allison & Busby	Since 1969, Allison & Busby has published quality books: from crime fiction to cosy and noir and literary fiction to classic, contemporary from writers of African and Caribbean origin.
Bogle L'Ouverture	Set up around the 1970s – publish Black and Third World political texts on Africa, Asia and the Caribbean.

Hansib Publications	Founded in 1971 – produces a range of titles on African, Asian, Caribbean and other people of colour worldwide, also Caribbean travel books and related literature.
Hawker Publications	Started in 1987 - publisher of at least half a dozen hair and beauty magazines.
Paublo Books	One of Britain's largest suppliers of multicultural books, listing of over 5,000 titles in 40 subject categories.
Tamarind Books	Began in 1989 – publisher of children's books, fiction and non-fiction material.
Xpress	Formed in 1992 – publishes classics, science fiction and popular fiction.
Mango Publishing	Established in 1995 in response to growing demand for small black press committed to publishing quality, first-time writers. Promotes writers work from British, Caribbean and Latin American literary traditions.

(Source: The Chronicle World, www.chroncileworld.org and the Gleaner, 28 November - 4 December 2003)

Besides, **Paublo** and **Tamarind Books**, along with the **X Press**, the older publications tend to cater for first generation African and Caribbean nationals and therefore have smaller, slimmer-type operations, while modern presses supply markets for younger readers and professional `browsers' who are more selective because of their hectic lifestyle and urbane outlook. The evolution of Xpress Publishing (1992), founded on a shoe-string budget, is a feat of vision, ambition and enterprise by founders - Steve Pope and Dotun Adebayo, both journalists. Pope used his flat to organize the business properly, before moving to larger premises.

After they were refused a start-up loan in excess of £10,000, the pair went ahead and published the controversial book, *Yardie,* by

Victor Headley in April of the same year. Within six months, the novel sold 10,000 copies and Pope and Adebayo never looked back. The publishing company has published over 160 different titles and in addition to attracting mainstream distributors (markets) such as Waterstones, W.H. Smith and Borders, Xpress has done business in America and the Caribbean. The owners of this innovative publishing house have invaluable advice for both would-be and existing (struggling) publishers?

- *Don't enter the business only to make money.*
- *Have a passion for literature.*
- *Explore alternative means to raising investment capital.*
- *Encourage talented writers to publish.*
- *Maximize profit advantage through export markets.*
- *Maintain trust and reliability in working relationships.*
- *Be committed to the aims and objectives of the business* **(Benjamin 1995: 2003)**.

Recently, there has been a new type of children's literature that borders on the superstitious and the (age-old) fairy tale tradition, influenced by J.K. Rowling's *Harry Potter* book series and films. The desire for children's literary entertainment however is not as simplistic, and according to the industry, more adults than children buy books. Books are bought as gifts and the choice is made according to adults' (own) taste. However, exclusive research conducted by a MORI poll on behalf of Nestle for its 2003 Family Monitor study, showed that young people were less inclined to read, or encourage children to read, than older persons.

In the 1980s, Grenadian Verna Wilkins, recognized the need for culturally diverse reading materials for children after she observed the difficulty her son had reading books that had no 'multicultural' input. She took 'affirmative' action 'by setting up (what is today) a formidable publishing company dedicated to producing multicultural books for children **(Minicase 5.11)**.

Minicase 5.11 Tamarind Books Ltd

Tamarind Books Ltd was set up in 1987 to plug the gap in the multicultural children's book market and founder, Verna Wilkins, has since been using a small overdraft to stabilize the operations. She learnt about the multicultural needs of the children's literature market through surveys involving parents, children and professionals dealing with diversity issues. With a staff of two, she developed a network of designers, marketers and writers and later, a core of editorial and book production personnel.

Wilkins' sternest challenge was persuading mainstream buyers, distributors and sales personnel who had no knowledge of the vast potential of the multicultural children's market, nor did they feel that Tamarind was going to survive in a segment of the publishing industry perceived to be non-traditional and different.

With an annual turnover of around half a million pounds, the company's strategy is to consolidate its operations, build a stronger clientele, and maintain a reliable network of artists, designers and producers for additional freelance work. A major plan is also to concentrate on improving children's material for the National Curriculum.

Today, black publishers are continuing the noble tradition of first generation journalists, writers and other artistic producers who were at the height of their literary powers during the intervening wars years, despite the lack of recognition. Importantly, too, while few minority writers feature prominently in the annual *Booker, Turner, Whitbread, Commonwealth* and other artistic and literary prizes, there is indisputable evidence that British Caribbean writers have contributed to more than 50 years of British literature. According to information obtained from the Arts Council of England, *Black and Asian British Fiction Writers* in the UK are characterized along the following lines: -

- 46% are of Caribbean heritage;
- 77% are males and 23% are females;

- They represent half of the Caribbean and Latin American Region;
- They are of African, Indian, Chinese, European and other mixed ethnicities;
- Over 5% reside abroad mostly in North America;
- They are ages 35 to 70 plus;
- About 75% are writers of fiction;
- An estimated 60% have published works reflecting their birthplace; and
- They publish themes on politics, culture, history and literature **(2005)**.

Veteran, prolific writers such as Edward R. Braithwaite, Kamau Brathwaite, Merle Collins, Frank Birbalsingh, David Dabydeen, Caryl Phillips, Samuel Selvon, Derek Walcott and Gordon Rohlehr, live outside of Britain even though they have made significant inputs into British fiction and non-fiction writing. Second generation artists – Fred D'Augiar, Alex Wheatle, Courtier Newland, Bernardine Evaristo, Naomi King and Karline Smith - are among the modern literary `giants' who are destined to sustain Britain's multiculturalism. Notably, just over half of all British Caribbean authors have published works that are (inclusively) representative of the Arts, Languages and Literature with respect to the British National Curriculum.

In addition, English publishing houses have collaborated with minority authors to publish works that reflect British and Caribbean environments respectively. These publications range from poetry and creative writing or short stories to semi-biographies and/or non-fictional works on the arts, culture and oral histories of minority communities in postwar Britain. The literature of the Brathwaites, the Dabydeens, the Naipauls, Selvon and Walcott particularly, is now integral to Caribbean Studies at British universities, the University of the West Indies and other tertiary institutions in the Americas. The success of British Caribbean cultural firms hinges on how effective owners can deal with challenges and at the same time, maximize opportunities to increase market share, thereby creating stability. A notable omission from the fertile British Caribbean publishing industry is the lack of data on the market value or the economic impact minority authors have on the UK literary market as a whole.

Challenges and Opportunities

On average, black firms experience formidable problems such as poor location, unsuitable premises, insufficient funding, lack of enterprise support and the volume of regulations. But perhaps the most hindrances owners face, are strategic in nature; they include dealing with large monopolies, entry barriers (restrictive prices) and balancing products and services range to meet the requirement(s) of segmented consumer markets.

Advertising

Challenges: This segment has a low take-up by British Caribbean firms, with most tending to be involved in PR – the value of this market is low, with the majority of firms located in the London Region. When this segment has a crisis, it affects the revenue of other media such as radio, television, newspaper and magazine publishing. Information on this sub-sector is hard to come by and the market is generally fragmented.

Opportunities: There can be collaboration or joint ventures between minority firms and mainstream companies on a subcontracting basis, targeting strictly minority consumers or complementary advertising involving consumer markets such as designer clothing, food and drinks, financial products for the elderly and mortgage for young first-time house buyers etc). Encouraging public institutions to set aside annual sponsorship budgets for recreational and social activities and events for inner-city youths experiencing long-term employment and those at risk of anti-social behaviour. A more strategic approach to competing in the open market is to Search, Analyze, Plan and Implement (SAPI) a diversity action plan.

Carnival Arts

Threats: This segment lacks sufficient resources to compete – virtually most firms are under-capitalized and are relatively micro in composition. They lack enterprise and funding support. Very few advisers in enterprise agencies have (expert) cultural knowledge and owners therefore rely on either colleagues or at best, are totally self-sufficient. This sub-sector is still largely fragmented because of its newness, apart from it being unclassified as a viable commercial entity even though potentially, activities around carnival arts have increased since the 1960s.

Opportunities: Since art is considered to be therapeutic in wider business circles, it might be useful for British Caribbean firms to persuade large companies to encourage staff in cultural activities to boost morale, cultural knowledge and productivity whilst reducing stress levels. This can be sold as an effective way of measuring mainstream companies' (proper) return on investment (ROI). The area of costume production is also potentially lucrative – firms can again engage companies especially those without a regular calendar of cultural events. Senior executives could be encouraged to organize events in conjunction with clients – these will help to add value to corporate (public) image.

Music

Threats: There are far less producers and marketers in this sub-sector than they are singers. There is no reliable database on the number of artists and therefore, a national policy for SMEs in music is piecemeal in scope, with the delivery of courses and routine training sessions by universities, colleges and community-based organizations. The rise of internet, mobile phone downloads and the mass marketing of CDs in big retail chains- WH Smith, Virgins, HMV and Woolworth – has crippled the profits of Caribbean record shops and musical producers. Set up costs are expensive for a record retailer and can be the biggest barrier to entry. Getting established takes a long time and certainly, location can have some advantage in terms of public image and popularity.

Opportunities: Success in the music business is possible if owners-producers target niches in calypso, reggae, soca, gospel or spirituals. Prime spots on the high streets are crucial and owners should make sure that firms have a proper cataloguing process. Community sponsorships are also attractive options; for example, award schemes for young achievers who are unknown and unsupported. Mail order and the use of web-based facilities are cost effective ways of managing music firms. The Internet enables consumers to access products and information on available services.

Publishing

Threats: Monopolies dominate the publishing market and while there is space for smaller publishers, they don't have the financial muscle for expansion. Minority publications run the risk of losing market share by imitating the content and presentational styles of mainstream. There're insufficient editorial, managerial and technical personnel in British Caribbean publishing houses. Well-equipped staff plus appropriate technology, can offer firms competitive advantage in segmented markets.

Opportunities: Publishers in London and the Southeast should set up branches in the Midlands, Scotland and Wales to maximize opportunities in ethnic markets. Encourage school-leavers to pursue media careers, thereby opening up the industry to brighter and more creative minorities. Owners should approach large companies to solicit contracts on the publication of prospectuses, annual reports, market strategies, newsletters and other corporate-type publications. Textbook publishing has lucrative prospects and it is a market that British Caribbean publishing firms need to exploit.

Design

Threats: Rapid decline in the number of enterprises across the UK because of changing fashions and the presence of low cost producers overseas. Black designers are not well connected with mainstream designers and there is pressure to compete with European styles and other products. Advertising new products is given low priority due to limited revenue for marketing campaigns. Few designers make use of exhibitions and trade fairs to promote products and services.

Opportunities: British Caribbean firms should research home and overseas markets to test product acceptance. Discussing ideas with the BERR's export promotion unit can be the first step towards selling products in mass consumer market. Membership with reputable trade bodies with an interest in the design trade is beneficial to image and reputation. Inviting large companies to engage in export trade agreements is also a useful way for minority firms to learn the principles and practices of '*Big Business*' and build on market advantage.

Broadcast Media

Threats: This segment is problematic in terms of start-up costs – entry barriers could be quite high depending on the type of media. Digital TV in the form of satellite communication is increasingly competitive and can drive smaller broadcast media agencies out of the market. The content of most black TV channels comprises cultural programs, music, religious activities and snippets of news. Investment in audience research, equipment and general programming is very limited. Not all community radio stations are fully licensed to enjoy high (public) approval rating and status.

Opportunities: British Caribbean media firms can expand coverage to other parts of England, Scotland and Wales to capture audiences in minority communities. The growth of multiculturalism in news and information services, also offers market advantage for firms to maximize existing funding opportunities for new media audiences, as a means of sustainable growth. In general, the challenges affecting British Caribbean cultural firms can be overcome if owners and managers take advantage of increasing opportunities in the CIS economy in Britain **(Table 5. 4)**.

Table 5.4 Summary of Challenges and Opportunities

(Source: Textual analysis of creative segments in chapter)

Segment	Challenges	Opportunities
Advertising	Poor take-up, with information difficult to obtain about this segment of the CIS.	Joint ventures with mainstream companies - complementary advertising and community sponsorships.
Carnival Arts	Micro firms lack funding and technical support.	Access to funding for arts initiatives; encourage large companies to buy-into carnival arts.
Music	Internet, CDs, and mobile phone downloads are crippling the profits of record shops.	Target niche areas, identify suitable premises and location, and develop an efficient cataloguing system.
Publishing	Management personnel in firms are scarce; firms unable to compete on price, quality and product volume.	Expand in minority markets; contract /subcontract with large companies in the production of corporate material.
Design	Competition from changing fashions and low cost overseas producers; lack of enterprise support.	Research home-overseas markets; discuss with the BERR export promotion prospects and take part in exhibitions and trade fairs.

Broadcast Media	Entry barriers are high; competition in the digital market; community radio suffers from poor program content.	Firms can expand into satellite market; implement suitable programs for different media audiences and take advantage of new investment opportunities for wider media schemes.

Added Opportunities

There is an obvious advantage to be gained by British Caribbean entrepreneurs in attempting to secure niche markets within the cultural economy, through the commercialization of ideas into marketable products and services. As such, the emerging strengths are evidenced by opportunities in other segments such as the antiques market, architecture and crafts. These strengths vary from medium to high for the Caribbean firms and they prove that as a section of the UK population, members of this group like other BMEs can make an exceptional contribution to an array of business and social enterprise activities. The commercial antiques market is worth around £900 million and there are signs that Caribbean students' attendance at architecture schools may increase from the current level of about 3% to 5% minimum.

In making a case for growth potential in the minority creative industry, one particular London study suggested that a clearer focus and better co-ordination is required for firms to achieve full potential. In the absence of any benchmark to measure 'distance travelled' by black cultural firms, it can be assumed that the potential exists for around 5,000 new enterprises if the ratio of BME-led ventures matched that of the total London population. The London study added that: -

If current BME led businesses in the creative enterprises matched all creative enterprises in London by turnover and employment, a further £500 million in extra revenues could be expected with extra 100,000 jobs. Many of these jobs would be in the more disadvantaged groups **(Respect 2005)**.

Cultural Regeneration

Since the 1980s, there has been much focus on culture as a contributory factor of regeneration and numerous studies have illustrated the importance of this sector to local and regional economies in the UK. However, these studies have failed to show the input of Caribbean peoples in changing the face of diverse communities with their brand of innovation, creativity and enterprise.

In the early part of this century, the DCMS reviewed the state of cultural regeneration with a view to look at indicators which showed evidence of high quality (cultural) input in various parts of the country. Apart from defining the term `cultural regeneration' and the methods used to identify areas of Best Practice, the review highlighted key schemes that impacted on economic and social development as a whole.

And whilst it is recognized that tensions between policies on the creative industries sector for global media businesses versus the support for small in local development exist, the overall aim for this industry is to increase jobs and GDP, whilst simultaneously resolving social exclusion and countering long-term patterns of uneven development (**Oakley 2004: 2006**).

Indeed, British Caribbean firms can tap into opportunities which regeneration schemes offer, along with other initiatives for emerging and existing cultural firms in the BME community. With increasing evidence suggesting growth in the cultural industries sector, the prospects for minority enterprises are excellent, providing that all-round support is given in areas such as quality location, premises, adequate human resources, funding, joint venture activities, market intelligence and access to highly competitive markets (**Minicases 5. 12**).

Minicases 5.12 Selected Cultural Sector Initiatives in the UK

- The **Custard Factory Quarter** in Birmingham is the largest single complex of creativity in Europe, providing 250,000 sq. ft of affordable workspace for as many as 1000 creative people from many different creative industries and sub-sectors. The development is privately owned by the Society for the Promotion of Artistic and Creative Enterprise (SPACE). This organization launched its first acquisition of premises for creative businesses with the development of Canalot Production Studios in North Kensington, 1986. Since 1990, SPACE has gradually acquired all of the land associated with the old Custard factory together with some adjacent railway arches.

- **The Chocolate Factory** which is designated the Cultural Quarter in Wood Green, north London, was opened in 1997. This development was inspired by Haringey Arts Council which leases and manages 5,000 square metres of floor space at the factory, a former sweet factory that provides studios for over 120 artists, film, video, music, theatre, photography, printing and craft industries. The site is shared with organizations and businesses.

- The Breightmet estate in Bolton, Greater Manchester is in the lowest 10% of deprived areas in the country. **Breightmet Arts** is an organization established by Bolton Community Education Services (part of Bolton Community College) and funded through Bolton Metropolitan Council's Housing Department's Percent for Arts scheme. It has worked with 71 partner organizations, 43 artists and worked with more than 5,000 individual participants, including adults and children. A long-term strategy has been formulated to use arts as a catalyst for positive change on the estate.

- **The Headland Café** is situated south of Bridlington harbour in Yorkshire. The facility is one element in a project which originated to reverse the decline in the popularity of the area as a holiday destination. East Riding of Yorkshire Council decided that the collapsing North Promenade should be repaired with the involvement of artists and designers. Following the sue regeneration of South Promenade with the involvement of artists, using quality materials and a high standard of modern design. Support for the project also came from European finding and the National Lottery Fund.

- **Mapping Scotland's' Cultural Future-** In January 2006, the Scottish Executive announced a transformation of the country's cultural landscape with a series of radical plans for the future. The plans involve an investment of an extra £20 million per year from April 2007 to support and nurture the best creative talent. To make this a reality, a new cultural development agency will be established, with the merging of the Scottish Arts Council and Scottish Screen. The aim is to develop talent and excellence in all branches of the arts, and the creative and screen industries.
- **Wales Cultural Industries –** In the mid-1990s, Wales carried out a major research into its cultural industries sector which showed that the sector employed 28,000 people or 2.6% of the working population. An estimated expenditure of £546 million was spent to boost creativity and this in turn, accounted for jobs and other wealth-creation activities through purchases and sales **(DCMS 2004: Scottish Executive 2006: Cardiff University 1998)**.

Conclusion

This chapter profiled the contribution of British Caribbean firms to the cultural industries sector within the context of the overall creative industries in the UK. The organization and performance of firms and their participation in key segments of the local and regional economies were emphasized. Notwithstanding its complex definition, using current industry statistics and independent research and sampled data, the market share of key segments of the CIS were presented. The contribution of Caribbean firms across sub-sectors was also highlighted through the use of case studies and other forms of evidence such as direct quotes from official reports and client responses.

The terms `creative industries' and `cultural industries' were used interchangeably to mean various forms of artistic and creative endeavours, including multimedia technology and other applications. An assessment of problem-issues affecting the sector was also discussed and reference was made to the impact these have on minority firms. The issue of limited data on Caribbean artists and cultural producers was also mentioned, since this reflected the nature of exclusion experienced by black businesses in almost every sector of the British economy today.

The range of challenges and opportunities was also mentioned as part of the dynamics of the sector, also in an attempt to focus on the pitfalls affecting the growth and stability of Caribbean cultural enterprises. Challenges were considered to be operational and strategic and they reflected the importance of owners cultivating a `learning enterprise' culture to compete in the marketplace. Opportunities in various segments and sub-sectors were demonstrated and how these could make a real difference to firm's profitability and general public image.

The chapter concluded by reviewing a study on the contribution of culture to regeneration that was commissioned by the DCMS in January 2004. Selected case studies were identified to showcase examples of best practice. They were also illustrated to provide further opportunities for British Caribbean firms to connect with other areas of the country, to consolidate their presence and increase market share in order to reflect quality levels of organization (structurally) and performance (outputs or profitability) in the cultural economy. In the next chapter the contribution of Caribbean firms to the construction industry in the UK, would be highlighted.

Chapter Notes

Caribbean Civilisation – a much discussed concept as Caribbean leaders seek to modernize the region, its institutions and educate domestic and overseas audiences about this community's complex history and its shared presence in a world that demands fresh thinking and decisive action for human advancement.

Cultural Impact – the Scottish Executive and the Welsh Assembly have made the creative industries a priority in their endeavours to measure the impact of this sector on their respective economies, and with the aim of unleashing the potential of talented, young entrepreneurs whilst boosting public confidence.

Artists Movement – visual arts also played a key role in the British Caribbean pioneering era in the early 20th century. Caribbean dentist and political activist, Ronald Moody was a pivotal figure in the mid-1960s Caribbean Artists Movement in the UK. Moody whose brother was the prominent Dr. Harold Moody, was reputed to be one of Britain's modernist sculptors and a number of his carvings were included in the 1939 exhibition.

Participation Rates – in the absence of formal data, it was necessary to use a conservative estimate to obtain a measured market share for British Caribbean cultural enterprises according to their industry segmentation and performance overall.

Desmond's – was a hit for nearly six years attracting millions of viewers worldwide. The award-winning show depicted the exploits of Desmond Ambrose, his family and all those who passed through his Peckham barbershop. It has been released on DVD and is broadcast twice daily on the satellitie channel, Trouble.

Lilt Ladies – this advertisement created much humour and intrigue as Jamaican-born Blanche Williams and Hazel Palmer were featured in the advertising campaign for the `Lilt' beverage. Both were discovered at auditions held at; a local bingo club and an Age Concern centre respectively. White advertising companies are slowly beginning to target influential minorities in Britain to improve their public image whilst maximizing the enormous potential that could be gained from these consumer markets.

Advertising First – ASAP Communications was the first black-owned and run consultancy providing advertising, sponsorship and PR to organisations interested in targeting minority businesses.

Founder-Director, Dr. Yvonne Thompson has a remarkable career treading between business and public life. She was awarded the CBE for services to women and business development.

Carnival Arts – apart from the Notting Hill Carnival event, carnival arts are now integral to different annual festivities throughout Britain. The growth of festivals and the trend towards including carnival processions within their programming is another important element of the promotion of this sector in the UK. Mahogany Arts Ltd has demonstrated the therapeutic value of this art form, helping young people to overcome their inhibitions and lack of achievement, thereby enabling them to use their artistic potential.

Decibel Initiative – a one-year initiative of the Arts Council of England that was aimed at promoting cultural diversity in the arts. The scheme invested more than £5 million in artists and a survey later showed, that 72% of black people read for pleasure and the Asian population 61%, whilst about 47% of minorities used public libraries compared to the national figure of 10%.

The Edric Connor Agency – was established by Trinidadian Pearl Connor-Mogotsi and her actor-husband Edric Connor in 1956 and it represented Caribbean, Malaysia, India and Africa, actors, writers and film-makers in Britain. In the early 1960s, the cultural activist was instrumental in setting up the Negro Theatre Workshop, one of Britain's first black theatre companies.

Horace Ove – is listed in the *Guinness Book of Records* as the first Caribbean director of a feature film (*Pressure*). As prolific film and documentary producer, he is well known in Europe. Pressure tells the story of a British-born black do-gooder teenager who joins the Black Panther movement in the 1970s in Ladbroke Grove after a series of humiliations at the hands of the white establishment. The British Film Institute that supported the production of the film initially banned its release for two years, fearing that its depiction of police brutality could prove counterproductive. Belatedly, the authorities permitted the film's release to widespread acclaim.

'Playing Away' – directed by Horace Ove in 1986, the cast also included well know figures Norman Beaton, Helen Lindsay, Nicholas Farrell and Brian Bovell. The Channel 4 film depicted a cricket match held in an idyllic Suffolk village, played by the local team and a visiting West Indian team from Brixton. The arrival of the team leads to new friendships but also unexpected hostility.

Lenny Henry – described as one of the leading black actors in Britain today and the first British comedian to make a live stand-up comedy film similar to the Americans, Eddie Murphy and Robin Williams. Henry's 1993 sitcom, *'Chef'* was unique for its humour, language and brilliance. It was later reported that in the guise of the character, Blackstock, Henry assisted Delia Smith to prepare one of the recipes she concocted for *Comic Relief* in 1997.

Floella Benjamin- a household name in children's television programming since 1987 when she co-founded Floella Benjamin Productions Ltd. In 2004, the company received the Royal Television Society award for the production, *'Coming to England'*, a similar title adapted for Benjamin's book which is used at universities to teach anti-racism, cultural studies and social history.

Global Commodities – Dr. Keith Nurse has researched extensively issues such as the global political economy of the clothing, banana, tourism, copyright and cultural industries. He is a proponent of artistic expressions and symbols of national and regional identify, as well as increasing the commercialisation of the arts and cultural industries to modernize Caribbean communities, universally.

Artistic Evolution – between the two World wars, Britain was a major centre for the recording and manufacturing of gramophone records. The recordings in London of African and Caribbean music (including

Cubans) demonstrate the important role and linkages played by migrant musicians in the evolution of the recording business in the UK. Other European countries; namely, Germany and France joined in this `bonanza.

Musical Diversity – Caribbean music is versatile, combining African, Indian, Latin American, European and other universal genres. It is now traditional to be entertained at Caribbean fetes, by a combination of calypso, reggae, soul and the African-Indian rhythm of chutney soca. Another fusion is gospelypso (a blend of gospel and calypso), made famous in the 1970s in Trinidad and Tobago and later became popular with the Barbadian community. Caribbean music is a global product that is marketed in Western capitals such as Holland, London, Paris, Toronto and New York. Artists like Sina Wayne also known as S.W. Storm (of Indian-Trinidadian parentage), is keen to promote soca, as well as forms of Caribbean music in the UK.

Jet Star Records – founded in the mid-1960s by the Palmer trio in west London, this company was dedicated to mainly US soul labels, but within 18 months the balance of their output shifted in favour of the emerging reggae and rocksteady sounds from Jamaica. The demand for this music was so great, that the Palmers had to develop other record labels. In 1984, Jet Star's popular *Reggae Hits* series were relaunched, with the first edition soaring the national charts where it remained for several weeks.

George Padmore – in honour of the brilliant Trinidadian writer and dedicated Pan-Africanist, George Padmore (1902-1959) the George Padmore Institute was set up in 1960 by a group of writers, educators, cultural, political and social activists at New Beacon Books Ltd, owned by the late Trinidadian John La Rose who was a cultural icon in the black community. Padmore was one of the most influential figures in the anti-colonial and independent struggles of the 20th century.

Selected References

1 Remarks by Dr. H.E. Edwin Carrington, Secretary General, Caribbean Community, at the *Alliance for Civilisation Seminar*, 25 September 2006, Saint Lucia.

2 Nurse, K (2000): *The Cultural Industries and Sustainable Development in Small Island Developing Sates*, University of the West Indies.

3 Dunlop, Stewart; Galloway, Susan; Hamilton, Susan & Scullion, Adrienne (2004), *The Economic Impact of the Cultural Sector in Scotland*: the Fraser of Alliance Institute and Centre for Cultural; policy Research, University of Glasgow.

4 *The Cultural Industries in Wales: setting the economic development agenda*, Cultural Enterprise Annual Report 2003-2004, Cultural Enterprise 2000, Wales.

5 *Mapping BME-led Creative Industries in London:* A final report, Respect August 2005.

6 *National Carnival Arts Strategy 2005-2007,* Arts Council of England, July 2005.

7 *Hard talk Extra* (with Bruce Oldfield), Interview with Gavin Esler, BBC 24 December 2005.

8 *First UK-based African and Caribbean general entertainment TV channel launches Digital Satellite,* College of North East London, 21 November 2003.

9 `The bigger picture, Film 24 Seven', *The Voice*, 8 September 2003 London.

10 Hines, Vince (2004): *Developing The Infrastructure of the Voluntary and Community Sector*, University of London.

11 Professor Ian Hall profile, *Caribbean Times*, 15 April 1994, London.

12 Cowley, John (1985): `West Indian Gramophone Records in Britain: 1927-1950', *Occasional Papers in Ethnic Relations*, No. 1, Coventry, CRER, University of Warwick, England.

13 Livingstone, Rochelle (1995): *Diachronic Study of the Evolution of Gospelypso in Trinidad and Tobago*, Arts & General Studies, Livingstone Enterprises.

14 Bilby, Kenneth (1985): *The Caribbean as a Musical Region*, The Woodrow Wilson International Centre for Scholars, Washington D.C.

15 Dawson, Christopher (1975): `Religion and Culture': *The Glifford Lectures*, Meridian Books Inc. London.

16 Bourne, C & Allgrove, S.M (1997): `Prospects for Exports of Entertainment Services from the Caribbean: The Case of Music', *Caribbean Dialogue* 3.3; pp 1-12.

17 Warner, Keith Q. (1982): *The Trinidad Calypso: A study of the Calypso as Oral Literature*, Heinemann Ed. Books Ltd, London.

18 `Jazzy Grooves for Newport City', *Ethnic Enterprise*, Autumn 2005, Wales.

19 `They were Britain's first black dance company', *The Guardian*, 5 August 1999, London.

20 Hines, Vince (1998): *The Rise of the Black Media in Britain*, Zulu Publications, London.

21 `20 Years of Campaigning Excellence 1982-2002', *The Voice Communications Ltd* 1982.

22 Benjamin, Ionie (1995): *The Black Press in Britain*, Trentham Books, London.

23 Cultural Diversity in Book Publishing Today, 12 March 2004.

24 Brown, Paul (2005): *Publishing*, Association of Graduate Careers Advisory Services (AGAS), University of St. Andrews, Scotland.

25 *A List of Black and Asian British Fiction Writers*, Arts, Language and Literature Service, Central Library, Birmingham, England, April 2007.

26 Oakley, Kate (2006): `Include Us Out – Economic Development and Social Policy in the Creative Industries', *Cultural Trends*, Vol. 15, No. 4 December 2006, pp. 255-273, Routledge.

27 Evans Graeme & Phyllida, Shaw (2004): *The Contribution of Culture to Regeneration in the UK: A Review of Evidence*: A Report to the Department for Culture Media and Sport.

Chapter 6

Construction Industry

Introduction

In the 1980s, the UK construction industry was hit hard by recession and by the 1990s employment fell throughout the industry but has risen over the past few years accounting for 7% of total employment. It has a high political and social profile, as a result of its key role in providing housing, its impact on the environment and its part as a major employer in contributing around 10% of GDP and employing over 2 million of which 2.8% or about 400,000 are from minority background. In 2005, the output of the construction industry in Britain was £107.01 billion and its diversity is evidenced by the number of contractors, consultants, building materials suppliers and product producers which are dominated by a relatively few large companies (*www.marketresearch.com*).

Estimates suggest that nearly 100,000 people would be required each year for the next five years. There are strong area variations on employment and labour, with all regions finding it difficult to recruit skilled staff to help employers deal with the volume of work which is expected to increase in the future according to projected increases in the number of regeneration schemes and related building activity throughout the UK. By 2010, the industry will need more of these: wood trades, managers, electricians, plumbers and bricklayers (**Goodwyn and Munn 2006**).

Like previous sections, information pertaining to this chapter was obtained from different sources; that is, utilizing datasets from directories, accessing material from press clippings, in-depth interviews, along with observational research to acquire anecdotal evidence vital to this growth sector. Where possible, information was obtained from experts and other industry related professionals.

Traditionally, the building trade is labour intensive but changes in technology and work processes have altered operations significantly. The issue of equal access to contract opportunities is a hindrance to minority firms with a combined market share of 2.3% or £2.23 million per annum. Independent estimates suggest that British Caribbean firms have a cumulative market share of 1% or £1.07 billion annually. Interestingly, a tiny fraction of firms in England, particularly in London and the Midlands, have surpassed this market share value by acquiring lucrative contractors or subcontracting into niche markets where there are elements of specialization.

Antiquity Period

In profiling the endeavours of British Caribbean operatives in the construction industry, it is vital to reflect on the African contribution to the building trade. Remarkable engineering feats such as pyramids, buildings and other structures were constructed in times of antiquity. Even with less sturdy materials at hand, Africans were still able to place their stamp of technological genius upon those materials. One of the great architectural wonders of the continent is Great Zimbabwe which has the most construction sites found outside the pyramids of Egypt. The great stone city, as it was called, is more than 800 years old. The African team, the Asantes, calculated that the work had approximately 4,500 stone blocks and it is estimated that 10,000 people lived in that city, making it one of the largest cities of its day (**Van Sertima 1985**).

Following in the footsteps of their African ancestors, Caribbean people also demonstrated great deeds in engineering that had a lasting impact on the technological environment of the Americas. The Panama Canal is a brilliant example and although their pioneering endeavours have been down-played by historians, it is known that without Caribbean skills, this waterway would have been in doubt. As it was, more than 20,000 people from Barbados, Jamaica, St. Lucia, Martinique, Guadeloupe, Cuba, the Dominican Republic and Puerto helped built the facility. Hundreds died in the process and according to officials, *`Latin America and Caribbean human resources are not limited to the less qualified positions, but also include engineers and experts, because there is a level of scientific expertise in the region which makes it competent to undertake work of this magnitude'* **(Valdez 2006)**.

In terms of Britain and Europe, there is evidence to suggest that there were early African entrepreneurs and state builders present. The legends of the mysterious `African sea-rovers', the Formorians, who had a stronghold in Ireland, verify the very early presence of people of colour in parts of the UK. In England, Stonehenge (meaning `hanging stones') in Wiltshire is one of the most brilliant, complex and mysterious architectural `wonders' in Britain. Although there has been stubborn resistance on the part of white historians to admit the possibility of African construction origins, there is general agreement that Stonehenge represents incomparable engineering by civilized people. Estimates of the construction phases range from 350 to 1100 BC. It was further stated that:

The construction was clearly beyond the skills of barbaric man and the theory is that the structure served as an astronomical observatory. There has been much debate over this issue, but there exists evidence to substantiate the observatory theory; and unless it can be refuted on mathematical ground such evidence must be accepted. This why Stonehenge remains one of the great mysteries of humankind, always challenging the mind to wonder about its mysterious and mystical past (**Rashidi 1985**).

Industry Classification

According to the BERR's `sector content' classification, `the building, construction and property services contains the following:

- Building and Construction Services;
- Building Materials and Products used in Construction;
- Construction Raw Materials; and
- Infrastructure **(Table 6.1)**.

The Construction Unit within the UK Trade and Investment is responsible for roads, bridges, tunnels, dams, architecture – residential, commercial and industrial buildings; regeneration, building products, building services, relationships with trade associations and professional institutions and generic construction issues.

Table 6.1 Sector Content of the UK Construction Industry

Building Services	Building Materials	Raw Materials	Infrastructure
Architectural	Cabling	Brick clay	Engineering
Builders	Central heating	Cement	Process plant
Building	Ceramic sinks/ baths	Aggregates	Public work
Civil engineering	Door frames, hinges etc	Quarrying	
Demolition	DIY tools, equipment		
Energy efficiency	Electrical installation		
Heating, ventilation etc	Street lighting		
House building	Domestic lighting		
Plumbing	Entertainment event		

(Source: UK Trade & Investment, February 2006)

Available evidence shows that minority firms are involved in maintenance and repair contracts with housing associations particularly those considered as social landlords'. In evaluating minorities' input into the construction sector, there is further proof of the British Caribbean firm's involvement in essential areas of the industry though on a relatively small scale. The statistics show that operatives are located in segments such as carpentry, designing, installation, plastering, maintenance and repairs. There are known cases where operators are engaged in several areas of construction on a yearly basis, a demonstration of their diversity and ingenuity **(Fig 6.1)**.

And yet, as far as the early 1990s, housing associations had relatively few African and Caribbean contractors on their books. Less than 10 were on approved lists, fewer than five were registered for maintenance and repair work, and only one association had about 27 approved black-owned maintenance and repair contractors registered. In fact that particular association (which was a minority-led London association) had spent 90% of its budget on African and Caribbean firms as a condition for meeting standard equal opportunities policy which is now being hastened by Government's *Rethinking Construction* that complements the best value principle.

Figure 6.1 Profile of British Caribbean construction firms

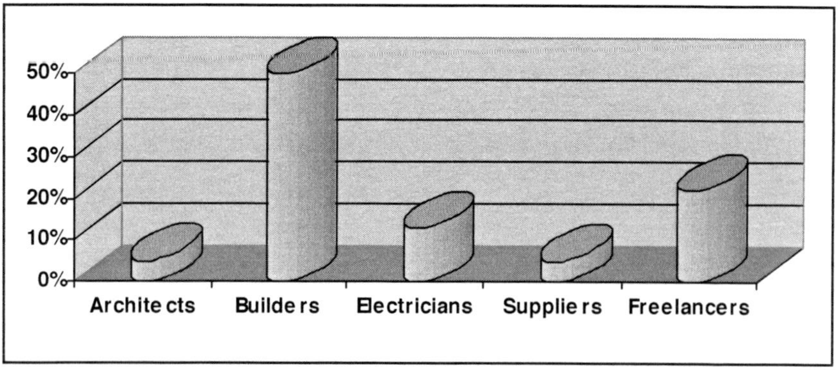

(Source: Black UK Net 2006)

Figure 6. 1 shows that although the national ranking for minority firms is low, there are hundreds of British Caribbean contractors located in England and Wales especially, with a market share of 5% in architectural services, half are in the building trade as plasterers, plumbers, designers and other contracting services; 13% are in the electrical/electronics field, 5% are building suppliers of plant materials and equipment, and nearly a quarter or 22% are freelancers or sole traders engaged in maintenance and repair contracts. The now defunct Black Contractors' Association (BCA) had a membership of over 300 with the majority of firms on the Approved List of Contractors in the London Boroughs of Lambeth and Southwark respectively. Through its advocacy and lobbying, the association enabled nearly 50% of its members to access procurement opportunities in London and the Southeast. Information was readily available and training for owners, managers and staff. It has been said repeatedly that the demise of the BCA in the mid-1990s is partly responsible for the further under-representation of black firms in mainstream construction schemes throughout England and Wales.

Location of Firms

In spite of this situation, British Caribbean firms are situated in London, the Southeast, the Midland Counties and Wales, securing small to medium-sized contracts ranging from £10,000 to £100,000 and between £200,000 to £500,000 plus. They have built a reputation over a number of years by undertaking work in multiple projects ranging from estate regeneration and civil engineering to enterprise development (more specifically incubator centres). Others are involved in routine or generic construction projects in local areas, whilst a few support DIY micro activity.

In almost every region, there are contractors classified as `general builders' and they consist of sole traders and limited companies, specializing in painting and decorating, plumbing and electrics. In the Southeast and the Midland Counties, there are exceptions, notably in medium-scale construction projects such as business incubators and community-type facilities. In Scotland and Wales, along with general trades, there are increasing trends in industry segments such as landscaping, roofing and tiling. One national directory highlighted a sample of British Caribbean construction firms this way:

- Builders - scaffolders, building and decorating, building services and developers.
- Building Supplies - doors and DIY store specialists.
- Carpenters and Joiners - designers, home carpentry and woodcrafts.
- Electrical Contractors & Suppliers - electronics and engineering.
- Electrical Appliances - electronics and videos (**Blacknet UK 2001**).

For the most part, these trades are attributed to migrants who arrived on the *Empire Windrush* in 1948 from the Caribbean with amazing skills in multiple trades. Their presence resulted from the invitation by authorities for `colonial' labour to help rebuild Britain's postwar reconstruction effort. Apart from the construction industry, skill shortages also existed in the health service and hotel industry and while the new migrants were self-made building specialists, some had experience in contract management and supervision. The only difference being, they had to translate such experiences within a British setting and cope with the culture shock that ensued. From all indications, Caribbean migrants performed well, with a great number who worked initially with mainstream companies, deciding to set up their own businesses. Indeed, firms that operate in various building trades make a positive difference to wealth creation, employment and add to new knowledge especially in locally, deprived and excluded communities in the UK **(Table 6.2)**.

Table 6.2 Location of British Caribbean firms by industry segments

(Source: Textual analysis based on informal sources)

Area	Segments
London/ Greater London	general builders, plumbers, electricians, decorators etc.
Southeast	general builders, roofers, tillers, window glazers etc.
The Midlands	general builders, engineers, plasterers, scaffolders,
Yorkshire & Humberside	general builders, decorators, designers, painters etc.
Scotland	builders, plumbers, decorators, roofers, DIY specialists.
Wales	builders, landscapers, decorators, maintenance specialists, etc.

Notes: Other regions such the North West, North East, South West, East of England also have similar but more micro construction firms. Their specialty is around repairs and maintenance, added to painting and decorating.

Indeed, there are over 500 black contractors operating in the UK, ranging from micro and small to medium-sized firms. Almost 10% are in the 50-60 plus age bracket with 15 - 20 years experience of managing their own firms and with 10 or more experience working in reputable construction firms such as Wimpey and Mc Alpine. And while the notion of consortia arrangements has been debated for years as a mechanism for improving the output of underperforming firms, it seems that 22% of sole traders are content on a tiny share of the market relative to their growth potential and industry experience, not forgetting the lifespan of their firms.

Property Services

Be that as it may, in their determination not be pigeonholed, a small percentage of British Caribbean professional builders have combined intelligence and the know-how of large companies, coupled with self-employment, to tap into both local authority contracts and the wider industry market, thereby providing a different perspective of the real status of British Caribbean-owned construction firms **(Minicase 6.1)**.

Still, by not having equal access to public contracts, several minority firms have experienced slow growth and those relying on housing association contracts, have suffered a similar fate. Since the majority of owners are dependent on these public-funded bodies for work, the question is, are these mainstream organizations (sufficiently) innovative in their procedures and general standards to support minority firms? Noteworthy, members of larger building associations in England, Scotland and Wales deliver multi-million contracts per year with the following networks dominating a considerable proportion of the UK building trade: -

- The British Woodworking Federation has annual sales of £200 million.
- Major Contractors Group has an annual turnover of £300 million.
- National Contractors Federation has a contracting turnover of £75 million.
- Scottish Building has over 85% of all building contracts in Scotland.

Minicase 6. 1 Sunshine Homes

Over a quarter of a century Grenadian Mike Harry, hasn't allowed age to impede his enterprise ambition. **Sunshine Homes** is a relatively new (starting early this century) firm with great promise. Harry who is a professional salesman, found a niche market for double glazing window products. He has vast knowledge of construction and property markets, having managed a construction training company in the 1990s. He has a good working relationship with his bank manager and believes in business plans that are realistic. Harry

is constantly developing new customers with the aim of promoting the business.
As a small firm, Sunshine Homes has equally, a small core of dedicated staff, with an inbuilt traineeship scheme for junior and senior staff. With a turnover of more than £400,000, Harry plans to "build on the existing client base and roll-out products and services" that customers need. He intends to increase the level of financial services to complement existing products, and according to him, "*Our customer base must broaden to generate a sustainable revenue stream for business growth and expansion*". That will be the real success for Sunshine Homes" (**Harry 2004**).

The UK contract system is complex and sole traders have little chance to accrue substantial returns unless they work in either partnerships or develop consortia-type arrangements with similar industry segments - plumbing, electrical engineering, maintenance, repairs and the like. Housing associations use various methods to work with minority contractors and yet public officials haven't developed appropriate strategies to optimize the diversity of black firms.

Indeed, very rare do mainstream construction companies include training and support for the development of British Caribbean subcontracting firms with expertise in painting and decorating. A notable example however, is the strategy devised by Miller Construction (UK) Ltd, a leading building firm, that dedicates 60% of its services to partnerships with small firms in areas of welfare, cleaning, temporary labour and security, an initiative that has been applauded by some public institutions (**De Montfort University 2006**).

Nevertheless, in other parts of the UK, Caribbean entrepreneurs have made good of the opportunities to change both the perception of their firms, as well as the economic landscape in inner-cities particularly. They have done so by competing with mainstream, proving that despite discriminatory and other practices, they can overcome and offer services that are tailored to meet the needs of various types of customers in the building industry. Some firms have developed specialized services to capture, small but growing niche markets in the building industry as well.

In Wales for example, although minority firms are not visible in urban areas such as Cardiff, there are some success stories in that country. The mere presence of commercial enterprises reflects the instinctive nature of minorities to maximize opportunities wherever they are despite adversity. In the Welsh Caribbean community owners have developed a range of service companies to maximize opportunities in diversified markets. Business services comprise cleaning, private hire (cab drivers), real estate, retailing, personal care, business support services, creative industries and construction (**Minicase 6.2**).

Minicase 6. 2 Leonard Lawrence in Wales

Leonard Lawrence came to Wales from Jamaica in the 1960s and before his retirement in 2002, ran a successful construction business. He worked as a civil engineer and started his business in the mid-1990s at age 57, employing at times up to 30 people. He managed the business for seven years before he retired and is involved in social enterprise.

"*When I arrived from Jamaica there was no bank that would sponsor you. But in the end I got to start my own business and wish I'd done it years earlier. When you go self-employed it is hard work, but the reward is greater because you control your own destiny.*" He rejects the view that people from African or Caribbean backgrounds are naturally less entrepreneurial than other groups, and called on young black people to consider starting enterprises of their own.

"I encourage the new generation to use the Ethnic Business Support Program in Wales to develop business plans that are likely to attract financial support'.

(Source: Grasp the Opportunity, Ethnic Enterprise, EBSP publication Autumn 2005, Wales)

Regeneration Schemes

Since the early 1980s, contracting firms have made use of urban renewal as a platform for securing lucrative public sector contracts in health, education infrastructure, road building, housing redevelopment and enterprise schemes – these have contributed to the creation of wealth and provided social amenities for deprived and excluded communities. Also described as local economic development, regeneration covers a broad spectrum of sectors which enhance the learning curve of minority firms, apart from adding to their profit margins and market share, locally. The issue has always been, what impact do British Caribbean firms have on procurement opportunities in the UK? And what are the constraints being faced? How can they be overcome? **(Minicase 6. 3)**

These issues can't be taken lightly since they can and do affect the credibility, profitability and lifecycle of firms. In examining the organization and performance of British Caribbean construction firms, there is overwhelming evidence that points to problems involving contract types, skills mismatch and tender pricing. As stated in the findings of one study,

Minority contractors can experience a mismatch between their preferences and the type of work on offer, difficulties in dealing with housing associations requirements for entry to approved lists and problems with tendering, including pricing. Availability of relevant training and advice seemed the exception rather than the rule, and communications with associations were often poorly developed **(Joseph Rowntree Foundation 1995)**.

Generally, contracts involving general construction work consist of:

- Site preparation and demolition.
- Building of complete constructions or parts thereof and civil engineering.
- Installation and completion (including wiring, insulation, plumbing, painting etc).

Minicase 6. 3 Rennie Building Contracts Ltd

Grenadian-born civil engineer and building contractors, Alexis Rennie established **Rennie Building Contracts Ltd** in 1979. The company which was a rarity in the British Caribbean community at the time specializes in modifications and alterations to hospitals, commercial and residential properties, listed buildings and also general building construction. Rennie's work was honoured by the George Padmore Institute in a series of life experiences shared by other Caribbean people, which were published in 1999.

Before becoming an entrepreneur, he worked as a `salaried' professional in the building trade and played a major role in the construction of the £30 million Thamesmead Housing Development Scheme, one of the largest of its kind in Greater London and the Southeast. The company has provided quality residential accommodation for customers over the past 21 years. In 2004, Rennie's firm designed and built the Monmot Hotel in Grenada where continues to provide quality housing for clients - at home and abroad.

The significance of British Caribbean firms' contribution to the housing sector should not be underestimated as this is directly related to owners' determination to rectify mainstream contract deficits, whilst adding to the improvement of social housing especially for deprived communities in UK cities. It is too, a very tangible effort towards strengthening their market position in the construction and property markets simultaneously. Ongoing research carried out among black housing associations show that growth has been maximized due to their management teams' ability to influence the provision of `private finance because of the Housing Corporation's policy of positive action (**University of Cambridge 1996**).

Housing development continues to be integral to regeneration policy and small firms are encouraged to participate in different schemes to ensure that capacity is maximized especially in the `*Local Labour in Construction'* initiative that has been in place over 20 years in England and Wales. This scheme allows public authorities, private landlords and housing associations to utilise local labour to boost housing and other building projects in neighbourhoods and districts. So, what is the real contribution to housing development by black-led housing associations?

In general, they are undersized service entities, with almost 80% owning or managing less than 300 homes and 50% having fewer than 100 homes **(Table 6. 3)**. Over 50% are in London and the remainder in the Midland Counties, Yorkshire and Humberside plus the North West. They're young and usually develop financial capacity after they have built up an asset base and cash reserves. According to the Cambridge University study in 1996, only 6% of African and Caribbean Housing Association were known and 4% registered before 1980. About 40% remain unregistered, but this snag has not affected growth trends.

Among developing associations, 50% have developed more than 75% of stock since the late 1980s, when new financial regulations required funding for new growth to come from both public and private sources also known as 'mixed funding', rather than depending on State subsidy. The figure below provides a snapshot of activity of black-led associations in Britain. Even though the data may have altered significantly since the 1990s, they represent more than a 'cautionary tale' of development within the Caribbean building trade in particular.

Table 6.3 Volume of housing stock Black Housing Associations in Britain

Region	1000 plus	250 to 999	100 - 249	Less 100	Total
East Midlands	0	3	1	3	7
London	3	4	11	28	46
Merseyside	0	0	2	0	2

North West	0	2	3	3	8
South East	0	0	0	3	3
South West	0	1	0	1	2
West Midlands	0	4	1	9	14
Yorkshire & Humberside	0	3	2	4	9
Total	**3**	**17**	**20**	**51**	**91**

(Source: Financing black and minority housing associations, Cambridge University and Federation of Black Housing Associations, May 1996)

Employment challenges

The construction industry is faced with many challenges and after a downturn in the 1990s, employment in this highly labour-intensive sector rose over the past few years. The increase in the use of technology such as improved building techniques and processes – has helped transform the industry in many ways. Stable employment is projected until 2015, but with significant variations at regional level.

Usually, construction activity is associated with economic cycles and tends to suffer peaks and troughs compared to other sectors. Large fluctuations in activity mean that in times when output is rising, skills shortage can build up quickly. The traditional `boom-bust' cycle has meant that a fall in activity tends to follow afterwards, which has resulted in a sharp decline in skills shortages as more labour becomes available. Consequently these shortages have not presented the industry with severe difficulties, as their duration has been temporary. In any case, the challenges for the industry are still great in so far as the numbers needed to fill vacancies in different categories in order to boost the projected output in the whole of the UK in the next two or so years.

Table 6. 4 illustrates that the UK sector will require nearly half a million employees to fill essential vacancies, with England alone needing 88% of the overall workforce, followed by Scotland 11.2%, and Wales and Northern Island needing to recruit 6.3% and 5.4%

employees respectively. The statistics also show that although Scotland is projected to have the highest increase in construction employment to the value of 18.1%, the Southeast will need the largest number of contracting employees throughout the entire country in terms of output required in specific areas of the UK.

The composition of the workforce in construction is different from most other industries, in that a high proportion (approximately 50%) of the labour pool is made up of people with well-developed manual skills such as bricklayers, steel erectors, roofers, carpenters, glaziers and so forth, compared to around 10% in the economy as a whole. Accordingly, employment is less concentrated on managerial, technical and professional occupations.

Table 6.4 Employment challenges in the construction industry

(Source: CITB-Construction Skills Regional Forecast, UK 2004)

Country/Region	Employees needed between 2004-08	% increase 2008
Greater London	35,300	0.9
South East	66,900	9.4
East of England	42,100	15.4
South West	19,850	7.4
West Midlands	36,800	15.6
East Midlands	32,500	13.6
Yorkshire & Humberside	40,200	19
North West	52,400	17.5
North East	10,400	10
Wales	27,550	6
Scotland	49,250	18.1
Northern Ireland	24,030 (between 2005-2010)	Not applicable
Total	**437, 280**	

Furthermore, market indicators show the greatest increase in the total industry requirements over the period 2003-2007 will be for:

- Wood trades
- Managers
- Electricians
- Clerical
- Plumbers
- Bricklayers (**CITB 2003**).

Sector Representation

Since the collapse of the BCA in the 1990s, there are few industry sector-based organizations that represent either the construction industry as a whole or segments of it. Representation is very important in the building trade particularly since the intensity of competition along with high barriers to entry in areas such as materials management, architecture, engineering sciences, to name a few, make it almost impossible for young, talented but inexperienced minority technicians to compete on a `level playing field'. The BCA's popularity was based on its capacity to include all segments of construction, along with other sectors comprising accountancy, business advisory and enterprise-related fields.

As an important segment in construction, architecture means different things to different people, and in today's fast-changing arena, it is part of a wider process of provision for the built environment. The role of architects in the last 20 years has changed from traditional draughtsmanship or design to one involving intensive project management. In June 1990 a group of architects founded the Society of Black Architects (SOBA). The aim is to integrate `fully the contribution of minority professionals as providers and consumers of architectural design services' (**SOBA's website**).

Since its formation, a business forum has been added, and the organisation's successes illustrate an exemplary approach to architectural innovation. The activities of the SOBA Business Forum consist of school workshops, visits to important sites, mentoring, network events, newsletter, exhibitions and field trips to places such as Liverpool and Wales on issues pertaining to education and sustainable development.

In the mid-1980s, minority professionals capitalized on the growing market for industry trades even though the construction industry was experiencing severe problems in structure and skills shortage. Like most construction firms in England, there is a high level of segmentation that lends itself to a combination of professionalism and entrepreneurship, a theme that is common among emerging British Caribbean firms operating in northern English Counties. Faced with competition from large reputable companies, but with the knowledge that the market is open to calculated risk-taking, professionals have turned their once `secure `paid employment into self-employment activity, motivated by self-reliance and a need to make a positive difference within their respective communities (**Minicase 6. 4**).

Minicase 6. 4 EAM Building Group

In 1983, electrician, Edwin Maxwell founded EAM Building Contractors Ltd, trading as **EAM Building Group**. The business has since developed into a general contracting company, providing excellent and consistent customer services by well-trained qualified and motivated staff. Building services include property refurbishment and maintenance, structural repairs extensions, electrical installations, gas installation and electrical installation emergency repairs.

The diversity of personnel is reflected in operatives; namely, bricklayers, electricians, joiners, painters, plasters and plumbers who are qualified at NVQ/City & Guilds level. The company invests in training managerial and supervisory staff in their respective disciplines, with ongoing support for career advancement. Due to the safety-sensitivity of the industry, site supervisors are trained specially in Construction Site Safety Awareness and they are regularly informed of changes in the Health & Safety at Work legislation. The firm undertakes projects as the `principal contractor' under the Construction Design Management or CDM legislation.

EAM recognizes the value of communication at all levels as a key element of good management. As such, regular monthly breakfast meetings are held to update staff of business developments, work issues and deliver `Tool Box Talks' and organizational systems training.

In recognition of its commitment to staff training and development, the company was awarded *Investors in People* status in March 2003 and was successfully reassessed in February 2006. EAM has an amazing client profile comprising universities, colleges, hospitals, local authorities and housing associations throughout the East Midlands. As part of its modernization strategy for procurement, it was among several participating companies involved in a procurement scheme led by De Montfort University, November 2005. EAM has a principled position on social responsibility; senior managers take part in civic activities aimed at improving the lives of various communities.

Indeed, the example set by minority construction firms illustrates the necessity, against the backdrop of economic and social disadvantage, for owners to contribute towards building social capital and boosting the economic asset (value) of inner-cities.

Training Requirements

Apart from their well-endowed talent, the successful market penetration of British Caribbean contractors like other minority firms depends very much on technical competence and the ability to adapt to new technology in an industry driven by process innovation. For the most part, a large percentage of first generation Caribbean builders are not altogether proficient with modern technology and hence will need to be fully equipped to adapt to modern trends in the building trade.

The representation of minority students in architecture for example, appears poor in relation to law and medicine and dentistry, but a comparison with all first degree students shows that the proportion of non-white first degree students in architecture is close to the average for all subjects in England. That is, in comparison with 18% in architecture, 16% of all first degree students are from non-white backgrounds. Based on the evidence in the labour market data, it could be assumed that each year between 400 and 500 plus Caribbean students enroll for construction trade-related degree and various other academic and technical/vocational courses per annum **(Table 6.5**).

Table 6. 5 Profile of architecture students

Ethnicity	Architec-ture	Architecture building & planning	Law	Medicine & dentistry	All students
White	73.8	81.6	66.3	61.1	78.1
Caribbean	**1.1**	**1.3**	**2.4**	**0.3**	**1.3**
African	2.0	1.8	4.9	1.2	2.0
Black other	0.6	0.6	1.1	0.2	0.7
Indian	3.5	2.3	7.4	14.0	4.7
Pakistani	1.6	1.1	5.0	4.5	2.2
Bangladeshi	0.7	0.4	1.4	1.0	0.7
Chinese	4.3	1.7	0.9	2.0	1.1
Asian other	1.5	0.7	1.8	5.0	1.3
Other	2.5	1.2	2.9	3.0	1.9
Non-white total	17.9	11.2	27.9	31.4	18.0
Unknown	8.3	7.2	5.8	7.5	5.9
Base	**4,325**	**17,236**	**29,080**	**20,016**	**729,179**

(Source: Architecture and race: A study of black and minority ethnic students in the profession, CABE, Research outcomes: 6, 2004, p13.

In spite of the low variations in construction-related areas, information from earlier studies explored long-term trends in the representation of minority students in architecture and its related areas. These developments showed that between 1992 and 2001, African and Caribbean entrants to architecture programs varied from 2% in 1992/1993 to 2.8% in 2000-2001(**RIBA 1992/93: 2000/01**)

Industry data also reveals that more than 5% of Caribbean people of working age are involved in construction, with a fair proportion of those who manage companies highly skilled (possessing academic and technical qualifications) whilst others have relevant accreditation from professional bodies in the industry, all in an effort to enhance their image and boost company reputation; that is, to be taken seriously by customers and mainstream agencies and institutions. Accordingly, the following qualifications are approved by industry standards including state-regulated bodies: -

- Level 1.2/3 General Construction Operations;
- Level 2/3 Bricklaying;
- Level 2 Roof Slating and Tiling;
- Level 2 Built-up Felt Roofing;
- Level 2-3 Scaffolding;
- Level 2-3 Carpentry & Joinery;
- Level 2-3 Demolition; and
- Level 3-4 Building Site Supervision/Management (***Construction News* 2002**).

Gender Issue

Gender imbalance is also a subject of tremendous concern to industry officials given that women account for 10% of those employed in the sector, 20% are pursuing construction related degree courses, 7% own micro-enterprises employing less than 10 people, and a high number or 81% are employed in the industry in secretarial and other trades (**CITB 2004-2005**). In the early 1990s, training providers considered women in construction as a priority and British Caribbean women were among those who turned to the building trade as a career path.

Skills shortages in four of the industrial sectors with construction having the highest number of skill vacancies out of 28 industries (38.2% against an average of 19.9%). This means that by recruiting more women in the industry, skill and labour shortages could be reduced whilst the principle of inclusivity could be guaranteed. Minority professionals and women have much to contribute and the industry cannot afford a skills shortage at a period when the industry has shown favourable growth over the past five years. With a strong economy, construction is competing with other industries for non-traditional groups, as evidenced by high-profile campaigns undertaken by diverse agencies such as the police, the army, nursing, teachers, banking and IT companies (**Gurjao 2006**).

The Women's Education in Building or `WEB' is at the forefront of this overdue initiative. Women received National Vocational Qualifications in all building trades and some trainees went on to set up micro firms. Bernice Lindsay, who was trained in fibrous plastering, is a self-employed tradeswoman, on the list of approved organizations that provided contracts from local authorities and housing associations. She spoke about her achievement this way:

I worked in telesales before going on the courses at WEB. I always enjoyed painting and decorating, and although I did odd jobs for friends, it was really only a hobby. I found getting my own business off the ground, getting registered and everything, quite hard. You have got to lay out a lot of money first, for materials and things, but luckily my family and friends were very supportive, so that made it possible. I prefer working for myself though I would like to be more established and employ other women to give them an opportunity - all they need is a break (**WEB 1994**).

The London Development Agency has also put measures in place to support women into construction and although evidence is sketchy, there are strong indicators that a significant number of British Caribbean women are involved in construction related (self-employment) activities ranging from architecture and engineering to technology systems modeling designed for building activities.

In general, the construction industry has great prospects for both promotion and monetary rewards based on flexible working practices and leading public agencies have begun to recognize not only the value of female involvement in the building trade, but implementing appropriate measures and schemes to facilitate more women with greater access to opportunities in this sector. This is the focus of the LDA's construction scheme for women's greater involvement:

We are helping to get more women and people from ethnic minorities into the construction industry where they are significantly under-represented. The Building Work for Women (BWW) project not only improves opportunities for those we help into work but also helps tackle the serious skills shortages in the industry. The LDA supports the aims of National Construction Week. We believe it is crucial to widen the pool of people entering the building trade, especially in the capital **(2002)**.

Quality Control

The issue of quality control is more than a paper exercise; it is central to planning, organizing and implementing various schemes, as well as delivering a range of products and services to customers of all types. The absence of monitoring procedures can have implications for health and safety at job sites, as well as undermine the profitability of firms coupled with their reputation to deliver efficient and reliable services. Quality standards guarantee trust from contractors, employees and the general public, and they represent an important yardstick for measuring organizational success. The sensitive and risky nature of the industry also implies that quality should be implemented in line with industry trends.

As a relatively new policy initiative, Rethinking Construction, benchmarks the modernization of local government where flexibility and the willingness to work in partnership with other industry sectors to provide maximum output, has become a prime consideration more so, in a world of increasing globalization. This policy derives from the Construction Task Force Report (1998) under the leadership of Sir John Egan. The idea is to encourage local authorities to achieve better quality construction at lower cost, with the potential community dividend being great. It is a policy that draws from the experiences of UK construction firms and it is primarily a replica of the USA where efficiency savings have gained currency in the construction process. Accordingly, the initiative sets out the type of targets that are applicable to the UK building trade:

- Reduce capital costs by 10%;
- Reduce construction time by 10%;
- Increase predictability by 20% per annum;
- Reduce defects by 20%;
- Reduce accidents by 20% per annum;
- Increase productivity by 10%; and
- Increase turnover and profits by 10% per annum.

Undoubtedly, this policy will affect the long term, as well as `spot' contracts (piecemeal work in painting, decorating or plumbing) in the building trade. It will involve information-sharing, greater communication links, capacity building and other requirements to ensure that contractors are aware of their responsibilities with respect to this new policy initiative.

But the quality issue goes further and in particular when it comes to architectural design and the use of it. Leading Caribbean architectural firms for instance, implement alternative assessments of quality and how they could be evaluated in the context of the profession, as well as the customer services delivered, using the formal business model. In the field of architecture, excellence is seen as the greatest advantage in terms of winning commissioned projects and maintaining a reputable image in the marketplace.

As a membership organisation, SOBA has encouraged affiliates to have a wide purview when dealing with designs that cover individuals and organisations from across the political and social divide. There is a growing body of opinion among non-European architects that structural designs should embody not only a project-oriented outlook, but must reflect the hopes and aspirations of the environment and its users. This approach is fast-developing among a new legion of architects in the African and Caribbean community (**Minicase 6. 5**).

Minicase 6. 5 Paul Henry Architects

Paul Henry Architects & Project Mangers Ltd was established in 1999 as one of East London's leading architectural practices. Prior to co-founding the firm, Paul Henry worked as an Architect for several reputable companies in the UK and Europe as well as the Middle East, and the USA.

PHA has an impressive list of residential, commercial, industrial and other related clientele, nationally and internationally. With its unique selling points being flexibility, innovation, reliability and good customer service, the practices' work is further underpinned by their sustainability, energy efficiency and environmentally-friendly designs (see their website at www.paulhenryarchitects.com).

Over the years, PHA has been a recipient of numerous accreditations and awards for its Architecture and contribution to the construction industry. Among some of its successes, has been: past consultants for the Arts Council of England; participated in a touring exhibition showcasing female and black UK architects' work in Asia, Australasia, Europe and the USA and received a special accommodation in the Waltham Forest Design Awards for a restoration/conversion project and many more. Recently, PHA (against a world-class catalogue of practices) was short-listed for a prestigious world Architectural design competition for the World Health Organisation's headquarters in Ghana, West Africa: a final decision is currently pending.

Apart from continuing to improve its quality of output; management plans to further diversify and expand its current organisational structure will ensure that the practice remains innovative, and continues to adhere to their motto of "excellence in design, service and delivery".

More than half of all British Caribbean firms have difficulty with tendering procedures – not only with the level of paperwork involved, but also industry jargon or vocabulary. It is important that owners develop contract management, technical specification, budgetary control, accounting and financial systems, project management techniques including conflict management and information-communication systems skills. The construction industry is pretty complex and varied, and firms can ill-afford to take unnecessary risks that will challenge their survival and competitive advantage in the marketplace.

The West Midlands firm of **Gilbert & Son Contractors Ltd**, profile is classified as 'general construction of buildings and civil engineering works' and although a small concern, the company has developed an excellent reputation in the urban regeneration and enterprise arena with quality control procedures. Set up in 1996 by C. E. Gilbert, the company has been awarded multi-million pound contracts, including the famous Black Businesses in Birmingham or '3b'.

A hallmark of Gilbert's success is learning from experienced industrialists and re-evaluating quality control in an effort to maximize contract opportunities and maintain the confidence of public sector and other commissioned bodies, as a consequence. Unemployed young peopled have developed skills in plastering, carpentry, plumbing, designing, roofing, tiling etc. With an annual turnover in excess of £2 million, the story of Gilbert's company is an 'enterprise legend', one that is committed to business and economic sustainability in the West Midlands.

Quality control in the industry also fits in neatly with the element of diversity and as was stated earlier in this book Caribbean people of all ethnic groups are very much involved in construction-related businesses. Their work in inner-city development has also won plaudits from public authorities as the Beharry family from Guyana confirmed (**Minicase 6. 6**).

In addition, sound risk assessment is vital to contract delivery (success) and even more critical to British Caribbean firms, struggling with a turnover of under £100,000 per annum. In particular, small builders have difficulty in handling new technology applications and these affect their firms' capacity to maintain high levels of output, thereby stultifying growth prospects. This situation is further compounded by the lack of enterprise support and technical assistance from mainstream agencies that should be supporting production firms such as the building trades.

Furthermore, risk assessment is crucial to the building trade since cost-based contracts may allow for *`open book'* accounting and guaranteed payment of costs incurred by the contractor whatever they may be. Reimbursable contracts require little information to define the scope of work, but they expose the owner to considerable risks since the temptation to cut corners is high when the likelihood of being discovered is too small. Minority construction firms need to conduct routine audits to determine the level of comparable risks, pricing mechanism, measurement in terms of duration and its effect on quality control, the level of incentives available and the cost-effective nature of the risk(s) incurred at every stage of the risk assessment process.

Minicase 6. 6 Atlas (London) Property Ltd

In 2003 a company that began in a phone box in North London, led the way as the fastest growing 100 companies based in the UK's most deprived areas. Atlas Property (London) Ltd had an extraordinary five-year growth rate of 10,496%, with an increase in profitability of over 300% in the same period. This translates into sales from £38,127 in 1998 to just over £4 million in 2002 (***Financial Times 2003***).

The company was also ranked as the 43rd largest in the new top 99 Estate Agents and positioned as the 23rd most profitable in England. Atlas is a provider of sales, lettings, property management, refurbishment, supported housing, rent guarantee, insurance and mortgage brokerage services.

Founder and director, Guyanese-born Harry Beharry and his wife, who are both qualified at Masters Degree level, set up the firm in 1986 with £600. The bank refused an investment loan of £15,000 to £20,000, referring to Beharry's lack of collateral and relevant business experience, even though he was part of the family business in Guyana at age 11. In the first few years, the first business cheque took three months to arrive and when it did, it bounced.

Despite setbacks, Atlas soon became a thriving business and subsequently, clinched a deal with landlords involving managing their properties and offering guaranteed rental incomes in return. Contracts were secured on the basis of efficiency and less bureaucracy. Over 80% of the firm's core business is generated from local authorities where Atlas supports housing for the homeless, asylum seekers and unaccompanied minors. The long-term plan is to build on these and expand the market base of the firm. However, the keys to Atlas' successes are:

- Detailed market research of both clients and competitors.
- Extensive knowledge and products.
- Understanding the micro and macro factors that impact on the business sector.

- Prepare a proper business and investment strategy and update it often.
- Recruit competent and experienced staff.
- Develop various high-order skills especially negotiating techniques.
- Be determined, focused and learn from successful business leaders.
- Listen attentively to customers; they know the market very well.
- Maximise the use of external resources – human, financial and technical.

Challenges and Opportunities in Construction

Indeed the challenges for the UK construction industry are great and so are the opportunities. As this chapter pointed out, on the one hand British Caribbean firms are contributing to the industry, and on the other, performance levels need to be improved. And yet their contribution is bound up with the various strategic features and mix of the industry in totality. In its own findings, the Adult Inspectorate claimed that there was no single cause of poor framework achievement in the construction industry, citing the difficulty small employers have in assessing the requirements of learners. The Inspectorate identified the following main strengths and weaknesses of current skills training:

Strengths:

- Increased demand for apprenticeships from school leavers.
- Good practical training in college workshops.
- Recent improvements in NVQ achievement rates.
- Good developments in colleges as a result of CoVE funding.
- Contribution of college staff and training providers' staff as assessors.
- Support for learners from all types of training providers.

Weaknesses:

- Complex apprenticeship framework requirements that deter employers.
- Low framework success rates as poor progression to higher-level students.
- Employers increasingly sidelined from training as private training providers.
- Very few apprentices trained by employer-led companies.
- Insufficient capacity in colleges to meet current demand.
- High proportion of inadequate training providers.
- Poor teaching of craft theory.
- Large number of poorly qualified entrants requiring basic training.
- Very few women in craft opportunities.

While the above analysis reflects the serious weaknesses as a whole, it is both the quality of personnel and output that are the main drivers of the construction industry. It is therefore important that the necessary steps be taken to reduce or alleviate altogether, the internal flaws that are associated with the British Caribbean segment of the industry. It was for this reason and more that, in progressing the *Rethinking Construction* agenda, the government set key performance indicators in early 2000, having recognized the importance of the building trade to the UK economy.

Our objective is to ensure an efficient market in the construction industry, with innovative and successful UK firms that meet the needs of clients and society and are competitive at home and abroad. The construction industry is central to the economy. It is this mechanism by which new homes, regional regeneration, modern transport facilities and a wide range of other public infrastructure activities are delivered" (**DETR 2000**).

Like other specialist industries, the building trade has enormous possibilities for British Caribbean firms, but it also challenges owners and managers to adopt a more professional and global approach to the management and delivery of products and services to wider sector markets rather than limiting contract value to non-lucrative neighbourhood community areas. The development of effective networks, coupled with improving organizational systems for effectively delivery of services, is essential to sustainability. Desmond Thompson, a leading London-based contractor, explained the value of industry sector networks,

We should move to a position where we develop a web of relationships with suppliers, developers, designers and customers through public-private partnerships. By investing our time and resources wisely, we can improve the image and general reputation of our businesses, and at the same time, we can gradually increase our market share **(Thompson 2004)**.

Nearly all contractors who were former members of the BCA have their businesses intact and are keen on reactivating this once well-known enterprise network. They are aware too, that to compete with large companies, not only involves putting their `houses in order', but also demonstrating a `critical mass' in the building trade at all times. Historically - spanning over 100 years - mainstream contractors have worked in partnership with other building specialists and industry officials overall, and this collaboration has worked remarkably well in so far as wealth creation, better public image and greater industry recognition are concerned, both nationally and internationally.

Moreover, greater success among British Caribbean firms is also possible if two principal positions are in place. First, owners should be more committed to repositioning their firms in lucrative markets, in addition to ensuring that efficient systems are in place to facilitate growth and domination of such markets. Second, the industry should offer greater opportunities to minority contractors to bid for public sector contracts, including housing association tenders for social landlords in excluded communities. Owners are aware that they alone cannot `crack the whip' and they feel that public authorities also have a responsibility to facilitate access to contract opportunities. The more experienced specialists know though, that these key factors will help to secure the benefits from the industry they are constantly seeking:

Setting realistic targets - improvement in the quality of service and creating performance targets and setting them against profits, safety productivity, and cost and client satisfaction.

Means of Delivery – routine research to improve competitiveness such as promotion, including sponsorship of community events, as a marketing strategy.

Innovation – the use of modern technology to enhance product performance and achieve better value for money.

Export Promotion – an increase in overseas Trade Missions involving more British Caribbean firms to access export opportunities in construction markets abroad in Africa, the Caribbean and Europe.

Management Practices – improve and build on internal systems of management, technical competence through the exchange of information and ideas on new products and services. Make full use of industry networking opportunities.

Procurement opportunities - making the contract system more open; simplify the contract tendering process from the beginning to the short-listing stages.

Effective Policy Research – examine the impact of British Caribbean firms' contribution on regeneration schemes, as well as profiling companies in key segments/sub-sectors of the industry, locally and regionally.

Approved List of Contractors - monitor the diversity contract performance of public authorities and private companies relating to construction contracts and related tenders.

Consortia Arrangements – public bodies should encourage more consortia arrangements for minority firms by creating viable partnerships with large companies and other mainstream organizations involved in the delivery of multiple construction and allied building contracts.

Future Trends

Above all, the future trends in construction will determine the growth and development of British Caribbean firms in general. Industry sources have predicted that consolidation is not common in the trade, but this may change, since at the moment, the industry remains fragmented with many smaller or micro players. The trend towards PFI schemes and greater private sector participation in large infrastructural projects, combined with the opening up of Government work to overseas competition as European Union markets become more liberalized, should create stability.

In the house building sub-sector, the trend towards Brownfield redevelopments stimulating a pattern of mergers and acquisition. The emphasis on high-density flats in city-centre sites, rather than on detached homes built on open field, also offers great employment opportunities. Other developments such as rising costs, skill shortages and legislation are serious considerations for owners of minority construction firms and ethnic managers in the building trade as a whole (**Fig 6.2**).

Construction activity is currently characterized by a shift from private work to public work, with implications for the workload of contractors specialized in different types of work. The large increases in government investment particularly in schools, health and road transport, should lessen the impact of the likely drop in commercial work in the short term, as weak profitability in the corporate sector is expected to affect private investment. However, there are clearly challenges for the workload of contractors specialized in different types of construction tasks (**CITB 2003**).

Figure 6.2 21st Century Trends in Construction

- Overall construction will avoid recession
- Growth will depend on government investment.
- The industry will be challenged by weakening private sector demand
- The sector will face rising energy, materials costs
- Long-term growth is projected around 22% until 2010
- Repair and maintenance represent 43% - 46% of construction output
- Further segmentation is expected
- Environmental legislation will affect material usage, waste reduction
- Smaller contractors will be in the majority
- Skill shortages will problematic unless resolved by training
- Numerous abound for overseas contracts

(Source: Textual analysis based on industry estimates)

Conclusion

This chapter dealt with the UK construction industry and the British Caribbean firm's sector professional input. This section of the book also dealt with growth opportunities in the building trade and a corresponding market for a variety of contracting specialists. The market share of Caribbean firms was assessed by the different segments owners operated in England, Scotland and Wales.

The industry has witnessed a resurgence in recent years, with employment at around two million people and a turnover of over £100 billion yearly. Although large companies dominate the sector, small firms are contributing to regeneration schemes involving local authorities, housing associations and other regeneration agencies.

Challenges such as new technology, procurement, competition and the rise of housing associations acting as social landlords, were also examined in much detail. The skills gap in the industry was also examined with an estimate of nearly half a million personnel required to fill vacancies in the years ahead. The low apprenticeship programs in construction by Caribbean youths was also looked at since training remains essential to the professionalism and financial stability of minority firms in the vital sector of the UK economy.

The input of firms in regeneration schemes in England was also highlighted, with examples of various industry segments presented through case studies and interviews. The need for a national authority to represent black builders and contractors in the form of the BCA was discussed in some measure. It was felt that the resuscitation of this organization is pivotal to the effective representation of black contractors in every segment of the construction industry at large. It was recognized that a considerable number of British Caribbean firms operated at the lower-middle and the bottom-end of the industry. Case studies proved though, that a growing minority of small firms had moved into mainstream contracting and were set to maintain quality standards in their overall performance in the industry.

The future trends in construction were summarized according to changes in the PFI arrangements, the high level of state investment in education, health and road communications, as well as the commercial benefits that would be accrued from larger public sector tenders and other annual procurement opportunities in the billion-worth construction industry. In the next chapter, the contribution of British Caribbean professionals to the personal care sector would be examined.

Chapter Notes

Housing Association – the Federation of Black Housing Association is an umbrella body for the black-led housing sector and black individuals involved in the housing field.

African Civilization – Ivan Sertima's *African Presence in early Europe* and Gerald Massey's *Book of Beginnings* produced evidence based on archaeological and anthropological to prove the enormous contributions by African people to the advancement of European civilization.

Panama Canal – until recently, very little was known about the remarkable engineering (waterway) feat. The first effort to build the waterway started in 1884 and was abandoned four years later, until tens of thousands of Caribbean people offered their services to help complete the project, with many sacrificing their lives to erect this historic landmark in the Americas.

Segmentation – apart from traditional areas, the construction industry is also categorized according to these segments: bricks and tiles, building merchants, building materials and over the years, market consultancy and accounting segments have emerged. Almost each segment or sub-sector could be classified as part of a mini-industry (on its own).

Local Labour in Construction – this scheme needs to be used more effectively by British Caribbean firms since it could produce additional economic and social benefits since local skills are utilized fairly and favourably to address issues around deprivation and exclusion.

RIBA – the Royal Institute of British Architects provides support for 40,500 members worldwide in the form of training, technical services, publications and events. The organization is involved in a national diversity campaign to improve the recruitment and retention levels of architects from minority communities, women and young people interested in the discipline.

Women Builders – the history of women builders can be traced to skilled manual jobs left vacant by men in the war periods which were filled by re-trained women. Females make up around 9% of the construction labour force (2002/03), representing trades, administrative and managerial occupations, secretarial and sole traders among others.

Professional Training – non-white postgraduate students are younger than their white counterparts, with exception of African and Caribbean students who were found to be older. It confirms that black students tend to benefit more from their combined levels of professional, academic and technical learning, all of which tend to put them in good stead at university.

Selected References

1 Goodwyn, F. and Munn, K. (2006): "Skills shortages: Crisis – what crisis?" *Contract Journal,* February 2006.

2 *Construction in the UK,* Trade and Investment DTI, February 2006.

3 Van Sertima, Ivan (1985): *African Presence in Early Europe*, Transaction Publishers.

4 Valdez, Ruben Sille Dr (2006): *The Latin American and Caribbean Panama Canal*, The Greater Caribbean This Week, 24 August 2006.

5 Rashidi, Runoko (1895): *Blacks in Early Britain* also MacRitchie, David, *Ancient and Modern Britons*, Vol 1, Los Angeles: Preston Associates, 1884, reprinted 1985.

6 UK Trade & Investment February 2006.

7 `*Meet the Buyer*', procurement seminar, CRÈME Initiative, De Montfort University, Leicester, England, 5 November 2005.

8 `Grasp the Opportunity', *Ethnic Enterprise*, Ethnic Business Support Programme, Autumn 2005, Wales.

9 *Financing black and minority ethnic housing associations*, Cambridge, May 1996.

10 The Blacknet. UK Directory, 2001.

11 *Ethnic Enterprise,* Ethnic Business Support Program, Autumn 2005, Wales.

12 `Alexis Rennie', *Changing Britannica: Life Experiences in Britain,* New Beacon Books Ltd, London, April 1999.

13 Construction Industry Training Board (2003a): Construction Skills Foresight Report 2003.

14 *Architecture and race: A study of black and minority ethnic students in the profession,* Centre for Education in the Built Environment, Research outcomes: 6, 2004, pp 13-15.

15 The Royal Institute of British Architects (RIBA) Education Statistics, 1992/93, 2000/01.

16 *Construction News*, May 2002.

17 CITB-Construction Skills Regional Forecast, UK 2004.

18 Gurjao, Sonia (2006): *Inclusivity: the Changing Role of Women in the Construction Workforce,* University of Reading & Chartered Institute of Building (CIOB).

19 Women's Education in Building (WEB), Annual Report, London 1994.

20 Graham, Vernon: 'I Did it my Way: Domestic services provider shows how it's done', *The Voice* 2 October 2006, London.

21 *LDA gets women into building industry in National Construction Week*, London Development Agency, October 2002.

22 Duff, Amy (2007): 'Partnerships, Paul and Rowena Henry', *Director Magazine*, March 2007.

23 'Guyanese wins Enterprise Oscar in the UK', *Indo Caribbean, Issue 5*, November 2004, London.

24 Risk Assessment vs. Contract Format, McGraw-Hill, London 1993.

25 *An Innovative and Efficient Construction Industry*: DETR, England, April 2000.

26 Interview with Desmond Thompson, London, 13 July 2004.

27 Construction Industry 2002-2007, South East England, CITB.

28 Egan, J. (1998) *Rethinking construction*, London: DTI.

29 Steele, Andy & Todd, Stephen (2005): 'The future of the black and minority ethnic (BME) construction sector in England', *Construction Management & Economics,* 2005, Vol. 23, Issue 10, pp 1017-1023.

Chapter 7

Personal Care

Introduction

In this chapter an outline of the organization and performance of British Caribbean firms in the personal care industry will be done. For the purposes of this section, personal care is referred to trends in the hair and beauty trade, along with aspects of fashion and clothing since these represent the main characteristics that underline the contribution of African and Caribbean communities to the personal sector in Britain.

Throughout this book, there is a recurring theme of British Caribbean professionals using self-employment activities to impact on the economic and social landscape of the UK. Effectively, such efforts give further rise to the dominant feature of black entrepreneurship in the country. Although personal care is sometimes linked to the creative industries because of its artistic and cultural composition, this sector should be given specific consideration and analysis so that operators, industry specialists, public officials and others can have a better understanding of the influence this sector has on the British economy, in multiple ways.

In the second half of the 20th century, minority communities in Britain were influenced by American values - (particularly those of African-Americans) - civil, cultural, economic, literary, political and social. These combined with `back home' and English traditions had a tremendous effect on cultural identity as far as British Caribbean communities were concerned. The growth and development of the ethnic beauty care industry in Britain, is therefore a direct result of both external influences and internal adaptations made by ethnic communities across England and Wales.

According to industry figures, the UK market for hair care products designed for black women is worth about £46.5 million, accounting for 70% of overall beauty spending by black women. The global market for black hair products is valued at up to £2.5 billion a year, with significant markets in South Africa, Brazil, the United States and Europe. The US market, valued by Mintel at £1 billion, has grown by 13% over the past five years, and is the most developed, with about 40% of the global black hair business. The UK is seen as the second largest growth market in this sector (***The Guardian*** **2005**).

The sector employs around 157,000 hairdressers and barbers in the UK, representing 6% share of the service industry and featuring micro businesses although they vary in size and composition (**HABIA 2004**). Franchising is on the increase and so is the trend of renting chairs or treatment rooms. In 2003, some 30% of hairdressers and 52% of beauty therapists were self employed. The sector profile reads like a roll-call of the '*University of Beauty Care*' (author's suggestion)

- Beauty and related sector – 34,000.
- Proprietors hair and beauty salons – 37,000.
- Self-employment hairdressers – 30%.
- Self-employment beauty therapists – 52%.
- Increase of hairdressers/barbers 1991-2000 – 18.7%.
- Increase in hairdressing managers/proprietors 1991-2000, 2.2%.

The industry is driven predominantly by black women who spend on average up to six times more than their white counterparts on hair and more than 50% regularly visiting a salon. On the one hand, Mintel researchers found that the average British woman spends £83.97 a year on beauty products and black women spend £117.44.

On the other hand, with the influx of barbers, the gender balance in beauty care has altered the industry's outlook.

British Caribbean Dimension

Black hair care products originated from the US and were designed for women with different shades of colour and texture. It was African-American, Madame C. J. Walker, who invented the *'hot comb'* in the early 20th century, and who became that country's first black millionaire. She influenced the birth of tens of thousands of salons and barber shops worldwide, including Caribbean hair stylists who own salons and barber shops. These represent a market share of 10% or nearly £4 million per annum and rising, and yet this sector is underperforming despite its latent potential. The beauty trade is still evolving, and it was only in the early part of this century that genuine efforts were made to address policy issues affecting minority hairdressers and barbers especially Caribbean operators in Britain.

Different sources confirm the level of segmentation in the British Caribbean personal care sector. Segments of beauty care consist of alternative therapists, beauty consultants, cosmetics, hairdressers and barbers, health clubs and fitness centres. It is clear that operators are no longer confined to the customary role of hairdressers/barbers, but are prepared to expand their services to accommodate growing niche markets. For instance, more than a third of British Caribbean salons provide European hair care services and specialist training for young and upcoming stylists in this field. **(Table 7.1)**.

Table 7.1 Selected databases of British Caribbean personal care firms

Habia	Business Directory	Independent Sources
Single salons (90%)	Beauty agencies (5%)	Hairdressers (75%)
Franchise salons (5%)	Beauty consultants 5%)	Producers (10%)

Mixed unisex & European Hair (35%)	Retailers (45%)	Manufacturers (2%)
4-10 employees (81%)	Beauty parlours (45%)	Beauty consultants (10%)
Urban location of firms (80%)	Not applicable	Therapy (3%)

(Source: HABIA, March 2006; Black Business Directory 2001; interviews and sampled data, 2000-2006)

In addition, hairdressing and barbering services are evident in the form of specialist sub-sectors within the industry. British Caribbean firms are noted for the following range of services: -

Hairdressers – hair relaxation – straightening services; thermal styling, braiding and weaving, as well as other services; and
Barbers – facial trimming, cutting/clipper sculpture, colouring and perming; hair and scalp analysis; face massage and wet shaving.

The impression of European culture in terms of hairdos and facials, has also added a new dimension to the increase in quality and volume of services provided by non-white beauty care firms in England and Wales. This situation is prevalent in salons and barber shops where `popular brands' such as conditioning treatments, neutralizing, colouring, relaxing and texturising are offered as both routine and complementary services. Interestingly, Europeans such as Bob Derrick and David Beckham also imitate the hairstyles of black people with braids, locks, weaves and other personal accessories, to add a touch of either ethnicity and/or a cultural stamp (of acceptance) to their appearance. Like music and sports, the grooming trade is fast becoming a `cross-over' industry where cultures collide and compete for quality, style and impressions.

In a study of the west London Borough of Brent, 30% of all Caribbean firms were in the grooming business, with women managing nearly half of all salons with services covering a multitude of areas. The

Harlesden neighbourhood which is described as one of the largest deprived inner-city areas in England has thriving beauty care firms. Caribbean people from all age groups from under 30s to over 50s own and manage salons and barber shops, offering a mixture of grooming and alternative therapeutic services. Such is the enterprise attraction that a small group of Oriental nail shops are located in the area, a trend that is commonplace in London and other parts of England where there is a large concentration of African and Caribbean consumers. Nearly three quarters of all customers considered these factors as crucial to their choice of a hairdressing salon or barber shop.

- Price of treatment;
- Location of salon;
- Staff treatment;
- Reputation of salon;
- Atmosphere at salon;
- Range of treatments;
- Location of salon;
- Quality of treatment;
- Opening hours;
- Appearance of salon; and
- Personal hygiene of staff (**Brent 2002**).

Growth and Development

The growth and development of the personal care industry in the ethnic community is attributed to the pioneering efforts of the British Caribbean firm of Dyke & Dryden. Its success acted as a catalyst for hundreds of men and women of colour who had a knack for beauty care, to go into business for themselves. It is estimated that more than a quarter or 25% of all beauty care firms in the African and Caribbean community have a lifespan exceeding 10 years. In his acclaimed book, *How they made a Million: The Dyke & Dryden Story* (**Hansib 2001**), businessman and author, Tony Wade gave a historic account of the growth and development of D&D, encompassing 30 years of challenges, opportunities and successes **(Case Study 7.1)**.

Case Study 7. 1 Dyke & Dryden Story

Dyke and Dryden (D&D) was established in 1965, beginning as a small retail shop in North London selling records and cosmetics to fellow Caribbean nationals. Jamaicans Leon Dyke and Dudley Dryden started the company and were followed by Montserrat-born Tony Wade. The firm became a leading manufacturer of over 500 hair care products sold in more than 15 countries worldwide including Africa, the Caribbean, Europe and the USA.

Yet, raising finance was a major problem. "The banks didn't have faith in us. They didn't see West Indians as people who would do well in business", said Wade. Then, there was a disastrous and costly sale to and buy back from the African American owned Soft Sheen, the first black-owned business listed on the Stock Exchange.

In 25 years D&D became Britain's first black-owned multi-million pound business supplying hair and beauty products to mainstream store outlets. Sales turnover mounted from £1 million in the early 1980s to £5 million by 1986. With a substantial volume of trade, the company had grown into a global ethnic hair and skin care industry, but it also had a social conscience. It provided cultural, educational and social services across the ethnic community including the funding of the West Indian Standing Conference (1958). The company also launched the Afro Hair and Beauty exhibition (1983), an annual event, in May, held at Alexandra Palace, north London. This weekend affair brings together manufacturers, distributors, hairdressers and professionals who celebrate and publicise their collective achievements in the beauty trade.

The company has been a recipient of prestigious awards – the *Sunrise Golden Awards* (1982) for business achievement, the *Revlon Awards* (1993) and the *West Indian Business Award* (1993). It was the first black-led enterprise to participate in a British Trade Mission overseas in 1984, and in that same year, the firm was rated the largest black hair care and cosmetics company in Europe.

Its unique mix of community focus and glamour was of course a perfect marketing opportunity. It spent approximately 30% of its revenue on marketing and research development and its corporate and social responsibility ethos was an immense source of pride for minority communities, especially African and Caribbean peoples. Wade's popularity earned him the leadership of the UK Caribbean Chamber of Commerce, director of a sub-regional training enterprise authority and head of a housing trust, apart from other distinguished posts he held during his entrepreneurial career.

At the time of writing the business was sold and the two original founders – Dyke and Dryden had died, with Wade publishing the groundbreaking book, *Black Enterprise in Britain* (**2001**) and other books, added to other enterprise pursuits. Sharing his insights into the hairdressing business, Wade agreed that competition such as the introduction of new brands, new `ethnic' players, variations in the distribution and supply chains, as well as changing customer trends, are factors that today's operators should consider seriously if they are to main their position in the marketplace.

And while start-up capital remains a sore issue, Caribbean business owners need to maximize training opportunities in areas such as leadership, management, IT, accounting and financial systems as well as advertising and promotion techniques to add to their creative abilities. With the increase in market segmentation too, owners will have to conduct routine research into new trends and adapt strategies to suit. According to Wade,

Despite pressure from financial institutions, manufacturers, retailers and bureaucrats, Dyke & Dryden had to control its operations. We motivated other businesses because of self-reliance and perseverance. We didn't believe in handouts because market opportunities were growing in the personal care market. At time, if large retail companies were receptive to the needs of the minority community, the industry's image would have been enhanced and the turnover in this sector would have also increased by 30% to 40%, almost overnight (**Wade 1998**).

British Caribbean-owned personal care firms can be found throughout the UK – full-time and part-time operators located in inner-cities. The idea is to stagger hours to either supplement daily income or utilize peak (evening) hours to generate higher returns by taking advantage of brisk business. There has been significant growth in industry segments; for instance, manicuring, pedicuring, as well as specialist services in aromatherapy and reflexology. Annual turnover is relatively low with micro firms accruing £20,000 to £50,000. Owners with more than one salon and a barber shop could earn roughly £50,000 to £100,000. Firms that are involved in manufacturing, distribution and the supply of beauty care products tend to have a turnover in excess of £200,000 because of the greater volume of products sold **(Table 7.2)**.

Table 7.2 Location of British Caribbean-owned personal care businesses

Barbers & Salons	Hair & Beauty	Distributors	Manufacturers
London	London	London	London
The Midlands	The Midlands	Southeast	Southeast
Yorkshire & Humberside	Yorkshire & Humberside	West Midlands	West Midlands
South West	South West	unavailable	unavailable
North East	North East	unavailable	unavailable
North West	North West	unavailable	unavailable
Southeast	Southeast	unavailable	unavailable
Scotland	Scotland	unavailable	unavailable
Wales	Wales	unavailable	unavailable

(Source: Independent research England, Scotland and Wales, 2000-2007)

The above figure illustrates that salons and barber shops are located across the British Isles (including Bradford, Doncaster, Coventry, Farnborough, Leicester and Liverpool). Distribution firms are dispersed in London, Greater London and the Southeast. Hair and beauty products manufacturers are situated in London, Greater London (Middlesex), the Southeast and the West Midlands (Birmingham). If Caribbean entrepreneurs have a 10% market share in the personal care sector, it means they are approximately 10,000 firms and if mobile hairdressers are added, the estimate could be much higher.

Skincare Market

In the mid 1990s, there were reports of fragmentation in the British skincare market and beauty parlours had to modify their operations to meet new customer demands. Since then, British Caribbean owners have introduced new product lines whilst others have set up alternative therapy firms throughout England and Wales, to maximize this niche market **(Minicase 7.2)**. Body Classic is one such firm that survived the shakeup in the skincare market and has progressed reasonably well.

Set up in 1994, the company specializes in skin creams, hair products and bath oils. Mail order is used to increase distributorship, thereby reducing overheads, maintaining competitive prices and quality at the same time. Its London shop offers inducement to customers traveling as far as Europe and Japan in the form of complementary services, such as aromatherapy. Proprietor Lisa Cookhorn offered valuable tips on operating an alternative beauty care shop:

The skincare industry is extremely competitive and sensitive and the needs of your clients are first and foremost. They must be given the opportunity to choose proper health remedies and this means you have to increase your knowledge of health and medicinal properties, skin textures, various therapies and existing services offered to clients by competing firms such as beauty parlours and health clinics. A caring and pleasant attitude to customers is vital, along with understanding the regulations of one's business (**Cookhorn 2001**).

Minicase 7. 2 Aurora– the Wales Connection

Barbadian Marcia Bennett, who grew up in Cardiff, founded **Aurora** recently to provide aromatherapy and holistic treatment services. A former hospital administrator, she went through the difficult process of setting up her enterprise with access to finance a major issue. With help from the Ethnic Business Support Program in Wales, she eventually succeeded. Her unique selling point is an `ultra-relaxed atmosphere' for clients.
Bennett chose self-employment after a succession of jobs spanning 20 years. Having developed a passion for health and beauty, she knew exactly what she wanted. *"I became interested in health and trade and later, I noticed a big demand for manicures and pedicure. The business employs a `cluster of associates' with complementary skills recruited to improve quality services*'. She is convinced that she did the right thing and said that, "*Before I had a job, now I have a career. I feel I am now home*" (***Ethnic Enterprise*** **2004**).

However, besides the customary salon and barber shop, there has been a noticeable growth in the alternative therapy market consisting of health clubs and fitness centres. Owners provide a combination of services – yoga, counseling, coaching, oral hygiene and fitness programs for both the young and the elderly. These can be found in London, Surrey, Cambridge and elsewhere in England. Perhaps one particular segment of the personal care industry that has introduced by some British Caribbean entrepreneurs is the health spa that facilitates a de-stressed environment for people who lead busy lives.

Only a few health spas for instance, are owned and managed by minority firms and yet, black women are among clients who frequent clinics to be pampered and seek `refuge from everyday stresses'. In east London, a British Caribbean firm decided to compete with The Sanctuary which attracts women from all cultural and social backgrounds. Junioros Relaxation is not only an innovation but the continuation of a survival strategy that is aimed at capturing markets that are external to `ethnic enclaves' **(Minicase 7.3)**.

Minicase 7. 3 Junioros Relaxation Centre

Junior Hart founded **Junioros Relaxation Centre**, a facility that is classified as 'the first UK day spa for black women'. It caters for groups, birthdays and 'hen' days and was set up in east London after three years of research to identify a facility that catered for predominantly black women.

Yet the story behind this enterprise innovation is quite interesting. When Hart's mother returned home from a disappointing health spa break five years ago in 2001, she had no idea she would inspire her son to embark on another business venture. The retreat was in the UK countryside and she had been the only black guest. After listening to his mother's laments, Hart decided to carry out research and recognized there was no such facility for women of colour. After renovating and joining two buildings, one of them a former mini cab office, the premises were designed to provide 'weary clients with a relaxing refuge from everyday stresses'.

The decision to locate a health spa in east London may seem odd, but Hart who is an experienced businessman has lived in the area for many years and believes that regeneration plans make it a pearl just waiting to be discovered. The firm's pampering packages include limousine transportation to and from the spa. Services on offer include reflexology, manicures, pedicures, massages and colonic hydrotherapy. All therapists are qualified and beauticians will be employed on a freelance basis. There are plans to introduce customized services for men to complement existing provision. According to Hart, "I think if people learn to relax, it can be very good for them. Well it's proven. It will be good for them. So, I just want to create Junioros to be part of that relaxation process."

One of the interesting features of Hart's firm is vertical integration which involves combining other business interests into the operational processes of Junioros. "*Everything is kind of entwined, you kow, Junioros is basically an extension of a business, coming from an investment side, and I am looking to incorporate music, with the chauffeured cars, so it is all part of the business.*"

(Source: Junior Relaxation: De-stressing in East London, Deborah Wong, Wellbeing editor, December 2004, London)

As was stated at the beginning of this chapter, the black community's contribution to personal care in the UK covers a broader spectrum. For the majority, beauty includes the total appearance of the individual - from hairstyles, clothing and fashion to a broader range of accessories. Of course, there is competition among various ethnic groups for appearance versus style. It is however in the clothing and fashion business that British Caribbean people have made their mark in an industry that signifies the real meaning of cultural diversity and market segmentation. It is this particular section of British society who will also define the future of the personal care sector, as owners strive to make their firms more open and marketable by targeting customers beyond their own ethnic (local) communities.

Clothing and Fashion Design

Clothing, footwear and fashion form one of the UK's largest export sectors totaling about £9 billion worth of goods and with exports valued at £6 billion. Overseas demand for British designs is rising, from the classic to the avant-garde. The estimated market share for British Caribbean entrepreneurs is about 4% or £5 million which represents a tiny fraction of their potential. This ethnic segment consists of clothing shops, modeling agencies and fashion designers operating on high streets and neighbourhood areas.

Today's cross-over of beauty care and fashion is not unusual for people of colour since historically, in communal societies, women worked as `supplementary' breadwinners and developed methods of thrift to cater for large households including extended families. Apart from the Caribbean Region, much of the fashion influences in the British Caribbean community today, originated also from Africa and the US (**Table 7.3**).

Table 7.3 International influences on the UK fashion industry

Types of Fashion	Period
Nehru Suit: Worn by Michael X who was part of the Black Power Movement; projected a strong black identity through the styling of the body and influenced by the racial struggle of African-Americans.	Late 1960s
Trilby Hat: integral to the image of poet, Linton Kwesi Johnson.	1970s -80s
African Shirt or the `Dashiki': Worn by African diasporic communities in Britain, the Caribbean and Europe, symbolizing Black Consciousness movements universally.	1970s
Afro Comb: Emerged at the same time as the Afro hairstyle, created in Africa and worn as a hair ornament by young British Caribbean men in a defiant gesture that magnified `blackness' of the wearer.	1970s
Leather coat: popularized by Richard Roundtree in the film, *Shaft* (1971) who wore leather jacket and tight polo-neck jumper. A British stylistic slant was to wear versions of the coat with a knitted tam, preferably in the Rastafarian colours of red, gold and green.	1970s

Indeed, cross-dressing influences are not only limited to Africa, Asia, the Caribbean and the USA, but `English' culture in the form of official dress, language and other traditions. These have a bearing on the way of life British Caribbean and other minority communities who interact with members of the UK host society as a whole. Much of these influences can be seen in more formal settings; namely employment and other official engagements involving mainstream organizations and minorities. But perhaps one the most enduring cultural influences that British society has benefited from over the past 50 years is ethnic food, a vital sector of the British economy that will be examined in **Chapter 9.**

In order to obtain a fairly balanced picture of the input of black firms in the UK's fashion designing industry, a number of independent sources were accessed, along with profiles of successful firms published via web directories and the media (**Fig 7.1**). One particular source demonstrated evidence of the diversity of this segment of the personal care industry.

Figure 7.1 Profile of the British Caribbean clothing design sector

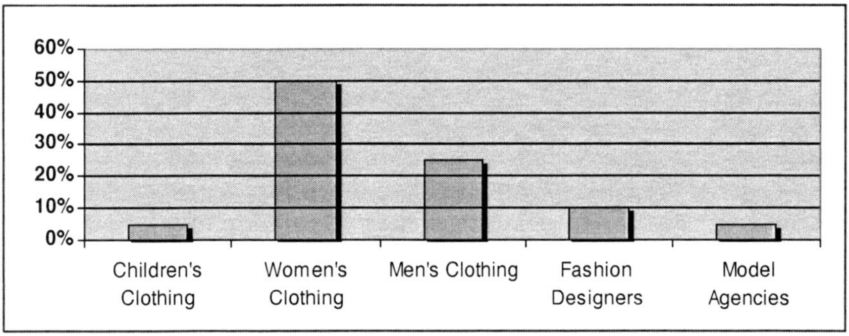

(Source: The Blacknet.UK Business Directory, 2005)

The above figure illustrates that an estimated 50% of all fashion houses sell products for women, 25% catered for men and 10% introduced segments for children and customers interested in designer clothing, while 5% of all firms had casting and modeling agencies in various parts of the British Isles (London, Essex and Cardiff particularly).

Essentially, having an ideal business location is very important to commercial success since this enhances business reputation and general public image, especially if there are proper facilities such as parking, access to transportation and other amenities for customers. A location that is unsuitable for trading activities can be disastrous for even the most knowledgeable of entrepreneurs, and this, along with ideal premises, makes for a promising enterprise of which the fashion trade fits neatly into the equation. Finding suitable premises in an appropriate location for trading is a formidable challenge for minority business owners because of the high cost of commercial properties and related expenditure for operating a thriving venture. Apart from these difficulties, however, there are notable exceptions in the British Caribbean garment trade **(Minicase 7.4)**.

Minicase 7. 4 Maurice Sedwell Ltd

Trinidadian-born Andrew Ramroop is an innovative entrepreneur who carved out a niche market in `bespoke' men's clothing in Savile Rowe, central London where few black businesses dared to trade. In 1988 he in **Maurice Sedwell (Savile Row) Ltd (MSL)** by purchasing 90% of the company shares and took over the business that was established in 1938. It was a landmark in the established tailoring fraternity especially since no other black-owned tailors dared to trade there. Before Ramroop owned MSL, he worked as a tailor after arriving from the Caribbean as a teenager and later studied at the London College of Fashion. The proprietor, Maurice Sedwell, was impressed with Ramroop's skill and work ethic and encouraged his understudy to buy shares in the company.

After Ramroop bought the company, 11 banks refused to help finance its expansion program during the recession of 1993; he turned to loyal clients for support and moved location from 500sq feet to 3,000 sq feet, of premises at 19 Savile Row. He then began focusing on growth and development of quality products and services to meet the demands of growing customers.

The firm had a small staff of 3 people and now has 14. Ramroop trains his staff to attain quality standards required to sustain the company's growth. MSL has customers in over 50 countries. The future of the business is essential, with annual growth pegged at over 5% since taking over the operations in 1988. The annual turnover has exceeded £10 million. MSL's market intelligence is geared to respond to changing trends in men's clothing. Support for aspiring businesses is paramount to MSL and this is evidenced by the new Savile Row Academy, an initiative aimed at training elite tailors for the future. Plans are in the pipeline to also train high quality tailors, cutters and designers to address the needs of the trade.

As a role model for the minority communities, Ramroop is active in the Masters Craftsmen's Association and retail Export Group. He is also on the Board of Directors of Harvard University Du Bois Institute. He spends much of his time sharing knowledge and experiences with students and young tailors. The Government of Trinidad and Tobago conferred on him the gold award for his contribution to commerce, industry and civic affairs, and he is also the first person in Britain to be awarded a professorship for `Distinction in the Field of Tailoring' by the University of Arts London and the only tailor to win the National Training Award (2007) and the Mayor of London Trailblazer award. His motto, "*All in all we leave nothing to chance, our main objective your image to chance*" is not only a commercial symbol, but one that truly befits an entrepreneur who is a leader in the British fashion and design industry.

Hair Products

A major disadvantage affecting the orderly development and overall expansion of small personal care operators is a lack of consistent and affordable range of hair care products, and since most are imported from Asian and US markets, it seems almost impossible for micro and small operators to compete. The idea of setting up a regional hairdressing school, fully equipped with modern facilities was suggested by operators in west London some years ago during a survey conducted by this author. More than 75% of operators favoured this venture because of the added value to the personal care trade (**TCS: Brent Council 2002**).

In the West Midlands, a similar view was expressed by traders who met to discuss the competitive challenges affecting their businesses. The more experienced owners clamoured for a distribution centre and a manufacturing company combined, specially designed for `ethnic' beauty care products. It was conceded that other competitors knew little of the `skincare' needs of African people and were thus reluctant to treat them with courtesy and consideration when purchases were made. There were suggestions that in some Asian retail outlets, the sales staff had no knowledge of the `composition' or `usability' of black hair care products and were therefore ill-equipped to offer quality advice on product guarantees etc. The issue of `under-pricing' or `under-cutting' essential beauty care commodities was also discussed at length (**BDA 2006**).

Just as there is a lack of official data on the number of black hair care manufacturers in the UK, there are a few, based on anecdotal evidence, pursuing an independent course of action by ensuring that the range of beauty products are available on Britain's high street stores. One prominent illustration is the **Urban Therapy** brand that was formulated by British-Caribbean economics graduate, Stephen Durham, in 2002. He is the proprietor of a few beauty salons and his products which are sold by Boots, Tesco's, Waitrose, Superdrug and Truvalu in Trinidad, are aimed at African and Caribbean men.

Durham's parents convinced him that his life was not complete without having a degree, and it was only in the last two years of his studies, that he decided to establish a business. His experience working at the department store of John Lewis instigated the idea of researching his `UT24/7' product which went on sale in April 2002. His product range consists of pre-shave scrub, shaving cream, moisturizer, body wash and shampoos.

The firm's long-term strategy is hinged on expansion into overseas markets, Australia and America inclusive. In terms of branding, Durham has plans to introduce other hair care and beauty products, complementing these with credit cards (as subsidiary goods). The young entrepreneur claimed that by taking a `common sense approach' to challenges rather than an `idealistic' one, Caribbean businesses can convert setbacks into lasting opportunities (***The Voice* 2002**).

Challenges and Opportunities

In this section, we will look at the issues facing the personal care trade and industry developments that may be advantageous to owners in their efforts to reposition their enterprises to increase market share and profit margins. Like other industry sectors in the UK, there are no exceptions to personal care in terms of the challenges facing it and opportunities which British Caribbean firms can maximize to gain further market advantage. Interestingly while there is little information on the organization and performance of ethnic firms in the hairdressing and clothing and fashion segments, there is information on the future trends and the steps that are required to make these possible.

Consumer Demand

Threats: The demand for basic hair cutting services tends to be constant, demand for additional services such as colouring and perming seems to be more influenced by cultural tastes and the economic climate. Consumers also tend to regard alternative therapies as a luxury item and as such, are particularly influenced by economic and social factors, apart from style. The constant change in clothing, fashion designs and their accessories will certainly place considerable strain on the resources of ethnic firms to adapt to consumer needs.

Opportunities: Yet, it is the growth in personal care markets –at home and overseas - that is creating greater opportunities for British Caribbean hair stylists and clothing designers to increase their market share and remain profitable enterprises.

Cost Factor

Threats: The hairdressing industry has a low wage image and there is no evidence suggesting that the minimum wage has affected any significant change in the composition of the workforce. Price standardization for hair care and beauty products remain problematic since competition by other ethnic distributors and suppliers has made it difficult for British Caribbean retailing firms to compete. Only 2% of all firms in this ethnic segment are involved in some form of manufacturing in spite of their huge potential. The fashion industry is also highly competitive and consumers tend to exercise an `economy prices' approach when making purchases.

Opportunities: Caribbean retailers should implement `a bulk-buying' method by using sector networks to create economies of scale in terms of products. Operators can also exploit the thriving market that caters for consumers who use various cosmetics for different shades of skin and hair textures and styles. This segment is lucrative but involves knowledge in trichology, chemistry, accounting, and commercial law. To guarantee success, owners would have to put efficient systems in place to monitor the volume of products and services traded, as well the procedures required, to conduct ongoing research on customers and the industry as a whole. Each firm ought to have a workable investment plan for each area of the business to facilitate growth and expansion over a medium to long-term period.

Skill Requirements

Threats: All segments and sub-sectors of this industry have severe skill shortages and the greater the demands by consumers, the greater the level of skills required. There are tens of thousands of vacancies in the personal care sector countrywide. British Caribbean firms bear the brunt of this situation as well, with over 50% of hairdressers and barbers finding it difficult to recruit staff with knowledge of the skin and hair, as well as employees with experience in `creating patterns in hair' and carrying out `facial treatments' including massage. There are also problems relating to firms that have fewer staff with experience in retailing European `hair' and `barbering' products respectively. Insufficient managerial and technical staff is also a grey area. The decline in the textiles and clothing industry has resulted in a loss of middle-management skills and not enough emphasis has been placed on attracting younger workers with a well-defined career path to create the next generation of senior technicians and managers.

Opportunities: British Caribbean owners should take advantage of education and training modules in the hairdressing, textiles and fashion design industry and ensure that employees are trained beyond the minimum requirements set by industry standards. Another way of improving staff levels is to identify apprentices who might be interested in work-study attachments. This will allow owners to make an informed and professional judgment as to the quality of potential employees in relation to their overall work ethic. Of course, researching new markets to improve the volume of products and services thereby securing greater revenue for staff and other resource investment for growth and expansion is highly recommended.

Business Planning

Threats: Only about 30% of British Caribbean hairdressers, barbers and clothing retailers have formal business plans or concrete ideas with projected aims and objectives over a five year period to deal with industry changes such as technology, customer profiling, market intelligence and organizational procedures, including management processes. The continued growth of the personal care sector has affected many firms in the areas of staffing (high turnover), use of information technology and loss of market share because of inter-ethnic and other forms of competition such as pricing and greater volume of products and services by rivals in the industry, as well as location and size of premises.

Opportunities: Owners should utilize agencies and organisations including Habia and the London Hairdressing Salon forum, among others, to access quality enterprise support to implement proper business planning systems. There is an urgent need for more technical support to enable operators to develop strategies for diversification such as new product(s) range in hairdressing and barbering, as well as clothing and fashion design segments. Enterprise support is necessary for marketing, PR, employment law and general business planning skills that need updating across industry segments.

Industry Partnerships

Threats: Only a few firms have either accreditation or membership with trade associations and other industry networks. Fragmentation makes it difficult for all segments of industry to work together since business, technical and organizational needs differ widely from one segment to another. Hairdressers and barbers have different needs than operators in the clothing and fashion industry.

Opportunities: Growth in various segments of personal care means that firms can link with Habia and other industry authorities to utilize their expertise and contacts, nationally and internationally. The science that is involved in hair care and beauty products including alternative therapies can be further examined with a view to generate viable projects for funding to stimulate increased product development. The modeling business is also a growth area and with annual beauty pageants for fully-figured women organized by a variety of organizations and international agencies, British Caribbean entrepreneurs can work in partnership with existing modeling agencies and or establish niche markets in this sub-sector of personal care. In the nature industry or leisure sector, beauty shows are now integral to what is described in modern terms as `cultural' or `pageant tourism', an enterprise that will be discussed in more detail in Chapter 11. Through effective collaboration with key industry partners, owners can have access to information and data on competitors' markets and therefore, better positioned to devise appropriate strategies for increasing market share and boosting profitability.

In addition, British Caribbean firms should examine export opportunities to take advantage of mass consumer markets. Dyke & Dryden, as a manufacturer of hair care and beauty products, showed how to compete with international giants. Maurice Sedwell remains a leader in men's clothing manufacturing and servicing mainstream markets in the UK and abroad because of its adaptation to customer trends. And the young Durham was successful in introducing the Urban Therapy beauty care products because he understood the demands of customers and the various interlocking forces at play in the personal care business. All of this means that owners should develop relevant market intelligence such as knowledge of the political climate, economic situation and the social trends in each exporting country. Making full use of BERR, the Export Promotion Council, the British Council and other such bodies, can prove invaluable towards capitalizing on overseas markets (**Table 7. 4**).

Generally, while the prospects for the personal care sector remain a challenge, there are useful indicators that reflect a positive side for British Caribbean firms. The market for beauty care products is likely to grow and the demand for quality clothing and fashion will also increase, as customers demand quality products at competitive prices and personalized services (**Table 7. 4**). As far back as the late 1990s, the Bank of England acknowledged that ethnic businesses were important to the UK economy.

Ethnic businesses can be a tremendous benefit to our economy. In a global market, having people with specialised knowledge of other parts of the world can only be to your competitive advantage. The challenge is to make sure that they are used to their full, because if you don't then you are wasting a big asset **(BBC 2004).**

The bank's views were echoed by a female fashion designer who produced clothes for the corporate market and who said that although she had won several contracts from companies around the country, the media's image towards black entrepreneurs hadn't changed much. She felt it was time for the black community to produce more entrepreneurs and at the same time, promote the message of enterprise success so that the ethnic contribution to the UK economy will be recognized more.

It is important that more people like us do start up in business. To be honest, the media is largely full of white people, but the more black people who make a success of business, the more the message will get across that people can be successful in whatever area they want. It will break down barriers in society and maybe stop a lot of talent from going to waste (**BBC 2004**).

Table 7.4 Competitive Framework of personal care in the UK

Issues	Challenges	Opportunities
Consumer Demand	Demand for basic haircutting services tends to be constant changes in fashion designs; place considerable strain on the resources of firms.	Growth in new consumer markets to provide growth opportunities for personal care firms.
Cost Factor	The industry has a low wage image – price standardization for beauty products is problematic.	Retailers should implement a `bulk-buying' method by using sector networks to create economies of scale.
Skill Requirements	Sub-sectors have skill shortages of personal care firms find it difficult to recruit general staff.	Owners should maximize education and training modules in the personal care industry.
Business Planning	About 30% of personal care firms have formal business plans.	Owners should utilize mainstream enterprise support agencies for technical advice on business strategy.
Industry Partnerships	Very few firms are accredited to reputable bodies in the personal care industry.	Firms should develop links with industry bodies and maximize their expertise and contacts.
Product Development	Firms have limited investment capital for new products and services.	Owners should develop an expansion program to generate more customers and generate greater revenue for investment and growth.

(Source: Analysis of various segments discussed in this chapter)

Conclusion

This chapter discussed the workings of various segments of the personal care industry and the market forces impacting on the organization and performance of British Caribbean hairdressers, barbers, alternative therapists, fashion designers, beauty care producers and industry-related operators. Whilst Caribbean-led firms have only 10% or about £4 million market share of the industry, it was revealed that black women alone spent in excess of £40 million per year alone of skin care products. Further, continental influences such as those in Africa, the Caribbean and the USA, have a bearing on culture, fashion and beauty care, and these impacts were assessed to show the measure of experience and knowledge operators have acquired over the past 40 years since Dyke & Dryden emerged as the first black-owned hair care firm in Britain.

Matters pertaining to location, premises, size of business and financial sustainability (based on annual turnover) of firms were examined to illustrate the diversity and the organizational dynamics of these entities. An evaluation was done to show the market value and the competitive advantage of businesses operating in these segments - hairdressing and barbering, clothing and fashion designing – of personal care. In this chapter various industry statistics were employed and case studies presented in an effort to provide factual accuracy and to show best practice. The idea behind the organization and performance of firms is made even more illustrative by the information and data on personal care enterprises across Britain. The composition, nature and ranging segments of personal care firms throughout the UK, attest to the creativity and enterprise of British Caribbean communities.

The growth of key segments or sub-sectors in the trade was emphasized in this chapter, with analysis of key challenges owners face, as well as opportunities to guarantee future success. Issues such as skill shortages, business planning, market research, product development, new services, scientific and technological advances, among others, were also mentioned to highlight stages of the planning process – from ideas-generation to implementation. The next chapter explores the role and function of the Caribbean firm sector in Britain's manufacturing trades.

Chapter Notes

Madam CJ Walker – born Sarah Breedlove, was described as an entrepreneur, philantropist and social activist since she was a pioneer of the modern cosmetics industry and her company created marketing schemes, training opportunities. In the 19th century her distribution strategies were as innovative as those any entrepreneur of her time. An early advocate of women's economic independence, she provided lucrative incomes for thousands of African-American women.

Habia – the Hair and Beauty Industry Authority was set up in 1997 to meet the needs of both the hairdressing and beauty therapy industries and it prides itself on being a dynamic and continuously evolving organisation. It is a non-profit, Government recognized Training Organisation. In 2002 the organization was set to merge with the Distributive NTO to create the consumer Services Industry Authority (CSIA) which will bid as a Sector Skills Council.

Dyke & Dryden- became Britain's first black-owned multi-million pound business supplying hair and beauty products to mainstream outlets, setting new business standards for services to the African and Caribbean community. Leon Dyke and Dudley Dryden MBE were community leaders in their own right, combining entpreneurship with community activities.

Selected References

1 Pool, Hannah: `Natural beauty', *The Guardian*, 22 October 2005.

2 *Skills Survey of the African Caribbean Hair Industry*, The Hair and Beauty Industry Authority (Habia), Doncaster, England March 2004.

3 Jewellery & Watches (October 2006), Men and Women's Buying Habits (October 2006), Men's Toiletries and Fragrances (2006), *Key Note* Market Report, UK 2005-2006.

4 Wade, Tony (2001): *How They Made A Million: The Dyke & Dryden Story*, Hansib Publishing (Caribbean) Ltd.

5 Clifton, Maughan (2000): `The Global Brand Scoreboard', *Business Week*, 2003.

6 Ethnic businesses thriving, *BBC News*, 20 September 2004.

7 Foulkes, Nick: `Andrew Ramroop: A First Smile for Savile Row', *London Standard* 1999

8 Sector profile of the UK hairdressing and beauty sector, 2003, National Guidance Research Forum, England.

9 Pryce, Scharene (2005): `Black British fashion designers prep-up for their own catwalk', *Colourful Network*, 2 August 2005 London.

10 Black Business Directory, England 2005.

11 Clothing, Footwear & Fashion, UK Trade & Investment, 2005

12 www.uktradeinvest.gov.uk/ukti/appmanager/ukti/sectors?

13 The Framework for Modern Apprenticeships in Hairdressing for Wales, Habia, Doncaster, England, November 2003.

14 Special Meeting with Birmingham Hairdressers, Black Business Association, West Midlands, February 2006

15 Impact Assessment of BME Business Programme, TCS Tutorial College and Brent Council, 2002-2005, London

16 Taylor, Kenneth (2002): `Groomed for success', *The Voice*, July 22, 2002.

Table 8.1 Profile of UK Manufacturing Sector

Segment	Value	Market Share	UK Region
Aerospace	£17.08bn	12%	South West, South East and North West of England
Automotive	£8.4bn	5.5%	UK wide
Biotechnology	£4bn	3%	North East, North West, East of England, London and Scotland
Chemicals	£5bn	11%	London,
Clothing & Footwear	£45bn		East Midlands, North West, Scotland, Yorkshire and Northern Ireland
Electronics & Engineering	£29bn	2%	UK wide
Food & Beverages	£64bn	17%	UK wide
Paper & Print	£14.3bn		North West, Yorkshire and Humber, The Midlands
Pharmaceuticals	£2.5bn	37%	London, East Midlands, North East
Plastics & Polymers	£17.5bn	2.1%	North East, Yorkshire & Humber, West Midlands and UK Regions
Shipbuilding	£2bn	2%	Poole, Southwest, the Norfolk Broads and Midland Counties
Steel	£10bn	2.3%	England, Scotland, Wales and Northern Island
Textiles	£7.62bn	7%	Midland Counties, North West, South West

(Source: Sector Briefings: Agcas Manufacturing Sector, 2005 England)

The above figure reflects the range of segments and sub-sectors of UK manufacturing, the volume of revenue generated annually, the market share for each segment and regional location where industries operate. As was explained earlier, new technology has resulted in the downsizing of several industries and `small is beautiful' is no longer a slogan, but an essential part of the mission statement of firms.

The industrial sector is therefore divided into multinational corporations, national firms and smaller or micro businesses that provide tailored products to meet the demands of customers. Smaller companies can be found in food and drink, paper and board, textiles, mechanical engineering, automotives, electronics and instrumentation.

Nevertheless, since the mid to late 1980s, the service sector has overtaken almost all production activities with a yield estimated in excess of 90%, and whilst the British Caribbean SME sector has less than 5% market share in manufacturing (black businesses have approximately 8.5% in all production activities), its potential in the cultural, food, technology, vehicular equipment and installation parts market is known, given also that the market for these segments of manufacturing are limitless due to a high degree of personalised service they attract.

Market Segments

The Royal Society confirmed that about 57,800 people from minority communities were represented in science, engineering and technology (SET) disciplines. Excluding `white' and `other' groups respectively, although statistically the overall figure is less than one per cent, when included as part of the total minority sector grouping, British Caribbean professionals represent 10% of the SET share of the mainstream market (**The Royal Society 2004**). This group also has a small market share in food (5%), cultural products (10% plus), garment production (3%) and related semi-processing activities (5%).

However, in other to gain further insights into the sub-sectors of Caribbean manufacturing firms, this author carried out a series of surveys in 2000-2006 involving 100 companies, to test the performance rating of various enterprises. These were done through consultations with owners, business associations, industry-wide networks, public authorities and policy makers. The surveys consisted of interviews and observational studies with a selected group of manufacturers and trades operators, with segmentation, market share, the use of IT and owners' views on networking featured as part of the initiative **(Fig 8.1)**.

Figure 8.1 Segmentation of British Caribbean Manufacturing Trades

(Source: Independent Research 2000-2006, England)

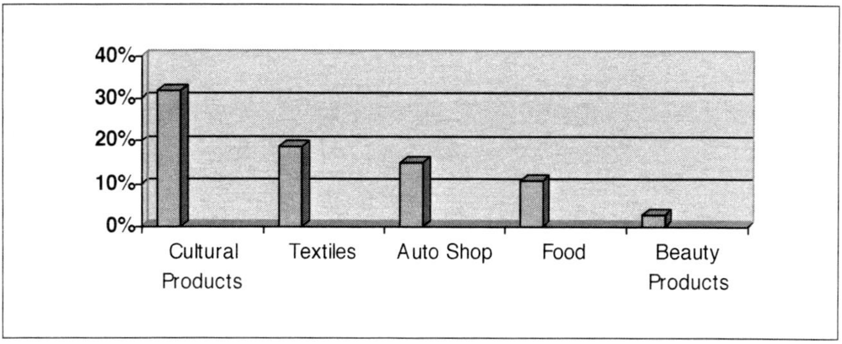

The above figure illustrates diversity features of Caribbean firms involved in segments of the manufacturing trades industry. In the cultural products segment, more than a quarter of all firms have niche markets in video production and craft designs. Textiles continue to increase in segmentation and nearly 20% of all products are related to fashion designs for all sexes and ages, with a small percent dealing with soft furnishings. The auto shop represents over a tenth of all manufacturing trades and there are signs of growth innovation with more mechanics specialising in vehicle maintenance, spare parts installation and offering advice to young drivers.

An examination will thus be carried out on the challenges and trends with respect to manufacturing-based activities involving this new core of `enterprise creators', with reference also to the traditional auto shop, vehicle repairs, maintenance and installation firms, all of which are integral to the fields of manufacturing and engineering.

Food Production

Even though the British Caribbean food market will be discussed at length in the next chapter, this section of the book will highlight how firms have developed an array of products over the past 50 years, with Caribbean foods alone, making up 10% of the total UK ethnic cuisine. There is a high level of specialisation in the food sector particularly as it relates to restaurants, take-aways and food factories located in various parts of England.

Specifically, there are two leading segments in the food trade; herbal seasoning and pastry products that Caribbean entrepreneurs have a considerable market share - between 15% and 20% respectively. Not only do these products show originality in their food processing techniques, but they also exemplify quality and distinction in British ethnic cuisine as a whole. To their credit, Dounne Alexander, and Wade Lyn (**Minicase 8.1**), are pioneers of ethnic foods in the UK today and their contribution is solid proof of food being a cultural unifier in an environment where class, colour and race `shake hands' daily.

Indeed, the stories of both Lyn and Alexander are bestsellers in the fictional business world where modernisation, market intelligence and grit are vital components of success. Alexander who is owner of Gramma's Herbal Foods was awarded the MBE for her contribution to the food industry and the Government of Trinidad and Tobago also recognised her work as a member of the Caribbean diasporic community. Her exploits as both a pacesetter and producer of herbal foods and drink will be elaborated upon in the next chapter.

Yet there are other unique industrial endeavours by Caribbean entrepreneurs including the oral hygiene product invented by Timothy Stewart. His `Agatha' toothbrush was designed for strokes sufferers and other incapacitated patients. Similarly, Clyde Pile's glass manufacturing business and Dalegety's Teas have shown the pace with which Caribbean food manufacturing is taking root in mainstream Britain similar to other ethnic foods now dominating the consumer market. Today, it is common to find on the shelves of supermarkets a range of spices, condiments and other seasonings as consumers appear to relish the novelty of ethnic foods in the UK.

Interestingly, Caribbean people who live in areas described as 'deprived and excluded' or who public agencies describe as 'hard to reach', tend to opt for micro/small units in textiles, fashion design, soft furnishings, engineering, electronics, light manufacturing dealing with housing accessories and other cottage-type trades such as crocheting or knitting of mats, pillow cases, etc. Much of these micro industries are operated by owners whose desire is to achieve financial independence and exploit market opportunities based on their sphere of knowledge and experience.

Minicase 8.1 Cleone Foods

For the past 20 years, Jamaican-born Wade Lyn has impacted on the ethnic food scene in England. After moving with his family to the UK in the 1960s, he qualified in Art and Industrial Design and went on to become a trained teacher.

In 1986 he began working with a family-owned food firm and was quickly promoted to General Manager, and three years later, he established **Cleone Foods**, producing beef and vegetable patties under the *Island Delight* brand and distributing his products to fast-food restaurants, convenience stores and supermarkets. He credits his mother and aunt for helping to make the business a success.

In 2001 his firm copped the prize for being one of the fastest growing 100 inner-city companies in the country. The business has a turnover worth millions and employs staff in excess of 40. Lyn is keen to pass on 'enterprise' wisdom to students by maintaining contacts with both the Birmingham City University and Aston Business School. He is keen to stress the value of entrepreneurship as an effective instrument to counter underachievement and underperformance of sections of black youths in inner-cities throughout England.

From all indications, Lyn is set to maintain high standards in his business activities. "I will continue to work closely with retailers to develop a definitive Caribbean segment by positioning our cuisine alongside other ethnic foods such as Italian, Indian and Thai. This can best be done by ensuring that Island Delight offers consumers a real alternative to traditional foods in the UK."

In continuing the enterprise tradition Caribbean people have pursued for ages, evidence of their input into industrial health products has been noticeable in the last century. A famous invention was a toothbrush specially made to assist stroke suffers and others experiencing disability due to various illnesses. Bermudan-born Timothy Stewart gained inspiration for his discovery after watching his mother unable to brush her teeth. The experience convinced him that the global oral hygiene industry can be transformed by innovation through the use of appropriate technology and market positioning.

The market for oral hygiene products has grown since the turn of the 21st century with an estimated value of £680 million alone in 2005. Two sub-divisions, toothbrushes and toothpaste, dominate the industry and continue to do so. As consumers realise the value of maintaining good oral hygiene and seek to attain white teeth, they are likely to spend on standard products such as toothpaste resulting in their value rising by 4% since 2003.

Midian International Inc now based in America, conducted product trials in the UK in the mid-1990s (that time the invention was said to be estimated at £35 million). The trials attracted enthusiasm and pride from the black community with professionals, ordinary folk and a broad range of investors keen on supporting the Agatha. Despite apparent setbacks, Stewart said in early 2007 that the Agatha Oral Hygiene System was on course for further development (**Minicase 8. 2**).

Limitations aside, the Agatha invention is a testament to the remarkable qualities of entrepreneurship by Caribbean people

For instance, Pile played a dynamic role in regenerating the Midland Counties at a time when recession forced the closure of large companies all over the country in the 1980s. Similarly, he led the way in promoting Best Practice models for urban renewal schemes in disadvantaged areas and notably, encouraged business professionals to support community-led initiatives such as the Community Roots Enterprise Centre and Black Business in Birmingham (3b) in the West Midlands. Fellow countryman, Tony Sealey, also believes that industries should work together to build strong and prosperous communities thereby removing the slur of `anti-social behaviour' that tend to be associated with Caribbean young men living in run-down estates.

Minicase 8. 3 UK Glass Manufacturer

Clyde Pile came to the UK from Barbados at age 16 and began working as a clerk. His next job was that of a salesman with Pilkingtons, the world-class glass manufacturer. Whilst working full-time, he obtained a Business Degree and he then moved to UBM Glass Group where he became Commercial Manager.

In 1985, he acquired the Welman's glass processing plant (one of his former client-subsidiaries) and established Glass Processing later renamed **Glass Tempering & Sealed Unit Production.** The company manufactured toughened glass for the double glazing industry. Between 1990 and 1994, the company invested nearly £2m towards improving competitiveness and increased plant capacity.

In the early part of this century, Glass Processing's annual turnover was in the region of several million pounds and a staff of around 150. After a five year pilot project, Pile launched the franchise company - Glassman UK Ltd, with a vision to build on existing franchises beyond Britain. Pile served on boards and committees that advice, support and finance black businesses including two major Community Finance Initiatives (CFIs) - Black Business in Birmingham (3b) and Community Roots Enterprise Ltd. With his formidable experience in business and industry, Pile will continue sharing his experience with owners of start-ups and existing firms to help them avoid the failure of market intelligence, an important component in the entire value chain of enterprises.

In the vein of their male counterparts, women have led the way in industry too, and whilst only a few are few represented in this sector, their value should not be discounted. Employment in manufacturing shows that just over 6% of the Caribbean workforce is engaged in this sector (**Manufacturing Industry Focus 2004)** and since the last century, more have developed an interest in vocational trades rather than the pursuit of office-type occupations. In effect, British Caribbean women are competing in commercial and industrial markets that were once perceived as a male preserve. Even more, they comprise over 25% of all self-employed people in the UK.

Industrial trailblazer, Sandra Croasdale, who found there is 'no glass ceiling when you are your own boss', left the nursing profession in the 1980s to manufacture glass and her company, Midland Board and Glass Ltd, captured awards in 1999 and 2000. At the beginning she was not recognised even by clients when they came to the office. In an exclusive interview with the *Voice* newspaper, she recounted her experience:

I found that people would come to the office and ask to speak with the boss and when they realised it was me, they were shocked. I am quite a strong character. I lived in that man's world and worked my business in that man's world. I think it was my attitude that made them accept this (***The Voice*** **2006**).

After a long stint in the industry, Croasdale moved on to set up **SC Associates**, a firm that provides business services in the West Midlands Region. Significantly, the Caribbean entrepreneur's unique selling points are to 'offer what the market needs; look at new technology, new markets and new ways of ensuring that you are ahead of the competition'. As a family company, she acknowledged that "we spend a great deal of time looking at the future."

Soft Furnishings

Another segment of the UK manufacturing industry that is partly owned by female entrepreneurs, is soft furnishings, a combination of the age-old hand woven products such as curtains, bedspreads, cushions, pillow cases, bread spreads etc. Other services associated with this industry are design, fitting, providing accessories such as tracks and poles, free measuring and estimates, cleaning, frame proofing and offering co-ordinating items such as wallpaper.

In 1988 it was recorded that the Caribbean clothing industry was among the world's fastest growth industry. Soft furnishings are grounded in originality; operations are usually cost effective and producers operate from home or in low-cost industrial units. However, this sector is confused with elements of the personal care industry since some products are frequently associated with `personal effects' in the form of jewellery designs and craft creations for living rooms.

And yet the ownership composition of operators in the soft furnishings trade can be either individual women or husband-and-wife teams who operate a division of labour scheme. The age group varies between 40-50 and 55 plus, with most operators being Caribbean-born nationals who came to the UK in the first half or middle part of the 20th century with exceptional skills and multiple (professional) experiences.

For the most part, operators utilise their time either away from full-time employment or when retired from active duty. They are determined to carve out vocational careers, by manufacturing curtains, drapes, blinds, cushions and other home furnishing products. In the process, they have acquired skills passed down by elders or by attending evening courses similar to modern British Caribbean women who attend cookery classes to upgrade their culinary skills at home, and for whom personal development is important. Currently, there are women in leading professions such as education, law, consultancy and healthcare, who are also actively involved in soft furnishings as a `side trade' while others have made it a full-time enterprise.

Independent estimates suggest that the average turnover for micro/small producers can vary between £10,000 to £20,000 annually depending on the nature of the business; that is, volume of custom, type of clientele and frequency of orders. If the division of labour is great; for instance where women manufacture the finished product(s) and men visit homes to erect curtains, hangers, deliver products and/or install house accessories, this can affect the volume of revenue generated. Generally, business is obtained through referrals, repeat custom, advertisement and industry sources. Custom is also obtained from boutiques, house designers, and reputable high street retailers that tend to purchase from small producers as part of their policy of supporting micro/small vendors.

The market for soft furnishing such as the manufacture of curtains, duvet covers, sheets, pillow cases and blankets, is affected by the state of the housing market since demand is greatest from new house owners. The made-to-measure sector of the industry is in decline due to the increased range of sizes of ready made curtains and available in shops and other small retail outlets (**Fig 8. 2**).

According to the UK industry classification, light manufacturers are highly segmented along the following product lines: -

Figure 8.2 Product Lines of Light Manufacturing in the UK

Antiques Bathroom
Retail Carpets and
Flooring Furniture
Retailer Gates and
Fencing Home
Accessories Home
Furnishings Hot
Tubs/Spas Interior
Design Lighting
Tiling Contractor

(Source: Light Manufacturers, DTI, 2005)

At the beginning of the 21st century, Government sought to enhance competition in the industry by broadening the scope for technical competence and vocational excellence. Driven primarily by market forces coupled with persistent underperformance, the authorities developed specialist centres of excellence to improve and support manufacturing businesses, and through the DTI, a network of technology institutes, manufacturing centres and centres of expertise in skills and training has been developed linked to university departments with particular manufacturing expertise.

Textiles and Clothing

The UK has a buoyant textiles industry with more than 3,000 firms operating across the country with exports worth £1.35 billion (2005 estimates). Although the main growth is around technical textiles, smaller companies have shown that innovation can bring about increased prospects for growth and development. Like other segments of the manufacturing sector, the textiles and clothing market is highly segmented – children, adults, professionals, sport persons, the elderly, retailers and other organisations provide either brokerage services or one-to-one consultancy services. The industry is faced continuously with tough competition from abroad, mainly from the Far East, India and Europe (Italy and Portugal).

And yet there are limitless opportunities, as the success of British Caribbean women show. One particular area is the baby market where Janet Theodore won the *British Innovators and Inventors Award* for developing a novel baby-feeding product with a difference. The West Yorkshire-based mother also has a previous creation, the Little Eaters Suit and Art Suit. The suits marketed as an all-in-one protective garment, are used to shield clothing at meal times and messy art play in nursery and schools, are available at Boots, John Lewis and other outlets. Indeed, Theodore's pioneering endeavours captured both the British invention and baby clothing market (**Minicase 8. 4)**

Textiles manufacturing and dress making are traditional industries that

Caribbean people have perfected. The first generation of Caribbean nationals for example, made a living by making dresses for private customers, usually for weddings and other special occasions. Designs were chosen from fashion books, magazines and/or were produced exclusively for customers.

The cost of this service varies according to affordability; that is, the ability to pay. Even less well off customers however are usually willing to pay extra when celebrating weddings, anniversaries and other social engagements involving family and friends.

However, there has been a slow take-up of this trade by younger British Caribbean folks. Apart from the social pressures associated with commercial and industrial initiatives, the main problem is that the demand for dressmaking services in recent years has suffered due to the shift in consumer preferences from expensive formal wear to casual clothes and classic fashions. Most Caribbean dressmaking businesses operate from home and on a part-time basis with little attention paid to macro market trends.

Consequently, the challenge is to research the market carefully and pit one strengths and knowledge against the specific (product) sector and allocate the necessary resources accordingly. Jamaicans - George and Cynthia Martin – are in the soft furnishings trade; they built the business organically for several years. In spite of a small operation, the business couple concentrate on high quality products at affordable prices, matched by consistency and style. Individual households, retail outlets and professional groups, as well as other consumer groups represent a long line of loyal customers who placed orders, frequently.

Indeed, the experience of the Martin family is not unusual, particularly amongst first generation Caribbean settlers, who countered racial discrimination by utilising their creative skills and (clever) adaptation of the British consumer market to develop products and services in niche markets. Unknown to many, the Martins combine their love of light manufacturing with food catering for two annual cultural events - the Notting Hill Carnival and the Glastonbury Festival. According to Martin,

Enterprise should have no boundaries, once you have the skills, the strength of commitment and the resources you can be the best you can. I started out operating an auto garage, then I went on to own a few shops and later, we started making curtains and blinds for retailers and private individuals (**Martin 2004**).

Minicase 8. 4 Tip Top Kids

Janet Theodore's passion for children has spawned a lucrative business that has already earned her company recognition from business peers and industry insiders after a few years of trading (established in 2004).

As a partner in **Tip Top Kids**, she has managed to penetrate a niche market that caters for the needs of parents and children alike. Her product differs from other producers in two ways; firstly, it allows young babies to lay in the foetal position close to their mothers where it feels most protected, and secondly, it features a protective blanket attachment that allows mothers to protect their privacy while breast feeding in public.

Similar to other businesses, Tip Top was faced with financial hurdles - initial capital investment - but with support from a personal business mentor and courses on business planning and accounting, she overcame this setback. "Running a business is new to me as my background is teaching. Without the necessary cash flow, it is hard to move to the next stage and one has to grow carefully", Theodore declared.

So having raised the barriers, how does Theodore view the future of her company? "Our sights are on conquering new frontiers. We hope to seek the world for products from inventors and develop them under our umbrella, at no cost to them and we'll provide distribution channels directly to the retail chain." (***The Voice* 2005**)

Motor Trades

Often described as the 'automotive' and vehicular' trades, the motoring industry is very complex and represents a range of engineering, machining and other technical sciences. In 2004, the automotive industry was estimated at 8.5% of the total manufacturing sector with the sales volume of rising from about just over £5 million in 1995 to £50 million nine years later. This increase resulted from consumer demands for vehicles, bodies, parts, tyres and other components **(ONS 1995-2004).**

There are more than 25 million cars on UK roads and the garage servicing industry is worth approximately £9.8 billion per year; that is around £350 per car. It is also said that the cost of shoddy repairs is estimated to cost drivers £170 million per year. There is no definitive estimate for the British Caribbean auto trades, but according to the UK Black Business Directory, the majority of firms tend to be involved in motor repairs, maintenance. Some are described as 'car centres', 'motor engineers' and 'auto centres'. Their work is strictly around bodywork, repairs, installations, test-drive runs, electricals, check-ups such as tyre-fixing, engine cleaning and other vehicle maintenance tasks. The Office of Trading has had 1.3 million complaints a year for poor workmanship from mechanics.

Trinidadians, Harry Singh and Seu Dyal Emrit, were experienced mechanical engineers who owned garages for over 20 years in London and were successful businessmen before retiring. Both men built sound businesses and their achievements were founded on:

- Quality customer care;
- Efficient and effective use of technology applications;
- A cost effective pricing system;
- The use of family networks; and
- Knowledge of the industry.

On the one hand, Emrit worked with a reputable auto shop and he used the exposure to develop his own business and pass on the experience to young mechanics. Singh's popularity, on the other hand, was noticeable among various communities in London and he created links with other garage owners to share best practice. "*We had a motto which said that all customers should be treated as part of an extended family. Our service was guaranteed by fairness, attention to detail and identifying proper solutions. We had to learn about the make up of every vehicle and offer advice to owners on licensing and insurance matters, and maintenance check-up periods.*"

Although both men didn't generate tens of millions from their trade, they set `gold standards' in the automobile industry for others to follow. Singh continues offering one-to-one advice to young engineers and entrepreneurs in other occupations. He admitted that car maintenance and the repair trade are both competitive because of new technology and the choices customers can make today.

A current trend in the car servicing market has been towards component replacement instead of repairs. As parts become more technically complex, the cost of labour needed for repair is too expensive compared to the cost of replacing the faulty part. This trend in part replacement has encouraged the start-up of specialist vehicular shops in the Caribbean community which focus solely on just one or a small number of component replacement parts at a lower cost (**Singh 2001**).

Paul Tate, who is a member of the second British Caribbean generation community, has operated **Paul's Auto Services** for nearly 10 years in Harrow. His firm provides all types of mechanical and electrical work and is dedicated to ensuring that clients are not frustrated by poor service. In 2004, he joined over 50 firms to form a local business network in Brent to support firms in accessing contract opportunities generated from the Wembley Stadium development programme and surrounding regeneration schemes. Tate's business success is measured by:

- Frequency of client visits to the garage;
- Knowledge of changing trends in industry;
- Quality of clients;
- Customer feedback about services;
- Advice from other businesses; and
- Level of turnover per year.

Owners of other surviving engineering firms made the point that offering an excellent service was critical to public image and market stability. Here are a few quotes taken from interviews with, and observation studies, at workshops/garages during my research into the (ethnic) motoring trades during the 2000-2006 period:

- *Starting this garage was as difficult as they come, no one was interested in helping me to finance the business; many people thought it was a no-go area for us - (***Auto Shop dealer).**
- *It was not easy, even members of my family felt I could not do it, but I believed in my ability and experience and having worked with a large company, I knew if they could do it, I could do the same and even better. Of course, if I didn't have my redundancy package and savings, there is no way I could have started and be here today* - **(Garage Owner).**
- *I thank God for my parents, they gave me a lot of support – none of the banks didn't want to know and even when I produced my business plan, they kept asking whether I was confident that the business would last for the first year. If I wasn't blessed and believed in perseverance, the bank would have won* - **(Auto shop Owner).**
- *You cannot succeed in running an auto garage shop if you don't plan carefully, make sure you know what the requirements are such as the right tools, equipment and the technology. You have to know much about the area you are going to be based and try and find out something about the customers. You need a proper plan with an alternative strategy in case the original plan fails. I was fortunate to be exposed to a large industrial firm and the*

> *manager taught me the basics and encouraged me to be always flexible, and so when I started my own firm, it was a lot easier. I got a bit of help from the bank because I looked different* - **(Car Garage Owner**).

The engineering industry is broadly defined to encompass the electro-technical sector; namely, electrical, electronic and mechanical industries, from capital power equipment to wiring accessories. It also touches on other areas such as `materials and engineering. There have been few inventions in recent times but in the late 1990s, the industry had the chance to reinvent itself.

Former Jamaican and West Indies opening batsman, Ron Headley, put away his bat to begin an industrial engineering career when he discovered the `*Ecocharger*', a device aimed at lowering emissions and bettering the performance in motor vehicles. If history is worth comparing, then Headley is probably in the league of African-American inventors - Madame C.J. Walker (the hot comb), Granville T. Woods (telephone transmitter), Elijah Mc Coy (lubricator cup) and Garrett Morgan (the gas mask).

Interestingly, it was during his break with cricket that Headley's idea was revealed. He worked as a car salesman and took time off to work on his discovery. Prior to that, he spent 20 years and over £1 million in perfecting his invention. When the banks refused to support him, he turned to friends in the sporting world - ex-cricket captain, Clive Lloyd and footballer, Cyrille Regis. Headley's company, **Headley Diesel Services**, has since attracted thousands of customers, including motor companies.

The Ecocharger is a cleaner diesel engine emission system which improves the performance of diesel cars because it reduces smoke emission, and according to the Caribbean industrial pioneer, "It works on the fuel before combustion, so there is no need for a catalytic converter to clean up the exhaust afterwards." In effect, his invention was a significant contributor to the 'breathing cleaner air campaign'. Headley was awarded a British patent in 1985 for his industrial feat.

Cultural Production

The UK cultural industries sector is constantly evolving as minority entrepreneurs display talent in creativity and adaptation to various product lines available in the market today. From costume designs, educational products and greetings cards to leather craft products, British Caribbean entrepreneurs have developed useable commodities that have influenced consumer's choice.

There is an evolving group of (second generation) entrepreneurs who are experimenting with handmade toys - glove puppets, dolls and children's furniture – and these goods are sold in high street outlets at affordable prices. There is likely to be a high level of artistic input, with toys well designed, original, skillfully decorated and finished to a high level of quality. Most of the trade can be found in UK Regions.

Other items for children such as board games, puzzles and skittles are also part of the British Caribbean contribution to light manufacturing, with a cultural touch, and as the Nubian Jak merchandising showed, there are no holds barred in the field of cultural products (**Minicase 8. 5**).

Minicase 8. 5 Nubian Jak Limited

Jak Mr Bubeula-Dodd owns **Nubian Jak Limited**, the largest company of its type in Europe. The company specialises in multi-cultural 'edutainment' concepts, providing for a balance for the ethnically diverse global village. Nubian Jak is the award winning board game which combines amazing pop trivia with historical achievements and facts. Prior to its official launch at Toy '95 (UK) the concept had already attracted an underground cult following and also fascinated the British media. The product was featured on the *BBC News, 11th Hour* and *Channel 1 News*.

Nubian Jak was recommended by the industry magazine, *Games and Puzzles*, as one of the top ten new games for that year and has since been dubbed "the most original board game concept of the 1990s". In 1996 a "*World Edition*" was introduced in New York and it created interest among (New York) African Americans.

Since 1995, the company has produced 4 editions of the game (European, World, Nu Millennium and International Anniversary Edition) selling over 115,000 to date. The firm also has the Americanised edition of the game distributed in the US by Temple Games.

In addition, Nubian Jak has set up a charity to honour famous people of BME descent. To date, plaques have been procured to commemorate Bob Marley at his first London home in Bloomsbury; Bicentenary (Slavery)Plaque in Luton Town Centre, Ignatius Sancho at the Foreign Office and Mary Prince, University of London.

With a small team and a turnover of about a million pounds, Nubian Jak is set to scale new heights in the cultural market. As a multi-talented artist, Dodd is a singer/songwriter, the medium most natural to him in expressing his creativity. He was born in London during the 1960s to parents from the Caribbean but was raised by his evangelist grandmother. He was leader of *The Conquerors,* a church band that gave him the chance to develop his musical creativity. His achievements are based on these guiding principles: -

- Follow your instincts and plan carefully;
- Never be fooled by initial success;
- Use faith as a guide;
- Work with like-minded people to succeed;
- Deal with differences through compromise;
- Say no to defeat and negativity;
- Strive to maintain dignity in failure and success;
- Confront challenges with determination;

- Never stop planning even when you think you've succeeded;
- Learn from other business experiences; and
- Develop strengths to cancel out weaknesses.

Product Value

Perhaps the most distinguishing feature of segmentation among minority firms, are owners broad appeal to both their communities and mainstream. In almost textbook fashion, owners have developed unique selling points in a range of products and services. By developing a self-made product-type differentiation based on cultural innovation, owners can and do influence their firms' chances of improved market share whilst generating tidy profit margins. Available business literature seldom mentions this important marketing feature.

The firms profiled in this book including light manufacturing entities, demonstrate a proactive customer strategy, a fact evident in the way products and services are advertised and promoted, either through informal or formal channels of communication. Cultural knowledge is a prized asset of most British Caribbean entrepreneurs and instinctive to their overall survival strategy in the UK. Using anecdotal evidence, this author sampled a group of entrepreneurs whose commercial success is hinged on marketing the unique selling point (USP) of firms.

The USP is critical to the image of firms operating in highly competitive markets. This marketing technique helps customers to make informed choices based on product knowledge. The unique selling point is also the centrepiece of marketing strategy since distribution and sales are built on the volume of particular brands sold, either as core products or value-added commodities especially for loyal customers.

Product features should be clearly defined and explained to customers via shop front advertising, industry media and a selection of personal selling including door-to-door advertising and promotion campaigns.

This makes it easier for customers to understand product features and enables business owners to offer additional inducements at discount prices (**Table 8. 2**).

Table 8.2 The Unique Selling Point of British Caribbean manufacturing segments

Business	Sector	USP
Cleone Foods	Food	The brand Island Patties is a definitive Caribbean segment of traditional patties (food) because it is now a feature of British cuisine.
Nubian Jak	Educational games	Fusing arts and culture to create games for educational purpose to satisfy the demands of a growing multi-cultural consumer market.
Midian International	Health	The AGATHA toothbrush with twin-features; cleaning solution and a waste disposal process that meets the needs of patients and the dental care industry as a whole.
Tip Top for Kids	Clothing	The brand Tip Top is a brilliant invention in the baby clothing market, featuring a protective blanket attachment that allows mothers to preserve their dignity while breast-feeding in public.

(Source: Adapted from information and case study material in this chapter)

Enterprise Battle Plan

Despite the fact that manufacturing appears to be underperforming according to national indicators, there are trends that suggest growth in key segments due to future regeneration schemes across the UK. Importantly, with the industry giving way to a rapid services sector, both areas will be competing for more gains than losses in the near future. In the main though, Caribbean firms have opportunities in the light manufacturing, soft furnishings, cultural industries, food and drinks, engineering, textiles and the educational materials market (books and other literature). The increase in technology products also provides a lucrative opportunity, but in all of this, owners and managers need to craft an effective battle plan to stay in contention and at best, to compete against major firms.

Every business must have a strategy to maintain a strong position in the marketplace of ideas, goods and services. And since industrial activities are underpinned by people, technology and consumers, plans have to be tailored to take into account these dynamics. The `battle' plan suggested here for Caribbean producers, is based on principles and practices that are applicable to even some of the most competitive industrial sectors in the UK.

- *Ideas Mapping* – this refers to discussing product ideas with friends, industry specialists who are knowledgeable about markets. This process helps to weigh the pros and cons of ideas-testing to determine whether the customary `gut-feeling' alone, is enough for the success of an invention or innovative product.
- *Pre-testing* – ensures that any new product is checked thoroughly for faults in durability, style or design; and in the case of non-industrial products, tough competition can affect successful market entry. There might be other factors too in the equation.
- *Business Start-up* – the founder and owner needs to be clear about the type of sector or segment he/she is operating and the notion of an organisation structure, materials and equipment, location and quality personnel, are among some of the critical areas to be considered from the outset. Understanding the competition too is very vital for a lasting presence in the market.
- *Premises and Location* – as stated above, there are important to image, reputation and the various organisation processes that relate to any industrial concern. It is advisable to look for areas that are accessible to customers and the wider public. If for

example, the area has no parking facilities, then the potential for (brisk) passing trade can be hampered by frustrated customers.

- *Operating Costs* – start-up costs such as labour, shipping and other essential expenses should be kept within budget though however, exporting costs might be incurred as a result of strikes, shipping problems, political crisis and other unpredictable circumstances.
- *Competent Evaluation* – for any new product, obtaining an expert evaluation can turn a potentially failed innovation into a successful one. For instance, developing an idea around an industrial product can prove costly from the point of view of filing a patent with the proper authorities and moving into full scale production.
- *Management Control* – a management control system ensures that the right things are done since its purpose is to provide staff with accurate information to make proper decisions, as well as correct weaknesses in approved policies, procedures or practices.
- *Quality Control* – allows for products and services to meet the right specification or requirement. Poorly made products can cause producers to lose customers and when orders are delayed, inventory piles up and this affect cash flow.
- *Promotion* – owners should give priority to the setting up of an efficient sales and marketing team before actual production starts, since from industry experience, sales are the lifeline of a company.
- *Customer Feedback* – is essential to the operations of any firm since a two-way flow of communication enables confidence-building and client trust. By inviting feedback from customers, the market share of the business can grow appreciably. The use of telephone interviews, mailshots to test product knowledge and warranty surveys are all workable methods.
- *Manufacturing Network* – involvement in a flexible and reputable manufacturing network offers tremendous opportunities to share ideas, experiences and even future strategies. The network can

also provide valuable advice on administrative functions such as staff recruitment, account reporting systems and purchasing from syndicated suppliers.

- *Monitoring* – constantly monitor and evaluate every department and unit of the firm; conduct a routine appraisal of the business plan to compare and contrast target failures or achievements.

Undoubtedly, the continued success of British Caribbean manufacturers is linked to their determination to develop new `strands' of learning by innovation, understanding various layers of world-wide legislation underpinning the sector and maximising opportunities for the creation of personalised markets that require a cultural touch and also those akin to the plurality of UK consumers as a whole. Thus far, this chapter has hinted at some of the challenges and opportunities which manufacturers will have to deal with in their attempts to keep pace with 21st century global standards.

Table 8. 3 demonstrates the challenges which small producers have to confront, as well as growth opportunities that exist to secure greater revenue and maintain comparative market share levels. Each segment is a growth area of manufacturing in the UK and it illustrates how important it is for operators to understand and value the varying market forces that could either create success or failure, based on the type of strategies implemented.

The competitive profile of the British manufacturing sector is vital because it provides the basis for targeting key sections in the production chain of any industry. In almost every segment, producers have to consider too, the volume of regulations from the EU, Britain or other international bodies dealing with patents, copyright and other regulations.

The need to focus on the impact large companies, department stores and specialist wholesalers have on the industry should not be underestimated. Consumer confidence such as purchasing power and choices made on luxurious goods such as manufactured products is also a key consideration in developing and promoting a new idea for product innovation.

Location is paramount because it determines the volume of trade, the level of accommodation or room to store materials, equipment and manufactured goods. Suitable and affordable premises are essential to house various administrative and other operational units of the business. If both premises and location are unfit, this situation can have a negative impact on the image of the organisation and cause the business to lose market share quickly because of a reduction in the expected volume of customers for a new product or service.

Additionally, research and development is necessary to all other functions within a firm (more particularly to do with manufacturing). Owners and managers cannot afford to `penny-pinch' this resource. Why? Most large manufacturers are frequently monitoring the market to discover trends in customer behaviour, demographic changes, distribution and supply chains, trading regulations, tariffs, developments in the domestic, commercial and housing market, as well as long-term investment strategies for the UK. These companies target members from minority communities who spend on luxurious products such as cars, home appliances and high-tech gadgetry.

Tapping into strategic networks is also important - British Caribbean firms can access training opportunities, information and advice on product development, coupled with regulations on other market trends, either through a sharing of experiences or formal sessions involving a network of industry segments **(Table 8. 3)**.

Dilemma versus Reality

In the more advanced areas of manufacturing such as biotechnology, chemicals, pharmaceuticals, aerospace and steel production, the barriers to entry are quite high and with a shortage of scientists and technical engineers, British Caribbean entrepreneurs find it increasingly difficult to maximise opportunities which these areas offer – both nationally and internationally. Students should be encouraged to pursue careers in science and technology and while more young people tend to be more computer savvy than adults, very few under-25s have recognised the various benefits of optimising modern technology (applications) for the world of business and industry.

There is little motivation for students attending college and university to think that far, particularly if they are considered too 'bright' or too independent-minded. The scale of prejudice against young Caribbean boys (attending secondary schools) in particular is so overwhelming, that their interest in scientific and technological issues is almost zero.

Expert opinion on this issue is divided on the basis of belief versus experience and interpretation. For the greater part, views are influenced by negative stereotyping of young people (of all races and cultures) by the mass media and amidst all this, the situation remains confused even to the most enlightened and or/ open- minded person. Barbadian-born Malcolm Cumberbatch, a specialist in economic affairs and social enterprise development, was part of a Loughborough University team that conducted a three-year national European-funded black business research project. He observed that the experiences of the Caribbean community differed from one to another and that facts and figures can't always explain the gulf between the (many interested in) social and (the few who are attracted to) natural sciences. He went on to make other compelling points:

We need to reinvent ourselves by developing and maintaining a learning excellence culture. We must sustain a constructive agenda in order to sufficiently exploit opportunities in the labour market, including operating our own businesses. One of the reasons why we have so few natural scientists could be the result of the choices some have made to pursue non-science courses at higher education institutions. Social welfare is a priority for many and this is *prevalent in areas where public officials describe communities experiencing `economic deprivation' and `social exclusion', as well as statutory agencies that claim repeatedly, that we are hard-to-reach. On the one hand, these situations lend themselves to welfare dependency and provide a backdrop to the way some react to learning and development. On the other hand, there is another group from the same community who believe in wealth creation as a vehicle towards removing unemployment, poverty, ignorance and lack of social status. These people are determined to make good of the opportunities on offer. There is need to investigate further, the probable cause for some young Caribbean people not engaging in economics, engineering, medical technology and the biosciences in particular* (**Cumberbatch 2007**).

Table 8.3 Competitive Profile of the British Caribbean Manufacturing Sector

Segment	Challenges	Opportunities
Clothing	Stronger competition from established companies, start-up costs may be prohibitive depending on the trade volume and location.	Diverse markets, personalised products that are affordable with back-up services.
Industrial Design	Larger firms with in-house design linked to departments and difficulty in striking a balance between good design and affordability.	The human factor is still important; operators can benefit from new technology and market innovation.
Food Production	Competition from other ethnic foods, food regulations and linking price with quality and consistency.	Skilled labour, technology and customer care can guarantee favourable returns.
Soft Furnishings	Competition in lower/middle end of market with large ready-made suppliers Harvey's/ Shopper Direct.	Growth in housing market, changing market trends, mail order targeting regular clients.

Textile	Sub-divided into smaller specialist groups, dominated by producers & label retailers Marks and Spencer, BHS, Littlewoods and John Lewis.	Links with local retailers and large manufacturers keen on buying from small operators.
Auto Shop	Independent maintenance and repair shops, fast-fit outlets, auto centres and franchised dealers who provide long warranty periods to car buyers.	Concentrate on niches, highly specialised work in one or two auto parts at lower cost, location is vital.
Leather Craft	Small and larger manufacturers who supply to large department stores and specialist shops with hand bags and other leather products.	Display shops to promote goods, advertise in Yellow Pages and local trade press, organise cultural and trade shows.
Cultural Products	Competition exists with established and reputable firms on the high streets; equipment can also be pricy and location too is critical.	Small producers can take advantage of cultural knowledge of communities, link with quality products, pricing and innovation.

(Source: Analysis of firms, 2000-2007, UK)

Nonetheless as was mentioned earlier in this chapter, there are positive signs of British Caribbean firms making advances in manufacturing and related production. Even though they relate to existing industries, independent research confirmed the likelihood of greater segmentation by firms in the near future.

Besides, food manufacturing is a specialist area covering herbal foods, drink (liqueurs and softer beverages), pastries and other condiments. The seasoning industry is a growth area and Caribbean food producers are capitalising on the British consumers' newly acquired taste for spices. The conflicting nature of the personal care sector sends mixed signals to operators, consumers and experts alike, but sampled data can usually provide some evidence about this highly segmented trade (and growing). Beauty products are the lowest on the British Caribbean manufacturing `radar' and yet evidence shows that there is much interest among operators to set up mini-factories to produce different brands of beauty products to complement their existing businesses.

In addition, there is a general perception and growing suspicion that other minority groups are cashing in on the popularity of black hair care products by appealing to low-pricing methods and bulk product inducements, whilst targeting African and Caribbean consumers who are not always in a position to pay for products sold at black beauty shops and salons. Yet, the value of the black hair care products is estimated at £46 million with Caribbean firms netting only 10% of the market that they, as consumer dominate. As was stated earlier, operators should form alliances within and across industry segments and develop proper distribution and supply (retail) chains in order to benefit from economies of scale; that is, reasonably priced products and accessories in the personal care sector.

Conclusion

This chapter examined the important role of British Caribbean firms to manufacturing and trades in the UK, showing its complexity and scientific nature by using combined methods of investigation to access relevant information and data. Interviews were conducted to test and verify factual accuracy on technical issues from an operational perspective. Observation studies were carried out also, to obtain a broader picture of issues and subject areas; namely, the composition of firms, organisational procedures, performance levels, customer relations, pricing strategies, production techniques and inter-personal relationship between owners, their staff and public authorities.

Information was also obtained from published sources – the press, websites, conferences and workshops, seminar papers – as well as collaboration with business leaders and enterprise networks. Of relevance, is the low level of representation in science, engineering and technology (SET) by Caribbean professionals. The Royal Society confirmed that less than one percent is involved in the sector, although when white scientists or technologists are excluded from the data, the evidence shows that Caribbean specialists represent up to 10% of the total minority represented in the industry. One year after the Royal Society study, a report published by the university of Warwick revealed that 2.3% of 'black' Caribbean professionals were represented in SET professions.

One of the UK's respected African chemical engineer, Dr. Elizabeth Rasekoala, is the founder of the **African Caribbean Network for Science and Technology** lamented the brain drain from the developing world and said that, 'In the UK, you have a huge over-reliance on importing highly skilled technical people from many developing countries, so this is making it very difficult for black people here to achieve education and skills (**BBC 2005**).

More specifically, data was compiled using numerous business samples obtained from consultancies involving performance audits and reviews, case studies, business planning sessions and information obtained from different segments of the industry, all in an effort to ensure factual accuracy and data efficiency, as humanely possible.

Judging from published labour market information (LMI), it is obvious that British Caribbean manufacturers and trade operators are not included in the body of national statistics. It is the case that their limited size and narrow composition, does not offer incentives for public mention and yet, this chapter demonstrated small, but significant trends among entrepreneurs who were determined to pursue their goal of financial independence whilst nurturing the unwritten aim of contributing to their communities and by extension, the UK economy.

It is hoped that this book will fulfil a long-held prophecy that the resourcefulness of the British Caribbean community should be celebrated, as more than just a pastime. Tony Wade of Dyke and Dryden and Dounne Alexander of Gramma's Herbal Foods received MBEs for their selfless contribution to industrial development (in beauty care and food respectively). By their example, the prediction of a dynamic group of manufacturers and trades operators in the Caribbean community may not be a pipe dream after all. In the next chapter there will be further evidence of entrepreneurs creating growth through innovation and an intelligent application of cultural knowledge to attain appreciable levels of market share in another highly segmented industry, food.

Chapter Notes

Manufacturing – remains a fundamental part of the UK economy, and the composition of the industry has changed due to demands by customers, modern technology and the overall impact of globalisation.

Diversity – Cleone Foods is an example of cultural diversity, employing Britons, Indians, Pakistanis, Bangladeshis and Caribbean staff who help to produce more than 100,000 patties per week.

SET – the reasons for the under-representation of Caribbean professionals in the science, engineering and technology sector is unknown. The **African Caribbean Network for Science and Technology** which is located in Manchester, is a national programme that encourages young people in the black community to show a greater interest in the science and technology including its vocational, educational, commercial and related benefits. Dr. Rasekoala has urged the government and media to prove more positive images of black people in the sciences, since these have an impact on young minds.

AGATHA – the oral hygiene invention remains a challenge for Timothy Stewart whose endeavours are based on securing guaranteed funding while maintaining a market presence in the modern world of dental care.

'Midlander of the Year' – an annual award, recognising people deemed to have made an outstanding contribution to the social, sporting, political or cultural life of the English Midlands. Clyde Pile is a recipient of this accolade.

Industrial Enterprise Careers – there are several opportunities for the graduate market regarding manufacturing segments including these positions: aeronautical engineer, distribution/logistics manager, electrical engineer, industrial/product designer, manufacturing engineer, mechanical engineer, process engineer, production manager, quality assurance manager and sales executive.

Baby Products – Janet Theodore's baby products invention typifies the British Caribbean flair for enterprise and conquering new frontiers in face of enormous challenges.

Selected References

1 *Trends in UK Manufacturing 1997-2005*, Benchmark Research Ltd, January 2006.

2 *Sector Briefings, Manufacturing Sector*, Association of Graduate Careers Advisory Services (AGCAS), 2005, England.

3 'SET and the UK's ethnic minority population' contained in *Digest of Engineering* Statistics 2003/4- Technologist Data Annex, The Royal Society Report, July 2004.

4 'Black businesswomen blaze a trail for success', *The Voice* 10 October 2006 London.

5 Stovell, Cathy (2001): 'Hospital dental care takes high tech twist' and 'Inventor may clean up with new toothbrush', *The Royal Gazette*, 22 January 2001.

6 *Oral Hygiene and Toothbrushes* – UK, Mintel International Group Ltd, 2004: 2006.

7 *Future employment in the engineering sector*, Working Future 2006, SEMTA 2006, Spilsbury Research/SEMTA 2004.

8 Hall, Jennifer (2005): 'Janet's Tip for The Top, Inventor Janet Theodore is making big waves in the market for baby products', *The Voice*, 26 September

2005 London.

9 Robson, Stephanie & Ortmans, Laurent (2006): *Economics Trends*, Office for National Statistics, March 2006.

10 UK Clothing & Footwear, Insight Report, Key Note Ltd UK, 2001.

11 Whitehead, Emmy, Purdy, David and Mascarenhas-Keyes, Stella (2006): *Ethnic Minority Businesses in England: Report on the Annual Small Business Survey 2006 Ethnic Boost*, Small Business Services, March 2006.

12 'Lack of Black scientists', *BBC News,* 15 June 2005.

Chapter 9

The Food Market

Introduction

This chapter looks at the British Caribbean food sector and its contribution to the UK economy over the past 30 years. No amount of challenges involving scare capital for start-ups, high-cost premises, fierce competition from supermarket giants and food monopolies, as well as inadequate enterprise and technical support, have prevented entrepreneurs from having a presence in the UK ethnic food trade. In fact since 2002, the market share for Caribbean food businesses increased from 5% to around 10% according to the market research company, Mintel (**2006**).

Estimates suggest that, that on the one hand, the UK food and drinks sector generates sales of £70 billion per annum and employs close to 500,000 people. In 2004, exports totalled £4.9 billion and registered a 4% growth in the first six months of 2005. On the other hand, based on the annual spend, the ethnic food market is worth just over £5 billion **(World Food Market 2006).** Almost 9 out of 10 members of the ethnic population consider their cuisine as an important part of their lives. As this population increase at a faster rate, the ethnic food market is expected to grow by 25% by the year 2010. However, these statistics underestimate the true size of the market, since micro producers in particular, process ethnic meals from scratch using their home-based units – activities which are scarcely recorded in official figures, either regionally or nationally.

Market research shows that white Britons have grown accustomed to

Caribbean, Chinese and Indian food similar to European cuisine (be it French, Italian or Spanish and recently Polish) and some of the meals in these sectors are now regarded as staples. Although Chinese and Indian dishes are market leaders, Caribbean food has become popular due to the annual Notting Hill Carnival and other similar festivities across the English Counties. Since the early 1960s, this festival has attracted millions of visitors across the world. The enchanting aroma and flavour of food and intoxicating smoothness of spirits and liqueurs, add to the excitement. The organisers of the carnival advertised *A Taste of the Caribbean Notting Hill Carnival* this way: -

- 1 ton of chicken curry
- 1 ton of (Jamaican) patties
- 15,000 deep-fried plantains
- 30,000 corn on the cob
- 1 ton of rice and peas
- 12,000 mangoes
- 16,000 coconuts
- 5 million hot and cold drinks.

Alongside this `sumptuous hit list', were the following participant indices: -

- 7,500 participants
- 65 Masquerade bands
- 10 steel bands
- 12 Calypso singers
- 35 static sound systems
- 20 Soca sound systems **(2003)**

Trade Promotion

The principal growth segments of the food trade are bakery products, confectionery, beverages (alcoholic and nutritious types), groceries, restaurants, take-aways or catering units and food retail consultancy. Despite its size and composition, the British Caribbean food market is valued at around £200 million (**World Food Market 2006)**. In recent years, producers have showcased their products to a wider mass market and in so doing, benefited from increased exposure which has translated into a rise in consumer appeal. Founder-owner of the **Caribbean Food Emporium**, Dawn Grant, believes that marketing is essential for Caribbean food producers to gain competitive advantage.

Effective marketing needs to compete with core ethnic segments such as Thai and Indian food. At CFE, we believe that the Caribbean food and drink industry is one of the most important and vibrant segments of the rapidly growing ethnic food sector. For this reason and more, we are proud to host a dedicated Caribbean food pavilion at the show in November (**CFE 2006**).

As part of its promotion campaign, the Emporium organises yearly conferences and seminar workshops to discuss issues affecting this sector. Celebrity chefs, owners and food scientists are among those who address meetings of producers and consumers. The primary objectives of the annual Caribbean Food conference are to:

- Celebrate Caribbean food heritage
- Encourage, support and promote businesses involved in Caribbean food
- Raise the profile of Caribbean food in the UK
- Network and communicate between suppliers and consumers
- Celebrate the diversity of Caribbean food
- Encourage entrepreneurs to start Caribbean food businesses; and
- Assist businesses to exploit market opportunities (**2003**)

In addition, a leading food publication observed the growing popularity of Caribbean cuisine by pointing out its exotic nature and product originality. Andy Mc Creath of Enco Products said that:

As growing numbers of mainstream UK consumers seek out new, exciting tastes and flavours, authentic Caribbean food and drinks are finding a fresh, wider audience and a greater presence on the shelf in UK multiple grocery outlets. Enco Products Ltd, the most dynamic name in the country's rapidly emerging Caribbean market, is actively driving consumer awareness and sales of these products outside the core ethnic market, in key categories such as carbonated drinks, sauces, dairy and sea food (**2006**).

In keeping with increasing developments in the UK ethnic marketplace, this chapter will examine trends in the British Caribbean restaurant, manufacturing and importing business sector. Known for their home-made cooking, presentation and style, food retailers thrive on low budgets and members of staff are recruited on the basis of culture, experience and the ability to be self-supervised. Bakeries, groceries and restaurants are located on high streets and suburbs, fulfilling a vital need that cannot always be met by other food houses **(Figure 9.1).**

Figure 9.1 Profile of UK Ethnic Food Market

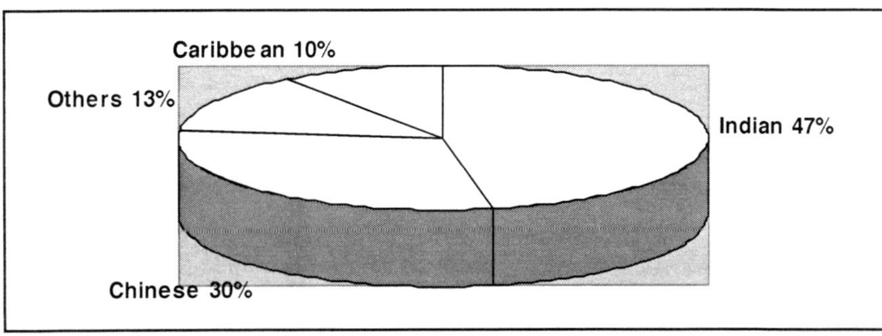

(Source: Keynote Report & Department of Trade and Industry, 2006)

Market Segmentation

However, the Caribbean food industry is largely segmented, with half of all retailing activities located in London and the Southeast, while less than half of all manufacturing and distribution operations in the Midlands and Northern Counties. Asian-Africans, Caribbean,

European and others trade in tropical produce, and almost in every inner-city area, supermarkets and greengrocer's trade in Caribbean special brands of food and beverages, as the information and data suggests:

- 50% of firms operate in London/Southeast
- 45% operate in the Midlands
- 5% are located in other parts of the UK
- 5% of firms export to Europe and North America
- About 30% of firms import raw materials from the Caribbean Region
- 70% of firms cash on in their country or origin's blends and distinctive tastes.

Whilst most Caribbean food enterprises are owned and managed by Jamaicans, other nationalities operate catering units, market stalls-type takeaways and personalised cooking services. For instance, raw materials for various products are imported from the Caribbean countries below, to satisfy a wide cross-section of the UK (mass) consumer market which has grown rapidly since the 1990s. The following is indicative of the importing countries and the products that originate from them: -

- *Barbados* – fruit juices from hilly areas
- *Bahamas* – cotton rum cakes – a famous recipe
- *Guyana* – herbal teas, sweetmeats, rum etc
- *Jamaica* – jerk seasoning, patties, buns, liqueurs, acckee and saltfish
- *Saint Lucia* – cooking utensils, decorative ceramics
- *Saint Vincent & The Grenadines* – food and drink imports
- *Trinidad & Tobago* – roti, curries, sauces and sweetmeats (**Table 9.1**).

Table 9.1 Major Suppliers and Manufacturers of Caribbean Food

Company	Description
Grace Kennedy (UK)	Leading international distributor and exporter of jellies, sauces, juices, meats, chocolate drinks and other drinks.
Walkerswood	First company to export Jerk Seasoning from Jamaica, over 15 Caribbean authentic sauces, spices, condiments and canned vegetables.
Wray & Nephew (UK) Ltd	Sole distributor of Jamaica's finest rums/premium spirits including international-award winning Overproof Rum, as well as Alize De France Red and Gold Passion.
Dees Caribbean Imports	Importers & distributors of non-perishable goods; ackee, callaloo, spiced bun, sauces and carbonated beverages.
Horizon Foods	Largest roti manufacturer in the UK and European market. Varieties include dhal phuri, aloo and paratha.
Enco Products Ltd	Portfolio brands comprise milk-based energy drinks such as Nurishment, along with Enco Hot Pepper sauces, Dunn's River ingredients and condiments and Mighty Malt tonic drinks.
Dalgety Caribbean Products	Highly flavoured herbal teas – peppermint, lemon, ginger, cerassie, lemon/fever grass. Dalgety also produces cassava and plantain chips (Minicase 16.1).
Cottons Rum Cake Ltd	Cakes are manufactured using the company's brand – made in The Bahamas from an authentic Caribbean recipe with the award-winning Don Lorenzo rum.
Sunrise Bakeries	One of the longest established ethnic bakers of breads, buns and cakes with a distinctive Caribbean flavour and taste.
Gramma's International Ltd	Manufacturers of herbal/pepper seasonings and sauces. Special brand of Zara's herbal tea (Minicase 9.2).
Cleone Food Ltd	Specialists in Caribbean patties, version of British pasty, filled with saltfish, vegetables, beef/halal meats (Minicase 8.1).

(Source: Caribbean Food Emporium, London 2006)

Generally, owners claim a certain speciality as their own. For Jamaicans, there is ackee and saltfish; Guyanese and Trinidadian food producers tend to reflect different dishes on their menu – Creole, African, European, Indian and Oriental dishes. Caribbean cooking has a distinct and unique flavour with an astonishing array of dishes: curried goat, mutton and chicken; crabs and lobsters; red beans and pigeon peas; meat or cooked fish in coconut milk or cream; black pudding and souse; rum and spices; macaroni pie and the list goes on. Other nationalities also exhibit the Caribbean's famous cuisine that combines the tastes of African, Amerindian, Chinese, Indian and European people respectively. It is for this reason why this sector of British industry should be carefully analysed in order to avoid a misrepresentation of the Caribbean contribution to the UK economy.

Geographic Location

Much of the information on ethnic foods is restricted to Chinese (Oriental) and Indian (Asian) cuisine with a token mention of Caribbean firms in the business of selling patties, condiments and beverages. In 1980, Rustie Lee who graduated from Birmingham College of Foods as a `master baker' and became a celebrity chef on television, opened her first restaurant, **Rustie's.** It became hugely successful and featured in *Britain's Good Food Guide*, and the BBC subsequently invited her to introduce Caribbean food to a wider audience. Since that time, Lenny Henry's *Chef* and Ainsley Harriot, *Ready Steady Cook* both highly acclaimed television programmes, have further stimulated consumer interest in Caribbean food.

There still remains though, a gap in the appreciation and understanding of this complex segment of the UK hospital industry. As was mentioned earlier, the industry is highly segmented across the country, including major cities and towns involving operations such as restaurants, private caterers, take-aways, groceries, manufacturers and retailers **(Table 9.2)**.

Table 9.2 Geographic spread of Caribbean Food in the UK

(Source: Independent Research, 2000-2007)

Regions	Towns/Cities
London/Southeast	All four sub-regions in London and Reading
The Midlands	Birmingham, Coventry, Derby, Dudley, Leicester
Yorkshire & Humberside	Blackburn, Leeds, Sheffield
North West	Liverpool, Manchester
South West	Bristol
Scotland	Edinburgh
Wales	Cardiff, Swansea
Ireland	County Down

The above figure illustrates the broad geographic spread of Caribbean food companies, representing more than 50% of the nine English Regions and an equal ratio of the entire UK combined. The annual turnover of this sector varies according to industry segments. The average restaurant generates a pre-tax revenue of £50- £100K and `middle-range' eating houses' generate roughly 75%% more of the total takings of the average eatery. Micro caterers earn less than £50K per annum but supplement their income with full-time employment. In effect, they invest a portion of their `paid' employment earnings into the business.

Conversely, due to the magnitude of their operations, food manufacturers accrue over £3 million per annum, with a healthy profit margin in excess of £100,000. Their products are exotic, original and demand-led and they maximise distribution and supply chains in co-ethnic markets; that is, buyers and sellers alike. Their main source of advertisement lies in the products they offer at affordable prices and quality customer service to match.

While researching this book, it was difficult to compute the total market share value of different segments of the British Caribbean food and drinks trade, but by using sampled data, estimates of industry segments were identified. This remains a critical area for additional scrutiny as the interesting work of **Caribbean Food Emporium** shows. By publishing success stories on the web coupled with regular networking events, the Emporium helped rekindle interest in the Caribbean food and drink trade in the UK (**Minicase 9.1**).

Minicase 9. 1 Caribbean Food Emporium

Founded in 1995, the **CFE** is the brainchild of British-born Caribbean entrepreneur, Dawn Grant, and since that period, the profile of Caribbean food and drink has been raised. The company publicises the work of producers, professionals and sector activities and collaborates with agencies and organisations to arrange yearly events such as the Food and Drink Conference and Exhibition. What was Grant's reason for setting up CFE?

It stemmed from the necessity for a holistic approach to Caribbean food in the UK. I was co-owner of a Caribbean restaurant and take-away in the early '90s and with an intense passion for ethnic foods, I was puzzled by the poor media coverage of an industry that we helped to define and develop. While researching on the Internet, I was also disappointed by the lack of information on this sector too, and I was determined to do something positive about it **(Grant 2002).**

The London-based businesswoman started the firm from scratch using an overdraft and other personal income, along with supplier credit. With a three-figure turnover, Grant stated that the volume of legislation and the compliance cost are challenges to the CFE. In an industry that is highly specialised, the retention of a small workforce and the frequent use of IT specialists and researchers to carry out `project-type' tasks, is of strategic benefit and value to the business, she observed.

She is convinced that `government funded business support', `enterprise education and training', `professional abilities and competence' and `general business advice' are essential to the survival and growth of Caribbean businesses. The strides that the CFE has made are both incredible and commendable and to date, it has weblinks with the *BBC, London Restaurant Guide; This is London, Black Britain* and *Blacknet*.

Seeking Opportunities

The food and drink industry is constantly evolving and as consumer tastes and interests change, the market adapts to meet such demands. Indeed, the requirement for ethnic foods in the UK over the past 30 years, begs the question; why aren't they more Caribbean food `houses' particularly since members of this community (first and second generation) are `relatively' good at catering and hospitality management? And even in spite of the proliferation of convenience foods, consumers still insist on `homemade-type' dishes to be served for the sheer pleasure and social interaction they provide. The adage that `variety is the spice of life' is therefore applicable to the food and drink sector, Caribbean-wise.

Contrary to media hype and sometimes inaccurate representation, Caribbean foods are rooted in spices and other condiments. The extensive ethnic composition of this community provides ample evidence of the degree to which caterers, restaurant owners and others in the hospitality sector, utilise a variety of peppers (chilli, black and white pepper and others) to `spice-up' dishes. For trained palates, curries, stews and other `gravy-type `meals are usually bland and `meaningless' if they are devoid of the correct application of (mixed) spices. The prevalence of *Jerk* seasoning and allied spices is proof of the creativity and versatility of the British Caribbean food sector in terms of its product range and the various uses of its `pepper or spice' ingredients (**Table 9. 3**).

Table 9.3 UK Market Share of pepper imports

Sector	1993 (£)	1995 (£)	1998 (£)	2002 (£)	2005 (£)	2007 (£)
Indian	171	205	240	274	308	342
Chinese	110	137	164	191	218	245
Mexican	45	52	59	66	73	80
Thai	20	25	30	35	40	45
Caribbean	10	20	30	40	50	55
Indonesia	7	9	11	13	15	17
Other	5	6	7	8	9	10

(Source: Understanding the Caribbean hot pepper market, Caricom Statistics, 1994-2006)

The above diagram illustrates the phenomenal increase in ethnic peppers to the UK from overseas with estimates ranging between 20% and 40% plus in the late 1990s to the present time. The estimates are based on actual imports in 1993-1995 and projections for 1998-2007. At the time of writing, the Caribbean market for peppers in the UK was expected to increase by 7%. Even so, the commercialisation of peppers and other spices is reflective of ethnic entrepreneurs, who when faced with restrictive practices such as racial prejudice and labour market discrimination, maximise their home-grown cultural ability to create both economic advantage thereby contributing to prosperous communities.

In terms of preparation, Caribbean food can be expensive than other ethnic dishes because of the nature of ingredients and supply costs. For example, Creole dishes vary from soups, to special stews and selected rice menus. Soups consist of ground provisions (cassava, plantains, eddoes, sweet potatoes etc), meat, vegetables and spices. Rice dishes comprise peas, vegetables and an assortment of meat(s). Bread, cakes and sweetmeats are produced on the basis of dough consistency and the balance between essences and spices.

One firm that pioneered the effective use of spices for both medicinal purposes and culinary delight is **Gramma's International Limited**. It is a market leader in the traditional herbal industry in an age where some consumers have seen the wisdom and necessity for `healthy' eating and drinking. To suggest that Gramma's may have contributed to this process of enlightenment could be perceived as an understatement judging by its success in the UK (**Minicase 9.2**).

Minicase 9. 2 Gramma's International Ltd

Dounne Alexander-Walker is founder-owner of **Gramma's UK Limited**, a company established in 1987 (in her Council flat), to manufacture hot pepper sauces and other herbal spices. Originally, her aim was to improve the quality of ethnic foods, whilst maintaining traditional herbal practices. The Trinidadian-born drew inspiration from her grandmother who was adept at herbal medicinal products – a renowned tradition of African and Caribbean societies respectively.

Initially, Walker had difficulty convincing medical authorities and health specialists about the invaluable `health properties' of her discovery even though she produced a potent herbal drink to cure the cancer of the family's pet dog, Zara in 1995. Other setbacks included lack of sufficient capital investment for research development, marketing and distribution activities. Her challenges were; firstly, to make a compelling case for Gramma's and its importance to the national health of Britain; secondly, to convince supermarkets of the importance of herbal products produced by a black firm; and thirdly, the limitations of operating from home.

Eventually, Walker's use of the media to launch a campaign to sensitise Britons about the importance of her discovery and its value to people suffering from illnesses, diseases and other medical conditions, paid rich dividends. Her company gained successful entry into mainstream markets - Fortnum and Mason, Harrods, Asda, Tescos and Sainsbury. The company's herbal seasoning became the first black food to receive `Jewish kosher' appeal and it is suitable for vegetarians, health conscious-people and weight-watchers.

With a healthy three-figure (yearly) turnover, the company has expanded production of herbal seasonings and a selection of herbal teas and drinks for diverse consumers. The provision of `health properties' through the use of herbal spices, is the unique selling point of Gramma's.

The pioneering British Caribbean firm has a definitive strategy and according to Walker, Gramma's will "*Expand market share by developing world class herbal food products; develop sounder technologies for further research in the field, coupled with stimulating young people in the food technology and manufacturing business, via mentoring, training and apprenticeship schemes.*"

It should be noted that prior to the establishment of Gramma's, Walker worked as a laboratory assistant and housing officer, and hence had practical experience in negotiating conflicts. After she learnt about market opportunities for herbal products, the next step was to convince the industry and lobby Government Ministers and officials, large companies, business networks and supporters to guarantee their support for the invention. In an effort to make her case consumer-appealing, she outlined multiple benefits of Gramma's products in this way:

- To create employment and job security;
- To improve food sales in the open market;
- To set up a herbal foods research centre;
- To boost quality in health food manufacturing;
- To help improve career prospects in the health foods industry;
- To provide complementary support to corporate Britain; and
- To strengthen racial harmony in the UK.

Beverage Industry

The UK food chain has a vibrant drink sector comprising manufacturers who produce different types of beverages that make up about 30% of all retailing activities in the industry. Expenditure on non-alcoholic drink increased by nearly 2% in 2003 as consumer demands resulted in a range of new 'brands' on the market. Increasingly, small ethnic firms with new products face tough competition in global markets and this could impact on their capacity for growth and sustenance. The issue of *Fair Trade* has meant that businesses operating in developing countries also have to operate on the basis of (strict) international standards; namely, quality control and compliance with a host of import/export regulations.

In the case of the Caribbean drink sector, some entrepreneurs have overcome this handicap by demonstrating innovation using their cultural heritage, and positioning their firms in diverse markets in the UK and elsewhere. Family-run firms especially, have capitalized on extensive networks involving personal contacts, `back-home' connections and business organisations to enter markets that were once the preserve of British and European conglomerates. One firm that is dedicated to global product excellence in the beverage segment is **Silverstone Tropical Foods**, with the owners sharing dual African and Caribbean heritage. The company was the recipient of the 2005 *International Business of the Year* award for its contribution to drink manufacturing. The UK-based family business began in 1996 and is managed by Nigel and Sonja Scantlebury.

The primary activity of the company is the sale of dried sorrel imported from West Africa and supplied to the UK and European consumers (Germany, Sweden and Austria in particular). The challenge for Silverstone is to change buyers' perception that sorrel drink `is a cold drink as opposed to one that can also be enjoyed hot, in tea form'. The Scantleburys emphasised that `many people are accustomed to having tea or coffee instead of the healthy benefits of a cup of hot sorrel'. This misperception of the product according to the owners, has led to inadequate support from lending institutions regardless of how `excellent our business plan is presented.' At the time of writing, the business was self-funded with product launches in Barbados, Jamaica and Saint Lucia. Plans are afoot for joint venture manufacturing in Senegal, West Africa, with additional plans to increase employment opportunities for local residents in North London through increased production. The firm is creating further opportunities for other Caribbean firms by introducing greater variety in the beverage market.

It is quite noticeable around the country that Asian firms supply the bulk of African and Caribbean food and this trend has presented a situation were there is undue pressure or dependency by (black) consumers to purchase commodities from Asian retailers thereby appearing disloyal to African or Caribbean businesses. Like other ethnic businesses, Asian suppliers enjoy a monopoly because of greater volume in their distribution and supply chains which contribute to seemingly lower prices for similar products sold by black retailers. Undoubtedly, such trend has a negative effect, leading to feelings of mistrust between Caribbean businesses and their customers. The saying that `money has no colour' is not always relevant when it comes to affordability, especially in markets where rivalry between buyers (products) and sellers (choice) collide. The owners of Silverstone have recognised this dilemma and responded by developing appropriate strategies to help other Caribbean producers to cope with this competition (**Figure 9.2**).

Figure 9. 2 Key business strategies for success

- Package community skills so that they become economically advantageous.
- Look for effective leadership in the community to support business excellence.
- Industry networks can break rival firms from exercising undue influence.
- Firms must campaign against restrictive practices in favour of `Fair Trade.
- There should be a balance involving social conscience vs. economic progress.
- Research markets by seeking information from industry specialists.
- Consult experienced and dedicated business advisers.
- Examine viable financial options before business start-up.
- Analyse strengths and weaknesses, be honest in business dealings.
- Cultivate effective business and social networks; and
- Develop a culture of learning to build on personal development.

(Source: Silverstone Tropical Foods, March 2005, London)

Championing Franchises

Franchising first became recognized in the UK during the 1970's, and according to the British Franchise Association (BFA), the total turnover of the franchising industry was estimated at £9.3 billion, with the number of businesses increasing by 3.6%.

The 27,000 individual franchised units in the UK have risen with total employment in the sector of more than 316,000 (**BFA 2005 estimates**).

In 2003, the BFA encouraged minority firms to maximise franchise opportunities in the UK "*The diversity of business sectors within the franchising industry makes it an accessible and realistic investment option for many groups that have a minority presence in business* (**BFA 2003**). The McDonald's fast food chain has been praised and ridiculed for being, on the one hand, an appropriate `business model' for franchising; and on the other, for being the `unacceptable face of American capitalism and culture' The evidence shows though, that the food giant's annual investment in the local economy and jobs, makes it a `good corporate citizen'.

Unlike other business communities, particularly Indian or Asian retailers, there is no official data on the number of British Caribbean-type franchise businesses in the UK. While it may not often be a vital consideration in terms of business start-up or expansion, they are plausible explanations as to why black entrepreneurs are not too keen to pursue this business arrangement. They lack technical experience, limited knowledge of franchising markets and the fear of risking slender resources on unknown ventures. Yet, information on growth prospects in key sectors like food, technology, professional services, healthcare, leisure and sports, is in abundance. And since supermarkets have discovered the opportunity and allocated more `fixture' space to Caribbean products out of their total world food and ethnic space, securing food and drink franchises can translate into greater sales and improved market share for minority entrepreneurs.

Described as the West Midlands Region's `*market champion*' for the Caribbean, Barbadian businessman Tony Sealey OBE, sits on public institutions in the West Midlands and encourages West Midlands companies to trade overseas. His exemplary leadership proves that for British Caribbean entrepreneurs, franchising can have tremendous impact in economic terms, as well as signify a considerable investment in communities. He provides the franchising (business) model for Birmingham, with two restaurants (in regeneration districts) that employ over 100 people, mainly young people and offer training programmes in catering, food preparation and presentation, customer care, money management and other skills required to operate an efficient restaurant.

Sealey described his business as `a conveyor belt. Kids will leave here and go and work for anybody – in good jobs.' He is convinced though, that McDonald's could do more to help disadvantaged communities and encourage minorities to take up franchises. From the perspective of hesitant members in the black community, the downside of franchises should not be confused with the advantages to be gained when enterprises are managed well. He agrees that franchising offers tangible benefits for ethnic businesses and their (local) communities than most critics would credit. Some of these benefits include: -

- *Better chance of Success* – research has shown that all businesses starting today, only 20% will be trading in 5 years time and with franchising these figures can be reversed.
- *A Proven Business* – with franchising an entrepreneur is buying into a business that is already operating. The franchisor will have made mistakes along the way and will have learnt from them. This knowledge is passed on as part of the franchise system. It enables one to start the business at a much higher point on the learning curve.
- *Organisational Support* – there is a great deal of help and support

available. From the start-up phase, the franchisee owner will receive training and will be reliant on the franchisor. As the new business becomes known, the owner will benefit from different types of support such as staff training. Opportunities to collaborate with other franchisees on larger projects are also likely.

- *Problem Solving* – the franchisors will provide the necessary technical support. However it is invaluable to be able to take things through with other franchisees, or the support team who may well have dealt with the same problem.
- *Management Support* – many franchisors hold review meetings to discuss all aspects of the business. The new owner will be able to check progress, celebrate successes and plan for the future. Experience has shown that many businesses have failed in the past due to lack of good business advice.
- *Product Research and Buying Power* – as part of a franchise network much of the product research and testing process will be carried out by the franchisor. It is also possible to take advantage of group buying discounts

All in all, the benefits of franchising arrangements tend to outweigh the disadvantage or the perception of failure as stated informally by sections of the black business community. If the success of this type of enterprise is anything to go by, then perhaps the only negation towards setting it up is the would-be franchisee (owner's) lack of knowledge, experience and lack of confidence and or mistrust in the processes involved in start-up. Such a notion of disadvantage that borders on the fear of failure should not be a problem since franchises are traditionally, ready-made businesses and known to have an excellent reputation and public image.

Grocery Trade

Like other UK industry segments, the grocery trade plays a vital role in national consumption patterns and is dominated by corporate entities which have up to 50% of the market. The top retail stores account for more than 80% of food sales with the largest chains being Tesco, Sainsbury's and Asda Stores. British Caribbean groceries have a relatively small share of the UK market that is equivalent to less than 2%, though in early 2000, the community's market share in peppers alone amounted to 3-4% (that is around £10 million to £20 million of the total product value imported into the UK (**Caribbean Agricultural Research Development Institute 2003**).

For the purposes of this chapter, two groceries have been selected; one in London and the other in the West Midlands because they mirror significant elements of supermarket chains in urban centres. Although both groceries vary in composition and size, their focus is on customer care, effective pricing strategy, proper location and courteous staff. **Lloyd's Groceries** (London) and **Russells Foods Trading Ltd** (Birmingham) have been preferred too, because they are most certainly, the longest surviving grocery outlets owned and managed by British Caribbean entrepreneurs who are inspired by a sense of family kinship and driven more so, by community self-help and pride.

Since 1978 when Lloyd's Groceries was set up, it has remained `a work in progress'. With a market share of 5% in the Brent area, the business continues to tick over, according to Lloyd Tate, founder of the family-owned shop. Below is a selected question and answer session carried out on the firm's premises in 2002.

- How many persons do you employ? 3
- What skills do your workers have? Customer care, supervisory and marketing.
- How many customers do you serve weekly? 200
- What is your average turnover per day? £700
- What is your greatest business expense? Business rates and refuse disposal.
- What are your views about the local council? Poor

- Which local services need improving? Premises, cleaning, advice/information.
- Who are your competitors? Other businesses like mine.
- How do you deal with competition? Reliability, customer care, business image.
- What problems affect your business? Lack of business support **(Minicase 9.3).**

Minicase 9. 3 Lloyd's Groceries

Lloyd Tate and his wife established the first Caribbean grocery shop in Harlesden, Brent in 1978. Apart from satisfying a `long-felt' desire for financial self-sufficiency, the overall aim of the Tates was to provide the black community alternative foods to meet their needs. Prior to setting up the business, Tate worked as a labourer and foreman with Wallis, the ice cream giant. His son Patrick co-manages the business and the other owns an auto shop in neighbouring Harrow.

The shop enjoys brisk trade from all sections of the community, attracting as much as 200 customers on busy days. On weekends and holidays, the number is greater. Neglected by years of mainstream support, **Lloyd's Groceries** now enjoy a measure of assistance from a local enterprise support initiative (2001-2004) as part of a neighbourhood renewal programme of Brent Council. So, what is Tate's formula for sustainability in the food trade?

As a family run business, we support each other in every way while emphasising on quality customer service. Harlesden is usually considered a poor area to live and run a business, yet we have shown, like others, that it is possible to succeed in both. If we maintain a disciplined management approach and continue focusing on building our customer base, we can achieve more. My greatest hope is to expand trade with the Caribbean Region. If we import more fresh produce here, we can strengthen trade relations between Britain and the Caribbean and create more jobs for a lasting prosperity **(August 2002).**

Russell's mini-supermarket is a household name in the city of Birmingham and the West Midlands and though surrounded by ever-increasing competition from other ethnic retailers, the business has grown from strength to strength. Similar to the Tate's grocery, Russell's is located in the heart of the regeneration district of East Handsworth. Elements of mystery shopping were used to obtain a reasonable view about the operations of the mini-supermarket including the customer base and the prevailing environment.

Expert-type observations were conducted for 20-40 minute intervals lasting up to four weeks and supported by informal `chats' with store assistants, along with shoppers' conversations involving the elderly, the young, professionals and the general `passing trade'. Interestingly, employees were of African, Caribbean and Chinese background.

The following information should therefore be regarded as a list of assumptions based on the research methods outlined above, methods of which are often applied when there are problems or barriers towards accessing factual information and data: -

- The turnover of Russell's appeared in excess of £150K per year.
- Purchases equated to roughly 100-200 customers daily, weekends more.
- The staff complement was roughly 12.
- The business had two sections – a grocery and butchery.
- A restaurant and bakery-takeaway were part of the supermarket.
- Most purchases were in excess of £20 at any one given time.
- Regular (Saturday) shoppers felt the supermarket had quality products.
- Over 40% of elderly Caribbean consumers appreciated the atmosphere.
- About a third visited the shop to enjoy social interaction with other shoppers.

- Customer care was premium with affordable prices set.
- The shop was accessible with the location said to `be just right'.
- Customer service was of a high standard and was valued by everyone. (**Independent Research: 2005-2007)**

If a ranking method was applied to both firms on organisational productivity, the London shop would receive 50-60% and the West Midlands-based outlet 70-80%. Although both shops vary in composition, size and operational profile, they provide consumer-led services. There was evidence suggesting a relatively high retention of staff according to the same number of `faces' present when visits were made to both shops. This was a firm indication of the commitment and dedication by staff to the business, especially supervisory and sales staff.

`Mother Nature' Trade

Between 2005 and 2006, television viewers had a rare opportunity to witness the ground-breaking efforts of Britain's lone Caribbean farmer, publicising the virtues of the farming trade to a group of youngsters who spent most of their lives in English cities. One of the programme details read like this:

Wilfred Emmanuel-Jones believes the British countryside is far too white, but he is on a mission to change that. This three part series follows Jones as he takes nine urban recruits on a life transforming journey on his farm in Devon. In a bid to reverse the segregation that has taken over the countryside and prevented ethnic minorities from settling outside urban Britain, Jones is launching a rural scholarship.

The Young ***Black Farmer*** *series documents the first batch of his rural rookies who spend the summer of 2005 living in a converted barn on his remote 30-acre farm and embarking on work experience placements in the local community* (**British Television 2005**).

Noteworthy, the Jamaican-born Jones' introduction of agriculture to deprived, inner city black and Asian teenagers is a scheme that is supported by Prince Charles. While agriculture represents about 1% of the total domestic earnings in the UK, it is of strategic importance to the economic, cultural and social well-being of the 60 million inhabitants in the country. It is this industry that provides commodities such as citrus, meats, vegetables and beverages. The UK Trade and Investment authority's recognition of Jones' contribution to brand innovation is a strong hint that farming remains a traditional and lasting enterprise in the 21st century (**Table 9. 4**).

The figure illustrates the value of agriculture to the food chain and although the UK's self sufficiency in `all food' was rated at 62% (**Defra 2003 estimates**), farmers and primary products imports were £18.7bn, with unprocessed food (£3.9bn), lightly processed food (£8.4bn and highly processed food (£6.4bn). In the second quarter of 2003, the agri-food sector provided a total of just fewer than 3.5 million jobs (equivalent to 14% of UK employees). The agricultural sector is defined in this book as forestry, fishing, livestock production, self- employed farmers, food enterprises and farmsteads.

Table 9.4 Sample of the UK Food Chain by employment and value

Sector	Enterprises	Jobs	Market Value
Catering services	104,200	1.4m	£67bn
Food and drink wholesalers	14,500	213,000	£8.8bn
Food and drink manufacturing	7,700	448,000	£19.3bn
Agricultural wholesalers	3,100	28,000	£675bn
Farmers and primary producers	303,000	550,000	£6.9bn
Fishing industry	4,200	18,000	£391bn

(Source: Department for Environment, Food and Rural Affairs – DEFRA – 2003)

There are thousands of allotments or home-gardens in the UK, a fraction of which are owned by older Caribbean residents. Therefore, Jones' ownership of a sizeable farm in the English countryside speaks volumes for the potential benefits others like him can derive. As an urban dweller who was born poor, his rise to `agricultural livestock' stardom is unique as his `*Fact File*' confirms below:

- 1957: Born in Clarendon, Jamaica, 1957;
- 1973: Joins the British Army;
- 1983: Accepted on the BBC Graduate Trainee Scheme;
- 1985: BBC producer/director;
- 1994: Founded food marketing agency Commsplus; and
- 2004: Launches `**Black Farmer'** range of farm produce.

His corporate products include brands of sausage varieties - *Premium Pork, Pork and Leek and Pork Onion and Chive* - and several delicious sauces, all of which are produced on his livestock farm in Devon. His brands are prominent in Asda stores in the Southwest. Jones' only experience of nature was working on his father's allotment weeding the sprouts and watering cabbages, but he had a dream that one day he would run his own farm. It took him over 30 years of hard work to fulfil that dream.

Notwithstanding the historic stigma that is associated with agriculture, due to slavery and colonialism which lasted more than 500 years in Latin America and the Caribbean, British Caribbean communities are aware of the difficulties plaguing the industry. Since the 1990s, these challenges have been discussed by the mainstream farming community.

For instance, the National Farmers' Union claimed that 99% of farmers were experiencing `the classic symptoms of stress' because of economic problems. The union's findings revealed that: -

- 62% of farmers had problems with record keeping and paperwork;

- 56% had difficulty understanding forms;
- 49% had problems arising from the effects of new legislation/ regulations;
- Nearly a quarter reported financial problems and were worried about money;
- Nearly a third had health problems which affected their work;
- 66% stated that their children weren't interested in the enterprise;
- 51% said that families hadn't taken a holiday over the last two years; and
- Over 70% had very low confidence in the survival of their businesses.
- 57% stated that they had considered quitting (**NFU 1999**).

Jones believed that his success was due to consumers who made `my business' and felt that the Northwest required economic regeneration, with agriculture as a mainstay (**Figure 9.3**). "This region is one of the least areas represented by minority communities who account for only 2.4% of the labour force and yet this region has many farms going out of business simply because young people are reluctant to take up farming as a way of life."

Figure 9.3 Business Tips from The Black Farmer

- Get customers involved in your product;
- Set up a dedicated website and include a petition page for support;
- Include email addresses of supermarket buyers as part of the wider network;
- Remember supermarkets are constantly monitoring consumers;
- Regard consumers as part of your firm's sales force;
- Consumers sell your brand(s) and are therefore very important;
- The most powerful persons in our lives are consumers;
- Research the market often and introduce new brand products;
- Organise product launches and publicise them effectively;
- Work with other food-related businesses and industry networks; and
- Don't concentrate only on home trade, venture into overseas markets.

(Source: The Black Farmer, Food Features, Agalinks.com)

Food Training

A constant lament from UK employers including the community/voluntary sector (which is also described as the social enterprise sector), is the lack of skills, formal experience, as well as a lack of motivation and confidence among young people and older workers particularly in areas where poverty and other forms of disadvantage are rife. A major barrier to the growth and expansion of the British Caribbean food sector according to owners and managers is poor staff training at the lower tier of the business operational chain.

Anecdotally, a quarter of all owners neglect formal staff training and instead, treat it is as a low priority. Some of the reasons given include; a very small staff, limited finances to invest in employee development programmes and a narrow customer base. Often on-the-job training is not adequate since employees need to be taught (formal) techniques like supervisory management, customer care, accounting and financial management, quality control procedures, as well as conflict resolution management.

Besides, there is a genuine shortage of chefs in the country with restaurants constantly looking for professionals to relieve overworked cooks in established kitchens. In recent years, there has been some relaxation in the laws on hiring overseas workers for the UK's hospitality sector. This system has been seemingly effective for Indian, Chinese and other ethnic eating houses, and to a large extent, the Caribbean food sector is still `playing catch-up'. Of course, there is greater co-ethnic diversity within the Caribbean food and drink trade than in any other ethnic firm sector (group). This is because of the community's historic cultural pluralism which is also evident in music, sports and other social activities. Unlike Britain though, Caribbean communities in Canada and the USA have a greater number of highly qualified chefs and caterers respectively.

In the early part of this century, the money transfer company, MoneyGram, carried out a survey involving Caribbean consumers in Britain to determine whether they `appeared in danger of losing their culinary traditions'. Thc research had mixed responses; more than half of the respondents preferred Caribbean food and over three quarters of 18-25 years said were interested in learning how to cook Caribbean food. The findings showed that the third generation of Caribbean people `would rather go and watch a football match than attend cookery classes'. The findings below made interesting reading at the time: -

Positive

- 72% believed eating ethnic foods was culturally important;
- 67% preferred Caribbean food; and
- 60% said they would like to eat more Caribbean food.

Negative

- 33% preferred convenience British foods;
- 40% said they would like to eat less Caribbean food;
- 47% admitted that they had never eaten Caribbean meals; and
- 83% said they were reluctant to learn to cook Caribbean dishes.
- **(MoneyGram 2002)**

Traditionally, the food industry has a high staff turn-over and this presents owners of small firms with a dilemma as to whether or not they should invest limited resources into full-scale training programmes, only to lose staff to the `highest bidder'. The situation is further compounded by a lack of training courses in the preparation of ethnic dishes. There are few institutions that teach Caribbean cookery, notably, Morley College, with the odd courses organised by mainstream organisations when there funding opportunities arise or when special requests are made by black community groups.

In an effort to resolve this intractable problem, some owners have been proactive in spearheading vocational courses in Caribbean Cuisine in London and the Midlands respectively (especially

Birmingham). Other initiatives include publishing recipe books and hosting television cookery programmes. Karlene Rickard has authored *A Child's Guide to Tropical Foods (2003)* containing lively illustrations of fruits and vegetables in the UK. Kenneth Gardiner has written *Creole Caribbean Cookery*, an authoritative publication tracing the origins of Caribbean food, covering ingredients, methods and recipes. Rusty Lee and Ainsley Harriot have successful careers in the hotel and restaurant industry. Harriot's own brand food products are popular in UK supermarkets and others worldwide. Sales have reached new heights, particularly in his cous-cous and soup range, with successful appearances at live events and on major television programmes in Australia, New Zealand, South Africa and most European countries. Through direct intervention from both British Caribbean experts, many consumers have learnt more about Caribbean food and the commercial benefits it has brought to the UK as a whole.

In researching this chapter, there was considerable evidence to imply that, despite a lack of formal qualifications, the average Caribbean person had working knowledge of and practical experience in food preparation. Noteworthy, in the mid-1990s, Middlesex University endorsed this view in a report recommending that dining and leisure facilities in community centres should be maximised to combat the shortage of culinary skills in the ethnic market. In effect, these centres should be utilised as a 'laboratory' in the production of modern food giants among sections of the British Caribbean community.

The community has a lot of cooking expertise that needs to be utilised. Recent press reports indicate that Caribbean chefs have achieved national reputations and it would be reasonable to suppose that they would be prepared to help in activities aimed at the betterment of their community. Speeding up the plan to provide short-term training programmes in cooking and food provision is important. The aim is to encourage youths who may wish to pursue careers in the food sector **(Middlesex University 1995)**.

Challenges and Opportunities

Like other industry sectors, the UK Food and Drink trade has numerous risks involving areas such as financial investment for start-ups, growth and expansion, proper premises, the right location, quality staff and a high volume of custom to sustain operations. Markets too are highly competitive and sophisticated with consumers demanding valued-added products and services, whilst owners have to deal with mounting regulations, each year.

But there are prospects too, judging by the collection of regeneration schemes that can provide opportunities for ethnic firms to introduce new products and services in the market. There are other advantages in the form of contracting with Local Authorities, private companies and collaborating with social enterprise and community-based organisations to deliver `commissioned-type' health food and `Healthy Living' initiatives in urban and rural parts of the country.

Other opportunities exist too, judging by the brand-labels depicting specific niche markets. Brands such as *`Refill'*, *`Calabash'*, *`The Ackee Tree'*, *`Cotton's'* *`Coco'*, *Mango's'*, and *`Xamacya'* illustrate the cultural, ethnic and heritage diversity of the British Caribbean food and drink market and its relevance to the UK economy. The CFE noted that 10% of all Caribbean restaurants in the UK are rated `Good' to Excellent' with a seating capacity of 30-200 diners **(Table 9. 5).**

With the increasing number of families eating out on a weekly basis and the rising trend of (traditional) 'packed lunches' in offices, as well as industrial premises, British Caribbean food operators can capture this market by developing an assortment of dishes specially adapted for different consumer tastes. Intensive research will be necessary to determine customer segments, product range, kind of presentation, purchasing frequency and other logistics to meet the demands of different client groups.

Table 9.5 Challenges and Opportunities for Caribbean Food and Drink

Sector	Challenges	Opportunities
Restaurant	Larger food companies operating with (high) economies of scale because of high volume of distribution and supply chains.	Specialist eating houses to service customer segments and secure access to lower cost (effective) supply chains by purchasing directly from `source'.
Catering	Cost of implementing regulations, poor quality staff, lack of capital investment and competition from reputable mainstream companies.	Public sector catering such as the NHS; mobile catering for special events, catering/ licensed bar for festivals and franchise operations.
Food Production	Appropriate premises, capital investment for machinery and equipment and other resources needed for start-up – competition from well known companies.	Light-manufacturing plants for general food preservation; joint ventures with large food companies targeting ethnic markets.
Drinks	Same as above	Target markets such as educational institutions, hospitals, youth clubs and other groups promoting `health living' schemes.
Agriculture	Access to farmsteads, adequate investment capital, no experience of UK-type farming methods and lack the knowledge of various regulations governing use of state (Crown) land and properties.	Small homesteads holdings involving cash crops (vegetables, seasoning etc) for domestic consumer markets; maximise local allotment schemes.
Franchising	No formal knowledge and experience of franchising arrangements and slender resources for investment.	Existing franchises in food, drinks, catering, healthcare activities, catering and agriculture.

Grocery Shop	Same as restaurant and food segments	Mini-supermarkets and retail units to provide specialist food, drinks and other consumables for customers with limited access to mainstream supermarkets and retail stores.

(Source: Tender Direct, Aberdeen, Scotland, 2007)

Conclusion

In this chapter, the UK Food and Drink trade was analysed to show the British Caribbean sector's contribution to the regional and national economy. Information and data on segments were presented to reflect the composition, size and performance of the Caribbean sector.

Food production was singled out as an area in which Caribbean businesses are growing at an average pace, and it represented over half of all activity in the hospitality sector, with a market share of 10% and an estimated value of £200 million according to the World Food Market indicators. Based on the annual spend of the ethnic population on ethnic food consumed at home, it is reckoned that this market is worth around £5.2 billion per annum. The annual Notting Hill Carnival and other festivities have given fresh stimulus to the promotion of new foods in the ethnic market, many of which feature on television and related media cookery programmes as highlighted below: -

Meaty mains and Barbie dishes

- Jerk chicken with rice and red slaw by Anthony Worrall Thompson, *Saturday Brunch*
- Caribbean pork spare ribs with celeriac dauphinoise by Ed Baines from *Saturday Kitchen*
- Trinidad and Tobago chicken wings by Ed Baines
- Cuban-style marinated lamb by Anthony Worrall Thompson

Festive Dishes

- Jamaican curried snapper with coconut and lime served with clap-hand roti, Ainsley Harriot from *Saturday Kitchen.*
- Spicy griddled snapper on pineapple salsa by Lesley Waters from *Ready Steady Cook.*

Veggies and Sides

- Rice and peas by Simon Rimmer from *This Little Farmer.*
- Curried vegetable and green banana bake with plantain salad and passion fruit vinaigrette by Orlando Satchel from *Veg Talk.*
- Roasted plantain with ginger and lime dressing by Tony Tobin from *Ready Steady Cook.*
- Callaloo bake by Anthony Worall Thompson from *Saturday Kitchen.*

Sweet Things

- Coconut bread by Bill Granger.
- Strawberry Hill pineapple with rum butter glaze by Ainsley Harriot from *Barbecue Bible.*
- Jamaican bananas from Burrastow Hotel.

Party Drinks

- Classic Mojito by Oz Clarke from *Saturday Brunch.*
- Rum and cola by Oz Clarke from *Saturday Kitchen.*
- Coconut milkshake by Anthony Worrall Thompson from *Ready Steady Cook.*

The segmented nature of the sector was also illustrated by the geographic spread of firms in the nine English Regions with a sprinkling of businesses in Scotland, Wales and Ireland. The product range included food seasonings, herbal drinks, condiments and sweet meats. In some of the food and drink products, the ingredients had their origins in the Caribbean Region. The brilliant work of the **CFE** promoting Caribbean food and drink on its website and organising network events with different sector agencies and organisations was highlighted.

Examples of franchising and the grocery trade were also given. The case of a local McDonald's franchise held by a Caribbean firm was included with particular reference given to the pros of such a business arrangement and the form it can take in the context of growth prospects in key sectors. Two shops in London and Midlands – **Lloyd's Groceries** and **Russell's Supermarket** respectively - highlighted the nature of operations such as customer care, staff retention and product quality.

The potential for agricultural production is indicative of the proven success of the pioneering efforts of the single **`Black Farmer'** in the British Isles and the contribution to the food trade, similar to the food seasoning, drink and beverage, manufacturing and franchising, useful tips were offered on how business owners and managers should operate in this segment.

The need for training and general orientation to improve the professional skills and competence of chefs, kitchen assistants and other technicians was emphasised. This was seen as important to the survival and viability of the Caribbean food sector. It is worth emphasising that Caribbean food and drinks firms have been established in the UK's larger cities for many years and in the last 10 to 15 years have seen the rise of the `drop-in' Caribbean takeaway. Joseph Quashie owns a Trinidadian takeaway in Shepherd's Bush for over 13 years and his regular customers include a mixture of Caribbean people, British, Irish, Africans and `new to London' Australians. According to Quashie, part of the appeal of Caribbean takeaways is that, `Our food is not bland and it is not fish and chips!' (**Quashie 2005**)

Finally, the growth of this sector was examined through key segments involving challenges and opportunities faced by owners. Undoubtedly, the unique selling point (USP) of the British Caribbean food and drink sector is its built-in heritage diversity that spans the range of products and services. Despite competition and sector limitations, members of this UK community have demonstrated resilience, a trait that is set to be maintained in the foreseeable future as owners seek to reform their operations to compete in broader co-ethnic markets to increase value and profitability. It is hoped that, similar to previous sections of this book, this chapter provides a comparable blueprint for further growth, development and expansion of the wider British Caribbean businesses community.

For readers who are interested in the food and drink trade, existing business owners and would-be entrepreneurs, information was accessed from official statistics, sampled data, business directories, case studies, formal interviews, observation studies, mystery shopping and other methods. I conducted food sampling sessions during shopping routine during much of the 2005-2007 periods to test consistency, and quality, as well as to obtain credible evidence on the food and drink trade in total. In the next chapter, the contribution of Caribbean entrepreneurs to the UK travel and shipping industry will be examined.

Chapter Notes

Mintel began over 30 years ago, providing food and drink research in the UK. Its leading analysts are world-renowned experts in diverse areas such as leisure, consumer goods, retail, financial services, sales promotion and social trends and its reach also extends into continental Europe, Latin America, Australia, Israel, China and South Korea.

The World Food Market is an event that focuses exclusively on global producers of food and drink who meet each year to showcase their products and services to consumers including distributors, suppliers and others in the industry. The event enables entrepreneurs to explore the wonderful world of international food with belief and originality.

The Grocery Trader is an independent monthly business magazine is aimed at grocery trade professionals and provides a valuable information channel for over 21,000 readers who subscribe to it. It covers news and features on food, drink, retail and non-food issues.

Famous Caribbean Rum Brands include Mount Gay (Barbados), Gold Magic Rum (Trinidad and Tobago), El'Dorado Rum (Guyana), Appleton Rum (Jamaica), River Antoine Rum (Grenada) and English Harbour (Antigua). There are other Caribbean-flavoured liqueurs which feature in the UK drink trade.

The Dalgety Group of Companies was founded in 1993 in Guyana and in 1995, the company commissioned a UK factory – Dalgety Teas and Herbs – its aim to produce introduce Europe to the authentic stronger flavoured herbal teas of the Caribbean. In 2001, the subsidiary of `Dalgety Caribbean Products', was set up to introduce gourmet Caribbean snacks and condiments – plantain chips, cassava crisp and extra hot pepper sauce to the British market.

Karlene Rickard – has over twenty years of expertise as a parent facilitator, trainer and counsellor working extensively in the UK, USA and the Caribbean.

Ready Steady Cook is a BBC daytime TV cooking programme first aired in 1994. The programme was hosted by Fern Britton from 1994 until 2000 when celebrity chef, Ainsley Harriott became the new host. The present duration of the programme is 45 minutes and it offers 3 million viewers plus insights into the preparation and presentation of various inter-ethnic dishes. Jamaican-born TV celebrity chef of the 1980s Rusty Lee, rose to fame on TV-AM with Anne Diamond. Lee has since shown an interest in politics.

Jerk is a Spanish word for jerked or dried meat which is also linked to the jerking or poking of the meat with a sharp object, producing holes which were then filled with the spice mixture. Like other Caribbean countries, Jamaican foods came from Spanish, East Indian, West African, Portuguese and Chinese. Jerk pork can be traced to the pre-slavery period of Cormantee hunters of West Africa through the Maroons who were Jamaican slaves that escaped from the British invasion of 1655.

UK Pepper Product Exports include hot pepper, hot pepper mash, hot pepper sauce, dried ground pepper and hot pepper extract. Their description and uses are renowned for sauces and pickles, restaurants and homes, food processing and catering industries, as well as mechanical, chemical and defence industries.

The Black Enterprise Awards scheme was founded by Kofi Kusitor, owner of the Colourful Network (an internet publishing site), in 2000. The aim of the annual event is to encourage the establishment and development of business leaders. It was postponed in 2006 to allow organisers to refine the awards process and re-emerge with a more focused, robust and better publicised event. Dozens of businessmen and women including young entrepreneurs have been recipients of various category-awards.

Fair Trade is about better prices, decent working conditions, local sustainability, and fair terms of trade for farmers and workers in the developing world. By requiring companies to pay above market prices, Fair Trade addresses the injustices of conventional trade which traditionally discriminates the poorest, weakest prices. It enables them to improve their lot and have more control over their lives.

The British Franchising Association was set up in 1977 to act in the interests of the industry as a whole. At least 20 different business sectors are represented with insurance services, hairdressing to quick print and designing all inclusive of the franchising industry.

The Black and Minority Ethnic (BME) Business Support Programme was a three year initiative (2002-2005) project initiated by TCS Educational Trust Ltd in collaboration with the Neighbourhood Renewal Team of Brent Council, West London. The programme provided nearly 60 firms with information and advice, skills training, capacity building and ongoing enterprise and technical support. At the end of the project, more than three quarters of all owners reported increased profits at 2-5%.

The National Farmers' Union has been established over 100 years and represents farmers and growers of England and Wales. Its central objective is to promote successful and socially responsible agriculture and horticulture, while ensuring the long term viability of rural communities.

Allotments are usually plots of land approximately 150 square years/125 square meters that are owned by Councils for the purpose of renting to local residents so that they may enjoy cultivating their own vegetables, plants or flowers in a quiet sand peaceful setting. Entrepreneurs can pool a portion of their profits to develop allotments to benefit the Caribbean community in the form of city farms, school farms, community gardens and or community-led allotment schemes as social enterprises.

Selected References

1 *The Grocery Trader News*, April 2006.

2 *The Economic Position of the Agri-Food Sector*: Quarterly Analysis September 2003, Department for the Environment, Food and Rural Affairs (DEFRA).

3 Wright, T & Pollert, Anna: *The Experience of Ethnic Minority Workers in the Hotel and Catering Industry: Routes to Support and advice on Workplace Problems*, Working Lives Research Institute, London Metropolitan University, July 2005.

4 Hamaker, Sarah Smith: 'A Balancing Act: Caterers do the impossible to make clients' dreams come true', *Restaurants USA*, September 2000.

5 Food and Drink Opportunities in the UK, UK Trade & Investment, 2006.

6 *Demand for Skills in the UK Food and Drink Manufacturing Sector*, Improve – Food and Drink Sector Skills Council, 2005.

7 Allotments Provision and Profile, Rugby Council, 2003.

8 World Food Market 2006

9 *Ethnic Food Supply Chains*: A Preliminary Assessment, The Knowledge Centre for Black & Minority Ethnic Businesses, September 2003.

10 *Proceedings of the Caribbean Hot Pepper Industry Workshop: Charting the way forward,* Caribbean Agricultural Research Development Institute (CARDI), Port of Spain, Trinidad and Tobago, November 2003.

11 Interview with Lloyd Tate, *Economic Research Project*, Brent Council: TCS Tutorial College, London, 15th August 2002.

12 Independent Research, Russell's Foods Trading Ltd, Birmingham, West Midlands, 2005-07

13 *Young Black Farmers*, Diverse Production, BBC 2005

14 *UK Food Industry*, Department for Environment, Food and Rural Affairs, 2003

15 National Farmers' Union Study of Farmers in England, 1999.

16 *The Viability of Commercialising the Restaurant, Bar and Facility Hall of the African Caribbean Leadership Council*, Centre for Ethnic Business Research, Middlesex University, 1995.

17 Rickard, Karlene (2003): *A Child's Guide to Tropical Foods,* BIS Publications, London October 2003.

Chapter 10

Business and Professional Services

Introduction

Business organisations do not only sell products, but they also advertise promise and trust to customers for business services rendered. Each party expects much from the other; customers expect to obtain products at affordable prices and businesses prefer customers to frequent their premises to increase turnover and market share. Companies that sell products or services must therefore take into account various considerations when dealing with consumer markets: profitability, cost effectiveness and the satisfaction of legal obligations.

Whether a business organisation is micro, small or medium-sized, there is need to establish services that are customer-oriented and as such, these should be carefully researched so that alternative brands could be made available to different customer segments. Furthermore, no two companies are alike and as such therefore, apart from the actual product, clients are interested in quality customer care, affordability, reliable service and reasonable guarantees for products and services.

In this chapter, we will look at the UK business and professional services (BPS) sector estimated at 7% of the GDP in the country. The major industries making up the British Caribbean business market in this regard are financial, legal, cleaning, consultancy, training, property development, recruitment and events management, among other micro-independent firms that operate on a part-time basis with owners employed with public agencies. Barclays Business Services reported that Caribbean firms had a market share of 8% in the finance and property market and about 5% of business and professional services overall (**Barclays 2006**). Given that 40% plus of this community own homes and in some parts of the country an excess of 50%, it is not surprising that business ownership in the financial and property market has been relatively consistent during the period 1999 and 2005.

The BPS sector is broadly fragmented and owners of firms rely on product knowledge, awareness of business regulations, efficient management systems, competent staff and valued custom to maintain market advantage. Much of the changes in the financial and legal services industry for example, are attributed to movements in legislation which can influence the difference between success and failure of existing and new firms. Proposed reform of the legal services sector could have wider implications for the professional services industry, with government planning to allow providers to establish multi-disciplinary practices to extend ownership rights.

The slowdown in the previously buoyant housing market had a negative impact on firms providing property-related services, notably the real estate sector. At the time of writing, the housing sector was experiencing difficulties resulting from high personal debts, unemployment, interest rate rises and affordability, all of which will affect house-building activity. Smaller firms that provide property-related services are therefore likely to experience less favourable trading conditions than larger firms although it is likely that firms can still benefit from growth in the commercial property market (buy-to-let and other such transactions) for a while longer.

Industry Portfolio

Financial services represent an economic powerhouse contributing over 5% to overall GDP and £17 billion a year with over one million people employed in London and other areas around the country.

Founded on a tradition of open competition, the industry provides unique and unrivalled expertise in banking, insurance, capital markets, securities dealing, foreign exchange, derivatives and fund management **(Fig 10.1)**.

The industry is supported by a robust professional services sector that is critical to competitive advantage. Accountancy and other related services generate net exports of £439 million and legal services generate exports totalling £1.8 million, although this industry generated an estimated £19.5 billion in terms of market share in 2004-2005. It employs about 267,000 people. The fund management sector contributes nearly £5,000 billion to the economy and it employs over 40,000 employees. Insurance generates a total of £152.7 billion, employing 348,000 people. Management consultancy is valued at over £10.1 billion (**UKTI 2006**).

Figure 10.1 Number of Business and Professional Services Firms

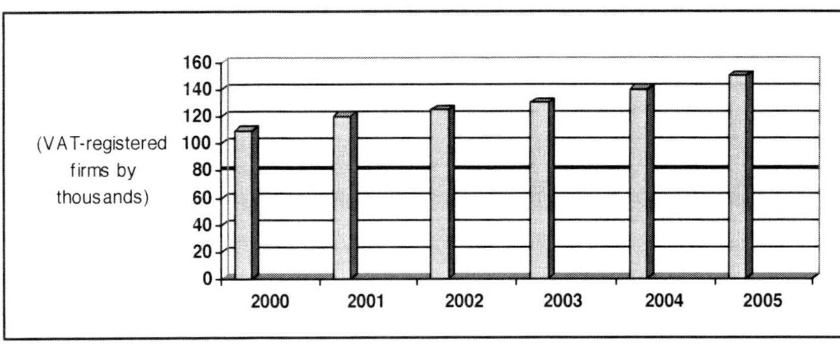

(Source: Professional Services Review, Barclays, June 2006)

The number of firms registered in the sector rose to 147,070 in 2005, according to the DTI. The figure illustrates that while the capacity of the corporate professionals sector continues to expand, the rate of new firm formation has grown fairly steadily since the early 1990s. The rate of expansion remains relatively high compared to sectors such as architectural services.

The British Caribbean BPS market is very dynamic especially when one considers that professionals contribute to the productivity of public institutions at a rate of 8-10% and over – mostly in the business, financial, associate professional and technical services either at middle management or supervisory and technical level respectively. Like other growth sectors, there is no reliable data on the output of Caribbean-owned firms in this sector, but estimates put the combined market share of 13% in financial and property services alone with a figure in excess of 10,000 companies which is roughly 50% of the total figure for the Caribbean SME sector in the UK. In relation to composition and size, firms range from micro, small to medium-scale; from 2-5 employees and 50-100 plus employees. The annual turnover of firms (or pre-tax revenue generated) varies from under £50,000 to over £5 million depending on the volume of services, size of the clientele market and the number of branches or units of companies in the UK or abroad. A common feature of a quarter of all firms is the establishment of social enterprises and community trading organisation to complement and supplement firms' activities and to demonstrate a level of corporate/social responsibility. In fact there is increasing evidence implying that a small fraction of black business start-ups `graduate' from social enterprise-type organisations to thriving commercial entities. These exist specifically among small and medium-sized companies that are market leaders in their respective sectors.

Market Leadership

The dynamic flair of the British Caribbean BPS sector is an important facet in owners' quest for market leadership. Prior to business start-up, professionals who served with distinction in public institutions at managerial level, and who felt they were victims of `occupational' discrimination (lack of promotional opportunities and salary inequality) maximised their experience and knowledge to go into business for themselves. Quite often, they are able to develop a client base in the first 18 months by appealing to co-ethnic markets. In this chapter, case studies would be produced of specialists in legal, financial, events management, consultancy training, marketing and other segments, who transferred brilliantly, their skills from public sector employment to an active career in self-employment whilst impacting on the prosperity of local economies in the UK **(Table 10.1)**.

Table 10. 1 Percentage of ethnic groups working in British industry

Sector	White	Indian	Pakistan	Bangla-deshi	Caribbean	African	Chinese
Production industries	25%	17%	16%	66%	14%	9%	7
Hotels, distribution & transport	26%	34%	46%	9%	27%	27%	47%
Private services	21%	22%	20%	-	22%	25%	23%
Public services	28%	26%	18%	18%	37%	40%	23%

(Source: Labour Force Survey, Spring 2005 to Winter 2005/2006)

According to the above figure, Caribbean professionals are the fifth largest employment group in primary, manufacturing and construction activities. Over a quarter are involved in the hotel, distribution and transport fields whilst just fewer than 25% are employed in private services. Similar to Africans, Caribbean people (37%) are more likely than any other group to work in public administration, education, health and social care. It is estimated that more than 40% of all Caribbean firms are located in the BPS sector.

Consultancy Services

The UK management consultancy market is valued at £6.94 billion **(2006 estimates**) covering an array of client groups, ranging from individuals and public institutions to private companies and sometimes, the community sector as well. Caribbean professionals opt for this type of business because it serves their vocational and commercial interests, thereby enabling them to make inroads into markets that are generally, the preserve of white companies. Apart from top class managerial competence, this industry demands extensive experience across mass markets, and owners of British Caribbean consulting firms are in the age category of 35-45 years and 45-55 years and over. They have either independent companies, sole trading units with associates, and/or partnerships involving two or more professionals with multiple skills (**Minicase 10.1**). Besides financial independence, there are other reasons for Caribbean professionals' choice of self-employment; they include:

- Fear of losing skills or becoming professionally obsolete.
- Want to be independent.
- Need to be valued.
- Need to do something after being made redundant or retirement.
- Like meeting people.
- Want to refine their competencies (**Interviews 2000:2007**).

Minicase 10.1 Focus Consultancy Limited

Political scientist, Professor Chris Mullard, created **Focus Consultancy** in 1986 to formalise his ideas on change management, equality and diversity. The company's organic growth is matched by its ethical principles which have resulted in an impressive clientele market including international governments and institutions.

The company employs in excess of 100 staff and operates in UK offices, as well as European sites, including Brussels, the home of the EU. In 1999, the British Army appointed Focus to assist with a national recruitment drive to enlist more minorities to the military. Though there is much to be done from the Army's standpoint, Focus' intervention has contributed to more members from the Asian and Caribbean communities joining the Armed Forces.

The Royally-appointed Professor blends politics with academia and enterprise brilliantly, and has set an exemplary reputation in the global consultancy market. As author of two seminal works, *Black Britain* (1973) and *Race, Power and Resistance* (1985), he has lectured at Universities in North America, the Caribbean, Australia and Europe. Recently, he chaired the Notting Hall Carnival Company that organises annual carnival festivities.

Focus' turnover exceeds £4 million and with a growing number of high-profile clients. Mullard's mission is to make a positive impact on equalities, particularly in areas where ethnic communities are disadvantaged and where policy direction requires a constant rethink.

'What gives me satisfaction, is knowing that our work is helping to bring about change in society. I like to see the big picture in everything. I need to see a vision and plan, I like to see things grow and evolve.' As an international company, Focus seems destined to maintain its position as a market leader in consultancy and change management for some time to come.

The consultancy industry is highly segmented with professionals identifying markets they feel comfortable with, and equally, those with few entry barriers. If there are restrictions in particular segments, owners tend to innovate by creating slimmer operations. Sustainable growth is hinged on quality services, product guarantees and the selection of lucrative markets that are accessible in range and scope.

Increasingly, British Caribbean specialists devote their energies and resources to proving innovative services, based on honed market intelligence. The financial company, **Euro Consultancy** of which Guyanese Arnold Narine was a co-partner, is dedicated to creating market opportunities for non-European economies including SMEs. With over 30 years business experience, including a five year stint with Price Waterhouse, Narine spotted a gap in the market for financial management services and acted decisively.

Most companies were quite weak and even the larger ones had no management accounts until the auditor came around – they had no idea of cashflow procedures either. The other advantage to accounting was that you saw the decision-making as part of a business at a very early stage in your career. For instance, with an engineering or marketing background, you arrive at that stage much later and you learn too late about the importance of understanding the figures **(*Caribbean Times* 1995).**

With a profile of international projects covering the Far East, the USA and France, Narine proved that, "Caribbean people were just as good as their European counterparts in presenting business and marketing cases for international funding assistance." Since its establishment in 1990, Euro Consultancy has offered financial, business management, training and related consultancy services for companies interested in contributing to the development of global economies.

In addition, competition drives the BPS sector and firms that lack the financial muscle, use their cultural knowledge and industry networks to access lucrative contracts. Firms outside of London turn to international markets to tap into new product and service types. With exposure to trade missions internationally, owners have embarked on a strategy of product differentiation as a means of penetrating overseas markets, especially those dominated by white expatriate companies. **Cole Consulting UK** has shown that, by employing a multidisciplinary approach to enterprise development, British Caribbean companies can access greater opportunities and play a decisive role in the revitalisation, and eventual stability of country economies (**Minicase 10. 2).**

Legal Services

The market for legal services is valued at £20 billion (***Ernst & Young, October 2002***; ***Department of Constitutional Affairs, London 2006***). There has been steady growth in this sector with legal firms switching their concentration from growth to profitability which means that there is a need to focus on cost structure and organisational management systems. Cultural barriers are the biggest obstacle to implementing such changes, with large firms still unable to meet their minority staff quota.

Minicase 10. 2 Cole Consulting UK

Incorporated in 1997, **Cole Consulting UK Ltd** is located in the West Midlands, and it provides multiple services; namely, criminology, marketing, education, enterprise support and community affairs. Founder-owner, Clarence Cole, is a criminologist and the company has a staff profile that resembles mainstream in relation to service provision:

- Strategic marketing, implementation planning and control
- Design of strategy to increase market share
- Business to business marketing
- PR and effective communications
- Educational teaching techniques
- Business planning and training
- Report writing
- Strategic marketing consultation
- Financial planning and forecasting
- The Criminal Justice System policies and practices
- English Legal System
- Criminological Theory.

Cole Consulting has serviced companies in the legal, criminal, local government, as well as non-governmental organisations in the UK and overseas. It has accessed and completed World Bank contracts in social governance, capacity building, as well as managerial and supervisory training to boost employee development. Its unique selling point (USP) is strengthening the capacities of human, technical and financial resources of diverse societies so that they can increase their competitiveness. The company's motto is, *`Helping communities to understand how to utilise their resourcefulness in a global environment'*.

In keeping with features of the US legal system, UK firms have examined partnership models such as Multiple, Multidisciplinary, and Limited Liability type organisation structures (**2005**). Owners have felt the effects of globalisation on their clients and have adopted new corporate structures whilst struggling to achieve attain return on investments (ROI) from new technologies. Key trends affecting the industry include: -

- Political – change in European legislation and threat of litigation.
- Social – clients are global and barriers to practising law overseas remain.
- Economic – fears around the consequences of economic pressures.
- Technology – presence of increased technologies weaken governance structure.

Conversely, while most of the challenges affect reputable law firms, ethnic firms are still struggling to compete in the billion-pound (dollar) marketplace. There are 11,098 solicitors from minority groups on the Roll, with 9% of all solicitors and 10% with known ethnicity. A total of just over 8,000 have practising certificates; that represents 8% of all solicitors with practicing certificates and 9% with known ethnicity.

The proportion of legal personnel from minority communities with practising certificates broadly reflects the proportion of the total population of England and Wales. Minorities comprise 8.7% of the total population in England and Wales, and 8.3% of solicitors working in private practice are from these communities. In the Eastern and South-eastern Regions, the number of solicitors from ethnic groups exceeds the proportion of the respective regions' ethnic communities. In these areas, British Caribbean professionals feature in the size of firm starting at a rate of just over 7% up to 40% and if the figure below is anything to go by, then the number of British Caribbean-owned legal firms is set to experience organic growth over the next 10 years, with elements of `*Sole Practice*' and `*Partnerships*' inclusive (**Table 10.2**).
The current presence of minority solicitors in this industry is mainly

due to a relative increase in the number of UK students accepted to do first degree law courses at universities and colleges. For example, in 2001 a total of 11,075 students were accepted to study law with a quarter of this number representing 2,733 students from a minority background. Industry trends showed that during the 1999-2001 periods, a total of 512 British Caribbean students were enrolled for law degree courses at even though this section of the community is 1% of the total UK population, it had a proportionate representation of nearly 2% of all law students attending courses at tertiary institutions in the country (**Law Society 2006**).

Table 10.2 Percentage of minority solicitors in the UK Legal Sector

Ethnicity	Sole Practice	2-4 Partners	5-10 Partners	11-25 Partners	26-80 Partners	81+ Partners
Caribbean	18%	40%	20%	10%	12%	12%
Asian	18%	38%	15%	14%	11%	15%
Chinese	21%	54	13%	6%	8%	10%
African	8%	25%	9%	23%	10%	32%
Other	11%	25%	13%	13%	14%	27%
All ethnic minority	17%	37%	14%	14%	11%	17%
White European	9%	22%	20%	19&	21%	27%
Unknown	11%	66%	15%	13%	13%	23%
All Trainees	10%	23%	17%	16%	17%	24%

(Source: Law Society, 2006 percentages have been rounded for uniformity)

The barriers around racial prejudice and market discrimination have not altogether dented the aspirations and general confidence of solicitors who have opted out from the mainstream to set up private practices. Notably, British Caribbean legal firms have attempted, with some measure of success, to achieve diversity through the identification of a pool of talented staff including paralegal personnel. Unlike like large companies, small firms have nurtured talent in the profession since they realise that the legal profession is uniquely placed to provide leadership in this area.

Indeed, issues around injustice could only be resolved effectively and efficiently, if there is the perception that the Justice System (whether public or private) is fair and equitable. In their efforts to contribute to justice and fairplay therefore, owners have developed specialist practices, and in the process, created niche markets to cover broad-based services such as: -

- Business and commercial;
- Commercial property;
- Crime;
- Employment law;
- Family law;
- Personal injury; and
- Residential conveyancing.

So, since ethnic law firms are set up to provide multiple services and benefits to their communities and the wider society, it is clear that owners and partners have accepted the notion that in order to compete, their organisations have to comply with industry regulations whilst developing services that are applicable to the demands of a broad client base even though specific services, as mentioned above, are inclusive of the total package.

This section will thus highlight the work of selected firms in London and the West Midlands particularly, to offer insights into the extent to which British Caribbean owners have gone to ensure that their firms remain competitive in legal services market.

Set up between the 1980s and 1990s, by qualified legal practitioners, these firms have represented hundreds of clients in the ethnic community and have collaborated with various public agencies and institutions to meet the demand for clients who feel a sense of failure by the Justice System.

The selected firms in Minicases 10.3 are indicative of changes that are constantly evolving in the UK's corporate market involving ethnic businesses. The evidence of family and partnership-type operations, also illustrates that more British Caribbean owners have moved beyond the *`I can do it alone'* culture and instead, have grown their businesses by including family members and like-minded partners at top level management in their operations.

Quite noticeably, there are several guiding principles that underpin the Caribbean legal services market in terms of organisation and performance. These principles mirror both the overall management style and leadership of the first and second generation of entrepreneurs in the UK. These principles are regarded as codes which are manifest throughout this book as: self-belief, pride in accomplishments, motivation, professionalism, integrity, enterprise and a co-operative spirit.

And contrary to existing literature on ethnic firms where little is mentioned about organisational systems and levels of production and productivity according to industry sector and segment, there is a strong case to be made around the management and leadership styles of Caribbean companies operating in the BPS sector particularly. In large measure, these styles can and do contribute ultimately, to the level of success members of this community enjoy in their quest to further the image and reputation of the UK, as a culturally diverse global (plc) market for innovative ideas, goods and services.

Indeed, firms such as Stennett & Stennett, Webster Dixon Solicitors and Toussaints Solicitors are among market leaders in the legal industry. Partners of these firms have staked their reputation on quality services for a mixed client base, irrespective of race, class and/or any other economic and social consideration. Through their example and others, there is greater recognition of the importance of minority-owned firms in the UK legal environment **(Minicases 10. 3)**.

Minicases 10.3 Selected British Caribbean Legal Firms

Stennett & Stennett - In 1989, Michael Stennett and Elaine Beckford Stennett started this London law firm with the aim of providing high quality service at an affordable price. The firm has a practical and modern approach while upholding the traditional standards of the profession. Its growth which has is client-led, has enabled management to set up a number of specialist departments to cater for additional services. Stennett invests in staff development and the practice as a whole, so that it can keep pace with the needs of customers.

The firms specialises in Conveyancing, Wills, Estate Planning and Probate, Litigation, Leasehold Extensions, Independent Financial advice, Family Services, Solicitors for the Elderly and Privy Council Agents for Appellants and Respondents throughout the Commonwealth.

Webster Dixon Solicitors (WDS) - In 1998, this firm was founded by two young legal practitioners, Michael Webster and Dawn Dixon. It is situated near the Royal Courts of Justice. It has a reputation for providing high quality legal services to its clients whether there are large corporations, small niche companies, partnerships or sole traders. The firm's greatest strengths lie in dealing with commercial and business disputes involving corporations, SMEs and other reputable clientele.

WDS' operations are underpinned by a campaigning edge, with high commendations from the Law Society and the CRE for it work in equality and diversity. The company received the Law Society's Race Equality Award in 2005 and recently celebrated 10 years in business. It is listed in both the *Chambers Guides* and the *Legal 500*.

Both partners are actively involved in various professional and community initiatives, with Webster the current chair of the Black Solicitors Network, board/council member of the London Law Society and member of the Law Society of England and Wales. Dixon was chair of the Association of Women Solicitors (2006-2007) and she also sat on the Diversity in Law steering group (***The Lawyer* 2004**).

Toussaints Solicitors – In November 1997, Mary Margaret Toussaint a graduate in Social Policy and Administration established Toussaints Solicitors in Birmingham in the West Midlands. The firm specialises in Civil, Family, Property, Probate and Criminal Litigation, Non-contentious Residential and Commercial Property matters.

Most of the firm's current work is generated from case referrals, repeat custom and in the case of criminal work from the Legal Services Commission with whom the Firm holds a Criminal Franchise.

The firm punches above its weight in the service delivery and other areas of work. Like other legal practices, the firm is affected by the current pace of regulations and technological innovations but management is embracing these challenges with a view to optimising the benefits to achieve further growth and profitability.

Toussaints Solicitors is a member of the Law Society of England and Wales, The Birmingham Law Society, The Black Solicitors Network, The Sole Practitioners Association, Association of Women Solicitors and The Federation of Small Business.

Financial Services

As was stated at the beginning of this chapter, the UK financial services market is valued at billions of pounds annually and contributes much to national productivity. The accountancy market increased in value by over 10% in 2004 alone to £16.01 billion. Though it is dominated by the '*Big Four*' Price Waterhouse Coopers, Deloitte & Touché, KPMG and Ernst & Young, the market is large enough to support a high number of small firms, most of which can be profitable.

Issues of concern to the accounting and financial sector include auditor liability, increasing regulation governing public companies and accountancy firms, and international accountancy standards. There is a view that the rising tide of regulations and standards may not necessarily result in lasting improvements in the industry.

Recent estimates show that the British Caribbean businesses have a market share of 8% in the finance and property market. The market comprises insurance, mortgage for both domestic and commercial properties, remittances and financial trading.

Prior to its receivership in 2000, **Versailles Group Plc** owned by Jamaican Carl Cushnie was the largest black business in the UK with a market value worth £630 million in 1995. As a financial trading company with affiliation to the London Stock Exchange, Cushnie established the firm after working for a large City firm for years. While sections of the community are disappointed over the fall of Versailles, there are valuable lessons to be learnt from trading in financial markets.

The property market is huge and it is estimated that over 50% of Caribbean people are home owners in the UK and many use a portion of their property portfolio as capital investment for business start-up (**Bank of England 1999**). The ownership of property is not new to Caribbean people especially those who migrated to the UK during the 1950s and 1960s. Stories have been told of migrants' purchasing power and their enterprising ability contrary to the myth peddled about the `laid back' attitude of Caribbean people in the media.

The late Randolph Beresford who was the first non-British mayor of a London Borough (Hammersmith and Fulham, West London), bought a property after arriving from Guyana (former British Guiana) in the 1950s. His action resulted in the consternation and frustration of nearly three generations of tenants who seemed content living in rented accommodation rather than purchasing their own homes.

As `traditional-type' entrepreneurs who were schooled in the virtues of land and property ownership based on a commercial and well-being necessity, it was not surprising that when all else failed, Caribbean people have tended to turn to the age-old property trade. Over half of all members of this community own homes throughout England and Wales and despite experts agree that this figure is low compared to the number of Caribbean people living in the UK, the fact is, this number represents 230,000 plus out of a total of over 500,000 plus residents.

Property Market

In further examining the property tenure in the English Counties, Caribbean people live in 43% social rented' and 6% `private rented' accommodation respectively (**2003**). It is therefore not unusual, for those interested in pursuing self-employment as an alternative to unemployment, to use portions of their property as collateral to acquire loans to finance business operations.

Yet interestingly, the same owners have difficulty in acquiring financial assistance from commercial institutions and enterprise agencies for business start-ups even though they don't seem to have much of a problem acquiring loans for house buying purposes.

For instance in London, studies have been done to determine the extent to which ethnic communities enjoy various levels of house ownership across the four sub-regions in the capital. As was stated before, the fact that just over half of all Caribbean people in the country own properties, there should be less of a risk for them to access the necessary funds for business start-ups since they already have a `guaranteed' form of collateral.

It is worth emphasising that homeowners find it relatively easy to meet their housing costs. Nearly half are satisfied with shared ownership and nearly three quarters have no problem in acquiring sufficient information on property ownership.

There is evidence suggesting that over 80% of all Caribbean house owners contend they have had no problems `getting a mortgage because of income or job, or their ethnicity'. Similarly, a high percentage does not have a problem with `legal problems due to solicitor's lack of knowledge of shared ownership'. The only downside to this type of property ownership, is that 97% of all Caribbean Londoners `have no shares in the property' market (**London Research Centre 2004**).

The determination to make good of financial opportunities in the property market is also evident in other parts of England where young entrepreneurs in the 25 to 35 plus age bracket are inclined to follow their parents' footsteps. They have learnt from the experiences of their parents during the 1950s and 1960s when trying to purchase their own homes. Racial prejudice was common in the formative years of Caribbean migrant's presence in Britain. White landlords in most of the English cities refused to sell or rent their property to black people even when migrants could afford to buy. The first generation of settlers used various ingenious means to survive and it was not uncommon in the mid-20th century to find sections of the Caribbean community living in poor housing conditions – cramped and often poorly heated.

Experiences such as the above was both a stimulus and inspiration to the second and third generation of Caribbean professionals who were determined not be daunted by their parents experiences, but instead maximise opportunities which the new set of circumstances offered to them. It was undoubtedly, a fine example of an abiding faith in their abilities to achieve financial independence and market success, in the process, as illustrated in Amanda Dinnall's case in Nottingham. Born of Caribbean parentage, she noted that after witnessing her parents' situation at age 12, she was determined `to be in a position to do better' (**Minicase 10. 4**).

Minicase 10. 4 Dinnall Property Services

Amanda Dinnall founded **Dinnall Property Services** (DPS) in 2005 to offer services in property location and acquisition. One year later, she opened up a division specialising in overseas property. "Our business plans anticipated us opening up to six offices throughout the UK. If things continue to go the way they are now, we will have to find ourselves new premises to accommodate growth and expansion," she explained.

DPS offers comprehensive property relocation and finding service for private and corporate clients looking to move or invest in property, both residential and commercial, across the UK. Clients include start-up businesses, ensuring they get it right first time. Dinall's extensive knowledge of the property trade has led the company to offer other services including corporate property management, to meet increasing client demands.

Dinnall had a flair for enterprise soon after leaving school and a passion for creativity which resulted in her working as a self-employed hair care and fashion specialist at aged 19. Though unqualified, she yielded the call of the property market and embarked on a career in the industry. After three years of rejection, she was recruited as a sales negotiator with an estate agency.

She then trained as a residential and property valuer and moved on to work for a property development firm and finally completed a Construction Management Degree which fast-tracked her career in the industry which is still dominated by white, middle-aged men. "*I built my business on passion, drive, determination and exposure to different professional fields where I developed excellent communication skills. I learnt that having the ability to listen, to understand the content and context of what is being said, responding diplomatically to win the respect and confidence of an audience. These skills became keys to my success with the individuals and companies I worked with and these attributes reflect the ethos of my work with clients*".

Dinnall's initial challenges were awesome; namely, negotiating full-time staff employment, undertaking part-time studies, planning the launch of DPS and raising her year-old son. `*Sometimes it is very hard to juggle my job, but remains at the back of my mind, is that ambition without knowledge is like a boat on dry land. The challenges I faced therefore, were merely a test of strength, self-belief and ability in the environment I worked in which is still dominated by white, middle-aged men. I found myself having to prove to contemporaries (all men) that I have the ability to perform to a high standard. The environment you choose to work in may not always be conducive to your growth potential but in the end, success depends on your ability to overcome odds, thereby making your dreams possible.*"

She encouraged young entrepreneurs to use their passion and ability to secure gains in the property market. `*I wasn't sure if I would really make it to this position, nut you cannot afford to be discouraged because anything worthwhile is hard to achieve.*

Remittances Flow

One of the less documented segments of the financial services trade in the UK is the flow of remittances among British Caribbean residents (around 40%) who send money to their families back home. Official sources point to a level of outward remittances close to £3.5 billion per year, while data from household surveys point to lower levels of £1.1 billion or less. The amount of remittances from immigrant households in the UK to their home-countries is likely to be closer to the amounts revealed by household surveys. On the basis of the available data and contacts with the remitting communities, the total money transfers flowing out of the UK can be estimated at £1.4 billion of which £0.5 billion flows out through informal mechanisms.

Estimates show that the value of British Caribbean remittances amount to over £400 million per year and notwithstanding its informal operations, this trade has attracted considerable interest among government agencies in the UK and overseas, including

World Bank institutions. Money transfers contribute to the less well-off in the Caribbean and other parts of the developing world. In part, they help support the welfare of individuals and their families most of whom live on either low-income or experience severe disadvantage in both economic and social terms. A potential benefit of this enterprise could be an arrangement between British-based Caribbean companies and their counterparts in the Caribbean Region for the creation of a revolving fund from remittances to finance the operations of micro firms and social enterprises in areas such as youth, women, health, community and other forms of social welfare activities for impoverished suburbs and rural communities.

The Caribbean communities in the UK have recognised the increasing demand for the overseas money transfers market. This area provides easy access, low costs transaction and rapid delivery, and currently, this demand is being met by a large number of informal value transfer systems (IVTS), including the notably hawala and hundi systems. The flow of remittances through these systems involves complex sets of transactions. A notable feature of the industry, are recipients' knowledge and understanding of contacts and agencies abroad, including the financial know-how of current exchange (conversion) rates and the like **(Table 10. 3).**

Table 10. 3 Baseline estimates of Total Remittances

Groups	% of total immigrant community	Total remittances (£m)
Bangladeshi	6.1	216
Chinese	5.3	187
Indians	22.7	803
Pakistanis	16.1	570
Caribbeans	12.2	432
Africans	10.5	372
Not included above	27.1	959
All Ethnic Groups	**100**	**3,541**

(Source: Informal Remittances from the UK, Overseas Development Group, Norwich, East Anglia University March 2004)

The above information on property value and money transfers proves that British Caribbean people have considerable material assets that are pivotal to successful business start-ups, as well as incremental growth and expansion of enterprise in key sectors of the UK economy. The information also illustrates the inherent self-reliance and single-mindedness of professionals to gain financial independence, values which have placed them in good stead particularly where commercial institutions have refused loans and other capital investment for business-start ups. Of interest, are the increasing number of Caribbean professionals in the UK who are prepared to work in paid employment (public and private sector) while operating micro to small part-time enterprises - either commercial and/or social enterprise-types.

Whilst there is no definitive figure for all home-based businesses in the UK, a reasonable estimate suggests that members of the ethnic community part-own and manage hundreds of `moonlighting' service firms to boost income or exploit opportunities in niche markets. This trend is prevalent among Caribbean women who balance public sector full-time employment with fostering and adoption, as well as other enterprise and socially-related activities.

The Cleaning Business

Another segment of the business and professional service sector that has shown tremendous progress in the last five years or so. Once regarded as insignificant in terms of commercial success, the cleaning industry is today a highly reputable service industry covering public and private agencies and institutions, comprising an array of cleaners employed and deployed to maintain quality hygiene standards and create a healthy working environment for all.

According to the Cleaning Industry National Training Organisation, the trade is worth £10 billion with an employment segment in the region of 820,000 people. In spite of growing competition, the contract cleaning market grew from £4 billion in 1996 to £6 billion in 2004. The industry is made up of domestic cleaners, office cleaners, hospital and school cleaners and other niche markets – carpet, window and vehicle cleaners.

The main difficulties facing the industry revolve around recruitment and staff retention of operatives than supervisory or management personnel. Basic skills, communicating skills, reading and understanding health and safety procedures and regulations and following instructions are widely recognised as skill gaps for operatives **(LMI 2003)**.

Undoubtedly, these challenges will continue affecting levels of production and productivity. Lack of basic skills can also impede profitability and severely limit opportunities for growth and expansion. Industry specialists say that more than 90% of employers report problems in recruiting part-time staff partly because of pay conditions. New cleaning firms in the minority community however, have their own share of start-up `blues' such as:

- Finding suitable premises in the right location;
- Limited supervisory staff;
- Banks' refusal to offer lending support;
- No enterprise and technical support;
- Meagre sector advice from public agencies;
- Inadequate business management skills;
- Insufficient knowledge of industry/market trends;
- Lack of trust in public institutions;
- Inability to link with viable industry networks; and
- Poor business planning.

Nevertheless, these drawbacks have not altogether prevented operators from penetrating contract cleaning markets they feel capable of, and sustaining over a considerable period. Through innovation, calculated risk-taking and adversity, British Caribbean professionals have carved out market niches in the industry and set examples for younger, would-be entrepreneurs to follow in this growing trade. Effectively, this new group of traders are making a difference to the dynamics of this segment of the BPS sector (**Minicase 10. 5**).

Minicase 10. 5 Universal Service Solutions (USS)

Universal Service Solutions is a market leader in the contract cleaning business and its growth in the last five years has surpassed few in the trade. Set up in 1995 by Jamaican-born industrial engineer, Lee Williams who received an MBE for services to business in the West Midlands (2006). With a staff of over 100, the company offers a one-stop cleaning service – janitorial, chemical and equipment supplies, office waste management and professional advice on industrial cleaning trends.

Williams established Universal owing to financial problems affecting a member of his family plus an opportunity that arose to start a business from scratch. His confidence to succeed was not enough for bank officials and he received instead a £500 overdraft facility. He eventually left his high-flying job and with a staff of two, including his mother and wife, used his home as an office to start the business, having had to convince clients that they would receive `guaranteed and cost-effective' cleaning services. A medium-term strategy was developed based on the first group of customers and quickly, Williams learnt the `ropes' of the trade by seeking advice from experienced industry operators.

Other initial difficulties involved recruiting a competent management and technical team with emphasis on ensuring that quality control systems were in place. Advertising and promotional activities were done using referrals and network marketing. The business grew with increasing staff, growth in annual turnover and cleaning contracts from private companies, all of which resulted in USS being singled out as one of the *Inner City 100* firms in 2002. The citation on the award read:

"Universal Service Solutions' managing director, Lee Williams has built his commercial cleaning, security and building care services company on entrepreneurial capacity and commitment to the local community. His strategy has been a resounding success, helping the company to make into the Inner City 100 for a second year, with a turnover rising 457% from £82,822 in 1997 to just under half a million in 2001. Williams is a pillar of the community having built links across Birmingham's media, business and social networks".

The company won its first public sector contract from the Environment Agency after attending one of the De Montfort University-led Supplier Development East Midlands (SDEM) events. Faced with stiff competition from national companies, Universal was awarded the contract on merit. According to Williams, "*The award of this contract is the first ever for Universal in the public sector. We are grateful to be given this opportunity through the SDEM initiative and we are look forward to delivering a first class service to the Environment Agency.*" The company enjoys an annual turnover of over £1 million which is set to grow dramatically, as efforts are made to maintain its position as an (innovative) market leader in contract cleaning.

The dynamism of the British Caribbean BPS sector can also be seen in recruitment, training, events management and marketing. Once dubbed as `soft-option' services, these segments have a high percentage of female ownership and represent unique strands of ethnic diversity in England and Wales. Business leaders are a blend of youth and experience, mostly graduates and seasoned (ex-public /private sector) professionals, determined to be hard-nosed businesspeople and implement a self-styled form of financial independence and collective action. A twin aim of these modern professionals also, is to create wealth and make a positive difference to their communities and the wider British society.

With the economic depression receding in the late 1980s, members of the Caribbean community who were faced with fewer promotional opportunities, redundancies and witnessed a shrinking public sector market, chose the enterprise option. Very timely, they made good use of their experience and skills for enterprise start-up whilst buoyed by the Conservative Government market-driven policies. All owners of British Caribbean-led firms in the PBS sector have enjoyed mixed fortunes, but have persisted with more than a third having in excess of 10-20 years in operation.

Recruiting quality staff - management, supervisory, technical and clerical – remains a bugbear. Family-owned firms have managed to tap into the commitment, skill and resilience of family relatives and friends to keep the business alive. Other founder-owners have combined the use of family members with industry specialists to strengthen core management teams. Advertising and marketing campaigns are done through word-of-mouth or referrals and membership of local business associations. Membership of trade networks is used for commercial opportunities and as an alternative to social interaction, the latter of which the majority of Caribbean business owners have little time for especially in the early stages of enterprise start-up.

Recruitment and Training

Firms in the recruitment, consultancy, events management public relations and the training market tend to grow reasonably well, with a significant number having an annual turnover of between £500K -£1M after the first five or so years. Profit margins are accrued by positioning firms in markets where owners feel their companies will fare well or where innovation in either a product or service can result in commercial success. The achievements of British Caribbean BPS however, are also due to owners' contacts within the public sector and their (growing) awareness of the necessity to link with key industry segments in the private sector where opportunities for enterprise growth and expansion are potentially great despite restrictive practices and stiff competition.

In addition, there is a realisation that operating a business can often be a gruelling experience, and that while leadership and managerial skills are essential, even more vital, are qualities of commitment and dedication in face of adversity. The ultimate success therefore depends on the founder-owner's willingness to take calculated risks and combine these with an excellent management team supported by a group of experienced and trusted administrative and technical personnel who in the main, are the mainstay of the business. The need for customer care is also important and apart from low-income business sectors, owners of high-income service entities are conscious that without proper customer care, accompanied by a carefully defined marketing strategy, the business could be undermined or face ruination.

In this section, we highlight the endeavours of owners who defied the odds by challenging market discrimination and established legitimate businesses with quality leadership and governance resembling those of large companies on Britain's High Streets. Apart from others, one extraordinary firm, **Nichols Employment Ltd,** exemplifies diversity in its range of business services **(Case Study 10.6)**.

Case Study 10. 6 Nichols Employment Agency (NEA) Ltd

With an excellent track record in administration and honed knowledge of the labour market, Joy Nichols founded **NEA Ltd** in 1984 after realising that her opportunities for advancement in a private company seemed destined to fail. With no support from commercial institutions, she promised a bank manager at the time, that he will `eat his hat' when she achieved her mission, and since that time, the business has grown into a thriving company with annual turnover of £3 million plus.

The company provides recruitment services for mainstream institutions such as the NHS, Social Services and private companies. In 2004, Nichols received a Queen's Award for Enterprise for promoting business success in the UK and was awarded the MBE (2006). She has been invited to sit on national Boards and Committees and has been a guest lecturer at Universities and colleges, spreading the `gospel' of enterprise to young people particularly.

NEA was part of a consortium awarded a million-pound LDA contract to offer advice, technical support and capacity building for ethnic firms involved in procurement and related contract tendering schemes in the capital.

However, it is Nichols' personality and commitment that are the main drivers of the company's success, apart from the phenomenal support the firm has received since its formation in the early 1980s. The NEA boos believes that whilst ambition is important, there are other vital ingredients that every entrepreneur should possess:

- Plan methodically and systemically and review plan(s) often with staff.
- Seek (high) quality advice from those in the industry and without.
- Recruit competent and dedicated staff including administrative personnel.
- Respect the wishes of customers – treat them well and they will reward the company.
- Create multiple partnerships, but only those that are sustainable.
- Look for opportunities in international markets – develop relevant negotiating skills.
- Develop a hard-nosed approach to marketing and sales- they make a difference to the firm.
- Develop sound market intelligence systems and review them regularly with your partners.
- Strive to maintain a balanced `work-lifestlye' if you can.
- Be flexible, honest and fair in your dealings with customers, suppliers and others.

Recently, NEA expanded its operations overseas by opening a South African branch based on its parental model in the UK, with the difference being that the public and voluntary sectors in that country would be serviced by a social enterprise-type organisation.

Due to the added value that the business sector has brought to black firms, owners are tapping into the lucrative segments of recruitment and training. The recruitment consultancy segment was predicted to grow by a moderate 3% to £25.98 billion as a result of slower growth in the domestic economy in 2005. The forecast is for an increase by 12% by 2010 with these segments increasing in value: blue collar employment, computing/IT, drivers, education, financial, hotel, catering, nursing, medical services, professional, managerial, secretarial and clerical, as well as technical engineering.

With the need for broad-based industry orientation, the UK training market is pregnant with opportunities to specialise and offer holistic services according to the volume of clientele and contract value. Industry figures revealed that between 2006 and 2010, training services will show modest growth, with a rise in 1% per annum in value to reach £18.44 billion by 2010 (**CIP 2005:2006**).

Events Management

This segment refers to organising public events such as book launches, cultural displays, exhibitions and other activities held either annually or on particular occasions. This activity is associated with PR and marketing research projects which usually have a short time-span, but may involve fairly sizeable budgets. Annual conferences, trade shows and other market-related events may also fit this enterprise segment. The London-based firm of Evolution Event Management Ltd is a pacesetter in the sub-sector of this industry (**Minicase 10.7**).

Recent studies have showed contrasting trends in business formation by first and second generation of African, Asian and Caribbean people. Initially, first generation Caribbean entrepreneurs set up businesses out of necessity; namely, the lack of alternative employment. Today, the situation appears quite different, with more than 80% demonstrating greater entrepreneurial activity in order to take advantage of market opportunities.

Minicase 10. 7 Evolution Event Management Ltd

Robert Bell founded **Evolution Event Management Ltd** over 10 years ago to provide top-notch services to clients from all backgrounds. The company's growth has been phenomenal with an annual turnover estimated at £2 million and increasing. It responds to gaps in the events management market including ethnic communities that may be desirous of such a provision.

As a member of the second-generation British Caribbean community, Bell operates his firm with professional flair and managerial flexibility. When he started the company, his game-plan was to `grow moderately' through gradual turnover, increase in profits and recruitment of highly trained and motivated staff to manage efficiently a greater volume of contracts. Although Evolution was generally dissatisfied with the quality of business advice and the `co-ordination of services' in the field of events management, Bell outlined the growth strategy for the company during its formative years:

Our growth has been realised through the increase in client spending and in profit margins. The company has limited bank overdraft facilities compared to turnover and has worked on organic growth to sustain and increase the firm's size. We recruit quality staff and encourage professional training and development at all operational levels since setting and maintaining high standards are important to remain competitive **(Bell 2004)**.

At the outset of this section, I stated that the BPS market share for British Caribbean firms varied from 8% to 13% with business, finance and property segments combined. With manufacturing output on the decrease since the 1980s, the services sector has become the most buoyant in the UK economy and has created added stimulus for non-white professionals eager to compete and challenge the system of racial prejudice and market discrimination.

In addition, British Caribbean communities, aware of labour market disadvantage and the failure of mainstream education to grapple with low educational attainment levels affecting some Caribbean boys, are prepared to maximise opportunities in the commercial market to make a positive difference. Whilst London and the Southeast have the majority of British Caribbean service firms, other parts of the country have witnessed the evolution of companies delivering various innovative services to meet the needs of co-ethnic markets.

In the Midlands Counties such as inner-cities in Birmingham, Leicester, Derby and Nottingham - where there is inadequate enterprise support or technical assistance by sectors - micro firms have mushroomed to offer tailored business services, including personal development training, market research, consultancy and selected funding advice for social enterprises. In Yorkshire and Humberside, areas in Northern and Southern England, as well as Scotland and Wales, there is a persistent core of British Caribbean entrepreneurs who are conducting a `silent revolution' to change the face of mainstream enterprise support for ethnic firms, by using a sector-by-sector model. Therefore, the geographic spread of firms in the British Caribbean community breaks the traditional mould of members sticking to so-called `ethnic enclaves' according to persistent claims in studies on ethnic firms in the British Isles (**Table 10.4**).

Table 10.4 Geography and turnover of British Caribbean PBS Firms

Segments	Regional Areas	Estimated Value (£)
Consultancy	London, Southeast, Midland Counties, Scotland	£100,000 - £5m
Legal Services	London, Southeast, West Midlands	£250,000 - £4m
Financial Services	London, Southeast, Midlands Counties, Yorkshire & Humber	£100, 000 -£500,000
Property	UK wide	£150,000 - £500,000

Remittances	UK wide	£432m
Contract Cleaning	London/Southeast, Midland & Northern Counties, Scotland/Wales	£50,000 - £2m
Recruitment	London/Southeast, Midland & Northern Counties	£250,000 - £4m
Marketing	London/Southeast, Midlands & Northern Counties, Scotland	£50, 000 - £2m

(Source: Independent Research and Interviews 2000-2007)

Challenges and Prospects

The BPS area is replete with challenges and opportunities all of which influence the way in which firms succeed or not. Start-up capital is not the only problem, but also the necessity for dedicated and competent staff to cover different areas of the operational chain. Then there is the mountain of regulations and ongoing competition from larger companies that pose threats due to their financial muscle and capability to create market monopolies.

Regulations are vital to ensure that firms comply with industry standards involving accounting and financial systems, quality management procedures, equal opportunities, customer care and statutory obligations in the form of National Insurance payments, taxes and other financial compliance issues. Micro firms have the most difficulty coping with the burden of regulations, and often, don't have appropriate staff and the organisational capacity to cope. For instance, laws on the environment and the registration of patents, copyright and other trademark rights can be difficult to preserve, if companies lack the flexibility and management capability. For British Caribbean firms, the concept of the 'learning firm' culture is a necessity in this regard.

Owners are expected to be acquainted with new trends in technology to compete effectively, since this can make a huge difference between success and failure. In every part of the operational chain, businesses require suitable technology and know-how. If applied correctly, modern technology can help reduce the amount of time and resources allocated towards dealing with cost and credit control management, customer segmentation, marketing, production and other processes associated with the proper management of a firm.

Conversely, the prospects for business and professional service firms are quite attractive particularly in leading niche markets: consultancy, recruitment, training, events management, the remittance trade and financial services. The fact that professionals take risks to set up a business, is indicative of the realisation and understanding that competition in new markets will always pose an equal risk (factor), and therefore, different methods are required to cope with different situations when they arise.

Opportunities for professional services are growing and though they have been problems in market segments such as real estate and financial services, increasing prospects abound. Entry into new areas requires analysis of market trends. For instance, the buy-to-let market is an attractive financial option, but a careful assessment should be made of clients and the general trend in this segment. Some might not be interested in the prospects of short-term investment as against others interested in long-term benefits. In each case, the cost and benefit must be weighed to determine outcomes or the desired results.

Contract cleaning is both a prestigious and a profitable enterprise and the demand for the efficient management of cleaning waste is now vogue particularly in hospitals, industrial sites and commercial premises where management is keen on maintaining a healthy work environment. While remittances represent an informal business, given the volume of transactions involved, opportunities for mobilising funds to enhance enterprise opportunities in the Caribbean are quite exciting. In effect, British Caribbean firms can create strategic links with Caribbean Governments through their London-based missions to introduce a long-term Micro Business Revolving Fund to facilitate the promotion of wealth creation in the suburbs and rural areas of the Caribbean Region **(Table 10. 5).**

Table 10.5 Challenges and Prospects for the BPS Sector

Segment	Challenges	Prospects
Consultancy	Industry conditions have become more difficult due to increasing regulations especially since the Enron fall-out in the US and the economic downturn in the market.	Increased demand for offshore banking, IT, market research and allied services; firms can be part of client organisations for periods.
Legal Services	New regulations, ongoing competition from leading city law firms; market intelligence for dealing with lucrative contract-deals.	Growth in consumer business and not-for-profit clients; cultural sensitive services; residential conveyancing growth due to a relatively dynamic housing market.
Financial Services	A risk for small business in an age where litigation is has increased; vendors need proper advice on how to benefit financially, from changes in the housing market.	Services for small firms burdened with increased regulations; franchising in real estate and the buy-to-let market is growing.
Remittances	Lack of mobilised capital for enterprise growth investment; resources are not centrally pooled; and informal channels will prove difficult to manage.	Viable investment schemes to resource micro enterprise in the Caribbean through informal financial networks.
Contract Cleaning	Low staff retention, low pay and owners and managers have difficulty coping with regulations; competition from reputable cleaning companies.	Management of cleaning waste; day time cleaning to provide cost effective service; contracts from local authorities, hospitals and other public agencies.
Recruitment	Competition and regulations: rights of temporary employees; established companies have a client list, experienced and reputable suppliers.	Demand for recruitment services in construction, education, financial services, the public sector and IT areas.

Events Marketing	Shift from traditional media advertising to on- line marketing; linkages between marketing and PR agencies, combining efforts to promoting more brand products and services.	Joint PR, events management and marketing activities; develop new client segments such as phone companies, IT firms and businesses catering for the youth, leisure and sports market respectively.

(Source: Textual analysis of various business and professional segments)

Conclusion

In this chapter, I examined the various segments that comprise the business and professional services sector and the British Caribbean firms' contribution to it. The key areas of the industry's portfolio are legal, accounting, audit and consultancy which amount to an increase in business formation with a market value of billions of pounds per annum in the UK.

We examined too, the estimated 13% market share of British Caribbean firms and showed their contribution to the financial and property areas (8%). More particularly, there was focus on growth areas such as cleaning, money transfers, consultancy, events management and legal services. These were analysed through case studies and data accessed from combined informal and formal research carried out mostly during 2004 and 2007.

Noteworthy, there was evidence of growth spurts in legal services with most firms concentrating on a range of personalised services to do with domestic property while others seek a resolution of legal matters. It was demonstrated that just over 50% of all Caribbean people are property owners and used a portion of their equity to finance business start-ups and/or introduce new brands in the market.

Reference was also made to the remittances trade since the volume (an estimated £432 million) show that there is an urgent need for this enterprise to be formally integrated into enterprise activities in the

Caribbean Region.

The evidence of growth trends in consultancy, recruitment, training and events management, was also shown. These trends were appropriated through selected profiles of industry segments and the geographic spread based on estimated turnover.
It is worth emphasising that location analysis is a vital instrument that should be used to study non-white professionals whose rate of business formation also include areas outside London and the Southeast.

As is customary, I looked at the challenges and prospects of each industry segment presented in this chapter. Issues around competition, regulations, organisational development and market intelligence were underscored. Based on industry trends, we suggested opportunities in key segments. These also relate to existing procurement opportunities evident in public sector agencies across the UK.

Generally, the BPS sector is integral to the UK economy and its growth is further reinforced by the recognition it enjoys from industry specialists, policy makers, government officials and the media. For British Caribbean firms, the major challenge is to develop appropriate market intelligence systems to compete a highly fragmented market. In the next chapter, I will examine the travelling and shipping sector and the impact Caribbean firms have on it.

Chapter Notes

Barclays Bank Plc – each year, Barclays conducts surveys of the business and professional services sector to measure progress including market share. Its work corresponds with related studies carried out by other public institutions.

Labour Market - since the beginning of the 21st century, there have been several changes in the pattern of paid employment versus self employment activities. British Caribbean firms have increased their

level of enterprise activity by £3% over the past five years.
Law Reforms - in December 2004, Sir David Clementi published a report on a new regulatory framework for legal firms in England and Wales. The report stressed the importance of competition and called for better representation for consumer interest groups.

Property Ownership – the Caribbean community's property ownership has been fairly consistent bearing in mind that many in the 1950s and 1960s experienced poor housing conditions. Property has often been used as collateral to set up business or expand on existing (domestic) property portfolio.

Cleaning Contract Market – the growth of this trade has been dramatic in the past five years. It is one of a wider range of services offered by facilities management companies. Other growth streams are security and property-maintenance markets.

IVTS – known as informal value transfer systems or underground banking systems that tend to characterise the alternative and informal remittance systems of Asian people.

Hawala – derived from the Arabic word, *`hawil'* in Somali means transfer – usually of money or responsibilities. The hawilaad is an informal system of value transfer that operates in almost every part of the world and perfected by Somalis.

NEA - Nichols Employment Agency has set a gold standard in the recruitment field. The company has broken into mainstream by capitalising on its niche markets in health and social care. Joy Nichols' own stature as a role model businesswoman is an added fillip to the firm's reputation.

Events Management – this growth segment that has a correlation with PR, marketing, conference and exhibitions services, and in time, become a monopoly that combines advertising and promotional facets. Owners recognise that collaboration is a meaningful strategy for greater market consolidation.

Selected References

1 Number of Black and Minority Ethnic businesses reach record levels, Barclays Bank plc, 2006

2 Private Equity's Impact as a UK Financial Service, British Venture Capital Association, January 2007.

3 Professional Services Review, Barclays, June 2006.

4 Financial Services Opportunities in the UK, UK Trade & Investment 2006.

5 Small, David; Ram, Monder; Deakins, David & Blackwell, Robert (March 2001):

6 Accessing Finance and Business Support by Minority Businesses in the UK, Centre for Enterprise and Economic Development Research, Middlesex University Business School, London.

7 Labour Force Survey, Spring 2005 to Winter 2005/2006, England.

8 Key Note Summary Reports 2005, 2006, 2007, UK.

9 International whiz kid placing the Guyanese economy on the world map, Caribbean Times, 17 June 1995, London.

10 The Future of Legal Services; Putting Consumers First, Department of Constitutional Affairs, England, October 2005.

11 An Insight into Legal Market Profitability, Cap Gemini Ernst & Young, October 2002.

12 Sir David Clementi's Report 2005.

13 Cole, B: Trends in the Solicitors Profession, Annual Statistical Report, Law Society, London.

14 The Lawyer, 12 January 2004.

15 The Financing of Ethnic Minority Firms in the United Kingdom, Bank of England, May 1999.

16 Survey of English Housing Provision Results, November 2003.

17 Shared Ownership and Black and Minority Ethnic Communities, London Research Centre, 2004.

18 House Proud Lady: Dinnall's property firm is only a year old and is already looking overseas, The Voice, January 3 2006.

19 Homebuy – expanding the opportunity to own: Regulatory Impact Assessment, Department for Communities and Local Government, London, May 2006.

20 Informal Remittances from the UK: Values, Flows and Mechanisms, Overseas Development Group Norwich, England, March 2004.

21 BME Remittance Survey Research Report, Department for International Development, London, 27 July 2006.

22 Race Audit of Social Policy Areas – A Snapshot of Black and Ethnic Minority Communities in the UK, The 1990 Trust, September 2006.

23 The Inner City 100 Winners, 2000, 2001, 2002.

24 The UK Cleaning Industry 2003, Labour Market Intelligence, England.

25 Chartered Institute of Personal Development, UK 2005:2006.

26 Interview with Robert Bell, Evolution Event Management, 13 July 2004, London.

27 Bourne, Clea: The UK's minority-owned PR firms –players without out networks? University of Stirling/Cardew Chancery Ltd, April 2003.

28 Business & Professional Services Cluster Opportunity Group, 3-Year Plan 2005-2008, Advantage West Midlands England, 2004.

29 Enterprising People Enterprising Places; Measures to increase Ethnic Minority

30 Employment and Business Growth, Report by the National Employment Panel, May 2005.

Chapter 11

Travel and Shipping

Introduction

Despite the 9/11 incident in the USA, the Association of British Travel Agents (ABTA) identified "significant trends and new business models" emerging in the travel agency sector in response to changing consumer requirements and supplier demands (**2002**). In particular, consumers grew in confidence with telephone bookings as a result of the rise in low-fixed cost telesales operators employing staff in high street retailing outlets. At the same time, the commission capping by suppliers and `no fee' low cost airlines have forced traditional high street agencies to start charging service fees, with significant improvements in profitability arising. A 2002 survey showed an encouraging future for agents with opportunities including: -

- Specialisation led to 24% profit improvement;
- Customer services peaked at 96% satisfaction;
- Staff achieved profits of 57% better than average;
- Agencies spending £500 per employee on training achieved 30% profits; and
- Product knowledge led to profit margins 16% above average (**ABTA 2002**).

The UK travel industry serves three main markets: domestic tourism by residents within the UK; outbound travel and inbound travel by overseas residents travelling to the UK. In 2005, total expenditure on travel and tourism was £69.11 billion, and a total of 235.2 million trips were made and 1.36 billion overnight stays were made. Between 2001 and 2005, the inbound sector was the best-performing of the three in terms of number of trips and bed nights spent (**Key Note Report 2006**).

High street retail travel agencies are facing a serious challenge, and over the past five years, the UK outbound market has continued to record healthy growth. However, this trend hasn't reflected in the turnover of travel agents and tour operators, due largely to the effect of Internet-based information and booking services, and the rise of the low-cost (budget) airline sector, both of which have encouraged a DIY approach to travel purchases. Some low-fare carriers have adopted a policy of only accepting website bookings, thereby boosting direct sales by virtually removing the role of intermediaries such as retail travel agents and tour operators in the booking process.

One of the main features in the travel sector is the increase in tourism and while Mediterranean destinations remain popular, the Caribbean has benefited most from this trend, with bookings up by 60% in 2003. Notably, worldwide tourism generated revenue totalling US$6.2 trillion of economic activity, with total demand forecast to grow to US$10.7 trillion by 2015. Tourism `products' alone, generated over £12 billion to the Caribbean in that period with 20 million tourists, a seven per cent increase over the previous year.

The prospects are even greater when one considers, that as the rest of the world comes to terms with political strife and the threat of the terrorism, countries such as Cuba, the Dominican Republic, the Cayman Islands, the Bahamas, Barbados, Jamaica and Trinidad and Tobago, are among favoured destinations in Latin America and the Caribbean (***Caribbean Times* 2004**). Apart from the odd election skirmishes and the drug trade, the region is a relative zone of peace where political and economic stability allows for investors to make good of their investment in a variety of tourist products and services. Therefore, it was no surprise when the Caribbean Hotel Association predicted that the number of visitors will increase to 30 million by 2010, a 50% increase in only 10 years. By 2015, travel and tourism demand in the Caribbean is expected to reach US$87.8 billion, generating over one million jobs in the process (**2005**).

British Caribbean Operators

The British Caribbean travel and shipping market is very dynamic with scores of travel agents and tour operators in England particularly. Its is estimated that in the transport and communications industry, businesses have a market share of roughly 5 per cent, representing the seventh largest area of self-employment activity according to sector participation (**Labour Force Survey 2001-2005**).

As a giant industry, international tourism, which also includes travel and shipping, did not fully develop until the 1950s, and apart from post-war British prosperity and the advent of the jet in 1958, a major factor that contributed to the birth of the Caribbean travel and shipping market, were restrictions with money transfers and the high cost of air travel experienced by Caribbean settlers in England.

Since the 1960s to the present, there has been an increase in Caribbean travel companies especially in London and other English Counties. This development has been marked especially, by companies devoted to transporting leisure and business travellers, tourists and freight to the Caribbean and other parts of the globe. Many of these companies today, have added shipping and money transfers as a package of integrated services. Personal travel or leisure tourism make up more than 50% of all activities of Caribbean travel companies, business is estimated around 15%, while 45% includes remittances and cargo services (**Fig 11.1**).

Indeed, this has been made possible with the introduction and expansion of all-inclusive hotels and resorts. The top five countries for UK visitors are Barbados (with a 10.4% increase between January and May 2003 year on year), Dominican Republic, Mexico, Jamaica and Cuba. Antigua is also placed high in the charts and St. Lucia with its Jazz Festival has enjoyed one of its most successful years, with 20% more arrivals from the UK alone.

The Spanish-speaking Caribbean or the Antilles also attracts considerable visitor interest, and despite their achievement, Caribbean travel and shipping companies are almost unknown to the general British public. If the estimated 5% market share in the travel market is indicative of British Caribbean operators, it means they contribute approximately £953 million to the UK coffers (that is, 5% of the total turnover for travel agents and tour operators which amounted to £19.06 billion in 2005). Harlesden in west London is home to the travel and shipping market, the fifth largest growth sector in that neighbourhood, generating around quarter of a million pounds per annum, despite the area being dubbed one the most deprived inner-city wards in England (**Johnson 2002**).

Figure 11.1 Major travel and shipping services

(Source: Evaluation of the Travel & Shipping Sector 2003-2007)

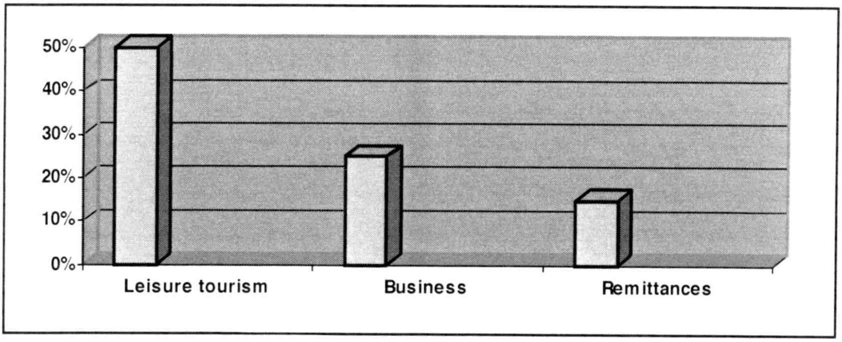

It should be noted that the UK tourism market is forecast to expand through to 2009, with the outbound market again expected to show the most growth. What the above figure illustrates, however, is the dynamic nature of British Caribbean entrepreneurs in endeavouring to create more product segmentation in the UK travel market. By studying their clients carefully and gathering vital information and data on market trends, operators can adapt their products and services to satisfy customer demands **(Table 11.1)**.

Table 11.1 Arrivals to Selected Caribbean Countries by Main Market – 2006

Destination	US	Canada	Europe	Other
Antigua & Barbuda	35,424	1,436	7,218	14,449
Barbados	130,969	49,317	241,575	141,328
Belize	150,560	15,551	34,085	46,288
Bermuda	227,716	27,674	32,347	11,225
Cancun (Mexico)	1,265,080	79,878	167,249	74,735
Cuba	-	382,929	428,985	316,347
Dominica	21,311	2,552	11,234	48,819
Dominican Republic	1,092,317	509,323	1,425,922	937,493
Grenada	27,121	6,334	32,496	52,539
Guyana	44,973	12,094	6,760	26,257
Jamaica	1,190,721	153,569	256,074	78,541
Montserrat	2,151	395	2,501	2,916
Puerto Rico	1,018,926	13,950	32,890	87,770
St. Lucia	117,450	17,491	85,565	82,004
St. Maarten	188,703	22,918	72,834	70,751
St. Vincent and The Grenadines	28,598	6,542	21,961	40,331
Suriname	714	-	22,850	11,323
Trinidad & Tobago	87,452	26,040	45,646	73,605
US Virgin Islands	518,006	4,148	11,952	64,152

(Source: Caribbean Tourism Organisation, February 16, 2007)

The data reflect tourist arrivals from the US, Canada, Europe including Britain and other parts of the world, to the Caribbean during the months of January to December 2006. This period includes winter time January to April and summer time - May to December.

Product Mix

The UK travel market is well suited for a variety of travel agencies and tour operating companies since it has the latest technology, a culturally diversified population, a world class financial centre - the London Stock Exchange - and opportunities for businesses in this sector to grow and expand beyond their potential. Generally, the product strengths of operators in tourism are:

- An abundance of worldwide destinations;
- Low cost pricing;
- Guaranteed destinations on time;
- Authenticity and unique experience of holiday packages;
- Customer care; and
- Knowledge of destinations and existing facilities.

Most of the British Caribbean travel firms use either their 'native' experience of home-countries or their wider industry knowledge of other overseas destinations to provide quality service. They compete by leveraging products and services in areas where a high degree of cultural sensitivity is involved. Three examples will suffice here; firstly, operators encourage clients to utilise 'one-stop shop' type services combining business with leisure; secondly, extending visitor stays and offering discounts on repeat visits; and thirdly, enhancing collaboration and partnerships between public and private sector bodies on special occasions including annual festivals around the world. This customer approach is evident among older Caribbean travel agencies that thrive on repeat custom, thus expending less on formal advertising and promotion channels **(Minicase 11.1)**.

Minicase 11.1 New Look Travel Ltd

Winston Pickersgill founded **New Look Travel** in 1971 at the height of Caribbean residents in the UK experiencing difficulty obtaining affordable travel and overseas holiday services. The elderly in particular, were keen on going home on holidays prior to returning permanently after retirement. Many hadn't returned home since they left in the 1950s and 1960s.

The company began as a partnership which lasted for approximately 22 years, until one of the partners retired and returned to the Caribbean about 15 years ago. Initially, the partners invested £3,000 to kick-start the business. Smaller travel firms benefited from New Look's generosity and according to Pickersgill, "*In an effort to provide a solid foundation for the travel and shipping sector, we supported owners through a ticket sale-commission system because many were unlicensed traders when they started the trade.*"

The multi-million pound company has various packages aimed at clients travelling to destinations in Canada, the Caribbean and the USA. It benefits much from repeat custom year-round, having built a sound reputation in the industry for over 30 years. New Look's accreditation includes ABTA, IATA and ATOL. The strategy is to consolidate its position as a leading travel and shipping company, by engaging communities through sponsorship, increase participation in the economic development of the UK and improve operational efficiency (**Pickersgill 2007**).

As was mentioned before, the UK travel market is highly segmented with the air freight segment worth £726.1 million (**2004 estimates**) and freight forwarding worth around £19.76 billion (**2006 estimates**). Air forwarding especially, is a niche market for British Caribbean firms. Poor economic conditions in some parts of the Caribbean have resulted in more UK-based Caribbean residents being involved in shipping or freighting consumables and thus using facilities such as warehousing, storage and customs-clearance activity.

Cargo Shipping

Although several larger companies have outsourced freight forwarding activities, a tendency that continues to grow, due to their size and composition, British Caribbean firms have decided against this approach. Rather, in an effort to reduce costs and improve productivity, owners have added this segment and developed a high level of specialisation, whilst maintaining awareness of security, consumer confidence and service reliability. Few brokers refuse cargo shipping which is an integral part of the travelling and shipping trade. Shipping also includes money transfers or remittances for personalised services involving families experiencing financial difficulty or in other instances, supporting older relatives who may need expensive medication and generally need income support. As Pickersgill of New Look Travel acknowledged,

We must build on our strengths in culture and knowledge of consumers to add flexibility to the services we provide. At New Look Travel, we are not carried away by profits; we believe in offering a reliable service that is cost effective to meet the needs and demands of our customers. We make it our duty to study our customers to understand if our services fit the profiles of different customers. For example, younger clients will choose different types of services than let's say, older customers who might just be interested in an ordinary holiday/ leisure package **(Pickersgill 2001)**.

Since the Caribbean travel companies in Britain cater for a predominantly Caribbean clientele, it is important that services are designed with this group in mind. Part of the value associated with travel agencies is the knowledge they possess about destinations. Customers expect firms to provide them with sound advice for competitive price. Cargo shipping was prevalent in the much of the 1980s as Caribbean countries like Guyana and Jamaica, were affected by the financial stringencies imposed by the IMF/World Bank. It was the so-called 'belt-tightening' period when the regional economy faced meltdown.

In Guyana's case, essential commodities such as wheaten flour and split peas were banned due to prolonged balance-of-payment difficulties. Foreign currency was scarce and the nation was urged to be increasingly self-sufficient. Families from all walks of life depended much on barrel imports to alleviate their economic and financial situation. The trade was so popular in the Caribbean, that teachers, public servants and other professionals operated part-time enterprises to supplement their meagre public sector wages. These micro trading units became part of a growing parallel economy which flourishes in part, today. Apart from food, clothing and footwear, other consumables were introduced in this fluid movement of goods and services, initially triggered by the cargo (shipping) trade.

For the past 30 years, the UK travel and shipping sector has grown dramatically, a beneficiary of innovation and driven by shifting consumer markets and global political and economic developments, and not the least, competition from mainstream travel agents and tour operators. Therefore, the achievements of British Caribbean operators should not be ignored since they have helped set new standards in the industry, as is in the case of (not only New Look Travel but) **Everton Forbes, MPS Travel** and **JJ Shipping (Minicases 11. 2)**.

Minicases 11. 2 Selected British Caribbean travel and shipping firms

Everton Forbes Travel Company Limited was established in 1968 and guarantees customer satisfaction with services ranging from cargo shipping and leisure travel to money transfers. The agency offers specialised eco tourism packages in parts of Latin America especially for travellers interested in visiting and benefiting from the scenery in the Amazon rainforest and other attractions in the Americas. According to Managing Director, Everton Forbes,

In keeping pace with new trends in the industry, we have extended our services to include more leisure travel. Customers request packages dealing with sight-seeing trips, especially Caribbean citizens who have been away from their home countries for years. There is also an increasing demand for high-income and budget-conscious travellers too, plus families, students and the elderly, most of whom travel regularly to renew their back-home roots.

MPS Travel was founded by Mark Loban in 1989 as a lead shipping company providing value for money services to countries worldwide. A flexible approach is matched by its commitment to customer care. Its diversification policy involves storing cargo until ready for shipment whether import or export commodities, with state of the art security system in place. A personal and professional packing service also exists and this allows customers access to weekly collection and delivery services.

The services are quite extensive – baggage, household and vehicle shipping; storage services, customs information, shipment protection, promotions, air and seas freight and customer packaging service producers, with agents located worldwide - Africa, the Caribbean and Europe inclusive.

JJ Travel and Shipping was established in 1992 by James Graham in another long line of innovative operators in the industry, and specialising in the field of international shipping. The company is committed to offering clients an optimum level of service that incorporates a highly competitive rates structure.

The firm maintains that shipping is about people and personal contact. It has a policy of recruiting staff with knowledge and experience of freight forwarding/liner shipping. With frequent changes in customers demands and the vagaries in the travel market, employing highly qualified staff with a wide cross section of commercial experience, is the only way to offer clients, the level of service required to develop business success in the 21st century.

British Caribbean travel agencies conduct an average of 55% of total business on the phone. Customers visiting offices account for an average of 40% of all transactions while about 5% are generated through the Internet. Leisure products make up nearly three quarters of all services provided by Caribbean travel companies. These products relate directly to international sales for the Caribbean region, Africa, the USA and parts of Europe and elsewhere. In terms of specialisation, there is an almost 60:40 ratio of travellers to the Caribbean and North America. Normal airfares range from £200 to £1000 plus, depending on circumstances such as:

- Time of year;
- Age of customer;
- Type of airline;
- Duration of travel or stay;
- Destination; and
- Nature of travel service.

Since the beginning of the 21st century, British Caribbean travel agencies have improved on specialisation, whilst introducing innovation for sophisticated clients. The Caribbean region attracts three quarters of a million UK visitors annually. Although the main attractions are undoubtedly the beaches, the differences of culture and the range of holidays people can go on, is immense. There are other competitive issues which include focus on providing excellent customer service, offering niche products and developing and retaining quality staff. In the main, small travel agents and tour operators consider competitive threats in the following order: the activities of larger companies and multinational firms, consumer Internet purchase, the introduction of travel shops on high streets, direct selling, commission capping and digital TV.

Corporate Responsibility

Society usually demands that businesses invest a portion of their resources to good causes. Contrary to the myth that only large companies are charitable in outlook, British Caribbean entrepreneurs are equally prone to render support to social programmes, a rather instinctive feature of most traditional societies. On the whole, minority communities exude civic pride and a desire to make good of their situation since the motivation is to overcome injustice and prejudice in their environment.

Throughout the 1960s to the present time, airline operators have used their services to create social benefits for both clients and others less fortunate. Ex-midwife, Jamaican-born Beverly Lindsay is one such pioneer of business success and corporate-social responsibility in Britain **(Minicase 11. 3)**.

The recently established firm, **Tropical Connections Ltd** (**2004**), is keen to help people based in the UK to realise their dreams of 'blue skies, palm trees and turquoise water'. Born in Britain to Barbadian parents, Maureen Smith who is the founder-owner of Tropical is an expert on property law and believes in blending estate development with leisure (forms of) tourism, thereby offering clients a chance to fulfil their dreams of visiting places in the Caribbean that most regard as 'paradise'. Hers is a continuation of the tradition that started more than

30 years ago by other Caribbean travel agents and tour operators.

With dual experiences covering both UK and Caribbean law and living, TCL is a specialist in property purchases (conveyancing and mortgage processing) and insists on high standards of customer care. Its services include: -

- Commercial Funding – helping developers to secure loans to develop and construct real estate projects
- Currency Transfers – transfer funds from the UK to the Caribbean
- Holiday Services - arranging self-catering accommodation and hiring vehicles for holiday-makers.

The success of the firm is attributed to client testimonials acknowledging the quality and efficiency of Tropical Connections' work. Referring to the products on offer, one client said, '*I could not have done it without Tropical Connections. I would always choose the firm if I had to do it all over again. Now I have my dream holiday in Barbados and the weather is great*' (**www.tropicalconnections.co.uk**).

Minicase 11. 3 Diamond Travel

Beverly Lindsay established **Diamond Travel**, a fully bonded travel agency in 1987. With its motto, '*A cut above the Rest'*, the company is one of Birmingham's leading independent travel agents, accredited by ABTA, ATOL and IATA, a member of the Elite Travel Group. Over the years, the agency has developed expertise in several areas, giving it the advantage of offering to repeat and new customers, the benefit of informed advice, specialist knowledge, and a service which is second to none.

The firm utilises the Internet and responds to customers requests, and constantly updates the website with special fares, package holiday deals and special offers based on availability.

Information on flights, accommodation and destination arrangements are obtained through a `booking request' form. With a small team of specialists in Internet booking, travel consultancy and accounts management, Lindsay has maintained a healthy annual turnover of more than £500,000 per annum. In 2002, 3b, a community enterprise agency, awarded her *Best Businesswoman of the Year*.

Although she manages a demanding business, Lindsay still finds time to participate in community activities by supporting many organisations. In 2001 she was recognised by the Jamaican Government for her invaluable contribution to community development. As head of the Institute of Jamaican Nationals, she believes that honouring successful Caribbean nationals is more than just a `one-off' affair.

It is not enough for us, to once a year gather to celebrate the achievements of our national heroes, if their legacy does not serve to inspire us to put personal differences aside and utilise all of our collective talents, skills and resources to leave behind something substantial that we as Jamaicans can be truly proud of (**Jamaican Government 2006**).

Real Competition

As in other industries, the travel sector is very competitive with large national chains, small-home based companies and travel agents focusing on all types of travel and tourism. Commonly, the industry is organised and represented by the national body - the Association of British Travel Agents (ABTA) and affiliated to other industry bodies such as the Confederation of British Industry. The Caribbean travel agency sector therefore has to deal with competition in the following ways: -

- *Large Companies:* well-known and respected in areas of adventure and travel in the world, especially those that have exclusive packages, successfully integrated travel agency services and adventure travel activities. This offers them complete control over the entire vacation.

- *Cruise-line Firms:* traditional agencies that have developed specialisation in global cruise-line tourism and are able to exploit their experience, reputation and financial solvency.
- *Travel Agents:* entrepreneurs with superior negotiating skills and extensive contacts with national and international travel companies to undercut small-based companies. Their successful marketing communications and marketing expertise is also a competitive edge to British Caribbean travel and shipping companies.

When interviewed for this book, the founder of JJ Travel & Shipping, James Graham, predicted that the standards set by British Caribbean travel agencies will remain the decisive factor regarding success or failure of their operations. J.J. Travel is located in south London, it provides an integrated airline and related travel packages that cater for both high-income and budget-conscious customers. Business travellers to the Caribbean benefit from `top-of-the-line' search for air travel deals to conduct activities such as research and field trips, as well as sabbaticals. The agency's value-added services offer knowledge, expertise, competitive rates and speciality focus on all-round travel, which translate into increased satisfaction for the customer. Graham outlined the keys to the success of his firm: -

We have segmented the travel business and targeted customers whose requirements are mutually beneficial to them and the business. We have repositioned the firm in the leisure, tourism and business market respectively and we communicate the differentiation of our products and their quality through personal interaction and leafleting. We have also developed a segment of loyally, repeat customers who have done business with the company in excess of 10 years. As a result of this trend, we have been able to maintain profitability over 5% **(Graham 2007).**

Tourism Product

The *Caribbean Times* reported that, as the rest of the world comes to terms with political strife and the threat of terrorism, the Caribbean is enjoying tourism revenue like never before'. The newspaper went on to state this:

Growth has continued during the first quarter of this year (2004); and the growth in tourism in the Caribbean has come in the face of 2.2 per cent decline in tourist arrivals for the hemisphere and a 1.2 per cent decline in world tourist arrivals. In Jamaica, as in Tobago and Cuba, the Dominican Republic and Cayman Islands, the Bahamas and other Caribbean territories, the increased arrivals and earnings mean the Caribbean is rebounding from the disaster after 9/11.

Clearly, North Africans seemed to have licked the initial fear of getting on an aircraft and the Caribbean is benefiting as a safe destination compared with the Asian and Pacific region, which experienced a 10% (**2004**).

Dominican tour operator, Courtney Love, is pleased with the growing prospects for tourism in the Caribbean. His Docklands-based firm, **Authentic Caribbean** is cashing on this trend. He believes that,

The Caribbean sales will definitely increase, with more destinations being introduced and lots of new resorts opening. We specialise in group and corporate bookings and they are increasing at a fast rate because the client is aware that the weather is likely to be excellent and the threat of terrorism is minimal' (***Caribbean Times*** **2004**).

In addition, there is European investment in the Americas, and in many Caribbean countries, the number of tourism arrivals by cruise ship exceeds the number of `stay-overs'. Cruise arrivals, usually only stay for a few hours – some passengers not even bothering to disembark. There are disgruntled feelings in Caribbean countries about the low share of revenue which remains in the region based on the large volume of profit that foreign operators and companies generate annually. And though governments have introduced relevant legislation to create a balance between commercial interests and the social welfare of citizens, it is often difficult to regulate every aspect of the tourist trade in light of the effects of globalisation.

The ability of countries to increase their share of this revenue is also frustrated by the perceived ease with which cruise lines can shift their schedules and play one country against another (**Pro Invest 2004**). While the cruise market is dominated by large US companies, there are potential opportunities for new partnerships between EU cruise ship operators and British Caribbean companies offering specialised cruise trips to ports which are too small for US giants.

In addition, there are also likely clusters of partnership opportunities for EU-British Caribbean enterprises in construction and development of port facilities, shore to ship communication and IT systems, as well as the development of shore excursions and duty free retailing. Some of these activities are being facilitated via British Caribbean tour operators.

Continuing along the lines of 'opportunity clusters', tourism around the world is built on international partnerships between elements in the process. These can take many forms such as creating linkages with hotels, transport companies, food businesses and a host of other business arrangements. Other valuable industry linkages that could be beneficial to ethnic operators are:

- Marketing arrangements;
- Franchising;
- Joint ventures;
- Licensing;
- Technical agreements; and
- Technology transfer.

This type of business model might be used to attract investors to finance hotel development in African, Caribbean and Pacific countries, using the `Buy-a-room-to-Let' concept, especially if combined with tax concessions (**ProInvest 2004**).

If however, ethnic airline tour operators are to improve their market share and enhance profit margins, they must streamline their operations to reflect a modern tourist trade which is driven by fast-changing customer needs, the stability of tourist destinations and the applied technology that is essential for building market segments. Industry linkages can thus be created using the framework below **(Fig 11.2**).

Figure 11.2 Structural linkages framework for tour operators

- *Hospitality Providers* - hotels, apartments, villas, resorts etc.
- *Attraction Providers* – golf courses, theme parks, casinos, national parks etc.
- *Infrastructure* – airports, roads, electricity, water, waste, medical, sea ports.
- *Local Transport Providers* – ferries, airlines, air taxis, buses, car rentals.
- *Construction* – contractors, materials, transport, surveyors, architects, valuers, engineers.
- *Hospital Supplies* – food, laundry, sanitary ware, alcohol and other beverages.
- *Property Sales* – estate agents, retirement, family holiday.
- *Financial Services* – credit cards, retail banking, insurance.
- *Marketing Services* – graphic design, advertising research, photography, PR.
- *Tourism Financiers* – merchant banks, private investors, investment funds.
- *Entertainment Production* – movies, music recording.
- *Media* – trade press, consumer media, and Internet publishers.
- *Professionals* - lawyers, taxi drivers, tourism consultants, accountants, investment analysts *(Source: Adapted from ACP Tourism Providers, European Union 2004)*

Therefore, it seems that to achieve market parity or establish a level playing field, British Caribbean travel companies should concentrate on consolidating gains with current customers, whilst conducting a campaign to target new clients. By investigating the demands of couples/families and individual adventure travellers by demography, agencies will be in a better position strategically, to allocate appropriate resources to meet such needs. The level of corporate advertising is equally important and annual sponsorship of high-profile events involving co-ethnic markets will enable companies to gain greater recognition all-round. Alternatively, collaborating with companies such as British Airways and Virgin Airlines is another way to strategically align the business with the market of international travellers.

Repositioning

Target marketing in the travel industry also includes repositioning, an effective approach to secure ongoing customers and introduce in the process, new product and service lines to satisfy customer demand. This requires constant reviews of the global market. Participating in exhibitions and trade fairs can serve too, the purpose of gaining public recognition and acceptance. Most Caribbean travel agencies have experience and contacts across the industry and these attributes should be used to offer unique services and core values that could help contribute greatly, to higher profits.

As far back as the mid-1990s, MPS Travel, known for its flexibility and innovation, modernised its operations to increase competitive advantage. The family-run company introduced new products to create greater customer choice. These products are supported by quality staff, flexible pricing, training investment and website improvement. Owner Mark Loban explained the process: -

Repositioning the firm is crucial to market presence and we have developed brand recognition through effective advertising, marketing communications and promotion. MPS has utilised the networking benefits of industry associations, trade shows and publications, as well as developed and promoted the company's website. Information is available to corporate and other type customers, and encourages regular feedback to plan better and introduce products and services to meet customer demands.

The company's marketing strategy mirrors the goals of reputation and customer care and our employees enjoy the challenge of serving clients. In return, the company promotes the benefits of services to staff through holiday entitlements, savings on vacation and reward them for improving the company's profitability. The key to competition is the volume of services offered at discount prices coupled with the way employees are treated; after all, they are the backbone of the business **(Loban 2002)**.

The travel agents and tour operators included in this chapter, operate small businesses with the average turnover of £300,000, and far higher in the more established travel companies. Operations are located across England (primarily in London, the Southeast and the Midland Counties).The Birmingham firm of **Travel Solutions Worldwide,** concentrates on low-cost fare provision for customers such as pensioners, `emergency-type' travellers (dealing with bereavement or family illness etc), the occasional business traveller, young people and regular holidaymakers. Their favourite destination is often the Caribbean and North America. Founder, Penny Howe who is a former nurse, said that clients tend to ask the following questions about travel agencies in an effort to assess the quality of service on offer; for example,

- How do you find a good travel agent?
- What should be the determining factor in choosing a travel agency?
- What special services do travel agencies offer?
- How do I know if my travel agent is consumer-conscious?
- How do I know if my travel agent is well trained?
- Who uses travel agents?
- Are travel agencies linked to an associated body? **(Howe 2006)**

Challenges and Prospects

Similar to other industries, the travel and shipping sector is constantly evolving, and its composition and size are determined by the level of product differentiation, customer segmentation and a pricing strategy to meet operational overheads whilst satisfying customer' affordability. The recruitment of experienced managerial, administrative and technical personnel is a necessity, since without a proper skills base, travel companies are destined to lose custom and eventually face closure. With small firms facing intense competition from big companies that introduce innovation in the form of (retail) travel shops on the high streets and linking their products to related companies, British Caribbean firms have to routinely evaluate their organisational structure and performance strategy to compete (**Table 11.2**).

Table 11. 2 Marketing framework for British Caribbean travel and shipping firms

Challenges	Opportunities
Monopoly: the market is dominated by British, European and American firms; they have a market share of over 80%.	British Caribbean firms can specialise in cruise line and adventure tourism, festival tourism, using their cultural knowledge of Africa, Asia, the Caribbean and Latin America, as well as the USA.
Skills: middle management and technical personnel are in short supply; they are fewer graduates in the industry today.	Firms can sponsor undergraduate training or offer bursaries for vocational courses in Travel and Tourism to professionals interested in a career; for example, Hospitality Management.
Inbound Tourism: dominated by large companies such as Thomas Cook and other agents that offer short-breaks and visits to historic/ heritage sites in the UK.	Caribbean operators can introduce new products in the inbound tourism market by engaging with educational institutions and social groups to facilitate excursions and heritage site visits to encourage settler communities to learn more about the UK.

Partnerships: multiple partnerships exist among European and mainstream operators, hoteliers, distribution and supply chains and other support services in the hospitality sector. .	Operators can maximise the presence of niche markets via franchising arrangements, joint ventures, licensing agreements and tourist hospitality services at the domestic and international level.
Profitability: larger branches are competing for a small share of the travel agency market and newcomers are prepared to pay high prices for good locations.	Owners must ensure that they have a proper licensing system preferably IATA affiliation since it does make it easier to trade and be recognised as a reputable operator, and it also allows for specialisation in products and services.

(Source: Textual analysis of firms 2000-2007)

Despite tough competition from mainstream companies, British Caribbean firms have a strategic advantage in terms of cultural knowledge or popularity with tourist destinations plus the fact they are located in high streets. Strengths apart, an average travel firm start-up operations require approximately £10,000 -£20,000 depending on the type of services earmarked and the volume of clientele being catered for, along with premises and location being sought. Financing 50% of travel agencies need new investment in order to compete with large companies.

Yet opportunities in the travel market are growing above 5% annually, with potential sales improvement due to growth in service fees or commissions. Caribbean operators in the UK can also develop strong agency management to produce top quality service and implement a vertical integration strategy that seeks to incorporate services to create branches producing different or similar products and services. Constant threats remain; namely, the Internet which provides a competitive medium for pricing; national and international competition involving larger travel conglomerates and unforeseen economic problems such as recession and currency devaluation, all of which can result in reduced revenue.

Niche Markets

Indeed, the tourism market is highly segmented and tour operators can maximise opportunities for travellers/tourists interested in `paradise' package tours, adventure or eco-travel and festivals, the latter of which are held annually across the world. And since the main role of travel agents is to provide a convenient location for the purchase of travel, it is vital that they provide specialist services for the benefit of consumers' tastes and general demands. The opportunities therefore a range of tourism products are thus limitless **(Table 11. 3).**

Table 11. 3 Examples of tourism products in the Caribbean

Products	Impact
Yachting	Popular in the northern Caribbean and the Grenadines.
Sport Tourism	Well known organised sporting events for example World Cup 2007.
Festival Tourism	St. Lucia's annual jazz festival; Carnival in Trinidad and Tobago, Caribana in Canada and other such festivities worldwide.
Ecotourism	Viable form of tourism protects the environment and involves local communities.
Pageant Tourism	Opportunity for countries to exhibit their `cultural wears' popular in Africa (especially Tanzania).
Health Tourism	Prevalent in the Bahamas particularly – climatic conditions in the Caribbean are appropriate for this form of tourism.

(Source: World Travel and Tourism Council 2004)

Certainly, there are other segments in the tourist trade that British Caribbean travel agencies should maximise using the tropical conditions in the Americas. Many destinations such as Greece, Spain and other Mediterranean countries have developed circuit partnerships in order to organise multi-country holidays. Tourism statistics show for example, that there is substantial travel between French citizens in France and the Creole speaking islands in the eastern Caribbean, and between residents in the Netherlands Antilles and Aruba. Such therefore is the competitiveness on the international tourism market that British Caribbean operators can, if they so desire, create guarantee' market space by utilising knowledge of culture and location.

Another important element of the travelling and shipping sector which is a rarity for ethnic firms is the provision of transport haulage services to mainstream and ethnic markets alike. Some British Caribbean firms are involved in this segment in a limited, but significant way, despite stiff competition from large haulage companies. Transport removals involve the provision of transportation services to both inbound and outbound destinations. This trade is a growth area in London particular among some minority enterprises and is integral to the physical distribution process of companies marketing value chain. The British Caribbean-owned firm of Benjamin Oswald in north London is a success story for those interested in setting up transport and removal businesses (**Minicase 11. 4**).

Minicase 11. 4 Benjamin Oswald

Entrepreneurs, Paula McGrowder and Daniel Henry, founded the `partnership' company of **Benjamin Oswald** in 1984 with the aim of providing `exemplary removals and delivery services to the London domestic and business community. The firm operates a large fleet of commercial vehicles from transit vans to articulated lorries nationally.

The founders started the business from scratch with a desire to `grow moderately' with a plan to achieve growth by increasing annual turnover, moving to new premises and ensuring that quality staff are in board. The use of overdraft facilities, family savings and personal savings have been used to sustain the business over the past 10 years, and according to the owners, `We don't rely on grants and hand-outs to progress.'

As a result of its commitment to quality, good work ethics, the firm is now a premier removal and logistics operator across London and the M25 Region. The company is the holder of BSI 9901 and Investors in People accreditated. It is a member of the national Guild of Removers and Storers.

With a small dedicated staff, the million-pound firm of Benjamin Oswald's unique selling point is its market intelligence system that has a tracking system for each client. '*We have developed a customer-oriented package that assess and evaluates the services we provide and encourage customers to offer feedback so that we can modify or add to the services we offer*,' Henry explained.

As the business progresses satisfactorily, competing in the market of larger haulage companies, Benjamin Oswald plans to expand in the European haulage market. In contributing to a segment of travelling and shipping sector, the London-based firm is equally adding to the physical distribution value chain of the marketing mix. '

Consumer Travel Trends

Changes in the travel market are impacting on the industry and operators have had to make significant adjustments in service delivery, to keep pace with such trends. The 2002 MORI survey showed the gap between the volume of bookings made with travel agents compared with tour operators was rapidly closing. In 2000 for example, 40% of respondents said they were 'likely to book direct with a tour operator'. The figure showed that this had increased by 7% to 47% (**MORI 2002**).

Commission capping and scrapping by the airlines is changing the face of the traditional travel agent. Increasingly, agents have to change service fees for their time, information ad expertise. In the early part of this century, information obtained from the industry, showed significant increases in the number of agents charging service fees. Service fees increased from 38% in 2000 for example, to 70% in 2002. **Fig 11.3** shows changing booking methods involving customers.

Figure 11.3 Changing Booking Methods – ever used by customers

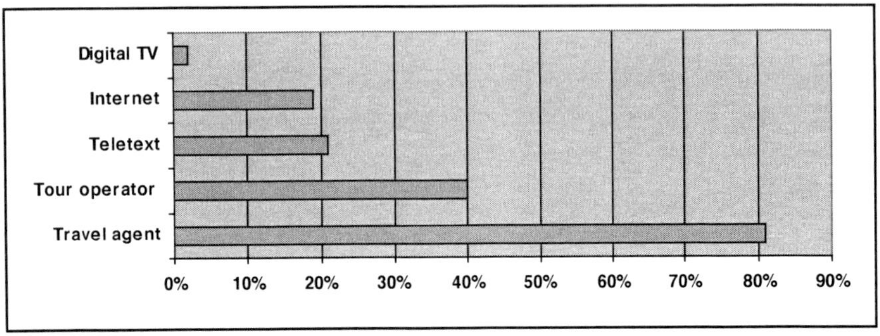

(Source: Consumer Travel Trends, MORI Survey 2002)

The above customers' responses followed questions about methods used to book package holidays as well as the likely methods to be used when thinking about booking holidays in the near future. In terms of `likely to use' the same number said they will use a travel agent, nearly half said they would use a tour operator by telephone, a quarter intended to use teletext, nearly half specified their preference of the Internet via a computer and nearly a tenth said they will use digital TV to book holiday travel.

Conclusion

In this chapter I scrutinized in some detail, the activities of the Caribbean travel and shipping sector and its contribution to the UK economy, to the value of over £953 million per annum (that is, based on the 5% market share as per the 2005 UK total figure of £19.06 billion). The presence of operators was due to lack of affordable prices for air travel and inadequate services to meet the demands of Caribbean immigrants who wanted to travel back home on a regular basis.

Since the late 1960s when the first Caribbean travel agency was established – Everton Forbes Travel – there has been relative growth in the number of ethnic firms in the travel and shipping industry. Operations could be found in city centres on the high streets across England – more particularly in London, the Southeast and the Midland Counties. The majority of operators are IATA affiliated and collaborate with major airline companies and tend to sub-contract with larger travel operators and the hospitality sector.

Issues around market trends, competition and the general operations of firms were discussed. It was stated that real competition came from large companies, cruiser-line firms and independent travel agents that have extensive contacts and the financial muscle to undercut smaller companies in the industry. Caribbean firms compete in the Caribbean and Latin American Region and there are growing signs that some companies have developed niche markets in Africa, the US and parts of Europe, in their attempt to grow the business through greater customer volume and a price differential strategy. **MPS Travel** for instance have agents in almost every continent and delivered services ranging from cargo shipping, money transfers, travel information and customer satisfaction to linkages with a range of hospitality industry segments.

The principle of corporate responsibility was highlighted and contrary to the myth that only large companies figured in this strategy, this chapter highlighted instances where British Caribbean travel agencies and tour operating companies are very much engaged with the community and keen on expanding their role and contribution across other ethnic communities. The brilliant work of Tropical Connections, Diamond Travel and to an extent, J.J. Shipping, MPS Travel and other operators both in London and the West Midlands, represented a comforting thought for potential travel owners to make a difference to the corporate landscape.

In an effort to develop viable operations, I also discussed the possibility of owners creating structural linkages throughout the value chain of the industry. As an adaptation of the European model, the suggestion is for British Caribbean operators to study carefully each segment of the tourism market and assess its viability and relate products and services to strategic areas within the value chain. For example, the success of tourism as a product was linked to local features such as property sales, a range of professional and business services, media, infrastructure and local transport providers, to name a few.

As a further complement, I detailed market reposition on the part of ethnic firms, citing the work in progress by MPS Travel to promote the benefits of the firm to both clients and staff. Proprietor Mark Loban insisted that clients and staff were the 'backbone of the business and without them, the business will falter' (**2002**). Further, understanding the varying needs of different clients by service type was equally crucial in the repositioning angle.

Finally, using a competitor framework, we determined the major challenges of and prospects for British Caribbean travel agents and tour operators in the matrix of intense competition from mainstream conglomerates. Challenges such as economies of scale, competition, location, affordability and location were examined. It was stated that British Caribbean firms will have to 'raise their game' by applying more of their industry experience, knowledge of the clientele, contacts at tourist destinations and better use of web-based market intelligence to increase market share and consolidate profitability.

Without a doubt, the UK travel and tourism market is forecast to show further expansion to 2009, with the outbound or external market expected to show the most growth. There is significant potential in the inbound or domestic market, however, with visits and spending from developing markets in Eastern Europe, China and South-East Asia expected to rise. One notable event that will contribute to an increase in travellers to the UK is the 2012 London Olympic Games. The event will benefit the whole of the UK, with each region likely to receive additional leisure and business visitors in the years prior, during and after the Games. British Caribbean operators can certainly maximise this historic opportunity by adapting their services to suit the (sector) demands of the occasion.

Information and data for this chapter were obtained from direct interviews with owners, questionnaire surveys, industry network sources, news features in the Press, site visits to operators and general discussions with travellers and tourists using travel agents and tour operators in the UK and abroad. Undoubtedly, the travel and shipping sector remains an unsung area of British Caribbean success and it is hoped that this chapter, like the overall book, will create greater awareness, a deeper understanding and an appreciation for the tremendous contribution this community and their ethnic cousins make to UK Plc. In the next chapter, I will assess the work of Caribbean firms to the knowledge sector also known as the computing industry or technology futures.

Chapter Notes

IATA – the International Air Transport Association was established over 60 years ago to represent, lead and serve the airline industry-94% of international scheduled air traffic.

ATOL – a consumer protection scheme (for passengers' flights and other travels) that carries out checks on tour operators and travel organisers, it licences, and requiring a financial guarantee called a bond which is lodged with ATOL.

ABTA – the Association of British Travel Agents was set more than 50 years and is an organisation which represents UK travel agents and tour operators responsible for the sale of around 90% of package holidays and approximately 45% of independent travel arrangements.

Sectoral Bodies – other organisations representing the travel and tourism industry include the Chartered Institute of Transport (CIT), the Hotel and Catering Institutional Management Association (HCIMA), the Institute of Travel and Tourism (ITT) and the British Hotels, Restaurants and Caters' Association (BHRCA).

Benchmarking Survey the Tour Operator's Benchmarking Survey provides practical data relating to both their financial and operational performance of tour operators and analysis on their success factors.

Private Airlines – the growth of this sector and the appearance of entrepreneurs such as Harold Laker aided the expansion of air travel after the war, which altered significantly too, the potential market for the airline industry.

Regulations and Controls – the 1970s were marked by a new direction in government policy towards regulations and controls when the Development of Tourism Act 1969 Act was introduced, along with the progressive introduction in the industry of the 1971 Civil Aviation Act that provided a system of licenses to control air tour operators in the UK.

Travel Retailing – new forms of travel retailing have been developed by the online travel/booking agents that are in competition with the established high street retailers; alternatively, they might be provided by the latter as part of their operation.

Package Tours – the origin of such activities can be traced to travel agent entrepreneurs who began operating foreign tours such as Thomas Cook who later expanded to sell a range of travel services – package tours were sold in turn through other travel agents.
The Caribbean Tourism Organisation - monitors the level of tourism performance in the Caribbean Region and provides information and data on trends in the trade by destination, countries' arrivals, main markets, frequency of travel and volume of visitors.

EU-Pro Invest Project – a joint initiative involving organisations from East Africa and Europe to explore and facilitate partnership and investment opportunities between companies from Europe and Africa in the ICT and digital media sub-sector market.

EU Tourism -principal European visitors to the Caribbean countries come from Germany, UK, Spain, Italy, with Scandinavian markets relatively small and French and Dutch visitors concentrate in the non-Caribbean French and Dutch speaking islands. European operators to the Caribbean operate by major cross-border operators and specialist companies that focus on the Caribbean.

Cross-border Operators – the major operators are Preussage, Thomas Cook and Rewe of Germany, MyTravel and First Choice, both UK tour operators.

ACP – the African, Caribbean and Pacific Group of States is an organisation created by the Georgetown (Guyana) Agreement in 1975, comprising 79-Members states which are signatories to the Georgetown Agreement or the Partnership Agreement between the ACP and the European Union officially called the ACP-EC Partnership Agreement or the 'Contonou Agreement'.

Caribbean Tourism Products – British Caribbean operators can maximise the various tourism products which exist in the Caribbean Region, with particular emphasis on natural assets (sea and beach). National parks sand historic and cultural resources remain relatively undeveloped as tourism attractions in the region.

Selected References

1 The 2004 Travel Agents' Benchmarking Survey, ABTA/Price Waterhouse Coopers, London, available from www.abtamembers.org/research.

2 Travel & Tourism, Key *Note Market Report*, October 2006.

3 Travel Statistics &Trends 2005, Association of British Travel Agents BTA.

4 The World's Leading Outbound Markets – Ten Key Facts, Mintel 2006.

5 Ethnic Minority Self-employment by sector 2001-2005, Labour Force Survey.

6 Johnson, C.A.: *Economic Research in Harlesden,* TCS Educational Trust ltd, November 2002.

7 *Tourist Arrivals by Main Market* (2006). Caribbean Tourism Organisation, February 2007.

8 Mason, Keith J ((2000): Marketing low cost airline services to business travellers, Air Transport Group, Cranfield University, Cranfield, UK.

9 `Changing the guard with black tourism', *BBC News*, 16 July 2003.

10 Holloway, J. Christopher (1983): *The Business of Tourism*, Macdonald and Evans, Plymouth, England.

11 Trinidad and Tobago: The Impact of Travel & Tourism on Jobs and the Economy, World Travel & Tourism Council 2004.

12 `A Day in the Life: Beverly Lindsay, Diamond Travel', Birmingham, England, *Travel Trade Gazette* UK & Ireland, 8 October 2004.

13 Tropical Connections Ltd website: http://www.tropicalconnections.co.uk

14 Interview with Winston Pickersgill, New Look Travel, 30 November 2007.

15 Jamaicans in the UK Honoured, 23 October 2006, Ministry of Foreign Affairs, Jamaica.

16 `Sunny Times', *Caribbean Times*, 4 June 2004.

17 Interview with James Graham, JJ Travel & Shipping, 17 January 2007.

18 Interview with Mark Lobban, MPS Travel, 5 March 2002.

19 Interview with Penny Howe, Travel Solutions Worldwide, 15 June 2006.

20 Profile of the Tourism Sector in the EU and Opportunities in Relation to the Caribbean Region, Pro Invest Europe, 2004.

21 Major, Bridget & Evans, Nigel (2003): *Graduates in the Travel Industry: A Reassessment of Employer Expectations*, Centre for Travel and Tourism, Northumbria University, England, September 2003.

22 De Villiers, D (2002) *Challenge of World Tourism*, address given at The International Investors Forum for the Tourism Sector AICC-Arusha, Tanzania, October 2002.

23 Boulton, R.E.S., Libert, B.D. and Samek, S. M. (2000): `A Business Model for the

24 New Economy', *Journal of Business Strategy*, 21 (4), pp29-35.

Chapter 12
The Knowledge Economy

Introduction

This chapter reinforces the initial notion of this book, that a sector-based model is appropriate and relevant to the overall analysis of minority businesses in the UK. Accordingly this chapter will persist with that trend by highlighting the contribution British Caribbean firms are making to the knowledge economy or the information technology and computing industry, as it is often referred to in wider circles. In today's global environment, knowledge-based technologies are vital to measure and sustain progress across industry sectors, especially in accessing markets with high entry barriers.

The term `knowledge economy' is used in this chapter to describe the emerging structure around the effective utilisation of intangible assets such as knowledge, skills and innovation potential as the key sources for competitive advantage. It also represents moving away from the economics of information age from those of the 20th century industrial era (**ESRC 2006**).

Developing economies are in the forefront of mobilising greater citizenship involvement and participation in the understanding and application of modern technologies for human progress. Such an encouraging trend is also applicable to businesses of all types; be they commercial, industrial and services. As far back as 2004, the Caribbean Community Secretariat acknowledged that Caribbean communities should develop a vested interest in information communication technologies (ICTs) because of their importance to global progress.

I believe the importance of this cannot be over-emphasised since it is well known that the information sector needs not only a solid information infrastructure and vehicles for universal access, it needs a strong state with solid regulatory capabilities and institutions capable of operating in the international market, promoting trade and tracking foreign investment for development. Strong leadership, efficiency in services delivery, transparency in government actions, investment in social services such as education and health, protection of the rule of law and a plurality of connected citizens are critical for democratic stability and are key to prosperity in this complex world (**Applewhaite 2004**).

The above comments are indicative of the view that the knowledge sector is critical to human development as a whole, with the UK Government's position on digital technology fairly consistent in so far as allowing the private sector to take the lead. National figures suggest that there are close to 100,000 companies in the software and computer services market, employing over one million people **(DTI 2004)**. Taken as a whole, there are over a billion Internet users in the world spreading across eight `World Regions' **(Table 12. 1)**.

Table 12. 1 World Internet Usage and Population Statistics

World Regions	Population (est.)	Internet Usage	Usage % of World
Africa	915,210,928	23,649,000	2.3%
Asia	3,667,774,066	364,270,713	35.6%
Europe	807,289,020	291,600,898	28.5%
Middle East	190,084,161	18,203,500	1.8%
North America	331,473,276	227,303,680	22.2%
Latin America/Caribbean	553,908,632	79,962,809	7.8%
Oceania/Australia	33,956,977	17,872,707	1.7%
WORLD TOTAL	**6,499,697,060**	**1,022,863,307**	**100.0%**

(Source: Internet Usage and World Population Statistics, World Gazetteer, 31 March 2006)

Table 12.1 above shows the continued growth in Internet users worldwide – a rise between 100% to over 400% during the 2000-2005 periods. The UK alone has 12.9 million or 52% of Internet users, while the Caribbean has 4.2 million or 11% of the total Internet users in that region.

The knowledge economy is subdivided with overlaps across industry segments thus highlighting its diversity regarding composition, size and market value of each segment or industry unit. In 2004 the computer industry entered a new phase of expansion, and as a result, the period 2004 to 2005 witnessed a recovery for the IT recruitment industry. The demand for IT professionals will increase while the flow of younger workers into the industry will fail to keep pace with demand. Yet, the competition remains, with the following segments set to continue raising productivity in the UK's knowledge economy:-

- Computer Hardware - £11.82bn
- Computer Software - £8.8bn
- Telecommunications - £65bn (mobile £13.6bn)
- IT Security - £1.44bn
- IT Training - £577m
- Office (ITC) Equipment - £3.7bn (**Key Note Report: DTI 2006**)

British Caribbean Sector

Research has shown that minority communities use their home PCs for education purposes more than white people. Information in 2003 revealed that South Asians (42%) were most likely to own a PC. Users in the Caribbean community were 37%, although respondents in the South Asian community were less likely to have an experience of the Internet than people from other ethnic groups (**University of Leeds 2003).**

In 2005, another survey was conducted among minority communities across the UK to enable Consumer Direct to raise awareness of services (and its introduction into four new regions) amongst the identified ethnic communities. The survey found that residents under

40 years old and over should be communicated via `mainstream media, supplemented by specialist TV, Press, radio and community radio stations, outreach and PR. The younger members of the Caribbean community should be communicated through tailored messages and channels to appeal to this culture (**Consumer Direct 2005**).

While there is no authoritative data for the British Caribbean involvement in the knowledge sector, evidence from the annual Labour Force Survey suggests that self employment activities in `*Other Services*' of 15.4% is indicative of Caribbean professionals' input into ICT services in the country (**Bradford School of Management 2001-2005**). In evaluating the sector more closely, independent evidence suggests that Caribbean firms feature in software programming, maintenance (cleaning) and repairs, IT recruitment and training. I will therefore present case studies in this chapter to illustrate the segments of the knowledge economy British Caribbean firms are known to be active producers.

Connectivity Innovation

Caribbean people are renowned for their artistic ability and use of technology applications, and in recent years, have utilised opportunities in the multimedia sector to set up innovative businesses and grow them as well, and in doing so, they have created a new dimension in the appropriate use of IT systems for both commercial and consumer purposes (**Minicase 12. 1).**

Minicase 12. 1 Epic Interactive Media

The multi-million firm of **XL Entertainment**, a media rights and holding company based in Chichester, was founded by St. Lucian-born Jim Brathwaite in 1997. The year before, he became Britain's first black CEO of **Epic Interactive Media** which he floated on the stock market to the value tens of millions of pounds. The company writes CD-ROM programmes and supplies interactive software to customers including NatWest and British Telecom.

At school and university, Brathwaite was keen on a career in marine biology, and later he joined Beecham Pharmaceuticals as an accountant, but when he applied to head the company's overseas branches, although qualified, he was refused because of race discrimination. Dejected, he left to work for another drug company and after eight years, decided it was time to go into business for himself.

With support from his bank manager, the company grew, eventually generating millions of pounds. Brathwaite's business empire comprises electronics, film, television and computers. He envisions owning a television station to promote the work of black producers in the UK.

Apart from his business activities, he sits on boards and committees including Business Link, the National Small Business Council, the Government's Export Advisory Committee for the Americas and educational institutions. In 2002 he received the CBE. One of his famous quotes is, '*I look forward to each day knowing that I will learn something new.*'

As was stated before, Caribbean IT firms are segmented, and according to independent profiling, owners operate the following areas of the industry with a percentage ratio: -

- Designing (2%) refers to various elements of web and IT related designing;
- Consultancy (4%) refers to ongoing advice and information on software products;
- Sales (6%) refer to old/reconditioned or new IT equipment; and
- Services (10%) include maintenance, networking and training (**BlackNet UK**).

Computer Training

Computer training is an attractive and lucrative segment of the industry, and while only few firms have attained profit advantage, others contribute to the expansion and viability of this sub-sector.

Services are offered to clients from community and mainstream companies, involving an initial client assessment to determine the availability of technology applications available and existing gaps in service provision. The assessment is important too, since this determines whether or not clients require language training to access IT software (programme) packages; that is, learning both theory and practice through English Language orientation **(Minicase 12. 2)**.

Industry sources reveal that the IT sector is highly competitive and this is best demonstrated by trends involving computer personnel switching sectors in non-IT professions. Managers have expressed the need for new recruits entering the labour market to improve their communications skills, bearing in mind that it was predicted some time ago, that over half of all computer professionals were likely to set up IT firms in five years time (***Computing Magazine* 2002**).

Minicase 12. 2 Interactive X Ltd

The London-based **Interactive X Ltd** was set up in 1998 as a multi-media company aimed at providing software designing and interactive services. The company has grown with a brilliant reputation to match, in quality computer maintenance services and technology training, with over 30% and 60% market share respectively. It has more than 500 clients, including local authorities, FE colleges and a host of growing micro firms.

Founder and director, Paul Muhammed, heads a small team responsible for administration, financial and legal matters, training and networking development. The firm has a consultative management style, since services are people-centred. For a relatively small business, the organisation is structured like a mini-corporate entity.

The half-a-million pound company remains dedicated towards shaping positive attitudes and images of the knowledge industry, by combining a mixture of sound business principles with a passion for community advances. In 2002, the founder was invited to chair a local enterprise network to offer greater representation for black firms in the run up to the opening of the new Wembley Stadium in 2007. The idea was also to reposition minority firms to access regeneration opportunities in the wider west London sub-region.

Muhammed is convinced that Interactive X has what it takes to remain a market leader in the IT field. The firm proudly boasts essential corporate values of competitiveness, creativity, information-driven, consistent quality, flexibility, multi-skilled staff and social responsibility.

IT Recruitment

This segment has experienced a rollercoaster journey over the past 10 years, from the peaks in demand in 1999 through the turbulence of 2000 to 2003, before a resurgence in 2004 and continued growth in 2005 and 2006. As a whole, the industry faces challenges around recruiting adequately skilled personnel to operate complex technology applications in both public and private sector. At the time of writing, vacancies had exceeded 3,000 covering about 11 occupational groups **(Table12. 2)**.

In addition, legislation continues to be tough as demand increases and agencies are faced with a wide-ranging compliance environment, needing to be aware of issues related to UK regulations, as well as international initiatives such as the EU Working Directive, which although frozen in 2006, could have affect the recruitment landscape in the future **(Key Note Report 2007).** IT recruitment agencies will need to be more creative in their recruitment and convince clients of the value of older, female and foreign workers.

Table 12. 2 Average earnings for permanent and contract IT staff in the UK

Occupational Group	Permanent IT Staff (first quarter 2004)	Contract IT Staff Average hourly rate (first quarter 2004)
Management	£52,000	-
Systems Design	£41,000	£39
Systems Developers	£37,000	£44

Programming	£32,000	£32
PC Support	£24,000	£15
Technical Support	£43,000	£43
Software Engineering	£36,000	£35
Database	£42,500	£50
Networking	£34,000	£27
Operations	£25,000	£20
Internet	£29,000	£29

(Source: Computing and IT in the UK: Basic Facts, Annual Business Inquiry Employee Analysis – www.nomisweb.co.uk/, 2005.

More and more females are making inroads into the knowledge sector especially within the recruitment field. The corporate image of many has inspired young entrepreneurs within the ethnic community to advance their own brand of professionalism. A small percentage of IT recruitment companies are run by British Caribbean women devoted to improving products and services.

In the main, target markets are dual in nature; client companies in need of IT staff on the one hand, and job-seeking candidates who can register their CVs and other (paper-based) expertise, on the other. Some firms have even achieved `approved supplier' status which means that they can work with large companies in several UK cities. Racial prejudice has been converted into a positive `weapon' to negotiate in a market that has less barriers to entry than other non-IT Plcs. The determination of minority women to succeed is further evidenced by their identical passion to create and develop new niche markets in the industry. Thus managing IT recruitment firms is seen as an `enterprise blessing' rather than the `curse' of unemployment and labour market discrimination as the owners of Alatron Limited so vividly demonstrates **(Minicase 12. 3).**

Minicase 12. 3 Alatron Ltd

Denise Lewis who founded **Alatron Limited** in 2002 has been driven by faith to achieve, and this has also helped her to cope with challenges in the formative period of enterprise start-up. With 17 years experience in IT, including 42 months in recruiting IT personnel, Lewis left to set up a private company. Her decision was based on a desire to secure financial independence and to have more stability in life.

After conducting four months of research, she set up the firm, insistent that she would not seek a loan from the bank or venture capital funds, but instead, rely on personal savings of £5,000 to set up the business. The firm specialises in SAP, Oracle, Globus & Peoplesoft and provides quality IT consultants covering the UK and Europe.

Lewis sought assistance from a London-based enterprise agency which proved helpful. The business plan was a valuable exercise for her and the British-born (of Grenadian parentage) commended her family and friends for supporting through the start-up phase.

One of the initial challenges she faced was adjusting to working independently after years of being part of a busy sales environment. To remain motivated was a learning curve, but once staff came on abroad, this became less of a problem although coping with the unpredictability of cash flows, was indeed a challenge too.

As activities in the business evolved, Lewis secured additional funds and took out a loan, using her property as collateral. Alatron has increased it staff component by recruiting administrative, marketing and public relations personnel. Clients include banks, blue chip companies and public sector organisations. The company depends largely on recommendations from clients and on advertising campaigns in trade magazines such as *Computer Weekly* and adverts on Jobserve, an online site for candidates. The firm also uses telesales, networking and participating in IT exhibitions as marketing tools to generate new business.

Alatron has survived because of its quality appeal to customers and the timely delivery of services as well. Lewis acknowledged though, that '*there needs to be more entrepreneurial seminars and access to business funding. At the moment, there is a lot of red tape in relation to gaining funding which can be off-putting to budding entrepreneurs*'.

(Source: Running her own show, 26 June 2003, Black Information Link, The 1990 Trust)

Database Management Systems

The computer software market is also competitive and the constant need to launch new products and titles, and to develop new technologies is intensifying. In this environment, scale advantages are increasingly. Although the market has always been driven by successful new products – which require significant investment in production and marketing – the amount of investment needed is growing, primarily as a result of the rising costs associated with the development and marketing of new software. Consequently, the availability of significant financial resources have become difficult to come by and a discriminating factor in the industry (**Key Note Market Report, 2005**).

Further, although businesses are now spending more on IT products, selling into this market has become more difficult, but minority firms recognise large companies' shrewd and methodical approach to buying software. The long held fashion and desire to have the latest products have replaced buying quality products with a track record on delivery and return on investment (ROI). Developments of this sort in the industry, has facilitated innovations and other forms of creativity among Caribbean-managed IT firms such as Enterprise Data Systems (UK) Ltd. The company creates opportunities for open-source software, with guarantees of quality maintenance support, as well as customised training in the use of modern IT applications.

Indeed, the marked difference with Caribbean computing firms, are owners' ability to tailor their products to suit various clientele (in the public sector) – where a significant portion of IT contracts are derived **(Minicase 12. 4)**. The emphasis on quality is particularly important in data management systems, given that poor quality equals poor returns which can eventually lead to a potentially successful IT firm going out of business.

Minicase 12. 4 Enterprise Data Systems (UK) Ltd

The 1992-founded West Midlands company **Enterprise Data Systems UK Ltd** (EDS) has partly revolutionised the commercialisation of technology systems, by combining personal touch with professionalism. Founder Andy Bailey, manages a small staff but, has an impressive client list - in excess of 200, with its philosophy, *'Our aim is to listen, respond and provide'.*

The lack of career advancement in previous jobs and limited financial prospects were the spurs to Bailey's quest towards business start-up. He also spotted an opportunity in the IT market for specialist technology products and services for small firms. Initial problems such lack of bank support and limited office space had to be overcome. Bailey's sheer entrepreneurial instinct coupled with useful advice from fellow IT specialists and business leaders in the community enabled him to persevere. *'The first thing the bank manger did was to stop my overdraft. I think that typically, Asians are seen as people with business sense - Caribbean people are not. We are not seen as serious business people,* Bailey declared.

EDS offers outsourced IT services to clients, with services including built computer systems, network design-installation, maintenance support, consultancy, data/network cabling and IT equipment security. Its networking cabling division is BICSI registered and in May 2001, the company achieved ISO 9001 certification as indicative of its commitment to quality customer care.

As part of the diversification strategy, Bailey set up the subsidiary firm of Kleen IT which provides cleaning and maintenance support services for companies' equipment, damaged and which tend to overheat because of bacteria (in the form of dust and dirt). A combined interior and exterior clean for PCs is guaranteed too.

In 2004, Bailey was part of a 15-member UK Trade & Investment (UKTI) team that visited Ghana in West Africa where he has established a social enterprise project involving HIV/Aids education awareness campaigns and a community IT initiative for people with no access to this provision. In June 2007, he was awarded the MBE for services to business in the West Midlands.

Electronic Commerce

The knowledge sector economy is filled with impressive profiles of e-commerce entrepreneurs staking claims in the industry to make good their creative talent and contacts in various communities. There are many unwritten stories of young British Caribbean professionals with original ideas that have potential commercial success, but who can't advance them because of a lack of technical support, or the reluctance of commercial institutions to invest in novel creations from the non-white community.

Nevertheless, it is the persistent attitude and a sense of self-reliance and pride that are the main drivers behind the eventual success of start-ups in the e-commerce world Because of the tremendous opportunities that the Internet offers, small IT specialists or operators with abundant ideas and experiences can convert these into commercial products and services. E-commerce is not new to inner-city communities and this is based on minority professionals represent a growing mass of intellectual and social capital that remains untapped and not publicised (**Minicase 12. 5).**

Minicase 12. 5 Innovation Station

In December 2005, Peter Morrison, a prolific inventor turned an everyday search for domestic tradesman into a thriving e-business, **Innovation Station, tradeof.com**, situated in Walsall, the Midlands. The company's cyberspace platform has created opportunities for members to their skills in exchange for those of fellow members. Transactions can be completed either as full trade – a direct swap; full invoice – a paid agreement for services rendered; or part trade/part invoice.

According to Morrison, the origin of the e-commerce business was quite unusual. '*It all started in 2001 when I needed a painter/decorator to do some work on my house. My money was tied up in another invention and it made me realise that each person is a commodity that someone else needs. I found someone in the end, but I started thinking about a mechanism that could trade services instead of money. A sales executive and two of my cousins were invited to come on board since we needed printing, web design and legal aspects of the enterprise*'.

The team developed a registration scheme to ensure administrative control and though it took the owner nearly four years to set up the business, the experience showed that the e-commerce market requires patient, tactful application. Morrison's philosophy centres on visualising ideas and working on at them until they become saleable commodities.

In the first six or so months, Innovation Station recorded nearly 200,000 hits and was scheduled to surpass a turnover forecast of £200,000 projected by the second year of trading. The e-commerce firm has stimulated business activity among UK companies and others that are primarily web-based in the US, Hawaii and Brazil. Membership consists of trades ranging from plumbers and electricians to accountants, blue chip companies, fitness trainers and football agents.

Innovation Station's medium-term strategy is to reproduce its site in other languages, recruit additional staff and up the volume of sole traders to secure the patronage of larger companies.

(Source: Trading places: Bartering online in the 21st century, The Voice 4 September 2006)

One noticeable trend in the knowledge sector economy also, is the evolution of web-based publications also known as 'electronic publishing', developed due to the scarcity of paper-based publications and the demand for specialist material dealing with issues affecting African and Caribbean communities. And whilst sections of the community have access to newspapers, magazines and other periodicals, a sizeable section of the youth population has limited access because of problems involving content and presentational style.

In today's world, African and Caribbean societies are continuously searching for meaning, ideas and the production of goods and services which are integral to a more progressive agenda. Professionals are acutely aware of the decreasing number of jobs in the public sector, along with the irony of persistent race discrimination and labour market prejudice, both of which are blots on the moral authority of Britain and its quest for global competitiveness despite the volume of legislation passed by successive Conservative and Labour Governments over the past 30 years.

Even more, are deficiencies resulting from poorly qualified people and inadequate social skills of new entrants in the labour market, all of which have placed added pressure on employers as they try to avoid inflated wage bills whilst endeavouring to maintain a cost-effective operation. With a doubt, this dilemma requires swift but appropriate action. There are vacancies for staff at all operational levels of business organisations in the UK and these include a demand for administrative personnel with computer-related skills. It is here that through their experience and competence, British Caribbean professionals are making significant inroads in the electronic publishing market (**Minicase 12. 6**).

Minicase 12. 6 Black UK (Online) Limited

Shirley Mc Greal established **Black UK Online Ltd** in 2003, with the aim of publicising the contribution of Britain's multicultural communities to the economy. She confounded the prediction of critics regarding failure, since it was felt that `the majority of black people did not have computers at home and still preferred reading newspapers.' Mc Greal used personal savings and factoring to start the online firm.

The original staff of two has now grown to more than five in a relatively short period, with honed expertise in web designing, editorial administration, marketing and public relations. With a fast growing clientele and an annual turnover of just under £500,000, Black UK Online has made immense progress in redefining the content and presentation of electronic newspaper publishing and other web-based literary endeavours.

The firm's contribution to e-commerce enterprise has attracted considerable interest across industry sectors over the past few years. Its Birmingham and Suffolk-based Black UK Publications, the parent company of blackukonline.com, has won several awards since launching. These include the *Suffolk Social Enterprise Award 2006, Highly Commended Finalist in the DTI-E-Commerce Award 2005, Best Use of Teleworking and Winner of the Windrush Small Business Champion Award 2004.*

The company acquired the monthly printed publication and website *Keep the Faith* in January 2005 which is distributed to nearly 2,000 ethnic churches and community groups in the UK, with a readership of over 200,000. The publication comprises news, information and features from the African, Caribbean and Christian communities respectively. A selected number of international development issues are also publicised.

Community Digital

As was stated before, 52% of UK households access the Internet from home representing a 4% increased from 2003. When one considers that the figure was first 9% in 1998, the increase has been very significant to this time.

As an extension of the knowledge economy, members of the British Caribbean community like their multi-ethnic cousins are keen to exploit commercial opportunities which today's Internet offers in the cultural heritage arena. There has been a considerable rise in the number of online publishing sites depicting either the heritage of individual Caribbean states or combining aspects of a Caribbean/ (Black) British traditions. The idea around these ventures illustrates the complexity and the diversity evident within the British Caribbean communities' input into the knowledge economy in the UK.

The presence of these sites also justifies the argument that Caribbean people in the UK are capable as their white counterparts, in adapting to the use of modern technology to set up and manage successful e-commerce ventures. One such site that is an evolving market leader is the online heritage publishing sector, Promoting Our Heritage (**Minicase 12.7**).

Minicase 12.7 Promoting Our Heritage

Advertiser and entrepreneur, Garfield Robinson set up the online business, **Promoting Our Heritage** in 2002 to promote Jamaican heritage by increasing access to spoken and written material about Jamaica and Jamaicans, done especially by not exclusively by Jamaicans. . The business began from scratch with a plan to grow it substantially by increasing annual turnover and improving research and development. Robinson used credit cards, a bank loan and personal savings to put the firm on a sound footing.

The site is divided into profiles of successful/high-achievers according to prescribed professional categories. Then there is an informative business directory with a sectoral outlook, featuring firms in almost every area of commerce and industry. An A-Z heritage shop is also part of the online marketing chain which has over 100 cultural books and numerous audio-visual products, offering customers an opportunity to purchase items from accessories and biographies to self-help books and selected videos.

The business also encourages individuals and small companies to advertise on the website and explains why they should: -

- Up to 4 listings of searches for Jamaican heritage culture;
- A home page/weekly report reflects visitors needs;
- The site is updated weekly;
- Listed in online directories - Yell.com, Thomson local;
- Over 90% of searches are UK based, US enquiries too; and
- Advertising rates are at £50 per year (13 pence per day).

Apart from offering commercial opportunities, Promoting Our Heritage's overall strategy is to ensure that that the traditions of Jamaican and Caribbean people in general, remain at the forefront of multicultural Britain for all to recognise and acknowledge.

Other elements of the community digital economy also exist in other parts of England including Northern cities, grappling with the `digital divide'; that is citizens unable to use IT and therefore face inequality in accessing basic web-based information on issues affecting their respective communities. Many need adequate information, advice and technical support to make informed decisions. More than ever, they need access to employment opportunities including guidance to become self-sufficient in terms of setting up businesses, even it means operating a social-type enterprise, as is the case with sections of deprived communities in inner-city England and Wales.

As result of the digital divide, there are unique ventures across the country aimed at creating advantage by linking public sector programmes with community initiatives through the facilitation of IT professionals, cultural experts and social entrepreneurs. This section of the book will highlight examples of best practice in this regard. The idea is to empower men, women and young people who represent diverse views of British society but who are interested in supporting community cohesion **(Minicases 12. 8).**

Minicases 12. 8 Selected British Caribbean Community Digital Media

Carlton Romaine of Bristol is in the forefront of **St. Paul's Carnival Project**, a new electronic media that helps us to present ourselves and highlight the best of our cultural heritage.' As proof of what he means, Romaine has a multimedia CR ROM showcasing the life and struggles of Africa Caribbean people in a city that has an 8,000-strong black population who want to access mainstream opportunities for secure employment and housing as well as cultural purposes. The project complements the Digital City Bristol initiative which is an exchange of information between town hall officials, business and the public sector using computer-diriven online facilities.

The **Black Information Link** or BLINK coordinated by John Adams, has established an important political presence on the Internet. This website sums up the rallying cry of the oppressed when it says, 'The inventions of humankind are not the prosperity of any one race to be used to gain artificial superiority. Technology can be as much an instrument of liberation as it is of domination. Liberators must gain control of these new technologies and employ them for the advancement of all humanity' (**http:///wwww.bristol.digitalcity.org**)

Patrick Vernon set up **Every Generation Media and Foundation** in 2002 with the launch of its first website www.everygeneration.co.uk. The Foundation's website has copped numerous awards, including the 2003 *CRE Race in the Media Award*, the 2004 *Windrush Award* and shortlisted for the 2005 *New Statesmen New Media Awards*. In 2003 the Queen selected Vernon as Pioneer of the Nation for Cultural History as part of her 50th anniversary and in that same year (October), the website and campaign, *100 Great Black Britons*, was launched. It represents an ongoing campaign to publicise the achievements of the African Caribbean community over the last 1000 years.

Since 2004, the enterprise has organised, in partnership with the National Archives, high profile events and media campaigns around Caribbean genealogy, serving as a catalyst in promoting family awareness in the black community. Material is also distributed to libraries and museums as part of their audience development.

In July 2006 his company published *When We Ruled*, by Robin Walker, with over 4000 copies sold in the UK and internationally, making it one of the most successful Black history books to be published in the UK. A major website celebrating black icons in film and television and over the last 100 years was launched, March 2007, in partnership with the British Film Institute (BFI). The campaign *100 Black Screen Icons* builds on the successful *100 Great Black Britons Campaign*. Every Generation Media's websites have monthly hits of 12 million. The organisation plans to develop new websites, books and produce films and documentaries in 2008 and beyond

Geography Landscape

The British Caribbean knowledge economy sector has grown considerably since the late 1990s and although this has not been fully acknowledged, the fact is that computer firms, software producers, maintenance support engineers, digital multimedia technicians and other equipment specialists operate in the UK mostly in the English Regions, Scotland and Wales. A reasonable estimates based on informal analysis (that is, case studies done and observations made) suggests that the market share for these firms is 2% with annual revenue of £66 million to the British economy.

Since a third of all Caribbean people have access to the Internet and only a small fraction are commercialising products and services from this medium, it means that there is a need to narrow or close the digital divide, ethnically speaking. Still, the number of computer-related businesses in the African and Caribbean communities is increasing yearly. While refugee communities from Central Africa are leading on Internet/multimedia technology services on the high streets and suburbs, Caribbean professionals are offering a variety of 'cultural brands' to meet the demands of a 'hungry' black community. Technology innovations are widespread and they are a testament to the '*Other Services*' (IT inclusive) that Caribbean men and women represent in the public/private sector to the value of 24% according to Labour Survey data **(Table 12. 3)**.

Table 12.3 British Caribbean Knowledge Firms in selected UK Regions

IT Segments	Locations
Software Programming	London/Southeast, Midland Counties, Scotland and Wales.
Maintenance Support	England-wide, Scotland.
Database Management	London/Southeast, Midland/Northern Counties, Scotland.
Training	England-wide, Scotland and Wales.
IT Recruitment	London/Southeast, Midland/Northern Counties.
Online Publishing	London/Southeast, Midlands/Northern Counties, Scotland.
Community Digital	London, West Midlands, East Midlands, Northern Regions.

(Source: Case studies and informal observation 2002-2007)

In each of the above segments, there are small firms that have a yearly turnover varying from less than £50,000 to £500,000 plus in the selected sub-sectors mentioned. According to the UK-wide Standard Industry Classification (SIC) there is evidence of minority representation in a variety of services – both public and private - and it is in some of these areas that ethnic communities have made significant inroads as this chapter attests.

More importantly, regional profiles have illustrated the extent to which minorities have blended cultural knowledge and professional experience to contribute to improved sector representation (by ethnicity) in inner-city areas. For instance, the Office for National Statistics highlighted representation of the black community under the *`transport and telecommunications'* sector in the following Regions by percentage ratios: -

- South East (3%)
- East of England (3%)
- West Midlands (9%)
- North West (2%)
- South West (1%)
- Scotland (1%)
- Wales (1%) (**ONS 2004/2005**).

Challenges and Opportunities

In market value terms, the competitive standing of British Caribbean firms in the knowledge sector remains under 5% and even though this is a reasonable comparison since Caribbean people comprise just over one per cent ratio of the total UK population by ethnicity, in relation to the projected growth rate in business formation, this figure could be higher, at least between 2% and 3%. The industry however, has many challenges as they are several opportunities as this chapter highlighted.

Whether it is software programming, maintenance support, training and IT recruitment or the community digital divide, there are challenges. The segmentation of the knowledge economy undoubtedly, creates more challenges. In computer hardware for instance, IT infrastructure is being centralised, with new concepts of delivery such as utility computing or service-centric computing coming into being. This, among other developments, will lead to a demand for low-cost ownership of client systems and desktop printer. The upside is that businesses are spending more on IT products and providers of software programmers can tailor-made products to suit customer requirements.

Computer software is competitive and the constant need to launch new product- brands, as well as develop new technologies is intensifying. Scale advantages are growing too, and the amount of investment required is proving formidable. Shortened planning cycles within organisations mean that IT budgets are evaluated on a short-term basis. Providers therefore need to keep track of organisational planning systems around IT equipment and tailor products and services with guaranteed outcomes and results that are cost effective to clients.

IT Recruitment is a challenge as well, with persistent skills shortage in the UK market, with legislation continuing to be tough as demand increases. Recruitment agencies need to be more creative in the flexible recruitment of older, female and foreign workers especially for end-user companies in the public and private sector.

The same goes for IT security which is very important to the stability of management of information systems (MIS) in any organisation. A large proportion of UK businesses still regard security as an overhead rather than an investment. IT security's increase share of total IT spending is due to the constant rise in the number, sophistication and threats faced by organisations plus the resultant growth in the number of breaches suffered. Providers of this particular service can therefore develop integrated security systems for end-users so that these systems could be integrated into the computer network at the planning and operation stage. The use of wireless and remote networking is fast becoming a necessity in the global technological environment.

The UK market for IT training is facing decentralisation as large companies consolidate their buying among smaller training vendors. Reputable companies have greater advantage when bidding for large contacts, particularly as major firms also seek to outsource all, or part, of their training management to vendors. Offering a broader range of training products and services is crucial and ethnic providers can thus target the ender user, rather than the IT professional.

The office equipment segment is developing with falling prices because of many competitors. Projectors for example have become smaller, lighter and brighter, and the market is polarising between ultra-portable models and powerful, state-of-the-art range fixed models, which sell in small volumes. Video conferencing equipment is a small area but promises future growth prospects **(Table 12. 4)**.

Table 12. 4 Challenges and Prospects for the UK Knowledge Economy

Challenges	Prospects
Database Management: increasing cost with competition from large companies dominating the field and more centralisation of IT systems.	Small firms can provide new software products for large concerns interested in training and marketing campaigns in a cost effective way.
IT Recruitment: problems with the recruitment of skilled personnel to operate in complex technological environments.	Firms can develop creative models in their recruitment packages and convince clients of the value of older, female and foreign workers.
IT Security: spending on IT is absorbing a large portion of IT budgets and there is still underinvestment in this vital area.	Firms can provide integrated network packages to improve security in large companies at planning and operating stage.
IT Training: major companies are consolidating their buying among small training vendors with large companies having an advantage when bidding for contracts.	Small providers can widen their range of training services – businesses and professional skills to IT staff, particularly project management, and aggressively target this market.

Office Equipment: divided between ultra-portable models and powerful, up-to-date equipment sold in small volumes; security in the public sector remains high.	Businesses can serve companies with binders, laminators and franking machines; the market for dictation machines is growing for public agencies.

(Source; Textual analysis based on IT industry segments)

Other existing opportunities in the knowledge economy are mobile telecommunications worth £13.6 billion (**2006 estimates**). Whilst the market is dominated by five main operators, with the value chain becoming more complex, the delivery of content over mobile networks grows in importance. Smaller operators can therefore offer specialist services in text or content presentation, advice on downloading graphics and audio/video elements. Affordable mobile telecoms products designed for students and the older children's markets are also another way of competing in niche markets. Teleworking is another growth area with nearly 3 million representing over a fifth of the UK workforce. Teleworkers are people who do work from home and could not carry out this type of work without the access to a telephone and a PC. The three broad categories of teleworkers are as follows: -

- Full time teleworkers who carry out their regular job from home for most or all of the time;
- Home-based teleworkers operating in various with home as their general base; and
- Occasional teleworkers who comprise the largest group, being based outside of the home but regularly carrying out work from home or at least one day per week.

However, there are negative views on teleworking such as the belief that employers wouldn't allow teleworkers to work from home, even where and when, it is possible. This flexible, relaxed approach to work is quite popular in private companies and public institutions especially when it involves complex contracts that are project-oriented, and may require managing and operating in less distracting surroundings.

This type of working approach is also beneficial to employees with childcare responsibilities.

Certainly, British Caribbean professionals can capitalise on the opportunities which this segment of the knowledge economy offers to either augment their income or establish a network of teleworking agency staff capable of delivering efficient (on time and within budget) services.

Conclusion

In this chapter the importance and relevance of the knowledge sector economy and the role of British Caribbean businesses in this, were discussed. The term 'knowledge economy' was defined as intangible assets of knowledge, skills and innovation that are keys to the competitive advantage of UK cities. The Government's often repeated position on digital technology was stressed in light of the presence of nearly 100,000 companies in the software programming and computer services market in general.

In the context of the millions of worldwide web users including 12.9 million in the UK where 37% are Caribbean `surfers', it was pointed out that there was still a growing demand for highly skilled IT technicians and computer operators in the industry. Growth segments in the industry were identified in namely, computer hardware, computer software, telecommunications, IT security, training and office (IT) equipment.

Minicases were presented to validate industry data and interviews from an assortment of knowledge sector enterprises operated by British Caribbean professionals and entrepreneurs, with 5-10 plus year experience in computer management and IT-related programme development skills. The geographic presence in the UK by firms was also highlighted to show the range and scope of representation by sections of the minority community although the percentage ratio averaged around 2% for self-employment as against 1% to 6%

and upwards in the public sector 'industry classification category'. Informal estimates suggest that the Caribbean firm sector's revenue contribution to the UK knowledge economy is worth over £60 million per annum; that is, when one calculates a percentage of this community's participation in the IT sector against the total market value of the industry.

Case studies were compiled to show the evidence of segmentation and demographic spread of firms, along with their level of organisation, composition and other operational management processes, often not considered by studies dealing with minority concerns in the IT/ knowledge or web-based creative sector in the UK. Since more than a third or 37% of all Caribbean people are PC users, it is clear that many are involved in different segments of e-commerce – both for commercial and social enterprise purposes, as highlighted in this chapter. There is also the obvious situation involving hundreds of minority professionals working from home on their PCSs either managing public/private sector contracts and/or engaged in a series of self-employment activities that entail the use of electronic activities and programming.

The segmentation of the knowledge economy brings its own challenges and opportunities, and by examining key segments, it was possible to indicate growth prospects in this sector comprising database management, IT recruitment, IT security, training and office equipment. Direct reference was made to trends (immediate and future) in mobile telecommunications. It is forecasted that the use of more wireless devices will (noticeably) change attitudes, corporate strategies and enterprise management processes in global technology. The next chapter will look at the endeavours of British Caribbean entrepreneurs in the education and training sector.

Chapter Notes

Regional Technology – the comments by Lolita Applewhaite, Deputy Caricom Secretary General reflected concern by officials in the Caribbean that people are important to development and as such they shouldn't be only beneficiaries, but also participants in ICT advances especially in the light of globalisation that will impact on the role of public services, businesses and civic affairs.

Global Usage – in Internet/web-based technology is increasing throughout the world including non-industrialised states where are using new technologies, overall, for the purpose of empowerment and securing commercial and social benefits for sustainability. For instance, between 2000-2005, more than a billion people the world over were Internet users, with a usage growth of 183.5% increase over that same period.

Consumer Direct – is a telephone and online consumer advice service supported by the DTI and operates in various UK Regions. Due to the demographic structure of the regions, the organisation is required to target minority communities beyond the mainstream media.

Kleen IT – one of few companies specialising in IT systems hygiene and security – a strategy that complements occupational health and safety in regularity terms. It is perceived in industry circles, that most computer cleaning companies are primarily cleaners with little or no knowledge of IT hardware maintenance and therefore suffer from `it was working before you touched it' syndrome.

E-Bartering – the electronic firm of Innovation Station has indeed brought the traditional system of bartering into the 21st century by encouraging traders of all descriptions and disciplines to trade on the Internet. The idea of promoting the value of small traders is commendable since it allows minority professionals to secure niche markets whilst operating their respective industry-sectors.

Faith Technology – the *Faith* publication by Black UK Online Ltd is an unusual endeavour that creates a channel for faith organisations, worshippers, interested communities and public institutions to interface on a variety of subjects and issues of mutual benefit. Its presence is a vindication that 33%-50% of Britain's one million strong African and Caribbean community worship regularly.

Selected References

1 *Knowledge Economy in the UK*, Economic and Social Research Council, 2006.

2 Applewhaite, Lolita (2004):`People First', *Caricom Perspective*, No. 72, Vol. 1, July 2004

3 *Businesses in the Digital Economy*, DTI 2004.

4 Computer Hardware (2005), Computer Software (2005), Domestic telecoms (2006), E-Recruitment Market (2006:2007), Mobile Telecommunications (2006), *Key Note Report*, UK.

5 `Information Technology Sector', *Understanding London's sectors* 2003, London Development Agency.

6 `Internet Usage and World Population Statistics', International Telecommunication Union & *World Gazetteer*, March 31, 2006.

7 `Ethnic minorities use IT more seriously', *The Reporter* 27 October 2003, University of Leeds newsletter.

8 James, Ross & Macauley, P (2005): *Communicating Consumer Direct to ethnic minority communities* Version Two: recommendations, DTI & COI, Spring 2005.

9 *Local businessman gets top job at South East Economic Regional Development Agency* (SEEDA), XI Entertainment plc, August 8, 2002.

10 *United Kingdom: ethnic minority self-employed by sector 2001-05*, Bradford School of Management, England.

11 *Computing and IT in the UK: Basic Facts*, Annual Business Inquiry Employee Analysis, 2005.

12 `Running her own show', *Black information Link* (The 1990 Trust), 23 June 2003.

13 Graham, Vernon (2006): `Trading places: Bartering online in the 21st century', *The Voice* September 4, 2006.

14 Dixon, Marcia (2006): `Words of Faith', *Faith*, Issue 22 May 2006, Black UK Online Ltd, Suffolk, England.

15 Promoting our Heritage – Profile Directory (www.promotingourheritage.co.uk/directory)

16 `Black Stars Rising', *KAL Magazine*, 16 May 2007.

Chapter 13

Education and Training Sector

Introduction

Since 1997, the Labour Government has presided over the largest investment programme for over thirty years in education, with an increase by nearly 50% and approximately 5.6% of the Gross Domestic Product (GDP) in 2007-08. This chapter will examine the education and training sector in the UK and British Caribbean firms' contribution to this 'human development' market. The £2.2 billion Building Schools for the Future programme is considered a major initiative, and the Department for Children, Schools and Families (DCSF) will utilise the services of contractors to deliver the 15-year programme.

Indeed, the current Private Finance Initiative (PFI) represents an innovation through which this investment will be channelled, to ensure that procurement delivers value for money and modern, well-designed learning environments. Ongoing investment in the public sector, and in particular education, is seen as a potential and attractive niche area for construction companies and independent providers, with levels of capital expenditure and services less affected by fluctuations within the economy as a whole.

In 2004-2005, there were around 4.7 million students in further education and 2.4 million in higher education. Estimates showed that £17.57 billion was spent on higher education and £7.9 billion on further education. The majority of students are full-time first-degree students, but adult learners make up an important part of the student community. In most of the top 30 universities, mature students account for around 8% to 10% of the total student population, and there around 20 universities where mature students represent over 25% of the total student body (**Key Note Report 2005).**

On the other hand, industry analysts concede that the training market is growing slowly. The key reasons appear to be that profitability in many of the UK's companies is severely under pressure and fees in the training sector are being reduced. The other reason is that this sector is struggling to make the economic case for training and development. Yet employer expenditure on off-the-job training in the UK accounted to £18.43 billion, a decrease of 0.3% on 2004-2005 (**Key Note Report 2006)**. The main source of public sector spending, the Learning and Skills Council, had a budget of £10.54 billion in the financial year of 2005-2006. It is projected that between 2007 and 2011, the UK training market, as measured by employer expenditure on external training, will experience modest growth, rising by 1% per annum from 2007-2008 upwards.

With respect to the nursery education market, the number of children aged three and four years old in early education, either on a part time or full time basis, is believed to have declined marginally in 2005 to 1.2 million children. England accounts for some 86% of the total number of children in early year's education.

In January 2005, the Market Business Development online publication stated that private sector nurseries accounted for 92% of the nursery market compared with 91% in 2001. The focus of market development has been in the private sector, with an estimated increased of 9% in the number of private sector nurseries, from 7,460 nurseries in 2001 to 8,164 nurseries in 2005. By 2010, the population of 0-5 year olds in England and Wales is expected to increase moderately whereas a reduction in the number of 0-5 year olds is expected in Scotland and Northern Ireland during the forecast period (**MBD 2005**).

With English Language being a corporate brand, the global value of education and training exports to the UK economy amounts to some £10.3 billion (**2002 estimates**). However, according to Lancaster University, the combined value of the sector including England Wales, Scotland and Ireland amounts to over £22 billion **(Johnes 2004).**

British Caribbean Education and Training

There has been considerable debate since the early 1960s on the variations in educational attainment of Caribbean people, especially young boys who experience the most school expulsions, in excess 2,000 per year than other students, thereby figuring prominently in the underachievement `league' tables of secondary education in Britain. Numerous studies on the underachievement of Caribbean boys have been done and they include the work of Grenadian Bernard Coard who exposed the failings of the English system of education in the mid-20th century. Other studies also examined this issue and gave reasons for the failure of Caribbean children in secondary schools:

- Family breakdown thereby creating one-parent households;
- Indiscipline behaviour by teenagers;
- Poor educational attainment by parents;
- Poverty involving low income families;
- Physical deprivation in inner-cities;
- Racial prejudice in schools;
- Parents lack of knowledge of the education system; and
- Reluctance by some parents to participate in PTAs.

Although parents and children acknowledge the persistence of racial prejudice in educational institutions – schools, colleges and universities – education authorities have expressed concern and intimated that appropriate action must be taken to remove this scourge from society. And so, there is some evidence that Caribbean boys in particular, are beginning to show signs of improvement in attaining higher GCSE grades. A main factor for this positive outcome has been attributed to the *Aiming High Programme* specifically targeted at black pupils.

Launched in November 2003, the programme aims to work alongside local authorities and schools to focus on raising the achievement level of all black pupils through devising leadership and management strategies to enhance effective teaching and learning, and was initially implemented in 30 secondary schools in 20 local education authorities.

According to recent reports, the percentage of Caribbean boys with five passes or more at Grades A-C had risen by 5.4% between 2003 and 2005, and for Caribbean girls 6.9%. The London Phoenix High School which has 75% of non-white pupils reported that in 2002, only 25% of students passed GCSE exams at Grades A-C and by 2006, the figure rose to an astonishing 77% which was way above the national average of 55%. Jamaican-born William Atkinson who is one of the UK's most successful school heads, based the results on *`residential study camps for pupils lacking motivation, setting up Saturday morning classes, taking students on day trips to universities to inspire them to strive for tertiary education and working with parents to encourage their involvement`* (***The Voice*** **2006).**

Typically, there are disparities in the representation of Caribbean professionals in public sector education employment. National reports on regional ethnic profiles show that in education, black people have just over a 1% percentage ratio. Yet when a closer examination is made on a region-by-region basis, the percentage ratios are different in almost each of the nine English Regions **(Table 13. 1).**

Table 13. 1 Caribbean education professionals in selected English Regions

(Source: Region in Figures Series, 2004-2005, Office of National Statistics)

Region	White	African	Asian	Caribbean	Mixed
Southeast	10%	1%	5%	1%	5%
East England	9%	3%	6%	3%	8%
West Midlands	9%	10%	7%	8%	

North West	9%	1%	8%	1%	11%
South West	9%	2%	1%	3%	7%
National Report	**93%**	**1%**	**4%**	**1%**	**1%**

Figures are rounded for uniformity

Market Segmentation

The dual aspiration of sections of the African and Caribbean community to pursue professional careers and set up enterprises is yet to be properly analysed in the context of the overall study of the broader UK minority business sector. The focus tends be on the underachievement of Caribbean students in education and their adult peers' underperformance in commerce and industry. While statistics can and do offer insights into the reality of enterprising communities, they can also disguise the real achievement of sections of the British population, subjected to prolonged racial prejudice, including labour market discrimination which lends itself to restrictive practices in certain industries such as those in science and technology.

Results from the graduate employment market show that most minorities opt for a variety of `employment status' based on study outcomes. For instance, degree students choose to work either in the public/private sector to gain relevant exposure, experience and skills and/or to secure further paid employment or self-employment. Others may identify a particular niche market and set up a business to service it. Studies between 2000 and 2006, illustrated the dynamics of minority graduate employment.

One study of nearly 1,500 in London showed that black students particularly used the graduate job market to prepare themselves for the real world of work in either paid work or self-employment. Though statistically black self-employment was less than 4%, it represented more than 2% percentage ratio than Asian students. A small fraction of African and Caribbean students are on postgraduate courses, a percentage operate a 'half-way house' type of employment; that is, working part-time in a public sector post and operating simultaneously, a part-time business a few days at a time or on weekends. Sectors often include cleaning, teaching/lecturing, social care, print journalism, radio communications etc (**Table 13. 2**).

Table 13. 2 Employment Status of Minority Graduates

Employment Status	White & Irish	Black	Asian	Total
Unemployed	4.8%	17.4%	11.7%	9.1%
Full-time employment	76.0%	63.2%	69.3%	71.8%
Part-time employment	6.3%	6.9%	5.6%	6.2%
Self-employment	5.4%	3.6%	1.4%	4.1%
In education/other outcomes	7.5%	8.9%	12.1%	8.8%
Total	**100%**	**100%**	**100%**	**100%**

(Source: The Graduate Labour Market in London, Focus Central London, March 2000)

The British Caribbean education and training sector is fragmented with varying degrees of segmentation. It is made up of nurseries, community-type schools known as supplementary schools, community-based colleges, semi-academies, training companies and independent consultancies, located mostly in England. The aim is to provide services to those who are unable to access adequately, mainstream provision, and who are generally dissatisfied by the way in which education services are delivered. Social responsibility is the overriding factor in enterprise start-ups rather than the profit motive.

However with education providers, clients expect quality and consistent service to students (young and adult learners), but there are some exceptions for training organisations. Minority professionals set up training firms to provide a service and make a profit to boost growth. A formal approach to planning and development is more pronounced, since the nature of the industry demands that operators maintain quality standards in dealing with customers and industry regulators alike. Market segmentation is therefore akin to the organisation and performance of the British Caribbean education and training sector, as the **Fig 13.1** shows.

Application methods in education and training provision are wide and varied and these differ from one group to another. Young learners for example, will obviously have different needs based on aptitude level(s). Adult learners have various needs too, but experienced professionals can easily detect subtle degrees of (low or high) aptitude among distinct groups. Experienced educators and trainers usually conduct an assessment/pre-lesson test to measure the aptitude of learners within a culturally sensitive, creative framework

Figure 13. 1 Snapshot of the British Caribbean education and training sector

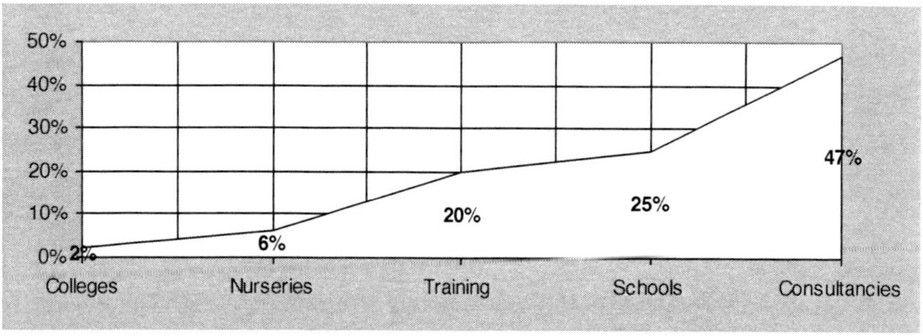

(Source: Black Net UK, 2002)

Figure 13. 1 demonstrates the diversity of the British Caribbean education and training sector, with nearly half being community schools and training firms, two per cent representing community-type colleges and just under half representing private consultancies. These statistics also illustrate the remarkable ability of professional entrepreneurs to compete in a sector dominated by large public and private sector agencies and institutions, and operated predominantly by white middle class educators and training specialists.

Nursery Segments

The nursery segment of education is sub-divided into kindergarten schools, childminders, after school clubs and other playgroup schemes. Charity by legality, they perform specialist and general functions; cultivating in young minds creative, emotional, moral, social and spiritual values. The idea is to ensure that every young `charge' is rounded so that he/she can become useful citizens in the future. Female-owned organisations for 0-5 year olds are located mostly in England **(Minicases 11. 1).**

Minicases 11.1 Geographic spread of British Caribbean nurseries in England

British Caribbean Francesca Muhammad, who is a devout Muslim, founded **New Mind School** in south London in 1996. The full-time independent school was established as a result of parents' requests for their children to acquire suitable academic and spiritual education to be able to function better in a multicultural society.

Archangels Montessori Day Nursery was opened in 1997 by Vera E. Jarrett to provide education and other provision for 26 children at any one time. The nursery supports children with learning difficulties and/ or disabilities and also children who speak English as an additional language. The institution was given a clean bill of health by the Social Care Inspectorate in January 2007.

SYAC Nursery was set up in 1991 to provide nursery education services to multi-ethnic children in the Sheffield City and its environs. It is operated by the South Yorkshire African Enterprise and Training Centre also known as SYAC. Other nurseries are located in London the Southeast and the Midland and Northern Counties, with nearly all serving broad-based communities' cultural, educational and social interests.

The customary structure of nurseries is a head, a deputy, specialist teachers, teaching assistant(s), cook and volunteers or paid helpers who have to be CRB-checked. The Social Care Inspectorate is responsible for ensuring that suitable regulations are in place, since children are vulnerable and can be at risk if nurseries fail to comply with procedural standards. Informal estimates suggest that Caribbean-led nurseries tend to last a decade and more, since founder-owners and staff take their responsibilities seriously and strive to uphold a proper working relationship with parents, relatives and stakeholders such as Social Services and other statutory bodies.

Community Education

The 1960s witnessed the rise of the Black Supplementary School Movement which has since become a major segment of the wider Caribbean education and training sector in the UK. This area provides alternative and complementary education for migrant children to help them develop positive and `grounded identity and to compensate for the failure of mainstream schools to offer children their educational entitlement (**George Padmore Institute 2003**).

Lately, this movement has become the subject of intense study since it benefits the very students whose parents were mainly from the second generation which the movement had within it is focus. There are hundreds of supplementary schools across the British Isles operated by men and women whose background consists of educators, community activists, cultural specialists and mentors. Sessions are held mostly on Saturday (weekly) while other organisations have week-long, after school homework clubs. They operate as registered or unregistered charities with a social enterprise outlook; that is, revenue is ploughed back into the organisation to purchase teaching material and cover expenses of voluntary staff.

As alternative education services, supplementary schools cover a broad range of subjects such as specialist language programmes multi-ethnic communities, cultural studies, history, English, Maths and Science, as well as SATs and GCSE revision support throughout England **(Fig 13. 2).**

Figure 13. 2 Examples of British Caribbean-led Supplementary Schools

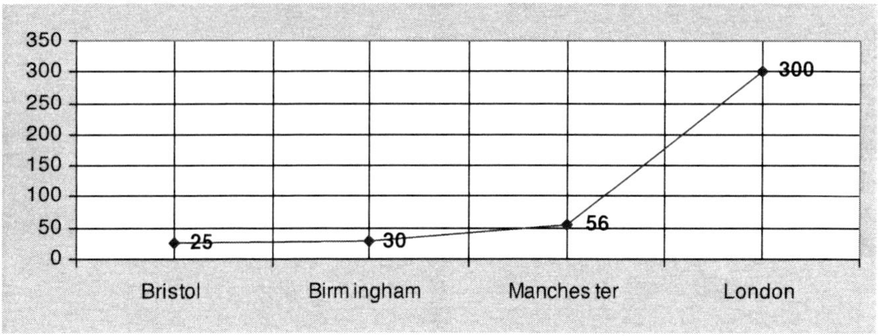

(Source: Adapted from information in the nine English Regions, 2006)

There has been support for the work of community-led education initiatives by both Central Government and local authority agencies. In 2000 the Supplementary Schools Support Service was launched as part of a national drive to offer capacity building for emerging and existing community-based education programmes aimed at improving the educational attainment levels of minority pupils particularly Caribbean children. The £1 million projected covered more than 500 supplementary schools across the country, and although it was short-lived, there was evidence of (shared) Best Practice among many schools in inner-city areas in England.

The city of Bristol's Renewal Programme invested £586,000 to improve the achievement rates of BME pupils, with a significant proportion allocated to supplementary schools. A forum has since been set up to allow providers to link with mainstream schools to support the increase in levels of educational attainment among black pupils particularly **(Bristol 2006).**

College-type Provision

In their endeavour to raise the standards of teaching and learning overall, British Caribbean specialists have extended the ambit of their services to reflect an emerging mainstream provision. This strategy has helped them to gain recognition as `level playing field' operators in the Government's quest towards maintaining premium standards in education. Market segmentation is also apparent here, since these community-based agencies have gained a somewhat competitive advantage in the Further Education market which remains a preserve of white institutions in the UK.

In this section, I will look at institutions that have earned national recognition for advancing new teaching methods, as well as instilling appropriate learning techniques in youngsters who are unable to access the National Curriculum, and at risk of exclusion. These organisations operate mini-academies, having dual charitable and (limited by guarantee) company status, with founders having extensive public sector experience coupled with specialist knowledge in education, literature and related social sciences. Many chose to set up independent institutions because of what they recognise, as a failure of the education system to deliver effectively and efficiently, on its target of enabling minority pupils, especially Caribbean children, to attain levels of educational attainment.

Perhaps more germane, is the perception of professionals that some school-heads are not too keen to grapple with the socially-related (extra curriculum, out-of-school) problems affecting young Caribbean boys in inner-cities, and since the main purpose of schools are to offer learning provision within the law, why should they have to deal with the social ills of their young charges? This debate has been intense and in recent years, starting in the early part of this century, a great deal of attention has been paid to this national scourge. Owners of education firms often ask, `Why does an advanced country like Britain has unusual high rates of student expulsions (particularly in secondary schools), possibly the worst in the whole of Western Europe? Critics argue that this trend is a result of growing multiculturalism which has placed undue pressure on policy makers, local government, teachers and learners alike, to meet targets. This system has created a clash of cultures in the British education system. In this section we will highlight examples of three pioneering education firms –**TCS Tutorial College, Global Graduates** and **Novas Academy** – that until recently were unknown to the public (**Minicase 13. 2**).

Minicase 13. 2 TCS Tutorial College

In 1994, Grenadian educationist and literature specialist, Dr. Roselle Antoine, after working as a University researcher and lecturer, founded **TCS Tutorial College** of which she is principal. The organisation was set up as a language school to offer tuition to home and foreign students whose native tongue was not English.

Despite initial setbacks, Antoine succeeded knowing that no other Caribbean person was operating a similar school in Britain. To some extent, this is still the case – it remains a preserve of white Britain. TCS is the first British Caribbean-led private English Language School with a mainstream syllabus in the UK. Students from over 40 countries including Africa, Asia and Europe, with a sprinkling of home students, were impressed by the curriculum, tuition and social atmosphere, fostered by a multicultural ethos. However, recession in the Far-East led to a reduction in student numbers and the business faced collapse.

By the late 1990s, the language school was transformed into a fully-fledged college as part of a diversification strategy, customer driven. The plan comprised an After-School provision, a Saturday School, an education trust and independent school, along with other social enterprise initiatives. The textbook strategy was a rarity in traditional language schools at the time, since they tended to maintain their core product - English Language. Sections of the Asian community have adopted elements of TCS' model by introducing complementary languages such as Hindi, Gujarat, Arabic, Mandarin and others, to their menu of courses.

TCS has perfected the Community Participatory Approach (CPA) model involving staff commitment to both the institution and learners alike. An assessment is undertaken at the beginning of students' enrolment, to determine their academic abilities, vocational potential and personality traits. There is ongoing evaluation of students to identify problem-areas and find practical steps to resolve them. *I Am Somebody Great'* is the motto of TCS, and this influences a positive outlook among staff and students, whilst annual graduation ceremonies reinforce this practice, as teachers, learners and community leaders alike, are given incentives for outstanding achievement in various fields of human endeavour.

Antoine has received numerous awards including the MBE in 2006, for her contribution to education and community affairs and the institution is a recipient of accolades too, for its work in education excellence. TCS' turnover is under £500,000, but it has viable partnerships with local education services and other public bodies, along with an excellent rapport with the general public. Since 1999, the organisation has maintained a consistent examination success rate of 95%-100%, and from all indications, the college is destined to remain one of Britain's premiere institutions committed to finding solutions to educational underachievement.

Academy Role

The Government's school academy programme is concerned with delivering quality education and these privately-sponsored state schools are located in deprived communities. The hope is that that some of the academies will partner with better performing schools locally, to form `trusts' or a federation and be lifted that way. Performance in the specialists schools especially at GCSE, has improved markedly – but the jury is still out on the academies **(*The Independent* 2006).** So how do minority education firms fare in all this?

The rise of educational entrepreneurship in minority communities was triggered by the 1960s Supplementary School Movement which began using a voluntary approach to learning and development, which gave way to formal methods of operation. The desire to achieve great things in Britain always remained a focus for first generation Caribbean nationals. Members of the second generation have witnessed first hand, the experience of their parents and their children and have realised that only by taking appropriate action consisting of workable solutions, can the endemic cancer of underachievement among Caribbean children be removed. The formula for success is being repeated, though using different methods, all over the UK **(Minicase 13. 3)**.

Minicase 13. 3 Global Graduates

'*Helping Talented Students Get Ahead*' is the slogan of **Global Graduates** set up by Yolanda Beckles in 1999 in her commitment towards providing equal opportunities for young people. The company works in London schools, offers support and advice about study choices as well as aiming to enhance career prospects of its student clients through personal and professional skills development and training.

Before Global Graduates, there was no other organisation that showed much attention towards the career prospects of students prior to leaving school. '*We grab inner-city kids from an early age and stay with them all the way until they are successful professionals. I am passionate about taking on organisations that say they want talent but never look outside their stereotypical box of recruitment. If you want talent, I'll give you talent,*' Beckles acknowledged.

Knowing that one day she would manage a business, Beckles who is of Trinidadian parentage, researched the market and set about acquiring the necessary experience. She turned down a job offer as a city dealer and went to work for the supermarket chain of Sainsbury's and after spending more than 10 years she left, satisfied that she was grounded in the principles of business management. '*In my days, you just needed ambition, drive, motivation and confidence and have some kind of intellectual know-how, and I had them all.*' Her next job with a charity opened her eyes to daily discrimination faced by talented, educated black people, and it was then she took an active role in diversity and equality issues (***The Voice* 2006**).

The self-made 'educational-social entrepreneur' had her company's work promoted on reality television 2006, but her unconventional style met with criticisms. She is convinced that her company's approach is workable in the circumstances. '*People might disagree but I make no apologies for not following the guidebooks that have been failing our children for years.*'

While researching this book, it was difficult to obtain factual data on the achievements of people of colour in the UK. It was obvious that spatial distribution, the lack of genuine interest in the work of the black community and the lack of public recognition for minority professionals in both the media and the public at large, gave way to cynicism and bewilderment, when successful entrepreneurs are mentioned in the ethnic Press. It is clear that an effective way to gather information and data on British Caribbean firms is to adopt a sector-by-sector approach, as well as examine the segmented nature of niche markets that demonstrate the unique selling point (USP) for most Caribbean businesses and social enterprises in Britain.

It is quite noticeable that in the area of education and training, white newspapers are reluctant to publicise stories of black achievement. Perhaps it may go against the grain of the perceived myth of underachievement versus achievement and underperformance versus performance. When the opposite is true, a problem arises. One typical example, was when an editor of a broadsheet was invited to publish a written (ready-made) feature on a renowned educator who was awarded the MBE, she refused to publish the story, saying 'we don't do guest pieces'. Yet, the very broadsheet published column-inches on gun crime and anti-social behaviour relating to black youths. It is these contradictions that inspire minority entrepreneurs to establish institutions to bring about stable and prosperous communities **(Minicase 13. 4).**

Case Study 13. 4 Novas Academy

In 1993, Gloria Hyatt of mixed background (Irish mother and Jamaican father) joined what was described as the UK's 'first independent school' for black children excluded from mainstream schools. **The Novas Academy** has been serving disadvantaged young black people from Liverpool since 1979, providing educational programs and resources for pupils excluded from mainstream establishments.

Hyatt helped transform the organisation from a small after-school club to a nationally acclaimed educational establishment recognised for its pioneering approach to working with children with emotional and behavioural difficulties. In 2003 she received an MBE for her services to education. .

Despite her troubled childhood, she excelled at school, showing tremendous academic potential and a talent for athletics. Her teacher's lack of faith in her aspiration to become a tutor strengthened Hyatt's resolve to maintain an ambitious path, and after leaving university, she worked as a social worker developing an affinity with young people since most had similar problems - single parented families and a sense of abandonment.

As head of the academy, she observed that, '*For the past 25 years we sought to deliver and develop innovative and sustainable solutions to overcome poverty and disadvantage for the black community in Liverpool. The achievement made by individuals over those years is a testament and credit to the academy, but also to the individuals themselves. Many defeated significant hurdles to attain levels of academic achievement they should be proud of, right through to learning English, becoming mentors and even going onto university*'**(*The Voice* 2005).**

Hyatt has since set up her own business with the aim of advising schools, supporting young people and being involved in regeneration and neighbourhood renewal. Changing people's lives for the better is important to her mission. The challenge she acknowledged, was exciting since it created opportunities and generated income to keep her in employment whilst surviving others. Due to her remarkable leadership, five educational projects were created to provide much-needed services for predominantly black children excluded from school.

Education Consultancy

One of the few segments that British Caribbean specialists occupy is education consultancy which is driven by issues relating to low educational attainment of black pupils especially, in the English Regions. These firms are dedicated centres of excellence, and while they have a corporate-type outlook in terms of quality standards, they nevertheless operate in a flexible manner according to client demands, and with a bias towards partnership working.

Contrary to the perceived view that black businesses overall, work in individual `silos'; that is, possess a tunnel vision, by their very nature, education institutions cannot afford to operate in isolation of the demands placed on them, by the teaching and learning environment. Noteworthy, is the link between education and employment that the Government has made for many years in its quest towards global competitiveness. This link is manifested in the relative success of *Partnership for Achievement*, a national education policy which the Birmingham firm of Visions of Esteem is a renowned market leader in the West Midlands Region **(Minicase 13. 5).**

Minicase 13. 5 Visions of Esteem

The veteran British Caribbean education practitioner, Paulette Wisdom, is the founder-owner of **Visions of Esteem** set up in 1998 to pursue the mission of, `*Your genuine partner of choice in supporting organisational growth and development*'. The company works with companies and organisations. The keys to realising its goals include are: meeting the challenge of diversity, increase effectiveness in internal practices and service delivery, raise standards and realise the potential of staff.

From the start, Wisdom knew that challenges had to be overcome and with limited finances and premises to operate from, she used her experience and contacts in the education system and broader industry, to convince buyers - Government Departments, Universities, Colleges and organisations working with children and adult learners – of her firm's quality education products and services. The core services of the business consist of:

- Audit, review and development of key equity strategy.
- Action research projects focusing on and/or identifying barriers to Best Practice.
- Professional staff development including those with leadership and governance roles.
- Strategy and operational development in raising achievements of Caribbean pupils.
- Evaluation of project/strategy/policy effectiveness.

With an annual turnover of less than half a million pounds, but which is set to grow over the next two to three years, VOE has membership with the local Chamber of Commerce and the Society of Education Consultants. Wisdom projected a positive future for the consultancy, with increased public sector contracts with emphasis on supporting national educational targets, a fact exemplified by Visions' research report in 2006 entitled '*The Context of African Caribbean Education and Employment in Birmingham*' which examined the link between learning achievement and the productivity output of Caribbean communities in the labour market.

From all appearances, VOE is on course towards a significant contribution to the Caribbean education and training sector in Britain, from a regional and national dimension.

Training Sector

The training sector is dominated by women from minority backgrounds who have a passion for equality in action rather than the customary (empty and cheap) political sloganeering of fairness for minorities. Women also believe that through expertise and commitment, the market can benefit them, both commercially and socially. Their sense of duty is measured by the positive results they gain and the challenges which test their endurance to remain focused.

In this section therefore, we will examine the work of professionals mostly highly educated and trained in diverse areas such as personal development or coaching, business development, management, human resources, administration, information technology and other disciplines, who have mapped a new terrain in commerce and industry through training and empowerment **(Minicase 13. 6).**

Minicase 13. 6 Platinum Employment Advice and Training Ltd

In 2001 **Platinum** was established to become a leading provider of people's development including training solutions in the West midlands. The organisation is committed to offering bespoke, demand-led programmes of support to local firms, individuals and communities.

Managed by highly-trained professionals - sisters- Georgina and Murett Mendez, the start-up challenges of the firm were acquiring suitable premises, generating enough clients and retaining suitably qualified staff to make the business profitable. Lack of genuine enterprise assistance and less-than-satisfied banking support, has not affected the growth and development of Platinum. Over the past five years, the firm has managed contracts on behalf of the European Structural Funds programme, the Department of Work and Pensions, Local Authorities, the Learning Skills Council and other public and private sectors agencies.

With an annual turnover of about £500,000 and its enviable portfolio and reputation for pioneering innovative projects. Platinum's long term strategy is to: improve its personalised service, training and development of techniques and resources, build on its accreditation status, deliver flexible and culturally sensitive provision, and provide a holistic service covering information, advice and guidance, as well as training, organisational development and capacity building support measure.

Aside of quality products and services at affordable prices, the success of any firm depends on effective communication including channels to transmit the message, be it an idea or commodity. In today's business environment, owners shouldn't ignore the importance of consumer's reaction to new products and services on the market. It is certainly true that whether a business is commercial, industrial or a service entity, a formidable challenge for founder-owners is their ability to be clear on the mission of the organisation. The more confident managers are, the greater the chances of motivating staff, thereby enhancing team building skills, all-round for achieving organisational goals and objectives.

Since the late 1990s, talented British Caribbean females have established training companies and organisations to address issues around interpersonal communication, media communications, confidence building, motivation, teamwork and other human resource management techniques. Once a preserve of white companies, this niche market is open to diverse specialists who maximise opportunities through targeted services to meet the specific needs of co-ethnic markets; that is, both community and mainstream organisations **(Minicases 13. 7).**

Minicases 13. 7 Prominent British Caribbean training firms

Former TV presenter, Jacqui Harper (of Jamaican parentage), is the owner of **Crystal Business Training,** a firm that delivers public speaking, presentation and communication skills programmes. It offers media tips to businesses of all sizes, banks, lawyers and other professionals.

Harper's flair for journalism was first noticed when she founded a newspaper at secondary school, age 16. In the 1980s, she joined Sir Trevor McDonald and Morita Stewart as one of few black TV newsreaders in Britain and by 2001, she was awarded an MBE for training and development and charity work.

Her idea of Crystal resulted from a gap in the market during her time in the media and the fact that business owners had difficulty cultivating proper relationships with the media. Her brilliant career is captured in the book, *Voices of Experience: The Professional's Guide to Making Great Presentations.*

As a young mother, she balances family life with managing a company. *I found it quite a difficult transition. I was full of self-doubt. I always thought I'd be useless as a mother. I think I'm quite a perfectionist. I get this endless ambition from my dad, he's restless, he always wants to do something else and sometimes I wish I could check this ambition and stop* it.' (***The Times* 2005**)

In 2001 Joan Blaney secured a CBE for her success in funding, signposting and building sustainable community projects across the West Midlands, after establishing the **Community Education and Training Academy** (CETA). She has considerable experience in the private, public and civic sectors and has founded a number of non-governmental organisations and registered charities for young people and women.

As an international NGO, the Academy promotes economic development in local communities and through its pool of professional trainers, the organisation inspires women from grassroots communities across Africa and Europe, to achieve personal goals. Blaney's most recent initiative was *Urban Dreams*, set up to help black entrepreneurs in the West Midlands to turn their business dreams into reality. The venture won support from multinational companies, stimulated viable businesses and gave jobless applicants the skills and motivation to find gainful employment. As Blaney pointed out,

`In reality, opportunities are not equal and the idea behind this is to help create a fairer society where people have real opportunities to succeed and are given access to those opportunities. It isn't because people in inner-city areas do not want to achieve but often they lack the connections to overcome the barriers in their way (***The Voice*** **2006**).

Vocational Training

With greater demand for suitably qualified labour to fill thousands of vacancies, there is a corresponding requirement for vocational skills to complement traditional academic certification. Profound changes in the labour market have created new approaches to teaching and learning development, and employers are conscious of cost effective leadership especially, when hiring managerial, administrative and technical personnel.

Having held influential positions in large companies and in local government departments, professionals from minority communities have converted their expertise into customised services, by going into business for themselves. Effectively, they have created unique segments of commercial training, bringing the industry closer to a `level playing field' ethos (**Minicases 13. 8**).

Minicases 13. 8 Vocational training firms

Yvonne Foster established **Lotus Training Limited** in 1994 in south London with much of its work focused on regeneration. Specifically, the company focuses on employment training minority communities and other excluded groups. Within a relatively short time the annual turnover of the firm moved from double-digit figures to nearly a million pounds (five years later).

As an accredited organisation, learners are trained in business administration, customer service and management. Eighty per cent of the company's business is commercially funded through contracts with local authorities and private companies. The multi-ethnic staff as role models for trainees and encourage them to take up studies relevant to their aptitude and aspirations as a whole. Promotion material uses positive images to challenge stereotypes.

In April 1999 Lotus started offering training through the modern apprenticeship programme and has since expanded this provision to cover advanced vocational training for supervisory and technical staff. The strengths of the firm are high standard of work placements, on the job training and good development of key skills.

The Jamaican Foster was the first British Caribbean woman to work with the construction firm Jarvis, as a trainer. Eminently qualified, she has demonstrated fantastic entrepreneurial ability in adapting to the vagaries of the labour market.

The Midlands-based professionals, Trudie Spencer and Linford Chambers, co-founded **Future Training 2000** to develop a community-based high tech learning centre. The company maps service provision by recruiting individuals who because of personal circumstances such as low esteem, loss of confidence and low educational attainment, mean that they are unable to achieve their personal goals including finding suitable employment or maintaining sustainable jobs.

Client needs are based on customer-orientated approach, rigorous assessment, quality assurance and effective partnerships. Training packages are tailored to suit individuals and business in most industry sectors. Qualifications are linked to the UK nationally recognised certification standards. In March 2005, Future Training was part of a trade mission to the West African state of Ghana, to explore `learning modules appropriate for the African market and transferable strategic partnerships (**Wolverhampton Chamber of Commerce 2005).**

Sector Geography

Contrary to the perceived legend that black businesses are located exclusively within London and Southeast, from Chapter 5 and onwards in this book, we have presented clear-cut evidence through case studies and industry data, to show the geographic diversity of the British Caribbean SME sector. And since these firms are not situated within the confines of retail units on the high streets, it is understandable that this situation will create some difficulty for policy makers and regional officials who might be unable to make proper assumptions or for that matter, identify sector location, as well as analyse structural composition and market output.

Consequently, in this section of the book, attention has been drawn to the various segments of the education and training sector in which British Caribbean entrepreneurs occupy in terms of geography. Of course, the broader aim is to demonstrate the impact these business organisations have on enabling regions to achieve targets set by Central Government. Though it was a challenge to capture all firms within this industry, it was important to present a menu of segments for readers to reflect on. As expected, many of the education and training firms are located in prominent British cities **(Table 13. 3).**

Table 13. 3 Key locations of British Caribbean education and training firms

Regions	Areas
London	All sub-regions, North, South, East and West
Southeast	Kent, Slough, Luton, Reading
East Midlands	Derby, Leicester, Nottingham
West Midlands	Birmingham, Dudley, Wolverhampton
Yorkshire & Humberside	Sheffield, Leeds, Kirklees
North West	Liverpool, Manchester
South West	Bristol

(Source: Textual analysis and case study material, England 2000-2007)

According to the above table, Caribbean education and training firms are located in over half (58%) of the 12 UK Regions, spread across inner-cities where there is a high concentration of minority communities. Studies done in other areas - Scotland and Wales inclusive - show evidence of growth in the training sector, though relatively micro to small in nature. For instance, most regions have long established community education ventures whilst independent consultants offer training to public sector agencies and community-voluntary organisations, on employment and career-related programmes.

However, in each of the regions, attempts are being made by local authorities in collaboration with various interest groups, to reduce levels of economic deprivation and social exclusion brought about by educational underachievement, mismatched skills and (labour) market discrimination. Yet in all this, sections of the Caribbean professional and business community play a pivotal role, one that is unknown to many in the UK today.

Challenges and Prospects

The education and training sector in the UK has grown considerably over the past decade with record levels of investment in education and skills training by the Labour Government. This twin priority has given fresh impetus to minority professionals concerned with investing their expertise and resources with a view to being self-sufficient and making a positive contribution to their communities. However, this sector has formidable challenges, as well as exciting prospects to develop niche markets in key segments – nursery education, primary and secondary education, further education, adult education, higher education and training in general **(Table 13. 4).**

Table 13. 4 Competitive framework for education and training in the UK

Segment	Challenges	Opportunities
Nursery education	High start-up costs, tough regulatory regime, skills shortage, other structural changes in the nursery market.	Demand for more childcare facilities, diverse course content, need for more specialist nursery provision.
Secondary education	High entry barriers, low attainment for Caribbean students, fragmented market with public, private and charity sector.	Community education provision, diversity in study programs, contracts with public and private agencies.
Higher education	High entry barriers, highly regulated, mainstream colleges have monopoly over stipulated courses and are publicly funded.	Scope for specialist institutions, links with colleges to achieve learning targets.
Adult education	Reduced expenditure and fragmented learning outcomes for adult learners in the workplace.	Residential training for the employed and jobless to attain qualifications - key partnerships a must.
Further education	Traditional institutions have monopoly over student intake and command resource allocation	Need for tailored courses from minority learners in partnership with institutions to achieve national targets.
Training	Human resources management, a low-keyed training priority, e-learning is a constant issue.	Urgent need for tailored employee programmes, demand for the outsourcing of e-learning contracts.

(Source: Research and Markets, 2005 and Key Note Market Reports, England, 2005, 2006)

Moreover, developing a culture of lifelong learning where adults can access education and training at any stage of their lives is a UK Government priority. It is stated that education and training should be available at work, at home, part-time or full time; at times and places which suit individual needs. Developments in the UK include:

- Open and distance learning.
- Accessible and flexible modes of study.

There are over 500,000 part-time students in the UK of all ages, with significant growth in short post-degree vocational courses to update skills, mainly in business, science and education; and

Modular courses.

British Caribbean firms can maximise opportunities in the various UK Regions where there are existing gaps between the acquisition of job skills and actual vacancies. These vacancies require both specialist and generalist skills for employees who are unable to cope with modern changes that globalisation brings in relation to how levels of production and productivity.

There are also excellent prospects for owners in the education and training exports market, a growth area that includes higher education, trans-national higher education, further education tuition, English Language teaching, examinations, private sector training, publishing, educational equipment and broadcasting, a billion-pound market.

Through links with the British Council, UK Trade and Investment (UKTI) and various education bodies, British Caribbean business organisations can become fully-fledged providers or sub-contract education products and training services that are akin to the services they offer, especially in markets where clients demand culturally diverse programmes. Other opportunities can be sought via World Bank, UN, Commonwealth and other international contracting agencies and institutions that work in Africa, Asia, the Caribbean,

Europe and Latin America, using again a multi-ethnic, sector-based model.

Conclusion

In this chapter some investigation was carried out on particular segments of the education and training sector in which British Caribbean firms are involved. It was emphasised that since 1997, the Labour Government made education a top priority and £2.2 billion was earmarked for a major schools building programme in the country. The percentage in public expenditure for education showed an increase by nearly half and approximately 5.6% of Britain's GDP.

The billion-pound training market was also discussed with growth trends in public spending – the Learning skills Council's budget – amounting to over £10 billion between 2007 and 2011. There was though, a sharp decrease in spending for on-the-job training at 0.3% during the 2004-2005 periods.

As a universal brand, English Language amounted to billions of pound and it represented one of the global exports that minority firms should exploit to their advantage.

A fairly detailed analysis, based on studies – past and present - was done on issues around the underachievement of Caribbean pupils and the recent positive outcomes attributed to the *Aiming High, Raising the Attainment of Minority ethnic Pupils*, specifically targeted at black pupils (**DfES 2006**). Regional variations regarding Caribbean education professionals in public sector were also mentioned and although the national picture showed an overall 1%, in some areas the ratio was three to five times higher.

In an effort to make a case for market segmentation, two examples were graphically illustrated. The first featured the contribution of African and Caribbean graduate students in the employment market which showed that overall, they represented the third highest `self-employment status, exceeding that of their Asian counterparts by more than two percent. The other scenario looked at the market share for consultancies (47%), schools (25%), training (20%), nurseries (6%) and colleges (2%), using the evidence from the Black UK Net. In a way, these two examples helped set the tone for the chapter.

In relation to education the following segments were touched on; namely, nursery, community education, college-type provision and the role of academies. These were identified because they highlighted the breadth and scope of the Caribbean education businesses and learning organisations that have developed a range of instructional products and in the process, added value to local and national targets, unknown to the authorities.

The training sector was explored around vocational training, subdivided around media communications, employee development, social inclusion training, modern apprenticeship and other job-related subjects. The evidence produced, bore little resemblance of the `news blackout' which minority firms are subjected to daily, even in their attempts to make a positive difference in British society through entrepreneurship and a sense of social responsibility.

Typically, a competitive framework has been devised, encompassing challenges and prospects within the education and training sector. The areas that featured in education were: nursery, secondary, higher, adult and further education, as well as training. The challenges centred on regulations, entry barriers, resource allocation and market intelligence. The opportunities highlighted the need for owners to look carefully at market opportunities in their respective segments and create partnerships with contractors/providers in mainstream public and private sector agencies. The potential for exporting education products and learning services was also pointed out since globalisation, apart from its down-side, also has prospects for innovation in emerging markets, worldwide.

Numerous sources were used to access information pertaining to this chapter; they consisted of industry figures, personal interviews, local business associations, random sample surveys and media profile of business organisations. The author applied expert observation on the operations of minority firms and a working knowledge of the national economy, to mirror objectivity. According to a leading Guyanese specialist on Workers' Education, "*Learning begins from the cradle to the grave, from the womb to the tomb and from the insurrection to the insurrection*" (**Denny 1981**).

It is anticipated that this chapter will create greater awareness of the contribution of British Caribbean professionals and their organisations to the national learning culture. Chapter 14 will showcase the input members of this community are making to health and social care in Britain.

Chapter Notes

Department for Children, Schools and Families replaced the Department for Education and Skills or the DfES, was set up by the Prime Minister in June 2007 build on the education and children's services over the past 10years.

Private Finance Initiative (PFI) – a special scheme introduced by the Government to create public and private partnership in the construction of schools, hospitals, railway and other State-run institutions. It allows for value for money and consumers expected quality services with this new venture.

English Language – is promoted as an export product by the British Council and UKDTI in countries worldwide, especially since English is a universal medium of communication for businesses transactions and other forms of human communication.

Bernard Coard – the Grenadian educator is renowned for his analysis of the British education system which labelled the children of Caribbean immigrants *'Educationally Sub-Normal'* (1971). His 'clinical' intervention generated considerable discussion and research over the past 30 years which shows that discrimination among succeeding generations of black pupils persists in the form of culturally unrepresentative curricula and low expectations for attainment and behaviour on the part of staff.

Aiming High, Raising the Attainment of Minority Ethnic Pupils' Strategy - a programme that began in 2003 to ensure that the needs of minority ethnic pupils were being met with effective and targeted mainstream provision. Every year 1,000 black pupils are permanently excluded and nearly 30,000 receive a fixed period exclusion. Although not given much coverage in the mainstream media, this programme has proven successful, with Caribbean pupils in some instances, having an average of over 50% passes in GCSE Grades A to C.

Minority Graduate Students – British Caribbean postgraduates are among 'senior' learners who upon leaving Higher Education, are keen to work and the choice of paid employment or setting up a business is quite a challenge. The percentage of black graduates into self employment has grown in the last five years.

Nurseries – in almost every English Region, there is a nursery provision or alternative childcare facility owned and managed by Caribbean entrepreneurs.

Montessori Nurseries – provide childcare requirements that a normal day nursery provides; they offer too, an environment alongside specially trained teachers which allows children to learn and develop naturally, free from routines and structure.

The Criminal Records Bureau (CRB) – is an executive agency of the Home Office that provides wider access to criminal record information by enabling organisations in the public, private and voluntary sectors to make safer recruitment decisions by identifying candidates who may be unsuitable for certain type of jobs especially that involve children or vulnerable adults. The main areas are education and training, financial services, legal and law enforcement, medical and health, public services, sport and recreation and welfare services.

Community Education – the modern equivalent of supplementary schools also known as `Saturday Schools' because tuition is held on Saturday. These `community' learning centres began in the 1960s after Caribbean families expressed frustration by the way in which their children and others were treated by the British education system. Some of these schools are now formal institutions, funded partly by either grant aid, commissioned contracts and/or self-financing.

George Padmore Institute – located at the famous John La Rose bookshop, north London and named after Trinidadian and Caribbean intellectual, George Padmore contributed to Pan-Africanism during the 1950s and 1960s. His works typified fellow pioneers Marcus Mosiah Garvey (Jamaican) and Cyril Lionel R. James (Trinidadian).

TCS Tutorial College – a unique private institution, offering public service education and training services, by fusing corporate excellence with social responsibility and driven by a learning ethos; that is, culturally based and community inspired and underpinned by partnerships with staff, students and various other stakeholders.

Global Graduates – an enterprise encouraging students to tap into their latent creativity through the acquisition of professional skills and training in preparation for the world of work.

Urban Dreams – scheme similar to the BBC television series, *Dragon's Den*. It has been so successful that local authorities in other parts of the country such as Haringey and Islington are interested in promoting its usage.

Selected References

1 `Training Market Report', *Research and Markets*, 2005.

2 Further Education, *Key Note Market Report*, September 2006.

3 Johnes, Geraint (2004): *The Global Value of Education and Training Exports to the UK Economy*, UK Trade & Investment, April 2004.

4 Higher Education Provision in the United Kingdom: An Analysis of HE Workforce Data, Lifelong Learning UK, December 2005.

5 `Top of the class, Programme targeting black pupils is raising standards in GCSE achievement', *The Voice*, 30 October – 5 November 2006.

6 The Graduate Labour Market in London, FOCUS Central London, March 2005.

7 Ethnicity and graduates' early outcomes (Winter 05/06), Prospects Careers Services', England.

8 `Cultivating new minds with intent to develop a bright future', *Black Heritage*, October/November 2003.

9 Recording the History and Development of the Black Supplementary School Movement, George Padmore Institute, July 2000, London.

10 `Supplementary Schools Significantly Contribute to Raising Attainment of Pupils in Central Bristol', *Supplementary News, Issue 1,* January 2006, Bristol.

11 `Ten years on, has Tony Blair fulfilled his pledge to improve education?' *The Independent* 30 November 2006.

12 Oswald, Janelle (2006): `A pleasure to mess with', *The Voice*, 10-16 April 2006.

13 Motune, Vic (2005): `Hyatt of her powers', *The Voice*, 18 July 2005.

14 The Context of African Caribbean Education and Employment in Birmingham: Research Report, Visions of Esteem for Partnership Achievement Ltd, October 2006, Birmingham, England.

15 Henry, William (Lez) `I'm fed up with Black Underachievement', *New Nation*, 9 October 2006.

16 Tikly, Leon, Haynes, Jo, Hill, John and Gillborn, David (2006*): Evaluation of Aiming High: Africa Caribbean Achievement Project,* University of Bristol, 2006

17 `Top Trainers', *Lewisham Life*, June/July 2004.

18 'Why it pays to talk', *The Times*, 24 August 2005.

19 Graham, Vernon (2006): 'Birmingham's Joan of Arc', *The Voice*, 16 May 2006.

20 '*Businesses take a bow*', Wolverhampton Chamber of Commerce, Summer 2005.

21 *The Education and Training Sector International Trade Strategy*, The British Council, October 2003.

22 Gundara, Jagdish S., 'Multiculturalism in Canada, Britain and Australia: The Role of Intercultural Education', *London Journal of Canadian Studies, Volume 17, 2001/2002.*

23 Denny, K.W.E: Industrial Relations and Sociology Course, Critchlow Labour College, Guyana, South America, March 1981.

Chapter 14

Health and Social Care

Introduction

In 2006, a historic account tracing the contribution of Caribbean professionals to the National Health Service (NHS) was published. In his foreword to the publication, Acting Chief Executive, Sir Ian Carruthers wrote, '*By making that long journey into the unknown on boats like the SS Empire Windrush all those years, Caribbean people were not only critical to the success of the NHS in its formative years, but also created a lasting legacy of diversity in its employees'* **(Kramer 2006).** Indeed, without the 'steady stream' of imported trained professionals, the health service would never have been able to meet Britain's growing health needs and maintain niche markets in diagnostics, laboratory technology and other non-clinical services.

However the question remains, did the contribution of Caribbean people to health and social care began in the 1950s and 1960s after the NHS was born in the late 1940s? This chapter will highlight how Caribbean professionals translated their knowledge and experience from working with the NHS into creating health and social care firms and other such organisations, capable of sustaining the British tradition of a global provider of quality healthcare.

Whilst much has been written about the NHS and its pioneering role in healthcare delivery, the efforts of Caribbean professionals have borne little public significance and where it has, token mention is given. In fact even though historically African people have contributed to scientific and technological advances and continue to do so, in today's media environment, these endeavours are scarcely acknowledged in spite of the so-called political correctness climate that prevails in multicultural Britain.

The NHS is the single largest public sector employer with staff in excess of one million, with people from black and other ethnic backgrounds representing over 14% of staff; that is, 180,000 people. The government committed a 43% increase in health expenditure in 2007; that is, up by £74 billion in 2005-2006, and this means that by 2008, public expenditure on health will be just over 8% of GDP.

The total value of the UK healthcare market is estimated at over US$10.5 billion and growing at a rate of 10% per year. The estimated turnover of UK manufacturers of healthcare products is US$7.9 billion, of which exports account for approximately US$5.3 billion. The market is divided into major products and services including radiotherapy, healthcare IT, on-clinical consultancy, advanced wound management, healthcare design, imaging techniques, in-vitro diagnostics (IVD) products, orthopaedics, among others (**UKTI 2005**).

African Genius

Africans were writing medical textbooks as early as 5,000 years ago, and according to sources, the Egyptians not only had a mature civilisation, but also a long period of medical development. It has been confirmed repeatedly, that much of the training and instruction of the healing priests were orally transmitted, as it is in the rest of Africa. It is likely therefore, that Western medical practitioners have only a partial grasp of the true scope of Egyptian or African (the author's emphasis) medical knowledge (**Finch 2000**).

Imhotep was the first architect and physician known by name in history - the founder of Egyptian medicine who is the author of a medical treatise, the so-called `Edwin Smith' papyrus, detailing anatomical observations, ailments and cures. The Egyptians had the capacity to produce a variety of pharmaceuticals derived from the animal, vegetable and mineral kingdoms. Western scicntists have confirmed that contrary to previous accounts, Imhotep is the original '*Father of Medicine* and not the Greek, Hippocrates who became famous for fusing philosophy with medicine in an effort to revolutionise the science (**Osler 2004**).

Migration of Professionals

Commonwealth migrants including Caribbean health specialists and ancillary personnel have been the backbone of the NHS for decades, and despite structural changes by successive Conservative and Labour Governments, non-white staff are still highly represented – men and women inclusive – within the service. By the end of World War II, a shortage of labour in the NHS, construction, transport and other sectors resulted in a British recruitment campaign for health workers from the Caribbean and other Commonwealth countries. British-born women couldn't respond to the hundreds of nursing vacancies because they were more interested in better-paid jobs. Recruits came from Barbados, Guyana, Jamaica, Trinidad and Tobago, Grenada, St. Christopher & Nevis, St. Vincent and The Grenadines, as well as other parts of the eastern Caribbean. After nearly 50 years, employment in health and social work among Caribbean professionals is still relatively high compared to foreign nationals now employed.

The NHS operates an international labour market to fill hard-to-recruit vacancies – both specialist and auxiliary nursing and medical personnel. According to the Nursing and Midwifery Council, 672,897 nurses were registered at March 2005, with overseas nurses accounting for nearly 12,000 or just over 1% of the total workforce. Although the migration of health professionals seemed to be more managed and targeted at key areas of critical care in the health service, between 1998 and 2005, more than 2,000 overseas-trained nurses from the Caribbean were registered in the UK, with flows and ebbs in the mid-1990s and the beginning of the 21st century. In terms of non-white Commonwealth countries and regions, the Caribbean contingent led the African and Indian sub-continent with higher levels of trained nurses, a pattern that began since the post-war period in the UK **(Table 14.1).**

Table14. 1 Overseas-trained nurses registered per annum in the UK 1998-2004

Country	1998-99	1999-2000	2000-01	2001-02	2002-03	2003-04	2004-05
India	30	96	289	994	1830	3073	3690
Philippines	52	1052	3396	7235	5593	4338	2521
Australia	1335	1209	3396	7235	5593	4338	2521
South Africa	599	1480	1088	2114	1368	1689	933
Nigeria	179	208	347	432	509	511	466
Caribbean	221	425	261	248	208	397	352
Zimbabwe	52	221	382	473	485	391	311
New Zealand	527	461	393	443	282	348	289
Ghana	40	74	140	195	251	354	272
Zambia	15	40	88	183	133	169	162
Mauritius	6	15	41	62	59	95	102
Kenya	19	29	50	155	152	146	99
Botswana	4	-	87	100	39	90	91
Canada	196	130	89	79	52	89	88
Nepal	-	-	-	-	71	43	73
Swaziland	-	-	-	-	-	81	69
China	-	-	-	-	-	-	601
Malawi	1	15	45	75	57	64	52
Sri Lanka	-	-	-	-	23	36	47
Lesotho	-	-	-	-	-	50	43
Japan	-	-	-	-	20	37	34
Singapore	-	-	-	-	-	-	28
Sierra Leone	-	-	-	-	-	-	24
Others	203	329	472	809	418	514	380
Total	**3479**	**5764**	**10473**	**20628**	**17143**	**16853**	**13248**

(Source: Nursing and Midwifery Council - NMC – September 2005)

In 2004, it was reported that the three largest categories of ethnic groups in the NHS were White (245,000), Black or Black British (21,000) and Asian or Asian British (19,000). The 2003 survey of Royal College of Nursing members reported that 9% of respondents were from minority backgrounds, of which approximately half were of Caribbean origin. Until the mid-1990s, there was no routine collection of national data, and the introduction of new ethnic codes in 2002 for England, makes trend analysis difficult (**Royal College of Nursing 2004/2005**).

The ethnic profile of medical staff is piecemeal, and at times, disjointed to the point of vagueness. Prior to the 1990s, information on Britain's medical health professionals was lumped into a mass figure, with a breakdown of categories in various specialities. Using published figures by the Department of Health, I have presented a fairly balanced picture of the Caribbean input into the medical profession in the UK.

Two significant trends have existed within the NHS since the 1960s, with the recruitment of medical practitioners from the traditional British Commonwealth (Africa, Australia, the English-speaking Caribbean, Indian-subcontinent and New Zealand) and later the Philippines and more recently, the EU. Firstly, non-white consultants who were trained abroad made up 11.9% of the consultant workforce. They were significantly over-represented in geriatric medicine (22%), genitourinary medicine (21.4%), paediatrics (17.2%), learning disability (36.2%) and old age psychiatry (18.4%), and were under-represented in general medicine and public health medicine.

Secondly, the percentage of doctors from minority backgrounds who were admitted to the UK medical schools in 1996, and therefore due to graduate soon after 2001, was nearly 27% as follows: Asian (20.7%) Chinese (2.1%), Black (1.5%) and other non-white professionals of African/Caribbean origin (2.6%) of the total number of medical students in the UK (***British Medical Journal 2004***). The authorities concede that the percentage of ethnic personnel in the medicare sector will soon rise from less than 2% in the early 1970s to 30%; that is in excess of current representation of people from minority communities in the general UK population.

A further argument is that monitoring ethnic groups and sex is generally undertaken in the expectation, that if there are concerns, they will be about under-representation of minorities – men and women. It should be stressed that in the mid-1990s, there was evidence of more data being collected on a segmented basis; that is, reflecting various health and medical staff employed in different parts of the NHS. For instance, medical doctors are a highly differentiated group – by their speciality, grade, gender, ethnicity and geographical place of work.

This presents the problem of narrowing down the groups of General Medical Practitioners including those working directly with the NHS. In 2004, the General Medical Council reported a total of 12,760 doctors were registered in the UK of which overseas qualified doctors made up 37% (4,721), compared to 19% and 44% qualified in the EU an UK respectively. Policies around equal opportunity are now in force and public authorities are expected to publish annual staff profile on the basis of ethnic origin, position and other occupational categories (**Table 14. 2).**

Table 14. 2 Percentage of Medical Staff by Ethnic Origin and Grade

(Source: Department of Health, medical and dental workforce census England, 2005)

Ethnicity	Cs	AS	SG	RG	SHO	HOFP
White	68.4	38.7	34.3	49.3	40.8	52.8
Black/Black British	2.2	4.5	6.2	3.9	3.8	2.8
Asian/Asian British	13.3	36.2	38.5	32.2	41.3	25.1

Mixed	1.1	1.7	2.3	2.2	2.3	3.1
Chinese	1.1	0.5	0.7	2.8	2.3	2.9
Other	1.2	10.0	9.3	4.8	4.4	3.9
N	31,993	2,554	5,527	18,006	21,642	4,663

Notes: Guide to the code groups: *Cs – Consultants, AS – Associate Specialists, SG – Staff Grade, RG – Registrar Group (SpR), SHO – Senior House Officer and HOFP – House Officer & Foundation Programme (year 1). The terms `Black' and `Black British' lumped as general ethnic data are misleading since to the casual observer, it underplays the true nature of the British Caribbean contribution to UK medicare. The same can be said for the presentation of statistics for (the rubric form of) `Asian/Asian British'.*

Whilst health officials claim that African and Caribbean people combined, have a `market share' of just over 2% in the medicare sector, by dividing the percentage by the number of each medical category above, a further analysis of the overall data presented, could be translated to the total number of black professionals represented in each medical speciality as follows:

- Consultants – 703
- Associate Specialists – 115
- Staff Grade - 342
- Registrar Groups – 702
- Senior House Officers – 822
- House Officers - 130 (***Department of Health 2005)***.

There is an obvious gender disparity in public health employment with the over-representation of women by over 80%, mainly due to the nature of the profession and the fact that more females are inclined to pursue healthcare professions than men. In relation to medical practitioners there is also an imbalance balance between men and women depending on the areas of speciality. Men operate as general practitioners (GPs) for the most part, while women opt for specialisation in midwifery, gynaecology, paediatrics and or related clinical and health care disciplines. Caribbean professionals have demonstrated commitment, dedication, knowledge and skill in their performance in the health and social care sector, qualities which often go unnoticed.

It is estimated that more than 25% of all doctors, nurses and ancillary staff are first generation Caribbean nationals who came to Britain in the mid-20th century to rebuild the NHS. Interestingly, contrary to the view that the first generation of Caribbean migrants was invariably unskilled and unqualified, evidence from the profile categories by the Department of Health showed otherwise. One study highlighted that out of a 2,701 Caribbean nurses, more than 70% had 15 years plus experience in health services and related areas of nursing care. Another 10% and more were also working in alternative health capacities – via an agency or `bank' set-up. Only about 11% or just fewer than 350 Caribbean nurses had one year's experience in the nursing profession (**Royal College of Nursing 2005**).

Jamaican-born Mary Seacole is the Caribbean's leading pioneer in the healthcare field, and her achievements are legendary. She is a member of the *`Hall of Fame'* in Jamaica, with her name inscribed in buildings, institutions and organisations in the UK and elsewhere. As a fitting memorial to her enormous contribution, the Department of Health launched the *Mary Seacole Leadership and Development Awards* in 1994 for BME nurses, midwives and health visitors. The scheme provides an opportunity for awardees to make positive and lasting contributions that promote high quality patient/client-focused care. It also facilitates recipients with an excellent gateway to develop leadership skills through innovative whist expanding their abilities to engage more fully in operational health management. This scheme is a testament to the recognition Seacole enjoys worldwide, both as a brilliant entrepreneur and natural herbalist. Hers is also a legacy that is destined to remain intact for succeeding generations (**Minicase 14. 1).**

Minicase 14. 1 Mary Seacole, the `doctress'

Referred to by different names, `another *Florence Nightingale'*, `*herbalist'* and `*doctoress'*, **Mary Seacole** was born Mary Ann Scott in Jamaica in 1805 to a black woman and a Scottish father who was a solider. She perfected the use of herbal or traditional medicine in the treatment of soldiers during the Crimean war in the 19th century. She learnt her medical skills from her mother. After she got married and her sickly husband died in 1836, she established a boarding house in Jamaica to deal with the cholera epidemic which swept the island claiming more than 30,000 lives.

Seacole worked with doctors and nurses and gained first hand knowledge of diseases and developed a medicine that produced remarkable results. It was said that many doctors felt threatened by her ideas of cleanliness, good ventilation, nourishing food and the separation of patients with contagious diseases.

She worked in the Caribbean, Latin America and parts of Europe, where she faced racial prejudice and other forms of abuse, but these setbacks didn't deter her mission. She once said, `*And wherever the need arises – on whatever distant shore – I ask no higher or greater privilege than to minister to* it'**(Alexander and Dewjee 1984**).

Seacole's boarding house provided for her personal expenses and financed her medical work. Her generosity was matched by her business-like approach; she often demanded strict payment for services rendered. She worked in her boarding house by day and volunteered with Florence Nightingale in the evening. She financed her practice due to owning and managing boarding houses and being an independent operator during the Crimea War. However, her labours did not prevent her from bankruptcy. In effect, she was left with expensive supplies that couldn't be sold at a fair price. After she returned to England, high-ranking military officials and others organised a benefit fund to help her financially.

A book written about her was well received and profitable. In 1867 another fund was set up, supported by Queen Victoria. The government awarded her the Crimea Medal for services rendered to the sick and injured and she also received recognition from other countries including France, Russia and Turkey.

> Both Nightingale and Seacole developed administrative and practical experience in handling tropical diseases and in so doing, contributed to nursing history. Undoubtedly, it was Seacole who combined her love of service with traditional medicine to produce a near perfect health care enterprise of the 19th century.

Perhaps unknowingly, the work of Seacole motivated other practitioners to develop low-keyed but successful enterprises in the health and social field. The acquisition of culturally sensitive skills is a major factor in the success or failure in the delivery of health care services to minority communities. These skills are in short supply within public health institutions and researchers are often ill-equipped to deal with the concerns of non-white people who need sensitive care provision. Although experts agree that this is the case, ethnic communities still experience variations in qualitative health care when compared to the majority population. Indeed, some minority communities have distinct health and social needs that require specialist forms of intervention and treatment rather than prescriptive types (**Higgingbottom and Serrant-Green 2005).**

Market Segmentation

It is issues like those above, that led Caribbean professionals to establish a variety of production units in healthcare. From medical practices, care homes and healthcare agencies to independent carers and day care centres, the majority of firms are micro to small, and since they are regulated by agencies such as the Department of Health, Social Services and the Commission for Social Care Inspection, staff complement based on experience and skill, is a necessity.

The unique selling point (USP) of many firms is their philosophy underpinning the diversity of staff and clients respectively. This has become almost a permanent fixture of care agencies in particular, that vie for different types of contracts – both in the statutory and the private/independent sector. The market for carers has grown with increasing segmentation and in the process, attracted minority communities from different age groupings. In such a sophisticated environment, a main concern is the way carers balance financial interest with the (social) responsibility of those within their care **(Table 14. 3).**

Table 14. 3 Percentage of Carers by gender and ethnicity

Men	Age Group 16-64 (%)
All Men	10
White (including British, Irish, White Other)	25
Indian	12
Pakistani	11
Caribbean	8
African	6
Chinese	6
Women	**Age Group 16-59**
All Women	14
White (including British, Irish, White Other)	33
Indian	13
Pakistani	16
Bangladeshi	15
Caribbean	10
African	8
Chinese	7

(Source: Carers UK, Sheffield Hallam University, 2005)

Estimates suggest that there are over one million men and 850,000 women who work full-time and provide unpaid care. Self employed Caribbean people who work part-time, are most likely to be carers like other ethnic groups. The figure above also illustrates that nearly a quarter of Caribbean men and women combined are involved in the care industry which is largely segmented around care for the elderly, terminally ill, sick and/or managing independent care facilities for paid clients.

Learning disability is a key segment in the healthcare sector and in the mid-1990s, it attracted considerable interest among minority communities faced with promotional restrictions in paid employment, not forgetting that they also learnt to maximise opportunities for social care entrepreneurship having benefited from exposure to mainstream agencies and organisations including Social Services and other statutory bodies. Instinctively, since the early 1990s, Caribbean migrants began establishing and appropriating models of commercial and social healthcare enterprises in London and other inner-cities throughout England. Regarded as a beacon in the learning disability segment, the firm of SFI Group Homes is also seen as a standard bearer for its culturally sensitive care delivery approach (**Minicase 14. 2**).

Minicase 14.2 SFI Group Homes

Striving for Independence Group also known as `SFI Group Homes' was founded in 1996 by Dorothy Pinnock, a social worker who was employed with the local authority for many years. The family-run west London business operates three homes, providing care and accommodation for adults with learning disabilities and challenging behaviours. Residents comprise a range of nationalities – white and non-white.

There is a self-contained day care centre for home residents as well as users from other homes in the area. A well-kept garden is seen as a useful resource for the residents, who have regular contacts with, and visits from families and friends. They are invited to events organised by SFI. Reviews are done yearly with six monthly updates carried out in the presence of care managers and local authorities - they contribute to meetings along with resident(s).

SFI contracts with health authorities, hospitals, rehabilitation and day-care centres and other agencies. Detailed action plans are prepared for each resident, outlining aims and objectives. These are supported by reviews that address specific needs of residents including the maintenance of medical records. More than 70% of clients have been in SFI's care for 10 years, a reflection of its excellent service provision.

The firm provides opportunities for residents in vocational training and they are also taught independent living skills such as shopping, budgeting and cooking. There are IT facilities on site and residents are encouraged to develop keyboard skills, as well as join local libraries. Reading sessions for residents are usually supervised by care workers.

In 2003 management undertook a performance review and formulated a business plan as part of a wider evaluation of its role in the care sector. The assessment was also designed to enable SFI to keep pace with regulations under the National Care Standards Act 2000. With a tailored structure comprising management, administrative and care teams, SFI promotes the service through referrals, repeat custom, direct contracts, *Yellow Pages*, NHS Direct and community links.

Between 1997-2001, profits rose by more than 80% as a result of increased contracts, and the company's turnover grew in excess of 100% due to a swell in homes/units and quality care staff. Although there was a marginal reduction in revenue due to a slight fall in users during 1999, profits have grown steadily over the past five years nearing the million-pound mark. The strategy is to consolidate operations by improving quality care services, thereby providing value for money for both residents and commissioned bodies.

Medical Practice

Prior to chronicling the Caribbean contribution to the NHS in 2006, it was assumed, that only people of Indian or Asian descent figured prominently in the (private) medical profession. When this author researched non-white medical practices across the UK, it was almost impossible to obtain official data on the presence and number of Caribbean professionals operating medical practices. Using anecdotal evidence from one-one-interviews and discussions with doctors, ancillary health professions, this book presents a sample of medical practices that complemented and acted in some instances, as alternative services for clients frustrated by the quality of public health provision.

From general practitioners, to specialists in dentistry, surgery, medicine, Caribbean people make an enormous contribution to the healthcare industry by demonstrating qualities of enterprise and professionalism in the medical field (**Minicases 14. 3**).

Minicases 14. 3 Selected British Caribbean Medical Practices (past and present)

- Trinidadian **Dr. John Alcindor (deceased)** was a health pioneer of the early 20th century working in hospitals in England before he set up his own practice in 1907, west London, one of the first black general practices at the time. Whilst his Pan-African ideals enabled him to fight for social equality, he also used his knowledge and experience in the medical profession to campaign on health issues such as cancer and tuberculosis.
- **Dr. Harold Arundel Moody (deceased)** of Jamaica was renowned for his creation of the League of Coloured People in 1931, but even though he was a qualified practitioner, racial discrimination prevented him from working in a hospital. He eventually set up his own practice in south London and represented hundreds of people to find suitable accommodation in the light of poor quality housing conditions for migrants from Africa and the Caribbean in the post-war period.
- Grenadian, **Lord David Pitt** (deceased) was a medical doctor and politician. After his studies in Scotland, he returned to the Caribbean to help form the West Indian National Party to lobby the British for self-government. He later returned to the UK and established a medical practice in London. He was a tireless campaigner for racial equality and was instrumental in setting up CARD. Although he did not win a parliamentary seat, he was appointed chair of the Greater London Council in 1974 and a year later, became a Peer in the House of Lords. He served as president of the British Medical Association in 1985-86.

- **Dr. Edward Adams** of Guyana worked for over 30 years in the NHS before setting up his south London practice in 1977. His `patient market' spans London, the Southeast and the Home Counties. His practice has grown from high levels of professionalism to a better understanding and knowledge of the medical and health care industry. His advice is, `*To survive in this industry, a great deal of effort and commitment is required. Customer care is important to a successful medical practice. I have dealt with thousands of patients and other clients from the NHS and private health care institutions* ` **(Adams 2004)**.
- Vincentian **Dr. Franklyn Jacobs** left the Caribbean to further his studies in anaesthetics and went into general practice within in the NHS including lecturing at the Royal College of Surgeons. In 1982 he set up his own practice in north London. He is a founder-member of the African Caribbean Medical Society that campaigns for a greater understanding of health issues in the black community.

A seminal work entitled *Many Rivers to Cross: Cross Caribbean People in the NHS 1948-69* by British author, Ann Kramer, in the conjunction with the NHS, was published by Sugar Media in 2006. Profiles of 30 health and medicare specialists from Barbados, Grenada, Guyana, Jamaica, St. Lucia St. Kitts & Nevis and St. Vincent & The Grenadines were in print. I viewed this rare but timely publication this way.

The health and medicare specialists featured, illustrated the well-known qualities of dedication, expert knowledge and resilience displayed by people of Caribbean origin for years, especially in their chosen station of life. The diversity of professionals as depicted from the Caribbean territories of their birth was essential to point out especially for members of the indigenous and wider migrant population in the UK. Such an approach will no doubt help to foster a better appreciation and further understanding of the immense social capital of Caribbean people so rarely publicised in an objective manner. The book provides useful anecdotes and refreshing insights into the challenges and future prospects for Caribbean people's involvement in healthcare, as well as other professional and entrepreneurial sectors. Quite remarkably, a significant number of those profiled were honoured by Royalty for their overall contribution to healthcare and civic affairs.

Far from highlighting their medical prowess, the above samples in the case study, offer valuable insights into the vital role Caribbean specialists played in their struggle - beginning since the 19th century - for economic independence and social justice in the Caribbean and Britain. Together with their male counterparts, female practitioners also left an indelible stamp on healthcare provision by leading on national initiatives and creating private initiatives to help reduce inequalities in healthcare delivery.

Professor **Carol Baxter** leads on equalities and diversity in the NHS; **Daphne Steel** was Britain's first black matron and was involved in community care projects. **Dr. Nola Ishmael** OBE is mentoring and coaching the next generation of NHS nurses and **Dr. Neslyn Watson-Druee** OBE, set up a career development company for minority professionals in 1988. **Sherlene Rudder** was awarded the MBE for her work in genetics in 2005 and Jamaican couple, **Doctors John and Jean Parboosingh** who contributed to the NHS for many years, emigrated to Canada in 1993 to continue their mission of medicare.

Domiciliary Care

As the UK population age rapidly, this will have a great impact on care services across the country since over £10 billion is spent on homecare services alone per annum. By 2020, it is projected that 16 million or 27% of the UK population will be 60 to 80 years plus which will certainly have implications for social care legislation, including the delivery of equitable care provision, as trends in Local Authority homecare provision in England suggest.

Changes to homecare provision also mean that hours will be increased considerably to take into account various types of medical and health condition affecting over 60s and even those within the middle age bracket. The main providers in all this are local authorities, private and community sector agencies and organisations.

However, it is professional-campaigners 'on the ground' who have made a difference by changing the face of domiciliary or respite care. In delivering community care to BME elders, there are still unfair assumptions and perceptions about these citizens (**Age Concern 2000**). In Haringey for example, adults and the elderly are among clients who benefit from domiciliary and other health care provision. Thousands of residents aged 65 plus benefit from *Older People's Services* whilst older residents, under 65 years receive supported housing, home care and day care services. Most of the 7% of Black and Minority Ethnic elderly receiving residential and day care services are very disabled or very frail.

Noteworthy, former NHS nurses, social care practitioners, community activists and other supporters have not only joined forces to advocate for quality care services for the elderly, but initiated positive action through the setting up of organisations to deliver holistic services - provision to match medical, health, social and cultural needs of residents.

Much of what is being done today in the social care market, reflect what professionals in the NHS did for many years coupled with the determination to make certain that various communities benefit from expert services for the greater good of those most vulnerable especially. The north London firm, **Satellite Consortium Ltd,** has a unique approach to domiciliary/respite care for the elderly in the sub-region. Its work has since been adapted as Best Practice by statutory agencies determined to reflect cultural sensitivity in their provision.

Elsewhere in England, solutions to healthcare concerns are being found too, with the creation of private firms to manage and deliver services to various ethnic communities. Caribbean healthcare firms have fundamental weaknesses such as their inability to make greater inroads into the newly-established Primary Care Trusts (PCTs), modernising technology applications for robust data collection systems and investment in lucrative tender-contracts involving clinical products.

Judging by this competitive gap between minority firms and mainstream companies, it is left to smaller units to play to their strengths in social care and implement services to meet local needs whilst maintaining market advantage in the realm of community care.

Independent Living

In attempting to support targets on community care including independent living schemes, there are different types of business arrangements set up by Caribbean professionals to take into account of the needs of the elderly population in various parts of the country. For those frail and housebound, there are essential services aimed at supporting their independence.

Described as a `serial entrepreneur' because of his passion for creating an assortment of enterprises, Leslie Fairclough is founder of **Higher Level Ltd**, a national care provider. In spite of the usual setbacks associated with start-ups, Fairclough has maintained the impetus of the business, with the aim of bringing quality care to clients who need it most, at affordable cost.

Children's welfare is essential to health and social care with a long-term strategy being to provide multiple services for those in care so that their cultural, education, moral, spiritual and social needs could be met. It is also another way of preventing young people from experiencing poverty, joblessness and related deprivation. Some British Caribbean firms are leading the way in providing solutions to help sections of the inner-cities' most vulnerable young (**Minicase 14. 4**).

Minicase 14. 4 Abronah Care Ltd

In early 2005 when ex-soldier Anthony Walters and his wife, agreed to set up a model children's home, **Abronah Care Ltd**, in the West Midlands, they didn't (fully) recognise that theirs was more than a `commercial concern', but a facilitator of social (care) change in inner-city England.

The firm's growth has been dramatic, with an annual turnover of over £600,000 in the first year of operation, an astonishing achievement for owners with no previous experience in healthcare, but who utilised the best experience and skills available in the community to make good of an opportunity in a highly-regulated environment. The ethnic diversity of the staff and clients underlines the philosophy of the founder and his determination to be integrated into mainstream.

To remain competitive, Abronah contracts with local authorities and other providers, thereby retaining excellent links with public and private agencies involved in implementing children's policies. The firm has regular consultations with community groups to access information on trends in the childcare market. By systematically evaluating the market, the company is better placed to adjust its products and services to meet changing client demands. Abronah's long-term plan is to set up a one-stop shop to offer holistic care services for young people, their families and professionals interested in improving the `Independent Living' status of young people from all backgrounds and circumstances.

The disproportionate number of black youths outside the education system and the labour market has prompted others to take appropriate action. A regional Connexions Service reported that thousands of `hard to reach' 14-19 year olds were out of school and lacked basic skills training. They are dissatisfied over their inability to access the National Curriculum more so being unemployed for long periods. Many also experience hopelessness due to low self-esteem resulting from improper role models and family breakdown. Their attraction to the `gang culture' is symptomatic of a need for recognition and social comfort.

Conversely, hundreds of graduates find difficulty adjusting to work life because of limited knowledge about employment practices. These constraints have a knock-on effect on the productivity of firms and the under-performance of regions that have large pockets of minority communities (**Verity 2007**).

It is in such circumstances, that British Caribbean-owned firms have come into their own, with cultural and unique services that are universal; that is, provision that takes into account the client market and the positive effect of partnership.

Independent living programmes are carried out by a competent management team supported by carers with multiple skills and experiences. The values of Abronah are based on moral and spiritual principles and are evidenced by programmes for users. The format has elements of the National Curriculum and follows guidelines stipulated by the National Care Standards Commission. External activities are also organised and regular assessments are conducted to measure progress by the young in care. The company plans to establish a healthcare facility on the high street to provide holistic services for companies working in community healthcare.

Older People Services

In their attempts to improve the quality, management and value of care for the aged, the disabled and vulnerable, Caribbean professionals have also embraced Central Government's policy of maximising the role of community enterprises. Through targeted services, the needs of older and fragile citizens are given priority through a range of measures, both informal and formal; that is, public agencies and community enterprises (**Minicase 14. 5**).

Minicase 14. 5 PJ Community Services Ltd

(Source: Race & Regeneration, Spring/Summer 2006, BTEG, London)

Claudine Reid is Director of **PJ's Community Services Ltd** established in 1992 in recognition of the need to provide an improved 'Home Shopping' service for older people in south London. The original founders also wanted to establish a business which provided opportunities for people who felt they had 'more to give' in terms of their potential, knowledge and experience, and were unfamiliar in their daily activities.

Start-up problems including many sleepless nights planning different approaches to public agencies did not dampen Reid's vision of growing the business on a large scale since the general idea was to offer local authorities alternative services which took into consideration the savings and improvements to home shopping service provided initially by Social Services.

A key aspect of the business is its flexible relationship with a number of local authorities which allowed the firm to deliver a more comprehensive service to customers. Reid explained one example of flexibility: -

A shopping visit to someone's home may also involve the changing of a light bulb, which may sound minor, but for our target market these minor household issues can cause problems and discomfort in the home. Our contract with the council is extremely strict in terms of what our service may or may not provide, and it does require some flexibility (**BTEG 2006**).

Another significant expansion for the £2 million per year turnover enterprise, was taking over a contract from a reputable retail outlet after it had disbanded its home shopping operation with 200 existing clients. The increase in capacity tested the resolve of PJ but management coped well by developing an appropriate strategy to deal with growth.

Whilst contract opportunities in the social care field are more demanding because of tougher regulations, Reid endorses the recognition by Government that there is a fundamental role to be played by social care firms in the UK economy. She has some useful tips for entrepreneurs who are in the process of making a transition towards developing a sustainable enterprise.

- Develop a clear vision of the type of service you want to supply;
- Always be prepared to take sound advice, drawn on expertise;
- Ensure that you think ahead, don't be complacent;
- Learn to develop a mindset of 'let's fund another client'; and
- Accountants and legal experts can help you manage business dealings with confidence.

Mental Health

This condition is associated with Caribbean people of African lineage living in Britain, and has its genesis in this description of the African man in 1792 by the Swedish botanist, Linnaeus, *Of black complexion, phlegmatic temperament, and relaxed fibre.....Of crafty, indolent and careless disposition, and are governed in their actions by caprice...Anoint the skin with grease.*

In his response to the Swede's racist description, mental health specialist, Colin Simms, said that, *"Perhaps this explains the rationale for the medical assumption and malpractice of forcing higher doses of medication and electric shocks on the unsuspecting black male living in Britain today* (***Church & Race* 2003***).*

The type of diagnosis and treatment has been a focus of intense debate amongst the African and Caribbean communities including churches, nationally. In 2003, AC churches and mental health workers discussed strategies for closer partnership to develop a suitable programme of welfare for mental health patients. It was agreed at the meeting that because patients experienced the harsher end of care treatment, religion and spirituality ought to play a critical part in helping them to cope with systemic injustices.

Aside from Simms, there are other independent-minded persons and social enterprise-type organisations that have assumed leadership roles in the campaign against the frequency with which black young men are misdiagnosed with a mental health condition. These campaigns range from specialists employed with public institutions to healthcare professionals who have set up autonomous organisations to ensure that the issue remains on the national agenda **(Minicases 14. 6).**

Minicases 14. 6 Profile of leading black mental health specialists

Dr. Kwame Mc Kenzie, consultant psychiatrist at the University College Hospital urged the government to target funding to help black mental health patients. There is need to build sustainable communities and this focus can assist in reducing illnesses within the African and Caribbean communities in the UK. Drugs and counselling Dr. McKenzie added didn't prevent mental illness, a fact that is acknowledged by the statutory sector and non-governmental organisations including black churches that deal with this issue.

Dr. Rosemary Mallet, medical sociologist, who was Chief Executive of Brent Mental Health Trust, highlighted research carried out by the Centre for Caribbean Medicine at King's College, London which pointed to the fact that schizophrenia is not simply the result of poor genetics or neuro-developmental patterns, but that the main reason may be social. Rates of unemployment, poverty and disadvantage were identified as factors contributing to incidences of mental illness affecting British African and Caribbean people.

Colin Simms, Servol Community Trust conducts action-based research on African Caribbean mental health and social care needs provided and managed supported accommodation for service users and developed a helpline, outreach and floating support for the community. He said that efforts must be made to bring a more harmonious approach to the treatment and understanding of mental health issues affecting the black and the wider community (***Church & Race* 2003).**

Unquestionably, statistics show that 50% of black people are likely to be sectioned, according to the first ethnic census of inpatiens published by the Health Inspectorate in December 2005. The census found that 9% of mental health patients were either black or of other ethnic origin. Black inpatients were 44% more likely to be sectioned under the Mental Health Act and half were subjected to control and restraint (**Black Londoners Forum 2005**).

In 2002, the Sainsbury Centre for Mental Health published a report entitled *Breaking the Circles of Fear*, the experiences of black people using the UK mental health services. The report examined the reasons why these residents are several times likely than average to be diagnosed with schizophrenia and generally sectioned under the Mental Health Act and treated in locked wards with high doses of medication. The recommendations were as follows: -

- Develop appropriate training for mental health staff and community leaders;
- Build the capacity of community and voluntary organisations; and
- Create regional networks of activities to promote better services.

Two other British-Caribbean healthcare specialists, Drs. Joanna Bennett and Frank Keating are in the forefront of training programmes to improve mental services, as well as evaluate areas of work and develop alternative methods of delivery to match client needs and general requirements. In 2004 the Government published a second draft of the Mental Health Bill which proposed sweeping changes to the way people are placed under compulsion for mental health assessment and treatment. It included broader conditions under which a person may be put under compulsion; the introduction of compulsory treatment in the community; and the creation of new safeguards including Tribunals and advocates **(Sainsbury 2005).**

And yet, other conditions relating to sickle cell, hypertension and diabetes are also integral to the wide-ranging work of scores of Caribbean health and social care groups in the British Isles. These organisations serve a dual purpose; firstly, they support different local and national healthcare initiatives in the UK irrespective of the cultural and racial background of service users; and secondly, these groups support their respective homelands in nation-wide campaigns, donating literature, medical supplies and equipment for children and young people, as well as the elderly.

Health professions have teamed with community activists to set up social care-type enterprises to heighten awareness and reduce incidences of sickle cell and other blood disorders experienced by members of the black community in the UK (**Minicase 14. 7).** Out of an estimated 750,000 donors on the four UK Bone Marrow and Cord Blood register, an estimated 20,000 are of African, Caribbean or Mixed Race descent. The figure is said to be relatively small compared to the current figure of around 50,000-60,000 cases of leukaemia, sickle cell, bone marrow and lupus suffers.

The ethnic numbers on the Anthony Nolan Trust are of 382,357 donors and the National Blood Service (British Bone Marrow Registry) 299,046 donors, mainly consists of white and northern European donors. Both registers have a shortage of donors from varying backgrounds. The bone marrow registers consist of donors in the following categories: Jewish (7,591), Mediterranean (3,377), Asian (11,495), African, Caribbean and Mixed Race (20,000).

Minicase 14. 7 The African Caribbean Leukaemia Trust

The **African Caribbean Leukaemia Trust** (ACLT) was set up in June 1996 by Beverley De-Gale and Orin Lewis, parents of former Leukaemia sufferer, Daniel De-Gale. On 7th April 1993 when he was six years old, Daniel was diagnosed with Acute Lymphoblastic Leukaemia (ALL – a childhood form of leukaemia) and had less than a week to live. He was placed on a two-year course of chemotherapy, but went to remission for 9 months and had to receive a further two-year course of similar treatment. Daniel's parents have been involved in media campaigns to raise awareness, organising bone marrow registration activities in the UK and taking part in TV documentaries. In June 1999, Daniel received a bone marrow transplant from an unrelated (female) US donor who is now part of the De-Gale Lewis family. The young Daniel however, succumbed to the condition on 8 October 2008.

The Trust assists families especially Black and Mixed Race sufferers of Leukaemia and related blood diseases with counselling, advice and moral support. Its main objectives are to:

Raise awareness in the black community, enable potential donors to be involved in offering hope and a healthy future to someone whose disease may otherwise be fatal;

Support and assist black people and people of Mixed Heritage suffering from Leukaemia and any other bone marrow related illnesses such as Aplastic Anaemia;

Educate the public about the need for better services for people suffering Leukaemia or any other bone marrow diseases.

The ultimate aim is to set up an International ACLT bone marrow UK-based register, to recruit potential donors for the Caribbean, UK and West Africa, and find matches for patients around the world.

Initially, De-Gale and Lewis knew that their son's survival hinged on bone marrow transplant, but because this tissue contains racially specific characteristics, the compatible donor for Daniel could only be found in the Black or Mixed Race population. At the time of his condition, there were about 285,000 registered potential UK donors, with only 550 of Black or Mixed Race descent. At the time, Daniel's consultant stated that he had a 1in 250,000 chance of finding a suitable donor. The young De-Gale finally died October 2008.

The ACLT conducts clinics in the UK to enlist donor support and organises charity events to raise funds to heighten awareness of its work. It collaborates various agencies and institutions including: the Fire Service, the Prison Service, the Black Police Association, corporate bodies, local authorities, trade unions, Government departments, Black Workers Groups, colleges and universities, plus several private individuals. In 1997 the National Lottery Charities Board provided a one-year grant to support the work of the Trust.

As a leading independent healthcare campaign organisation, the ACLT has filled a void regarding a blood condition that for years, was perceived as not on the `high' list of health priorities, nationally. The Trust and other campaigners have partially helped to bring Sickle Cell Anaemia to the fore and it is hoped that the organisation's work will stimulate further research, deepen the awareness of many and develop a possible cure for this debilitating, hereditary condition affecting the lives of members from the African, Caribbean and Mixed Race communities in the UK and the world as a whole.

There are hundreds of other groups often described as '*hometown*' organisations that work in partnership with various government and non-governmental agencies back home and overseas to provide much-needed materials, equipment and services in the healthcare sector. Much of the work is driven by former NHS employees and related social care experts. One such organisation in the UK is the **Grenada Voluntary Hospital Committee** or the 'GVHC'.

In mid-2007, the organisation celebrated its 40th anniversary, and since its creation in 1967, members have donated cash, materials and equipment to residential homes and hospitals in the Caribbean, including Grenada. As a registered charity, GVHC was originally formed by a group of Grenadian nurses whose interests were the:

- Relief of sickness in the state of Grenada, Carriacou and Petit Martinique;
- Relief of sickness, hardship and distress in Caribbean territories; and
- Raise awareness of health issues amongst the African and Caribbean community.

It is worth repeating that Caribbean healthcare firms are highly segmented and though estimates vary in terms of actual market share overall (18% self-employment activity recorded by the ONS), there are other indicators that make interesting reading. Information is piecemeal and data is either ambiguous or non-existent. The impression given too, is that black-led firms are insignificant to the UK healthcare sector because of their composition and size, and as such they are not really valued for what they offer.

Nevertheless, there is no denying the extent to which these enterprises are making a positive difference to client choice(s) particularly those who demand culturally sensitive and specific provision. This approach is not restricted to the needs of first generation migrant communities, but also second and third who obviously recognise the disparities in healthcare delivery in cities and rural areas of the UK.

Allied Sciences

As was stated at the beginning of this chapter, the British Caribbean contribution to the healthcare industry is wide and varied, and besides health and medicare segments, there are other areas in which professionals have turned their attention in their quest to redefine `independent' choices in heath services, locally and nationally. Quoting figures obtained from the online publishing company, Black Net UK, the evidence suggests that Caribbean enterprises have market shares in counselling (5%), residential homes (6%), fostering and adoption (10%) and childminding (30%)
(Fig 14. 1).

The data reflect a silent revolution taking place in the health sciences field among non-white specialists/practitioners and activists who are dispelling the notion that despite setbacks, they are capable of competing in a sector that is still perceived as the preserve of white institutions. The statistics below are also indicative of the rapid growth, the increase in segmentation and the corresponding demand for additional care services from the independent sector, a fact borne out by the increasing choice made by users of healthcare provision all over the UK.

The estimates point further to the theory that Caribbean professionals maximise opportunities in the healthcare market, as well as enhance linkages between public and private sector by offering a package of high quality provision which meets industry standards from the perspective of the sector and users alike. Almost in textbook fashion, these small independent units are forging a renewed pathway in the delivery of high quality provision for the nation's sick, weak and others who are in need of healthcare to improve their general well-being.

Figure 14. 1 Estimates of British Caribbean healthcare firms' market share

(Source: Independent analysis obtained from BlackNet UK, 2002)

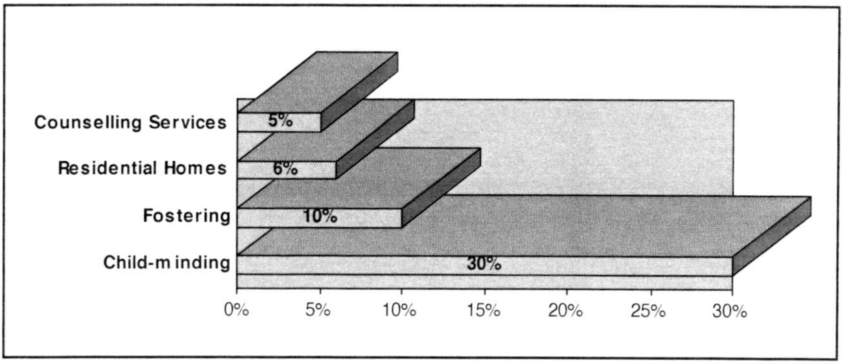

In addition, even though quantifiably the market share of various segments might be small compared to traditional mainstream, the presence of segmented units of British Caribbean health and social care enterprises in the British Isles should be a comforting thought for authorities in light of growing pressures on the NHS and Social Services to widen the breadth and scope of healthcare and community-based provision to guarantee equity and fairness, in accordance with Central Government's healthy living agenda.

Service Philosophy

With a doubt, the success and longevity of health and social firms in the British Caribbean community have much to do with owners desire to maintain a distinct set of services, coupled with a viable partnership model. In recognising the value of the NHS and its relationship to providers and client-users, ethnic enterprises acknowledge that apart from providing selective or holistic services tailored to meet specific user markets, it is also about image and reputation, all of which have to be packaged in an attractive and competitively priced manner. The values therefore, that underpin Caribbean business success in healthcare services are:

- Links with health authorities through previous contacts and/ or association with statutory bodies as managers or other supervisory, technical posts;
- Industry networking skills through ongoing campaigns for equal access to public health provision, as well as advocacy on national issues such as cancer, diabetes, hypertension, HIV/Aids, mental health etc;
- Knowledge of client needs and user expectations, coupled with appropriate interventionist strategies involving cases of critical care that require a specialist, but culturally sensitive approach;
- Flexibility in procedures involving expert evaluation, diagnosis, treatment and after-care services to ethnic clients and users of statutory medical and health care provision;
- Professional-type organisational structures and systems appropriate for contracting requirements and delivery of broad-based services to multi-ethnic clients; and
- Track record of achievement including accreditation and other professional awards, in heath-related institutions and/ organisations over an extensive period. Almost every founder/ owner of Caribbean health and social care enterprise has a minimum of 10 years' experience in a health-based industry sector or segment in Britain or overseas (**Minicases 14. 8**).

Minicases 14.8 Leading British Caribbean Medicare Pioneers

Dr. Annabelle Burnham is a consultant in Obstetrics and Gynaecology with over 15 years experience in her respective field. Her special interests include minimal access surgery, contraception, menopause and gynaecological scanning. She has treated hundreds of patients using an integrated service approach. Her professionalism relies on achieving a high standard of care, a minimum of delay in relaxing, friendly surroundings. A regular audit and review of outpatient and inpatient practices and procedures are performed.

Dr. Nelda Elizabeth Frater is a GP with a medical practice that specialises in detoxology. She believes every client is an individual whose treatment and substance abuse rehabilitation package must be specifically designed to suit individual needs. Rehab treatment covers alcohol, drug, or substance abuse.

Professor Cynthia Pine is the first black woman to head a major UK Dental School (Liverpool University). She was also elected as the first female president of an international association involved in dental research, 2000-2001. She has supervised numerous research projects in her field, as well as co-authored the UK Review of *Behavioural Science Teaching.*

Dr. Mahendra Persaud Deonarine is a celebrated scientist who has conducted a successful experiment using the cassava plant to develop a cure for cancer. Using the root crop, he genetically engineered it with tumour-targeting antibodies to kill cancer. He confirmed that the treatment had successfully targeted and killed bowel cancer cells in cell culture. His work attracted considerable attention in the British newspapers and the reputable Scientist journal.

Dr. Samantha Tross is the first female Orthopaedic surgeon of African ancestry in the UK. As a Fellow of the Royal College of Orthopaedic Surgeons, she specialises in Adult Reconstructive (commonly referred to as hip and knee replacement) Surgery. In 2001, the publishing firm, Tamarind Ltd, released a fictional biography of the young doctor's achievements. According to the Caribbean-born medicare specialist, "*Young black people in the UK are not exposed to enough positive examples of black achievement; they are not given the right encouragement to believe that they can become doctors if they want to.*"

Exposure to the NHS and other corporate-type bodies, offers senior practitioners a wealth of knowledge, skills and opportunities to be more competitive in the marketplace. This in turn, has led some to establish firms to improve employee development programmes in the healthcare sector. Like much of the public service today, the modernisation of the NHS is paramount since customer choice, changing market trends and the need to be cost efficient and effective in management terms, are all factors that need consideration. The struggle within the healthcare sector for additional resources versus positive outcomes is set to continue even when financial and material resources are evenly matched by a strong desire to train and retrain staff at all levels of the organisational chain. In effect, flexibility remains a strategic tool.

The independent sector is seen as the `heart and soul' of ex-NHS personnel who can utilise their competence, experience and extensive contacts to negotiate lucrative contracts either through the provision of personalised services or health management consultancies. Critical in all this, is the consistency of maintaining quality industry standards, coupled with the satisfaction of client needs at affordable costs. Inter-personal skills and knowledge of healthcare are not sufficient credentials, but rather the ability to adapt services to specific client needs outside the traditional public sector, can be a formidable challenge for new entrants in the healthcare market.

Furthermore, in today's environment where web-based technology or e-commerce has made information far more accessible and quick, it is equally important for healthcare entrepreneurs to appreciate the value of building on their knowledge of organisational management systems and quality control procedures, since depending on the type of market one enters, contracting from commissioned bodies, could impact on results thereby posing risks to relatively new firms in the healthcare sector. **(Minicase 14. 8).**

Minicase 14.8 Beacon Organisational Development Ltd

Ex-NHS health specialist, Dr. Neslyn Watson-Druee who was awarded the MBE for nursing leadership, established **Beacon Organisational Development Ltd** to provide personal development and leadership training for chief executives, leaders and team managers in the health, other public and financial sectors accordingly. Her transition from the NHS to an independent businessperson was supported by an industrial management development Esso Scholarship.

Utilising much of her experience, she employed the *Management-McCann Team Management Profile*, a leading psychometric tool for identifying individual and team work preferences. This model earned Beacon a proud reputation for mainstreaming strategic management services in the independent healthcare sector.

'I start by drawing out the job holder's Team Management Profile major and related roles followed by a review of their key targets and critical success factors, and the results from their Types of Work Profile. This reveals each individual's area of preferences for those tasks needed for high performance, 'she said, explaining how the model works.

Beacon uses this scientific model to make the transition between the identification of strengths, areas that prove challenging and the job demands. Feedback from the profile, prepares delegates to return and have a constructive conversation at work, particularly where there significant gaps in the line manager's and job holder's perspectives exist.

Another important segment in which British Caribbean professionals are making progress, is in health staff recruitment, as the crisis surrounding staff retention in major sectors of the UK economy intensifies. Whilst maintaining staff levels at the supervisory and lower end of the organisational scale remains problematic for many organisations, accessing top management and technical personnel can also be tricky. The attraction for higher salaries, improved conditions of work and service (holiday entitlements, study leave etc) and more friendly working environments, as well as increased promotional opportunities, tend to attract high-flyers or dedicated, career-minded people.

Medicare scientists such as pharmacists are in short supply. They are a source of scientific and technological advancement for healthcare. Thousands of practitioners migrate each year to *'Greener Pastures'* to enjoy better living and working conditions. The pharmaceutical industry is very complex and experts say that it takes around 10 to 12 years and a reported hundreds of millions of pounds to develop a new medicine before it becomes a commercial success. The industry employs around 73,000 people and generates another 250,000 jobs in related industries. Of the major medicines sold in the UK, around half were developed in British laboratories. Twelve of the 25 medicines prescribed by GPs on the NHS are British. The industry exported in 2005, £12.2 billion creating a trade surplus of £3.4 billion.

Health Care Location

Since healthcare services are important to the needs of every citizen, it is understandable that British Caribbean firms will try to locate enterprises is as many areas as they possibly can despite the risks involved in competing with large companies that have carved-out niche markets. As more than half of all care homes, independent consultancies and medical practices are situated in London and the Southeast, there are other industry segments spread throughout England in particular.

Evidence from the case studies included in this chapter shows that privately-owned firms are keen on spreading the market risk by operating in areas where there is a demand and also where services could be delivered in a more targeted way. The idea of pricing services to suit the conditions of commissioned bodies is also a perquisite for market entry by Caribbean-owned healthcare enterprises in Britain.

In areas where there is a predominance of ethnic communities, including African and Caribbean residents dispersed in wards and districts, there is a tendency to divide services according to market demands and use grassroot networks to obtain information and data to position firms. For instance, Abronah Care utilised multiple links – both statutory and non-statutory – to set up operations in the West Midlands, recognising that competition with monopoly care agencies was possible if a proper strategy targeting `at risk' and vulnerable children and young people described as `hard-to-reach' by authorities, was properly implemented with due regard for the expectations held by education, health, and Social Services' authorities.

As well as London and the Southeast, other parts of the country have long-standing independent organisations. The traditional enterprise model is often matched by a host of loosely co-ordinated network schemes that provide services specifically aimed at sections of the elderly population. For instance, there are several day-care centres and related facilities in inner-city locations; namely, Birmingham, Bristol, Cambridge, Cardiff, Dudley, Glasgow, Leicester, Liverpool and Manchester. These enterprises provide quality support to service-users suffering from diabetes, cancer, heart disease and hypertension, to name a few illnesses. However, with the creation of '*BME Elders' Forums*' in recent years, it is difficult to determine both the efficacy and quality of care provision offered to people of Caribbean origin since figures for members of that community are literally subsumed or at worst, hidden in multiple datasets.

Additionally, as in education and other statutory services, location is fundamental towards shaping the type of services that are offered by firms to differing ethnic markets. Ownership of healthcare businesses, variations in service delivery as well as the structural composition of firms and market output, are equally essential. It is therefore necessary for owners to consider the critical factors that impact on the delivery of quality healthcare services especially at the pre-start up phase. These factors include:

- Diversity of communities such as cultural and ethnic composition.
- Demands for specialist health and medicare services generally.
- Quality of healthcare provision and the relevant agencies that exist.
- Cost of delivery and the competition in surrounding areas.
- The regulatory nature of the environment or practices governing services.
- Type of contracts, their duration and main providers; and
- Life expectancy of the local population - children, young people, older people.

The very nature of the healthcare sector means that in identifying a location for enterprise start-ups, serious consideration must be given to local regulations such as planning permission, signage, parking etc. Owners of residential homes for older people and children ensure that choice of premises is in keeping with planning laws and other stipulations. The choice of premises is also a key ingredient in the marketing mix of healthcare firms. Operators in the Midland Counties have positioned their businesses near to high street locations in premises that are visible, accessible and user-friendly. Apart from spending less on corporate advertising, owners have made sure that their companies remain permanent in the eyes of both clients and `passing trade' (potential customers).

Since a market is defined as a set of arrangements by which buyers and sellers are in contact to exchange goods and services, British-Caribbean and other minority-owned healthcare entrepreneurs are constantly making efforts to ensure that the location they choose for business is compatible with the expectations of users and the wider demands of potential clients.

Challenges and Prospects

So far, we have learnt about the dynamics and complexity of the health and social care sector, and as an important institution of the economy, the challenges are many, as they are prospects. The industry is highly regulated and operators' success depends on effective and efficient management of change in legislation, technology, type of staff and broader competitive factors such as the effects of international finance and trade markets.

And though the sector as a whole is a reputable global brand, minority firms are still struggling to compete. Whilst there is no guarantee that equality laws will ever create a level playing field in business and industry, market forces will nevertheless dictate as an intervening mechanism, the way British-Caribbean and other ethnic firms strive to maintain and ultimately improve their market share in key segments of health and social care in Britain (**Table 14. 4**).

Table 14. 4 A Competitive Grid of the UK Healthcare Industry

Segment	Challenges	Opportunities
Nursing	Low retention rates, the demand for staff in critical care and other serious health conditions.	More nursing agencies targeting recruits with key skills in critical care, health-related expertise; partnerships with PCTs, NHS Trusts and other statutory agencies.
Medicare	Shortage of medical doctors and allied clinical practitioners to deal with diseases and illnesses in the modern age.	Setting up polyclinics in inner-cities with links to commissioned agencies and recognised medicare networks to boost healthcare.
Disease Management	Growing demand for biotechnology to treat suffers affected by HIV/Aids, Sickle Cell, Alzheimer's, Lupus and Cancer to name a few.	British-Caribbean scientists can establish firms, linkages with large firms to produce innovative products and services according to cultural sensitivity.
Social Care	High demand for care workers, recruitment problems, poor pay and stressful working conditions and little recognition status.	Small care firms can develop quality, customer- centred care training NVQ Levels 2-4 or the equivalent, to produce an army of carers that can add value to the industry.
Healthcare Training	Restricted opportunities for senior positions in the national health service for African/Caribbean nursing and clinical care graduates.	British-Caribbean professionals should set up consortia firms to facilitate employment for black graduates in nursing, clinical and non-clinical professions.

Fostering &Adoption	Growing demand due to family breakdown, general dislocation of society, leaving children vulnerable and lacking parental support.	Caribbean foster-parent agencies and adoption network enterprises can develop culturally specific provision for African/ Caribbean children needing proper parental guidance and support.

(Source: Textual analysis of healthcare firms based on industry trends 2005-2007)

In the face of a nursing shortage – an estimated 180,000 nurses expected to retire in the next 10 years - and ongoing changes in the NHS structure, independent providers can maximise opportunities by competing for a share of the market. The shortage of professional health care workers are due to factors such as institutional discrimination, market forces, as well as deficit-led redundancies totalling more than 20,000 involving staff in NHS Trusts, Mental Health/Learning Disabilities Trust and Primary Care Trusts throughout England. With additional investment in healthcare set to rise from £764 billion in 2005-2006 to £92.6 billion in 2007-2008, it means that funding has been allocated to provide higher volume and quality of care **(Royal College of Nursing 2007).**

In terms of medicare, the main challenge is to improve the number and quality of Caribbean medical students. Since 2001, the *Access to Medicine Project* at King's College London has worked to encourage and enable young people from the inner-London schools to train as doctors. Nearly 200 local students have begun their training as a result of this initiative. The success of the scheme has faltered somewhat with the continued under-representation of young people of Caribbean and dual heritage background. British-Caribbean healthcare businesses can therefore collaborate with the Centre for Caribbean Health and the University of the West Indies to promote joint research and development activities to benefit people in the Caribbean and of British-Caribbean people in Britain.

In addition, the opportunities for private medical practices still exist, with the establishment of polyclinics or community-style health centres that can benefit diverse communities, some of whom might be unable to access traditional healthcare facilities because of distance, low income or lack confidence in the quality of provision by local institutions. The training of more community health workers is also an important factor in maintaining a durable healthcare delivery system – whether public or privately owned and managed.

The medical field has tremendous prospects for young and experienced British Caribbean professionals – recent graduates and more recently established practitioners. Areas of speciality could involve oconolgy, dentistry, ophthalmology, cardiology, radiology, gerontology, paediatrics, pharmacology, orthapaedics etc. For these segments in the medical field, professionals can operate as contracted as follows:

- GPs - practitioners who have contracts with PCTs;
- GMS Other – salaried doctors who work in partnerships, known as assistants;
- GP Retainers - practitioners provide service sessions in general practice.

Under disease management, independent firms can also capitalise on increasing trends in communicable diseases such as HIV/Aids, venereal infections among others, affecting an increasing number of inner-city children and young people, particularly teenagers. Possible cure for terminal illnesses like cancer, hypertension, sickle cell anaemia and leukaemia, could also be examined through collaborative action-research with science institutions, the Royal College of Physicians, the General Medical Council and the Department of Health.

As an enterprise, social care has great prospects both in terms of children in care and domiciliary services for the elderly. With a fast, aging population coupled with the breakdown in families and the growing moral and social decay in society, Government will look to private initiatives for solutions and the development of culturally sensitive and culturally specific provision for the UK's minority communities. The steady growth in the childminding business since 2001, demonstrates the demand for this service, and the existing African and Caribbean (firms') under-representation in this area could be reduced, with the creation of more units. The market for children's homes is £850M; that is, expenditure by local authorities and fostering agencies, that deal with clients aged 10 to 15 years old.

Health Initiatives

Boosting market share within the British Caribbean independent healthcare sector will depend on a greater understanding of diversity and race initiatives implemented by NHS Trusts. The Department of Health contends that health policies on equality and diversity make a difference and though these recent changes may be unknown to a sceptical public, it is important to give recognition to these initiatives since they signify changes to the operational culture of the National Health Service, for the best in the long term **(Table 14. 5).**

Table 14. 5 Diversity and race initiatives in selected NHS Trusts

Trust	Initiative
South Yorkshire Ambulance Services	`Race to Train', the use of drama to highlight equality, diversity issues to enable staff to understand the need for such a strategy.
North West Region	Diversity Training – appointment of three Diverse Workforce Facilitators to assist and support NHS organisations in managing diversity and equality.

South Birmingham PCT	Positive About Human Rights – a refugee health professionals steering group based on a partnership model between organisations willing to help with the integration of refugee health professionals.
South London & Maudsley NHS Trust	A Positively Diverse Initiative – a component of this initiative has a specific focus on the career development of nurses, with systematic processes aiming to offer staff support.
The Royal Berkshire/Battle Hospitals NHS Trust	The Initiative – training program with external trainers to help staff deal with verbal and physical aggression; a conflict resolution approach.

(Source: NHS Employers, 2005b: 2006, Department of Health, England)

The competitive factors relating to ethnicity in healthcare can also be seen by the way in which communities have taken into consideration the national '*Healthy Living*' policy, a scheme that encourages residents to benefit from regular (physical) exercises, excellent nutrition and other activities to impact positively on their general well-being. The setting up of enterprises in support of this scheme is set to continue. In accessing material for this book, there were some interesting trends in the healthy living market involving women who operate as independent distributors of companies in the Wellness industry, a relatively new phenomenon in the UK and a by-product of the American health and fitness trade. As micro units, these enterprises complement existing businesses specialising in healthcare treatment with a socio-cultural touch.

Although there are no definitive figures on this particular growth segment, informal estimates suggest that there are groups of Caribbean women in the 35 to 45 age bracket who are carving niche markets and in the process, transforming the social care market by embedding a cultural sensitivity ethos. As an experienced manager with public and private sector experience, Janet Smith is a talented professional who believes in maximising opportunities in the healthcare market with an innovative edge, as her micro firm, **Lighter Life**, illustrates (**Minicase 14. 9**).

Minicase 14. 9 Lighter Life

Entrepreneur Janet Smith founded **Lighter Life** in 2004 with the aim of providing healthy living services to people experiencing problems with fitness, weight increase and related health imbalances. The enterprise is relatively small, but in the first two years, it had a reasonable turnover of £150,000-£200,000. A one-to-one service is offered to clients on an appointment basis. Each client is assessed using a `track record of history' in relation to nutritional standards, general eating habits, frequency and type of (outdoor) exercise including relaxation techniques.

Smith's early beginnings were challenging and since she started the healthcare enterprise in her front room in west London, it was difficult promoting the firm's highly personalised services since first-time customers were keen on value for money after recognising that the services on offer, would `work wonders in reasonable time'**(Smith 2005)**.

With no business advice and funding support available, Smith started the firm using overdraft facilities, credit cards, personal savings and other investment income. Using her range of contacts in family circles, along with friends and colleagues, Lighter Life's boss started with less than half a dozen clients and steadily gained popularity within a year by extending services to professionals in the commercial and industry sectors. The new firm utilised the system of customer referrals and repeat custom, a common feature of Caribbean firms in their formative years of trading. Smith's long-term plan is to advertise in the trade Press, although initially, she had to capture new customers using the personal touch in order to build a credible image portfolio.

Lighter Life has a small team of advisers and instructors offering complementary healthcare support services, including advice on the use of food supplements and regular exercises. The firm's strategy is to expand across London and enlist quality customers and empower them to contribute more to the business, by devising healthcare networks and customer referral groups.

Conclusion

In this chapter we examined in some detail, the UK healthcare industry and its operating systems within key segments of the British-Caribbean firm sector. The NHS was identified as the largest employer with a market projected at over £10.5 billion, a growth rate of 10% per annum and exports accounting for billions of pounds. The market is divided into major products and services with large companies, medium-sized suppliers and other smaller suppliers of NHS and Social Services-commissioned tender-contracts. Statistics show that the British Caribbean contribution to the healthcare sector is 18% with a market value estimated at £1.89 billion per annum.

The origin of traditional medicine was sourced from ancient Africa in which Egyptians such as Imothep was the true `*Father of Medicine*' compared to the proclaimed version of the Greek, Hippocrates, for whom the Hippocratic Oath was made famous. The use of herbal medicine for treating illnesses, diseases, fractures and other human condition was also discussed briefly to demonstrate that people of African heritage have contributed to inventions and innovations in the world of science and technology long before Western science claimed its (exclusive) origins.

The efficacy of traditional medicine was evidenced in the work of health pioneer, Jamaican Mary Seaole, the equivalent to English nurse, Mary Nightingale. Seacole's work was legendary during the Crimean War in the 19th century. Since the early 1990s, the Department of Health has hosted an annual award scheme in the honour of Seacole to celebrate the endeavours of healthcare professionals, who by their example, have boosted the image of the NHS in terms of diversity and racial equality. Many Caribbean professionals have gone on to set up independent units and community-based organisations offering alternative and complementary healthcare services.

The same can be said for the medicare segment, with hundreds of Caribbean practitioners contracted with the NHS and managing private practices and specialising in areas of health and medicine. The contribution of Caribbean migrants to the NHS was captured in the book, *`Many Rivers to Cross'* authored by Ann Kramer, in conjunction with the NHS and published by the multi-ethnic publishing firm, Sugar Media.

The importance of Caribbean-owned and managed residential care units involving the elderly, children and people with varying degrees of disabilities, was also highlighted. Much of the work in these areas dealt with domiciliary or respite care. Independent living schemes were also mentioned, involving children in the 11-19 years category experiencing disaffected lives because of family breakdown, unemployment, lack of schooling and `at risk' of offending.

Other segments were also examined including the enterprising work of mental health practitioners and campaigners who are working in partnership with public health authorities and agencies, to reduce the incidences of black men being sectioned and prescribed large doses of medication as part of a social control mechanism under the Mental Health Act. This important work has been commended by large companies such as the supermarket chain, Sainsbury's which has a centre for the study of mental health.

The activities of social enterprises in campaigning for a possible cure for sickle cell anaemia, lupus and other blood disorders, were also featured in this chapter. The commendable work of the **African-Caribbean Leukaemia Trust** bore much significance since the organisation has a long history of promoting awareness of the plight of sufferers.

There was a cursory look at how Caribbean women are capitalising on the national Healthy Living initiative inspired by Central Government. The work of **Lighter Life** was singled out because of its personalised approach to dealing with conditions relating to overweight, fatigue and other imbalances experienced by professionals.

The characteristics underpinning the work of firms were also pointed out. These referred to the high level of expertise, experience, contacts and the partnership culture embedded in the operations of British Caribbean health entrepreneurs. The choice of location was deemed important to the competitiveness of firms especially in light of increasing demands for quality services by consumers.

It was stressed that the regulatory environment and access to public amenities played a crucial part in the successful delivery of healthcare services in local areas. Again it was emphasised that Caribbean healthcare organisations could be found in major cities in Britain, and they included an array of day-care centres for the elderly.

Like other chapters, the challenges and prospects of the UK healthcare sector were examined according to key segments – nursing, medicare, disease management, social care, healthcare training, fostering and adoption. It was demonstrated that client demands throughout the country will impact positively on opportunities in either the development of new service segments or boost current initiatives. The suggestion for Caribbean practitioners to set up polyclinics or mini-medicare centres in the community to complement the work of PCTs and NHS Trusts was also stressed in light of the idea gaining currency within Government circles.

Finally, practices in diversity and racial equality were identified in a sample of NHS Trusts in an attempt to give new meaning to the fairness doctrine in the '*Health for All*' campaign that the NHS is legendary for since its 1940s creation. This chapter is aimed at nurturing a further understanding and appreciation of the involvement and overall contribution British-Caribbean professionals and independent providers have made (are continuing to make) to modern healthcare delivery in the UK. Where health is concerned, *`all are involved and all are consumed'*, to quote the poetic words of the late Guyanese-Caribbean poet, Martin Wylde Carter. In the next chapter which is the penultimate one in this book, we will look at the inspiring work of some of Britain's leading social entrepreneurs, including youth enterprises, as they fashion more innovation this time, in the **Social Enterprise Sector**.

Chapter Notes:

Caribbean Contribution - Health Minister, Rosie Winterton acknowledged that the NHS had become a high quality service in large part because of the commitment, skilled and dedication of health professionals from the Caribbean and other parts of the world, from its inception in 1948 to the present time.

African Medicine – scholars have been baffled by African medical science because of the misinterpretation of `magico-spiritual' and `rational' elements. In 2001 it was reported in a science journal that numerous Greek philosophers including Pythagorous and Plato studied in Egypt and that they were no sharp demarcation between the fields of study in religion, philosophy, science, astronomy, mathematics, music and hieroglyphics.

Imhotep – the Egyptian had titles such as *Chancellor of the King of Lower Egypt, Chief Sculptor* and *Maker of Vases in Chief* and was one of a few commoners ever to be accorded divine status after death. He is the acclaimed inventor of the Papyrus scroll, the oldest known bearer which was probably written around 1700 BC.

NHS Market – globalisation including the enlargement of the EU has impacted on the migration of nurses from outside Europe to the UK;

EU Directives ratify free mobility within the countries of Europe for professionals with designated qualifications including nurses. Nurses from countries outside the EU however, have to apply to the UK governing body for nursing for verification of their qualifications in order to be on the register.

Information Gap – the RCN has acknowledged the scant information and data on the number of people joining and leaving the NHS. This means that the authorities cannot measure accurately the current basis of recruits and destinations of nurses leaving the NHS.

Mary Seacole Leadership Award – set up in 1994 by the Department of Health to recognise health professionals from the ethnic community who have excelled in the areas such as mental health, sickle cell and sexual health, to name a few. One of the 1997 winners of the award, Dr. Gina Higgingbottom MBE, is a leading researcher into hearth health promotion and BME health issues. Her work entitled *`Heart Health Promoting Behaviour'* has improved the knowledge base on health issues affecting African and Caribbean young people.

The African Caribbean Medical Society (ACMS) - was formed in March 1981 by a group of black doctors to act as a support network for black doctors and medical students and to strive to improve the health of the black community by liaising with policy makers. It is a forum for discussion and dissemination of medical information to the communities in the UK.

Black Matron - Guyanese-born Daphne Steel was the UK's first black matron. She came to Britain in the 1950s and rose through the ranks as a midwife at St Winifred's maternity hospital, West Yorkshire and was appointed matron in 1964. She died in the early part of this century.

Chief Nursing Officer - . Dr. Nola Ishmael who was born in Barbados was appointed the first non-white director of nursing in

London (1995-2003). As a nursing officer, she championed minority staff development and was a key figure in the Mary Seacole Awards. She is an independent healthcare consultant and patron of the Sickle Cell Society. In 2000 she received the OBE for her contribution to nursing and in the same year, the Windrush Award for work in healthcare. She was awarded an Honorary Doctorate in 2003 for her work in policy development in nursing

Mental Health – *Breaking Circles of Fear* is a national programme that aims to improve mental health services for African and Caribbean communities. The project is based at the Sainsbury Centre for Mental Health which was established as a charity to improve the quality of life for people with mental health problems. The charity carries out research, policy work and analysis to improve practice and influence policy in mental health.

Sickle Cell Anaemia - is a disease of red blood cells that is hereditary. People with the condition have sickle haemoglobin, a protein of the red blood cells, which is different from normal haemoglobin. The disease is common among people of African, Caribbean and Asian descent. In 1979 another campaigning organisation, the Sickle Cell Society was set up with Dr. Neville Clare as head and a group of patients, parents and health professionals concerned with the lack of understanding and the inadequacy of treatment for sickle cell sufferers.

Female Surgeon - Dr. Samantha Tross is among a small but growing number of female surgeons now practising in Britain, and although nearly 50% of medical graduates are women, most enter general practice. The figure for those going into surgery is below 5%.

Cancer Cure – the British-Caribbean biochemist, Mahendra Persaud Deonarine used the cassava plant to develop tumour-targeting antibodies to destroy cancer of the bowel. The hope is to acquire sufficient clinical data to begin treating people in the near future.

The Inner City 100 - was devised by the New Economics Foundation and supported by the Royal Bank of Scotland and NatWest and launched in 2001 by the then Chancellor of the Exchequer, the Rt Hon. Gordon Brown MP. The award covered 15 inner-city areas in the UK, with aim of recognising the success of businesses by tracking and measuring the development of firms, making this the first UK-wide indicator of inner city business activity and growth.

Selected Publications:

1 Kramer, Ann (2006) *Many Rivers to Cross: Caribbean People in the NHS 1948-69* in conjunction with the NHS, published by Sugar Media, London, England.

2 *Health Minister celebrates Caribbean contribution to NHS*, Department of Health, 2 April 2007.

3 *UK Healthcare Excellence*, UK Trade & Investment, November 2005.

4 Osler, William (2004): *The Evolution of modern Medicine*, Kessinger Publishing, p12.

5 Alexander, Z & Dewjee, A (Eds). *Wonderful adventures of Mrs. Seacole in many lands,* Bristol, England: Falling Wall Press, 1984.

6 Finch, Charles Dr (2001): *The African Background of Medical Science,* International Department of International Medicine, The Morehouse School of Medicine, USA, 19 July 2001.

7 *Black and minority ethnic and internationally recruited nurses*, Royal College of Nursing Employment/Working Well surveys, 2002:2005, England.

8 *Of Germs, Genes and Genocide: Slavery, Capitalism, Imperialism, Health and Medicine,* United Kingdom Council for Human Rights, 1989: 2003.

9 *Past trends, future imperfect? A review of the UK nursing labour market in 2004/2005,* Royal College of Nursing, London, England.

10 *British Medical Journal, Vol. 329*, September 11, 2004.

11 Grainger, K (2006): `Equal access to training for black and minority ethnic nurses', *Nursing Standard*, 20, Pg41-49, Vol. 20, No 42, United Kingdom.

12 Baxter, Carol Professor (1988): *The Black Nurse: An Endangered Species*, National Extension College for Training in Health and Race, Cambridge, England.

13 *Black and Ethnic Nurses, Midwives and Health Visitors Leading Change:* A Report of the Mary Seacole Leadership Award- the first five years,

Department of Health, November 2000.

14 Higgingbottom, Marie-Awoko G & Serrant-Green, Laura (2005): *Developing Culturally Sensitive Skills in Health and Social Care with a Focus on Conducting Research with African Caribbean Communities in England*, Universities of Sheffield & Nottingham, England, December 4, 2005.

15 Carers UK, Sheffield Hallam University 2005.

16 Goldacre M. J, Davidson J. M, Lambert T. W (2004): Country of training and ethnic origin of UK doctors: database and survey studies, *British Medical Journal* 2004, 329: 597-600.

17 McNeill, Helen E (2000): `Biting back at poor oral hygiene', *Intensive and Critical Care Nursing,* 2000, 16, 367-372, England

18 The Social Care Sector in the UK, Universities and Colleges Admissions Service (UCAS), Press Release, 14 February 2003.

19 Labour Market Information (LMI) Review, February 2003.

20 Verity, Paul (2007): Presentation on the `*Role of Birmingham and Solihull Connexions',* Institute of Asian Businesses Special Dinner, July 18, 2007, Birmingham, England.

21 `Delivering the enterprise: the reality behind the rhetoric', *Race & Regeneration*, Spring/Summer 2006, Black Training & Enterprise Training Group, London.

22 Children's Nurseries, UK Market Report 2006, Laing and Buisson, England.

23 Ambler, Mark; Armstrong, David & Hawksworth, John: *Costs and Benefits of Universal Childcare,* 2003, Daycare Trust, London.

24 `Black men: misrepresented, misdiagnosed and misunderstood', *Church & Race*, Vol. 18, Summer 2003.

25 Breaking the Circles of Fear, *The Agenda*, Issue 1, Spring 2005, The Sainsbury Centre for Mental Health, London.

26 Our NHS today and tomorrow, Royal College of Nursing, April 2007.

27 Black Net UK.

28 `Celebrating black and ethnic minority women business owners', *Prowess Profile*, Issue 5, Autumn/Winter 2005, England.

29 Placement Statistics 2005-2006, British Association for Adoption & Fostering.

30 2002/2003 Childcare and Early Years: Workforce Survey, Sure Start May 2004, London.

Chapter 15

Social Enterprise Sector

Introduction

In this final part of Section II of this book, the role of the social enterprise sector and the part played by British Caribbean people since the 1930s in the UK would be examined. There are many ways to define a social enterprise particularly in light of the frequency with which activities of all types are associated with this traditional undertaking. One consistent definition is the trade in goods or services linking that trade to a social purpose, with the need to deliver on both financial and social performance targets. In other words, having a double `bottom line'.

Social enterprise is a relatively new term for a type of business that has existed for at least a century. The term *social enterprise* relates to *social entrepreneur,* the name originally given to 19th century philanthropic business people and industrialists, who had genuine concern for the welfare of their employees. Today it varies from country to country. In Britain, the focus is on the use of surplus as the defining characteristics. In North America, there is less emphasis on generating a surplus and more of the double bottom line nature of the enterprise. European usage tends to add the principle of social rather than individual ownership.

It is estimated that there are more than 50,000 social enterprises in the UK, generating more than £27 billion turnover and contributing more than £8 billion to the economy- this represents about 5% of all economic activity in the UK alone. Social enterprises are diverse, ranging from small, community-owned shops, faith groups to large companies winning multi-million pound contracts (**Small Business Service 2005**).

The Charities Aid Foundation reported that individuals and companies give £300 million to thousands of charities. It also offers award-winning financial services to charities, and today, charities and donors have over £2.2 billion of charitable funds in the Foundation's services. There was an increase in donations paid from charities and trust accounts from £107 million in 2004/2005 to £126 million in 2006/2007, an increase by nearly 20% (**CAF 2006: 2007**).

The National Council for Voluntary Organisations or the `NCVO' which is the largest umbrella body representing voluntary and community organisations in the UK stated that 90% of its members are registered charities, with over half focused on improving education, health and/or social support for people in need. In England, nearly 274,000 employees as well as millions of volunteers. These charities generate over 40% of the sector's £22.6 billion annual income. The London region has the highest number of members, with 32%, with the lowest being the North East with 3%. Member's income range from £10,000 to £5 million (**NCVO 2005).**

Other indicators show some 3.2% of the working age population is engaged in social entrepreneurial activity. This represents nearly 1.2 million people although the rate is low compared to the formation rate for traditional business engagement (6.2% of the working population). British Caribbean social entrepreneurs have a market share of over 6% which means that members of this community own and manage in excess of 3,000 social enterprises in the UK (**Global Entrepreneurship Monitor 2006).**

The sector has changed dramatically, and since the early 1990s, there has been a significant expansion in terms of numbers, roles and responsibilities since the establishment of the first benchmark of general charities was introduced in the same period. For instance, there was an increase from 98,000 in 1991 to 169,000 in 2004, nearly 100%, and more recently, since 2000 the sector has seen a net increase of 28,000 organisations. Nevertheless, small charities constitute the vast majority of the voluntary sector population and much of the growth since the 1990s. It is still the case that over half (56%) of the voluntary sector has an annual income of less than £10,000 (**NCVO 2004**).

Caribbean Social Enterprises

The history of Caribbean settlement in Britain can be divided into a number of phases. Initially, the first arrivals had been slaves, imported as domestic servants. After the end of slavery, during the 19th century, those who stayed on were scattered seamen, students and entertainers. They lived near seaports though they were not noticeably, a separate community.

After the beginning of the World War 1, however, thousands of Caribbean migrants arrived in the war industries and merchant navy. They established themselves in the seaports and major cities, where their presence sparked race riots in the years immediately following the war.

Many remained in Britain, forming the nucleus of substantial, but ghettoised communities in cities such as Cardiff, Liverpool and London. The final phase of Caribbean settlement took place after World War 11, when approximately a quarter of a million arrived to settle permanently in Britain between 1955 and 1962. But the necessity for community self-help was inevitable after many Caribbean settlers, unable to prove their status, were either threatened with deportation or denied employment. This situation posed a challenge to members of this community, but it was one that they confronted in a constructive manner.

In response to the situation, Jamaican physician, Dr. Harold Arundel Moody, founded the **League of Coloured People** (LCP) in 1931 and its journal, *The Keys* in 1933. The organisation helped African and Caribbean people who were in trouble. Dr. Moody came from a family of entrepreneurs, his father being a chemist and it was therefore natural for him to help those less unfortunate. The League represented sacked seamen to Parliament, defended people in court, raised funds to help hundreds of destitute black children and ensured that children in homes had holidays. The organisation also found work for the jobless. So influential was the organisation, that it was invited to give evidence to a Royal Commission on conditions in Jamaica.

Social Organisations

Long before the term `*social entrepreneurship*' became part of the economic vocabulary, Caribbean settlers have always exercised the culture of giving for centuries. In fact, the unfriendly conditions that confronted settlers, tested their ability and capacity to join forces with other migrants to create viable organisations in the first half of the 20th century through to the 21st century **(Minicase 15. 1).** This chapter will capture a mixture of social enterprise segments that British Caribbean entrepreneurs are renowned. These segments contribute to the lifeblood of all communities in the UK and they comprise the following: -

- Social Organisations
- Community Centres
- Community Associations
- Cultural Segment
- Enterprise Agencies
- Trade Associations
- Professional Networks
- Education Organisations
- Housing Associations
- Credit Unions
- Social Care
- Training Organisations
- Youth Enterprise
- Faith Organisations

Minicase 15. 1 The West Indian Standing Conference

The **West Indian Standing Conference (WISC)** was formed in 1959 to represent Caribbean people living in the UK, to promote justice and fairplay. Founder-Director, Montserrat-born William Trant OBE (for services to community relations in 1999), leads a small dedicated team that champion issues such as immigration, economic inequality and social injustice. Trant is a recipient of other awards; namely, the 1996 Montserrat Certificate of Honour by Queen Elizabeth II in recognition of valuable services to his country in the field of National and Humanitarian Service during Hurricane Hugo, 1989 and the onset of the volcano in 1995.

The Standing Conference of West Indian Organisations later known as WISC, was created due to the 1958 Notting Hill civil disturbances, which had repercussions for areas such as Bristol, triggered by racism involving `skinheads' and `teddy boys' that singled out members from the African, Caribbean and Asian community for unwarranted hostilities. Of course, WISC has several challenges including calls for a name change which is being addressed during its 50th anniversary, 2008. As the longest non-white managed voluntary sector organisation in the UK after the League of Coloured People, WISC promotes and supports education, training, counselling, advocacy, legal service and social research. The organisation work had a positive effect on migrants who experienced poor social housing on their arrival in the UK in the 1950s and 1960s.

Recent funding from the Community Fund has strengthened WISC's position in advocacy and networking. The newsletter, *Teamwork* is circulated widely to members and network organisations. From all indications, WISC appears destined to remain a potent symbol of hope, justice and fairplay for peace-loving peoples in the UK and elsewhere.

Community Centres

WISC's creation stimulated centres across England to service the welfare needs of others, including the elderly and the young from African and Asian communities many of whom came as contracted workers and students in the UK. Community organisations paid peppercorn or low rents (avoiding grants to cover market) rents for Council-owned facilities and as a result of this financial concession, most organisations survived their formative years in fairly good health. Facilities were managed by voluntary Boards/Committees, along with paid project workers and voluntary staff, with local government offering annual grant-aid and technical support for the upkeep of organisations.

Obviously, new legislation in the 1960s and 1970s, restricting the number of Commonwealth citizens to the UK, created fresh challenges, but unique opportunities for migrants to give of their time and resources to good causes to complement paid or full-time employment in the construction, health, public transport, textiles, hotel and other service sectors in the economy. Community centres were set up in several cities to cater for the welfare development of settler communities. **(Minicases 15. 2).**

Minicases 15.2 Selected British Caribbean-owned Community Centres

The West Indian Cultural Centre was set up in 1976 by the African Caribbean Leadership Council in north London. Founded by Caribbean settlers, it was originally identified as a resource to provide community education, entrepreneurship and of other community activities. It is grant-aided by Haringey Local Authority, with services provided to the elderly, young people and the wider community. The centre is grappling with matters relating to organisational modernisation, under-utilisation of facilities and limited funds for its expansion programme. The multipurpose centre could be used to train young people in various types of enterprise development, and in fact, Middlesex University suggested in the 1990s that management should develop an ongoing training programme for young African and Caribbean chefs because of a shortage of skills in this trade.

The African Caribbean Millennium Centre (ACMC) in Birmingham was set up in 2001 replacing the African Caribbean Resource Centre. It provides welfare and employment support services such as a community radio training programme for the black community. The ACMC is funded by the City Council and at the moment, it has workspace for multimedia recording, business units, a digital café, arts education and cultural resource. Additional support comes from other agencies and institutions; the European funding, the Arts Council, the Millennium Commission and Cadbury Trust

The Sheffield and District African Caribbean Community Association (SADACCA) was founded in 1986, incorporating the West Indian Association which was formed in 1955-56 by a group of dedicated Caribbean people who were determined to improve general living conditions for themselves and children. The founders approached the City Council for larger premises since there was demand for additional facilities to provide additional services for the elderly and young people, along with organising cultural events and running training programmes for the unemployed. The design and transformation of the current facilities was aided by black architects who gave most of their time freely. They were also skilled workers from the Caribbean community, operating as carpenters, painters and decorators who were previously unemployed, but for whom the project was a lifeline for improving their job prospects. The all-purpose centre is also used by public and private agencies for conferences, seminars and other public engagements.

As stated above, Caribbean-owned community centres are operated by voluntary Committees or self-styled enterprise Boards especially where a dual status of charity and Limited Company by Guarantee status exists. A major challenge facing the management of some centres is the case involving founder-members who relish occupying executive positions over a lengthy, unstipulated period (10 years continuously). The reason for this state of affairs varies from senior activists' mistrust of `newcomers' vying for leadership and fear of embarrassment if the organisation collapses, to the lack of understanding the importance of proper succession planning.

Besides the deadening effect on growth potential, this situation has a negative impact on the image of organisations since potential members and donors question the integrity of the leadership as well as the system of accountability in place to monitor and avoid such discrepancy.

However, from the foregoing, it can be said that community centres act as a magnet to attract older people, the young, professionals and the wider community, a fact that is not often acknowledged, but stated implicitly when conditions are laid down by funding bodies in awarding grant-aid or inviting groups to compete for commissioned contracts according to best value principles.

Nevertheless, these community centres have a pivotal role in helping to change relationships between public agencies and diverse communities, based on the realignment of public services that are fair and equitable, coupled with the access to job, training, career advancement and related opportunities for minority communities. And since they are compelled by the desire to make a real difference, as well as the demands for equitable services for ordinary citizens, the task of improving systems of governance and ensuring that a proper image is maintained, are formidable tasks for founders, management teams, staff, volunteers and supporters generally.

The Garveyist philosophy of self-help and group power is the focus of associations complementing and/or supporting social enterprise activity in the UK. The aims of these loosely co-ordinated bodies comprise mobilising communities around social events, hosting epochal events such as 'Black History Month' observances, Kwanza', and (inter-territorial) 'Independence' celebrations and related activities. These associations were formed to meet different community needs and though criticised for a low retention of young people, there are signs that this attitude is changing, though slowly, in organisations that have redefined a new social enterprise pathway.

Again these organisations have a lifespan of 20-30 years plus in areas where there is a concentration of non-white communities and where social welfare services are inadequate. The leadership of community associations vary in type; some are operated by community activists whilst others recruit professionals with extensive experience in community affairs and/or competence in other disciplines. These associations collaborate with like-minded bodies with the aim of securing the confidence and guaranteed support from local institutions including city councils and funding agencies. Whilst associations have been slow to change their structure to reflect the new social enterprise culture, their practices reflect much of this approach today

This principle is a stipulation of various funding agencies as well as commissioned institutions, and one which social enterprises in minority communities heed as they attempt to secure 'competitive' funding and other resources (**Table 15. 1**).

Table 15.1 British Caribbean Community-type Associations

Name	Location	Activity Profile
African Caribbean Community Centre	Cambridge	Health, social, cultural matters for older, retired and disabled people.
Afro-Caribbean Care Group for the Elderly	Manchester	Provides a caring and supporting service for older people.
United Caribbean Association	Leeds	Social (health) care provision in the BME community.
Gloucester West Indian Association	Gloucester	Social events, education, welfare services for the young and older people.
Bexley African Caribbean Community Association	Kent	Social activities, donations to recognised charities, cultural/ sports events, sightseeing, and education sponsorship.
African Caribbean Project	Warwickshire	Advice and support to parenting, health issues, education, employment, training and behaviour.
African Caribbean Women's Association	Scotland	Inclusion of women in employment, training, facilitates joint working and influencing policy and provision in all areas.
African Caribbean Central Point	West Midlands	Keep fit classes, luncheon club, social events, fun-days, education trips, other activities.

Caribbean Island-Territory Associations	England-wide	Education, culture, health, donations, tours, conferences, exhibitions, partnership with UK organisations, Caribbean Governments and non-governmental organisations.

(Source: Independent survey of community associations, 2000-2006, UK)

The above figure illustrates the similarity and diversity of the community groups profiled. It partly explains too, the reason why Caribbean people strive to maintain independent organisations, capable of partnering with like-minded bodies whilst teaming with public and private sector agencies and institutions to make a positive impact on various communities, as well as boosting local regeneration outputs. There is a history of Caribbean-island type associations in England and their chief aim is to represent their respective nationals and work with UK-Caribbean Government officials and non-governmental organisations to improve public services and add vitality to social welfare provision in cities and villages in the Caribbean where such provision is limited or non-existent.

Ever since their formation, volunteers and professionals representing Caribbean associations have raised cash and other donations to support healthcare, education, cultural and other important initiatives for the elderly, the young, the disabled and other less fortunate. In some instances, professionals are actively involved in setting up initiatives and ensuring that systems are in place to achieve planned targets. With the involvement of second-generation professionals particularly, there is evidence suggesting a growing socially entrepreneurial outlook for most of these groupings. This fact is evident by regular events to celebrate community achievements including awards to individuals and organisations for their contribution to `good causes' in specific areas of charity `giving' in various parts of the UK.

Throughout the nine English Regions, social enterprises reflect a dynamic composition in terms of their nature and types. For instance, in London and the South East, there are over 200 organisations bearing titles such as: *'health foundation'*, *'information centre'*, *'community centre'*, and *'Women's Association'* among others. In the Midlands and Northern English Counties, such as Birmingham and Bristol respectively, scores of groups link arts, culture, training, information, advice, advocacy and capacity building to their list of priorities.

In Glasgow and Scotland the **African and Caribbean Network** is an umbrella body for the communities of the same name in the city. Its aims are all-embracing and the organisation has a constructive approach to integration according to its primary aim, *'To promote the inclusion of African and Caribbean residents as equal and valued members of their communities, alleviate and eradicate discrimination through raising awareness of the issues, facilitate a joint working approach, influencing policy and provision at all levels and empowering African and Caribbean people to contribute to these processes.'*

Cultural Segment

This segment of social enterprise is the nerve centre of minority communities and is vital because of the continued quest for individual and collective identity that prevails. Culture is necessary too, because it fosters understanding and appreciation of a society's past and present such as African, Indian and other people of colour who contribute to universal progress. There is some recognition of minority-led initiatives and their impact on British society, but the ongoing struggle to overcome vestiges of racial discrimination and institutional prejudice tends to dwarf this fact in the eyes of the majority.

The creative talent of Caribbean people is known and yet, there is an urgent need to further publicise their endeavours to reinforce the veritable history of their contribution to the UK. This section of chapter

15 will highlight sampled organisations that showcase the African and Indian dimensions of the Caribbean community, as a people of artistic expression and cultural plurality **(Minicases 15. 3)**.

Minicases 15. 3 The Drum and the Caribbean Indian Dance Troupe

The Drum was established in 1986 in Birmingham to create a fusion of African, Indian or Asian, Caribbean, Chinese and other cultures. Activities and events such as poetry reading, book launches, comedy nights, meetings, plays, public discussions, seminar/workshops, and business meetings are held year-round. A variety of organisations and groups use the facility as well.

As a leading cultural centre in the Home Counties, the facility hosts national and international events such as the 2006 Trinidad Carnival diasporic festivity, annual Black History Month observances and concerts involving church groups and other social organisations. The Drum is supported by local authority grants and funding agencies. The long-term plan is to promote the use of the centre to wider audiences as a sustainable measure, and according to the head of The Drum,

We can accommodate large audiences since there are sufficient culture performance areas, meeting rooms, exhibition facilities, along with scope for a host of other artistic and cultural activities. We're keen on tapping into the diverse talents of ethnic communities in the West Midlands and neighbouring English Regions. The 21st century is the ideal time to grow and expand since history has shown that culture is a powerful, unifying force for change and progress, universally (**The Drum 2007**).

The Caribbean Indian Dance Troupe (CIDT) was launched in 2001 at the Irish Cultural Centre in Tottenham, north London, by Trinidadians Fidel Persaud, his wife Isha and daughter, Chandani. Although the dance troupe is relatively young, it has grown in stature. All three Persuads are trained in the Kathak style of Indian classic dance by eminent teachers from India. The husband and wife team placed second in the Grand Finals of the popular TV show, Mastana Bahar in 1988, winning a scholarship to further their dance technique.

The troupe has performed in the Caribbean, the UK, France and the US. They presented with The Mighty Sparrow and Misteeq, the popular British group. The organisation conducts dance sessions in London schools, with the purpose of sharing cultural experiences through an Indian Caribbean perspective. The troupe has received slight assistance from Caribbean individuals and businesses that are of Indian Caribbean origin in the UK. Due to its origins, the CIDT works in conjunction with faith organisations in the Indian and Asian communities, performing at weddings, concerts and other celebratory occasions. Another major highlight of the organisation's work was its performance at the opening of Caribbean Expo 2001 at the Excel Centre, Docklands before an audience of over 700. The organisation trains dancers as young as five and is opened to persons interested in learning Indian Dance with a touch of Caribbean Chutney folk. According to the Persauds, '*we would like to see more unification of the UK Caribbean people of Indian descent considering that they are about 75,000 in the UK; we can surely make an impact'* (***Indo Caribbean* 2003).**

Whilst the emphasis on culture among Caribbean people in the UK especially, has emphasised the dominance of Africentricity or African philosophy, because of the strong ancestral ties to the African Continent, it is equally important to reconnect the Caribbean's history based on its current multi-ethnic composition and cultural types. Slavery and indentureship played a huge part in the origin, growth, development and expansion of Caribbean people at home and in diasporic communities in Africa, Asia, Britain, Europe, Latin America and North America. The cultural mix has thus enabled this particular community to adapt and recreate traditions with variations in meaning, interpretation and actual reality in host societies. Intrinsically, these variations have become part of a survival strategy in the face of prejudice and discrimination – individually and institutionally.

The increasing growth of cultural synergies in the UK resulting from artistic notions of self and their ethnic composition, is both a welcome sign of potentially, stable communities. But this also presents a real challenge for those reluctant to recognise and appreciate that universally, while cultures collide, they also have a meeting point in their respective struggles for appreciation, preservation and respect from the presumed majority (that is, black versus white). So that both the celebration and tensions that exist in today's' UK cultural environment is perhaps an acid test for both migrant-settler communities and their counterparts – the host society.

Also, cultural issues are frequent in organisations that aim to meet the aspirations and needs of minority communities across the country. One aspect of culture that is noticeable in much of the work done on ethnicity and regeneration is the performance of community enterprises led by, and for the benefit of black entrepreneurs. Cultural issues dominate because mainstream agencies set up with a remit to service all communities are unable to do so adequately, because of a lack of understanding on how to tailor services to meet the culturally sensitive and culturally specific needs of ethnic communities. Today, this remains a national problem in spite of reforms to the Equalities Act and related social reform policies. That said, in an ethnically diverse setting, no institution can categorically argue, that it has the wherewithal to deal with inequality and unfairness in the distribution of resources for economic and social development. However, institutions can collaborate with groups and organisations that are better placed to deliver public services aimed at all citizens (based on a culturally sensitive provision).

Enterprise Agencies

Whilst much of the information on the history of Caribbean community enterprise is limited to the post-Scarman era, there were two important ventures that not only demonstrated the resilience, but also the ability of Caribbean people to collaborate across the political and social divide. For some time prior to the 1980s, The First Partnership Bank Project and the UK Caribbean Chamber of Commerce made media headlines with their innovation and extraordinary potential to change the economic landscape of African and Caribbean communities for good.

Before its demise, **The First Partnership Bank Project** or the 'FPBP', researched by Equinox Consultants and Cooper and Lybrand Associates, as the 'Afro Caribbean Bank Project', was launched by Sir George Young, the Conservative MP. The project sought to address problems faced by minority entrepreneurs in setting up businesses, by the creation of a financial institution specially designed to service their needs. The proposition was for a minimum of £5 million be set aside as investment capital and deposits of £50 million within three years. On the basis such level of deposits, a loan portfolio to businesses and individuals would be developed, building up to about £1.5 million. The Bank of England approved the main objectives of the financial institution as they were then:

- To establish a financial institution to serve the needs of Afro-Caribbean and other minority communities in Britain, through the provision of high-street banking facilities, including the taking of deposits and the encouragement of savings amongst members of those communities.
- Through such an institution, to develop understanding of, and positive assistance to, the business development needs of members of minority communities who wish to establish or expand business enterprises in Britain.
- To enhance the expectations of the black and other minority communities by establishing a financial institution staffed progressively by members of the communities.
- To ensure as far as possible, through its financial structure, that such an institution is primarily owned and controlled by the black and ethnic minority communities themselves.
- To increase wider awareness of the status and economic importance of the communities themselves.
- To seek to influence the criteria and lending activities of existing banks, by evidence of the success of such an institution **(Hansib 1987)**.

Apart from eliciting the views of sections of the black community, African and Caribbean banks were sought and support was received in principle for both equity participation and reciprocal banking arrangements. Unto this day, there are still lingering thoughts as to why this (potentially viable) enterprise failed, and if there are chances for its resuscitation anytime in this century.

The mid-1980s saw the birth of other community enterprises after the Scarman Report which recommended that in the wake of the civil disturbances in Birmingham, Liverpool and London, public authorities had to reassure black communities that everything possible would be done to avoid the repeat of such incidents in the future. Enterprise development agencies were first set up in various parts of London, with the **North London Business Development Agency** and **Deptford Enterprise Development Agency** in south London among the most popular ones in the capital.

Elsewhere, **Community Roots** and **Black Business in Birmingham** or `**3b**' are the `agency-engines' for small enterprise in the West Midlands, whilst **Cariocca Business Parks** (Manchester) and **South Yorkshire African Caribbean Training and Enterprise Centre** (Sheffield), are the main drivers behind enterprise assistance and technical support for minority business development in parts of the Northern Counties, largely in economically deprived and socially excluded areas. Not only do these areas require adequate public services provision, but small firms need targeted assistance and support if they are to recover firstly, from structural poverty and secondly, the vicious cycle of racial prejudice and restrictive practices, resulting from limited access to public and private sector contract opportunities, along with the prevalence of piecemeal policy-making which restrict a proper assessment of the organisation and performance of minority firms (particularly those with the potential to compete) in local and regional sector markets in the UK (**Minicases 15. 4**).

Minicases 15. 4 Selected Community Enterprise Agencies

The North London Business Development Agency or the NLBDA which was set up in 1995 with its motto, *Helping businesses Grow*, was managed by a team of Caribbean specialists including St. Lucian born, Emmanuel Cotter MBE and Jamaican, Elsa Redwood. The agency created over 2,000 start-ups through a series of information, advice, skills training and financial support, over 4,000 jobs and 30,000 plus business counselling sessions. It had a turnover of more than one million pounds but generated several millions more from public funds including the Single Regeneration Budget. The NLBDA had strong links with local providers and international minority supplier councils, and led trade missions involving hundreds of business owners and professionals to the USA, annually.

The **South Yorkshire African Caribbean Training and Enterprise Centre** (SYAC) was set up in 1991 by Caribbean professionals who recognised the need for a facility to house Caribbean and other minority-owned firms in Sheffield and South Yorkshire generally. It has about 22 incubator units and other workspace facilities including a nursery and office site. It has an annual bursary for potential young entrepreneurs to fund short training schemes. Unlike other enterprise agencies, SYAC is self-financing with plans to redevelop the centre to boost its turnover of under £250,000 per annum. The expansion will create an enterprise assistance and technical support program for businesses and maximise regeneration opportunities. At the time of writing, the centre was recovering from the June-July 2007 flood that left businesses and properties in the region devastated.

Community Roots and **Black Business in Britain (3b)** were established in the mid-1980s as part of the Conservative Government's Community Finance Initiatives to regenerate run-down inner-city areas where structural poverty and reduced public investment threatened to blight the lives of communities and scupper business renewal. Both agencies are managed by Boards comprising African and Caribbean business owners and professionals. The agency provides support to start-up firms while 3b offers advice and technical support for existing businesses and others with growth potential. Funded by the public purse, together, both agencies have created hundreds of businesses and equally more jobs across Birmingham and West Midlands Region.

As a dynamic agency, **Cariocca Business Parks** was set up in 1986 with the object of developing enterprise initiatives that are beneficial to residents of Manchester. A group of six founder-members of mostly Caribbean origin planted the original idea of training Caribbean youths through the utilisation of workspace facilities. The Urban Aid Programme provided £1.9 million to fund the construction of the existing facility. The agency has a Management Board comprising professionals and business people, and has achieved its principal objectives through the management of two business incubators parks in the city. It provides business premises and support services for small firms and in 1991, the project won the prestigious *Community Enterprise Award* and *Charles Douglas Award* for the most outstanding example of community enterprises. Cariocca's sterling endeavours are attributed to the persistence and energy of community workers who gave their time, knowledge sand skills for the success of the company and who later became unpaid directors of the company.

The establishment of community enterprise agencies in key English cities during the 1980s and 1990s was a reflection of the state's recognition that public agencies were unable to offer adequate business support to minority firms in the country and this rebounded on deprivation and exclusion in urban communities where underinvestment in new start-ups was seen as problematic. The reasons given for this situation were that business advisers lacked the cultural skills and market intelligence to deal with the evolving, dynamic minority enterprise sector. Owners are often stereotyped and discriminated against even when they have sound commercial ideas backed by workable business plans. The presence of a few `ethnic' advisers in the formative years of the enterprise development agency system was, also cause for concern by the authorities and client-businesses alike.

Yet state intervention was premised on a methodical approach towards enterprise support services. The original idea was to investment millions of pounds into the construction of well-endowed incubation centres or workspace units with affordable rentals in deprived English wards and districts. These facilities were expected to mirror a dual legal status – charity and Limited Company by Guarantee - in short, a social enterprise model. Owners would benefit from a menu of information, advice, training, capacity building and related services, and after a three year period or so, they would be transferred into larger accommodation with improved services such as product development, market intelligence, promotion, leadership training and coaching in contract management and negotiating techniques. The expectation was for these `new graduating firms' to compete at the growth/maturity lifecycle stage.

Reports from centres confirm that hundreds of businesses have benefited from support, along with employment running into thousands more, along with tens of thousands of training hours and business counselling sessions accordingly. There has been a succession of intangible benefits for business owners also: greater self-confidence and worth, improved inter-personal communication skills and knowledge on how and where to access public information.

That said, at the time of writing, there was no consistent method used by incubation centres at Broadwater Farm Estate (London), SYAC (Sheffield) and Cariocca (Manchester) to assess the organisation and performance of firms. It is difficult to access `hard' data on `graduating' firms that are still resident in incubator units over 10 years, in many instances. Whether this situation is due to the absence of a coherent enterprise strategy, underinvestment in market intelligence for small firms or the need to maintain a relatively stable, business occupancy level remains a matter of speculation. It is important however, for enterprise agencies to implement a system that can routinely appraise the performance of firms including African and Caribbean enterprises.

In addition, since Caribbean or other minority ethnic-led enterprises follow a traditional pattern of enterprise support, attempting to alter or modify aspects of it, may have implications for the level of public funding, as well as the inability to achieve targets set by funding agencies' contractual arrangement. By today's standards, the number-crunching game continues involving minority firms, and very little attention is paid to the organisation and performance of these firms using a sector based model. It was predicted that with the presence of business associations, this strategy had a relative chance of success, but the jury is still out on this one.

Trade Associations

Quite interestingly, much of the preliminary work done to set up Caribbean-managed enterprise agencies was undertaken by community activists and business professionals who formed networks to represent the interests of diverse communities including theirs. It was another manifestation of Caribbean leadership, creating an enduring influence on the system of governance and broadening the scope of involvement and participation for other communities interested in business enterprise development. (**Minicases 15. 5**).

Minicases 15. 5 British Caribbean-led Trade Associations in the UK

Previous to the formation of business associations and other enterprise networks, the **UK Caribbean Chamber of Commerce** (UKCC) pioneered the start of formal trading bodies among Caribbean entrepreneurs particularly. Set up in 1976 by men and women from all fields of business and professional life, the Chamber dealt with the tasks of market research and providing information and support on various aspects of business and enterprise. Its role was `: -

To preserve, protect and defend the rights of its members in the development and prosperity of their businesses and, however controversial, strive to achieve a better deal for members and the community they serve, from governments (both local and central) and financial institutions'. In part, the British Government's recognition of the Chamber provided the stimulus needed to establish enterprise agencies in blighted inner-city areas.

Black Business Associations (BBAs) were formed during the 1980s and the early part of this century to lobby mainstream institutions to allow business owners to secure procurement opportunities and take part in enterprise promotion, in the UK and abroad. Many owners have limited access to traditional markets and they encounter difficulty when trying to obtain finance from lending institutions.

There are other trade associations representing different client firms in predominantly inner-city areas where exclusion is common. They include the **Black Business Association (Walthamstow)**, **Bristol Black Business Association**, **Leicester African Caribbean Business Association**. The **African Caribbean Business Network** (ACBN) in London and the **Black Business Association (Birmingham)** have enjoyed popularity at local and national levels. The BBA in Birmingham was launched in 2002 to represent nearly 2,000 firms in the West Midlands, and was involved in projects such as the Phoenix Fund for business development. It was in forefront of two national priorities; a national council for African and Caribbean firms and the formation of a national young entrepreneurs' network in Britain. Founder-members of the BBA, Lee Williams and Andy Bailey, are recipients of the MBE for their contribution to business development in the West Midlands.

The ACBN was a Greater London Authority initiative of former London Mayor, Ken Livingstone. The network represents 18,000 AC businesses in the capital, and it is involved in different activities around enterprise support and procurement opportunities, to name a few policy matters. Founder-member and businessman, Michael Webster said that, '*The ACBN will be pivotal in raising the profile of African and Caribbean-owned businesses in the 21st century. This LDA network will provide support for owners and encourage other individuals of African and Caribbean origin to get into business for themselves*' (***AC Business News* 2003**).

In addition, there are other business networks performing the role of mini-enterprise agencies and acting for the most part, as conduits for Business Links and Chambers of Commerce. Examples of these are the **South London Ethnic Minority Business Association** (SLEMBA), **Black Business Initiative** (BBI), the **African Caribbean Business**

Forum in Birmingham, the **African Caribbean Enterprise Consortium** (ACE) in Nottingham and others. With the advent of the RDAs, each agency was advised to encourage to set up minority business forums to be integral to Regional Development Plans to reflect an inclusive approach to policy development. According to the new arrangement, business associations and other enterprise networks should be members of these regional bodies although such a relationship is yet to be formalised. Why? On the one hand, there is a distinction between the ethos of business associations and the workings of minority business forums on the other. Business associations are driven by a commercially, corporate agenda, whilst minority business forums are influenced by mainstream priorities; that is, they are instruments of RDAs. This poses a dilemma for both parties since they rely on each other for the sharing of information and Best Practice pertaining to minority business advancement in specific regional localities.

The issues which are of grave concern to black business associations comprise supplier diversity; that is, public sector contracting opportunities for Caribbean firms, tailored enterprise support and technical assistance for firms operating in growth sectors and underperforming in others, broader representation of ethnic personnel on regional and state boards and more targeted investment in local areas where African and Caribbean enterprises contribute to urban regeneration. As contentious as these issues are however, British Caribbean businesses are also aware that their resolution is possible through painstaking advocacy and working across the political and social divide. Success is also likely if entrepreneurs are willing to develop strategic alliances with reputable professional organisations. In the new climate of partnership, this has become a trademark of British Caribbean social enterprises.

Professional Networks

Further to the exemplary way in which social organisations were set up from the 1930s through to the present time, as well as the steady growth in community enterprise agencies and business networks, there has been a corresponding rise in the volume of professional bodies founded by entrepreneurs, covering several disciplines. Some represent gender priorities involving female entrepreneurship and women's welfare issues even as others merge commercial aspects with social responsibility principles.

Studies fail to capture these variables which are important towards a better understanding of the quantitative and qualitative contribution of Caribbean people to the social enterprise sector, principally as they relate to key segments. Clearly, the union between business and social enterprise is even more apparent among young, budding entrepreneurs within African and Caribbean communities, a trend that would be revealed in the section on youth enterprise. The value of pooling resources to form co-dependent professional networks should not be underestimated since it enables organisations and businesses to work more resourcefully within a broader strategic framework of mainstream representation and market (re)positioning.

Caribbean professional networks have mushroomed over the past 30 years and they tend to operate differently than let's say, conventional businesses in terms of segments and/or sub-sectors. The difference lies in their structure, activity profile and various alliances they seek to be engaged with. Their motivation lies in making a positive difference to members and equally, that of the broader community interest. Another objective is to ensure agendas are firmly placed in the context of mainstream priorities and whilst most networks are keen to remain independent, management realise that working exclusive of the system can result in regression. Networks which have an ideological or political mission are usually partial in dealing with public agencies but they too are interested in collaborating with mainstream, if the agenda is similar in outlook or mutually beneficial in terms of achieving end-term objectives.

Due to the range and scale of organisations and subgroups

within, I will sample broad-based professional networks; that are, representing sectional interests, led by British Caribbean entrepreneurs, as well as highly acclaimed professionals in a number of disciplines **(Table 15. 2)**.

Table 15. 2 Profile of leading Black Professional Networks

Networks	Purpose
European Federation of Black Women Business Owners (EFBWBO)	Set up in 1996 by Yvonne Thompson to increase the economic visibility of black women in Europe and their access to information and resources.
African Caribbean Diversity	Originally named the African Caribbean Finance Forum in 1990. The ACD promotes entry, development and advancement of members into business organisations through education, employment and professional development.
Society of Black Lawyers	Founded in 1973 by lawyers from the ethnic community including Rudy Narayan and Sighbat. The Society promotes the rights and welfare of minority lawyers as well as those in the community who require protection by the law.
African Caribbean Associations	Pioneered by Caribbean professionals from 1970s and present in city/regions in the UK. Priorities are culture, education/training, employment and other welfare issues. Contracted to deliver public services to boost local initiatives.
The 1990 Trust	Increase the participation through capacity building, the aspirations of minorities including Caribbean communities. Campaigns for racial equality, economic inclusion and social justice.
Union of African and African Caribbean Organisations	Formed in 2001 to promote the involvement of membership-organisations in the regeneration of Stoke on Trent and North Staffordshire, especially in areas of health and social care, education, training and employment.

(Source: Published information 2000-2007)

The influence of professional organisations is felt across the UK, with branches or units in the Southeast and Midland Counties, Scotland and Wales. For example the **Black Solicitors Network** (1995) promotes the interests of African, Asian and Caribbean solicitors and participates in consultations initiated by the Law Society and other Government bodies regarding matters which black solicitors are involved. The BSN was recognised as a Law Society Group in 2003.

In the Home Counties, these organisations and others profiled in the above figure are part of a wider network representing the collective interests of Caribbean and other diverse communities. Much of the activities emphasise inclusion and ensuring that members are aware of changes in legislation and their affect on clientele. Almost each London Borough has community-type professional organisations embodying the hopes and aspirations of their communities. **Barnet African Caribbean Association** and the **Watford African Caribbean Association** play an active role in the civil rights of its members. Like other organisations, they're linked to Voluntary Service Councils, the umbrella body for all community and voluntary sector organisations. Education moreover, is the cornerstone of many partnership networks that were established in the last century, and it remains a focus of discussion and for appropriate action by professionals and campaigners alike.

Education Charities

One of the prerequisites of any society is the right of citizens to acquire a sound or reasonable education or alternatively, training in particular technical or vocational skills in order to access employment opportunities in either the public, private (self-employment inclusive) or the community-voluntary sector. Indeed, education is the foundation upon which communities use to compete but this fundamental right has been constrained in some respects, by the below average learning attainment of some Caribbean students. Given the complexities associated with education policy, underachievement among black pupils in public institutions, seems to remain a contentious issue for families and authorities respectively.

Grenadian-born Bernard Coard's seminal text entitled, *`How They West Indian Child is Made Educationally Subnormal in the British School System'* (**1971**) expressed the irritation of African and Caribbean parents over the uneven number of their children who were described as `educationally sub-normal' (ESN) and expelled due to racism and cultural stereotyping. This problem has been addressed repeatedly in subsequent studies. The Rampton Report (**1981**) and the Swann Report, *Education for All* (**1985**), were two policy documents focusing on black communities, plus recent works identify approaches to dealing with underachievement (**Cork 2005**).

However, there are differences in levels of educational attainment vis-à-vis the rates of expulsion, and according to a 1997 report, about 0.78% of Caribbean children were permanently excluded and by 2001/2002, the proportion had fallen to 0.4%. The figure for white children was still much lower at 0.13% and, by 2002-2003, permanent exclusions for Caribbean children fell further to 0.25% compared to the proportionately lower figure of 0.12% for white children. Hence, despite the improvement, Caribbean children are still substantially more likely to be excluded (**DfES, 2003b: 2004**). This persistent trend is a cause for grave concern, especially for those who value education as a means to successful youth transition into adulthood (**Joseph Rowntree Foundation 2005**). Officials commented on the reasons for this situation:

Exclusions (the author's emphasis) are rarely clear cut, but many Black pupils who find themselves subject to disciplinary procedures perceive themselves to have been unfairly treated. Black pupils are more likely to be excluded for what was defined by schools as `challenging behaviour'. The length of fixed term exclusions varied considerably in the same school between Black and white pupils for what are described as the same or similar incidents (**Ofsted 2001**).

Exceptional Initiatives

Notwithstanding the stream of national policy measures including the highly publicised, *Aiming High, Raising the Attainment of Minority Ethnic Pupils' Strategy,* Caribbean communities have pioneered initiatives to help reduce the estimated 30,000 black pupils who receive a fixed period of exclusion every year **(Minicases 15. 6)**.

Minicases 15. 6 Key community education innovations in England

Len Garrison co-founded the influential **African Caribbean Education Resource** (ACER) in 1976 in London. His organisation promoted cultural and literary talent among Caribbean young people, by publicising their endeavours. He believed that groups such as supplementary schools were ideal channels to enhance black pupils' education and compensate for their lack of cultural support and miseducation in schools (**1993:269**)

Chapelton Parent's Action Group was set up in Leeds, in the 1970s to try and improve attainment levels of African and Caribbean secondary school students, through enhanced school facilities. The aim was to developing joint working partnerships with parents, teachers and young learners themselves.

Mediaid is a registered charity which has been in operation since 2000. It was founded amidst concerns over the high rates of exclusion of African and Caribbean students. It covers schools and colleges and has developed a range of preventive and intervention strategies for families. It has moved from a voluntary status to a more diversified funding base.

Advocaid which was established in 1989 provides support for schools in the form of advocacy to parents in their interaction with educational institutions. From the start, education has been the core of its work and the organisation has established an excellent reputation for supporting black families with children experiencing exclusion from schools.

100 Black Men of London was formed in 2001, with a similar chapter in Britain by a group of concerned men whose mission was to respond to the challenges experienced by black youths and provide leadership and support, by creating an environment to motivate young people to become economic and moral stakeholders in the communities they serve. The organisation enjoys recognition and respect from the community and other sections of British society, including public institutions and private agencies.

(Source: Independent research, 2000-2007, England)

British parliamentarian, Dianne Abbott's annual conference, '*Education and the Black Child*' has attracted wide media coverage annually while **The Gus John Partnership** collaborates with agencies and organisations to address educational underachievement among Caribbean boys and other equality issues. In various English Regions, there are networks, alliances and other private initiatives aimed at offering education services to meet the national curriculum. Communities are also encouraged to learn more about their ethnic, cultural and social heritage. In response to these initiatives, a national resource centre to support and promote supplementary schools in England was established in 2000.

In addition, the commitment to find alternative solutions to underachievement is a major focus of leading education charities that operate in diverse communities; that is, areas where economic exclusion and social deprivation are rife. These charities believe that with the right approach, underachievement and large-scale expulsions could be reduced or alleviated altogether, in a gradualist manner (**Minicase 15.7**).

Minicase 15.7 The Roselle Antoine Foundation

The Roselle Antoine Foundation (RAF) was established as a charity in 2001 by Caribbean educator and literature specialist, Roselle Antoine, to be a model institution for solutions to educational underachievement. The Foundation collaborates with parents, children and young people, as well as public and private institutions, along with professionals in Africa, the Caribbean, France and England. Its motto is, *Action for Education Rights*.

A top priority is to promote learning for the disadvantaged and employment skills for the jobless and develop the capacity of excluded communities. The activities of the Foundation are informed and guided by multiple concerns which are translated into plans on education, training and enterprise development. The Foundation is resourced by small grants and regular fund-raising activities, and it has a solid partnership with TCS Tutorial College, an independent institution of which Antoine is Principal.

The charity has a unique structure, blending youth with experienced professionals and volunteers who work through a broad-based committee system, which has a Cabinet-style leadership. Management and committee heads plan youth leadership, gender (men and women forums), welfare matters, cultural and educational events and activities. Special occasions include annual *Celebration of Achievement* ceremonies to reward members and the wider community. The *RAF Young Ambassadors* programme reflects a genuine interest in cultivating leadership skills among young people to make them useful citizens in society. Each ambassador is responsible for a Chapter and organising area activities.

The Foundation has experimented successfully with a culturally sensitive model combined with a Community Participatory Approach (CPA), in an effort to find practical solutions to educational underachievement. It involves encouraging African, Caribbean, Asian and other communities to mobilise families, friends and supporters to participate in national and international events and activities. This method has inspired confidence among members and fostered renewed trust within communities. A long-term strategy is to develop alternative solutions to underachievement affecting Caribbean children in the UK and build on the organisation's international partnerships with a focus on education, training and leadership development.

Social Housing

Like other social amenities, housing has long been linked with discrimination and prejudice, and it has taken a considerable time for issues relating to this human necessity to be resolved, although not quite. Caribbean migrants who came to Britain in the post-war period experienced poor housing conditions as racist signs, *'No Irish, No Blacks, No Dogs'* were erected by white landlords across the country. Even when foreign settlers showed proof of (guaranteed) affordability and good character, proprietors prevented them from buying properties. Stories were told of white landlords' refusal to allow Caribbean migrants to purchase homes that were on sale in inner-city areas. The few landlords who were slightly liberal and recognised the financial gain, reacted differently although they still possessed an inherent prejudice to their non-white clients.

As a result of this condition, hundreds of migrants lived in cramped accommodation particularly those who worked with the transport, NHS and other essential public services. Students who came from other parts of the British Commonwealth to the UK to further their studies also experienced overcrowded living conditions. In an effort to overcome this dreadful circumstance, Caribbean settlers maximised the use of informal financial measures known as *pardner, su-su, box-hand*, and along with formal banking methods to secure their own homes, thereby proving the historic legacy of enterprise built on self-reliance and thrift. Despite the many challenges, more than 40% of this British community live in properties as *'still-paying mortgagees'* or *'paid-up mortgagees'* with the remainder in rented private, housing association and Council-owned accommodation.

Dedicated campaigns by activists such as Julienne Etienne, Lee Samuels and others in the minority community, spurred the Housing Corporation into action, and in 1986 and 1991, strategies for minority housing associations were developed to empower communities to be directly involved in the provision of housing. The birth of these housing associations has made an obvious difference to the way in which housing resources are allocated to ethnic communities throughout England. It has also made a great impact on the public understanding with regard to equality issues on social housing and their corresponding link with local economic development in inner-city areas where exclusion and deprivation blight the lives of residents.

The strategy for establishing a minority housing association in the UK has been met with considerable success, and according to public officials, this approach has become a model for other countries, especially in mainland Europe (**Department for Communities 2006**). The concept of self-help and the desire to work with other nationalities as well as the authorities, proved very effective for minority communities who felt disadvantaged by the system. By playing a leading role in the reshaping of the housing sector in inner-cities, Caribbean migrants demonstrated initiative and drive, and the overall impact their collective actions could have on a vital strand of social policy legislation in the country. It is also a testament to first generation nationals who were determined (probably unwittingly) to pass on the traditions of financial independence and co-existence in a complex, but highly diversified industrialised nation such as Britain in the first half of the 20th century.

In this section on social housing, I will show examples of black housing associations and their effects on housing provision, based on their community-based origins and their desire to meet the needs of social rented housing and redressing the historic inequalities of minority communities in the social housing field. The sample of housing associations below, emphasise the significance of community enterprises working with their client base and maintaining viable partnerships with statutory agencies to achieve long-term goals and objectives. The sample also offers insights into different market segments targeted by housing associations, in meeting growing demands for social housing provision in diverse communities (**Minicases 15. 8**).

Minicases 15.8 Samples of Black Housing Associations in England

Black Housing Associations (BHAs) were initially set up to provide `affordable and quality housing' for predominantly African and Caribbean residents, but by the mid-1980s and amendments of the Race Relations Act (2000), these bodies were advised to extend services to other minority communities. The Housing Association's first five-year strategy in 1986 focused on encouraging the development and registration of minority housing. Subsequently, the number has increased at a slow, but steady pace, with non-housing activities and services included as a part of the wider profile of black housing associations:

- 70% offer development and management services;
- 50% corporate services;
- 90% domiciliary care and support services;
- 50% regeneration and community development;
- 50% non-residential units; and
- 10% offer other services (**University of Cambridge 2005**)

Ujima Housing Association was founded in 1977, London by a group of black housing workers concerned about the housing needs of young, single black men and women. It has one subsidiary, Lien Viet Housing Association in Hackney working with Vietnamese community. Ujima has nearly 200 employees at its west London headquarters, plus 13 other locations. Services include regeneration, elderly care, mental health, low-cost home ownership and accommodation for single homeless, refugee and other vulnerable groups. The association has a Community Development Unit partnering with agencies and organisations on different mainstream and community priorities. With an annual turnover of £25 million, it the largest enterprise of its kind in Britain and Europe (***The Voice* 2006**).

Nehemiah was registered in 1989 after it was founded by the Church of God Prophecy. It offers housing services to the predominantly black population in the West Midlands and works in conjunction with several housing associations. Statistics reveal that over 70% of lettings go to people aged 65 plus, but the acquisition of schemes for families and single people, mean that services will increase, with the likelihood of elderly provision reduced considerably. Over 80% of African and Caribbean residents are offered `homes-let' provision and just over 10% white and European residents benefit from such services.

Reading Afro Caribbean Elderly Housing Association (RACE) was opened in 1993 operating one-30 unit sheltered scheme. The scheme targets African and Caribbean residents, but it also has nearly half a dozen white tenants **(Jones 2004).**

Arawak Walton Housing Association was formed in 1994, Manchester – fusing two groups Arawak and Walton. The association specialises in meeting the complex housing needs of diverse communities. One of success keys, is the professionalism and dedication of the management and general (staff) team which allows for a financially strong organisation. The organisation's culture is one of flexibility and commitment to embrace new initiatives including new construction, stock transfers, short-life properties and leasehold improvements.

Significantly, the enduring struggle to improve housing conditions among Caribbean people at the start of the 20th century, was also connected with the wider campaign for social justice and economic inclusion for others experiencing comparable disadvantage. Furthermore as the case study depicts, black housing associations with Caribbean-inspired leadership, have demonstrated their credentials in corporate responsibility; by firstly, ensuring that their managerial structure is flexible and open, and secondly, their service operations are diversified to such an extent where various communities irrespective of ethnicity, culture and other persuasions can benefit. In some ways, leaders of the profiled housing associations have redefined multiculturalism in the context of an essential segment of the social enterprise sector, social housing.

Credit Unions

Credit unions act as co-operatives and are owned and managed by members, offering accessible saving facilities with low interest loans to members. The formation of these enterprises is another feature of community self-help by British Caribbean people, prior to their arrival in, and settlement in the UK in the mid-1950s. The custom of thrift is a progressive strategy dating back to the Emancipation era when freed slaves and indentured labourers in (the colonial) West

Indies had to find ways to co-exist with slender resources pertaining to land, property and money.

In what appeared to be a mechanism for short term investment, Caribbean people utilised the informal banking system of `*pardner*' or `*su-su*'. There are unwritten but instructive accounts of this investment scheme undertaken by first generation settlers. These stories which are contained in oral history projects in the UK, offer insights into a variety of experiences by migrants including their lives in pre-independent West Indian surroundings, the circumstances that led them to emigrate to Britain and North America (the US inclusive) and the means used to exist in a racially, divisive environment.

Thus it could be argued that credit unions have their genesis in the pioneering endeavours of Caribbean settlers, who in attempting to secure a return on investment (ROI), expended a portion of their income by opting for a method that was person-centred, accessible, uncomplicated and less risky. The expectation was that each `*pardner round*' will be available at the end of each investor's claim period. The key to this unwritten arrangement was the `word' of the `*holding partner*' or individual `banker' or `bankers'. It was said that this arrangement had enterprise features, typical of Caribbean people universally such as:

- Small groups involvement in this enterprise;
- Operators partnered with mostly folks `back home';
- Personal savings and other individual amounts were agreed on;
- Savings were used to buy property, furniture and pay for Christmas holidays etc;
- Drawings and their specific time and round were agreed;
- Changes to the drawing period and amount had consensus; and
- Very few reports of abuse of trust and other illegal activities.

Given that credit unions began in 19th century Europe during the depression, they were virtually unheard of in the UK until the late 1960s and most were linked to churches in the African and Caribbean communities. A credit union offers a maximum interest of 1% per month on loans, spreading across a year with no hidden cost and loan protection included. It also offers free insurance over, not just on loans but savings also. The major advantage of a credit union however, is that it allows those who are disenfranchised by banks to be able to save and borrow on an equal footing, pushing out loan sharks out of business, plus keeping money in the community it came from. So we can safely say that the history of credit unions in the UK has its genesis in the enterprise culture of people of Caribbean background **(Table 15. 3)**.

Table 15.3 Caribbean Confederation of Credit Unions

Affiliates	Members	Total Assets ($)
Antigua & Barbuda	12,939	20,342,681
The Bahamas	26,657	134,957,282
Barbados	107,796	321,764,154
Belize	28,586	29,156,150 (estimates)
Bermuda	4,561	7,226,141
Cayman Islands	7,072	66,237,806
Dominica	73,550	102,219,535
Grenada	22,854	44,354,723
Guyana	27,248	5,506,778
Jamaica	728,447	393,170,570
Montserrat	4,130	3,696,815
Netherland Antilles	18,346	48,402,930 (estimates)
St. Kitts and Nevis	11,703	18,982,226
St. Lucia	37,461	67,710,084
St. Vincent and the Grenadines	34,576	59,972,079
Suriname	10,305	471,370 (estimates)
Tortola	310	40,040
Trinidad & Tobago	339,378	493,409,095
Total	**1,495,919**	**1,810,660,459**

(Source: Consolidated Statistics, Caribbean Confederation of Credit Unions, 2003)

The figure above is a snapshot of the number of credit unions (under 400) in the Caribbean with assets of nearly $130 million, but which excludes share deposits, loans, other reserves and total reserves. At the time of reporting, credit unions in Barbados, Jamaica and Trinidad and Tobago were moving towards Central Bank `prudential supervision', as part of a reform strategy by the CCCU in the management, technology and member-driven products and services of the enterprise (**Caribbean Confederation of Credit Unions 2003**).

British credit unions are part of a world-wide movement covering 80 countries, with over 40,000 credit unions and an estimated 120 million individual. These co-operative-type bodies operate under the provision of the Credit Unions Act 1979 and are regulated and supervised by the Financial Services Authority (FSA). There has been limited media coverage on the contribution of minority communities to this UK enterprise though some studies acknowledge that credit unions serve multiple functions especially for Caribbean communities. They offer a facility for people to meet and interact, as well the provision of financial services suited to the needs of the communities in which they live and serve.

A study in the West Midlands showed that 13% of Caribbean residents were members of credit unions which suggested that a much higher level of African and Caribbean organisations as a whole, responded to social enterprise activities more than any other non-white group in the region. Yet missing from this vital assessment of community financial services was the (percentage) level of investments, loan portfolio and the overall assets in which Caribbean `investors' contributed towards. It was clear that members of this community recognised credit unions as a third factor in `alternative service providers' with regard to community financial provision (**Olatundun 2004**).

Social Care

Apart from being complementary to the healthcare industry, social care is also a vital segment in the social enterprise sector. It is founded on the principles of equity, fairness and the broad inclusion of communities from different backgrounds. This segment covers units in childcare, day care centres for older people, children and young people among others and responds to mainstream priorities such as: -

- Working with a diverse community of older people to offer healthy living services.
- Offering advice and support to parents, carers and children with special needs.
- Stress management provision for people recovering from drugs and alcohol.
- Developing positive initiatives for young people excluded from mainstream.
- After care mentoring services for long-term unemployed residents.

In this section, organisations that impact on social care programmes in various communities across the UK would be examined. In each area of the country, there are numerous Caribbean-owned organisations operating a range of social care and related services for both members of their community, as well as other diverse groups. They have voluntary sector management committees with registered charity and limited company status or operate as a social enterprise.

A sub-committee system is optional for these organisations particularly when dealing with complex issues affecting communities. It is customary for most minority voluntary groups to dictate their agendas due to the history of discrimination and racial prejudice experienced by members and their communities as a whole. This approach has been tempered somewhat by the recruitment of professionals to sit on boards and committees in trusteeship and related advisory capacities. In effect, sentimentality has given way to rational judgement.

Historically, funding has been a major obstacle for community groups countrywide, but Caribbean social care agencies maximise home-grown resources and explore wide-ranging opportunities within local authority commissioned contracts and other social care initiatives in respective regional areas. With the introduction of the *Best Value* principle and the *Local Compact,* Central Government mandated Social Services throughout the country to strengthen relationships with independent providers who are experienced, competent and enjoy the confidence of interest groups; healthcare trusts, GPs, nursing bodies, network organisations, individual healthcare professionals and related personnel in the health and medicare field. In this way, the philosophy of social care is better served when an amalgam of agencies and institutions – public, private and community/voluntary – work together to achieve common objectives. For the most part, funding is secured through a combination of local authority grants or subvention, sub-contracting or direct commissioning, Lottery and other charity resources, as well as fund-raising events, along with sponsorship. Each social care agency tailors its services to suit area residents and other surrounding communities **(Table 15. 4**).

Table 15. 4 Profile of Social Care Organisations in England

Organisation	Area	Major Services
Organisation of Blind African Caribbeans	London	Information and advice, housing, befriending and reader service, job club etc.
The Manchester Black Health Forum	Manchester	Community care, home care support, counselling, mental health support, seminars and conferences, health information advice.

Black Carers Project	Bristol	Information, advice, advocacy and emotional support and free respite service for carers of African and Caribbean background.
African and Caribbean Community Centre	Cambridge	Health, social and cultural matters concerning older, retired or disabled people of west Indian and similar backgrounds.
Future Health & Social Care Association	Birmingham	Ex-offenders' project, family services, social housing, mental health services, learning disabilities and social enterprise project (Case Study).
African Caribbean Mental Health Association	Sheffield	Research contributory factors regarding diagnosis and misdiagnosis of mental health suffers; promoting awareness among the black community and agencies.
Caribbean Elderly Hairoun Day Care Centre	Buckinghamshire	Day care centres for clients from all backgrounds/nationalities, social care and mental health provision.

(Source: Directories of Local Authorities, Associations & Community Centres, England 2000-2007)

The social care organisations sampled in the above profile, are a reflection of the diversity in this area and the extent to which professionals, volunteers and campaigners have gone to offer services that are representative of the needs of ethnic communities. Possibly a unique selling point of the majority of community enterprises, is highlighted above, are the widespread involvement of public agencies in the consultation process where it involves enlisting trustees to advice on more effective ways of delivering multiple services. Securing this level of participation is also important because organisations are likely to secure additional financial and technical support to add value to existing provision.

By targeting services over several areas, Caribbean social care organisations can identify trends in client markets and adapt services to suit. Quite often, it is not about the type of services that are on offer, but the way in which they're advertised and promoted to users, mostly for older people, children, people with disabilities and others with more complex conditions. It is these situations that usually present formidable challenges for minority social care organisations in the UK.

It is therefore admirable that Caribbean enterprises have lasted over a prolonged period, from 10 to 15 years plus. The 1990s-established social care agencies have a new dimension to their operations, assuming a traditional approach to social care management and delivery of services, as well as introducing mainstream elements to compete in growth segments of the social care market (**Minicase 15. 9**).

Minicase 15.9 Future Health and Social Care Association

Future Health and Social Care Association (1996) was established in Birmingham and founder-member, Roger Telphia is CEO. The association was set up to meet the housing and support needs of adults, particularly those with a history of mental health issues and learning difficulties. It is directed by a Board of Trustees and supported by a senior management team, administrative and other staff, totalling a workforce in excess of 140.

It supports vulnerable members of the community by providing training, homes, care facilities and education and is the leading social enterprise on the current Inner City 100 index. According to Telphia, '*Our philosophy is to main a self-sustaining position rather than relying on grant funding. We knew that only a few BME organisations were involved in delivering social care services and we recognised that the opportunities for us were limitless since we were targeting a client market that was not adequately serviced. As an organisation, we have a strong business ethos and we are striving to maintain this culture.*'(**Telphia 2007**)

The enterprise principle reflects the CEO's experience in offering financial advice to small firms prior to establishing the association. Starting the firm was a struggle since there were insufficient funds, but Telphia provided initial capital via his credit card. The key to the company's success is a hard-nosed, sustainable business approach to running a social enterprise. FHSCA has expanded without recourse to public funds, with a definitive management structure with services delivered through a multi-departmental unit system and backed up by appropriate operating procedures.

The association has a turnover exceeding £1.6 million while retaining the primary focus, an enterprise led by black people but working across diverse communities. Its long-term strategy is to invest in a new social enterprise to provide domicilary care, with a plan to employ over 200 people. Being a black-led organisation has given the association a competitive advantage in the social care market since its services are culturally sensitive. As an advocate for third sector organisations, the association is playing a leading role in delivery of health and social care services, and in doing so, it is developing the organisation into a national provider.

Training Organisations

When aspects of the British Caribbean community are recorded, there is a tendency to be preoccupied with incidents of racial prejudice and discrimination, and much of the history is limited to ordinary self-help organisations involved in issues that are beneficial to communities in their local areas. Little is mentioned about the diversity in essential services that professionals have infused in community enterprises they lead and the impact these have on mainstream provision.

In this section, I will examine briefly aspects of the British Caribbean contribution to training development as an integral part of the social enterprise sector. The last 10 years have witnessed an increase in the number of personal trainers, community-based organisations and social enterprises dedicated to capacity building involving a multi-cultural approach. The desire to sustain an enterprise culture within an entirely community-focused and client-centred manner, has initiated a debate on whether businesses and charities are very similar in today's complex market. Apart from its tradition of competitiveness, trade in goods and services is expected to reflect a set of commercial and social principles with customer care and sensitivity at the very heart of service delivery.

Now that government is commissioning charities to run public services in areas as diverse as childcare and employment programmes, job opportunities have diversified and multiplied beyond recognition. The growth in professionalism in British Caribbean training organisations means that social enterprises need different skills from their staff and it also shows a demand for improved services, tailored to suit the ever-changing needs of clients and other users of mainstream services. The training segment is increasingly seeking people with private sector experience to bring transferable skills such as finance, human resources, policy and IT (***The Guardian* 2006**).

Like other segments discussed in this chapter, minority training enterprises are present in almost all 12 UK Regions, serving communities across the cultural and social divide. The structural composition of these organisations varies in terms of size and performance though much depends on the volume of services and the equal number of client-beneficiaries using the service. In London and the Southeast where ethnic communities are more disperse in larger numbers, providers tend to structure their services towards end-users, and therefore maximise organisational systems and procedures to ensure that services are delivered efficiently. In the Midlands and other Home Counties where communities are far more complex and widespread, providers make sure that their operational and delivery systems are flexible enough since they may have to cater for clients outside their service areas.

Principally, the average Caribbean training organisation has two types of structures; one that is basic in definition and the other, complex in terms of multi-tasking departments or operating units. Small training firms dealing with regeneration contracts such as skills training and employment schemes usually have a flat organisation structure; that is, one or two directors, supported by a project administrator, possible part-time trainer, outreach worker and a few volunteers to help with either capacity building and/or clerical/reception duties.

The other structure is semi-corporate consisting of a Board of Trustees, an executive director, along with a tier of administrative and operational staff, with volunteers to match. These organisations may have branches or units in more than one locality and may also have a membership base in order to benefit from the experiences, skills and expertise of various communities represented on various sub-committees of social enterprise organisations (**Minicases 15.10**).

Minicases 15.10 Selected British Caribbean Training Enterprises

The Black Training and Enterprise Group (BTEG) was set up in 1991 as a national organisation providing a voice to government for BME service providers. Founder-member and director, Jeremy Crook, is a social policy practitioner and a recipient of the OBE for services to community development. BTEG advises public sector agencies and institutions and non-governmental bodies, provides technical assistance and support to voluntary and community groups, with links to over 600 third sector organisations in the UK. All sector organisations can join the network by subscribing to BTEG's quarterly publication, *Race and Regeneration*.

BTEG has an efficient management and operational team and has three strategic centres responsible for education, regeneration and technical assistance. Capacity building remains a trademark and this has won plaudits in wide circles. With a turnover of nearly one million pound, the enterprise has a mixture of funding from charities, government departments and other donors. Its has delivered contracts on behalf of Jobcentre Plus, Connexions and the Learning and Skills Council.

Positive Action Traineeships in Housing (PATH) West Midlands was set up in 1987 by a group of concerned individuals and employers to address the under-representation of people from minority ethnic communities in professional fields. It offers information, advice and guidance which involve working with people to help them access work opportunities via positive traineeships with partner organisations such as Birmingham Children's Hospital.

Initially specialising in providing training in housing management, the organisation succeeded in recruiting 129 trainees by 1997, of which 104 were successful in obtaining employment. With a small operating staff, the organisation has achieved more than 80% success rate in its apprenticeship programme. The housing learner's scheme attracts over 50% of successful Caribbean applicants who express interest in securing housing management, administration and various technical positions in the industry. PATH received the matrix accreditation in 2002 for its external services. It has a turnover of over half a million pounds and plans to widen its *Fast Track Scheme* to cover other areas of employment training and job prospects.

PATRA East Midlands Ltd is located in Nottingham and was set up in 1996 as a premier capacity building and regeneration agency to deliver services to the African and Caribbean community. It offers traineeships with employers which allow learners to study for academic and vocational qualifications. The aim is to provide sections of the community opportunities to improve their skills to compete in the labour market.

PATRA undertakes research which identifies gaps in policy and prospects relating to issues such as housing, health, employment and social care within diverse communities and how these reflect on public sector services. The hope is that apart from delivering alternative service, the organisation will be in a better position to influence policies and strategies for the regeneration of Caribbean and other minority groups.

If the few training agencies profiled in the case study are anything to go by, then there are indicative of the exciting prospects for sustainable growth in the social enterprise sector, with training and capacity building being the cornerstones for diversification, change and flexibility as they relate to essential public services with a culturally specific touch.

Youth Enterprise

In contrast to the persistent, negative reporting on Britain's inner-city youths, it would be thoughtless to exclude the brilliant efforts of Caribbean young entrepreneurs particularly, in this book. Whilst there is a preoccupation with the gravity of anti-social behaviour and other ills affecting a fraction of black youths for instance, there is another side of the story that remains untold. The creativity and innovation among young entrepreneurs could be seen as a media prize, that is of course, if newspaper editors and television producers are interested in publicising solutions to youth achievement among sections of the UK population destined to become future leaders.

The importance of celebrating the achievements of young minority entrepreneurs was made possible when the Treasury hosted an event to launch the first national young entrepreneurs' network, bringing together 150 businesses and social enterprises from six UK Regions, including Scotland and Wales in June 2007. The event was organised by the Black Business Association (West Midlands) in conjunction with Enhanced Consulting Ltd and it exemplified the maxim that public institutions can collaborate (effectively) with independent organisations to showcase and reward the talent of the young.

The launch of **Inner City Enterprise (ICE) UK** saw an estimated half a dozen industry sectors represented including 70 businesses, five public sector institutions and six social enterprises. Of the total number of businesses that participated in the launch, over half (52%) were owned by people aged 18-30 years and nearly half (47%) were managed by individuals aged 30 plus. A quarter of all firms represented the cultural-creative industries and business and professional services respectively, even as another quarter mirrored information technology, social enterprise, personal care, as well as education and training sectors in that order **(Fig 15.1).**

Figure 15.1 Profile of industry sectors at ICE UK's Launch

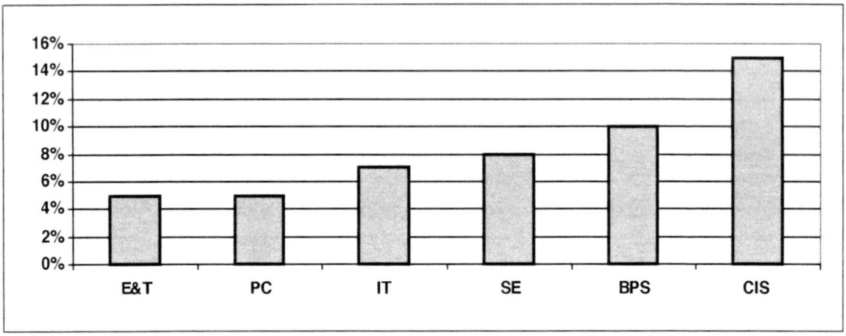

(Source: HM Treasury, June 2007

Sector guides: E&T – education and training, PC – personal care, IT- information technology, SE – social enterprise, BPS- business and professional services and CIS – cultural industries sector.

The mantra of `think small first' has become a well-known phrase in response to criticisms from small business owners and lobby groups that the public sector is not doing enough to develop the capacity of small firms in order for them to access contract opportunities to allow for growth and expansion. In recent years, the flurry of activities to include minority firms in the procurement process has not met with much success. There is no evidence to suggest that young entrepreneurs had access or benefited from national scheme. The two Office of Government and Commerce- sponsored procurement projects piloted in London (Haringey) and the West Midlands (Birmingham) were aimed at promoting best practice in public sector procurement, and many ICT-related projects to public contracts. To date, there isn't any real evidence as to how many black businesses benefited from this national `exercise' as well.

Ethnic businesses make up 10% of the small business population, with Caribbean firms demonstrating a market share of 11% of all businesses nationally. The Global Entrepreneurship Monitor carries out annual surveys of economic activity across the UK and it acknowledges that youth entrepreneurship has increased since 2000. Data from mainstream institutions and information obtained from the ICE-UK event, corresponded with a consistent pattern of entrepreneurship among Caribbean people especially in the 25-35 age categories, as highlighted in *The Voice* newspaper between 2005 and 2007.

The newspaper published business features on recruitment, property, food and drinks, publishing, education and training, showcasing the range and scope of British Caribbean trading activities in the country. Twenty five (25) of these firms were sampled to compare their sector representation with those evaluated at the ICE event, along with other enterprises included in this book. The findings from *The Voice* sample revealed the following: -

- 62% of enterprises were owned by under-30s.
- 56 % of the businesses were owned by males.
- 44% of all enterprises were owned and/or managed by females.
- 11% of the enterprises were located in the education and training sector.

In general, the statistics also justify the heights young Caribbean entrepreneurs are capable of achieving either at the same level or beyond those of their older counterparts. Thus the perception that `young people don't have appropriate role-models' is a failure of critics to recognise the success patterns across sections of the ethnic community. This belief is fuelled by expert opinion that magnify the use of television celebrities to test, justify and make reference to the suitability of role-models young people tend to admire and follow in terms of conduct and general behaviour. This is further manifested by the glorification of disorderly conduct and other vices involving TV stars in the mass media. Yet, the young business people interviewed for this book offered compelling views about their motives for self-employment as an alternative to either working for others, being unemployed and/ or indulging in anti-social behaviour **(Minicases 15. 11)**.

I was quite impressed with my father and his desire to see our family create wealth and I though well, there must be something good about that. Why should I not try to do likewise? (**Proprietor of Auto Shop, London 2004**)

Our parents struggled a lot to lay a foundation and today, we have to make good those opportunities to succeed. We have to learn from their mistakes and also understand the reason why they had to develop different survival strategies (**Owner of Personal Care Firm, Southeast 2005**).

Minicases 15.11 Young British Caribbean Entrepreneurs - a sample

Enhanced Consulting Ltd was established by Merisha Stevenson in 2006 to provide personal development training and generally develop the capacity of individuals and sector organisations in the West Midlands Region. Stevenson is a trained business consultant, a free-lance radio producer and founder-member of the recently-established National Inner-city Young Entrepreneurs' Association. She is a recipient of 3b's *Young Business of the Year* 2006. ECL also offers advice on PR, money management, job opportunities and networking.

In 2006, Joel Graham-Blake launched **Cultiv8**, a recruitment agency which won acclaim for encouraging large corporations to recruit young African and Caribbean professionals. Prior to setting up his business, Graham-Blake took part in Urban Dreams and was a mentor for New Deal and co-wrote a mentoring volunteer's course for the Open College Network. The company's plan is to become a viable global recruitment agency (***The Voice* 2006**).

Chevreen Wisdom owns **Lady Pineapple Entertainments** and she is was a recipient of two successive awards - the 100 Black Men of London's *Youth of the Year Community Service* award (2003) and the Black Enterprise Awards for *Young Entrepreneur of the Year 2004*. The firm organises cultural entertainment for a variety of organisations including popular charities, with audiences varying between 2,000 and 3,000 at a time. Wisdom's aim is to be an expert in cultural artistry (***The 100* 2004**).

Gordon Bennett is owner of **Charles Gordon** (a firm named after him). He is a property developer, music promoter and business consultant. He is reported to have made his first million age 21, and although he had no formal education, his instincts were always around running a business. He financed his enterprise using his home as collateral and his business has grown. He plans to set up other projects including a magazine, a drinks label and train singers in order for them to compete for major record labels (***The Voice* 2006)**.

Natalie Smith is the founder of **Passionet (2003),** a specialist bookstore offering black urban fiction and other books written by black authors and multicultural literature, through its online facility. The general idea is to encourage young African and Caribbean children to read quality material in order to raise their literacy levels, with an added incentive of them understanding their culture. Passionet has been involved in reading campaigns, including a project in association with Black History Month in secondary schools, and another aimed specifically at boys aged 11 to 15. Smith believes that her enterprise will grow to become a household name. Her tips for success are, *`be prepared to struggle and you need to keep an open mind and be prepared to learn the long the long way – through experience'* (***The Voice* 2005**).

At the age of 20, Carey Williamson of **Willaf Ltd** scooped the Young Entrepreneur of the Year Award in 2003. His company provides critical e-business and networking solutions. A steady- growing company, Willaf delivers a complete hardware procurement services and partners with IBM, serving clients in London. The company has formed a separate arm to offer telecommunications services to its growing client base and is in partnership with IBM.

My mother inculcated in me financial discipline and self-reliance, but also that I should help others who need support most. That I should not shirk from the responsibility of `earning my keep' where necessary since society doesn't owe me favours (**MD, Training Firm, Midlands, 2005**).

There are hundreds of us doing lots of great things, but not everyone knows. I believe in making a difference is vita. Managing your own business can help change other people's opinions about us. We have achieved a lot of good things in the past, so why can't we do the same today and always? **(Owner of IT Firm Yorkshire 2007)**

These comments further emphasise that young people are aware of the struggles of first generation Caribbean settlers who arrived in the first half of the 20th century to help rebuild post-war Britain. The prospects for change are possible because of ongoing campaigns against injustice, the fact that Britain has become more tolerant and liberal, coupled with a fast changing global environment in which parts of the developing world are becoming dominant players in the global economy. Young, minority entrepreneurs are also highly qualified professionals and technologically savvy. There are calculated risk takers who are capable of negotiating with larger institutions and companies to strike `better deals'. In effect, there are maximising opportunities provided in growth sectors of the UK economy.

Faith Organisations

Like most other initiatives in the UK, Caribbean people have been associated with the establishment of churches and other faith-based organisations over the past 50 years. Initially treated as outcasts in white-dominated churches such as the Roman Catholic, Anglican, Methodist and other denominational sections of the Church of England in the 1950s and 1960s, members established churches all over England. They persisted with strands of evangelicalism including Pentecostalism and Seventh Day Adventist Baptism. Religion provided Caribbean communities the opportunity to counter the scourge of racial prejudice and help them to remain somewhat sane in an environment that proclaimed Christian values, but in practice, demonstrated the opposite.

Gradually, the new churches grew to act as social centres for the community even though the manner of worship was akin to that of African-American practices rather than traditional Anglican or Catholic liturgy. Gospel music came to play a part in British cultural life and it was again Caribbean worshippers who were instrumental in establishing British Gospel choirs, most notably the London Community Gospel Choir. Black worshippers account for more than two-thirds of all church-goers in London and 7% of worshippers nationwide. Through their adherence of faith, Caribbean communities have shown their willingness to help preserve communities in which they live through diligent service.

In this section of the book, the contribution of Caribbean-led churches and other faith organisations would be assessed, to show their impact on the wider community in which they operate, particularly in light of recent years when leading British politicians have been courting spiritual leaders and their congregants to 'make their vote count'; meaning to be more involved in the political affairs of the country. A former prime minister even acknowledged that, '*It wouldn't surprise me if that within the next five years you see more church leaders being more political* (**Blair 2006**).

Apart from their vitality as moral and spiritual vessels, faith organisations are change-agents in the development process. They actively encourage members to act in the best interest of their environment and in the process, empower others to promote social governance in community affairs either (directly) through faith enterprises or other area-associated bodies (**Minicases 15.12**)

Minicases 15. 12 Major British Caribbean-led Faith Enterprise Organisations

The New Testament Church of God (NTCG) was founded in 1953 by Dr. Oliver Lyseight who was also the first national overseer of the organisation. The church served as a haven for thousands of Caribbean migrants during the 1950s and 1960s. They were offered hope and support to cope with the hardship they experienced as new British Commonwealth settlers. Before his death in 2006, Dr. Lyseight also founded the Afro West Indian United Council in 1976 to promote a representative and united voice for the emerging black churches at the time. Today, the church has over 107 branches, 2 missions and over 10,000 members with a further 20,000 adherents, along with assets in excess of £20 million.

The Pentecostal Credit Union (PCU) was set up from virtually nothing in 1979 and is now one of the greatest and most successful credit unions in the UK. Rev. Carmel Jones has been the driving force behind the organisation. `*The two entities of the Pentecostal Church and the credit union movement fit well together. They reflect principles of fairness, helping one's neighbours, justice and working to make the world a better place in which to live,* ' he explained. The PCL was set up because minorities were turned away by the banks and other lending institutions, also as result of other bitter experiences black had with money lenders and shady banks. The organisation had supported the growth of black majority churches and has developed a range of community activities and support in local neighbourhoods. The credit union has an asset value running into of millions of pounds.

The United Evangelical Project (UEP) was initiated in the late 1970s to respond to the increasing problems experienced by Caribbean young people. Church leaders identified the lack of relevant facilities for young people, which inhibited their growth potential and created further burdens for them and others. Since churches in the UK did not have the expertise to support young people in this way also, churches came together and establish UEP with a view to `working together to fulfil our potential and bring hope of a better community'. The faith group provides accommodation, education, youth discipleship, legal support and prison link services respectively. It has a turnover exceeding £500,000 generated through fund-raising, project development and contract delivery.

The African and Caribbean Evangelical Alliance (established in 1984) is a national umbrella organisation for black majority churches in the UK. The organisation is a source of support to churches, organisations and individuals by providing a voice for black Christians in the media and to statutory agencies such as the Home Office and the Charity Commission. As a membership organisation, the Alliance offers training, resources, advice and guidance to churches and Black Christians on diverse issues. Rev. Joel Edwards who was probation officer and who services on several faith, government and public agency advisory groups, is the first black director of the Evangelical Alliance UK.

> Other Black-majority Churches such as **Cherubim & Seraphim Council of Churches, the Seventh Day Adventist, Council of African and Caribbean Churches, International Ministerial Council of Great Britain, Joint Council of Afro-Caribbean Churches, New Testament Assembly and Wesleyan Holiness Church** are among countless other faith organisations providing a variety of support services to both members and diverse communities throughout the UK.

There are other faiths that merit inclusion since they also contribute to the moral, spiritual and social dimension of minority communities. Often described as `minority' faiths because they figure less in the overall affairs of mainstream religion, these non-Christian-beliefs are integral to Caribbean settlers since the 1940s. Rastafarianism is allied to the Ethiopian Orthodox Church and the practices of adherents are different to other religions. The popularity of this religion is considered more of a `socio-cultural' identity than a religious faith since there is a prevalence of Christians, sports people and others wearing dreadlocks, signifying style rather than substance (**Aldred 2005**).

There are other forms of religious practices that reflect a sense of identity and belonging for sections of the British Caribbean community. For instance, the vitality of Hinduism and Islam is not only due to the `traditional' presence of settlers from the Indian sub-continent (India, Pakistan and Bangladesh and Sri Lanka) but also that of Caribbean migrants from Guyana, Trinidad and Tobago, as well as the wider Caribbean Region. So that festivals such as Youman Nabi, Eid-ul-Fitr (Muslim), Diwali and Phagwah (Hindu) and Chinese New Year (Chinese) and Hanukkah (Jewish), have become acceptable `ethnic-religico norms' (the author's emphasis) similar to annual festivities to commemorate Easter, Christmas and New Year.

Whilst other faith organisations contribute to the moral and spiritual empowerment of their devotees, they also have an impact on economic and social development which is manifested through organisations as diverse as the Maha Sabha and the Islamic Anjuman – two respected

Hindu and Muslim groups which include Caribbean people, either at the helm or facilitating the process. Perhaps the most remarkable factor in the equation is the double impact of Muslim and Hindu commercial organisations on British institutions particularly in the areas of banking and multi-faith cultures. In fact, the success of enterprises led by individuals of either faith is underlined by culture, religion and other ethical codes. The giving of Zaka (a third of income donated to charity) by Muslims for instance, represents an essential part of Islamic traditions.

In addition, although their supporters tend to have greater advantage in terms of identifying with a `common cause', non-Christian faith enterprises create potential space for wider diversity with their special `brand' of social entrepreneurship. This is further evidenced by their utility of ethnicity, religion, social mix and cultural-rootedness, values which have cemented their place in British society, and which also have resulted in `mini-crossovers'; that is adaptations by some sections of the Caribbean community - Indian, mixed or other ethnic backgrounds.

It should be emphasised that whilst they are fundamental differences in worship between African and Caribbean congregants respectively involving Africentric beliefs on spirituality vis-à-vis Eurocentric religious practices, there are clear signs of religious leaders beginning to combine theology or divine teaching with *`faith economics'* (author's emphasis). Aspects of this are resonant in case studies involving the PCU and the UEP. Churches also recognise that the spiritual well-being of their communities cannot be divorced from economic and social welfare. The activity of the UEP is a classic example of a group of churches joining forces to develop a wide range of projects to cater for the needs of the community.

As was stated earlier, non-Christian organisations do affect aspects of culture and faith in British society, but they are also in the forefront of faith economics and this principle has been mirrored by succeeding generations of Hindus, Muslims and Jewish devotees for some time. In addition to temples, mandirs and synagogues, this practice is transmitted through daily teachings, religious literature, the family and support structures. And yet, the examples in the **Minicases 15. 12**, illustrate that there is a necessity for churches to enhance their profile by widening consultation beyond their congregation, routinely assessing the various problems in their locality and surroundings, developing a flexible approach and tone in terms of the 'message' and working in partnership with other faith and non-religious groups, to achieve broad-based community objectives. More than ever, there is a need for faith enterprises to play a greater role in regeneration schemes in inner-city areas.

Perhaps instinctively and contrary to opposing views, much could be said about faith organisations that are making efforts to cushion sections of their community from the debilitating effects of discrimination and prejudice which at worst, could impinge on the moral sanctity on even the most inspired of religious devotees among us. It reinforces the known principle that every faith-based organisation ought to consider in the modern world which is that the link between spirituality and materialism cannot be ignored (**Johnson 2007**).

Policy Initiative

As the growth of social enterprises highlight variations in type, composition and performance across the UK Regions, government officials have been examining support measures to help maintain the viability of this sector. There is recognition from all sides that social enterprises are a force for change and for good especially in communities where structural poverty and other social ills exist. Reasons given for their importance and relevance include: -

- They tackle some of society's most entrenched social and environmental challenges;

- They set new standards for ethical markets, raising the bar for corporate responsibility;
- They improve public services, shaping services design and pioneering new approaches; and
- They increase levels of enterprise, attracting new people to business (**Cabinet Office 2005**).

With the creation of the nine English Regions, along with the other three – Scotland, Wales and Northern Ireland – there is a broad commitment to deliver business support through the information, diagnostic and brokerage model relevant to SMEs, including social enterprises in England. In the early part of 2007, most of the (original) Business Link services were ceded to the regions and it was hoped that such a move would result in greater success for social entrepreneurship in the 12 UK Regions. Implicitly, there are expectations on both sides; firstly, minority communities expect that the new system will deliver and that the current policy framework for social enterprise development will act as a catalyst for improving the image and credibility of this evolving sector in the UK economy. Secondly, regional officials hope that beneficiaries will grow to trust the new system and support enterprise initiatives, by offering feedback and being more involved in the policy and decision-making process in every region throughout the UK. At the time of writing, it was reported that RDAs had invested £74 million into special support activities for social enterprise so that greater ties could develop between the agencies and the wider specialist support market **(Table 15. 5)**.

Table 15.5 Social Enterprise Policy Initiatives in selected UK Regions

Region	Policy Initiative
London	Social Enterprise London promotes networking opportunities, best practice and representation to achieve an inclusive robust and creative social enterprise community.
Southeast	Exploring the potential for social enterprise to bring innovation into public service delivery. The agency leads the Cultural Shift partnership that comprise social entrepreneurs, policy makers, academics and community groups interested in reforming public services.
East Midlands	Mapping the minority voluntary and community sector to assess issues affecting the sector and invested £2 million to simulate both the supply and demand side of the sector; maximising capacity building, research and policy and sports development to promote the area.
West Midlands	Advantage West Midlands is one of the first agencies to establish a regional strategic social enterprise network, and it is predicted to invest over £25 million to support the sector by the end of 2008-2009.
Yorkshire & Humberside	Yorkshire Forward has supported major awareness-raising initiatives to encourage new and existing social enterprises with opportunities to trade and promote their products and services to procurement professionals across the public and private sector.
South West	The RDA invested nearly £2 million pounds in the Regional Infrastructure for Social Enterprise known as `RISE' to lobby on behalf of social enterprises. It offers women training for jobs, including access to business opportunities.
Scotland	Scottish Social Enterprise Coalition was set up December 2005 to change grassroots culture around social enterprises which contribute £1.2 billion, with a view to consider them as integral, as well as a norm in the Scottish economy.

(Source: Nurturing Social Enterprises in the Regions, Regional Insight, November/ December 2006)

Major Characteristics

As was stated throughout this chapter, Caribbean-led social enterprises have a distinction in entrepreneurship and civic service beyond the confines of their respective locality. This distinction is further evidenced by a majority that comprise an active management and sub-committee system dealing with specific issues on welfare, youth, women, fund-raising, marketing, policy etc. Nearly a quarter of enterprises have dual legal status – charity and company limited by guarantee. This provides an opportunity for commercial and social trading, whilst maintaining the not-for-profit aim or purpose.

Contrary to literature on community organisations and more recently, entrepreneurship, Caribbean-led organisations consist of activists and professionals. Distinguished medical practitioners, Dr. Moody and Lord Pitt were initiators of divergent groups and professional organisations that represented multiple communities, beginning in the 1930s through to the present.

In the formative years, there was a gender disparity (favouring men) in most social organisations although women played what was sometimes described as an `*invisible*' but `*important supporting roles*'. As a whole, women, feature prominently in faith organisations and the success of churches, temples, synagogues and other places of worship, owe much to their unswerving dedication to progress even in times of difficulty or crisis. Youth representation varies depending on the type of organisations; that is, aims and objectives or for that matter, their general mission. Primarily, cultural, faith, youth clubs and related groups tend to attract young people in the under-30 age category.

International organisations such as the **International Association of Lions Clubs**, the **Rotary**, **Toastmasters/Mistresses** and the **Jaycees** have variations in youth and women sections. The traditional youth wing of Lions, the **Leos,** initiates members in their tender years to assume leadership of the Lions fraternity in future years. The women's wing, Lioness(es) is also integral to the organisation although in recent years, women have been accorded equal status in terms of the title `Lion' that precedes their actual name. Critics have likened this approach to the campaign for greater gender equality and recognition in reputable civic organisations that traditionally tended to exclude women and younger people.

Social enterprises operate in areas where poverty, run-down estates, poor public services, social disorder, crime and other ills are prevalent. Mistrust among sections of the minority community persists, but as this chapter revealed, the desire for `all-inclusive' partnership has become the key to successful participation in the workings of local economies by social enterprises. Indeed, the features below are a reflection of the new dynamics of British Caribbean social enterprises:

- 80% have traditional Management Committees and voluntary staff.
- 20% operate Social Enterprise-type Boards and paid staff.
- Led by community activists and in recent times, trained professionals.
- Relative gender balance of men and women (50-60 plus age group).
- Membership includes a small proportion of 45-55 age groups.
- A very tiny fraction of affiliates are under 30 years old.
- Operate from a mixture of publicly and private-owned premises.
- Turnover varies from under £50,000 to £1m plus in the case of church groups.

Challenges and Prospects

Like other sectors, there are formidable challenges and exciting prospects ahead for British Caribbean social enterprises operating in a wider UK context. Challenges have to do with the issues that confront operational management in competing with larger, established community organisations. Opportunities pertain to advantage to be gained in the marketplace because of branding products and services that are both commercially and socially acceptable to clients from multiple backgrounds. This section will focus on community centres, enterprise agencies, trade associations, education organisations, housing associations, credit unions, youth enterprises and faith organisations (**Table 15. 6**).

Table 15. 6 Social Entrepreneurship - Challenges and Opportunities

Segment	Challenges	Opportunities
Community Centres	Dependent on grant-aid with little access to ownership of premises.	Develop special 'brand' products and services; develop partnership initiatives to generate additional revenue to acquire premises.
Enterprise Agencies	Competing with Chambers of Commerce, Business Link and other public agencies.	Examine sectors and segments that are under-serviced and tailor specific services to access clients.
Education Organisations	Government-funded institutions and emphasis on national priorities and local authority imperatives.	Identify local needs, obtain information on national education and training programmes and develop suitable projects in conjunction with multiple agencies.
Housing Associations	Large associations, regeneration agencies with capitalised budgets and local authority contracts.	Discussion with public authorities, sub-contracting arrangements with large associations unable to satisfy specialist social housing services for minority communities.
Credit Unions	Poor publicity, limited resources, too few trained personnel in credit control and financial risk management	Business owners and social entrepreneurs can set up a revolving fund for credit union activities and sponsor training courses in credit control/ financial risk management.

Youth Enterprises	Disjointed policies, scanty media coverage, and perception of being under-valued.	Mature business owners can mentor young entrepreneurs, use trade associations to lobby for resources and relevant media publicity for successful enterprising young people.
Faith Groups	Christian groups tend to encourage congregants to focus mainly on aspects of religion and spirituality.	Deploy more social capital in regeneration, social enterprise activities in local areas – encourage enterprise spirit in all communities.

(Source: Textual analysis based on trends in the social enterprise sector, UK, 2000-2007)

Conclusion

In this penultimate chapter, social enterprise was defined as a commercial set of activities with a social benefit result. It was prevalent in 19th century UK as part of the altruism of business people and industrialists. In North America there is less emphasis on the use of excess profits and more on the `double' bottom line, while the European meaning is about adding the principle of social rather than personal ownership.

The number of social enterprises and their market value were also examined, along with their diversity ranging from small, community-owned shops and faith groups to large companies operating multi-million pound budgets. An estimated 3.2% or 1.2 million of Britons economically active population are engaged in social enterprise activity. British Caribbean people have a market share of 6.9% which means that this community own and manage in excess of 3,000 social enterprises in the UK.

A fairly detailed analysis was done on about 14 segments of the British Caribbean social enterprise sector; they included social organisations, community centres, community associations, cultural segment, enterprises agencies, trade associations, professional networks, education organisations, housing associations, credit unions, social care, training bodies, youth enterprise and faith groups. This approach allowed greater insight into the workings of the various segments which make up social entrepreneurship within the Caribbean community in Britain. The information and data were captured via case studies, charts, figures, anecdotes and (interview) quotes from the estimated 100 organisations featured in this chapter covering all of England and parts of Scotland and Wales in that order.

A framework of challenges and prospects was devised according to key priority areas involving community centres, enterprise agencies, education organisations, housing associations, credit unions, youth enterprises and faith groups. This framework forms an essential part of this book, starting in Chapter 5 through to 15, to help readers recognise how British Caribbean business owners and social entrepreneurs managed to compete in a complex and increasingly diversified UK economy. The final section and chapter of this book will outline a strategy for British Caribbean firms in the 21st century in light of the effects of globalisation on UK plc.

Chapter Notes:

The Charities Aid Foundation was set up in 1924 as a department initially, to encourage more efficient giving to charity, and since 2000, the organisation has helped to set up the UK's first charity bank, *National Giving week* (2004) and *Sharing the Caring* (2005) campaign to encourage more salaried employees to donate a portion of their earnings to charity.

After the League of Coloured People, the **West Indian Colonial Club** was also set up in the late 1940s, with the premises used by ex-servicemen and `early arrivals' from the Caribbean. The British Government provided non support systems for nationals who came in response to the jobs advertised in the West Indies, and many entertainment houses in Britain operated a colour bar.

The West Indian Organisation Co-ordinating Committee (WIOCC) was formed in 1964 as an umbrella organisation for six Manchester-based West Indian societies and associations; the Trinidad and Tobago Society, Jamaica Society, Leeward Islands People's Association, Guyana Association, Barbados Association and the Grenada Association.

Caribbean communities could be found throughout the UK and by the largest concentration is to be found in London, Birmingham and the broader West Midlands conurbation. Significant communities exist in other population centres, notably Manchester, Nottingham, Leicester, Bristol, Leeds, Sheffield, Luton, Derby and Cardiff.

Best Value was introduced in 1998 by the Labour Government, replacing Compulsive Contract Tendering or `CCCT', as a means of improving equality access to procurement opportunities for minority other excluded groups in the country. Best Value is founded on the principles of *Compare, Compete, and Consult.*

The Black Community Forum Ltd in Sheffield, set up in 1991, was another umbrella organisation comprising over 90 affiliated groups from Africa, Pakistan, Yemen, India, Chile, Eastern Europe and elsewhere. The principle of collective responsibility has been a unique selling point of Caribbean generations since their arrival in the mid-20th century in the UK.

Caribbean settlers of Indian origin made a significant contribution to the UK, with young women coming to Britain to train and work as nurses in the NHS, while men found employment in public institutions, and after many years of study practised as lawyers, medical doctors, dentists and lecturers, to name a few professions.

The Indo-Caribbean Association was set up in the 1970s and it sponsored sports and cultural events, including the Indo-Caribbean cultural festival in 1986 in London. The organisation received a Caribbean Times Community Award, sponsored by Hansib Publishing Ltd.

Black Rights (UK) was established in 1982 following the civil disturbances in Brixton. It was conceived by Guyanese barrister, Rudy Narayan, along with other Caribbean professionals, Roy Sawh, Sam Springer, Sam Springer and Harold Mangal.

Scarman Report – produced by Lord Leslie Scarman, recommending that urgent steps be taken to address poverty and lack of facilities for economic and social progress for the black community. The report followed civil disturbances in 1981. Besides Brixton, the disturbances spilled over in other parts of England; namely, Toxeth in Liverpool and Moss Side in Manchester.

The Indo Caribbean newsletter promotes the culture and heritage of people of Indian origin from the Caribbean.

Eid-ul-Fitr – also spelt `Eid-ul Fitr', the first day of the succeeding month of Shawwal, Muslims attend Salah at the mosque to celebrate the end of the fast.

Diwali- the Hindu *`Festival of Lights'* which marks the New Year and falls in October. People light candles or lamps in their windows to welcome Rama home to his kingdom and a rightful king. Lakshmi, the goddess of wealth, is also worshipped on this occasion and many businesses open new account books at this period.

Phagwah- also known as `Holi' the start of India' hot season in February and a joyful time dedicated to Krishna. People throw coloured water or `abeer' and bright powders at each other with no barriers of rank or caste. Families and friends visit each other exchanging good wishes and sweetmeats.

Hanukkah- the Jewish *`Festival of Lights'* in November/December celebrates the winning back of the temple in Jerusalem 2000 years ago, its eighth day duration being symbolic of the miraculous story of how the supply lamp oil lasted much longer than expected.

Selected Publications:

1 Annual Report of the Charities Aid Foundation, 2006/2007, England.

2 *NCVO's Vision for the Future*, September 2005, London.

3 *A Survey of Social Enterprise across the UK*, Small Business Service, London, IFF Research, 2005.

4 *Exploring the Role of the Third Sector in Public Service Delivery and Reform*, HM Treasury 2005.

5 *Measuring Enterprise Impacts in Deprived Areas*, Small Business Service, December 2002.

6 `Nurturing Social Enterprises in the Regions', *Regional Insight*, November/December 2006.

7 Harding, R (2006) *Social Entrepreneurship Monitor*, GEM, United Kingdom 2006.

8 *Working Together: A Strategy for the Voluntary and Community Sector and the Learning and Skills Council*, LSC January 2004.

9 Hylton, C. (1999): *African Caribbean Community Organisations: The Search for Individual and Group Identity*, Trentham Books, England.

10 Ali, Arif (1987) *Third World Impact*, 8th edition, Hansib Publishing Ltd.

11 ACBN launches at City Hall, *AC Business News*, Summer 2003.

12 African Caribbean Diversity webpage, 31 August 2006

13 `Caribbean Indian Dance Troupe', *Indo Caribbean* newsletter, Issue 2, April 2003.

14 Cork, L (2005): *Supporting Black Pupils: Understanding and Improving Home-School Relations*, Routledge, England.

15 Wright, C, Standen, P, John, G, German, G & Patel, Tina (2005) *School exclusion and transition into adulthood in African Caribbean communities*, Joseph Rowntree Foundation, England.

16 *Growth and diversification of Black and Minority Ethnic housing associations*, University of Cambridge; also Paper on the topic presented by D. Harris and F. Lyall-Grant, at the European Network for Housing Research, 29 June – 3 July 2003, Iceland.

17 `Mission possible; Ujima to give a hand-up not hand-out', *The Voice, June-26-July 3, 2006.*

18 Nehemiah Housing Association, Annual Report 1992, England.

19 `Ethnicity and Housing: the contribution of housing associations', *Core analysis,* Issue no 5, August 2003.

20 Jones, P: `Towards Sustainable Credit Union Development', Association of British Credit Union Ltd, 1999.

21 Olatundum, D, Black and Minority Ethnic Participation in Credit unions in the West Midlands, Advantage West Midlands, England.

22 *Consolidated Statistics, 31 December 2002 and 31 December 2003*, Caribbean Confederation of Credit Unions.

23 Reynolds, T: *Caribbean Families, Social Capital and Young People's Diasporic Identities*, London South Bank University, September 2005.

24 *Keep the Faith*, Issue 27 December 2006/January 2007, Black UK Publications, Suffolk, England.

25 *Faith and Service to the Community*, Report on the National Meeting of The Inter Faith Network for the UK, 2001.

26 `It's Time to Move Mountains', First National Black Empowerment Conference, Employment Forum (UK), 5 April 2002, Croydon, London.

27 `It's Make or Blake' *The Voice*, May 17, 2006.

28 `Lady Pineapple wins Black Enterprise Award' *The 100,* Vol. 1, Issue 6, November 2004, London.

29 `Bookworm Venture', *The Voice*, December 1, 2005.

30 `Charles Gordon made his first million at just 21', *The Voice*, January 18, 2006.

31 Aldred, J. D. (2005): *Respect: Understanding Caribbean British Christianity*, p 107, Epworth, England.

32 *Social enterprise action plan: Scaling new heights*, Cabinet Office, 2005.

33 `Nurturing Social Enterprises in the Region', *Regional Insight*, November/December 2006.

Chapter 16

A Blueprint for Sustainability

The contribution of the British Caribbean SME sector is yet to be fully recognised and it is in the interest of all concerned to try and create awareness in order to bring about a real sense of economic and social justice, in a society that prides itself on fairness, freedom and tolerance. For over a century, Caribbean migrants have shown the most amazing level of entrepreneurship, by creating jobs, introducing new products and services, added knowledge and skills, as well as helping to cement communities and building prosperity, especially in deprived inner-cities throughout the British Isles **(Johnson 1997).**

In this final chapter, we will outline a plan of action for British Caribbean business enterprises for the 21st century and beyond. In the introduction, the stated purpose of this book was to examine the organisation and performance of the British Caribbean SME sector during the last 100 years, by profiling key industry sectors owners are engaged in. In concluding therefore, this strategy is to provide the foundation upon which further development and sustainability can be possible for the tens of thousands of businesses and social enterprises owned and managed by Caribbean people. Since this book is the first of its kind, it was vital to obtain relevant facts and figures to determine the challenges affecting owners, as well as prospects for improving market share in key sectors. This book was written using a sector excellence model (SEM); that is, examining each sector and categorising them into segments according to the operations of the firm. Through this method, a better understanding of how British Caribbean SMEs function in relation to the organisation structure and level of output against the background of intense competition emerged.

To reiterate, `*British Caribbean business or enterprise*' has been defined as any commercial firm or social enterprise, owned by persons born in either the Caribbean or the UK (of Caribbean parentage). It is hoped that this definition will offer greater clarity on the contribution firms make to the economy within a British context. The reason for this is simple; the estimated 18,000 firms (commercial and social enterprises combined) are located in the UK, with main offices here. The terms `*West Indian*' and `*Caribbean*' were used interchangeably to explain the process of development and change in the Caribbean and the diaspora. In order to provide an objective view of this progression, along with trends and events that led to the migration of Caribbean people to the UK and other Western societies, this book is divided into three sections. **Section I** consists of 4 chapters; **Section II** covers chapters 5 to 15 and **Section III** contains a strategic blueprint for the British Caribbean SME Sector.

Chapter I traced the history of the Caribbean against the backdrop of slavery, (Indian) indentureship and Political Independence. For centuries, European powers fought over the Caribbean, exploiting its resources to help propel the Industrial Revolution. The forced removal of millions of Africa to the Americas and the subsequent damage to the psyche of succeeding generations is perhaps one of the most dreadful events in human history. Added to this, indentureship helped to create conditions for divide and rule whilst developing a system of class, race and other forms of division. These turbulent events among others did not daunt the spirit of the region's emerging leadership and its people, to press ahead with changes, even beyond limited expectations, for eventual self-government and economic integration, a work still in progress.

Chapter 2 looked briefly at the Caribbean Regional economy, showing the effects of free-market policies that stimulated enterprise among urban and rural folk. The challenges and successes of these policies were seen too, in light of the struggle for self-determination and a fully integrated regional economy. The evolution of a Single

Market economy was mentioned to illustrate the degree to which the Caribbean has made advances in revitalising its democratic institutions to keep pace with globalisation.

Chapter 3 focused on the origin of the United Kingdom including its political, legal and social value system. The presence of settlers from the former British Commonwealth – Africa, Asia, the Caribbean and elsewhere – was highlighted. The minority population is diverse, making up more than 6% of the total UK population. Caribbean residents consist of over 1% of the country's population and over 12% of the total minority community combined. This section also explored the different regions and cities Caribbean firms operate and the obstacles they encountered in their quest towards financial independence.

Chapter 4 covered the strategic and operational challenges affecting owners, and it was felt that a proper market intelligence system should be put in place so that firms of all sizes and types can cope with different threats in the business environment.

Chapters 5 to 15 were the centrepiece of this book's title, *'British Caribbean Enterprises: A Century of Challenges and Successes'*. These sections covered 11 industry sectors and over 70 business segments, involving numerous commercial firms and social enterprises respectively. Information was obtained from current databases – official, private (independent), questionnaires, interviews, expert observation (studies), case studies, industry sources, conferences and seminar/workshops, consultancies and media profiles. This book was researched over an eight-year period (1999-2007), with the last two years, 2006-2008, spent compiling drafts including this final chapter, for publication.

Revelation

Evidence from a collection of sources – formal and informal - showed that more than a third of all Caribbean people have an enterprise tradition tracing back to their homeland. And though ethnic monitoring has been used to determine the racial origin or nationality of business owners over the past 20 years, official statistics have done little to explain broadly, the organisation and performance of British Caribbean firms. The first real attempt at enterprise was in 1907 when Trinidadian, Dr. John Alcindor, set up a private medical practice in Paddington, west London. By the mid-1960s, the first black business, Dyke & Dryden, with an international reputation, emerged. It was pivotal to the transformation of the hair and beauty care industry, spawning hundreds of personal care firms in the UK. Entrepreneurs were continuing the pioneering work of African-American, Sarah Breedlove also known as Madame C J Walker, who invented the hot comb and made a fortune from the manufacturing of beauty care products. The current market share for British Caribbean firms is estimated at 11% (**2006 estimates**).

In addition, while social enterprises began in the first half of the 20th century, as community and voluntary groups, they grew alongside commercial firms and vice versa. This trend too, was not publicised widely until the early part of this century when GEM carried out a study showing an increase in social entrepreneurship among minorities, including (African) Caribbean operators with a market share of 6.9%. In all, the findings revealed several key trends within this minority business community (**Fig 16.1**).

Figure 16.1 Major Trends in the British Caribbean SME Sector

- 58% of men, 38% of women are founder-owners of commercial firms.
- 68% of males, 32% females own-manage social enterprises.

British Caribbean enterprise started in 1907, with the community's

- Contribution to Healthcare spanning 100 years;
- Cultural Industries are 80 years;
- Social Enterprises are 75 years;

- Education and Training & Travel and Shipping 40 years respectively;
- Food and Personal Care 35 years respectively;
- Construction Industry and Manufacturing trades 30 years respectively;
- Business and Professional Services 20 years; and
- Knowledge Economy or Computing 10 years.
- 11% of firms are commercial and 6.9% are social enterprises.
- British Caribbean firms contribute an estimated £5 billion to the UK economy.

(Source: Adapted from research findings, 2007)

There was significant growth potential in all sectors by at least 1%-2% per year. The cultural industries, construction, health and social care, social enterprise, travelling and shipping, as well as personal care are the oldest of all start-up sectors – from 1907 through to the 1960s. During the 1970s and 1990s, there was evidence of the growth and development of the food, business and professional services, computing, education and training and the manufacturing (vehicular) trades. The beginning of the 21st century showed a rise in youth entrepreneurship with under-30s setting up enterprises in the knowledge sector and the creative industries. Others ventured into personal development services, specialising in graduate recruitment, job skills training and business support, mostly for the young unemployed.

Why a Strategy?

For the purpose of this book, we define strategy as a process that involves careful, methodical and systematic planning for all aspects of a business organisation. It involves the skilful application of human, financial, technical and other resources to ensure that the organisation achieves its goals and objectives. Strategy is therefore different from tactics which relate to short or medium-term methods to achieve for example, an operational goal or aim. A strategy for British Caribbean firms is therefore critical and important for its value-added nature since such a strategy will benefit various stakeholders – public, private and other statutory sectors.

Recurring studies show that these firms operate in low-income markets and owners are therefore unable to grow viable firms. Yet the evidence in Chapters 5 to 15 illustrated that entrepreneurs are performing across industry sectors and segments, some of which were originally the preserve of white-dominated companies. Nearly a third or 30% of firms could be considered part of the UK's traditional SME sector since they have staff levels ranging from 50 to 100 plus. Another 50% of micro firms have almost 50 employees (full and part-time), a trend that is noticeable in healthcare, education and training, as well as social enterprises and other emerging sectors.

Given the practicalities of business performance in key industry sectors, it is prudent for government agencies and enterprise development agencies to obtain data by assessing firms, using the traditional case history framework; that is, recording the organisation and performance of firms, over a medium-term term period of 5 years, as a first step.

Moreover, this strategy will give fresh impetus to technical support from agencies responsible for delivering services to improve the production and productivity of firms. It will also give a clearer meaning to terms such as *`diversity'*, *`inclusion'*, *`level playing field'* and *`multiculturalism'*, often used by politicians, the media and policy experts. For those concerned with fair trading and sound economic practices, this strategy represents a unique opportunity to change the corporate landscape of Britain for good.

The importance of analysing the number of firms and quality of output to the UK economy is crucial to policy-making. Any evaluation should thus establish certain facts. Did additional regeneration funding cause the formation of more businesses and social enterprises? Did financial incentives cause firms to undertake additional investment in other markets? Did training courses in leadership and management cause companies to adopt new business practices? Did regulatory changes result in the improved performance among firms in a particular region or inner city area in the UK? These questions are vital because they can yield the desired results from any organisation and performance review that is carried out. Evaluation of minority firms is also intended to provide credible evidence to demonstrate whether government-sponsored initiatives are working or whether business development services are realistic in terms of a sector-based approach.

The Context

A definitive strategy will influence British Caribbean firms' integration into the global market. In its current form, equalities legislation cannot effectively remove or alter levels of discrimination and restrictive practices affecting minority businesses. Instead, a greater effort towards creating inclusiveness - encouraging greater participation among Caribbean people in all areas of national life - is an intelligent approach.

The introduction of a merit system rather than US-styled *Affirmative Action* is urgent since Britain's tradition of patronage, an unwritten constitution and a complex law-making process, all make this move difficult to be affirmed. With the best will in the world, it is virtually impossible for the British Establishment to legislate for changes in behaviours on the basis of race, colour, class or creed by society as a whole.

Millions of pounds are spent on capacity building but with limited impact on African and Caribbean enterprise performance in local economies in the UK. Studies have shown that these communities are often unable to access capacity building schemes, aimed at equipping them with the technical knowledge and skills to manage regeneration programmes **(Fig 16. 2).** In evaluating ESF funding, the Government Office for London said:

Black groups still appear to be slightly under-represented according to the evidence.

Project managers should be aware of recording ethnicity using the new breakdown to allow a full evaluation of programmes to impact on identified groups.

Currently, structural and cohesive funds represent over 30% of the EU's budget, and rules for the 2007-2013 round were expected to be finalised in 2007. These funds comprise only a small part of public spending, but their influence goes beyond size because they address inequalities and engage partnerships.

Figure 16. 2 Impact of ESF Funds on beneficiaries

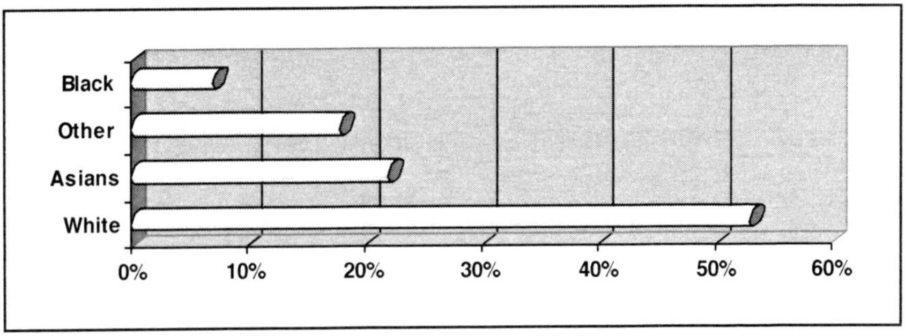

Source: Evaluation of the ESF London Bidding Rounds, Government Office for London, January 2001

Economic Dimension

Globalisation affects the operations of every firm and whilst large companies in construction, food, technology, and logistics, manufacturing, healthcare and business services dictate consumer choices, market share and above all, prices, the existence of regional trading organisations, is a formidable challenge for minority firms. Because of their make up, these trading blocs wield great influence on national (Governmental) policies. There are regional trading blocs in Africa, Asia, the Caribbean and Latin America, Europe, the Middle East and North America. Some have sub-divisions such as Africa which has about four, while South America has a few. Market strategies should therefore be informed and guided by these economic trends worldwide and owners should conduct a mapping of regional and international trends to secure market advantage (**Table 16. 1**).

Table 16. 1 Major Regional Trading Blocs in the World

(Source: CIA World Fact Book, IMF Database 2006)

Trading Blocs	Member States	Population
The Arab League – March 1945	Algeria, Bahrain Qatar, Comoros, Djibouti, Egypt, Iraq, Jordan, Kuwait, Lebanon, Libya, Mauritania, Morocco, Palestine, Saudi Arabia, Somalia, Sudan, Syria, Tunisia, Yemen, UAE	1,467,255, 669bn
Association of South East Asian Nations (ASEAN) – August 1967	Brunei Darussalam, Cambodia, Indonesia, Laos, Malaysia, Myanmar, the Philippines, Singapore, Thailand and Vietnam.	553, 900,000m
Caribbean Community (CARICOM) – August 1973	Anguilla, Antigua & Barbuda, Bahamas, Belize, British Virgin Islands, Cayman Islands, Cuba, Dominica, Grenada, Guyana, Jamaica, Haiti, Montserrat, St. Kitts-Nevis, St. Lucia, St. Vincent and the Grenadines, Suriname, Trinidad and Tobago, Turks & Caicos Islands.	14, 565,083m
European Community (EU) – March 1957	Belgium, Bulgaria, Cyprus, Czech Republic, Denmark, Estonia, Finland, France, Germany, Greece, Hungary, Ireland, Italy, Latvia, Luxembourg, Malta, Netherlands, Poland, Portugal, Romania, Slovakia, Slovenia, Spain, Sweden, United Kingdom.	496, 198,605m
The African Union (AU) – July 2002	Angola, Benin, Botswana, Burkina Faso, Burundi, Cameroon, Cape Verde, Central African Republic, Chad, Comoros, The Congo, Côte d'Ivoire, Djibouti, Egypt, Equatorial Guinea, Eritrea, Ethiopia, Gabon, Gambia, Ghana, Guinea-Bissau, Kenya, Lesotho, Liberia, Libya, Madagascar, Malawi, Mauritania, Mauritius, Mozambique, Namibia, Niger, Nigeria, Rwanda, Sahrawi, São Tomé and Principe, Senegal, Seychelles, Sierra Leone, Somalia, South Africa, Sudan, Swaziland, Tanzania, Togo, Uganda, Zambia, Zimbabwe	800,000,000m

North American Free Trade Agreement (NAFTA) - January 1994	Canada, Mexico, USA.	430, 495, 039m
South Asian Regional Community (SARC) – December 1985	Afghanistan, Bangladesh, Bhutan, India, Nepal, Pakistan, Sri Lanka	1,467,255,699bn
Union of South American Nations Unasur)– December 2004	Argentina, Bolivia, Brazil, Chile, Colombia, Ecuador, Guatemala, Guyana, Honduras, Nicaragua, Paraguay, Peru, Suriname, Uruguay, Venezuela.	379, 782, 748m

Notes: Population figures are rounded for uniformity. An African Common Market is due 2019. Unasur is the creation of South American states, including Guyana, an English-speaking Republic and a former British colony.

Sector Growth

As was stated in preceding chapters, the first sign of enterprise involving members of the British Caribbean community was 1907 when Trinidadian doctor, John Alcindor, established the first black medical practice in London. This was followed by various social enterprises including the **League of Coloured People**, the first black ballet company, **Les Balles Negres** and the **West Indian Standing Conference**. By the 1960s, Britain observed the growth of a new wave of business formation with the establishment of the hairdressing firm of Dyke & Dryden, followed by a succession of food shops, travel agencies and a host of other firms dotted around urban centres in England.

With case histories of firms in leading sectors and segments of business and industry since the early part of the 20th century, coupled with information pertaining to the rising levels of social entrepreneurship in the early part of this century, added to data from public sources, a gradual representation of the organisation and performance of British

Caribbean SMEs gradually unfolded. This depiction also revealed budding growth in the 11 sectors profiled in this book, from about 7% in 2001 to 11% in 2006, according to ONS figures (**Table 16. 2**). It further signified the importance of conducting definitive analyses on minority firms in both local and regional economies to obtain a robust account of their activities for the purpose of central economic policy.

Table 16. 2 Industry Sector Leaders and their Geographic Spread

Sector	Geography	Turnover (estimates)
Cultural Industries	UK-wide	£20,000 – £500,000
Construction	England, Scotland, Wales	£50,000 - £5m+
Personal Care	UK-wide	£20,000- £2m+
Manufacturing Trades	England mostly	£100,000 - £5m+
Food Market	UK-wide	£20,000-£5m+
Business & Professional Services	UK-wide	£50,000 -£5m+
Travel & Shipping	England mostly	£100,000- £3m+
Knowledge Economy	England, Scotland and Wales	£50,000 - £5m+
Education & Training	England mostly	£100,000 -£500,000
Health & Social Care	England mostly	£100,000 -£1m+
Social Enterprise	UK-wide	£20,000-£1m+

(Source: Independent Business Surveys, UK 1999 – 2007)

The above data represent sampled case studies, reviews and appraisal of business associations, coupled with one-to-one discussions with business owners participating in conferences, symposia, and seminar-workshops. Primary information was obtained from questionnaires that were piloted to owners who expressed an interest in being included in this book.

Significant Progress

Chartering the work of minority firms can be problematic if vital information is unattainable and data sources are at worst, unreliable. A strategy for British Caribbean firms therefore, should consider the value of a strong, quality-based information and data collection system to enable policy makers to make informed decisions on the operations of different segments of minority firms in the UK. The proper allocation of resources for inner-cities is best served, if not valued, when every effort is made to secure as much information and data as possible, to produce an efficient system in the way public revenue is spent particularly for enterprise support, regeneration and overall economic development programmes.

One of the unique features of British Caribbean companies is the quantum of activity that far outweighs their structural size and composition. For instance, some firms are considered small, but their core businesses comprise high-profiled events that resemble those of mini-corporations. This is quite noticeable in cases involving `charity arms' that complement core activities of firms and where social enterprise is recognised as a means of diversifying or adding `product layers' to existing commercial portfolios.

It is absolutely necessary that a sectoral model be applied for a better understanding of the contribution members of this section of British society are making to UK plc, according to the annual market value of the industry sectors below: -

- *Cultural Industries sector* is estimated at £112 billion;
- *Construction* is estimated at £107.01 billion;
- *Personal Care* is valued in the UK at £1 billion;
- *Manufacturing Trades* generate £15 billion per year;
- *Food* is worth £5 billion (ethnic foods alone);
- *Business and Professional Services* are largely segmented and

represent a multi-billion currency industry in the UK with financial services contributing £17 billion a year, management consultancy £6.94 billion, legal services £20 billion and remittances £5 billion and cleaning £10 billion;

- *Travel and Shipping sector* is worth £69.11 billion;
- The *Knowledge Economy* or computing is also a multi-billion currency area;
- *Health and Social Care* sector £20 billion or US$10 billion per year; and
- *Social Enterprise* is worth £27 billion to the UK economy (***ONS 2005-2007***).

The British Caribbean business community has made small, but important strides over the past years. As these firms expand, their founders and MDs will emerge as an insightful and powerful cadre of business and civic leaders in their own communities and the wider British society. Even though they don't always contribute to the shaping of national policy, their presence tends to influence local and regional priorities. Minority business leaders hold the key to the improvement of economic success because they serve as the bridge between the corporate world and minority groups. They usually inject a fresh perspective and new approaches into the overall business and enterprise sector. Their input to cultural, education and broader social welfare issues should not be underestimated or ignored either. They can link their communities with much-needed corporate resources: capital (financial, human and technical), markets, jobs and skills. By having access to the market share of minority firms, a better appreciation and understanding of the organisation and performance of British Caribbean commercial and social enterprises, can be possible (**Fig 16. 3**).

Figure 16. 3 Estimated market share of British Caribbean firms

(Source: ONS and independent research 2002-2007)

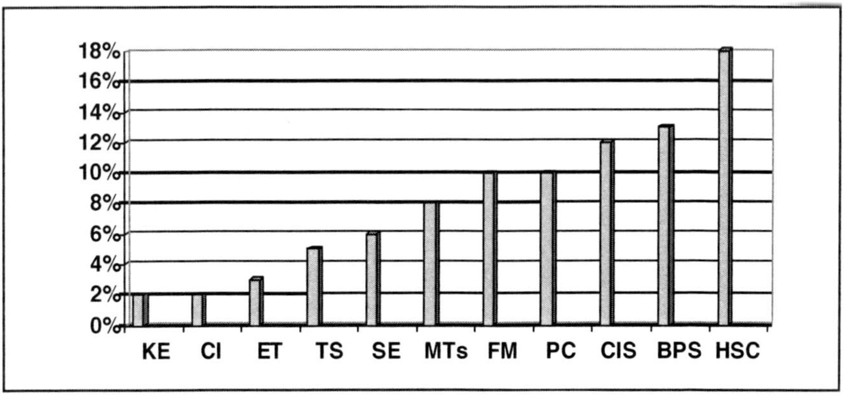

***Guide to Sectors**: KE- knowledge economy or computing 2%; CI- construction industry 2%; ET- education and training 3%; TS – travel and shipping 5%; SE- social enterprise 6.9%; MTs – manufacturing trades 8.5%; FM- food market 10%; PC – personal care 10%; CIS – cultural industries sector 12%; BPS – business and professional services 13% and HSC – health and social care 18%.*

The above estimates are actual data from the Office for National Statistics, coupled with conservative projections using sampled firms to test their market share during 2002 and 2007. For instance, the market share for travel and shipping, manufacturing trades, personal care, business and professional services, as well as health and social care, are consistent with data from the ONS and other independent sources such as business reviews and sector audits on trade associations, as well as individual entrepreneurs.

Strategy formulation

The impact of a comprehensive strategy for the British Caribbean SME sector is also premised on several key elements that are necessary to support a systematic plan for various industry sectors and segments such as those outlined in this book. These elements are: -

- Enterprise Support;
- Urban Regeneration;
- Cultural Sensitivity;
- Human Resource Management;
- The Learning Firm;
- Investment;
- Marketing;
- Research and Development;
- Legal; and
- Financial.

Enterprise Support

Enterprise support is a vital area that lends itself to the stability of firms in any society. The lack of it or its partial delivery can impede the orderly development of SMEs. Small firms that operate in highly competitive markets require sound advice, technical assistance and support. In instances where restrictive practices are the foremost challenge to owners, support is even more critical.

Currently, billions of pounds are spent on promoting the creation of business for a `strong enterprise economy' across all regions. A further objective is to ensure that all government departments and agencies can deliver better regulation for the private, public and third sectors. The new Department for Business, Enterprise and Regulatory Reform (BERR) has as one of its goals, to *`deliver free and fair markets, with great competition, for business, consumers and employees*' (**BERR 2007**). If the existing evidence is true, then previous economic reforms in enterprise support have not benefited minority firms in so far as improving levels of production and productivity as the 2007 Comprehensive Spending Review pledges (**Fig 16. 4**).

Figure 16.4 Additional funding for business and the promotion of enterprise

(Source: Creating Conditions for Economic Growth', BEER 2007, England)

- The 2007 Comprehensive Spending Review provides BERR with a total budget of £3.3 billion in 2008-2009, £3.2 billion in 2009-2010 and £3.2 billion in 2010-2011. BERR will deliver key priorities within a budget fixed in nominal terms on average over the 2007 period including: -
- Continued support for business and the promotion of enterprise, including the allocation of a total of three rounds of Enterprise Capital Funds at £50 million per year;
- An ambitious better regulation programme that reduces unnecessary regulatory burdens and works for everyone in the public, private and third sectors;
- Additional funding for the Nuclear Decommissioning Authority of £338 million by 2010-2011 to ensure the continued safe management of nuclear waste liabilities; and
- Funding from BERR/Defra Environmental Transformation Fund.

It is hoped that this new booster fund will benefit all sections of the SME sector in the UK including British Caribbean firms that are often excluded from major allocations of funding for technical assistance and enterprise support, as a large body of evidence has shown for many years. A consistent, reliable and genuine form of support can help business owners to achieve, among other things: -

- Strengthen organisation structure;
- Recruit quality staff;
- Develop sustainable marketing plans;
- Put in place quality control procedures and systems;
- Introduce standardised products and services;
- Boost export markets; and
- Create effective links with various industry sectors.

Urban Regeneration

A strategy for firms should consider this aspect of economic development. Urban renewal benefits communities typified as 'deprived' and 'excluded'. Social enterprises have a reputation for resolving inequalities affecting various communities. Some of these organisations are recipients of UK and EU capacity building funding 'streams'. These enterprises have the cultural sensitivity, the know-how and are usually well connected at grassroots level unlike statutory agencies and institutions.

The Campaign for the Protection of Rural England has said that regeneration needs to be recognised as a major industry in the UK alongside leisure and tourism. The charity estimates that over 500,000 people are employed in local economic projects, and it was forecasted at the beginning of this century, that employment in this sector would increase by 627,000 in 2006. Urban projects contribute about £12.5 billion to the UK economy or fewer than 3% of the GDP (**CPRE 1999**).

Capacity building is integral to urban regeneration and organisations such as WISC, BTEG, SYAC and local business associations are leading on schemes aimed at strengthening the capacity and performance of community groups added to different enterprises. Faith groups such as churches with an asset base often running into millions are also involved in the provision of moral, religious and spiritual support to whole communities.

If social enterprises are to be effective in the delivery of urban regeneration initiatives, they need institutional support to strengthen organisational capacity such as the retraining of staff – managerial, administrative and technical personnel altogether. However, for the process to have any meaningful impact, the following questions need to be answered; for example,

- What is the community sector?

- Why develop its capacities?
- What kind of problems exists?
- What help do social enterprises need?
- How can capacity building be used to help?
- What methods of intervention are required?

Motivating social enterprises in the Caribbean community is an initial step in reaching 'hard to access' groups, and according to a leading specialist on capacity building,

Capacity building is the business of equipping all actors to perform effectively both in doing their own thing in their own field and level of operations, and in working in collaboration or partnership with others operating in other fields and other levels. It is an essential component of both empowerment and enabling. Enabling is about ensuring that those who are empowered have the information, technology, skills and support to exercise their authority (power) responsibly. It is about roles: who should do what and in partnership with whom. Therefore it is about relationships and interfacing between the different fields and the different level of responsibility **(Wakely 2003**).

Cultural Sensitivity

Most settler communities, who came to the UK prior to the first half of the 20th century, have integrated relatively well. To their credit, it is their cultural strengths that have helped them cope with racial prejudice and institutional discrimination. Cultural sensitivity has proven effective in areas where public officials tend to ignore the values of minority communities in favour of pushing through reforms to achieve national targets – outcomes and outputs. Much of this is prevalent in inner-city areas where there is a high concentration of these particularly new migrants, unable to adjust to their new environment.

Cultural sensitivity is a strength and an asset for Caribbean people and it is one that informs and guides enterprise principles and practices as evidenced by the manner in which owners operate their firms. Micro traders in particular, use informal channels of communication such as word-of-mouth and referrals, as part of the marketing process. Generally, culture remains integral to the socialisation process of Caribbean people and other minorities in the UK.

Owners should conduct routine checks on the environment they operate, to keep informed about changes in customer's needs that might be dictated by cultural and social attitudes. Producing regular news bulletins to exchange best practice and publicise generally, the work of the firm, is another effective tactic. Encouraging employees to take part in community events is an excellent way of allowing them to gain fresh insights into the cultures/sub-cultures of the working environment. Visits to large companies to learn about new technologies, management techniques, corporate governance, along with partnerships, are important in terms of developing ideas on how to manage conflict, changes and other trends in the business world.

Another approach is that of strengthening market intelligence by ensuring that information-data collection procedures are watertight. This is a formidable challenge particularly for new start-ups or firms less than five years old operating in healthcare, training, business and professional services, and social enterprises. In a dynamic economy, owners cannot afford to ignore cultural sensitivity; they do so at their peril.

Human Resource Management

Human resource management or `HRM' is a process of recruitment, selection and placement of quality staff in managerial, administrative, technical and related positions in the firm. It also includes staff appraisal in punctuality, courtesy, customer relations, absenteeism or lateness and overall job performance. The quality of workforce can determine the perceived image consumers and the wider public have of organisations. Apart from professional competence, other qualities such as commitment, dedication and loyalty are vital too. Respect for authority is a continuous problem for firms recruiting staff in today's labour market.

In addition, discriminating against employees is both unethical and illegal. Hiring someone without a skill because he or she is a close friend is inappropriate. Since competition among firms is part of the economic process, British Caribbean firms have to gear their operations to deal with this marketing challenge. New regulations involving wages and working conditions such as the EU Working Directive and others like it also require careful consideration. If an owner/manager pays an employee less than he or she deserves simply because the employee is in a difficult position, this action might be deemed unethical (**Fig 16.5**).

Figure 16.5 Managerial relationships involving ethical responsibilities

(Source: Adapted from Griffin, Ricky W: Management, 6th edn, Houghton Mifflin Co., 1999 USA, p106)

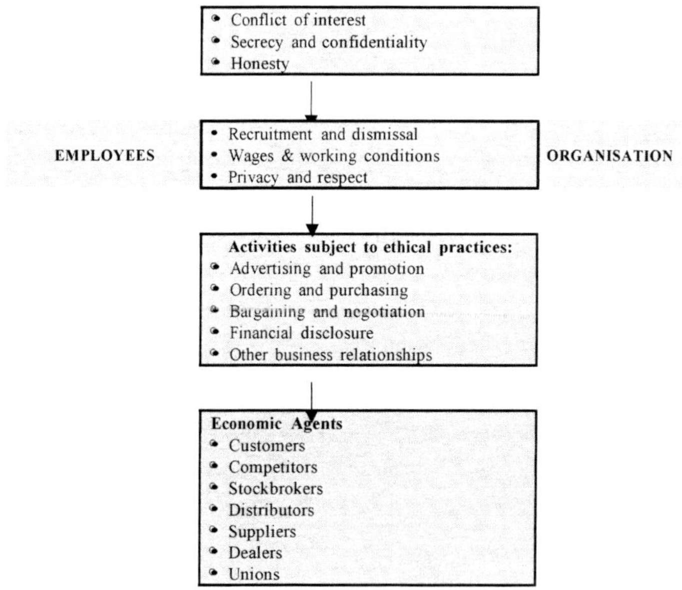

As **Figure 16. 5** illustrates, the standards of behaviour set by owners can enable staff to improve their performance. There is also a flip side to this however – employees have a duty and responsibility to honour contracts with their employers. If there are conflicts of interest involving secrecy, confidentiality and honesty, these will not be beneficial to the broader interests of both employers and staff since this may have damaging consequences to the reputation of the firm. The above figure highlights areas of concern that owner-managers and staff need to consider, along with the impact economic forces have on the firm's position in the marketplace. A strategy for British Caribbean firms should therefore analyse these relationships to ensure that management functions are carried out according to sound ethical principles and practices. In effect, the implementation of an effective HRM strategy will help firms resolve conflicts such as:

- Problems with staff;
- Various economic trends;
- Changes in the trading environment;
- Consumer spending patterns;
- Limited market share; and
- Lack of scientific and technological innovation.

Owners should also seek expert advice and guidance on strategic issues affecting their operations. Apart from annual profits, it is the image of firms that is equally important. Maintaining excellent relations with different stakeholders in a range of corporate sectors is indeed the crux of real business success.

The Learning Firm

The idea of the learning firm relates to the processes management put in place for continued growth, development and sustainability. These processes include enhancing the knowledge and technical competence of staff at all levels and implementing relevant procedures to achieve market advantage.

The success of the learning firm is dependent on an owner's commitment to change in sectors where consumer markets are constantly changing such as in the IT, travel and shipping, education, manufacturing, as well as business and the professional services sector. Proper market intelligence is the most effective means of avoiding problems that firms have when dealing with competition. Not only does competition affect new products and services, but also new technology, highly skilled personnel, financially endowed companies and reputable distribution supply chains, along with market intermediaries such as brokers.

The British Caribbean learning firm should therefore take into account all aspects of the value chain in relation to the strategic and operational nature of the business. A learning firm is capable of achieving the following: -

- A proper system of market intelligence;
- Constant upgrade of staff training;
- Regular review of systems and procedures; and
- Accreditation from recognised industry bodies (**Table 16. 3**).

The process of education and skills training is essential to the learning firm and this is particularly relevant to service companies delivering public sector contracts. They are expected to have regulatory procedures such as effective monitoring controls and other forms of accountability. As a private institution, TCS Tutorial College is committed to delivering quality education services to young and adult learners. Its motto, `*I Am Somebody Great*' captures the excellence model it is renowned for in parts of London, as well as its organisational culture, as a learning firm.

Table 16. 3 TCS' elements of a Learning Organisation

Procedures	Mechanism
Recruitment	Libraries, referrals, school, social events to attract clients.
Personal Plan	Assess ability levels to ensure program suitability
Induction	Enabling clients to fit into new surroundings.
Exams	Tests/routine assessments of learning goals and future aims.
Achievement Events	Incentives for students, teachers, community leaders, others.

Civic Functions	Community support for learners, families, staff and others.
Evaluation	Learning aims and objectives and overall programme success.

(Source: Evaluation of TCS Tutorial College learner's assessment procedures, London 2007)

The TCS *'community participatory'* model is designed to resolve problems associated with educational underachievement affecting many Caribbean children, especially boys in England. The institution has perfected the learner assessment principle, which integrates the cultural and social background of clients from diverse backgrounds. This enables a correct evaluation to be made when measuring aptitude levels of both young and adult learners. A personal action plan is then drawn up to form part of the overall assessment process and is monitored regularly. Learners are involved in work trials and take part in community events, to help build self-esteem and confidence, so that they can contribute to community kinship.

Investment

Although scarcely acknowledged, immigrant companies have helped shape the economic power of the UK over a century. Often described as 'outsiders', these firms are dedicated to investing labour, financial and technical resources to secure material benefits whilst providing lasting benefits for whole communities.

In researching sections of the Caribbean community, we found that almost 100% of owners expressed confidence in doing business in the UK, a fact that is evidenced by the thousands of firms operating for many years throughout the British Isles. Mainstream agencies and institutions should invest in these firms for these principal reasons: -

- There is limited paperwork involved;
- Innovation exists in products and services;
- Cultural sensitivity in dealing with customers;
- Companies are well-connected with communities;

- Firms have established bases;
- Owners are socially responsible;
- Founder/owners are dedicated to the elimination of social inequality; and
- Businesses are flexible –management can adapt to changes.

Judging by the number of locations British Caribbean firms are based, there is a case to be made for a viable investment strategy in the creative industries, business and professional services, food, healthcare and social enterprises, all of which can add value to existing public services and complement the activities of mainstream companies interested in expanding into minority communities.

As mentioned earlier, these firms comprise 11% share of the market, with a market value estimated at £5 billion per annum. Mainstream investors therefore cannot ignore this fact in their efforts to target potential growth sectors in the Caribbean SME sector in Britain.

Regarding expectations of high profitability, construction, manufacturing trades, food, the knowledge economy, health and social care, and business and professional services, have tremendous potential for sustainable growth, thereby allowing for greater profit retention. Market entry is an important element of investment strategy and business owners have established firms according to the following: -

- Previous experience with public/private institutions;
- New product idea;
- Joint venture concept; and
- Through an agent and distribution agency.

Marketing

British Caribbean firms tend to use informal channels to advertise and promote new products and services. In recent years however, there has been a growing realisation that formal channels of marketing are equally vital to gain greater recognition and public acceptance. A marketing strategy should contain segments in terms of brand name, new product types, quality services, advertising and promotional media, distribution networks and market share portfolio of various segments.

The food sector which consists of retail sales and manufacturing has its own product lifecycle and is considered relatively short in Caribbean communities, and yet operations need to maintain high market shares in order to compete effectively. In other sectors, owners have improved standards in the range of products and services because they recognise that quality and reliability are twin essentials for a reputable image.

Understanding the dynamics of financial, product and consumer markets is essential to marketing and can determine whether or not firms are capable of competing in areas where there are high entry barriers; namely in science, technology and large-scale manufacturing. Although their operations might be limited to food production and business and professional services, some Caribbean companies have bucked the trend by accessing lucrative (sellers) markets. **Grace Kennedy, Wray & Nephew, Cleone Foods, Focus Consultancy, Cole Consulting, Dalgety Teas, Universal Service Solutions** and other multi-million pound firms in construction and engineering have accessed mainstream markets, once the preserve of large companies.

Analysing market forces including their impact on products and services is key towards a better understanding of globalisation. A policy for British Caribbean businesses should recognise the necessity for an export-based skills programme for management and technical personnel particularly. Owners should invest in technical and vocational courses to complement traditional academic programmes. In the absence of a coherent policy, some owners have applied innovation by combining cultural traditions with the marketing mix (price, place, product and promotion) to optimise trading opportunities. Blue Mountain Coffee Limited, MPS Travel and Shipping are among firms pursuing this approach, resulting in job creation and limitless opportunities for wealth creation in deprived neighbourhoods **(Fig 16. 6)**.

Figure 16.6 Competitive influences impacting on British Caribbean Firms

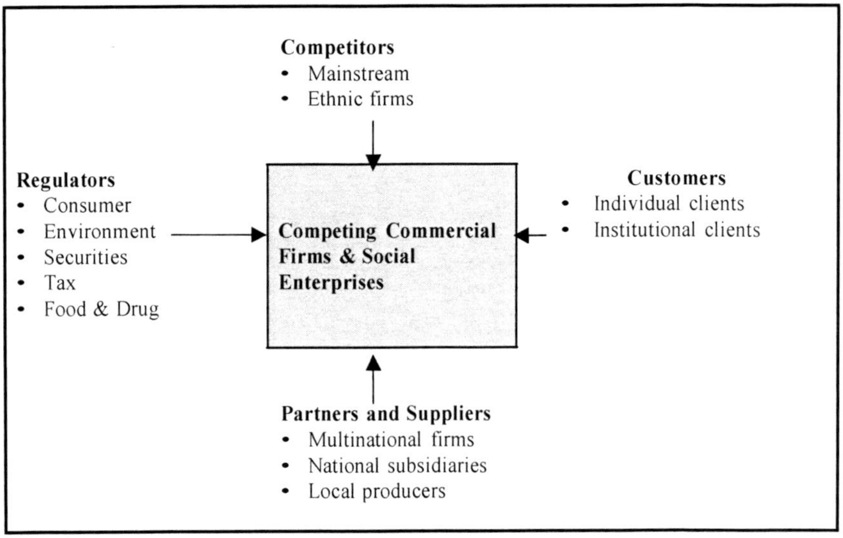

(Source: Adapted from surveys of Caribbean firms 1999-2006, UK)

According to the above figure, there are multiple factors affecting the performance of firms. Owners should consider carefully each market influence since it determines the extent to which companies can either gain successful market entry or develop innovative products and services to satisfy customer demands in existing markets.

Research and Development

In order to be successful in the UK and global markets in general, it is vital for British Caribbean firms to have a local base for R&D facilities. In Chapter 4, we stressed that one of the challenges facing minority firms is market competition and with the constant influx of new products and services, owners have to adapt their processes to suit national and international market requirements.

One way of showing commitment to consumers particularly in the manufacturing and services sector, is to develop tailor-made services in collaboration with large, established companies, with a strong research and development component. This is possible in key sectors such as food, production, multi-media technology products and semi-processing industries.

Perhaps the best example of British Caribbean firms' efficient use of R&D, is in the food sector where owners are propelled by market forces to add value to products and services via presentation, style, affordability, taste and related cultural attractions. Other methods include intensive advertising and promotion campaigns consisting of taster sessions, pre-purchase samples of new products and routinely evaluating product launches by competitors. Information on these is obtained from the industry press or visits to restaurants and high-profile luncheons to product-test new recipes and menus.

British Caribbean businesses have the potential for increasing market share in a range of consumer products, but they require substantial investment and knowledge capital to gain entry into industrial, manufacturing and other technologically based industries. Specialist training for young people in science and technology must be intensified to prepare a new generation of technicians to establish companies, thereby boosting levels of representation among minorities in the field of science and technology in the UK.

By establishing R&D, firms can participate in markets where new technologies and know-how are constantly developing. For firms to be successful in European and other international markets, owners have to become part of a wider research network or prepared to work with relevant institutions such as laboratories, universities, manufacturers and other such organisations. With only about 4% of all British

Caribbean firms in the manufacturing sector, the potential exists for a new cohort of entrepreneurs to be blooded for the manufacturing and related production sectors. The advantages of pursuing an R&D strategy are many and they include: -

lowering costs for new products;

- shorter delivery time;
- increase use in meeting quality and specific product requirements;
- quicker pre- and after sales service;
- creation of commitment to customers;
- overall boost to profitability; and
- greater advantage in dealing with industry competition.

Failure to put in place efficient R&D systems could result in several disadvantages such as:

- a negative effect on competition;
- problems in achieving satisfactory profit margins;
- inability to develop well-known brands;
- inferior marketing capabilities;
- poorly qualified and talented personnel; and
- lack of total commitment to penetrating national-international markets.

And yet, the unsung national achievements of food companies such as **Gramma's, Cleone Foods** and **Dalgety Teas** all attest to owners' desire to continuously improve the quality of products and services to enhance profitability, increase market share and maintain a sound reputation in the food trade (**Minicase 16. 1**).

Minicase 16. 1 Dalgety Herbal Teas Ltd

A leading London publication described British-Guyanese, Mark Dalgety, as the `*Master Tea Blender*'. His tea company, **Dalgety Herbal Teas Ltd**, is the only black-owned company in the UK with in-house manufacturing facility capable of producing three million teabags per day. It has a customer base in excess of 3,000 independent retailers along with major supermarket chains such as Sainsbury's and Tescos. World export markets include the Caribbean, North America, Europe, the Middle East and China.

A chemical engineer by profession, Dalgety was forced to use his credit card to set up his tea business because his bank refused a loan. `*I did approach my bank but they thought it would be ludicrous for a Caribbean man to sell tea to the English, who are considered as the connoisseurs of tea.*' The firm has grown from strength to strength, with Dalgety claiming 1,000% growth. The company produces a range of herbal teas and recently, two new varieties were launched - `Instant Ginger Tea and Caribbean Classic, a fusion of leaves blended from the Caribbean and Kenya.

The teas grown in the Caribbean Region and elsewhere are shipped to the UK for processing. The finished product is chemical-free. Dalgety is constantly looking to identify products that could excel in niche markets. His firm competes on (100%) quality and claims its teas are superior to other brands on the market. The pricing strategy is tailored for average customers. Apart from the R&D strengths of Dalegty Teas, the company has a proud record of paying farmers well for their produce. According to Dalgety, `*farmers are properly compensated for their farm produce and in return, we receive superior tea for less than we had to pay tea syndicates*' (***Knowledge Fountain Magazine 2007***).

Legal

A strategy that frequently assesses laws and various regulations in the UK, Europe and elsewhere, is also important to owners' quest for proactive management. Businesses are constantly faced with legal barriers such as government licence, charter or patent. Manufacturers especially, have to pay attention to new trademarks and other international standard requirements for new products,

Experts claim that e-commerce can offer opportunities to reduce cost and build better relationship with customers. Many owners are still reluctant to fully engage in electronic transactions. Among the most popular reasons are uncertainties around fraud, unaware of the relevant e-commerce legislation. Access to simple and practical information on the main legal and regulatory aspects of e-commerce is therefore crucial in order to remove existing barriers.

Large companies involved in drug manufacturing are in a position to protect their products from competition by use of patents. Other legal barriers relate to environmental and safety standards particularly when new organisations enter some industry markets. Regarding climate change and other environmental hazards, firms should review their procedures and systems to confirm with current legislation (**Brooks, Weatherston & Wilkinson 2004**).

Business owners should make sure that they acquaint themselves with regulations and general laws governing their specific industry sector. Whilst this may incur costs, it is better for firms to take the necessary precaution than to be subjected to financial penalties that could leave owners bankrupt.

Financial

This is a major issue for SMEs including British Caribbean firms since the early 20th century when settlers began setting up enterprise organisations. Since that time, thousands of entrepreneurs have relied on personal savings, credit cards and `borrowings' from relatives and friends for start-ups. Even with fairly detailed business plans, they are refused loans and other forms of financial capital. With few exceptions, enterprise agencies have been found wanting too, with advisers' perception of business ideas as either 'too ambitious' or `unrealistic', responses which owners describe as `naked prejudice' rather than a genuine desire for agencies to be supportive.

Waldinger, Aldrich and Ward (**1990**) acknowledged that bankers have well-developed `stereotypes of success of Asian business and lack of success among Caribbean firms'. These firms depend on business and advice agencies to assist in processing applications for loan finance. While information on the number of British Caribbean firms that have benefited from start-up capital vis-à-vis those who haven't, remains patchy, independent research confirms that more than half of all new African and Caribbean firms experience similar problems.

Financial capital is the lifeblood of new firms that require materials and equipment to set up proper offices or factory sites. Then there is the expenditure for the recruitment of relevant staff and the payment of professional fees, accounting and legal costs, and more. Budgeting for business start-ups is tricky since owners have to balance between income and expenditure, bearing in mind that they are likely to be managing loss-making operations for at least the first six to eight months, depending on the laws of supply and demand in various consumer markets. Yet, with a sound, but flexible business plan and a bit of luck, owners can make significant progress in the introductory phase of the business than they can ever imagine.

Most firms tend to have standard accounting practices; that is, income and expenditure, including fixed and removable assets, along with information showing a reasonable balance or deficit. Companies with more than 10 employees produce in-depth accounts, detailing information on salaries, fixed assets and their value, contracts or sale agreements, as well as items subjected to depreciation such as computers and other office equipment that may lose capital value after a year. This information is critical since it can be used to measure the performance or the gearing ratio of firms. A balance sheet therefore can indicate the following:

- The profitability of firms;
- Staff profile including their professional competence;
- The level of accountability and systems within firms;
- Volume of marketing via advertising and promotion;

- Assets versus liabilities and their impact on firms' resources;
- The market share portfolio of firms;
- The overall image and reputation of firms; and
- The general case history of firms.

As a general rule, the greater the current assets compared to the current liabilities, the safer the firm should be. However, the more powerful the company the less relevant these ratios are. Large firms such as supermarkets and Internet giants will not have to repay short-term liabilities quickly; they will have the power to say `no'. Small firms on the other hand, will not have this power and so, for them, these ratios might be a matter of life or death (**Fig 16.7**).

Figure 16.7 Example of calculating the gearing ratio of a firm

(Source: adapted from information and data analysis contained in this book)

$$\text{(Gearing) Ratio} = \frac{\text{Current assets}}{\text{Current liabilities}}$$

The ratio gives a measure of the short-term safety of the firm and the current assets are those that could be turned into cash in a short period of time, while current liabilities are those which might have to be repaid at short notice, thereby putting a drain on the limited resources of the company. The key to maintaining reduced liabilities is to conduct a regular evaluation of each unit of the firm to determine its overall `gearing' position. Real estate companies and other such service firms experience cash-flow problems often and the view of a seasoned property dealer is worth reflecting on, in this situation: -

Updating and regularising your firm's accounts, helps business owners to have accurate information and data on the volume, type and level of sales accrued over a period. This process can also help management to analyse customer trends for example, as well as market trends in your sector. With proper accounts management can allocate the necessary resources and target them efficiently **(James 2003).**

Capital Fund

Whilst the national budgetary allocation for enterprise promotion and technical assistance is likely to increase considerably over the next five years, history has shown that minority firms hardly benefit from this public resource. In an effort to implement an efficient financial strategy for British Caribbean businesses, the establishment of a special capital fund, complementing existing resources, is urgent. The idea of a bank to serve black firms was floated in the 1980s, and so was the formation of the UK Caribbean Chamber of Commerce – its aim was to advocate and represent broad-based concerns of minority firms in the UK (Chapter 15). These initiatives failed because of personality conflicts and unforeseen circumstances.

Indeed, the level of funding allocated to regional business associations is inadequate and it can't achieve the maximum results, perceived or expected by public agencies, in their usually wide economic regeneration remit. Lean budgets of approximately £100,000- £300,000 or there about, per annum cannot develop fully, the organisational capacity of tens of thousands of minority firms in the 12 UK Regions, which have diverse needs since they operate in highly segmented industries. Neither can this level of resources monitor effectively, the organisation and performance of firms on an annual basis. A capital development fund for the British Caribbean SME sector and other minority firms will do the following: -

- Contribute greatly to inward investment schemes in the UK;
- Create opportunities for new products and services;
- Entry into new markets by owners;
- Participation in employment schemes aimed at the young unemployed;
- Improved incentives for staff training; and

- Enhance technology capacity through R& D.

Though this might be a bit tricky to accomplish, a share option scheme (SOS) is another financial strategy that could be introduced by more established and reputable Caribbean firms such as food and drink companies, business and professional services that access public sector contracts, as well as manufacturing firms producing innovative products for the benefit of diverse communities. The SOS initiative will challenge the relationship between firms and customers. It will test the confidence, trust and the ability of both parties in supporting each other's aspirations - one that is commercial (the seller) and the other value for money (the buyer). It is another way of encouraging, empowering and stimulating sections of the (hesitant) Caribbean community to invest in business ventures, in a very big way.

In addition, this initiative will challenge the competence and professionalism of founder-owners because they will be entering new territory, which so far, has remained the preserve of white middle-class company bosses. British Caribbean business owners will have to devise relevant company prospectuses, investment documents, to attract potential shareholders. The following information should be included as well: -

- The type and nature of company;
- Ownership of properties, materials and equipment;
- Staff salaries, pensions and other incentives;
- Details of directors, management and administration;
- Corporate governance of the organisation;
- Risk factors;
- Shares proposed including their categories;
- Current trading position and prospects;
- Business strategy;
- Relationship with Government and other public institutions;
- Operating and financial review documents;
- Financial information in general; and

- Other related information for public consumption.

The benefits of the SOS scheme are undoubtedly advantageous. Companies will be in a better position to grow much quicker. Opportunities for expansion will be much greater. Companies will be able to strengthen their procedures and systems including market intelligence. With quality investors, firms can access multi-sector markets thereby increasing their market share and cutting liability to a bare minimum.

Organisation-Performance Framework

In this section, an introduction to the organisation and performance framework for the British Caribbean SME sector which is essentially, the major theme of this book, will be examined. We will outline the elements to be incorporated to make this framework viable and recognised as an important strand of economic policy, regionally and nationally. Since the historic 1971 Bolton Report on small firms was published, there have been numerous reviews and enquiries on problems and issues affecting SMEs in the UK.

In addition, in the early 1980s when there was civil unrest in English inner cities because of unemployment, deprivation and exclusion affecting sections of the black community, other studies were done on minority firms within the context of immigration, race and discrimination. Very little evidence has been produced to show firstly, where key firm sectors are located and secondly, the segments they represent in the 12 UK Regions.

Moreover, studies have shown little contrasting features between firms operating in London, the Southeast and other parts of England and Wales. Very little has been published until recently, on the contribution social enterprises make to the economy. Again too, a bit of statistics exist in this respect, with little by way of case studies. The reason given is that social enterprise is a relatively new area of study even though this segment of the economy has evolved since the early part of the 20th century in Britain, Europe and the US.

To enhance understanding it is advisable to examine the elements that resemble this framework closely. The model that will be illustrated brings together many elements of commercial and social enterprise activities that have their origins in 1907. The suggested organisation and performance model is therefore predicated on the following:

- Objectives of Framework
- Why Organisation?
- Performance Route
- The Process

Objectives of Framework

Setting out the aims and objectives makes the framework easier to understand and appreciate in the context of various sectors and segments British Caribbean firms operate within. The main objectives of the framework are:

- To measure the composition, size, profits, survival, growth, competitiveness, as well as image and corporate responsibility;
- To test the various measurements of economic performance through the performance of sampled companies operating in various sectors and segments; and
- To draw conclusions on relations between mainstream institutions, business performance and economic welfare.

Why Organisation?

The organisation of firms is of particular interest to society since consumers especially, can make informed choices as to the type of firms they ought to engage with in terms of products and services. If the information is unavailable, it is difficult for them to make the right choices. While company advertisements may help with public image, large companies receive unfettered media coverage, and it is therefore fair that minority firms receive similar recognition.

On a broader level, policy-makers can make credible assessments on resource allocation in regions where there is evidence of underperforming firms or those at risk of closure. The organisation of firms includes existing management and staffing levels, organisation structure and the relationship with industry alliances, consumers, public institutions and other agencies involved in the distribution and supply chain process.

Evaluating the organisation of SMEs is critical to understanding their case histories according to a sector-segment axis, whilst being able to diagnose problems more effectively. The desire to stereotype or create `myths' about firms on the basis of ethnicity and or/diversity, becomes less of an issue since this method helps to raise the profile of minorities regarding their contribution to the UK in general.

Performance Route

The performance of minority firms is critical to overall planning especially since in almost every region, pockets of businesses receive little or no technical support from public agencies. An independent survey demonstrated that more than 50% of all minority firms had no access to mainstream support in Britain during 2005-2006. instead, owners relied on advice and technical assistance from independent accountants, solicitors, family and friends. British Caribbean businesses have an estimated market share of 11% per annum and only half of all owners in London, the Midlands and the Northwest of England, had some type of statutory support to enhance growth and expansion (**Fig 16. 9**).

Figure 16. 9 Percentage of Caribbean firms accessing enterprise support

(Source: Independent study of Enterprise Support Agencies, England and Wales 2006)

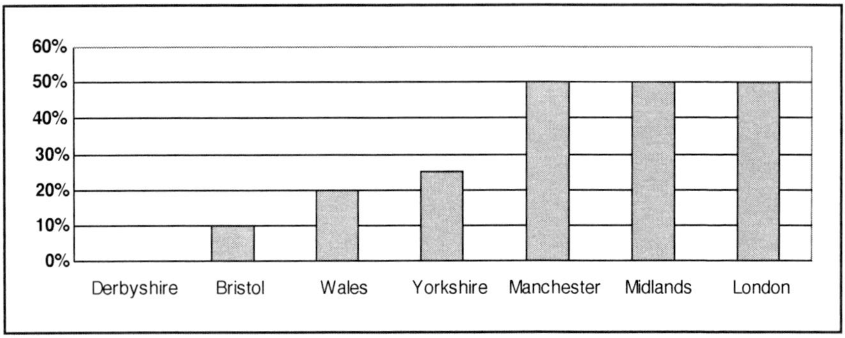

The Small Business Service has been conducting surveys of SMEs over the past years, but information is often limited to the number of firms, selected sectors excluding growth in industry segments and their potential. Other statistics comprise estimated turnover and other basic data. The surveys are unable to determine for instance, the number of firms in each of the 12 UK Regions and with the absence of performance ratios in relation to industry sector markets, purchasing power of consumers and other indicators, it is difficult to understand the real impact these firms have on the UK economy.

In addition, there are no case studies to support the evidence presented and the annual exercise appears to be a simplified version of number-crunching rather than a rigorous attempt to examine and analyse the organisation and performance of minority firms on a sector-by-sector basis. The surveys exclude the estimated value of each minority firm by ethnicity too. This information is essential because it enables public institutions in particular, to have a balanced picture on the state of minority firms at any given time. Moreover, it helps to facilitate medium and long-term planning, thereby preventing politicians making uninformed disclosures, or worst, making empty promises.

The Process

The time is right for intensifying the evaluation of SMEs in the UK since Britain has slipped from fourth to nearly the 12th position in the Organisation for Economic Co-operation and Development (OECD) countries. To regain its competitive advantage, greater emphasis must be placed on monitoring the key players of wealth-creation including African and Caribbean firms and social enterprises. All three political Parties have said little about the importance of evaluating the organisation and performance of minority firms which comprise a substantial portion of the GDP, let alone employment, new technology and innovation, along with stability and the prosperity they have brought to once blighted neighbourhoods.

The rich blend of youth and experience that characterise the ownership of minority firms in the UK, is a major cause for celebration, more so the organisation and performance of these concerns. This framework will serve as a barometer to determine fairness, equality and tolerance, values that are glorified by political leaders as British in every regard. The importance of assessing the organisation and performance of minority firms can't be discounted from the equation of diversity. The process of implementation should be done this way instead: -

- Every Region should be encouraged to develop a comprehensive database of firms operating in wards and districts by (carefully defined) ethnicity;
- There should be a national sector-based approach to evaluate minority firms to obtain information that may appear problematic;
- The use of community expertise is also important – the training of lay researchers is a useful way of supplementing untrained or non-existent professional staff;
- Co-ordinating research activities with central governments, universities and other documentation centres is critical to this; and
- Annual evaluations and study sessions with sections of the minority community are also appropriate means to obtain and test results (**Table 16. 4**).

Table 16. 4 Excellence Model of British Caribbean firms

Performance Indicator	Impact
Ownership and location	Establishes type of ownership and where firm is based.
Strategy	Describes the growth and development process of firm.
Structure	Organisational composition and layers of firm's authority.
Management and staff	Information on number and levels of staff determined.
Employee development	Assesses frequency, type of training offered to all staff.
Market share	Share of the major product or service locally/ nationally.
Partnership arrangement	Existence of special agreements with major companies.
Mergers and acquisitions	Plans for joint ventures or buying into other firms.
Investments	Value and proportion of direct investment taking place.
Research & development	Volume and type of R&D and duration of investment.
Lobbying	Management representation in business associations.

Source: Adapted from research findings of Caribbean firms, 2000-2007, UK

By linking the history of the firm into a set of performance indicators, this approach provides a specific input for the business history of the firm, whilst highlighting the various elements that comprise the organisation and performance of the firm as a whole. The above sector-based framework will determine the competitiveness of the British Caribbean SME sector in a global UK economy and also address in principle, some of the major issues around market competition, corporate responsibility and social inequalities.

Yet, an informed guide towards understanding the British Caribbean SME sector is also possible if practical measures are taken to assess start-ups and existing firms; namely, commercial, industrial and social enterprises. The sector-based approach is a useful option to apply. Measures used should be qualified as well as quantified. By using this method of intervention, policy makers and others responsible for business and enterprise development can monitor the organisation and performance of minority firms more effectively since information and data will be more accessible. The suggestion is for the following measurements to be considered as part of an integrated model for analysing the performance of minority firms in total:

- Number of business start-ups by sector and region;
- Type of industry sector/segment;
- Number of small to medium-sized firms;
- Number of social enterprises;
- Jobs created per industry sector/segment;
- Turnover of businesses per year;
- Volume of loans to business owners including women;
- Volume of financial support for young entrepreneurs;
- Types of business support and duration;
- Number of premises-facilities acquired by owners;
- Number of businesses offered contracts/tenders;
- Number of customers purchasing products/services;
- Number of under-performing firms;
- Number of 'at risk' firms assisted;
- Number of firms with growth potential;
- Number of industry sectors/segments with growth potential; and
- Number of firms assisted with competition challenges.

Improving Competitiveness

A definitive strategy for the British Caribbean SME sector is designed to strengthen the organisational structure of firms, improve competitiveness, enable owners to access markets, increase market share and enhance profitability in various industry sectors. The strategy is all-embracing; that is, it covers public, private and civic bodies that are involved in diverse policy initiatives around political engagement, economic empowerment, social equality, financial inclusion, cultural synergy and community cohesion.

Firstly, such a strategy will enable Central Government to frame appropriate legislation and procedures to ensure that firms are properly analysed to take into account their organisational composition and levels of production and productivity.

Secondly, a strategy will enable public bodies such as the Regional Development Agencies, Local Authorities and allied statutory bodies, to better understand and appreciate the contribution of minority firms including social enterprises, as well as their overall impact on inner-city local economies especially as they relate to regeneration schemes.

Thirdly, a strategy will facilitate positive action on the part of policy-making institutions such as Universities and research centres of excellence and independent think-tanks, since they will have access to factual information and reliable data on the organisation and performance of the minority firm sector in the UK.

The strategy will further reinforce the importance of including British Caribbean-owned firms and other minority enterprises in key policy initiatives such as economic affairs, education, social development, healthcare, science and technology, as well as manufacturing.

Fourthly, a definitive strategy will help business owners to be equipped with requisite skills, experiences and techniques to evaluate their organisational structure and (growth) performance in order to keep pace with trends in the micro and macro environment, thereby improving their competitiveness.

Generally, it is hoped that a strategy for the British Caribbean SME sector will have multiple benefits by impacting on activities of key stakeholders operating at different operational and strategic levels of the UK society (**Table 16. 5**).

Table 16. 5 Impact of British Caribbean Business Strategy in the UK

Stakeholders	Impact
Central Government	Effective policy and planning based on the ability of the authorities to analyse complex sets of information from businesses and social enterprises in the UK Regions.
Public Bodies	Appropriate intervention with regard to economic regeneration, contract compliance and overall understanding of the needs of different industry sectors and segments.
Policy-Makers	Availability of reliable information and accurate data to facilitate the implementation of local and national policy priorities and measures.
Business Owners	Improve overall strategy planning and development processes of firms according to their respective sectors and segments.

(Source: Adapted from the Rummler & Brache Improving Performance model, USA 1995)

The above table illustrates that a strategy is not one-dimensional, but it encompasses various interest groups with Central Government acting as the main stakeholder, by facilitating multiple partnerships with a view to ensure that there is effective co-ordination between and among public agencies policy-makers, commercial firms and social enterprises or third sector organisations in the British Isles.

Product Lifecycle

There was small but significant growth spurts in British Caribbean commercial firms and social enterprises in key sectors and segments over the past 10 or so years. Ideally, market growth in industries occurs where product innovation is a dominant element of the process marketing chain. Geographic differences accounted for the dispersal of firms in the nine English Regions and parts of Scotland and Wales respectively.

The study of the British Caribbean firm sector showed that whilst 1907 was the first phase of real business activity with the establishment of a private medical practice in London by Dr. John Alcindor, business formation rates among Caribbean settlers grew substantially in the 1980s through to the 1990s. During this period, there was relative growth in half of all sectors with manufacturing trades, food retailing, personal care, business and professional services, education and training, healthcare, construction and social enterprises, evolving.

Business owners should be aware of the lifecycle that their products face because competitive conditions can be very different at each phase of this process. Figure shows the different stages in the product lifecycle of the Caribbean SME sector, each with its own characteristics based on entry points in terms of sector development **(Fig 16.10)**.

Like most other small firms, British Caribbean businesses operate in industries where there are fixed and variable costs, but members of this community also experience the most acute form of institutional prejudice, apart from routine market pressures. These situations have therefore given rise to variations in the overall product lifecycle of this business community during the last century (1907-2007), unlike other minority firms.

Figure 16.10 The product lifecycle of British Caribbean SMEs

(Source: Adapted from International Business Environment, Pearson Education, p69

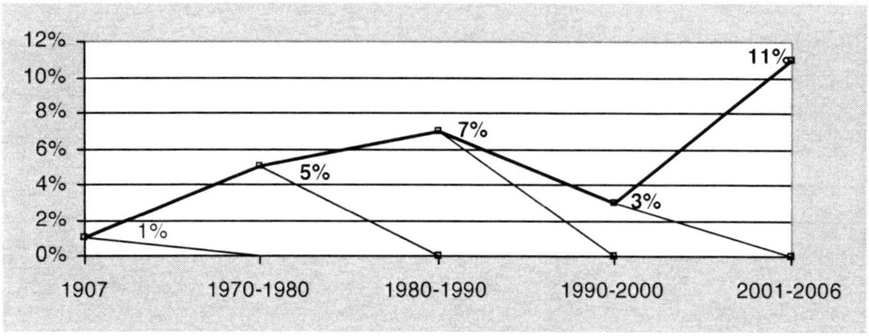

Figure 16.10 explains the periodic lifecycle of the Caribbean SME sector over the past century. This trend reflects combined political, economic and social pressures owners, managers and staff are subjected to in their attempt to maintain viable enterprises in a country that they consider `home' and a place to earn a decent livelihood. The following lifecycle periods highlighted the circumstances that led these firms to experience variations in their overall market share performance: -

- *Introduction* – in 1907 few firms were established with limited market entry due to racial prejudice and the fact that Caribbean settlers were relatively new to the UK economic environment.
- *Growth* – during the 1970s and 1980s, there was evidence of growth by about 5% representing more than half of all business activity over the period. There was a great desire to operate companies and manage social enterprises as the recession of the 1980s created enormous opportunities to fill the gaps left vacant by tens of thousands of industries that collapsed throughout England.
- *Maturity*- between 1980-1990, British Caribbean firms showed maturity levels in terms of productivity, with market share increasing from 4% to 7% as owners competed for high stakes in mainstream markets using the mechanism of pricing, product

quality and cultural knowledge to gain entry into food, healthcare, businesses and professional services and other emerging sectors. This period was marked by flexible and innovative services offered by professionals acting in some instances as independent consultants or through a partnership arrangement with private and public sector agencies.

- *Decline* – the 2000-2004 periods saw glimpses of decline within the British Caribbean SME sector especially in the food, semi-processing, textiles design, and information technology sectors. The decline was apparent in much of the late 1990s and the beginning of the 21st century as new brands in clothing, computer software and the supermarket monopoly took hold. About 3% of firms couldn't cope because of limited financial capacity and a narrow market base – restricted to low-income minority communities.
- *Recovery* – 2004 to 2007 witnessed a remarkable improvement in British Caribbean SMEs market share from 7% in 2001 to 11% in 2006-2007. This trend was due to the development of firms in health and social care, personal care and social enterprises that were established by a young group of entrepreneurs between the ages of 25-35 and in some other instances, younger (**See Chapter 15**).

Diversity Firms

Minority-owned businesses operate in a variety of industries, but they tend to concentrate in low-income to middle-income growth sectors. These market variables illustrate the necessity for statutory agencies to act decisively to help owners take aggressive entrepreneurial actions that will propel them into high-growth sectors. Specifically however, 11% of all British Caribbean-owned businesses, compared to other minority-owned businesses, participate in 11 categories of traditional and non-traditional sectors, with supported segments:

- Cultural Industries
- Construction Industry

- Personal Care
- Manufacturing Trades
- Food
- Business and Professional Services
- Travel and Shipping
- Knowledge Economy
- Education and Training
- Health and Social Care
- Social Enterprise

The level of representation and under-representation of this SME sector varies. For instance, firms are fairly well represented in the food, health and social care, social enterprise, cultural industries, personal care business and professional services respectively. In construction, manufacturing, travel and shipping, knowledge economy, education and training, there are degrees of under-representation in terms of segments.

Furthermore, it is quite common for business owners to go for '*cross-over*' sector-markets; that is, maximise opportunities in other industries to improve profitability and increase market share. It is also another effective way of building on broad-based industry experience for ultimate growth and expansion (**Table 16. 6**).

Table 16.6 Diversity of the British Caribbean SME Sector

Industry sectors	Key segments
Cultural Industries	advertising, carnival arts, broadcasting media, music, performing arts, publishing.
Construction	architecture, general building, electrical, engineering, independent consultants and allied builders.
Personal Care	hairdressing, barbering, fashion design, clothes manufacturing, alternative therapy, consultancy.
Manufacturing Trades	food production, inventions, cultural products, technical designs, auto trades.

Food Market	restaurants, groceries, take-aways, manufacturing, catering, retailing.
Business and Professional Services	legal, financial, consultancy, cleaning, market research, advertising, training, events management and more.
Travel and Shipping	airline travel, cargo shipping, tourism, remittances.
Knowledge Economy	general computing, business information systems, e-commerce, IT training and other segments.
Education and Training	supplementary schools, independent schools, training firms, independent consultants, nurseries.
Health and Social Care	private medical practice, children's homes, respite care for the elderly, childminders, adoption and fostering, training units.
Social Enterprise	social organisations, community centres, enterprise centres, professional networks, business associations, youth enterprises, housing associations, credit unions, social care, training organisations, faith organisations.

(Source: Independent evaluation of firms 2000-2007, UK)

Targeted approach

The growth and sustenance of British Caribbean firms is possible when a greater effort is made by owners to develop more efficiency systems to deal with high overheads and low-income markets. Growth is driven by information technology, innovative products and services, as well as support from staff. Owners should be careful to differentiate between operational management and strategic management. Operating the business on a daily basis is different to formulating long-term strategy for the firm. Positioning firms in potential growth markets can help secure substantial revenue to grow the business. Owners have to therefore tailor their products and services to meet these new challenges. Of course, customer care should be top priority as well.

Conversely, minority-owned industries require constant support from public agencies and investment by large mainstream companies.

The classic example might be the new Business Link Brokerage identifying a group of `corporate stars' among British Caribbean firms in about three to six English Regions and evaluating their market performance through a series of procurement sessions with large companies, using a sector-based model. After a few sessions, mainstream companies can take on these firms and product-test owners with contracts between £100,000 and £250,000. An enterprise service mentor should be appointed to assess and evaluate investment-market risks and so forth.

Experience shows that when minority-firms confine investment to traditional segments or the ones they are good at (despite low profit margins); it is often difficult for owners to position their firms for higher-growth opportunities. The more financially-endowed and more connected British Caribbean-owned firms are however targeting niche markets where few if any minority-owned companies are involved and or competing in industries where significant growth opportunities exist. Classic examples are **Universal Service Solutions** (cleaning and facilities management), **Nichols Employment Agency Ltd** (recruitment and healthcare), **TCS Tutorial College** (education), **Platinum** (training and capacity building), **Maurice Sedwell Ltd** (clothing) and the **EAM Building Group** (construction).

In addition, the success of minority firms in national and international markets depends on the quality, consistency, reliability and range of scope provided by multiple agencies and institutions, funded by government and public agencies. Targeted strategies for business success should be delivered by local and regional organisations. There are hundreds of support agencies in the UK set up to provide technical assistance and enterprise support to SMEs in rural and urban areas, including communities experiencing deprivation and exclusion.

However owners lament the poor quality of support including lack of cultural sensitivity and incompetence by some advisers, especially in dealing with start-ups. I instigated a three-year (2001-2004) economic programme for over 50 micro and small firms that never accessed technical assistance and enterprise support even though they were established for some time; that is, over 30 years. The level of satisfaction by owners was evidenced by the following results: -

- 53% said they were able to `set proper' goals for their firms.
- 45% said they are `focusing on objectives-setting'.
- 32% said they have been able to `motivate staff' greatly.
- 32% claimed that they could `anticipate client needs' better.
- 23% could `use new technology' applications to improve market intelligence.
- 23% have learnt `new ways of conducting business' (**Brent Council: TCS 2005**).

Funding remains an issue for new firms with little capital to set up operations. Existing firms need substantial funds to develop either a new product or service, and/or expand in lucrative markets. Either way, British Caribbean-owned firms seem to suffer the most even when they have fairly sound business plans. There are numerous sources of funding that could be accessed and though information is much easier to come by than 20 years ago, quite often, owners are frustrated by the time spent looking for appropriate finance and the number of intermediate agencies to be contacted for the desired results **(Table 16.7).**

Table 16.7 Profile of major funding streams for SMEs

Type of source	Features
Own resource	Personal savings or redundancy payments –funding the business from personal savings can offer owners greater chances of success.
Banks	Overdrafts – a source of short-term finance normally for working capital; loans – long-term finance for purchasing capital equipment.
Small Firms Loan Guarantee	Assists businesses in raising commercial finance from other approved lenders when an applicant lacks assets as security for a loan.

Small Business Finance	A source of loans for small businesses in different cities and regions through the UK, especially that offering business-to-business service.
Reinvestment Trusts	Independent loan providers, capital comes from private/public sources.
The Prince's Trust	National organisation operating with area offices, the Trust has helped young people successfully to set up in business.
Business Angels	UK's specialist in raising funds for early stage business opportunities seeking an initial investment of under half a million pounds.
Early Growth Fund	Exist in some English Regions (different names), a venture capital co-investment fund financed by Government and RDAs, capital to assist early stage firms and it matches risk capital by businesses angels or private sector investors on the same terms.
Other Funding Sources	Hundreds of schemes and programmes to help social firms particularly; include the Big Lottery, Heritage Lottery Fund, Awards for All and a range of funding regimes such as European/UK funds. Information on types of funding can be found on the Internet or from local enterprises agencies, Council One-Stop shops or other business agencies.

(Source: Small Business Guide, 2007/8, England & Wales)

Growth Projections

In this section we shall examine the prospects for growth in the British Caribbean SME sector according to the information and data obtained from official and independent sources, all in an effort to justify the necessity for an organisational and performance model for this vital section of the UK economy. By evaluating numerous studies on minority-owned business and in the process, conducting practical reviews of large segments of minority firms in the UK, there is every reason to suggest that British Caribbean-owned firms will demonstrate future growth.

The available evidence is reassuring and it is reasonable to assume that firms will experience small, but significant growth spurts over the next five to 10 years. Judging by the partial decline in the late 1990s to the resurgence in 2004 from 7% to 11% market share in 2007, there is every indication that advances will be made in the product lifecycle of firms. This growth will be linked directly to changes in contract tendering procedures, enterprise support, economic trends, consumer spending patterns and other expected chain of events such as the effects of energy prices.

This situation will help galvanise the competitive spirit of Caribbean people in areas where there strengths are the greatest, and where investment opportunities exist, particularly if strategic alliances are possible and workable. The prospects for growth are further reinforced by recent studies showing that Caribbean people are among the most entrepreneurial in the UK, with more than a third likely to set up a business within two to five years' time.

Other studies point to the growing interest in student-youth entrepreneurship among third-generation minorities aged 20-29 and in some instances younger, as they continue to be `enterprise standard-bearers' similar to first and second-generation migrants. If these and other trends are anything to go by, then the overall picture for the British Caribbean population is not bleak, as perceived by critics (**Fig 16. 11**).

Figure 16.11 Projected growth of British Caribbean-owned firms

(Source: Independent analysis based on sources using data contained in the 1991 and 2001 Census)

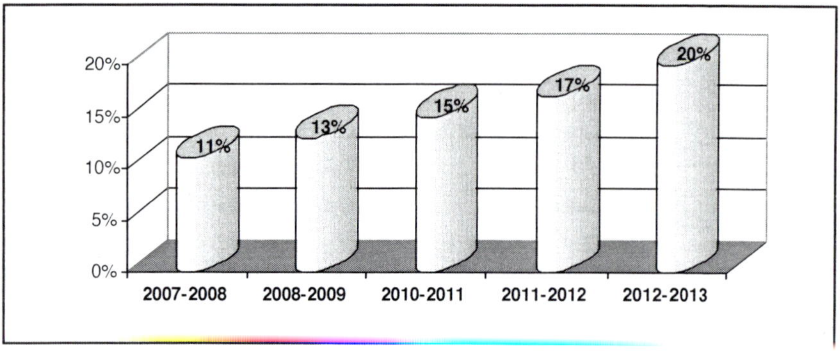

The above projection is in line with similar growth patterns since 1979 through to 2004 when the market share of firms rose from 2%-3%, 5%-7% and from 7% to 11% despite lack of enterprise support from mainstream agencies. The market will reflect current trends experienced by firms. For example, 30% of owners researched for this book, showed interest in medium to long-term strategy planning. This means that 1 in every 30 firms is likely to have a 5-10 year strategy which will undoubtedly impact on sales and profits.

More than a tenth of all owners have projected minimum, but stable growth, leading to gradual expansion. Some like Aimex International are examining different options for revenue generation from other income streams based on equal projected sales income. The market share of 2%-5% is significant since this will impact on the UK economy in terms of additional jobs, wealth creation, new skills and knowledge and greater market segmentation in urban and suburban areas (**Minicase 16. 2**).

Sustainability

Noteworthy, an organisation-performance model is also necessary because of the extraordinary lifespan of British Caribbean SMEs; that is, the overwhelming number of industries that are sustainable over a generation. Apart from the newest of them, the knowledge or computing sector (10 years), others have been around between 20 and 100 years old, making the total British Caribbean-owned business enterprise sector in the UK, nearly five centuries or 465 years old.

Significantly, the leader of the `pack', is healthcare which is 100 years old, followed by cultural industries 80 years; social enterprises 75 years; education and training, along with travelling and shipping 40 years respectively; food and personal care 35 years accordingly, coupled with business and professional services 20 years (**Fig 16.12**). Such factual evidence demonstrates that despite the lack of industry acknowledgement and national recognition, business owners have continued pursuing commercial and social enterprise activities, thereby illustrating the real meaning of diversity in terms of ethnicity and economic development in the UK

Figure 16.12 Longevity of the British Caribbean SME Sector

(Source: Independent analysis of firms based on start-up periods)

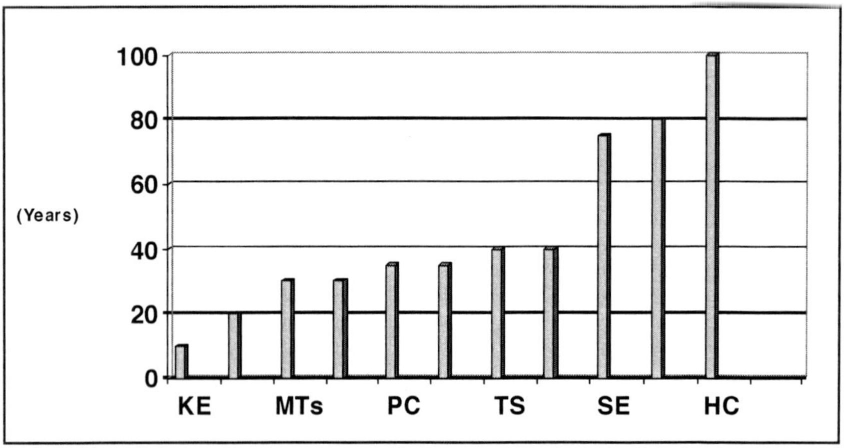

Sector guide: *KE – knowledge economy; BPS – business and professional services; MTs- manufacturing trades; CI- construction industry; PC –personal care; FM – food market; TS – travel & shipping; ET- education & training; SE- social enterprise; CIS – cultural industries sector and HC –healthcare.*

Case Study 16.2 Aimex International

Patrick Frederick is Chief Executive of Aimex **International** which he established in 1996 to provide corporate funding and technical advisory & business support services for Small & Medium Sized Enterprises (SMEs) and International clients. It focuses on organisational structures and performance processes using a sector- based approach, along with a value-added principle that ensures that enterprises remain sustainable. The company operates within the Commonwealth and other parts of the world.

Prior to setting up the firm, Frederick worked with two major international companies, holding senior positions in engineering and corporate finance respectively for over 21 years. Later, he established a financial management consultancy to provide business and investment advice to high net worth individuals and SME clients. He is currently establishing a new company to directly fund projects and support businesses in developed and developing countries worldwide.

As a highly qualified and experienced business executive, with a Bachelor's Degree in Mechanical Engineering (Middlesex University) and an MBA from Cass Business School in the City of London, the Dominican-born didn't experience the usual problems associated with minority start-ups, but instead overcame setbacks by developing a track record of client trust and confidence in product and service delivery. He asserted that *"In essence, I consider my unique selling point as myself because people relate to people. I guarantee customers high quality delivery, at an agreeable and affordable price with an exemplary after-care service. Technical competence and Customer care is essential to the services sector and if you can provide 100% customer satisfaction, your reputation will remain intact and your business will continue to grow"* (***Frederick 2007).***

His leadership skills and entrepreneurial business acumen are widely respected and these have led to current appointments including a Board Executive Committee member of the MENA-OECD Enterprise Financing Network for the Middle East and North Africa, resulting in him sitting on the Advisory Council of the Bahrain MENA Investment Centre. He participates actively and leads on various enterprise initiatives with African and Commonwealth states, and is also a member of the British All-Party Parliamentary Group on Entrepreneurship. Fredericks' leadership is also evidenced by his political interests as Chair of the UK Conservative Party Business Relations for South East England and former Director of Business Affairs for the Boris Johnson Conservative Campaign for Mayor of London in 2008. He has also been a member of the Mayor's Forensic Audit Panel which reviewed the financial and operational effectiveness of the Greater London Authority and the London Development Agency.

Previous appointments have included inaugural Chair of the African Caribbean Business Network in 2001, memberships of the London Corporate & National SME Councils for the Confederation of British Industry and Private Investment & Creative Industries Commissions for the London Development Agency.

Fredericks' excellent contribution and leadership in promoting SMEs globally earned him the *International Non-Governmental Organisation World Bank Group* and *IMF African Society Achievement Award* for 2007 from Washington D.C.

His long term plan for Aimex International is to position the company worldwide with the goal of delivering improved relationships and SME services between states, donor institutions and the enterprise marketplace including the World Bank, United Nations and throughout the Commonwealth. He firmly believes that the firm is capable of successfully working and competing with international organisations, whilst succeeding in helping economies grow through increased enterprise activity.

The Caribbean-born entrepreneur is currently discussing with influential African and Commonwealth organisations areas of economic development and technical co-operation, encompassing the private sector for both corporate and enterprise along with the requisite global multilateral agencies.

Perhaps even more interesting, is the fact that the Caribbean contribution to healthcare began prior to the inauguration of the 1940s-NHS, not forgetting that members of the community also pioneered innovations in enterprise culture as early as the 1930s. Later, the country was to further witness the evolution of minorities' contribution to early 20th century culture with musical recordings involving African and Caribbean artists and the establishment of the first black ballet company, Les Balles Negres.

Other noticeable trends were the setting up of social enterprises by Caribbean people in the 1930s with the League of Coloured People, founded by Dr Harold Moody; the advent of the Supplementary School Movement and the beginning of the non-white travel and shipping industry in the 1960s.

Challenges and Prospects

From available evidence of national and regional initiatives and forecasts on government's spending priorities, current investment is likely to be in strategic sectors of the UK economy. It is expected that there will be a deliberate attempt to engage minority firms in

London, the Southeast, the Midland and Northern Counties, as well as Scotland and Wales respectively.

Moreover, national priorities and programmes will determine the effectiveness of businesses and their impact on the economy such as those relating to regeneration or urban renewal, healthcare, culture, sports and leisure, business services and social enterprise among other areas. These initiatives will help create opportunities for minority firms to invest in (market) growth and expansion. The existing procurement policy will be tested for its fairness and equality as it seeks to offer British Caribbean-owned firms a `level playing field'.

Challenges

In all of this, there are operational as well as strategic challenges owners will have to face; they are: -

- Working continuously to ensure that premises are environmentally friendly;
- Maintaining a professional atmosphere in the workplace;
- Developing effective customer care charters;
- Routine reviews of quality control procedures;
- Ongoing testing of products and services for market approval;
- Developing sound information-market intelligence systems to monitor trends;
- Strengthening links in the industry through membership of trade bodies;
- Organising regular staff development programmes;
- Advertising and promoting the firm using various media channels;
- Inculcating effective leadership, management practices to deal with industry changes;
- Developing flexible approaches to transact business with large companies; and
- Preparing the firm for export opportunities in overseas markets.

Equally, there are challenges for mainstream companies interested in growth and expansion strategies within national and overseas markets. Shedding inherent prejudices and media-influenced stereotypes of minorities particularly African and Caribbean entrepreneurs, will be the initial test. Their ability to assess and deal with minority firms on merit will also be a challenging prospect such as: -

- Trusting and confiding relationships with business owners;
- Demonstrating cultural sensitivity in transactions;
- Valuing enterprise diversity as positive not negative;
- Pre-test minority markets prior to dealing with minority-owned firms;
- Supporting minority sectors with potential and lucrative, growth prospects;
- Creating investment opportunities in `interested' minority communities;
- Appointing senior managers to facilitate access to British Caribbean-owned firms; and
- Set up flexible, but industry-type mentoring schemes for minority owners.

Opportunities

There are exciting prospects for large companies and minority firms to develop strategic alliances without losing face or affecting each other's profit margins. The growth in various industry sectors is an encouraging sign for business owners in the UK. It means that mainstream companies can engage in cross-industry partnerships with minority firms that have similar operational processes, whilst sharing Best Practice with minority enterprises in general.

However, trust, honesty and fairness in information-sharing and product knowledge among other business practices, are essential qualities that management of both mainstream and British Caribbean firms should inculcate if are to become mutual beneficiaries of their firms' resources of time such as labour, finance and technical expertise. Above all, understanding the importance of British Caribbean entrepreneurship to the SME sector means that there are fundamental issues that need consideration including: -

- Impact of legislation on business development since the 1970s.
- Economic importance of minority business development to UK businesses.
- Level of annual growth of minority firms versus population growth in the UK.
- Effects of public procurement on minority firm's production and productivity.
- Level of corporate investment in minority firms and annual growth patterns.
- Annual revenue of minority firms and the percentage of jobs generated.
- Qualitative and quantitative comparisons with British Caribbean-owned firms and the total UK business community.
- Volume of selected regional programmes for disadvantaged businesses so that a clearer explanation of current British Caribbean and other minority business activity could be presented.

It seems therefore that the major industries in which the British Caribbean SME sector can make considerable progress are healthcare, business services, construction, financial services, information technology, education and training, as well as travel and shipping. These sectors are crucial because of their (growth) forecasts ranging from 5% to nearly 20% altogether.

Growth is hinged on a combination of high capital investment, product and service diversification, scientific and technological innovations, improved quality assurance systems, market expansion overall, joint ventures, market expansion, cost effective leadership and greater segmentation to maximise opportunities in global markets. The benefits for business owners will be tremendous, since their firms can collaborate with national and international industry players to build market share and increase profit margins (**Table 16. 8**).

Table 16. 8 Industry sectors beneficial to British Caribbean business growth

Industry	Challenges	Benefits for businesses
Healthcare	Growth rate in excess of 10% - dominated by primary care, clinical excellence, palliative, hospice care. Conditions are difficult for small operators.	Links with local/regional bodies to maximise older people and children services - culturally sensitive provision.
Business Services	Moderate growth; specialisation becoming more important; larger companies involved in global positioning –local/ regional services are vital for new clients.	Position firms for growth via links with companies with similar services, unable to gain entry into minority markets.
Construction	Solid growth, job prospects to rise by 22%, repair maintenance output projected up to 46% of total construction output. Customers are looking for smaller contractors to demand prompt, reliable services.	General construction and project management firms can maximise opportunities in construction, education, health and social housing projects.
Financial services	Growth in banking, insurance, fund management/securities, excellent market share. Regulations from UK/EU adding to increasing costs.	Develop solid brokerage relations with banks, building societies and other institutions to access clients excluded from needed provision.
IT	Increased growth forecast of 17%. Heavy demands on Internet capabilities; demand for security systems to detect and prevent fraud.	Negotiate with companies to outsource IT solutions; introduce freight invoices and supply-chain management solutions for firms.
Education and Training	Investment to rise by nearly 40% by 2015, method of procurement to deliver value for money – only some minority firms are involved.	Joint ventures with education-training agencies to enhance curriculum strategy; build learning centres for student population.

Travel & Shipping	Set to rise by more than 5%, expenditure on holidays abroad 41% by 2010. Large companies have a monopoly.	Specialised services for consumers including festival tourism for national/overseas clients.

(Source: Textual analysis and evaluation of industry sectors 2005-2007, UK)

A New Agenda

An organisation and performance framework was recommended as an evaluative tool to monitor the annual contribution firms make to the UK economy. The formation of a business council will enable this process to be a lot smoother and effective. The success of this venture depends however, on the will and commitment of owners, along with their ability to mobilise the necessary resources to make this project a long lasting goal.

The idea of an institution rather than a community-type organisation with limited authority or influence is both puzzling and interesting. Firstly, there is no single organisation that adequately represents the hopes and aspirations of the Caribbean community, more so commercial firms and social enterprises, which comprise part of the lifeblood of the UK economy. Secondly, there has been a constant (national) clamour for minority communities to be more actively involved in the decision-making process of Britain.

In Chapter 1, reference was made to the formation of a national business council to implement a business and economic agenda for the nearly 15,000 businesses and 3,000 social enterprises altogether. Since there are various business associations and related community groups involved in social activities, with very few influencing policy making in a big way, it is opportune for a business council to be part of the solution to facilitate business growth and market expansion, rather than experience symptoms of underperformance or potential risk of closure.

Rationale

There are numerous reasons for the establishment of a business council to represent British Caribbean businesses. Some of these are historic; others have their origin in culture, whilst others relate to a sense of both independence and inter-dependence; that is advancing an economic agenda that is premised on individual initiative and collective achievement.

Epochal events such as slavery, indentureship, persistent struggle against racial prejudice and discrimination have affected Caribbean communities for over a century in the UK and these attitudes are dramatised in various political, economic and social value systems in Britain. It is absolutely necessary for a British Caribbean business strategy that is located within a formal institutional context.

Constant reference to the achievements of African-Americans and British Indian/Asians poses a dilemma for Caribbean people who find difficulty being accepted and acknowledged for their contribution to British society. They also have to prove that they can excel in several disciplines and of course, sustain commercial ventures, once they begin.

Undoubtedly, this pattern of proof-showing has a delibitating effect on owners who have the potential to succeed in a big way. The emergence of the *African Renaissance* is also a comforting thought for Caribbean people who perceive the struggles of continental Africa and its diasporic communities as a wider struggle for *Black Economic Liberation.*

A national business council must be policy-oriented, authoritative in range and scope, reflecting the widest possible representation for African and Caribbean businesses and social enterprises generally. It must have a clear mission and value statement, with defined aims and objectives. It must be a `stirring' advocate for reform, acting as a conduit between firms, the government and the rest of civic society. It must be a viable arbiter on issues affecting members and be proactive on business and economic affairs in Britain and elsewhere.

Policy Strands

Features such as collaboration, unity, plurality, sector modelling, harmony and tolerance and integration should form the core values of the organisation from its inception. The council should partner with like-minded organisations, with membership drawn from entrepreneurs and professionals. A sector-based model for research and development is vital and links should be made with international bodies including regional trading blocs, educational institutions, industry associations and others. A plan of action defining routes to finance, trade and general economic engagement, is also important in pursuing a global strategy for British Caribbean firms. These links will help firms to improve brand image and product development similar to other businesses worldwide.

In addition, the council should incorporate a business strategy that embodies a broader agenda with suggested strands being:

- Education and Training;
- Cultural Industries;
- Business and Professional Services
- Manufacturing;
- Healthcare;
- Science and Technology; and
- Social Enterprises.

By including these as part of a broader strategy, firms will be better placed to supply high quality goods and services at competitive prices. This in turn, will boost their image and reputation as authentic producers of wealth rather than marginal *'units of production'* operating in *'ethnic enclaves'* in the UK economy as a whole.

Conclusion

This book focused on the organisation and performance of British Caribbean firms in key sectors and segments in the UK over a century. The aim was to highlight the challenges and successes of owners of commercial firms and social enterprises combined (**Table 16. 8**). In all, 16 Chapters were included, detailing the organisation and performance of industry sectors and segments. Several issues such as leadership and management, marketing, product development, service expectations, the role of public institutions and quality control among other others, were discussed.

Observation studies were also conducted in almost every sector and segment profiled. Information and data collected were cross-referenced with the Office for National Statistics and Regional Intelligence Observatories (on-line population Census libraries). In the absence of relevant data, we conducted sample-sized or mini surveys to determine the organisational capacity, as well as the performance dynamics of British Caribbean firms in the 12 UK Regions. Much of the information on minority firms are located in hidden datasets; that is, data located or buried within a statistical time series to be used for `selected' official purposes. This situation created much difficulty in accessing consistent information and reliable data to support claims for example, of underperforming firms in certain sectors.

Due to the complexity of the subject and the issues therein, it was decided not to write a (traditional) narrative account on the Caribbean community since much of this could be found in various studies on cultural, social and related issues involving diverse communities across the UK since the 1960s. The recognition that minority communities are contributing to economic advancement in the UK over two generations, means that it is prudent to critique the organisation and performance of British Caribbean SMEs using a sector excellence model (SEM). Therefore this book has a dual historic and modern enterprise framework, drawing from culture, economics, ethnography, geography, history, industrial relations, management, sociology, politics and other disciplines.

By drawing on these disciplines, relevant facts and figures were included, to serve as an informed guide to the contribution of critique the organisation and performance of British Caribbean SMEs using a sector excellence model (SEM).

Caribbean firms to the UK economy. Yet, unlike other literature on minority communities in the UK, the phrase '*British Caribbean*' was deliberately appropriated to give recognition to the locational presence of Caribbean business owners and secondly, to illustrate the fact that they were born in both the Caribbean (about 40%) and in Britain (60%). This created a twin-heritage implication since existing terminology confined Caribbean people in the UK to '*African Caribbean*', ignoring the truth about the effects slavery, indentureship and colonisation had (and still have to some extent) on the ethnographic composition of Caribbean peoples. Descendants of polyethnicity – those of African, Chinese, Portuguese, Indian and other mixed heritage - find it difficult to relate to this form of historic misrepresentation by Western historians, in particular.

Conversely, the term '*settler*' was also prescribed since historically, there has been persistent use of the phrase '*immigrant*' to describe non-European minorities who migrate to the Western metropolis. As one example, traditional literature described Europeans as '*settlers*' in the '*New World*' (the pre-independent period of the West Indies). Caribbean people who migrated to Britain should therefore be accorded equal status-rights, since like other progressive nationalities, they have staked their claim, and in the process, made a significant contribution to the political, economic and social lifeblood of the UK.

Reference was also made to the responsibility of government and other decision-makers in their role as bridge-builders of minority communities, in order to create a climate of confidence and greater trust. Making effective use of the procurement system was regarded as a positive way of ensuring British Caribbean firms can access lucrative contracts. Business owners' responsibility to be informed on issues to do with corporate governance was also looked at. There was focus too, on key sectors where survival was dependent on having proper systems and procedures in place. Notable examples were construction, healthcare, technology, education and training and manufacturing.

However like most works, this book has drawbacks, as information pertaining to British Caribbean firms was problematic due to insufficient data and profiling of firms. There is no proper sector representation of minority firms in the whole of the UK. In short, official records are piecemeal, with little or no monitoring carried out on business founder/ owners who have dual heritage such as African, Chinese, Indian and other mixed ethnicities. Identifying these intricate layers of ethnicity is crucial because it provides a clear explanation for the recurring difficulties researchers face in reconciling information and data across racial boundaries in areas as diverse as politics, economics, business, welfare, regeneration, gender and so forth.

In addition, there is no official data on British Caribbean firms and their contribution to the UK economy (based on a regional segmentation model). Policies on these firms are almost non-existent although the LDA has included a black business policy as part of its overall agenda for the capital. Yet much of the research on minority firms has an unfocused approach to the organisation and performance of non-European businesses, let alone their impact on urban renewal. There is also increasing exclusion of this sector in local regeneration schemes in areas where a high concentration of minorities or where the demographics reflect the potential of enterprise among young Caribbean professionals.

On the business side, some owners were undecided about providing information on their firms' revenue and annual turnover, and sought assurances that this information would remain confidential. Over the past 30 years, business owners in both the (British) African and Caribbean community, rightly or wrongly, have perceived mainstream providers to be using them as information fodder or *`subjects'* for *`box-ticking'* exercises; that is, to achieve Government-stipulated BME annual targets. Owners contended that while they were not indifferent to policy initiatives, they nevertheless questioned the validity of enterprise support schemes which did little to help either business growth or boost market opportunities in their respective sectors.

Some were concerned about the use to which information would be put and whether their disclosures might expose them to security risks. Surprisingly however, the majority of businesses were happy to participate and offered information willingly and frankly to ensure that this book was a success. Many went to great lengths to ensure that case studies mirrored their firms' image and personal experiences in developing coping strategies to deal with competition and commercial institutions that failed to offer start-up (investment) capital, as well as funds for expansion.

At the Labour Party Conference held in September 2007, the British Prime Minister emphasised that his Administration was keen to utilise the talents of every person in Britain and he explained what he meant by this affirmation:

So this is the next chapter in our progress. The next stage of our country's long journey to build a strong and fair society. I want a Britain where there is no longer any ceiling on where your talents and hardwork can take you. Where what counts is not where you come from and who you know, but what you aspire to and have it in yourself to become. Past generations unlocked just some of the talents of some of the people. In the new Britain of this generation, we must unlock all the talents of all of the people. Not the old equality of outcome that discounted hard work and effort. Not the old version of equality of opportunity – the rise of an exclusive meritocracy where only some can succeed and others are forever condemned to fail. But a genuinely meritocratic Britain, a Britain of all the talents. Where all are encouraged to aim high. And all by their efforts can rise (**Brown 2007**).

Indeed, the Premier's all-embracing speech represented the `finest hour' for majorities and minorities alike in Britain. From all indications, the future of the British Caribbean SME sector remains a challenging quest for owners, managers, staff and customers alike. However, these relationships hinge on a series of contractual obligations, bounded by partnerships and trade loyalties with respect to each stakeholder. Perhaps this is the litmus test for Caribbean people and other minorities in the UK and the world over.

Chapter Notes

EU funding – the NCVO's paper agrees that Structural Funding should be focused on the most disadvantaged Member States, but called for significant proportions of funding to continue for social programmes in the poorest areas of the 15 original members states.

Competitiveness – the *White Paper on Competitiveness* was published by the Labour Government in 1998 to set out a programme for economic reform including business support and enterprise promotion throughout the UK.

EU Working Time Directive – the main objective of this European policy is to promote health and safety at work, given the clear evidence that people who work long hours run higher risks of illness and accidents.

BERR- the Department for Business, Enterprise and Regulatory Reform was created by the Prime Minister in June 2007 to lead the Government's work to raise the rate of UK productivity through the creation of conditions necessary for business success and to ensure the UK responds effectively to the challenges of globalisation.

OECD- the Organisation for Economic Co-operation and Development is an international organisation of 30 countries that accept the principles of representative democracy and a free market economy. It originated in 1947 by Frenchman Robert Marjolin to help administer the Marshall Plan for the reconstruction of Europe after World War II.

CPRE- Campaign for the Protection of Rural England was set up in 1926 as a registered charity to champion the English countryside, with members and supporters over 6,000 and living cities, towns, villages and the countryside.

The African Renaissance - a late 1990s concept popularised by South African President, Thabo Mbeki in African nations were called upon to solve the problenms troubling the continent; this philosophy remains a key part of the post-aprtheid intellectual agenda.

Black Economic Liberation – refers to the principle of African people recognising that for political independence to be meaningful, it should be complemented by susbstantial forms of economic empowerment and finanical self-realiance in order to for Africans universally, to achieve ultimate freedom.

Selected References

1 Johnson, Christopher A (1997): Redefining Enterprise Culture in Britain, a Position Paper, Goldsmith's College, University of London, 13 January 1997.

2 Waldinger, Roger, Aldrich, Howard & Ward, Robin (1990): Ethnic Entrepreneurs: Immigrant Business in Industrial Societies, Sage Publications, p106.

3 Okokon, Susan (1998): Black Londoners 1890-1990, Sutton Publishing, Gloucestershire, England.

4 Evaluation of the ESF London Bidding Rounds, Government Office for London, January 2001.

5 UK sector fights for EU funding levels, National Council for Voluntary Organisations, 2005-2007.

6 CIA World Fact Book, IMF Database 2006.

7 Paliwoda, Stanley (1993): Identifying International Market Opportunities, Thompson Publication, UK.

8 Brock, Colin (1986): The Caribbean in Europe: Aspects of the West Indian Experience in Britain, France and the Netherlands, Routledge.

9 Promoting Prosperity, A business agenda for Britain, Commission for Public Policy & British Business, Vintage 1997.

10 `Creating the Conditions for Economic Growth', 2007 Pr-Budget Report and Comprehensive Spending Review, Department for Business, Enterprise and regulatory Reform, England.

11 Growth Patterns of Urban Regeneration 1999-2006, Campaign for the Protection of Rural England, April 1999.

12 Wakely, Patrick (2003): Capacity building for better cities, University College, London.

13 Rummler, Geary A & Alan P. Brache (1995): Improving Performance: How to Manage the White Space on the Organisation Chart, San Francisco, Jossey-Bass.

14 'Managerial relationships involving ethical responsibilities', Griffin, Ricky W (1999): Management, 6th edn, Houghton Mifflin Co, USA, p106.

15 Khan, Sikander, Yoshihara, Hideki (1994): Strategy and Performance of Foreign Companies in Japan, Praeger/Greenwood, pp 82-84 &112.

16 Brooks, Ian, Weatherston, Jamie and Wilkinson, Graham (2004): The International Business Environment, Pearson Education Limited, England, pp 73-74.

17 Interview with Lloyd James, property agent, 15th October 2003, London.

18 'Mark Dalgety', Master Tea Blender', Knowledge Foundation, Issue 5 February-May 2007, London.

19 Business Development Services for Small Enterprises: Guiding Principles for Donor Intervention, Committee of Donor Agencies for Small Enterprise Development, February 2001, World Bank Group, Washington, DC, USA.

20 The Performance of European Businesses in the 20th Century, Business History Unit, London School of Economics, 2002.

21 Cashin, Paul (2004): *Caribbean Business Cycles*, IMF Working Paper, WP/04/136, International Monetary Fund, July 2004. USA.

22 BME Business Programme Harlesden 2002-2005, Impact Assessment Report, Brent Council & TCS Tutorial College, May 2005, London.

23 The Birmingham and Solihull Small Business Guide, 2007/8, West Midlands, England.

24 The New Agenda for Minority Business Development, The Boston Consulting Group, June 2005, USA.

25 Indo-Caribbean people & Indo Caribbeans, wikipedia.

26 Greene, F (2005): *Youth Entrepreneurship: Latent Entrepreneurship, Market Failure and Enterprise Support*, National Council for Graduate Entrepreneurship, Policy Paper No. 002, May 2005, UK.

27 Interview with Patrick Frederick, CEO of Aimex International, 19 November 2007, London.

28 Exploring 'Britishness', Summary Report, RSA, October 2004, England.

29 Prime Minister, Rt. Hon. Gordon Brown MP Labour conference speech, Labour Party Conference, Bournemouth, 24 September 2007.